Douglas Johnson

A COMMENTARY ON
EXODUS

KREGEL EXEGETICAL LIBRARY

A COMMENTARY ON EXODUS

DUANE A. GARRETT

A Commentary on Exodus

Published by Kregel Publications, a division of Kregel, Inc., 2450 Oak Industrial Dr. NE, Grand Rapids, MI 49505-6020.

The English translations of the original Greek or Hebrew texts of the Bible are the author's own.

The Hebrew font used in this book is NewJerusalemU and the Greek font is TeubnerLSCU; both are available from www.linguisticsoftware.com/lgku.htm, +1-425-775-1130.

ISBN 978–0–8254–2551–6

Printed in the United States of America
14 15 16 17 18 / 5 4 3 2 1

For Patty

CONTENTS

PREFACE

I owe thanks to many people for seeing this commentary through to completion. I must first thank my wife Patty for her patience as I spent many hours closeted away with my research. Paul Hillman of Kregel shepherded the manuscript through the typesetting and proofing process. My student Andrew King read through an early set of proofs and spotted many problems and errors. Lori Shire did a heroic job of editing, proofing, and generally improving the work. I also owe a debt of gratitude to the students who took my class, "Hebrew Exegesis: Exodus," at the Southern Baptist Theological Seminary. Their enthusiasm encouraged me greatly, convincing me that the project really was worth the time and effort. Many fine commentaries on Exodus are readily available, but I have intentionally written this work to fill certain gaps within the literature. To this end, I have been selective and have not dealt with every possible issue.

First, I have sought to give readers a short, basic introduction to Egyptian history, culture, language, and geography. I studied this material first to educate myself, and then I endeavored to communicate it to my readers. My desire is that they would appreciate the context of the biblical story. It has astounded me that many treat Egyptology as a matter of no importance whatsoever for the interpretation of Exodus.

Second, I have sought to convey to readers the state of the evidence and arguments over crucial historical questions. Difficult issues include but are not limited to the following: the date of the exodus, the genealogy of Moses (Exodus 6), the location of the sea that Israel crossed, and the location of Sinai. I have argued for a specific solution where I thought it was warranted, but I have tried to treat evidence as even-handedly as possible. Critical scholars tend to dismiss these questions as meaningless (asking about the location of Mount Sinai being on a par with asking where Calypso's island is located). Confessional interpreters tend to grasp at solutions too quickly (there are some noteworthy exceptions). My goal has been to try to walk readers through the complexities involved, affirming the reliability of the text without dismissing or distorting pieces of evidence.

Third, I have tried to illustrate the importance of analyzing Hebrew prose on a clause-by-clause basis. To this end, I have translated every clause on a separate line. This commentary is not a full discourse analysis of the Hebrew text, but it does seek to demonstrate that by considering each clause and its predicate separately, one can gain a better appreciation of how the language flows and communicates.

Fourth, I have sought to demonstrate that Exodus contains a series of poems (and not just the one "Song of the Sea" at Exodus 15). This entails proving that the various texts are indeed poems and showing how they work and why it matters.

Fifth, I have sought to make this commentary useful for pastors and Bible teachers without neglecting to deal with thorny problems. To this end, readers will find that reflection on the biblical text within the main body of the commentary is often fairly short. I do not want anyone to have to wade through pages of discourse to find out what I think a passage means. I have placed a great deal of the technical discussion in the footnotes. Thus, the reasoning behind my interpretation is often found in the notes.

Sixth, I have tried to read Exodus as a Christian theologian. To this end, I have given a good deal of attention to relating the book to the New Testament and to Christian doctrine. This, too, reflects my desire that the commentary be serviceable to Christian ministers.

ABBREVIATIONS

AB	Anchor Bible
ABD	*Anchor Bible Dictionary*
AEL	*Ancient Egyptian Literature*
ANE	Ancient Near East
ANET	*Ancient Near Eastern Texts Relating to the Old Testament*
AOAT	Alter Orient und Altes Testament
AYBD	*Anchor-Yale Bible Dictionary*
BA	*Biblical Archaeologist*
BAR	*Biblical Archaeology Review*
Bib	*Biblica*
BSac	*Bibliotheca sacra*
CBQ	*Catholic Biblical Quarterly*
CEV	Contemporary English Version
COS	*The Context of Scripture*
CTA	*Corpus des tablettes en cunéiformes alphabétiques découvertes à Ras Shamra-Ugarit de 1929 à 1939.* Edited by A. Herdner. Mission de Ras Shamra 10. Paris, 1963.
CTJ	*Calvin Theological Journal*
D	Deuteronomist
E	Elohist source
ECC	Eerdmans Critical Commentary
ESV	English Standard Version
ExpTim	Expository Times
GKC	Gesenius' Hebrew Grammar. Edited by E. Kautzsch, translated by A. E. Cowley. 2nd ed. Oxford, 1910.
H	Holiness Code source

ABBREVIATIONS

HALOT	*The Hebrew and Aramaic Lexicon of the Old Testament.* L. Koehler, W. Baumgartner, and J. J. Stamm. Translated and edited under the supervision of M. E. J. Richardson. 4 vols. Leiden: Brill, 1994-1999.
HAR	*Hebrew Annual Review*
HBT	*Horizons in Biblical Theology*
HCSB	Holman Christian Standard Bible
HS	*Hebrew Studies*
HTR	*Harvard Theological Review*
HUCA	*Hebrew Union College Annual*
IBHS	*Introduction to Biblical Hebrew Syntax*
IBC	Interpretation: A Bible Commentary for Teaching and Preaching
Int	*Interpretation*
ISBE	International Standard Bible Encyclopedia. Edited by G. W. Bromiley. 4 vols. Grand Rapids, 1979-1988.
J	Yahwist source
JAOS	*Journal of the American Oriental Society*
JBL	*Journal of Biblical Literature*
JBQ	*Jewish Bible Quarterly*
JETS	*Journal of the Evangelical Theological Society*
JITC	*Journal of the Interdenominational Theological Center*
JNES	*Journal of Near Eastern Studies*
JNSL	*Journal of Northwest Semitic Languages*
JSOT	*Journal for the Study of the Old Testament*
JSOTSup	Journal for the Study of the Old Testament: Supplement Series
K&D	Keil, C. F., and F. Delitzsch, *Biblical Commentary on the Old Testament*
KJV	King James Version
KTU	*Die keilalphabetischen Texte aus Ugarit.* Edited by M. Dietrich, O. Loretz, and J. Sanmartín. AOAT 24/1. Neukirchen-Vluyn, 1976.
lit.	literally
LXX	Septuagint
MT	Masoretic Text
N	Nomadic source
NAC	New American Commentary
NASB	New American Standard Bible
NEAEHL	*The New Encyclopedia of Archaeological Excavations in the Holy Land.*

ABBREVIATIONS

NIDOTTE	*New International Dictionary of Old Testament Theology and Exegesis.* Edited by W. VanGemeren. 5 vols. Grand Rapids: Zondervan, 1997.
NIV	New International Version
NJB	New Jerusalem Bible
NJPS	*Tanakh: The Holy Scriptures: The New JPS Translation*
NRSV	New Revised Standard Version
NTS	*New Testament Studies*
OTL	Old Testament Library
P	Priestly source
RB	*Revue biblique*
ResQ	*Restoration Quarterly*
RSV	Revised Standard Version
SEAJT	*South East Asia Journal of Theology*
SOTSMS	Society for Old Testament Studies Monograph Series
SP	Sacra pagina
TJ	*Trinity Journal*
TNIV	Today's New International Version
TynBul	*Tyndale Bulletin*
VT	*Vetus Testamentum*
Vulg.	Clementine Vulgate
WBC	Word Biblical Commentary
WTJ	*Westminster Theological Journal*
ZAW	*Zeitschrift für die alttestamentliche Wissenschaft*

INTRODUCTION

Exodus is the true beginning of the story of Israel. Genesis is essential to the story, but it is a prologue, describing the lives of individual patriarchs rather than the history of a people. With Exodus we begin the story of the national entity called Israel. Exodus is also where the reader comes to understand the nature of YHWH. He keeps his covenant to the patriarchs, he reveals himself as "I AM," and he shows his power as the deliverer of his people, breaking the power of Egypt in the plagues. Exodus contains the initiation of the Sinai covenant, the governing document in the relationship between YHWH and Israel. With that, the nation receives the first presentation of the laws, statutes, and ordinances that were to be normative for every aspect of Israelite life. Finally, Exodus includes the establishment of the fundamental institutions of Israelite worship, the Aaronic priesthood and the central shrine. In short, Exodus is the beginning of everything that is distinctively Israelite, and it is the fountainhead of most of the literature of the Old Testament that follows, including the rest of Torah, all of the Prophets, and a good deal of the Writings.

THE SOURCES AND COMPOSITION OF EXODUS

Since the development of the documentary hypothesis, scholars have expended much effort attempting to show what sources lay behind

Exodus. They are concerned to show whether a given text is from J, or E, or P (or even D),[1] or whether it is from a source outside of the standard four documents. In a study that combines source criticism with tradition criticism, George Coats attempts to untangle what he believes are the threads of the traditions about Moses in Midian narratives.[2] William Propp subjects every passage in Exodus to a documentary hypothesis-driven source analysis, and he generally sticks with the traditional J, E, and P. Unlike many contemporary scholars, he believes it is possible to distinguish Exodus E from Exodus J.[3] Thomas Dozeman, on the other hand, rejects the existence of E altogether (at least for Exodus), and in his source analysis he focuses primarily on P and the "Non-P History." The latter is a kind of amalgamation of more recent interpretations of J and of the Deuteronomist; it is said to have been completed in the postexilic era. He essentially divides all of Exodus between these two sources, the "P History" and the "Non-P History."[4]

Some parts of Exodus come in for more severe documentary dissection than others. Considerable attention, for example, is devoted to the attempt to discern what sources lay behind the plague narratives.[5] For example, J is said to refer to the hardness of Pharaoh's heart with the

---

1. For example, Anthony C. Phillips, "A Fresh Look at the Sinai Pericope, Part 1," *VT* 34, no. 1 (1984):39–52 and Phillips, "A Fresh Look at the Sinai Pericope, Part 2," *VT* 34, no. 3 (1984): 282–94, in a study of the Decalogue and the Book of the Covenant, seeks to distinguish what in the text is pre-Deuteronomic, what was contributed to Exodus by the "Proto-Deuteronomists," and how the theology was recast by the Deuteronomists. On the other hand, Thomas B. Dozeman, *God at War: Power in the Exodus Tradition* (New York: Oxford University Press, 1996) argues that an ancient liturgy on YHWH as a God of war was refashioned by Deuteronomistic *tradents* into the salvation history of the Exodus.
2. George W. Coats, "Moses in Midian." *JBL* 92, no. 1 (1973): 3–10.
3. William H. Propp, *Exodus 1–18: A New Translation with Introduction and Commentary,* AB 2 (New Haven: Yale University Press, 1999), see especially pp. 47–52; and Propp, *Exodus 19–40: A New Translation with Introduction and Commentary,* AB 2A (New York: Doubleday, 2006).
4. Thomas B. Dozeman, *Commentary on Exodus,* ECC (Grand Rapids: Eerdmans, 2009), 35–43. Dozeman gives two lists describing, respectively, which texts he believes to be from the "Non-P History" and which texts he believes to be from P on pp. 48–51.
5. For such a study, see Samuel Loewenstamm, "An Observation on Source–Criticism of the Plague Pericope (Ex. VII–XI)," *VT* 24, no. 3 (1974): 374–8.

verb כבד, while E uses the verb חזק.[6] Stephen Geller believes that there are two sources and two distinct theologies, one "covenantal" (C) and one "priestly" (P), behind the Sabbath legislation in Exod. 16.[7] In another intramural squabble, scholars wrestle over the relationship between P and H,[8] a debate that to me seems analogous to rivals within a millenarian group heatedly arguing out fine points of eschatology.

Much of this discussion is of doubtful value, either in terms of gaining better tools for interpreting the text or in terms of finding criteria for dividing it into its supposed sources.[9] It maintains only a shell of intellectual coherence; scholars continue to use the terms P and J (unless the latter is jettisoned in favor of the "Non-P History") while no longer holding to anything that may be meaningfully called a consensus. The theory is not based in any ancient Near Eastern analogies but is from start to finish an analysis based in extrinsic and peculiar criteria. For example, it is supposed that an ancient author who believed that the divine name YHWH was not revealed until the time of Moses would never use that name in his narrative until after he had reached the point in his story where the name is revealed. But as long as his readers knew the name, there is no reason for the narrative to have avoided it. Similarly, the whole concept of "doublets" as evidence of multiple sources shows no appreciation for the importance of repetition and "seconding"[10] as a literary device in the ancient world. Many particulars of source criticism are unpersuasive or even odd. Even if one accepts the idea that both J and E had a plague tradition, is it not

6. Robert R. Wilson, "The Hardening of Pharaoh's Heart," *CBQ* 41, no. 1 (1979): 22–3.

7. Stephan A. Geller, "Manna and Sabbath: A Literary–Theological Reading of Exodus 16," *Int* 59, no. 1 (2005): 5–16.

8. See Saul M. Olyan, "Exodus 31:12–17: The Sabbath according to H, or the Sabbath according to P and H?" *JBL* 124, no. 2 (2005): 201–9.

9. Against John I. Durham, *Exodus,* WBC 3 (Waco: Word Books, 1987), xx–xxi; and Brevard S. Childs, *The Book of Exodus: A Critical, Theological Commentary,* (Philadelphia: Westminster, 1974), throughout his commentary.

10. The term refers to what is often called "parallelism." It is a poetic device based on repeating or restating points that have already been made, often with additional information given in the second line. James Kugel, *The Idea of Biblical Poetry: Parallelism and its History* (Baltimore: Johns Hopkins University Press, 1998), developed the notion of seconding in his analysis of Hebrew poetry. The poetic use of seconding points to how important repetition was in the rhetoric of ancient Israel, but it is not evidence for multiple sources.

peculiar that both had a tradition that Pharaoh's heart was hardened, and yet that they used different verbs to describe this?

The Book of the Covenant is widely supposed to be a collection of various laws from different times and places in the history of Israel. Here again, however, this consensus was reached without real reference to the analogies in ancient Near Eastern law. Raymond Westbrook's arguments on this issue are worth hearing:

> Conventional wisdom regards the Covenant Code as an amalgam of provisions from different sources and periods, the fusion of which has left tell-tale marks in the form of various inconsistencies in the text. . . . Interpreters of the Covenant Code need to come to terms with the fact that it is part of a widespread literary-legal tradition and can only be understood in terms of that tradition. The starting point for interpretation must therefore be the presumption that the Covenant Code is a coherent text comprising clear and consistent laws, in the same manner as its cuneiform forbears.[11]

Joe Sprinkle, similarly, demonstrates that one may read the Book of the Covenant as a coherent whole without recourse to explaining difficulties via competing sources.[12]

Finally, the whole effort is fraught with contradictory conclusions and a general lack of clarity. Whatever consensus there once was has only diminished with the passage of time. T. D. Alexander, for example, demonstrates that there is more unity to Exod. 19:1–24:11 than earlier scholars recognized, and along the way he describes the conflicting conclusions of scholars committed to the documentary hypothesis.[13]

Beyond being a dubious enterprise, source criticism of this kind is of doubtful heuristic value.[14] That is, it does not help us to understand

---

11. Raymond Westbrook, "What is the Covenant Code?" in *Theory and Method in Biblical and Cuneiform Law: Revision, Interpolation and Development*, JSOTSup 181, ed. Bernard M. Levinson (Sheffield: Sheffield Academic Press, 1994), 36.
12. Joe M. Sprinkle, *The Book of the Covenant: A Literary Approach*, JSOTSup 174 (Sheffield: *JSOT* Press, 1994).
13. T. Desmond Alexander, "The Composition of the Sinai Narrative in Exodus XIX 1–XXV 11," *VT* 49, no. 1 (1999): 2–20.
14. Curiously, Daniel B. Mathewson, "A Critical Binarism: Source Criticism and Deconstructive Criticism," *JSOT* 98 (2002): 3–28, argues that source criticism and deconstructive criticism are very compatible. That,

what the book means.[15] To the contrary, source analysis has often hindered the literary and theological interpretation of the text. A distressing and inevitable outcome of analysis based on some version of the documentary hypothesis is that it leads to commentaries that have more to say about the supposed sources of Exodus than they do about the canonical text. That is, we come away with little in the way of an interpretation of the one document that we know to be real, the book of Exodus.

Yet another unfortunate aspect of documentary analysis is its tendency to date texts very late. John Van Seters, an adherent of the documentary hypothesis who nevertheless has revised many of its once established conclusions, maintains that the simplicity of the Exodus covenant code argues against it having an early date (the older documentary hypothesis considered this to be a mixture of J and E material and therefore from relatively early in the Israelite monarchy). In his view, the more streamlined covenant code of Exod. 21–23 implies a postexilic date and indicates that it was meant for diaspora Jews without priesthood or temple.[16] But this is only one example of a trend in recent studies to push more and more of the material of Exodus into the postexilic.

A discussion of the origin or sources of Exodus should not remain trapped in the nineteenth century, continuing to talk about J, E, D, and P as though those terms actually mean something real and historical. That path is a dead end. If one wishes to speak of the origin of the book, one should look in a new direction. One newer analysis is that of David Wright. He argues that the laws of Hammurabi and the laws of the Covenant Code of Exod. 21–24 so strongly parallel each other in content and structure that the similarities cannot be coincidental or a reflection of general similarities in the ancient Near Eastern legal traditions. Rather, the author(s) of the Covenant Code must have had direct access to the Hammurabi texts. Wright accepts a late date for the Covenant Code (740–640 B.C.) and argues that Israelite scribes could have come into contact with the code during the period of domination

---

in my view, can hardly be considered an endorsement for either method. Mathewson uses Exod. 14 to try to demonstrate his point.

15. For example, the lengthy discussion over sources (J, E, P, or N) behind the Passover text (Exod. 12:1–13:6) found in Childs, *Exodus*, 184–95, contributes little to our understanding of the passage or even of the origin of Passover.
16. John Van Seters, *A Law Book for the Diaspora: Revision in the Study of the Covenant Code* (Oxford: Oxford University Press, 2003).

under the Neo-Assyrian Empire.[17] This latter point is certainly debatable. Evidence for knowledge of Akkadian cuneiform by Israelite scribes during this period is very thin, and is there little reason to suppose that Neo-Assyrian archivists would have shared Hammurabi's text with subjugated provinces on the western frontier of their empire. Furthermore, it is not at all clear why orthodox Israelite scribes from this period would want a copy of a thousand-year-old Babylonian text as the basis for their religious law. One could argue, to the contrary, that the evidence from Hammurabi points to a much earlier provenance for the Covenant Code (although I shall attempt no such project here).

The main point I wish to make is that investigation of the sources of Exodus, if such is to be attempted at all, should be done by an avenue more up-to-date and potentially more fruitful than what we see now. Continually flogging the dead horse of the documentary hypothesis is pointless. At any rate, I am already on record with my reasons for abandoning the documentary hypothesis,[18] and I will proceed no further in this vein. I will, however, from time to time in the commentary discuss passages that are thought to be evidence for various sources.

The authorship of Exodus is traditionally assigned to Moses, but the book is anonymous. It never states who wrote the book, although it often asserts that the legislation within the book was given by God to Moses, and that should be the starting point for a confessional view of the origin of the book. From that perspective one may reasonably contend that Moses was responsible for the compilation of this book. This does not reject the possibility that sources were used or that there has been editing; for example, it is reasonable to assume that Exod. 6:14–25 is based in preexisting and extrinsic genealogical records. But for the most part, there is very little basis for distinguishing sources within Exodus, and the effort gives few benefits in terms of an enhanced understanding of the book. The full process whereby the book was composed is unknown to us, but it is a unity. It bears the marks of being a late second millennial text (see "The Suzerainty Treaty Form" below), and it was written by someone who was familiar with the circumstances of Israel in Egypt. We may continue to view Exodus as the "Second Book of Moses."

---

17. David P. Wright, *Inventing God's Law: How the Covenant Code of the Bible Used and Revised the Laws of Hammurabi* (Oxford: Oxford University Press, 2009).
18. See Duane A. Garrett, *Rethinking Genesis: The Sources and Authorship of the First Book of the Pentateuch* (Grand Rapids: Baker, 1991).

THE TEXT OF EXODUS

In describing the state of the text of a book of the Hebrew Bible, we must first describe the general characteristics of the language (whether it has marks of being a particular Hebrew dialect, or has a large number of loanwords, or is marked by a high number of difficulties and idiosyncrasies). Then, we must take note of how well it has been transmitted (whether there are indications of a high number of scribal errors, so that there are grounds at various points for emending the text, and whether the Masoretic Text is generally in agreement with the versions). Finally, because this commentary includes an original translation of the Exodus, I also describe the translation method I have followed. The translation is clause-by-clause for prose, but for poetry it breaks the Hebrew text down according to its stichometry as I understand it.

The Hebrew Of Exodus

Exodus is written in classical Hebrew in a clean, narrative style using what is often described as "standard biblical Hebrew." It is grammatically consistent with what we see in preexilic texts of biblical Hebrew, and it has no particular idiosyncrasies. The vocabulary consists primarily of common words, and rare or obscure words seldom stand as the *crux interpretationis* of a passage. A few common words, in addition to a fair number of toponyms and personal names, may be of Egyptian origin. Even these words are generally not exotic, and they pose little difficulty in translation (for example, the Hebrew measure זֶרֶת ["span," Exod. 28:16] is probably derived from the Egyptian *ḏrt*).[19] Technical vocabulary relating to the construction of the tabernacle and of the priestly vestments naturally poses something of a challenge. On the whole, however, the Hebrew of Exodus is straightforward. This is not to say that there is no room for disagreement about the precise significance of a given passage, but in contrast to a book such as Hosea or Job, few passages in Exodus are truly obscure.

Text-Critical Issues

The transmission of Exodus appears to have been remarkably clean. Fragments of the book found in the Judean desert (the Dead Sea Scrolls and related texts) are generally in agreement with the MT.[20]

19. James K. Hoffmeier, *Ancient Israel in Sinai: The Evidence for the Authenticity of the Wilderness Tradition* (Oxford: Oxford University Press, 2005), 220.
20. Durham, *Exodus*, xxvii.

In the scholarly treatment of Exodus, the text receives a fairly small number of suggested emendations. In a study of the text of the plague narratives (7:14–11:10), B. Lemmelijn found that in the overwhelming majority of cases, variants in the ancient versions could be explained by contextual consideration (and not by a different Vorlage) and that the MT was the preferred reading.[21] There are minor differences between the MT and the ancient versions such as the LXX, but it is not the purpose of this commentary to list them. In comparison with what we see in many other books of the Bible (Jeremiah or Job, for example), differences between the MT and the LXX are minor indeed. As a rule, text critical issues will be discussed only in the rare cases where, in my judgment, emendation may be called for. For those who desire a catalogue of significant variant readings that occur in the Hebrew manuscripts and in the ancient versions, Propp's two-volume Anchor Bible commentary is highly recommended.[22]

The Translation Method of This Commentary

In interpreting a book of the Bible, the most important single issue is the obtaining of an accurate translation. As such, the translation occupies a major place in this commentary. The procedures I have adopted are as follows:

- In prose, each clause is translated on a separate line. These lines are numbered by chapter, verse, and lower case letter. Thus, "1:12c" is chapter 1, verse 12, clause c.

- Relative clauses, which function grammatically as adjectives, direct objects or prepositional phrases within a larger clause, are not put on a separate line.

- Narrative is distinguished from "reported speech" (a direct quotation of a character in the narrative). Reported speech is indented in the text to distinguish it from the main narrative. Furthermore, a quote within a quote is further indented (as when the text says something like, And YHWH said, "You shall say to them, 'Do not come up the mountain.'"). See, for example, the translation of 3:13.

---

21. Bénédicte Lemmelijn, *A Plague of Texts? A Text-Critical Study of the So-Called 'Plagues Narrative' in Exodus* 7:14–11:10 (Leiden: Brill, 2009), see especially p. 212.
22. Propp, *Exodus 1–18* and *Exodus 19–40*.

- In footnotes, I have explained the translation wherever necessary, commenting on grammatical and lexical features in the text. I have also made some comments about the discourse-level function of various clauses.

- For poetry, I have given the entire text of the poem in English and Hebrew. I have divided the poems into lines according to the following rules.

  1. The major disjunctive marks of the cantillation system are taken into account.[23] In the majority of cases, line breaks occur at the *silluq*, the *athnach*, and the *zaqeph qaton*, with some breaks occurring at the *pashta*, *revia*, or *tifha*. As a general rule, when a disjunctive accent serves to mark a line break, it will have a weaker disjunctive accent within its domain. As is done here, names of accents are given in italics in a simplified transliteration.

  2. The "line constraints" as described in O'Connor[24] and refined in Holladay[25] are taken into account. These constraints state that in any Hebrew line of poetry, there must be:

     - *From 0 to 3 clause predicators.* A line may have no predicator, but it should have no more than three. A clause predicator may be a finite verb, an infinitive absolute that functions as a finite verb, an infinitive construct phrase functioning as a finite verb (for example, an infinitive construct that has a suffix functioning as the subject of the action), a participle functioning as a periphrastic finite verb, and the particles אֵין and יֵשׁ. O'Connor also counts the vocative as a predicator, and I have followed that rule.

---

23. See Raymond de Hoop, "The Colometry of Hebrew Verse and the Masoretic Accents: Evaluation of a Recent Approach"; "Part 1," *JNSL* 26, no. 1 (2000): 47–73; "Part II," *JNSL* 26, no. 2 (2000): 65–100.
24. Michael P. O'Connor, *Hebrew Verse Structure* (Winona Lake: Eisenbrauns, 1980).
25. William Holladay, "Hebrew Verse Structure Revisited (I): Which Words 'Count'?" *JBL* 118, no. 1 (1999): 19–32; Hebrew Verse Structure Revisited (II): Conjoint Cola, and Further Suggestions." *JBL* 118, no. 3 (1999): 401–16.

- *From 1 to 4 constituents.* A constituent is a word or phrase that fills one grammatical slot. Examples would be a subject, a predicate, or a prepositional phrase. Although it has more than one word, a construct chain functioning as a subject or vocative, for example, is a single constituent.

- *From 2 to 5 units.* A unit is basically a word, but small particles such as כִּי or אִם or prepositions such as אֶל do not count as units. One may debate what does or does not count as a unit. I treat לֹא as a non-unit, and only count כֹּל as a unit if it is absolute.

3. In the presentation of the poems, the number of predicators, constituents, and units is indicated. For example, in the poem that I believe exists in Exod. 6, the line 6:5c is said to be "1–2–2" (1 predicator, 2 constituents, and 2 units).

4. Comments are made in footnotes if, in my opinion, the line structure of a poem does not agree with what one would expect from the accentuation or line constraints.

5. Poems are also divided into "stanzas" and "strophes." Stanzas are here understood to be the major divisions of a poem, and strophes are the major divisions of a stanza. I use the term "verse" only in reference to numbered verses, not in reference to poetic subdivisions.

EGYPT

Exodus opens its story in Egypt, and the history and culture of Egypt form the backdrop for the whole of the book. But the average person, and this surely includes the average pastor or Bible teacher, knows no more about ancient Egypt than that they built the pyramids, wrote in hieroglyphs, and oppressed the Israelites. Beyond that, what most people know about Egypt comes from watching motion pictures such as *The Ten Commandments*, or *The Prince of Egypt*, or even *The Mummy*. It is essential, however, that anyone who seeks to teach or proclaim Exodus have some understanding of the nature of the land, its history, and the possible setting for the exodus events.[26] Some treatments of

---

26. For an understanding of Egyptian history and culture beyond the limited survey presented here, the following texts are recommended. John Baines and Jaromír Málek, *The Cultural Atlas of the World: Ancient Egypt*,

Exodus, even some major and scholarly commentaries, treat the book as though awareness of its Egyptian setting were a superfluous matter. This is surely misguided.

The Land

The Nile River made human habitation of Egypt possible. With its annual floods, the Nile not only provided water for drinking and agriculture but also cast up black, alluvial soil on its banks to provide fertile ground for the planting of crops. Thus, Egyptians called the land immediately adjacent to the Nile the "Black Land," and the desert beyond the reach of its flood waters the "Red Land." Except at a few oases, human civilization was impossible in the harsh desert away from the Nile. It is important for the modern reader to realize that the Nile River valley *was* Egypt; almost everything else was wasteland. This means that a large part of the ancient kingdom of Egypt—everything south of the Delta—was hundreds of miles long but only about five miles wide! The Nile also neatly divided Egypt into two parts. The Delta region (in northern Egypt) is known as Lower Egypt, while the Nile south of the Delta is known as Upper Egypt (so-called because it is upriver since the Nile flows from south to north).[27]

---

rev. ed. (New York: Checkmark Books, 2000); Rosalie David, *Handbook to Life in Ancient Egypt* (Oxford: Oxford University Press, 1998); Rita E. Freed, Yvonne J. Markowitz, and Sue H. D'Auria, eds., *Pharaohs of the Sun: Akhenaten, Nefertiti, Tutankhamen* (Boston: Museum of Fine Arts, Boston, 1999); Nicolas Grimal, *A History of Ancient Egypt,* trans. Ian Shaw (Oxford: Blackwell, 1992); Kenneth A. Kitchen, *Pharaoh Triumphant: The Life and Times of Ramesses II, King of Egypt* (Warminster: Aris & Phillips, 1982); J. E. Manchip-White, *Ancient Egypt: Its Culture and History* (New York: Dover, 1970); Barbara Mertz, *Red Land, Black Land: Daily Life in Ancient Egypt* (New York: William Morrow, 2008); Barbara Mertz, *Temples, Tombs & Hieroglyphs: A Popular History of Ancient Egypt* (New York: William Morrow, 2007); Ian Shaw, ed., *The Oxford History of Ancient Egypt* (Oxford: Oxford University Press, 2000); Ian Shaw and Nicholson, *The Dictionary of Ancient Egypt* (New York: Harry N. Abrams, 1995); David P. Silverman, ed., *Ancient Egypt* (Oxford: Oxford University Press, 1997); William K. Simpson, ed., *The Literature of Ancient Egypt: An Anthology of Stories, Instructions, Stelae, Autobiographies and Poetry*, 3rd ed. (New Haven: Yale University Press, 2003).

27. Sometimes Egypt is divided into three parts: Lower Egypt (the Delta), Middle Egypt (the northern half of the Nile valley below the Delta), and Upper Egypt (the southern half of the Nile Valley).

Egypt enjoyed great security within its environment. It was all but impregnable from the east, where deserts and harsh, rocky mountains terminated at the Red Sea. Similarly, to its west was the vast Sahara Desert. To the south, Nubia could and occasionally did pose a threat, but for the most part Egypt dominated Nubia. Also, the cataracts (waterfalls in the southern part of the Nile) made riverborne invasion or migration from the south difficult. To the north was the Mediterranean, a fairly secure border since seaborne invasion was very difficult in the ancient world. Threats could come in from the northwest, from Libya, but the most vulnerable spot for Egypt was the narrow corridor to its northeast linking Egypt with Canaan and beyond that with the great powers of Mesopotamia, Syria, and Anatolia. This land bridge did provide access for trading and diplomatic contacts. Still, migration and invasion by Semitic peoples via the northeastern corridor would be a standing concern for Egypt throughout its history.

The agricultural benefits of the Nile were enormous. Every year the river would flood and, besides providing the water that was essential for life, cast up alluvial soil along its banks, making the land extremely fertile. The annual inundation did not render the land invulnerable to famine (a flood that was too high or too low could be catastrophic), but for the most part this resource allowed the Egyptians to grow grain and vegetables in an abundance that was the envy of the rest of the world. It is not without reason that the hungry Israelites in the wilderness longed for the Egyptian Delta. This land was, by comparison with the wilderness, a paradise providing food without end. Egypt also had relatively easy access to precious metals (especially gold[28]) and semi-precious stones. Using these materials, together with pigments available for making paint, the Egyptians produced works of art of great dignity, delicacy, and beauty.

On the other hand, Egypt had virtually no hard metal (iron, or copper and tin for bronze) for making tools and weapons, and very little timber for construction. Buildings were thus made of sun-dried brick or, in the case of great monumental structures, of stone. The remains extant from ancient Egypt today are thus almost entirely monumental, as mudbrick buildings would eventually dissolve back into the soil (especially those that were located in the wet Delta region). This feature of Egyptian archaeology has a parallel in what remains of Egyptian writings. Many texts were carved into stone monuments, but the vast

28. For a summary on the mining and use of gold in ancient Egypt, along with a brief survey of relevant geological data, see Colin Reader, "Pharaoh's Gold," *Ancient Egypt* 9, no. 2 (2008): 15–21.

majority of Egyptian texts were written on papyrus, a paper made from the papyrus plant, which grew along the Nile. Papyrus was a great benefit to Egyptian scribes, but it, too, was perishable. Thus, a large number of surviving texts from ancient Egypt are monumental; almost all of the papyrus documents have disappeared. By contrast, the clay tablets popular for documentation in Mesopotamia could last for millennia.

Egypt was divided into 42 "nomes" (provinces or districts), with 22 in Upper Egypt and 20 in Lower Egypt. The word "nome" comes from Greek; the Egyptian equivalent is *sepat*. The local lords that governed the nomes, traditionally called "nomarchs," could pose a challenge to royal authority and at various times contributed to the breakdown of an effective central government.

There are a few places in Egypt that every reader of Exodus ought to know. These include:

- *The Delta*. Already described above, this triangular, northern part of the Nile is where the river breaks into several smaller streams. It is the focal point of Lower Egypt, and its southern point is at about 30° N.

- *The Faiyum*. This is a fertile oasis area located west of the Nile and about 60 km (37 miles) southwest of modern Cairo. It includes Lake Moeris, which is connected to the Nile by a stream called the Bahr Yusuf ("River of Joseph").

- *The Great Bend of the Nile*. This is a place in Upper (southern) Egypt where the Nile, as it flows north, suddenly turns east, then bends back to north, then back to west, and finally resumes its general northward flow. It is in the vicinity of 26° North.

- *The First Cataract*. This is the first of a series of cataracts (waterfalls and rapids) as one goes up the Nile toward the south. It marks the boundary between Egypt and Nubia, and is located at 24° N. Elephantine, a city near the first cataract and at the southern edge of the first nome, marks the traditional southern border of Egypt.

- *The Gulf of Suez*. The Red Sea forms a great "Y," with one arm to the west of the Sinai Peninsula and one arm to the east. The Suez is the elongated gulf that is west of the Sinai.

- *The Gulf of Aqaba*. This is the other arm of the Red Sea's great "Y," on the east side of the Sinai Peninsula.

- *The Wadi Tumilat*. This is a wadi (a seasonal stream) that goes from the Nile Delta toward due east at about 30°5´ N. It empties into Lake Timsah, north of the Gulf of Suez. The Israelites took this route out of Egypt, and Pithom, one of the store cities that they built, was located on the wadi.

- *Thebes*. Sometimes the capital city of Egypt, this was the cult center of the god Amun and contains the most extravagantly built-up temple complex from the ancient world, at Karnak. It was located in the southern part of the Great Bend, at 25°4´ N.

- *Memphis*. This was the traditional capital city of unified Egypt. It was at the junction of Lower and Upper Egypt, just south of the Delta, at 29°45´ N. It is at the southern edge of modern Cairo.

- *Saqqara*. This is the site of some of the oldest (3rd dynasty) pyramids, such as the step pyramid of Djoser. It is west of Memphis.

- *Giza*. This is the site of the great pyramids and the sphinx. It is west of modern Cairo.

- *Avaris / Pi-Riʿamsese / Tell el-Dabʿa*. This is the vicinity of the Hyksos capital (Avaris), and later of the capital city of Ramesses II (Pi-Riʿamsese; it is the biblical "store-city" Raamses). The modern name of the site is Tell el-Dabʿa. The Israelites lived in this general area during their sojourn in Egypt. It is in the eastern Delta at 30°47´ N and 31°50´ E.

Chronology and History

It is astounding that pharaonic Egypt endured more or less unchanged for some 3,000 years, and that for much of that time it was a dominant world power. One could almost say that the history of Middle Eastern and Western civilization is divided into two parts: first, Egypt, and then, everything else.

There are two methods of breaking up the 3,000 years of ancient Egyptian history into manageable segments. The first, following the work of the Egyptian historian Manetho (3rd century B.C.), is to break the history up according to the dynasties (Manetho said there were 30 dynasties of pharaohs; today that is extended to include a "dynasty 0" and then up to the 33rd dynasty).[29] The second method is to partition Egyptian history into major eras that describe whether the nation was powerful and united or was weak and divided, or was under foreign domination. The major eras of Egyptian history with their respective dynasties are described in Table 1.

Establishing the chronology of ancient Egypt is difficult and complex, but one can appreciate the rudiments of how this is done by getting acquainted with the Sothic calendar. The ancient Egyptian civil calendar consisted of twelve months of 30 days each. In addition, there were five intercalary days added every year, bringing the total to 365. But there were no leap years to correct for the additional ¼ day of the solar year, and thus every four years the civil year fell one day behind the solar year. This meant that the civil calendar would progressively be further off from the solar year, until it had gone through a cycle of 1,460 years (4 × 365), bringing it back, for one year, into agreement with the solar year.

But the Egyptians did have a way of recognizing when one solar year had passed: it was marked by the first rising of Sirius, the "dog star," as a morning star. Sirius disappears from the Egyptian sky for about 70 days per year. Its annual reappearance marks one full solar year. This event is called a "heliacal rising" of Sirius (or, after "Sothis," the Egyptian name for Sirius, a "Sothic rising"). Thus, the New Year's Day of the civil calendar would correspond to the Sothic rising once every 1,460 years (this lengthy period of time is a "Sothic cycle"). From Roman records, we know that a New Year's Day and a Sothic rising were on the same day in A.D. 139. Working backwards through one Sothic cycle, therefore, we know that another such year was at about 1321 B.C., and that the prior convergence of New Year's Day and the Sothic rising was in around 2781 B.C. (we cannot be precise because we don't know exactly from what latitude in Egypt Sirius' rising was observed in the various records, and this can make a difference of more than a decade). But if, for a given year of a pharaoh's reign, a record tells on what day in what month the Sothic rising took place, one would know where that specific year was set within the Sothic Cycle, and one could determine reasonably accurately what year that was according to the Gregorian Calendar. We do have two such Sothic risings recorded; these come from Year 7 of Sesostris III (about 1856 B.C.) and from

29. The total number of dynasties may vary; not all scholars include up to a 33rd dynasty.

Year 9 of Amenhotep I (about 1516 B.C.).[30] These years then become linchpins that hold the chronology of Egypt, as it is known from king lists and other official records, to an absolute chronology based on the modern calendar.

The Sothic cycle is but one tool that Egyptologists use, and it sets the timeline on a fairly solid footing. One should not, therefore, treat Egyptian chronology with undue skepticism. There are still uncertainties about Egyptian history, and it is not possible to be absolutely precise, but the chronology of Egyptian history is not arbitrary. Except for the early dynasties, it is not likely to be off by more than a few decades, at most. The dates listed in Table 1 follow the low chronology of K. A. Kitchen;[31] other chronological reconstructions of the history of Egypt will have slightly higher dates. As a general rule, uncertainty about the dating of Egyptian epochs becomes greater as one goes further back in time. Thus, the dates for the Ptolemaic period are quite precisely known, but the dates for the Archaic period are less precise.[32] On the other hand, a recent study that applied carbon-14 dating to Egyptian artifacts supplied by major museums from around the world largely confirmed the standard dating system for Egyptian chronology.[33] Skepticism about the reliability of standard Egyptian chronology is unwarranted.

We should also note that not all scholars agree regarding what dynasties belong in what eras. Thus, for example, some place the 3rd dynasty in the Archaic period, but others, as is done below, place it in the Old Kingdom.[34]

---

30. The absolute dates mentioned here follow the low chronology of Kenneth A. Kitchen in "Egypt, History of: Chronology," in Freedman, ABD Vol. 2, 321–331. Earlier dates (1872 and 1541) are given in Shaw, *Oxford Egypt*, 11.
31. Kitchen, "Egypt, Chronology," 321–331.
32. For an alternative date scheme, see Shaw and Nicholson, *Dictionary*, 479–83.
33. Yves Miserey, "Égypte: la chronologie des dynasties revue au carbone 14," *Le Figaro* (June 18, 2010).
34. For example, Kitchen ("Egypt, Chronology") puts the 3rd dynasty in the Old Kingdom, but Baines and Málek, *Cultural Atlas*, 36, put it in the Archaic or "Early Dynastic" period.

TABLE 1. THE CHRONOLOGY OF ANCIENT EGYPT			
Major Eras	**Dynasties**	**Dates**	**Remarks**
Predynastic	n/a	prior to 3000	Egypt not unified
Archaic	"0" and 1st–2nd	3000–2700	Egypt unified and classical Egyptian culture established
Old Kingdom	3rd–8th	2700–2160	Pyramid age; Egypt powerful and united
First Intermediate	9th–10th	2160–2010	Political chaos; Egypt not unified
Middle Kingdom	11th–12th	2106–1786	A second era of power and unity; overlaps with the First Intermediate
Second Intermediate	13th–17th	1786–1550	Weakness and division; this period includes the Hyksos dynasties (15th and 16th)
New Kingdom	18th–20th	1550–1069	Egypt's imperial age; the exodus probably took place in the 18th or 19th dynasty
Third Intermediate	21st–25th	1069–656	Approximately coincides with Israelite monarchies; Egyptian power waxed and waned
Saite-Persian	26th–31st	654–332	Foreign domination of Egypt
Ptolemaic	32nd–33rd	332–30 B.C.	Greek domination after Alexander the Great and subsequent rule by Ptolemaic kings
Roman	n/a	After 30 B.C.	Decline and end of classical Egyptian culture under Roman domination

Predynastic Egypt

This is essentially prehistoric Egypt, as there are no written records with which to construct a history. Knowledge of conditions at this time is dependent on finding the archaeological remains of communities at individual sites. The cultures that emerged were essentially regional; there was, as yet, no pan-Egyptian society. An important transformation of the land took place with the end of the last ice age. Exceptionally heavy rains and flooding south of Egypt, in East Africa, broke open channels that allowed the White Nile to begin to flow. The Nile River thus took on the characteristics that it has to this day. At the same time, there was very little rainfall in Egypt itself, contributing to the desertification of the land (prior to this, Egypt and even the Sahara were composed of grassy plains and even some large lakes). These two factors—a desert land, and a great and seasonally flooding river flowing through the middle of it—would allow for the creation of classical Egypt. On the one hand, the river both made agriculture possible and unified Egypt. On the other hand, the desert isolated Egypt in the manner described above and contributed to the creation of a homogenous culture.

Predynastic cultures are identified by the sites at which their remains have been found. For example, the Badarian cultural phase (which flourished about 4000 B.C.) is named for the place at which remains from this culture were found, at el-Badari in the northern half of Upper Egypt. Amratian culture (which flourished about 3600 B.C.) is named for a site called el-ʿAmra further to the south. Human civilization began to flourish during the late predynastic period. Agriculture is known to have been practiced in the Badarian culture, and the delicate Badarian pottery was of very high quality (some even regard it as the finest pottery ancient Egypt ever produced). Amratian pottery was decorated with various human and animal motifs, and the making of stone monuments was well-established by the end of this period. It may be that loose confederations existed in Egypt and that gradually power became more centralized.

Archaic Egypt

The historical process in which Egypt was unified between 4000 and 3000 B.C. is not fully understood.[35] Two factors appear to have been decisive: the military success of the kings who unified Egypt, and the

35. For a recent analysis of this problem, see Kathryn A. Bard, *From Farmers to Pharaohs: Mortuary Evidence for the Rise of Complex Society in Egypt* (Sheffield: Sheffield Academic Press, 1994).

organized irrigation of the soil (which allowed for large scale agriculture, brought about population increase, and functioned best when there was a strong central government to insure cooperation in irrigation maintenance). King Narmer, a semi-legendary predynastic (or "dynasty 0") king, appears on a famous stone palette with images of himself on both sides. On one side he is wearing the red crown, and on the other the white crown (the ruler of Lower Egypt wore a red crown, and the ruler of Upper Egypt wore a white crown). The red and white double crown became the abiding symbol of pharaonic rule over the "Two Lands," Upper and Lower Egypt. On the other hand, a king named Meni (or Menes) is said to have established the 1st dynasty, and it may be that Meni and Narmer were one and the same. Be that as it may, the country was unified under a single pharaoh by about 3000 B.C. Memphis, on the southern tip of the Delta and thus at the junction of Lower and Upper Egypt, became the capital city. The distinctive Egyptian style in art and writing (the hieroglyphic script) was well-established by the end of the Archaic period. This is, of itself, an astonishing achievement: the political, artistic, literary and religious culture established by the end of the Archaic period would endure virtually unchanged for 3,000 years.

Old Kingdom

The unification of Egypt naturally led to its becoming a great power and arguably the first nation (as opposed to city-state) in history. The names and chronology of the pharaohs of the first five dynasties are known from the Palermo Stone, a black basalt stone inscribed with parallel lines that list the kings from this time. Pharaohs maintained the security of Egypt by leading military campaigns to the Levant and to Libya, and they maintained control of the nation by, among other things, seeing to it that the lands held by any individual baron were dispersed across Egypt. Thus, no member of the aristocracy had his land concentrated in a single location, from which he could set up a rival dynasty. This policy would fail in the 6th dynasty, however, as provincial governors became local warlords. The 7th and 8th dynasties were a series of ephemeral kings.

The monuments that the world identifies with Egypt, the pyramids and the Great Sphinx, were built during the Old Kingdom period. The first major pyramid was the Step Pyramid built by Djoser, the first pharaoh of the 3rd dynasty, and his architect Imhotep (this scholar-architect was so renowned that he was eventually deified). The zenith of pyramid building was the Great Pyramid of Kheops (Khufu), which was constructed in the fourth dynasty. Some of the finest statuary of

Egypt comes from the Old Kingdom. Some classic works of Egyptian literature, such as the proverbs of Ptahhotep, also date from this period. We should note that all of these achievements were already hundreds of years old when Abraham was born.

First Intermediate Period

The 9th dynasty consisted of rulers who claimed power from the city of Herakleopolis Magna (this city, located on the west side of the Nile and just south of the Faiyum, was the cult center of Herishef, a ram-headed creator god; the Greeks identified Herishef with Hercules, and thus the name Herakleopolis). But during the Herakleopolitan 10th dynasty, a rival dynasty, the 11th, was established at Thebes. Central authority thus had collapsed. Few monuments survive from this time. Even so, this era produced some significant works of literature (all of it in a pessimistic tone), such as the "Song of the Harper" and the "Admonitions of Ipuwer."

Middle Kingdom

The 11th dynasty can be considered the end of the First Intermediate and beginning of the Middle Kingdom, and central authority was gradually reestablished during this time. The founder of the 12th dynasty, Amenemhet I (reigned 1963–1934) moved the capital city to Itjawy, close to the traditional capital city of Memphis. In the 12th dynasty, Egypt had a series of strong and for the most part long-lived pharaohs (Amenemhet I, Sesostris I, Amenemhet II, Sesostris II, Sesostris III, Amenemhet III, Amenemhet IV, and Sobeknofru). As such, the 12th dynasty is the glory period of the Middle Kingdom. Quarries were reopened and monumental works were again produced. The beautiful White Chapel was built at the temple complex at Karnak by Sesostris I (reigned 1943–1898). The army was rebuilt, and Sesostris III (reigned 1862–1843) won significant victories against Nubia in the south. Amenemhet III (reigned 1843–1798) greatly expanded the development of the Faiyum by extending irrigation works and building a great mortuary complex at Hawara (called the "Labyrinth" by classical authors). He exploited the Sinai Peninsula for minerals, especially turquoise, and in the center of the peninsula at Serabit el-Khadim he enlarged a great shrine to Hathor. Canaanite workers in these mines gave us the first true Semitic alphabet, the Proto-Sinaitic script, which is the precursor to the standard Hebrew alphabet. Amenemhet III also established a city for "Asiatics" (Canaanites and other Semites) in Lower Egypt.[36]

---

36. Orly Goldwasser, "How the Alphabet was Born from Hieroglyphs," *BAR* 36, no. 2 (2010): 36–50.

Some important literature comes from this time. The most important of these is the autobiographical "Tale of Sinuhe," in which the protagonist, Sinuhe, tells us that he was an attendant of Nefru, wife of Sesostris I. When Sesostris died, however, Sinuhe feared that he would be killed in the subsequent political turmoil, and he fled Egypt. On his way out of the country, heading toward Canaan, he passed by fortifications built along Egypt's northeastern frontier; these, he tells us, had been put in place to keep the "Asiatics" out of Egypt. This is a valuable piece of information, as it illustrates how the Egyptians felt themselves to be under constant pressure from invaders or immigrants from Canaan. Sinuhe, now in self-imposed exile, took up residence in Canaan, which he describes as a good land, abundant in figs, wine, oil, honey, grains, and cattle. In this, and in his dealings with local kings and warlords, he provides us with a firsthand account of life in Middle Bronze Age Canaan. In an episode reminiscent of David and Goliath, he tells how he entered into single combat with a mighty champion and defeated him.[37]

Second Intermediate Period

The stability of the Middle Kingdom collapsed rather abruptly with the advent the 13th dynasty (1786–1633 B.C.), in which 70 kings ruled within about 150 years. Especially catastrophic for the country, however, was immigration (or invasion) of Semitic peoples from the Levant. These outsiders naturally congregated in the eastern Delta, at their point of entry, and they were soon numerous and powerful enough to seize control of Lower Egypt. The kings of the 15th and 16th dynasties (1648–1540 B.C.) were Semitic rather than Egyptian, and they are known as the Hyksos (from the Egyptian *heka khaswt*, "foreign rulers"). They established their capital at Avaris, in the eastern Delta. Not surprisingly, the Egyptians came to hate the outsiders who had taken control of at least part of their country. The Egyptian 17th dynasty (1633–1550 B.C.), ruling from Thebes in the south, set about driving out these foreign overlords.[38] On the other hand, the Hyksos

---

37. Miriam Lichtheim, *Ancient Egyptian Literature: A Book of Readings* (Berkeley: University of California, 1973), 1: 222–35.
38. A list of the kings of the 17th dynasty is found in Jürgen von Beckerath. "Theban Seventeenth Dynasty," in *Gold of Praise: Studies on Ancient Egypt in Honor of Edward F. Wente*, ed. Emily Teeter and John A. Larson (Chicago: University of Chicago, 1999), 21–26. This essay, focused entirely on constructing a sequence of 17th dynasty pharaohs, is a good example of

did bring new technologies into Egypt, such as improved metallurgy, new livestock breeds, and apparently also the military chariot.

New Kingdom
Ahmose I (reigned 1550–1525 B.C.), founder of the 18th dynasty, succeeded in driving out the Hyksos and establishing the New Kingdom. Egypt thereafter became an empire that reached through Canaan and into Syria. This was not an empire, however, in the sense that the Roman Empire was, with occupation, colonization and often direct governance of the conquered territories. The Egyptians preferred to remain in their own territory except for short campaigns and the establishment of a few fortified barracks in the region. In Canaan and Syria, local governments remained intact and demonstrated their submission to the pharaoh by the payment of tribute and by the submission to him of local disputes for adjudication.

As the New Kingdom is not only the greatest chapter of Egyptian history, but also the time in which the exodus probably took place, its pharaohs deserve special attention. From the 18th dynasty the following pharaohs are noteworthy.

- *Amenhotep I* (reigned 1525–1504): He is best known for a successful military campaign into Nubia in the south, from which he brought a great deal of wealth into Egypt. He also opened or expanded mining operations (for example, reviving turquoise mining in the Sinai), and he engaged in monumental building projects, especially at the temple site of Karnak, near Thebes. Devotion to the sun-god Amun and expansion of the temple facilities at Karnak, which became the center of pharaoh veneration, were marks of the 18th dynasty.

- *Thutmose I* (reigned 1504–1492): He continued the subjugation of Nubia, partly because of the threat the Nubians posed and partly to get his hands on the gold of that land. He also continued the expansion of the temple precinct at Karnak. To the northeast, Egyptian power extended as far as the Euphrates River in Syria, where Egypt came into conflict with the kingdom of Mitanni in northern Mesopotamia. While Nubia was directly administered by Egypt as a colony, however, Egyptian power in

---

the kind of puzzle Egyptologists must unravel and of the limitations of the data at their disposal.

the Levant was probably limited to making certain city-states into tributary vassals.

- *Thutmose II* (reigned 1492–1479): The length of his reign is actually much in doubt. Although the son of Thutmose I, his mother was a secondary wife. To strengthen his claim to the throne, therefore, he may have married his half-sister Hatshepsut, who was fully royal.[39] Be that as it may, Thutmose II was Thutmose I's designated heir, but a powerful faction coalesced around Hatshepsut at Thebes. And Thutmose II had a short time on the throne. Apart from his putting down a rebellion in Nubia, there is little that scholars can confidently ascribe to his reign. When Thutmose II died, his son and heir (by a harem girl named Isis) was only twelve years old.

- *Hatshepsut* (reigned 1479–1457): She was the most famous woman pharaoh of Egypt. At the death of Thutmose II, the crown passed to his son, Thutmose III. Hatshepsut (his aunt) was powerful enough to direct the government as regent. After a few years, however, she openly claimed the throne and governed as king, even taking a throne name for herself (Egyptian pharaohs had royal wives, but there were no governing queens, and thus she was in effect not "queen" but "king"). She did not set aside or do away with Thutmose III, however; he was regarded as her coregent. She expanded the commercial contacts of Egypt and is famous for having built a magnificent funerary temple for herself and her father (Thutmose I) at Deir el-Bahri. In popular Christian preaching, one may sometimes hear the claim that she was the "daughter of Pharaoh" who drew Moses from the Nile; there is absolutely no evidence to support this. A powerful pharaoh would have scores of daughters by his minor wives and concubines; even if Moses's birth was contemporary with Hatshepsut (and this cannot be established), there would have been many princesses of various rank at this time. Hatshepsut is an intriguing if somewhat enigmatic figure. After her death, her name was chiseled out of many inscriptions, while others were hidden or destroyed. Traditionally, this has

39. But some say that Thutmose II was not Thutmose I's son at all, but only his son-in-law. Also, evidence that he married Hatshepsut is thin (Hans Goedicke, *The Speos Artemidos Inscription of Hatshepsut and Related Discussions* [Oakville: Halgo, 2004], 107–12).

been attributed to the malice of Thutmose III, who supposedly hated her for exercising power while he was the rightful pharaoh. More recently, this theory has been questioned. It may be that the idea of a female pharaoh was regarded as unnatural.[40] Hatshepsut's mummy was recently discovered. She died in her early 50s perhaps of cancer or of diabetes complications. She was severely overweight at the time of her death.[41]

- *Thutmose III* (reigned 1479–1425, partly as coregent with Hatshepsut): He began to reign in his own right when Hatshepsut died around 1457. He became sole ruler at a moment of crisis—the king of Kadesh in Syria (probably with the prodding of Mitanni), had put together a powerful, anti-Egyptian coalition of Syrian states. Thutmose took the army north and won a great victory at Megiddo, a city in the Jezreel Valley in Canaan. He subsequently subdued the coastal cities of Canaan and also took Kadesh. In the 33rd year of his reign (about 1446) he crossed the Euphrates River and decisively defeated the king of the Mitanni in a pitched battle. Indeed, he was away on military campaigns throughout his reign—usually in Syria and Canaan but also in Nubia—and he seems to have chalked up one victory after another. He established Egyptian garrisons across the Levant and took tribute from subject kings. He also did great building works, especially at the temple of Amun at Karnak. If the "Early Date" for the exodus (1447) is correct, and if the Egyptian dates here are also followed, then the exodus took place in the middle of his reign, just around the time he was defeating the king of Mitanni in Syria. This seems implausible, suggesting that either the Early Date of the exodus or the chronology of the 18th dynasty is wrong.

- *Amenhotep II* (reigned 1427–1400): His reign was occupied with maintaining Egyptian hegemony over the Levant. To this end, he waged several campaigns to keep the empire from slipping away. Even so, the Egyptian Empire in Syria lost ground to Mitanni. Curiously, he is famous for having been very

40. Joyce A. Tyldesley, *Hatchepsut: The Female Pharaoh* (London: Penguin Books, 1998), 225.
41. Ayman Wahby Taher, "The Mummy of Hatshepsut Identified," *Ancient Egypt* 8, no. 2 (2007): 10–13.

athletic; he boasted, for example, of having been a terrific archer. Some believe that Amenhotep II was the pharaoh of the exodus, based partly on the lack of military campaigning late in his reign and partly on an anecdote concerning Thutmose IV, described below. To sustain the claim that Amenhotep II is the pharaoh of the exodus, however, one must adjust the date for the exodus (normally dated to about 1447 if the Early Date is followed), or for Amenhotep II's reign, or for both.

- *Thutmose IV* (reigned 1400–1390): Like his predecessors, Thutmose IV tried to maintain Egypt's empire in the Levant. Near the end of his reign he negotiated a peace treaty with Mitanni, and his successor, Amenhotep III, took a Mitanni princess as his wife. A peculiar fact about this pharaoh is used to make the argument that Amenhotep II was pharaoh of the exodus. As a young prince, he had military duty at Memphis, near the pyramids. He had a dream, he claimed, in which the god Horus told him that he would become pharaoh if he freed the sphinx from the sand in which it was trapped (in ancient Egypt even great monuments could be swallowed by the shifting sands of the desert). It is thought that Thutmose IV told this story to legitimatize his claim to the throne, and that he needed to do this because an elder brother, who should have become the pharaoh, suddenly died. This brother could have been, it is suggested, the firstborn of Pharaoh, who died in the last plague. If so, this sets the date for the exodus. This is a possible scenario, but it is impossible to prove, and it is a very slender basis for dating the exodus. Many pharaohs were not succeeded by their firstborn sons; Ramesses II's successor, Merenptah, was his thirteenth son!

- *Amenhotep III* (reigned 1390–1352): Peace having been established with Mitanni, he devoted himself largely to building up the great city of Thebes. His reign was long, peaceful, and prosperous. Two famous individuals from his reign are his chief wife, Tiy, and his master builder, Amenhotep son of Hapu. The former was the daughter of a commoner but came to be a favored and competent political adviser to the pharaoh. The latter directed the great construction work of this time.

- *Amenhotep IV/Akhenaten* (reigned 1352–1336): He was the famous "heretic" pharaoh. Although he at first continued to build up the temple complex at Karnak, he soon underwent a religious transformation and became in practice, and possibly in theology, a monotheist. He disregarded all the cults of the other gods, began to build a grand new city and worship complex at el-Amarna, and devoted himself to the worship of the sun-disk Aten (he also changed his name to from Amenhotep to Akhenaten; he called his new city Akhetaten—both of the new names honored Aten). During his reign the empire in the Levant deteriorated, and local kings throughout Canaan sent him correspondence begging for assistance. Perhaps he was too preoccupied with his new city and religion to be bothered with these matters. Also, in the north, the power of Egypt's ally, Mitanni, began to fail under the onslaught of the emerging Hittite Empire, coming out of central Anatolia (modern Turkey). Shortly after Akhenaten's death his new city and religion were both abandoned. The correspondence he received from Canaan had been inscribed on clay tablets and mostly written in Akkadian, the diplomatic language of the day. Some letters date from the reign of his father, Amenhotep III, and the latest letters date from the first years of his successor, Tutankhamun, but most are from his reign. Also, some letters are from Mesopotamia or Mitanni, but most are from the Levant. They were found by a peasant woman in 1887 (382 tablets were eventually recovered). These letters are of enormous importance for the study of Canaan in the Late Bronze Age, and they are known as the Amarna Letters.

- *Tutankhamun* (reigned 1336–1327): He was a boy when Akhenaten died, and the country was governed by a regent. The Restoration Stele, a monument from his reign, describes how terrible conditions were under the heretic Akhenaten and how the new pharaoh restored order. Tutankhamun died at about 18 years of age and his reign was otherwise unremarkable except for the fact in 1922 the English Egyptologist Howard Carter discovered his tomb basically intact—that is, although grave robbers had found it, they had left a great deal behind (all other pharaonic tombs had been thoroughly plundered). Thus, from the treasures that were placed in his tomb, modern people were able to get a glance at the wealth and treasure of Egypt. At Tutankhamun's death, a period of confusion followed, in which a courtier named Ay, Tutankhamun's widow Ankhesenamun, and a general named Haremhab struggled for power. Eventually Haremhab won out, even though he was by his own admission without royal blood. He was the last pharaoh of the 18th dynasty.

- *Ramesses I* (reigned 1295–1294): He had been Haremhab's vizier, and as the former died childless, he was made Haremhab's heir. He begins a new dynasty, the 19th.

- *Seti I* (reigned 1294–1279): He restored Egypt, repairing the damage done in the latter years of the 18th dynasty. He finished the work of restoring the traditional religion. He resumed the work of building up the temple precinct at Karnak. At Abydos, a little to the north of Thebes, he built a grand mortuary temple for himself. He also set about rebuilding Egypt's empire in the Levant. When he came to the throne, Egypt's holdings in Palestine had been reduced to three fortified cities at Beth Shean, Rehob, and Megiddo. Egypt's chief rival for control in this area was now the Hittite Empire, against which he fought at least one war. Also, although he maintained Thebes as his capital city, he recognized the need for a royal presence in the north and built a royal palace near Avaris, the former Hyksos capital, in the eastern Delta.

- *Ramesses II* (reigned 1279–1213): The most famous of the pharaohs, he reigned for 67 years and fully restored the glory of the Egyptian Empire. He led a series of campaigns into the north to regain full control of the Levant. He encountered the Hittite army in a great battle at Kadesh, on the Orontes River in Syria. In this battle, Ramesses was cut off with a small number of men by a much larger Hittite army, but by personal valor (so he claims in his monuments) he held off the enemy onslaught until Egyptian reinforcements arrived. The Egyptians failed to take Kadesh and the battle was for them at best a narrowly escaped catastrophe, but the pharaoh's courage was celebrated in numerous inscriptions. Egypt and the Hittites made peace in 1258, and Egyptian suzerainty over Palestine was restored (Ramesses II campaigned, for example, against Moab and Edom). He went on to be one of the greatest builders of all the pharaohs, constructing or enlarging temples and monuments all across Egypt, especially in Thebes and Abydos. He had colossal statues built to himself at Abu Simbel, far to the south (these statues had to be moved away from the Nile in the 1960s, during construction of the Aswan Dam, to save them from the waters of Lake Nasser). He also built a new capital city for himself at Pi-Riʿ*amsese* (the biblical store-city of Raamses) at the site where Seti I had built a palace, near Avaris. In the Late Date model for the exodus, Ramesses II was the pharaoh of the exodus.

- *Merenptah* (reigned 1213–1203): The thirteenth son of Ramesses II, he took over the kingdom after his father's 67-year reign (many of Ramesses's 150 children having predeceased him). Egypt's military prowess had declined with the increasing age of Ramesses, moreover, and thus Merenptah faced a number of challenges when he took the throne. He had to put down rebellion in Canaan, and he faced an invasion from the west of Libyans and Sea Peoples. The latter group refers to Indo-European peoples, some of whom were Greek, who pushed south across the Mediterranean during the 13th century. Making good tactical use of his archers, Merenptah slaughtered the invaders in the western Delta area and so saved Egypt. Already about 60 when he became pharaoh, however, Merenptah died as an old man and Egypt fell into confusion. The 19th dynasty thus came to an end. For biblical studies, the most important record of Merenptah's reign is a monumental stele he erected to commemorate his victories in Canaan. It includes the line, "Israel lies waste, its seed no longer exists," and this constitutes the first extrabiblical reference to Israel. We thus know that Israel was settled in Canaan by 1209, when the stele was written. The exodus, therefore, can be dated no later than the reign of Ramesses II.

After a period of civil war and usurpers, the 20th dynasty was established by Setnakht (reigned 1186–1184). Order was reestablished by the end of his reign, and his son, Ramesses III (reigned 1184–1153), inherited a fairly unified Egypt. He soon faced the challenge of renewed invasion from Libya in the northwest and from Sea Peoples in the northeast. He successfully beat off both attacks, and his defeat of the Sea Peoples was commemorated in a great inscription at his mortuary temple at Medinet Habu (in the area of Thebes). The repulsed Sea Peoples almost certainly included a group known as the Pilisti, who settled in the southwest part of Canaan and became the biblical Philistines. After the death of Ramesses III, the 20th dynasty went into a long decline, and by the time it ended (in about 1069 B.C.) the New Kingdom era was over.

Third Intermediate Period
Egypt was no longer politically unified. Pharaohs of the 21st dynasty ruled from Tanis in the Delta (the capital at Pi-Riʿamsese having been abandoned due to silting up of waterways). But parts of Egypt were effectively independent; much of southern Egypt, for example, was controlled by Theban high priests. Not all the dynasties were made up of native Egyptians. For example, the Libyan pharaoh Shoshenq I (reigned 945–924) established the 22nd dynasty. He sought to bring all of Egypt under his control, and he was in part successful. He also conducted an expedition into Israel and Canaan that stripped the land of its wealth (he is the Shishak of 1 Kings 14:25[42]). The record of his achievement is inscribed on the "Bubastite Portal" at Karnak, in Thebes. The 25th dynasty (780–656 B.C.) was Nubian and included the pharaoh Taharqa (690–664 B.C.), famous from 2 Kings 19:9. At times there were rival dynasties in Egypt.

The Remainder of Ancient Egyptian History
Egyptian power briefly rose again under Psammetichus I (reigned 664–610 B.C.), who expelled the Assyrians and Nubians and also reunified Egypt. He established the 26th or "Saite" dynasty (so-called because they ruled from Sais, in the western Delta). He was followed by Necho II (reigned 610–595). Hoping to curb the rising power of the Babylonians and Medes, he moved his army through Israel, defeating and killing Josiah of Judah along the way (2 Kings 23:29). Necho II was defeated at Carchemish (605 B.C.) and driven back into Egypt by Nebuchadnezzar II of Babylon. Egypt was annexed into the Persian Empire by Cambyses in 525 B.C. The fall of the Persian Empire to Alexander the Great led to the Greek takeover of Egypt in 332. After Alexander's death in 323, Ptolemy I (one of Alexander's Macedonian generals) seized Egypt, and his dynasty ruled Egypt until the death of the last Ptolemaic ruler, the famous Cleopatra VII (reigned 52–30 B.C.). After Antony and Cleopatra were defeated by Octavius (the emperor Augustus) in 31 B.C., Egypt was placed under imperial rule as a Roman province.

A Word about the Egyptian Language
Readers of this commentary will in a few places encounter transliterated Egyptian, and thus it is advisable that they be acquainted

42. The dates for the reign of Shoshenq I, as well as his identification with the biblical Shishak, are fairly well-established. See A. J. Shortland, "Shishak, King of Egypt," in *The Bible and Radiocarbon Dating*, ed. Thomas E. Levy and Thomas Higham (London: Equinox, 2005), 43–54.

with basic issues concerning the language. Egyptian is classified as an Afro-Asiatic language, having some traits in common with Semitic languages, but other traits in common with African languages such as Cushitic and Berber. It is a dead language today, except as it survives in the liturgy of the Coptic Church.

As is well known, classical Egyptian was written in hieroglyphs. These were pictures that served either as phonograms (signs indicating sounds, just as Roman letters indicate sounds), logograms (signs indicating specific words), or determinatives (signs that classify the meaning of a sign to disambiguate it). For example, if English used such a writing system, a picture of an eye could mean the noun "eye" (this would be a logogram), or it could be used to be the sound of the English long "i" (ī; it would here be a phonogram). Similarly, a picture of waves could mean "sea" when used as a logogram, but as the sound "sea" when used as a phonogram. Therefore, a picture of waves with a picture of an eye below it could be used for the verb "see" (the waves representing "sea" would be the phonogram, indicating how the word is pronounced, but the eye would be a determinative, telling the reader that this word is related to vision).

Egyptian hieroglyphs number in the hundreds, and these are organized into standard categories. Used as phonograms, some hieroglyphs represent a single consonant, while others represent two or three consonants. Unfortunately, hieroglyphs do not represent vowels, although some letters represent semi-vowels, similar to the English "y." And since ancient Egyptian had no tradition to preserve the pronunciation of the words, scholars are not entirely certain how the words were pronounced (although there are certain scholarly conventions for pronunciation, such as inserting the vowel "e" after certain letters). For this reason, the English spelling of Egyptian proper names and words can vary from one scholar to the next. For example, many Egyptian tombs contain little figurines of men and women. In the afterlife, these were supposed to become servants who would do work for the deceased. These figures are variously called by the name "shabti," or "ushabti," or "shawabti." Because the script has no vowels, no one can be sure of the pronunciation of the word. Similarly, the spelling variants for the names of pharaohs and gods can be quite confusing.[43]

Ancient Egyptian could also be written in a shorthand kind of

43. For the sake of consistency in this text, place names follow the spelling in Baines and Málek, *Cultural Atlas*; pharaohs follow the spelling in Kitchen, "Egypt, Chronology"; and deities follow the spelling in Barbara Watterson, *The Gods of Ancient Egypt* (London: Sutton, 1984).

hieroglyphs called hieratic, or, beginning about the 7th century B.C., in a cursive hieratic called demotic. Hieratic and demotic are difficult to work with, and scholars typically transcribe these into standard hieroglyphs and use that as a basis for translation work. In addition, scholars use a standard set of transliterations when discussing Egyptian words. It turns out that in spite of the large number of hieroglyphic signs, Egyptian writing can be reduced to a transliteration system of consonants. These are given in Table 2.

TABLE 2. TRANSLITERATION OF EGYPTIAN CONSONANTS

Sign	Value	Sign	Value	Sign	Value
ꜣ	Weak glottal stop	*n*	N	*ḳ*	Q
j	Weak glottal stop	*r*	R	*k*	K
y	Y	*h*	H	*g*	G
ꜥ	Strong glottal stop	*ḥ*	"throaty" H	*t*	T
w	W	*ḫ*	German ch	*ṯ*	Tj
b	B	*ẖ*	German ch + y	*d*	D
p	P	*z*	Z, S	*ḏ*	Dj
f	F	*s*	S		
m	M	*š*	Sh		

The values for the letters given above are simplified, and the transliteration follows the European transliteration system used by James Allen.[44] In an older transliteration system, *j* is transliterated as *í*, *z* is transliterated as *s*, and *s* is transliterated as *ś*. The Egyptians no doubt had slightly different pronunciation for each of the four "h" letters, as

44. James P. Allen, *Middle Egyptian: An Introduction to the Language and Culture of Hieroglyphs* (Cambridge: Cambridge University Press, 2000), 14–7.

suggested above. A "glottal stop" is like the Hebrew א or ע. The first glottal stop (ꜣ) is something like the א; it is not the number 3! When you come across a word of transliterated Egyptian, it is not necessary to try to pronounce it. In fact, nobody today really knows how to pronounce it.

THE REALITY AND DATE OF THE EXODUS

The exodus of Israel from Egypt is historical and occurred as described in the book of Exodus. Today, however, many scholars believe that the exodus tradition at best has only a small kernel of truth and at worst is entirely fictional.[45] To be sure, they are aware that the exodus event dominates the Israelite consciousness of their history (Amos 9:7, for example, makes no sense unless one understands that the prophet is speaking to people who believed that the exodus made them different from every other people). Scholars who believe that the exodus is a myth need to account for this.

Ronald Hendel, for example, embarks on a new kind of tradition criticism to explain elements of the exodus story. The notion of enslavement in Egypt, he says, arose from the many experiences of western Semites with enslavement to Egyptians. But there were many small examples of such slavery through the centuries, and not one great example of the enslavement of one people, Israel. Similarly, the tradition of the plagues of Egypt is a gathering together and retelling of many examples of plagues, famines, and disasters in Egyptian history. The story of Moses is greatly expanded and folded into the traditions of enslavement, plagues, exodus, and wilderness wanderings. Of the man himself, Hendel claims, we can be sure of little more than that he had an Egyptian name and that he is associated with Midian.[46] Against

45. E.g., John J. Collins, *Introduction to the Hebrew Bible* (Minneapolis: Fortress, 2004), 108–10.
46. Ronald Hendel, "The Exodus in Biblical Memory," *JBL* 120, no. 4 (2001): 601–22. Hendel builds upon the reseach of Jan Assmann, *Moses the Egyptian: The Memory of Egypt in Western Monotheism* (Cambridge, MA: Harvard University Press, 1997), who describes his approach as "mnemohistory," which focuses not on what actually happened but on how ancient peoples remembered their past. On the other hand, Hendel's analysis is reminiscent of the now discarded tradition history of Martin Noth, except that Noth's work was based more in the analysis of the biblical text, and Hendel (following Assmann) makes a case that is more rooted in archaeology.

such a radical recasting of the exodus, what may one say in defense of the historicity of the narrative?[47]

Ideally, we ought to consider whether the exodus is a historical fact before we consider when it occurred. It turns out, however, that a number of the arguments for establishing the date of the exodus are also critical for establishing the reality of the exodus. For the sake of presentation, moreover, it is easier to comprehend some of the data first in relation to the date. Therefore, we begin our study with an examination of the date of the exodus.

As is widely known, the exodus is often dated either to about 1447 B.C. (the "Early Date") or to the mid-thirteenth century, about 1250 B.C. (the "Late Date").[48] This is not to say that these are the only two possibilities, and we will also consider two other alternatives (see below, "A Very Early Date or a Very Late Date?"). Nevertheless, we will begin with the standard Early Date and Late Date to give focus to our discussion.

The Late Date

Although the Late Date for the exodus once dominated the field,[49] it lost a great deal of support with the collapse of the Albright model.[50]

47. I will not concern myself with alternative theories for accounting for the origin of Israel, such as the partial exodus theory, the native revolt theory, or the gradual migration theory, as that would take me too far afield of my main purposes.
48. One can find a variety of opinions among the commentaries. Douglas K. Stuart, *Exodus,* NAC 2 (Nashville: Broadman & Holman, 2006), 24, supports an Early Date, while R. Alan Cole, *Exodus: An Introduction and Commentary,* TOTC (Downer's Grove: InterVarsity, 1973), 43, prefers a Late Date, as does Nahum M. Sarna, *Exodus: The Traditional Hebrew Text with the New JPS Translation, Commentary,* The JPS Torah Commentary (Philadelphia: Jewish Publication Society, 1991), xiv. Others are hesitant to ascribe a date to the exodus or set its events against events known from Egyptian history. See Terence E. Fretheim, *Exodus,* IBC (Louisville: John Knox, 1991), 9–10; Peter Enns, *Exodus: From Biblical Text to Contemporary Life,* NIV Application Commentary (Grand Rapids: Zondervan, 2000), 23–5; Durham, *Exodus*, xxiv-xxvi; Cornelis Houtman, *Exodus,* trans. Johan Rebel and Sierd Woudstra, Historical Commentary on the Old Testament (Kampen: Kok, 1993), 175–9.
49. For a succinct presentation of the classic arguments for placing the exodus in the late 13th century, see Nahum M. Sarna, "Exploring Exodus: the Oppression," *BA* 49, no. 2 (1986): 68–80.
50. This was an attempt, at the middle of the 20th century, to bring about a grand unification of biblical history and archaeological data. It is named for the great polymath William F. Albright. As part of the synthesis, it

Critical scholars began to move away from the historicity of the exodus entirely, and conservative scholars tended toward the Early Date model. Thus, in recent years it has had few vocal advocates. K. A. Kitchen, however, continues to support the Late Date model; he has made a strong case for this position in *On the Reliability of the Old Testament*,[51] and he is by no means the only contemporary evangelical defender of the Late Date.[52] As such, we must reopen the question of the date of the exodus.

Biblical Data

Exodus 1:11 states that the Israelites worked on the construction of a city called Raamses. We know that this city was built by and named for Ramesses II (reigned 1279–1213). Taken at face value, this indicates that the Israelites were present and working in Egypt during the reign of Ramesses II in the 13th century. Therefore, the Israelites could not have already left Egypt in the 15th century, as the Early Date for the exodus demands. Although the significance of Exod. 1:11 is debatable (see the discussion below of "The Store Cities"), as a piece of evidence it must be reckoned to be supportive of the Late Date.

Two other biblical passages are often cited as evidence for the date of the exodus, however, and these are problems for the Late Date. 1 Kings 6:1 tells us that the construction of Solomon's temple began in the 480th year after the exodus; dating the former to about 967, the latter figures to have taken place in 1447. In addition, in Judg. 11:26 the Israelite "judge" Jephthah asserts to the Ammonites that in his

---

postulated an exodus during the reign of Ramesses II. The historical synthesis is capably presented in John Bright, *A History of Israel* (Philadelphia: Westminster, 1959). This historical reconstruction, which at one time was dominant in American scholarship, had a number of weaknesses. By about 1980 it had largely been abandoned in mainstream scholarship.

51. See Kenneth A. Kitchen, *On the Reliability of the Old Testament* (Grand Rapids: Eerdmans, 2003). Kitchen's main point is not to defend the Late Date but to defend the historicity of the Old Testament. But for the exodus, he does this entirely within the framework of a late-date model, and his arguments support that reconstruction of events.
52. See Iain W. Provan, V. Philips Long and Tremper Longman, *A Biblical History of Israel* (Louisville: Westminster John Knox Press, 2003), 131–2; Ralph K. Hawkins, "Propositions for Evangelical Acceptance of a Late–Date Exodus–Conquest: Biblical Data and the Royal Scarabs from Mt. Ebal," *JETS* 50, no. 1 (2007): 31–46; and James K. Hoffmeier, "What is the Biblical Date for the Exodus?" A Response to Bryant Wood," *JETS* 50, no. 2 (2007): 225–47.

lifetime Israel had already been settled in the land for 300 years. If Israel did not enter Canaan until the latter part of the 13th century, they obviously could not have already been there for 300 years at the time when Jephthah spoke. Kitchen must deal with these two passages if he is to sustain his claim that the exodus did not take place until around 1250.

Regarding the 480 years of 1 Kings 6:1, an old explanation is that the number 480 refers to twelve generations, and that each generation is by convention set at 40 years (thus, 12 × 40 = 480). But in the ancient world the actual time from the birth of one generation to the next was in reality probably about 23 years. Thus, twelve generations is really about 276 years, which works well as the chronological gap between the exodus and the temple for the Late Date. The difficulty here, of course, is that the text never speaks of a "twelve-generation" gap, only a gap of 480 years. We should observe, however, that 1 Chron. 6:3–8 indicates that the high priest Zadok (living in the reign of David) was a tenth-generation descendant of Aaron. Although this is conceivable with a 15th century Aaron, it is more reasonable with the 13th century Aaron of the Late Date.

Kitchen, however, prefers to believe that the author of kings has given us a figure of 480 by selectively using the chronological data of Exodus–Judges. Specifically, he thinks that the figure refers to the aggregate of all years during which Israel was not under oppression plus years for the wilderness wandering and for the reigns of the early kings. He suggests that the source for the figure 480 may have come from the data outlined in Table 3.[53]

This is, to say the least, a creative way of looking at the data; the assignment of 5 years to the period of Joshua's leadership is arbitrary, as Kitchen acknowledges. We should not automatically assume, on the other hand, that biblical writers reckoned time as we do (see "A Caveat on Early Biblical Chronology" below). As Kitchen notes, if we add up all of the years mentioned in the Bible from the exodus to Solomon, we actually get 554 years plus an unknown number of years for the governments of Joshua, of Samuel, and of Saul. Advocates of both the Early Date and the Late Date try to find some way to compress this span of time. A period of over 554 years is certainly not compatible with an exodus at 1447, and those who protest that they read the Bible literally at 1 Kings 6:1 find themselves reading the Bible in a nonliteral manner in Judges. Kitchen also tabulates the data for the years of the judges in a manner that plausibly sets it within a framework of about

53. Kitchen, *Reliability*, 308–9.

1200 to 1000 B.C.[54] His proposal cannot be proven, but it should not be dismissed as mere cleverness. It is reasonable and is respectful to the Bible, reading it as an ancient book which presents data in a way meaningful to ancient—not modern—readers. One must say that, as a piece of evidence, 1 Kings 6:1 favors the Early Date, but also that Kitchen's argument is plausible when seen against the backdrop of ancient historiography and of the fact that the literal reading of the years given in Joshua–Judges–Samuel chronology is incompatible with the *prima facie* interpretation of 1 Kings 6:1. Kitchen's interpretation may be the only one that actually finds a way to reconcile the chronology of Joshua–Judges–Samuel with 1 Kings 6:1.

TABLE 3. THE 480 YEARS OF 1 KINGS 6:1 ACCORDING TO K. A. KITCHEN

Years	Source
40	Egypt to Jordan (Num. 11:33)
40	Othniel (Judg. 3:11)
80	Peace after Ehud (Judg. 3:30)
40	Peace after Deborah (Judg. 5:31)
40	Gideon (Judg. 8:28)
48 (3+23+22)	Abimelech, Tola, Jair (Judg. 9:22; 10:2–3)
31 (6+7+10+8)	Jephthah, Ibzan, Elon, Abdon (Judg. 12:7; 9, 11, 14)
40	Eli (1 Sam. 4:18)
40	Samson and Samuel (Judg. 15:20; 1 Sam. 7:2)
32	Probable years for Saul (see 1 Sam. 13:1)
40	David (1 Kings 2:11)
4	Solomon's years prior to beginning temple
5	Proposed years for Joshua and elders
480	Total years

54. Ibid., 202–9.

Kitchen fairly disregards Jephthah's claim that Israel had in his day already been in the land for 300 years (Judg. 11:26) on the grounds that Jephthah was a blustering brute who did not really know or care how long ago Israel had settled in Canaan.[55] He was, after all, only interested in shouting down the king of the Ammonites. Confidence in the authority of the Bible does not require us to believe that Jephthah was correct in what he said, only that he really said what he is claimed to have said. There is some support in the text for the view that Jephthah did not know much about the local history and culture; he refers to Chemosh as the god of the Ammonites (Judg. 11:24) when in fact Chemosh was the chief god of Moab (Num. 21:29). Milcom was the chief god of the Ammonites (2 Kings 23:13). On the other hand, Jephthah does display fairly good knowledge of the stories of the Israelite conquest (Judg. 11:15–22). Thus, we cannot treat his claim that Israel had been in the land for 300 years as worthless. As a piece of evidence, his testimony favors the Early Date.

Historical Arguments

An interpretation of 1 Kings 6:1 and Judg. 11:26 that sets aside the apparent literal meaning is only necessary if there are important historical reasons for doing so. Several such arguments, which support the Late Date, may be brought forward.

Archaeology of the Israelite Hill Country

Although it is not an absolute diagnostic indicator, a combination of two factors generally indicates that remains from Iron I sites in Palestine are Israelite settlements and not Canaanite settlements. These are (1) the presence of a kind of an inferior, utilitarian pottery, and in particular the "collared-rim" pithos,[56] and (2) a type of house floor plan commonly referred to as the "four-room house." Kitchen, following the reports of I. Finkelstein and of A. Zertal, observes that there was a sudden appearance of settlements in the Ephraim hill country at the beginning of Iron I, around 1200. Diagnostic indicators, including pottery, building construction, and even diet (the lack of pig remains among these settlements) implies that they were occupied by Israelites rather than Canaanites. Alternative theories of where these Israelites came from (such as Finkelstein's view that they arose from the indigenous population) do not work. Thus, there is little in the way of a

55. Ibid., 209.
56. See Amihai Mazar, *Archaeology of the Land of the Bible: 10,000–586 B.C.E.* (New York: Doubleday, 1992), 345–8.

realistic explanation for this situation except that they came in from the outside.[57]

This implies that the biblical story—that the Israelites invaded the land from without—is true. The data, however, most clearly supports the Late Date for the exodus, since there is no evidence for an Israelite presence from an earlier time, around 1407 B.C., when the early-date theory claims the conquest took place. Any attempt to advocate for the early conquest must account for how the Israelites remained invisible for 200 years. One can make arguments along these lines: perhaps the Israelites continued to live in tents or occupied existing housing (Deut. 19:1), and perhaps they initially used pottery similar to that used by the Canaanites. If so, they would be archaeologically invisible. Still, it is hard to see how they remained in this status for almost 200 years. All in all, the settlement data from archaeology favors the Late Date.

THE LOCATION OF THE EGYPTIAN CAPITAL CITY

The capital city during the 18th dynasty was Thebes, in Upper Egypt and 500 miles south of the Mediterranean. Goshen, where the Hebrews resided in the northeastern Delta, was therefore two or three weeks travel time (by river along the Nile) from the Egyptian capital. In this situation, it is difficult to understand the frequent contact between members of the royal household and Israelites described in Exodus. Moses makes many visits to Pharaoh. It is true that the pharaohs had several palaces and were sometimes in residence at Memphis, just south of the Delta, but even that city was well south of Goshen. An 18th dynasty pharaoh may have maintained a palace in the northeast Delta and may have been in residence when Moses was there, but this is all speculation. By contrast, the royal residence of Ramesses II at Raamses (or Pi-Riʿamsese) was close by Goshen and thus the constant interaction between Moses and Pharaoh needs no explanation. This favors the Late Date.

JOSHUA'S ALTAR ON MT. EBAL

From 1982 to 1989 Israeli archaeologist Adam Zertal excavated a site on Mt. Ebal dating to the Iron I period (1200–1000). Most significantly, Zertal believed that he found the very altar of Joshua's covenant ceremony described in Josh. 8:30–35. On the basis of pottery and scarabs found at the sight Zertal concluded that the altar should

57. Kitchen, *Reliability* 224–30. For an alternative approach to the problem, see William G. Dever, *Who Were the Early Israelites and Where Did They Come From?* (Grand Rapids: Eerdmans, 2003).

be dated from the 13th to 12th centuries B.C.[58] If this is Joshua's altar, then plainly the conquest could not have taken place in the late 15th and early 14th centuries, as the Early Date requires.[59] Not surprisingly, Zertal's claim to have found Joshua's altar on Mt. Ebal has been challenged.[60] Needless to say, those of us who believe that the Bible is true would love to see Zertal vindicated (the notion that Joshua's very altar may have been found is truly exciting). On the other hand, if one is convinced that the Early Date for the exodus is the only viable option, one is in the unusual position, for an evangelical, of wanting to see his claim overturned. Zertal, at any rate, responded to his opponents and argues that the ceramic evidence indicates that the Mt. Ebal site is indeed Israelite and from the 12th century.[61]

The Problem of Shechem

Shechem is a special problem for the Early Date. Located in the hill country between Mt. Ebal and Mt. Gerizim, Shechem is where, according to Josh. 8:30–35, the Israelites renewed the covenant, proclaiming the curses and blessings of the Law. Again, in Josh. 24, Joshua gathered the people at Shechem to give them his valedictory address. The book never states that Shechem was destroyed or conquered; it is as though there were no Canaanites in Shechem at all. Deuteronomy, moreover, appears to put the first sanctuary of Israel at Mt. Ebal, right by Shechem.[62]

Arguing, as it does, that the conquest occurred in about 1407, the Early Date model has a significant problem here. The Amarna Letters indicate that Shechem, under its king Labayu, was not only occupied but was one of the most powerful states of Canaan at this time, in Late Bronze IIA. For example, in EA 244 (among the Amarna Letters), Biridiya, king of Megiddo, is fearful that Labayu, king of

58. Adam Zertal, "Has Joshua's Altar Been Found on Mt. Ebal?" *BAR* 11, no. 1 (1985): 26–43.
59. See Hawkins, "Evangelical Acceptance," 36–46.
60. See Hershel Shanks, "Two Early Israelite Cult Sites Now Questioned," *BAR* 14, no. 1 (1988): 48–52. Describing the review of the Ebal site by Michael Coogan, Shanks reports that Coogan concluded that it was indeed cultic but not necessarily Israelite.
61. Adam Zertal, "Israel Enters Canaan—Following the Pottery Trail," *BAR* 17, no. 5 (1991): 29–49, 75.
62. See Sandra L. Richter, "The Place of the Name in Deuteronomy," *VT* 57, no.3 (2007): 342–66.

Shechem, will come and conquer his city.[63] Excavations at the site confirm that Shechem was a strong city around 1400 B.C. This period of Shechemite glory came to an end between 1350 and 1300; the city was destroyed, and the Late Bronze IIB Shechem was a shoddy, insignificant site.[64]

Kitchen suggests that this fits the biblical portrayal of the 13th century, when he believes Joshua was there. Shechem was a village without a king, and it was too insignificant to merit mention in Joshua other than as a location.[65] If Joshua arrived at Shechem around 1407, however, according to our present knowledge it should have been one of his most formidable enemies. One may try to save the Early Date by suggesting that the Shechemites allied themselves to Israel, but this is an ad hoc solution and unsatisfactory. Joshua 9 is fairly clear that Gibeon was the only city in alliance with Israel, and that only by deceit. Thus, our current understanding of the data strongly favors the Late Date for the exodus.

The Suzerainty Treaty Form

The "suzerainty treaty form" refers to the formal elements and the sequence of those elements in a treaty between a greater power, the "suzerain," and a lesser power, the "vassal." For example, the Sinai covenant, as presented in Deuteronomy, is a treaty between a suzerain (YHWH) and a vassal (Israel). It contains a number of formal elements. These include a title (1:1–5), historical prologue (1:6–3:29), stipulations (5–26), blessings and curses (28), rules for the depositing of the text (31:9, 24–26), a provision for witnesses (31:19–22), and so forth.

In 1954, building on the work of other scholars, George Mendenhall noted that these elements in the biblical covenants have parallels in suzerain-vassal treaties found in the ancient Near East.[66] Many copies of treaties from the Hittite Empire have been recovered, along with treaties from Babylon, the Third Dynasty of Ur, Mari, and elsewhere. These suzerain-vassal treaties may be very similar, in form, to the biblical covenants, having many of the same elements in the same order. Or, they may have only a few elements in common with the biblical examples. But the presence or absence or a given element (for example,

63. "EA 244," translated by W. F. Albright and George E. Mendenhall (*ANET* 485).
64. See Itzhak Magen, "Shechem," *NEAEHL* 4:1345–59.
65. Kitchen, *Reliability*, 162–3.
66. George E. Mendenhall, "Covenant Forms in the Israelite Tradition," *BA* 17, no. 3 (1954): 50–76.

whether it has or does not have a stipulation for witnesses) is not a random matter. Treaties did not arbitrarily include or exclude formal elements. They followed standard patterns, like the standard forms for modern legal contracts, and the inclusion or exclusion of a given element was determined by what was in fashion, so to speak, at the time. Thus, one can uncover a clear chronological typology, whereby any given treaty or covenant follows the pattern used in the era from which it came. In short, the formal structure of a treaty is a useful tool for dating that treaty.

As a result of this, scholars began to debate whether formal parallels demand that the book of Deuteronomy be dated to late 2nd millennium, rather than to the mid-1st millennium, where critical scholars had generally dated the composition of Deuteronomy. For example, Meredith Kline used the parallels to argue that Deuteronomy is from the time of Moses.[67] D. J. McCarthy[68] and Moshe Weinfeld,[69] on the other hand, argued that the data does not require a 2nd millennium date and placed Deuteronomy in the Neo-Assyrian (1st millennium) context. Kitchen, however, after making an exhaustive comparison of the Sinai covenant form as it exists in the Old Testament (in Exodus–Leviticus, in Deuteronomy, and in Joshua 24) with all extant suzerain-vassal treaties from the ancient Near East, shows rather conclusively that these three presentations of the covenant cannot possibly be from the 1st millennium. On formal grounds, he claims, the Sinai covenant must come from the late 2nd millennium, about 1400–1200 B.C.[70] This favors the late exodus date. By contrast, he argues that treaties from 1600–1400 (corresponding to an early exodus) lack certain elements, such as the historical prologue. Against Kitchen, I am not completely convinced that a formal analysis can adjudicate the dating of the Sinai covenants in so narrow a range, whether they date from the late-15th century or the late-13th century.[71] But since Kitchen has done exten-

67. Meredith G. Kline, *Treaty of the Great King; the Covenant Structure of Deuteronomy: Studies and Commentary* (Grand Rapids: Eerdmans, 1963).
68. McCarthy 1963.
69. Moshe Weinfeld, *Deuteronomy and the Deuteronomic School* (London: Oxford University Press, 1972).
70. Kitchen, *Reliability,* 283–94.
71. Hoffmeier, "Biblical Date," 246, notes that Kitchen himself warns that the data cannot be read too precisely, since the biblical texts are records and not actual covenant documents.

sive research with the original sources, his conclusions must be taken seriously, even if they are not unassailable.[72]

The Early Date

The Early Date for the exodus has long been maintained by many conservative Christian interpreters on the grounds that it is most compatible with the biblical data.[73] It is not clear, however, that this consensus will stand much longer, or even if it still stands today. In 1972, Bruce Waltke argued that biblical and archaeological data made a date of about 1407 for the conquest to be all but a certainty.[74] In his 2007 *An Old Testament Theology*, however, he showed that he had lost this confidence about the dates for the exodus and conquest, and he even followed K. A. Kitchen in dating all of the judges to the 12th century, after the Late Date model for the conquest.[75]

Biblical Data

The Early Date begins by assuming that the 480 years of 1 Kings 6:1 are strictly sequential and neither an aggregate nor representative of an artificial convention of 12 generations multiplied by 40 years. It

72. Bryant G. Wood, "The Rise and Fall of the 13th Century Exodus-Conquest Theory," *JETS* 48, no. 3 (2005), 479–83, stoutly attacks Kitchen's use of the covenant structure, stating, "Kitchen has merely manipulated the biblical data to support his pre-conceived conclusion as to when the exodus took place" (p. 480). But except for his analysis of the biblical text, Wood's understanding of the ANE texts is entirely dependent upon Kitchen's work and does not come from a firsthand analysis of the evidence (all his references to texts other than the Bible cite Kitchen's work as their source). And Wood's analysis of the biblical texts is itself very peculiar. For example, he regards all of Deut. 1:1–4:43 as "admonitions" and only treats one verse of the entire book, 5:6, as "Historical Prologue" (p. 482), even though all of Deut. 1–3 is narrative history! This is quite arbitrary, but it allows Wood to fit Deuteronomy within Kitchen's formal analysis, in which treaties from 1600–1400 make little use of the historical prologue. It seems that Wood himself came to the texts with a "pre-conceived conclusion as to when the exodus took place."
73. Charles H. Dyer, "The Date of the Exodus Reexamined," *BSac* 140, no. 559 (1983): 225–43 is a good example of this viewpoint.
74. Bruce K. Waltke, "Palestinian Artifactual Evidence Supporting the Early Date of the Exodus," *BSac* 129, no. 513 (1972): 33–47.
75. Bruce K. Waltke, *An Old Testament Theology: An Exegetical, Canonical, and Thematic Approach* (Grand Rapids: Zondervan, 2007), 589 n. 1, 592, and 592 n.13. In n. 13 he calls the date of the exodus "uncertain."

also assumes that Jephthah knew what he was talking about when he claimed that the time from the conquest to his own day was about 300 years. For reasons described above, these two biblical texts do not make the Late Date impossible. On the other hand, it is always best to begin with the simplest explanation of a passage. In this case, the simplest explanation is that numbers can be taken at face value and that the exodus took place around the year 1447 B.C.

This obviously favors the Early Date, and with this chronology, one can attempt to synchronize the date of the exodus with Egyptian history. William Shea, for example, argues that Thutmose III was the pharaoh of the exodus. Following a high chronology for Egyptian history, he contends that Thutmose III died in the year of the exodus at the crossing of the sea and that his successor, Amenhotep II, showed a marked hatred for Semites in his reign.[76] We should note that today many Egyptologists hold to a later date than 1447 for the end of the reign of Thutmose III, placing it at about 1425,[77] thus too late for Shea's reconstruction to work.

We should also bear in mind that the simplest or most "obvious" interpretation is not necessarily correct. For example, the straightforward reading of Exod. 12:40 indicates that Israel was in Egypt for 430 years, but the Apostle Paul interpreted the 430-year gap to refer to the period between the giving of the promises to Abraham and Israel's arrival at Sinai (Gal. 3:16–17). This indicates that the Egyptian sojourn was much shorter than what "the simplest explanation" of Exod. 12:40 would require (Paul was following a standard Jewish interpretation; see "A Caveat on Early Biblical Chronology" below for further discussion). As E. Thiele demonstrated for the dating of the Israelite kings, biblical chronology can be highly complex and, against a naïve reading of the Bible, counterintuitive.[78]

Finally, we should be careful about claiming more for the evidence than it actually bears. In particular, we really do not know when the Jephthah episode took place. If, for example, he judged around the year 1250, then by stating that Israel had been in Canaan for 300 years he was actually claiming that the conquest took place in 1550 B.C., or 150 years before the Early Date conquest! To put it another way, it is not legitimate to postulate a date of approximately 1100 B.C. for Jephthah's

76. William Shea, "Exodus, Date of the," in Bromiley, *ISBE*, 1.230–38.
77. Shaw, *Oxford Egypt*, 481.
78. Edwin Richard Thiele, *The Mysterious Numbers of the Hebrew Kings: A Reconstruction of the Chronology of the Kingdoms of Israel and Judah* (Grand Rapids: Eerdmans, 1965).

claim, and then assert that his testimony supports a conquest at approximately 1400 B.C., because in fact we have no way to verify when he judged.

The Habiru

A people designated the "Habiru" appear in Akkadian tablets from the 2nd millennium B.C. The term first appears in texts from the 18th century; the latest cuneiform occurrence of the word is in a text from the 11th century.[79] The name is intriguing. Were the "Habiru" connected to the "Hebrews"? The precise orthography (spelling) of the term is debatable; sometimes they are called "Hapiru" or "Apiru," but "Habiru" is the most probable. Similarly, although one cannot say that the linguistic connection between "Habiru" and "Hebrew" (עִבְרִי) is beyond question, it is certainly reasonable. The Habiru appear across the ancient Near East, showing up in Egypt, in the Mesopotamian cites of Mari and Nuzi, and even as far away as Boğazköy, the capital of the Hittite Empire in central Anatolia (modern Turkey). They especially appear in Canaan and are mentioned prominently as a presence in Canaan in the Amarna Letters from the late 18th dynasty of Egypt. They appear as early as the 19th century but are most commonly encountered in texts from the latter half of the 2nd millennium, and especially from the Amarna Age (c. 1350 B.C.). They disappear as a social phenomenon by the end of the 2nd millennium.

Habiru are essentially people whose lives have been disrupted by war, famine, high taxes, and other natural or man-made calamities. They are not members of a single ethnic or linguistic group. Although many Habiru were West Semites, we know from Alalakh texts that some people of Hurrian background were Habiru. Instead, the term "Habiru" seems to refer to outsiders, especially foreigners, who live on the fringes of society; they are often brigands who move about in gangs, are sometimes refugees or fugitives, are generally of low status, and are often perceived as a threat. They could be employed in the service of high officials and could attain to fairly high status, although that would be exceptional. Idrimi, King of Alalakh, says he rose to power in his city after living for seven years among the Habiru.[80] Some Habiru

---

79. Nadav Na'aman, "Habiru and Hebrews: The Transfer of a Social Term to the Literary Sphere," in *Canaan in the Second Millennium B.C.E.* (Winona Lake: Eisenbrauns, 2005), 253. See also Niels Peter Lemche, "Habiru, Hapiru," in Freedman, *ABD* Vol. 3, 6–10.
80. "The Story of Idrimi, King of Alalakh," translated by A. Leo Oppenheim (*ANET,* 557).

among the Hittites were held in prison but others evidently had high rank, as they were addressed in very respectful terms. Habiru were highly mobile. From Nuzi, evidence indicates that they could enter into contractual service with local citizens and thus be tolerated as a presence in society. They could be employed as unskilled laborers or as mercenaries.

In Canaan, from the evidence of the Amarna Letters, they were concentrated in the hill country. It is debated whether all occurrences of the term "Habiru" in the Amarna Letters actually refer to the class of people known as Habiru or whether the term is simply used as a pejorative by one king to describe another. That is, when one king says that another is a "Habiru," he may simply mean that the other king is behaving in a lawless manner. On the other hand, an Egyptian stele set up by Seti I (19th dynasty) refers to an expedition against gangs of Habiru living in the mountains around Beth Shean.[81] It is clear that the Habiru were a significant threat; in EA 271 (in the Amarna archives), Milkilu of Gezer pleads for the pharaoh to deliver him from the hand of the Habiru.[82]

An obvious question is whether the Habiru of the Amarna Letters, who are plainly creating a great deal of trouble for the Canaanites, can be identified with the biblical Hebrews. For chronological reasons, one cannot argue that Joshua's conquest is reflected in the Amarna Letters. If the conquest began in 1407, then by the time Akhenaten began to reign (1352) Joshua would have already died. The Bible indicates that at the end of Joshua's life Israel already had "rest" in the land (Josh. 23:1–2). But the text also indicates an ongoing struggle against the Canaanites (Josh. 23:5), and one could argue that this is the situation reflected in the Amarna Letters.

Plainly, one cannot say that all Habiru everywhere were Israelites. The Habiru existed long before the Israelite Hebrews and are found in places where Israelites did not live. It remains an open question, however, whether Israelites were a subset of a larger phenomenon of the 2nd millennium, the Habiru, and whether the name "Hebrew," as a derivative of "Habiru," somehow stuck to the Israelites. If so, then it may well be that the Habiru of the Amarna Letters refers at least sometimes to invading Israelites. If that is the case, then the Early Date for the exodus, or some variation of it, must be correct.

---

81. "Beth-Shan Stelae of Seti I and Ramses II," translated by John A. Wilson (*ANET,* 255).
82. "EA 271," translated by William F. Albright and George E. Mendenhall (*ANET,* 487).

The term "Hebrew" (עִבְרִי) in the Old Testament almost invariably refers to the Israelites in a foreign context or as viewed through the eyes of foreigners. Among themselves, by contrast, the Israelites were the "Sons of Israel" or "Israelites" (בְּנֵי־יִשְׂרָאֵל). The overwhelming majority of occurrences of the term Hebrew/s are in two contexts: in Genesis and Exodus, where the native Egyptians speak of the Israelites as Hebrews, often using it as a term of derision (Gen. 39:14,17; 41:12; 43:32; Exod. 1:15,16,19; 2:6,7,11), and in 1 Samuel, where "Hebrew" is the designation used by Philistines for the Israelites. In 1 Samuel, the term often carries a derisive meaning (1 Sam. 4:6,9; 13:19; 14:11,21; 29:3); the Israelites in turn disparaged the Philistines by calling them "uncircumcised Philistines." YHWH, the God of Israel, is always called "the God of the Hebrews" when Pharaoh is addressed (Exod. 3:18; 5:3; 7:16; 9:1, 13; 10:3). This usage should be considered ironic, as it probably carries the connotation, "the God of lowlifes and slaves," and yet this God turns out to be far more powerful than the gods of the Egyptians, who were the more sophisticated "master race." After the departure from Egypt, YHWH is never again called the "God of the Hebrews."

Several other occurrences of "Hebrew" in the Bible are noteworthy. Abram is called "the Hebrew" in Gen. 14:13; in this context, he is designated as an outsider or resident alien in Canaan. The term does not seem to be racial, since Abram's racial designation would have been "Aramean." In Gen. 40:15, Joseph says he is from "the land of the Hebrews." Joseph is not claiming that his family possesses all of Canaan, and he is probably not even speaking of the particular territory where his father sojourned. Rather, he seems to be using the term in the way that the Egyptians used terms like "Asiatic," as a semi-pejorative designation for the Semites of Syria-Palestine. When Jonah is designated as the guilty party among a ship's company of Gentiles, he calls himself a "Hebrew" (Jonah 1:9). Probably this indicates not just a racial or national identity but describes how the sailors would view the Israelite who had brought so much trouble down upon them. Also, as stated above, the Israelites normally designated themselves the "Sons of Israel," a term which carried national pride and identity. They might refer to an Israelite slave, however, as a "Hebrew" (Exod. 21:2; Deut. 15:12; Jer. 34:9, 14), a designation that suggests that an Israelite who falls into slavery has reverted to his former, disgraced state.

We should also note that the term "Hebrew" as a designation for the Israelites is quite old. Apart from the 10th century usage of the term by the Philistines, most are from the patriarchal period or

Egyptian sojourn. The 8th century usage in Jonah is exceptional and does not reflect normal usage for the monarchy period. After the exile, the Israelites are called "Jews" (יְהוּדִי [plural: יְהוּדִים]; see 2 Kings 25:25; Ezra 4:12; Neh. 1:2; Esth. 2:5 etc.). On the other hand, under the influence of Old Testament texts such as Exodus, Jews also began to be called "Hebrews" (Phil. 3:5).

All of this suggests that the term "Hebrew," for the Old Testament period, is very close in meaning to what we see of "Habiru." It is a term for aliens, troublemakers, lowly people, and slaves. Abraham was "Habiru" in the sense that he was a landless alien. Calling the Israelites "Hebrews" (or "Habiru") in Egypt reflects their status as foreigners, refugees, and then as slaves. It seems certain that 2nd millennium Egyptians would have regarded a refugee West Semitic "Asiatic" population in their midst as "Habiru" (the stele of Seti I refers to his enemies both as "Habiru" and as "wretched Asiatics"). The Philistines perhaps preserved the usage of "Habiru"/"Hebrew" into the 10th century as a way of expressing disdain for the Israelites. In the account of Joseph's life—a Hebrew slave and prisoner in the service of the native population who rises to a level of prestige—we can see parallels, described above, to what is known of the Habiru. The timeframe for the biblical occurrences of the term "Hebrew," mostly from the 2nd millennium but with some 10th century usage in the Philistine context, is consistent with what we know of the chronological distribution of the term "Habiru." The concentration of references to Habiru in the hill country of Canaan (from the Amarna Letters) coincides with the Israelite homeland in the hills of Ephraim, Benjamin, and Judah. The claim that the term "Hebrew" is derived from "Habiru" is at least arguable. Such a claim would not imply that all Habiru were Israelites, but that the Israelites were perceived to be a nation made up of Habiru.

One should be aware that a number of scholars deny any connection between Israel and the Habiru.[83] Anson Rainey argues that there is no linguistic relationship between the words "Hebrew" and "Habiru," that the term "Habiru" describes a social and not a racial group, and that the Egyptians knew the Israelites not as "Habiru" but as "*Shasu*,"

83. For example, Oswald Loretz, *Habiru-Hebräer: Eine Sozio-Linguistische Studie über die Herkunft des Gentiliziums ibrî vom Appelativum Habiru* (Berlin: Walter de Gruyter, 1984), 181, concludes that all biblical references to "Hebrew" are postexilic and therefore too late to have any connection to the Habiru.

a term they regularly used of West Semitic pastoralists.[84] N. Na'aman suggests that "Hebrew" is linguistically connected to "Habiru," but that the use of "Hebrew" in the Old Testament is essentially a literary move: the older meaning of "Habiru" was eventually applied to all Israelites who lived outside their homeland, as in the exodus narrative. But for Na'aman, this linguistic move took place in the 1st millennium,[85] too late to be of any significance for the date of the exodus or conquest. In a dated but helpful study, Mary Gray argues that there is an undeniable connection between "Habiru" and "Hebrew," although she states that one cannot equate the two or use the connection to date the conquest.[86]

One must be clear that if there is a connection between "Habiru" and "Hebrew," it is not one of equivalence. It would rather be a matter of a name that was broadly associated with a class of people throughout the Near East becoming affixed as a gentilic to one people in particular, the Israelites. By analogy, a Boeotian tribe called the Graikoi migrated to Italy in the 8th century B.C. Thereafter, the Romans called all peoples of that race and language the "Greeks," even though the "Greeks" called themselves the "Hellenes." Those who deny any connection between "Hebrew" and "Habiru," moreover, need to account for "Hebrew" as a designation for Israelites in the biblical texts. Even so, we cannot say that a link between the two terms is established or that the Habiru of the Amarna Letters definitely included Israelites, and we cannot specifically identify any action of Amarna Habiru with any Israelite action in the aftermath of the conquest. But it remains a tantalizing, and I think real, possibility.

Akhenaten's Failed Religious Revolution

As described above, the pharaoh Akhenaten of the 18th dynasty attempted to eradicate the worship of all other gods and establish Aten, the sun-disk, as the sole god of Egypt. It is quite strange that in the middle of three millennia of history, during which time Egyptian religion continued essentially unchanged (notwithstanding the fact that various gods would rise and fall in popularity), there should have been a brief—and even spectacular—attempt to establish monotheism. Why did Akhenaten do it? One might suggest that the astonishing power displayed by the God of the monotheistic Hebrews shook the Egyptians

84. Anson Rainey, "Shasu or Habiru: Who were the Early Israelites?" *BAR* 34, no. 6 (2008): 51–5.
85. Na'aman, "Habiru and Hebrews," 269–72.
86. Mary P. Gray, "The *Ḫâbirū*-Hebrew Problem in the Light of the Source Material Available at Present," *HUCA* 29 (1958): 135–202.

rather badly. If so, it might be that Akhenaten and those around him were so unsettled by what had happened that they felt that they needed to adopt a version of monotheism themselves. If so, the exodus obviously happened some time prior to Akhenaten's reign, and this reconstruction of events excludes the Late Date.

There are two problems with this theory, however. First, the dates of his reign (1352–1336) are seemingly too late for the early exodus. If the events of the exodus, according to the Early Date, took place almost 100 years prior to Akhenaten's inauguration, it is hard to see why the reaction they provoked would take so long to develop. On the other hand, our knowledge of social conditions prior to Akhenaten's reforms is limited; it may be that there was a grassroots movement toward an Egyptian monotheism that began to develop soon after the exodus but was embraced at the highest level of society, by the pharaoh, only after about a century had elapsed. This interpretation only requires that a significant and perhaps influential minority were drawn toward monotheism as the movement grew. It was beaten back afterwards by the majority of Egyptians and the entrenched priesthood of Amun, who held to the older ways. On the Late Date exodus theory, we should note, Akhenaten's religious revolution took place while the Israelites were still in Egypt.

The other problem is that nothing from Egypt clearly links Akhenaten's reformation to the Hebrews and their monotheism. Thus, the idea that the two are related is pure speculation. We do not know why Akhenaten did as he did. An old explanation for Akhenaten's heresy is that he embraced the Aten cult in order to draw people away from the worship of Amun and, thus, from the powerful priesthood of Amun at Thebes. That is, Akhenaten's religious revolution was essentially a political move and an attempt to weaken his priestly rivals. But this is an unsatisfactory explanation for such a far-reaching change as the embracing of monotheism. In the world of Egyptian polytheism, monotheism was alien to the point of being incomprehensible. It is hard to understand how it arose in such a context in the absence of some significant, external influence. If political power had been the issue, Akhenaten could have easily patronized the shrines of other gods while ignoring the cult of Amun; there was no need for such a radical step as monotheism. For that matter, the Amun priesthood did not become a true rival to pharaonic power until about 400 years after Akhenaten; the claim that the pharaoh was combatting the priesthood is actually anachronistic.

Some argue that the monotheism of Akhenaten was purely an internal, Egyptian development, since the god Amun, like the god Aten, is sometimes referred to as the sole god. But Amun religion was never a true monotheism, whereas the Aten cult was. If the cult of Amun sometimes embraced all the deities of Egypt and claimed to be the highest expression of religion, it never denied the validity of the worship of the other gods. This kind of syncretism, in which the identities of several gods could be merged into one, was common in Egyptian religion throughout its history.[87] Akhenaten's cult of Aten actively sought to bring devotion to all other gods to an end, and it reached a high degree of theological abstraction, conceiving of its god simply as the solar disk and not as an anthropomorphic or zoomorphic deity.[88] This level of abstraction, a movement away from an idol-centered religion, together with its intolerance of the other gods, marks the Aten faith as true monotheism.

A few scholars have sought to make a connection between Israelite monotheism and the Akhenaten heresy, but all have argued that the influence went from the Egyptian version of monotheism toward Israelite religion rather than the other way around. That is, Israelite monotheism is said to have been derived from Akhenaten's monotheism. The most famous proponent of this idea is Sigmund Freud, who argues in *Moses and Monotheism* that the original "Moses" was in fact an Egyptian, a priest of Akhenaten's monotheistic cult who led a group of Semites out of Egypt after the collapse of the Aten movement. After a series of events dimly and confusedly remembered in the biblical account, Israelite monotheism emerged under the leadership of a second "Moses," a Midianite.[89] This is, to say the least, a highly fanciful reconstruction, and no scholars follow it today. William Propp, however, has argued much more carefully and tentatively for the thesis that Akhenaten's monotheism is the source of its Israelite counterpart.[90]

An important argument for the idea that Israel learned its monotheism from Akhenaten is in the similarity of Ps. 104 to the one Egyptian text that has survived from Akhenaten's religion, the famous "Hymn to

87. It would not even be correct to call Amun worship henotheism; it was sometimes a syncretism, but even then it operated alongside of the separate cults of the other gods.
88. Prior to Akhenaten, Aten was sometimes shown in human form with a hawk head, but in Akhenaten's religion, the deity was simply the disk of the sun with beneficent sun-rays, ending in human hands, reaching down to earth.
89. Sigmund Freud, *Moses and Monotheism,* trans. Katherine Jones (New York: A.A. Knopf, 1939).
90. Propp, *Exodus 19–40*, 762–94.

Aten." This hymn, possibly written by Akhenaten himself, was found inscribed on a wall of the tomb of Ay in Amarna. Notwithstanding major differences in essential theological outlook, it does have some striking parallels to Ps. 104. For example, the hymn says of Aten: "When you set in western lightland, / Earth is in darkness as if in death; / One sleeps in chambers, heads covered, / One eye does not see another. / Were they robbed of their goods, / That are under their heads, / People would not remark it. / Every lion comes from its den, / All the serpents bite."[91] Psalm 104:20–21 similarly has, "You set darkness, so that it is night, in which all the animals of the forest come creeping out. The lions roar for prey, seeking their food from God." This and a few other parallels do indeed suggest some level of influence, and as it is highly unlikely that Akhenaten was influenced by the psalm, one might conclude that the psalm drew upon the "Hymn to Aten." There is not nearly enough evidence, however, to demonstrate that the psalmist worked with a copy of the hymn before him, and the differences in outlook and content between the psalm and the hymn are so numerous and striking that it is far more likely that the psalmist did not have direct knowledge of the hymn. Indeed, the Akhenaten cult was heavily suppressed in Egypt after the pharaoh's demise, and it is not at all likely that the psalmist would have had a copy of the hymn available to him unless he lived in Amarna during the short-lived period of the cult's flourishing (recall that the hymn was found in an Amarna tomb). It is more likely that elements of the hymn resurfaced in later Egyptian and perhaps Canaanite religious poetry,[92] and that these later poems may have been known to the psalmist. In short, whatever influence the hymn may have had on Ps. 104 was purely literary and not theological, and it was indirect, being derived from secondary, intermediate sources. Therefore, the relationship of the Aten hymn to Ps. 104 has no bearing on the claim that Egyptian monotheism brought about Israelite monotheism.

This much we can say with certainty: the monotheism of Akhenaten was a bizarre and short-lived phenomenon in Egyptian religious history. By contrast, devotion to YHWH alone, despite the occasional aberration, was the single most dominant phenomenon of Israelite religion throughout their entire history. It therefore seems intrinsically unlikely that monotheism arose spontaneously in Egypt and in opposition to their entire culture, and that it then spread to Israel, where it became a permanent fixture. It is more reasonable to suppose that the

91. "The Great Hymn to Aten," translated by Miriam Lichtheim (*COS* 1.28.45).
92. See the discussion in Leslie Allen, *Psalms 101–50, Revised*, WBC 21 (Nashville: Thomas Nelson, 2002), 39–41.

fixed devotion of Israelites to one God so impressed certain Egyptians that for a time they abandoned their traditional ways.

It is striking that most of the Amarna Letters, with all of their distress over the Habiru, come from Akhenaten's reign, and that we see in this period his failed attempt at monotheism. It was, at the very least, an interesting period of Egyptian history. At the same time, we have no direct evidence that the Hebrew religion or the exodus event influenced Akhenaten's religious revolution. We should also note that the idea that Israelite monotheism influenced the Akhenaten cult does not of itself require an Early Date for the exodus. It is possible that Akhenaten and like-minded Egyptians were influenced by Semitic monotheism while the Israelites were still among them, well before the exodus. Thus, a Late Date for the exodus would still be possible. We simply do not know.

The Soleb Inscription

Far to the south, on the west bank of the Nile in Upper Nubia (at 20°27′ N) at Soleb, Amenhotep III, father of Akhenaten, set up a temple. He portrayed himself in the temple inscription as a god-king; Amenhotep III is pictured wearing a lunar headdress and holding the divine scepter. In the accompanying text he made typical pharaonic boasts, showing subjugated peoples with arms bound behind their backs. The historical accuracy of his boasts is open to question; pharaohs routinely claimed to have conquered all of Egypt's enemies, regardless of whether they had actually done so. One of the places that the text mentions, however, is "the land of the *Shasu*, (those of) *Yhw*."

The *Shasu* are a pastoral people of Syria-Palestine, and *Yhw* is by nearly universal consent YHWH (a minority opinion is that *Yhw* is a geographical term). These *Shasu* were, it appears, a YHWH-worshipping people. The Israelites would have been regarded by the Egyptians as one of the *Shasu* peoples. One might suggest, therefore, that the Soleb inscription refers to the Israelites, and that they were at the time of its composition living somewhere in the area of Canaan. This would in turn imply that the exodus had already occurred sometime prior to the inscription, and would require a date for the exodus either early in or prior to the reign of Amenhotep III. Once again, however, we need to bridle our enthusiasm. Donald Redford argues that the *Shasu* mentioned at Soleb were a clan living in the southern Transjordan, possibly in Edom. He concludes that they were a pre-Israelite group of YHWH-worshippers.[93] Redford may be completely

93. Donald B. Redford, *Egypt, Canaan, and Israel in Ancient Times* (Princeton: Princeton University Press, 1992), 272–3.

wrong, and the *Shasu* mentioned at Soleb may in fact be the Israelites, but we do not have sufficient information to settle the matter. If not definitive, however, the Soleb inscription at least may be cited as evidence favoring an Early Date exodus.

Other Related Issues and Theories

Beyond the matters discussed above, there are several other issues that are important for the date of the exodus. There are also alternative theories and other pieces of data that pertain to the reality of the exodus event. These are as follows.

The Store Cities

According to Exod. 1:11, Hebrew slaves were employed in constructing the store cities of Pithom and Raamses. The identification of the sites of these cities is critical to the question of the date of the exodus, since—obviously enough—the Hebrews could not have been working in those cities at a time when the cities did not exist. If we can determine where the cities were and when they flourished, then we have a window within which we can place the exodus event.

Raamses

The city Raamses is equated with the Egyptian name Pi-Riʿamsese, the great capital city of the 19th dynasty pharaoh Ramesses II (reigned 1279–1213 B.C.). But where was Pi-Riʿamsese? Scholars once thought that it was at Tanis on the grounds that statuary from the time of Ramesses II was found there. Archaeologists believed that the city had been founded by Ramesses II and that it had not existed prior to his reign. That being the case, it was thought, the exodus could not have possibly taken place prior to the 13th century since, until that time, there would have been no city of Raamses for them to have worked in. Scholars now universally acknowledge that the identification of Raamses with Tanis was a mistake; the statuary from the time of Ramesses II had been moved there by Egyptians when they abandoned Pi-Riʿamsese and built up Tanis. This process began in the 20th dynasty (1186–1069 B.C.), and Tanis became the Egyptian capital city in the 21st dynasty (far too late for the exodus). Tanis was never known as Pi-Riʿamsese.[94]

It is now fairly certain that Raamses or Pi-Riʿamsese was located at a site called Tell el-Dabʿa or Qantir (this site is quite close to Avaris, the capital city of the Hyksos pharaohs, and thus Raamses

94. Kitchen, *Reliability*, 256.

is sometimes said to have been at Avaris). Located on the Bubastite branch of the Nile in the eastern Delta region, the city here was very old; perhaps having been founded in the Old Kingdom period of Egypt (3rd millennium B.C.). This area was controlled by Semites by c. 1650, and eventually Avaris became the Hyksos capital city. When native Egyptians under Ahmose drove out the Hyksos and founded the 18th dynasty (around 1540 B.C.), Avaris was destroyed. But Ahmose rebuilt its fortifications and palace buildings.[95] These sites were short-lived, however, and evidence indicates that for much of the 18th dynasty Tell el-Dabʿa was abandoned. In the 19th dynasty, however, Ramesses II made the city his capital and built there a splendid palace. One may obviously conclude, as advocates for the Late Date do conclude, that the Israelites worked on this city and remained there until the exodus, sometime during Ramesses II's reign.

To assess this, we must ask two questions. First, since it is certain that the city at Tell el-Dabʿa was not called Raamses or Pi-Riʿamsese until the reign of Ramesses II, does the fact that the Bible says the Hebrews built "Raamses" (by name) mean that the Hebrews were there up until the time of Ramesses II? If so, then the Early Date cannot be correct. Second, was there significant building activity at Tell el-Dab*ʿa* in the 18th dynasty (1550–1295), prior to Ramesses II? We know that Ramesses II did a great deal of construction work there, and this fact supports the Late Date. An Early Date requires that there was construction work there also in the 18th dynasty.

Regarding the first question, B. Wood states, "It is clear, then, that the name Rameses used in Exod 1:11 is an editorial updating of an earlier name that went out of use."[96] What Wood is suggesting, in order to sustain the Early Date, is that a later editor revised Moses's text. Wood's interpretation is coherent, but it is only "clear" that the text has been revised if one has already determined that the exodus took place long before the time of Ramesses II and that the *prima facie* evidence of Exod. 1:11 can therefore be set aside. If one simply reads the text as it is, without a preconception of when the exodus took place, it is "clear" that the Israelites worked on a city called Raamses and therefore were

95. Shaw, *Oxford Egypt* 216. Strangely, the Ahmose palace at Tell el-Dabʿa was decorated with frescoes in the Minoan style famous from Knossos in Crete. See especially Manfred Bietak, *Avaris: The Capital of the Hyksos: Recent Excavations at Tell el-Dabʿa* (London: British Museum, 1996), Plates IV and V and pp. 73–6.

96. Wood, "Rise and Fall," 479. Wood uses the spelling "Rameses" for both the pharaoh and the city.

present at its construction in the 13th century. Of course, one can point to evidence that place names in the Bible were from time to time revised for the benefit of later readers. This apparently occurred in Gen. 14:14, which refers to Abraham pursuing the captors of Lot up north to "Dan" (the site called Dan did not receive that name until the time of the judges; prior to that it was called Laish [Judg. 18:29]). One may argue that after the name Raamses or Pi-Riᶜamsese became world-famous as the celebrated city of Ramesses II, and that because the former name of the site had become obscure, the biblical text was revised to reflect the name that readers recognized. As such, the name itself does not demand a late exodus. Even so, the name does favor a Late Date, as a late exodus does away with any need to postulate a revision of the text.

The second question is more difficult to answer. On the one hand, it seems that the city at Tell el-Dabᶜa was largely abandoned during the 18th dynasty, and this would imply that no work was done there with which we can accommodate the Early Date. On the other hand, there is some evidence of activity there. It appears that at least for a short time after the fall of Hyksos Avaris, there was an 18th dynasty royal citadel there, although this may have been abandoned during the 18th dynasty. Manfred Bietak observes that east of an area that he calls Platform H/I, there was a middle-class settlement at which royal scarabs from Ahmose to Amenhotep II were found.[97] There is also evidence for a military camp in the area.[98] We should remember that mudbrick construction does not survive well in the Delta, and thus the lack of archaeological evidence for mudbrick warehouses is not surprising. Even so, the lack of clear proof for construction work in the 18th dynasty favors an exodus in the reign of Ramesses II, when we know that there was a great deal of construction there.

There is, however, another consideration. What does Exod. 1:11 mean by calling Pithom and Raamses "store cities" (עָרֵי מִסְכְּנוֹת)? The term plainly refers to locations that serve as depots for supplies of various kinds, possibly attached to temples[99] or possibly for military use[100] (see 1 Kings 9:19; 2 Chron. 16:4; 17:12). A capital city could also be a store city (1 Kings 9:19), but it seems odd that Raamses would be called a "store city" and even listed after the much less significant Pithom if at the time of building Raamses was in fact the capital of Egypt's greatest pharaoh. The capital center at Raamses was enormous and

97. Bietak, *Avaris*, 72.
98. Ibid., 81–2.
99. Hoffmeier, *Ancient Israel*, 63.
100. Houtman, *Exodus*, 1:244.

lavish, being heavily adorned with monumental works. If the Hebrews were working on the city at the time of Ramesses II, we might expect the text to have said something like, "the Hebrews built Raamses, the city of Pharaoh, and they also built the store-city Pithom" (a king's capital city was sometimes referred to as "the city of X," as in Num. 21:26; 2 Sam. 5:9). The very magnificence of Ramesses II's capital seems to speak against the idea that the Bible is referring to his construction of this city, unless it is merely asserting that the Israelites built storage facilities in the vicinity of his palace city.

In summary, and in support of the Early Date, there is a little evidence that Tell el-Dabʿa may have been a storage depot in the 18th dynasty. In addition, one may argue that the language of Exod. 1:11 is ill-suited to refer to the magnificence of Ramesses II's construction work. On the other hand, the fact that the site is called "Raamses" favors the Late Date, as does the fact that we know that massive construction work was done there in the reign of Ramesses II.

Pithom

Pithom was once identified with Tell el-Maskhuta, a site on the Wadi Tumilat a few miles west of Lake Timsah (in the southern area of the modern Suez Canal). The foundation of the major city at this site dates to the reign of Necho II (reigned 610–595 B.C.), a date obviously far too late to be the city that the pre-exodus Hebrews worked on. Donald Redford, we should note, does claim that Tell el-Maskhuta was Pithom, and he argues that the Jews at the end of the biblical period, as they constructed the legend of the exodus, simply identified Necho II's city as the place in which their ancestors had worked.[101] That is, the account of Hebrew slaves building Pithom is fictional, but the Jews who created the story did not realize that Pithom was actually unoccupied during the time of the supposed Hebrew enslavement.

In fact, however, evidence indicates that Pithom was at Tell el-Rataba, a site in the Wadi Tumilat a few miles west of Tell el-Maskhuta, and it is probable that Tell el-Maskhuta was Tjeku, the place called Succoth in the Bible. Ramesses II built a temple at Tell el-Rataba, and thus it is clear that some construction work was done there during his

101. Redford, *Egypt*, 451. For a report of material evidence found at Tell el-Maskhuta, see John S. Holladay, Jr., *Cities of the Delta, Part III: Tell el-Maskhuta* (American Research Center in Egypt Reports. Malibu: Undena, 1982).

reign.[102] Thus, the identification of Pithom with Tell el-Rataba poses no difficulty for the Late Date. But was Tell el-Rataba occupied during the 18th dynasty? Almost certainly it was; it had a long history, being occupied as early as the Middle Kingdom. Evidence for an 18th dynasty presence includes architectural remains from that time as well as scarabs with the names of Thutmose III and Amenhotep III.[103] As such, Pithom allows for either an early or a late exodus.

The Archaeology of the Conquest

The date of the Israelite invasion of Canaan is obviously related to the date of the exodus. It is helpful, therefore, to have a cursory look at the archaeology of Canaan in the relevant periods. Also, two cities that the Israelites conquered under Joshua, Jericho and Hazor, are frequently called upon to arbitrate the date of the exodus and conquest. Basic issues are described below.

Broad Patterns in the Archaeology of Canaan

Although there is some difference among scholars regarding nomenclature and the precise dates, Table 4 presents what can be regarded as a standard model for our period.

The Middle Bronze Age was an era of great prosperity for Canaan. The cities were numerous, relatively large, and walled. The population was relatively dense. Material culture was generally of a high quality. The use of the fast potter's wheel allowed for the creation of delicate pottery, and a burnished, red slip characterizes many vessels.[104] The Middle Bronze came to a fairly abrupt and dramatic end. A number

102. See Hoffmeier, *Ancient Israel*, 58–65. It may be that the biblical Pithom was little more than a storage facility and that its precise location will never be known, but Tell el-Rataba is the best candidate. The claim that the Saite occupation of Tell el-Maskhuta is the best candidate for the biblical Pithom is definitely wrong. See also Kitchen, *Reliability*, 256–9.

103. James K. Hoffmeier, *Israel in Egypt: The Evidence for the Authenticity of the Exodus Tradition* (Oxford: Oxford University Press, 1996), 119. Tell el-Rataba has been excavated several times, most recently by Michael Fuller in 1977, 1978 and 1981. Unfortunately, in 1981 the Egyptian government laid water conduits directly through the middle of the Tell, using backhoes, bulldozers, and other pieces of heavy machinery, and doing a great deal of damage (see http://users.stlcc.edu/mfuller/retaba.html). It is unlikely that further meaningful data will be forthcoming.

104. Mazar, *Archaeology*, 182–3.

of major destruction layers are found at important cities, including Jericho, Shechem, and Hazor, and these are dated to around 1550 B.C.[105]

The Late Bronze Age is often regarded as a period of Egyptian domination in Canaan, as it is at this time that we have the major campaigns of pharaohs such as Thutmose III and Ramesses II, as well as the Canaanite vassalage to Egypt represented in the Amarna Letters. Late Bronze I is the period of Canaanite collapse. Many cities were violently destroyed at the beginning of Late Bronze I and not resettled until much later.[106] Settlements in the hill country declined markedly. The heaviest concentration of cities during the Late Bronze Age was in the lowlands, in the Shephelah and in the Jezreel and Beth-Shean valleys.[107] The use of the fast potter's wheel was abandoned, and local pottery subsequently was somewhat cruder than before. On the other hand, there is continuity with earlier Canaanite material culture where urban life persisted, that is, in the lowlands, at cities such as Megiddo.[108] There is a marked increase of settled, urban sites during Late Bronze II; these are mostly along the coast.[109] The Amarna Letters describe a civilization that is still thoroughly Canaanite (not Israelite).

The beginning of Iron I, around 1200, marks the collapse of major civilizations all across the region. Hittite, Egyptian, Mycenaean, and Mesopotamian powers all go into decline, although the nature and extent of their troubles were not uniform.[110] At the end of the Late Bronze and beginning of Iron I, Merenptah conducted what was apparently one of the last successful incursions into Canaan. Subsequently, Ramesses III fought to defend the homeland in Egypt rather than to extend the empire. The Sea Peoples and the Greeks made a series of migrations (with one group apparently becoming the biblical Philistines). Settlements began to be observable in the hill country and, as described above (see "The Archaeology of the Israelite Hill Country"), these can be considered Israelite.[111]

---

105. For descriptions of the period, see Mazar, *Archaeology*, 174–231, and Anson Rainey and R. Steven Notley, *The Sacred Bridge: Carta's Atlas of the Biblical World* (Jerusalem: Carta, 2006), 50–60.
106. Rivka Gonen, "The Late Bronze Age," in *The Archaeology of Ancient Israel*, ed. Amnon Ben-Tor, trans. R. Greenberg (New Haven: Yale University Press, 1992), 216.
107. Mazar, *Archaeology*, 240.
108. Ibid., 257–74. Late Bronze Megiddo also gives us some famous ivory pieces.
109. Gonen, "Late Bronze," 217.
110. See Rainey and Notley, *Sacred Bridge*, 104–9.
111. Mazar, *Archaeology*, 328–55. For an account of the current debate over this issue, see Dever, *Early Israelites*.

TABLE 4. CANAANITE PERIODS RELEVANT TO THE CONQUEST		
Period	**Dates B.C.**	**General Description**
Middle Bronze II	2000–1550	Large, walled cities; large population, high material culture
Late Bronze I	1550–1400	Cultural collapse; many cities destroyed; population reduced
Late Bronze IIa	1400–1300	Recovery begins; Amarna age
Late Bronze IIb	1300–1200	Recovery continues; age of Ramesses II and Hittites
Iron I	1200–1000	Merenptah encounters Israel; collapse of Hittite and Egyptian New Kingdom empires; Israelites visible in hill country; Sea peoples ("Philistines") settle in SW Canaan

It is difficult to see how a conquest at about 1407 (the Early Date) fits into this overview. We have already pointed out that the emergence of identifiable Israelite sites in Iron I favors the Late Date. More than that, the Early Date has significant problems with the archaeology of the Late Bronze Age. The collapse of urban population in the hill country took place at the end of the Middle Bronze, in 1550, around 150 years before the proposed Early Date conquest. At the end of Late Bronze I, the hill country was so sparsely occupied that it seems inconsistent with the conquest account given in Joshua, where the Israelites faced fairly stiff resistance and defeated numerous foes who operated from significant cities (such as Ai, Bethel, Debir, and Jerusalem, as well as numerous cities in the Shephelah).[112] The continuing scarcity of observ-

112. Interpreters debate the location or occupation history of sites such as Ai and Bethel. For a small sample of differing views on just the city of Ai, see Joseph A. Callaway, "New evidence on the conquest of 'Ai,'" *JBL* 87, no. 3 (1968): 312–20; David P. Livingston, "Location of Biblical Bethel and Ai Reconsidered," *WTJ* 33, no. 1 (1970): 20–44; Leonard Allen, "Archaeology of Ai and the Accuracy of Joshua 7:1–8:29," *ResQ* 20, no. 1 (1977): 41–52. Debir, assuming it can be identified as Khirbet Rabud, did not become a walled city until Late Bronze IIa (Moshe Kochavi, "Rabud, Khirbet," *NEAEHL* 4:1252), too late for the Early Date conquest. Obviously, the

able settlements in the hill country during Late Bronze II is difficult to reconcile with an Israelite settlement beginning in 1407, when this area should have been repopulated. Egyptian domination of Canaan, a characteristic of the Late Bronze Age, is not reflected in Judges, where the Egyptians are notable only for their absence. Finally, it seems odd that the Canaanite civilization would begin to revive in Late Bronze II, beginning around 1400, on the very heels of the Israelite invasion. This is, to say the least, counterintuitive. One could answer these arguments by contending that the Israelites were more or less confined to the hill country in the Late Bronze, that the Egyptian interaction was only with the Canaanites in the lowland,[113] that the Israelites were still more pastoral than sedentary (thus leaving no archaeological footprint), and that the Late Bronze II Canaanite resurgence was in the lowlands, away from the Israelite center. Still, the archaeology of Canaan, as we understand it at this time, favors the Late Date, as it does not have to account for so many archaeological anomalies.

Jericho

Theoretically, archaeological evidence for the date of the destruction of Jericho under Joshua could settle the matter of when the exodus and conquest occurred. Unfortunately, the history of the excavation of Tell es-Sultan, the site of Old Testament Jericho, has been anything but helpful. The first diggings at Jericho were done by Charles Warren (1868) who sank several shafts to bedrock. These were followed by excavations done by Ernst Sellin and Carl Watzinger from 1907 to 1913. Although their work initially supported belief that Jericho had been destroyed by Joshua, Watzinger in 1926 revised his analysis to conclude that a major destruction had occurred around 1600 B.C., too early for Joshua's time. The site was then excavated again under John Garstang between 1930 and 1936. Garstang believed that the destruction of what he called "City IV" could be dated to about 1400 B.C. This seemed to confirm the Early Date for the exodus. However, a fourth major excavation was carried out under Kathleen Kenyon from 1952

---

history of each city must be determined on a case-by-case basis, and some will argue that specific sites do favor the Early Date invasion. But the point here is not to adjudicate each site, but that the broad contours of the Late Bronze Age, as understood by the majority of archaeologists, do not favor the Early Date.

113. On the other hand, there is evidence the Merenptah did make it into the hill country. See Gary A. Rendsburg, "The Date of the Exodus and the Conquest/Settlement: The Case for the 1100s," *VT* 42, no. 4 (1992): 519–20.

to 1958. She concluded that Middle Bronze Age Jericho had come to a violent end around 1550 and that during the Late Bronze Age the city was either unoccupied or too modestly occupied to merit the description of it given in Joshua (she does, however, allow for a Late Bronze II destruction of Jericho, which she says may have been the basis of the account in Joshua).[114]

It is generally agreed that the city suffered a cataclysmic destruction (Garstang's "City IV" or Kenyon's Middle Bronze II city), and many elements of this destruction layer work well with the Bible's account of the city's fall. The problem is its date. John Bimson attempted to remedy the situation by redating the end of the Middle Bronze Age to 1400.[115] That is, he acknowledged that the city was destroyed at the end of the Middle Bronze Age but argued that the age itself was dated wrongly. Few scholars are persuaded that this redating is valid. Bryant Wood, on the other hand, has tried to show that the pottery of Jericho's great destruction is from Late Bronze I and does indeed come from c. 1400 and, therefore, that it establishes Garstang's date for the destruction of the city.[116] Most archaeologists are not convinced, however, and the current consensus remains that the cataclysmic destruction of Jericho to which archaeology attests took place around 1550.

A significant development in this regard is the dating of charred grain from Jericho. The existence of this grain is frequently cited as part of the evidence that City IV was destroyed by Joshua's forces, since the invasion took place after Passover, during the grain harvest time in Canaan, and since Israel was commanded not to plunder Jericho but to burn it. However, two recent radiocarbon analyses of grain samples (done in 1993 and 1998) indicate that Jericho's fall dates to the mid-16th century, or c. 1550 B.C.[117] This independent confirmation of the date for the destruction of City IV undermines efforts to redate the fall of Jericho to 1400, whether by redating the end of the Middle Bronze Age (Bimson) or by redating the fall of Jericho (Wood). Unless one can demonstrate that the radiocarbon dates are inaccurate, the evidence

114. Gideon Foerster, "Jericho," *NEAEHL* 2:679–80.

115. John J. Bimson, *Redating the Exodus and Conquest,* 2nd ed. (Sheffield: Almond, 1981).

116. Bryant G. Wood, "Did the Israelites Conquer Jericho? A New Look at the Archaeological Evidence," *BAR Electronic Archive*, Vol. 19.2 (March/April 1990).

117. Barbara J. Sivertsen, *The Parting of the Sea: How Volcanoes, Earthquakes and Plagues Shaped the Story of Exodus* (Princeton: Princeton University Press, 2009), 9 n. 39.

requires that either the Jericho that Joshua destroyed was not City IV or that, if he did destroy City IV, the Israelite invasion was far earlier than we have allowed for—almost 150 years earlier than even the "Early Date," but more in line with the chronology of Judges (when read literally and not compressed).

We should bear in mind that Jericho, as archaeological sites go, is in terrible shape (this is obvious even to the untrained eye when comparing Jericho to sites such as Megiddo, Hazor, or Beersheba). Every archaeological dig to some degree ruins evidence, and this site has been dug repeatedly (and at least sometimes with primitive methods). Furthermore, erosion at the site has been extremely severe. Kitchen suggests that there may have been a city there that Joshua destroyed in the late 13th century (following the Late Date), but that the sad state of the site makes it very unlikely that it will ever be found.[118] It is, at present, not possible to justify using Jericho to establish either an Early or Late Date for the invasion of Canaan. This is not to say that both of those dates must be wrong; for myself, I do not have confidence that our archaeology-based understanding of Jericho's history is certain. We know that at some point Joshua's armies crossed the Jordan and destroyed Jericho. But chronologically Jericho remains a problem and does not establish the date of the conquest (unless one dates it to 1550).

Hazor

Hazor, along with Jericho and Ai, is said to have been destroyed by Israelite forces under Joshua (Josh. 11:10–11). Located at Tell el-Qedah, north of the Sea of Galilee, it was examined by John Garstang in 1928 in a very limited way and then was excavated in a much more thorough manner between 1955 and 1958 by major Israeli archaeologists under the direction of Yigael Yadin. Further work was done in 1968–69, and excavations are still carried on there. It was a major Canaanite city and at the crossroads of trade routes between Canaan and Egypt to the south and Syria and the Euphrates valley to the north. An unusually large city, Hazor at its height, during the Late Bronze Age, had both an "upper city" and a "lower city." During this time, Hazor was destroyed and rebuilt several times; it reached its zenith in the Amarna Age, during the 14th century. After a major destruction of Hazor in Late Bronze II (13th century; the destruction layer is at stratum 1-a in the lower city and stratum XIII in the upper city), the lower city was never rebuilt (thus, this destruction level is the surface stratum, 1-a, of the

118. Kitchen, *Reliability*, 187.

lower city). After a gap of some time, there was a small occupation at upper city stratum XII; the upper city eventually became an Israelite stronghold under Solomon (stratum X).

The massive, Late Bronze II destruction of the city is attributed by many scholars, including Yadin himself, to Joshua's destruction of the city.[119] This interpretation supports the Late Date for the exodus.[120] A problem with this analysis is that, according to Judg. 4:2, Jabin, king of Hazor, was an oppressor of Israel during the judges period. One wonders, if Jabin was an oppressor of Israel, how it is that there is no major fortified city at Hazor after the destruction of stratum 1-a and stratum XIII until Solomon's upper city stratum X. Wouldn't Jabin have had a great city, and shouldn't it have been found between the Hazor that Joshua destroyed and the Hazor that Solomon built? Thus, it may be that Joshua's destruction layer is actually earlier than stratum 1-a and stratum XIII, and that this city (1-a / XIII) was Jabin's Hazor.

Lower city stratum 3 (end of Middle Bronze II), it turns out, also suffered a major destruction. This enables some to argue that the large conflagration layer at lower city stratum 1-a and at upper city stratum XIII, the layer that ended the Late Bronze II city, was the work of Deborah and Barak rather than of Joshua.[121] If so, Joshua could have been responsible for the burning of the city at lower city stratum 3. Here, however, we have the same problem encountered at Jericho: the destruction layer at lower city stratum 3 dates to about 1550, and this, in the Early Date chronology, is too early to be Joshua's city.[122]

Furthermore, it is possible that Jabin in fact did not occupy a large or fortified Hazor, since his army commander Sisera actually resided in a different city, Harosheth-hagoyim (Judg. 4:2). The fact that Jabin "reigned in Hazor" (Judg. 4:2) may simply mean that it was his command center. Support for this also comes from the peculiar title given to Jabin, "king of Canaan." This sounds like the self-aggrandizing claim of a warlord; until the Israelite monarchy, Canaan was never under a single king. In addition, Jabin's army was highly mobile, consisting of 900 chariots (Judg. 4:3). All in all, it sounds as though Jabin was a

---

119. Amnon Ben-Tor, "Hazor," *NEAEHL* 2:603.

120. Hoffmeier, "Biblical Date," 245–6, argues that the destruction of shrines and shrine images from this layer accords well with the conquest under Joshua, since Israel's armies were charged with the task of destroying pagan shrines. In the ancient Near East armies did not typically desecrate sacred locations and objects.

121. E.g., Wood, "Rise and Fall," 487–8.

122. Ben-Tor, "Hazor," 2:595.

warlord with a mobile force who terrorized Canaan but used Hazor as a base of operations rather than as a fixed, fortified city-state. Also, if Jabin had no walled city, this would explain why Judges does not mention the destruction of Jabin's Hazor, but only of Jabin himself (see Judg. 4:24). Therefore, we have little basis for asserting that Joshua destroyed the older stratum 3 while Deborah and Barak brought about the massive conflagration at stratum 1-a. The Bible never says that Jabin's Hazor was destroyed.

We should also note that there is a destruction layer at lower city 1-b, dated to the latter part of the Amarna Age (late 14th century).[123] This sits in between the Early and the Late Dates for the exodus and conquest. In short, there is no shortage of destruction layers at Hazor, but none, in the current state of our knowledge, fits a conquest under Joshua in 1407. On the other hand, the city of strata 1-a and XIII does fit the Late Date. If one is looking for the simplest solution, it is that Joshua destroyed this Late Bronze II city and that Jabin had a command post but not a fortified city there.

The Problem of the Hyksos

We have already seen that the Hyksos were Semites who migrated into or invaded Egypt during the first half of the 2nd millennium B.C. They eventually brought Lower Egypt (the Delta area) under their control, and they had their capital city at Avaris. The 15th and 16th dynasties, ending about 1540, were Hyksos. Not surprisingly, biblical scholars have sought to explain the role the Hyksos played in the story of Israel in Egypt. Four opinions are possible.

A Hyksos Pharaoh Ruled in the Time of Joseph?

A Hyksos pharaoh promoted Joseph to power: the appeal of this suggestion is that it seems to make the story of Joseph more plausible. Who would be more likely to promote the Hebrew slave Joseph to power than a pharaoh who was himself a Semite and who spoke (almost) the same language and had the same cultural background? If Joseph served under a Hyksos pharaoh, his career had to have been around 1600 B.C. This requires the patriarchs to have lived later than traditionally assumed (they are usually dated around the turn of the millennium, around 2000 B.C.). On the other end, it requires somewhat of a shortening of Israel's time in Egypt and the wilderness wandering,

123. Ben-Tor, "Hazor," 2:596. From Yadin's account, however, this destruction layer (stratum 1-b) was apparently not nearly as massive as that at stratum 1-a.

since the Merenptah Stele unambiguously shows that Israel was established in Canaan by 1209.

Apart from these problems, this interpretation of the Hyksos does not agree with the biblical narrative, which strongly implies that the pharaoh who knew Joseph was Egyptian. In the Genesis narrative, when Jacob and his sons migrate to Egypt, Joseph must act as an intermediary, explaining his family's customs to the pharaoh and telling his family how to respond to the pharaoh's questions. The stated reason is that shepherds are an abomination to the Egyptians (Gen. 46:28–34[124]). It is hard to imagine how the diplomatic introduction of Joseph's Semitic family would be necessary or even appropriate if the pharaoh himself were Semitic. The text plainly presents the pharaoh and his aristocracy as Egyptian; Joseph must find a way to mitigate the disdain they will feel for these Semites.

A Hyksos Pharaoh Enslaved the Israelites?

A Hyksos pharaoh was the pharaoh of the oppression: in this interpretation, the pharaoh who did not know Joseph (Exod. 1:8) was himself an outsider and therefore unfamiliar with the historic ties between Egypt and the Hebrews who lived among them. Chronologically, it might make sense with the early exodus, as it allows for about 200 years of slavery for Israel before the exodus. In reality, however, this model is completely implausible. Exodus 1:8–10 portrays the pharaoh's hatred for the Hebrews as—like the hatred that all the Egyptians felt—a visceral fear and loathing of a foreign people. It is also very difficult to see how the Hyksos, trying to rule over a large and resentful native population, would focus their antagonism on a people who were their natural allies (culturally and linguistically, the Hebrews were probably almost indistinguishable from the Hyksos). Finally, if the Hebrews, like the Egyptians, had been oppressed by the Hyksos (and therefore were the natural allies of the Egyptians), it is unclear why the Hebrews would still be slaves after the Hyksos were expelled.

The Israelites Who Departed Egypt Were the Hyksos?

The Hyksos can be identified with the Israelites: this theory asserts that the expulsion of the Hyksos by the Egyptians and the exodus of the Israelites are actually one and the same event. This view finds

124. Although Egyptians kept livestock, they were primarily grain farmers. Semitic shepherd clans, with their large herds, did great damage to the fields.

support in Josephus, *Against Apion* 1:81–91. It might be that what we have is one incident presented from two points of view. The Egyptians claim that they successfully drove out the hated Semites, while the Hebrews claim that they were saved by their God from slavery to their Egyptian overlords. From the standpoint of historical context, this model has one advantage. As we have seen, Ahmose, founder of the 18th dynasty, completed the work of driving the Hyksos out of Egypt around 1540 B.C. Most archaeologists date the fall of Jericho to the end of the Middle Bronze Age, about 1550 B.C. Although there is still a problem in correlating the exodus with the fall of Jericho, it is much easier in this model than is the case with either a 1447 or a 1250 exodus.

Nevertheless, this model, too, has significant problems. First, it requires a date that is at least one hundred years earlier than even the Early Date, following a literal reading of 1 Kings 6:1. Second, the expulsion of the Hyksos and the biblical exodus have nothing in common beyond the fact that both the Hyksos and the Hebrews were Semites. The Hyksos expulsion came at the end of a protracted struggle. The 17th dynasty pharaoh Tao II (Seqenenre) waged war against the Hyksos and was killed in battle. He was succeeded by Kamose, father of Ahmose, who waged war against the Hyksos for some years before handing the fight to his son. Ahmose was able to achieve final victory. The process of driving out the Hyksos took many years, therefore, as opposed to the relatively short period (a year at most) between Moses's return to Egypt and the exodus. The Hyksos history involved foreign warriors who dominated Lower Egypt, but the exodus involved slaves who never waged war against their Egyptian masters. Certainly their time in Egypt did not end with a war in which the Hebrews were the losers. The two events are simply too unalike to be competing descriptions of one event.

THE HYKSOS PROVOKED ANTI-SEMITISM AMONG THE EGYPTIANS?

The Hyksos experience exacerbated the Egyptian hatred of the Israelites: this interpretation asserts that the Egyptian experience with the Hyksos gave them good reason to fear Semitic foreigners who resided in their country. In reality, Egypt already had a long history of having to contend with immigration and infiltration by Semites, whom the Egyptians called "Asiatics," from the Levant. The period of Hyksos domination would have only convinced the Egyptians that things would get very bad if they allowed these Semitic interlopers to get out of hand. From this standpoint, the Egyptian fear expressed in Exod. 1:8–10 makes good sense. Indeed, Exod. 1:10 actually expresses the fear that the Hebrew slaves would rise up and take over the land of Egypt (see commentary), just as the Hyksos had done. Thus, the most reasonable scenario is that the Hebrews were enslaved after the Hyksos were defeated. The Israelites were not the Hyksos, but they were seen to be very much like them. When the Hyksos were defeated, the Israelites were immediately viewed with suspicion and fear.

With this understanding of the Hyksos, it is possible to make sense of Josephus's equating the Hyksos with the Hebrews. If the Hyksos and the Hebrews were together a dominant Semitic power in Lower Egypt, then it follows that after the defeat of the military power of the Hyksos, the civilian Semitic population that did not flee Egypt would have been enslaved. From the Egyptian perspective, the Hyksos and Hebrews would have been part of the same population group. But the defeat and expulsion of the Hyksos royalty and warriors would have been entirely separate from the exodus of the Hebrew slaves.

Eccentric Theories

There are many peculiar theories about the time and circumstances of the exodus. Some are from amateurs and quacks, but others come from respected and accomplished scholars. The latter are instructive even when the actual theories are implausible. Two such theories are presented here.

The Speos Artemidos Inscription

The Speos Artemidos is located near Beni Hasan in Upper Egypt, roughly halfway from Memphis to Thebes. The name is Greek; it means, "Grotto of Artemis." It is a rock temple to the goddess Pakhet, whom the Greeks identified with Artemis, and thus the name. Pakhet was a feline deity, similar to the ferocious lioness-goddess Sekhmet and the more protective and maternal Bastet, a goddess whose animal was the domestic cat. Pakhet may have been an amalgamation of the two. The Speos Artemidos contains an inscription by Hatshepsut; it honors Pakhet and (as all such inscriptions do) boasts of the greatness and accomplishments of the pharaoh.

The temple and its inscription have been known for over a century, but the inscription is somewhat enigmatic, and recently a new translation has been proposed by Hans Goedicke, Professor Emeritus at Johns Hopkins University. Goedicke has produced a detailed treatment of the text, laying out all the difficulties it contains and defending his own rendition.[125] His interpretation, whatever one may make of

125. Goedicke, *Speos Artimedos.*

it, is fascinating, and for a time it gained a following.[126] The following summarizes Goedicke's interpretation.

Hatshepsut, after the introductory lines, in the first section speaks enigmatically of troubles that beset Egypt. There was a "Lord" who was "over the coast-line" and whose flames were "outside the Two Mountain-ranges."[127] This means (according to Goedicke) that fire was visible across the Mediterranean; the latter phrase means that the locus of the troubles was outside of the area between the "Two Mountain-ranges," that is, outside of Upper Egypt, which was flanked by hills and cliffs. The crisis was centered in the marshy flatland of Lower Egypt, from which one could see the flame on the northern horizon of the Mediterranean Sea. Hatshepsut then indicates that areas around the shrines of the gods were darkened, and that lamps had to be placed within them. More than that, many of the gods themselves (that is, their images) had to be moved to temporary shelters, apparently because of some local calamity.

In the second section of the inscription, Hatshepsut insists on the legitimacy of her seizure of the throne, claiming that it was the will of the god Amun. The third section is pure political propaganda: Hatshepsut claims that all of greater Egypt, including the Sinai and the southern regions down to the fourth cataract, submit to her and prosper. The army, which previously had been badly equipped and demoralized, is reinvigorated. In the fourth section, she asserts that she restored a decaying temple of the goddess Hathor at Cusae, about 40 miles south of Beni Hasan, and she claims to have brought embezzlement of temple funds under control.

In the fifth section, Hatshepsut describes her newly built temple to Pakhet. She praises Pakhet because the goddess opened "roads for the water-torrent"[128] so that Hatshepsut (or Egypt) was not drenched. In section six, Hatshepsut claims she distributed foods to several towns in Upper Egypt that had experienced an influx of refugees who came from Lower Egypt and needed food. In the seventh section, she indicates that the temple of Thoth, who was especially worshipped in Hermopolis Magna,[129] had been ransacked. This could be attributed to the desperation of the refugees from the north. Hatshepsut declares

126. A popular presentation of this theory is Ian Wilson, *The Exodus Enigma* (London: Weidenfield and Nicolson, 1985).

127. Goedicke, *Speos Artimedos*, 6.

128. Ibid., 17.

129. The scribe-god Thoth was associated with the Greek god Hermes, and thus the name Hermopolis.

her intention to restore the temple and to provide an allowance for the ritual services there. The eighth section is badly worn, but she appears to address troop grievances about garrison duties.

In the ninth and last section (still following Goedicke's interpretation), Hatshepsut asserts how great is her power, saying that she was a "born conqueror"[130] and that the uraeus (the cobra worn on the pharaoh's crown, and a symbol of Lower Egypt) sprayed fire on her enemies. She then describes the situation in Avaris, the old Hyksos capital in the northeastern Delta at Tell el-Dabʿa: "I levied the first draft since Asiatics have been at Avaris of the North Land."[131] In other words, she subjected the Semitic inhabitants of the eastern Delta to forced labor. This could be taken to mean that the forced labor system imposed on the "Asiatics" (Semites) had been allowed to lapse for some time, but that Hatshepsut reinstated it. She speaks of the Asiatics as "resident aliens"[132] (Egyptian: *shemau*, a term that describes foreigners who have been granted the right to live in a designated area of Egypt with freedom to establish their own settlements and maintain their own economy). She says that the *shemau* thought that she would be weak and unable to rule effectively. But apparently her bid to control them by forced labor failed. And so, she says, she sent away these people, whom she also calls the "abomination of the gods."[133] More than that, she says, "the (flat) land removed their sandal imprints."[134] This is an odd choice of words; it usually describes the ritual whereby a priest, after giving an offering to an Egyptian god, walked backwards and swept away his footprints from the sanctuary. Here, it suggests that the *shemau* left Egypt completely.

Goedicke argues that the inscription is an attempt to validate Hatshepsut's seizure of the throne. More specifically, it is a defense of her right to rule in the aftermath of a recent calamity. Goedicke believes that this calamity was the eruption of the volcano on Thera (also called Santorini). Thera is the southernmost Greek island of the Cyclades group in the Aegean Sea. At some time in the Middle or Late Bronze Age[135] the mountain exploded. It ejected approximately

130. Goedicke, *Speos Artimedos*, 91.
131. Ibid., 25
132. Ibid., 23.
133. Ibid., 27.
134. Ibid., 28.
135. The date of the eruption is debated. Some place it around 1500, while others set it earlier, around 1600. Bietak, *Avaris*, 78, on the basis of pumice deposits, dates it "sometime after the reign of Ahmose and before that of

14 cubic miles of rock, or about four times the amount of the famous Krakatoa eruption of A.D. 1883. This eruption has been linked to the fall of Minoan civilization on Crete, and even to the fall of the Xia dynasty in China (Chinese records suggest that a "volcanic winter" may have played a role in the latter event). Goedicke believes that the "glow over the coastline"[136] in the inscription refers to observation of the event from the north shore of Egypt. He thinks that the eruption triggered a tsunami, which is the source of the great water torrent that Hatshepsut refers to. Possibly a wadi helped to divert some of the waters and so spare Egypt further devastation, and it is for this that Hatshepsut offers thanks to Pakhet for saving her (or Egypt) from getting drowned (Pakhet's alter ego, the goddess Bastet, was revered in the eastern Delta). The darkness that required the lighting of lamps at the shrines would be a result of the darkening of the sky in the aftermath of the eruption, the air being filled with heavy clouds of soot. The flight of refugees to the south would be a natural result of so much distress in the Delta. This could result in the pillaging of a temple along the refugees' route into Upper Egypt, and it would have put a strain upon local resources in the south.

Goedicke is not unaware of the similarities between his interpretation of the Speos Artemidos inscription and the exodus. The soot-like dust that filled the land and caused boils (Exod. 9:8–11), the ferocious and unnatural storms (Exod. 9:20–25), and the darkness that filled the land (Exod. 10:22) could all be aftereffects of the eruption. Furthermore, he suggests, when the Israelites left Egypt, they turned north toward Lake Manzala, a large and irregularly shaped bay above the eastern Delta that opens into the Mediterranean Sea. They became trapped with the sea north, south, and east of them and with the Egyptians to their west. But, as a result of the powerful winds stirred up by the unnatural weather, and especially because of the tsunami, the waters temporarily drew back for the Israelites but then swamped the pursuing Egyptians.[137] Goedicke thus sees not only the Thera eruption but also the Israelite exodus reflected in the Speos Artemidos inscription.

Thutmose III." On the other hand, Frank Yurco, "End of the Late Bronze Age and other crisis periods: A Volcanic Cause?" in *Gold of Praise: Studies on Ancient Egypt in Honor of Edward F. Wente*, SAOC 58, ed. Emily Teeter and John A. Larson (Chicago: University of Chicago, 1999), 455–463, asserts that the Thera eruption is securely dated to 1628 B.C., during the Hyksos period.

136. Goedicke, *Speos Artimedos*, 6.

137. See Goedicke, *Speos Artimedos*, 102–4.

There are grave objections to this scenario. The Bible indicates that the Israelites departed by way of the Wadi Tumilat, considerably south of the Mediterranean. What were they doing so far north, by Lake Manzala? Although we must allow for a margin of error in both the geochronology of the Thera eruption and in the chronology of the pharaohs, Hatshepsut's reign (1479–1457) appears to be too early for even the Early Date exodus, and Thera seems to be too early for Hatshepsut's reign. Strong evidence places the Thera eruption at about 1628 B.C.[138] It is true that Manfred Bietak examined the pumice at Tell el-Dabʿa and dated it to a time very nearly consistent with Hatshepsut's reign, but this is not decisive.[139] Also, the Bible indicates that there was some time between the plagues and the subsequent crossing of the sea. This is not consistent with a tsunami, which would have hit the coastline very quickly after the eruption, even before the sooty clouds and storms made their way into Egypt.

In the final analysis, this entire scenario is most likely to be completely wrong. Goedicke is a serious scholar, and his analysis of the inscription is detailed. Even so, his translation is not the only, or even the standard, interpretation of that text. In a recent analysis of the inscription by James P. Allen,[140] Goedicke's "glow" is simply the beneficent rays of the sun. The shrines are doing well and are not sitting in darkness or being moved to temporary locations. Hatshepsut does restore temples and send provisions to needy areas, but not because they are in chaos and overrun with refugees. Temple maintenance and local food shortages were routine problems that every ancient ruler had to face. Hatshepsut's references to Asiatics, in this interpretation, are primarily a retrospective look back at the damage done to Egypt by the Hyksos, and there is no reference to placing them under forced labor. She does, however, speak of expelling the Hyksos, whom she calls the "abominations of the gods."[141]

---

138. Sivertsen, *Parting of the Sea*, 23–7.

139. Bietak, *Avaris*, 78. But Yurco, "End of Late Bronze," argues that the pumice evidence is not conclusive.

140. James P. Allen, "The Speos Artemidos Inscription of Hatshepsut," *Bulletin of the Egyptological Seminar* 16 (2002): 1–17. See also James Henry Breasted, *Ancient Records of Egypt* (Chicago: University of Chicago, 1906), §§296–303.

141. This interpretation of the text, to be sure, has a problem of its own: it has her taking credit for the departure of the Hyksos. How could Hatshepsut boast of this, an event that took place some 80 years before she wrote this inscription? Pharaohs did tend to try to grab glory from their predecessors' accomplishments, but this seems a bit much. On the other hand,

Goedicke's is a fascinating but unlikely historical situation for the exodus.[142] If nothing else, it is a tale worth telling to illustrate the dangers of speculative and eccentric interpretations that seek to sweep away all the problems of dating the exodus by means of one grand theory.

The Sivertsen Hypothesis

A new theory based in part on the Thera eruption has been proposed by geologist Barbara Sivertsen. She argues that there were two exodus events; the first was in 1628 B.C. and coincided with the eruption of Thera, and the second took place in 1450 and coincided with the eruption of Yali (another Aegean volcanic island). She believes that proto-Israelites living in the Wadi Tumilat area during the Second Intermediate period were forced out of their homes by the effects of the Thera eruption and that, under the leadership of Moses, they went to Mt. Sinai in 1628. She argues that the first nine plagues (except for the locusts) were the effects of the volcanic eruption. Three generations later these Israelites invaded Canaan and destroyed Jericho in about 1550. In this, she affirms that Jericho City IV was in fact destroyed by Israelites at the end of the Middle Bronze Age. She bases her belief that Israel was in the wilderness for four generations on Gen. 15:16. She believes that the second exodus was made up of Israelite captives who had been taken to Egypt early in the reign of Thutmose III. She credits the Yali eruption of c. 1450 with causing the plague of the firstborn, and she believes that the Israelites fled Egypt at this time by the "Way of Horus," near the Mediterranean coast, and that pursuing Egyptians were drowned in a tsunami caused by the Yali eruption. The two exodus events were merged, she says, in Israelite oral history. As people repeated the stories, they were melded into one, coherent tale.[143]

Hatshepsut may be claiming merely that she removed the last vestiges of the Hyksos' presence in Egypt, not that she personally drove them out. See Allen 2002, 17.

142. In addition to chronological problems attendant to dating Thera as late as Hatshepsut's reign, and to questions raised about Goedicke's translation of the inscription, there is an alternative theory that associates the Thera eruption with the reign of Ahmose. Based on the "Tempest Inscription" dated to the year 22 of Ahmose (c. 1530 B.C.), this interpretation asserts that widespread flooding in Egypt described in this text corresponds to the eruption of Thera. See Karen P. Foster, Robert K. Ritner and Benjamin R. Foster, "Texts, Storms, and the Thera Eruption," *JNES* 55, no. 1 (1996): 1–14.

143. Sivertsen, *Parting of the Sea*.

Sivertsen's study is erudite and is worth reading if only for the enormous amount of information she has accumulated. The most obvious problem with her work is that she is highly arbitrary in her use of biblical data, taking some details very literally, modifying others, and rejecting others outright as nonhistorical. She justifies this by appealing to studies in oral history on what details are likely to be lost or remembered, and on how memories can be merged. But one cannot help sensing that biblical data that do not fit her theory are simply tossed aside. For me, her hypothesis is another example of the kind of eccentric exodus theory that the reader should avoid.

Chronological Conundrums

In addition to specific issues related to the circumstances at the time of the exodus and conquest, a theory for dating these events must also take into account events prior to the exodus. Can the price for which Joseph was sold as a slave date the exodus? Who was the pharaoh when Joseph became vizier? When and for how long were the Israelites enslaved? How long were the Israelites in Egypt? Most importantly, are we sure that we understand the biblical use of numbers?

The Price of a Slave

The purchase price for Joseph, when his brothers sold him into slavery, was 20 shekels (Gen. 37:28). If the Late Date for the exodus is correct, this took place sometime after 1700 B.C. After a survey of the prices paid for a slave in the history of the ancient Near East, Kitchen argues that this price is right for this time.[144] The average price for a slave in Mari or Old Babylonia, for example, is at about 20 shekels at this time, but a slave's price was lower at earlier times (8 to 10 shekels in the Third Dynasty of Ur, just before 2000 B.C.) and higher at later times (30 shekels in Ugarit or Nuzi, from the 15th to 13th centuries, and 50 shekels or above in 1st millennium Assyria). Thus, the price paid for Joseph dates this event fairly precisely to about 1800–1600 B.C.

There is, however, a significant flaw in this argument. As Kitchen himself notes, the actual price paid for a slave could vary greatly; the figures he gives are only averages. In short, Kitchen concerns himself with only one economic factor: long-term inflation. But several other economic factors go into determining the price paid in an individual purchase. First, there is short-term inflation or deflation. In ancient Rome, the price of slaves plummeted when Caesar flooded the market with captives from his wars with Gaul. Second, there is the

144. Kitchen, *Reliability*, 344–5.

quality of the individual "merchandise." A young, strong, or skilled slave could fetch a high price, but an unskilled, aged, or sickly-looking person would only command a low price. From the records of Caecilius Jucundus, a businessman of ancient Pompeii, we know that a woman named Umbricia Antiochis in A.D. 56 sold a slave named Trophimus for 6,252 sesterces. But another slave just two years earlier sold for just 1,500 sesterces; obviously Trophimus was a slave of high value.[145] Third, there are the individual circumstances of the buyer. A rich man infatuated with a beautiful slave girl might pay an exorbitant price to have her; a shrewd merchant with no emotional stake in the purchase would know how to buy the same girl for as little as possible. Fourth, there are the circumstances of the seller. If a person was for whatever reason desperate to unload a slave, he would take a very low price. Which of these factors apply here?

The short answer is that we do not know. Perhaps the brothers were anxious to get rid of Joseph (since their alternative was to kill him), and so they took a low price. On the other hand, perhaps the price of 20 shekels was a high price for a slave at this particular time and place. If this is the case, the text could be implying that the high price paid for him showed that Joseph was an outstanding individual, both talented and handsome (this is sustained both by how Joseph's masters invariably put him in charge and by the sexual desire of Potiphar's wife toward him). But the reality is that we cannot say whether the narrator expects us to be struck with how cheaply or how dearly Joseph was bought, or whether this is just an incidental detail and that Joseph brought in an average price. The price of Joseph tells us nothing about the date of the exodus.

The Pharaohs of Joseph, of the Enslavement, and of the Exodus

A significant problem for both the Early and the Late Date schemes is postulating which pharaoh enslaved the Hebrews and which pharaoh ruled Egypt at the time of the exodus. In the Late Date model, of course, the latter question is answered decisively: the pharaoh of the exodus was Ramesses II. On close inspection, however, this does not settle matters at all. Ramesses II was one of the most powerful pharaohs of all, and he ruled an empire that included Canaan. How are we to square this with his being the pharaoh whose power was broken by the plagues? K. A. Kitchen not only supports the Late Date for the exodus, but he is also the world's foremost authority on Ramesses II. Yet

145. Mary Beard, *The Fires of Vesuvius: Pompeii Lost and Found* (Cambridge, MA: Harvard University Press, 2008), 179.

he makes little attempt to set the exodus in the context of Ramesses II's reign; he merely argues that it happened perhaps sometime after regnal year 15 and notes that Ramesses's treatment of other foreign laborers is analogous to what we see in the Bible.[146] On the other hand, the Early Date also has a problem with identifying the pharaoh of the exodus. The date of 1447 sets it in the middle of the reign of Thutmose III, but he, too, was a great warrior pharaoh who dominated Canaan. It may be that our Egyptian chronology is wrong, but interpreters with no expertise in Egyptology cannot pick and choose dates that favor their particular theory.

The pharaoh of the enslavement is somewhat of a problem for the Early Date. If we assume for Israel an enslavement of 80 years and a 1447 exodus, we have the slavery beginning right after the expulsion of the Hyksos. No time could be better suited for postulating the enslavement, but it only works if the enslavement period was right at about 80 to 90 years. The length of the Israelite enslavement is not given in Exodus, but it seems to have been at least 80 years, since the Israelites were already enslaved when Moses was born and since they were not released until he was about age 80. If the period of slavery was longer than that, one has a Hyksos king enslaving the Israelites, and that makes little sense. The Late Date could also postulate an enslavement at the time of the expulsion of the Hyksos (that would make for an enslavement of almost 300 years), but it could also set the enslavement anytime within the early 18th dynasty.

The identity of the pharaoh who elevated Joseph is also somewhat of a problem for the Late Date. If we assume that Israel had been in Egypt for 430 years at the time of the exodus (on the basis of Exod. 12:40), and if we assume that the exodus occurred in about 1250, then Israel entered Egypt in 1680. This suggests that the pharaoh who knew Joseph was Merneferre Ay, who reigned 1691–1668. The difficulty is that this pharaoh ruled Egypt at the end of the 13th dynasty, as the Middle Kingdom ended and the Second Intermediate began. With his death Egypt fairly fell apart; the next major event was the rise of the Hyksos. But Genesis implies that the Joseph's pharaoh ruled all of Egypt (see Gen. 41:29–30) and that Joseph, by his able administration, only made Egypt all the more unified and under the pharaoh's direct authority, as all real property was sold to him for food (see Gen. 47:13–23). This seems a far cry from the political chaos that Egypt was sinking into during the 13th dynasty.

Having Joseph present in Egypt in the reign of Merneferre Ay is

146. See Kitchen, *Pharaoh Triumphant*, 70–1.

not impossible. It is conceivable that although a capable vizier, Joseph's administration allowed large numbers of Semites to immigrate during and after the famine. Evidence does indicate a sizable Semitic presence in the eastern Delta during the 13th dynasty.[147] If so, this would have set up Egypt for the time of Hyksos domination. Also, we might say from an economic standpoint that leaving all the property of the kingdom concentrated in the hands of one king, while the mass of the population was enslaved, may not have been such a good thing. Thus, although Joseph's administration was a great success from the standpoint of the royal house, we cannot be sure that Egypt remained politically and economically healthy after Joseph's death.

Using the Early Date, on the other hand, and still working with a 430-year sojourn, Israel entered Egypt about 1877 B.C. This coincides with the reign of Amenemhet II (1901–1866), a 12th dynasty (Middle Kingdom) pharaoh, who ruled at a time when Egypt was unified. This agrees better with what we gather about the political situation during Joseph's time. There was a process of unifying the kingdom and dismantling the power of the nomarchs during the Middle Kingdom; Sesostris III (also called Senusret III; 1862–1843) is often credited with bringing the power of local lords under control. The main title used by nomarchs, "great overlord," came into disuse during his reign. But the actual demotion of the nomarchs may have occurred prior to his time. But even if this is so, we are far from demonstrating that the increased centralization of power that took place during the Middle Kingdom was the result of Joseph's administration. The diminution of nomarch power may have been the result of prolonged royal policy in the Middle Kingdom,[148] and not due to something as dramatic as a seven-year famine. Also, the Genesis narrative appears to say that Joseph bartered food for land with common people, not with the high nobility. In fact, Joseph specifically exempted the priests (who in Egypt were aristocrats and not a purely religious order) from having to sell their land (see Gen. 47:20–22). That is, unlike the Middle Kingdom consolidation of pharaonic power, Joseph does not appear to have been in a power struggle with the nomarchs.

In summary, the data concerning Joseph, the oppression, and the exodus do not strongly favor or exclude either a Late or Early Date. Also, as described below, one should be wary of trying to resolve such

147. Manfred Bietak, "Canaanites in the Eastern Nile Delta," in *Egypt, Israel, Sinai: Archaeological and Historical Relationships in the Biblical Period*, ed. Anson F. Rainey (Tel Aviv: Tel Aviv University, 1987), 41–56.

148. See Shaw, *Oxford Egypt*, 174–6.

questions by simply adding up years. Our computations may in fact be based on a faulty reading of the Bible.

A Caveat on Early Biblical Chronology

When discussing biblical chronology, we cannot always be sure that we are interpreting the various numbers of years mentioned in the Bible in the manner that the authors intended. We have already seen, for example, that there are alternative proposals about interpreting the 480 years of 1 Kings 6:1. In the above section, I have used the 430 years of Exod. 12:40 as a guide to setting up a chronological correspondence between Egyptian history and the exodus narrative. But Jewish interpretation, as preserved in the Talmud, asserts that the Egyptian sojourn was not 430 years but 210 years. Following talmudic texts, one can find the exact chronology for all of biblical (Old Testament) history, beginning with the year of Adam's creation (in year 1 of the calendar, or 3760 B.C.). According to the rabbinical reckoning, Jacob and his family entered Egypt in 2238 (1523 B.C.), and the exodus took place in 2448 (1313 B.C.).[149] Exodus 12:40, which seems to demand a 430-year Egyptian sojourn, is given an entirely different interpretation that essentially cuts that time in half. The 430 years of Exod. 12:40, according to talmudic teaching, actually go from God's covenant with Abraham (Gen. 15) to the departure from Egypt.[150]

The talmudic interpreters and the traditions they represent maintained unimpeachable respect for the veracity of the text. They did not come up with their interpretations in order to accommodate modernity. Most importantly for Christian readers, the Apostle Paul gives the 430 years of Exod. 12:40 the same interpretation. He asserts that there were 430 years between the giving of the promises to Abraham and the arrival of Israel at Mt. Sinai (Gal. 3:16–17). In Acts 13:17–20a, Paul mentions a 450-year span of time from the time God chose the patriarchs (which begins at Gen. 12) to the beginning of the judges period.[151]

---

149. Following this system, and because of the long lives of the patriarchs, there was a direct line of tradition from Adam, to Lamech (in the Seth line), to Noah, to Abraham, to Jacob, to Jochebed (mother of Moses), and to Moses. That is, Moses could have heard stories from his mother that had been handed down through a very few persons, going back to Adam himself (Mattis Kantor, *Codex Judaica: Chronological Index of Jewish History* [New York: Zichron, 2005], 69)!

150. Kantor, *Codex Judaica*, 70.

151. See the NIV and ESV, which properly render the Greek of Acts 13:20a. The 450 years covers the whole span of time for the events of vv. 17–19.

This is plainly impossible if one reads Exod. 12:40 to mean that Israel was in Egypt for 430 years, as it would require compressing all of the patriarchal period plus the years of the conquest into twenty years.

The talmudic chronology places the entrance into Egypt at a time corresponding to the beginning of the 18th dynasty, has David establish his capital in Jerusalem in 2892 (869 B.C.), has the fall of Jerusalem in 3338 (423 B.C.), and places the Nehemiah mission to Jerusalem in 3426 (335 B.C.). The whole history of the Persian Empire from Cyrus's conquest of Babylon to Alexander the Great is compressed into about 60 years (from 3389 [372 B.C.] to 3448 [313 B.C.]). As a chronological reconstruction, this is oblivious to well-established facts of ancient history and is, plainly put, impossible. Of course, the fact that many aspects of talmudic chronology are wrong does not mean that their interpretation of the length of time between Abraham's covenant and the arrival at Mt. Sinai is wrong. In light of Paul's use of these dates, we should hesitate to insist that there must have been a 430-year sojourn in Egypt or that there must be 480 years between the exodus and Solomon's temple. We cannot be sure that we understand those figures as the authors intended.

The point here is not that we must or must not adopt the talmudic interpretation for the length of the Egyptian sojourn. The point is that there is an ancient tradition of interpretation that reconstructs the chronology of biblical history in a way that would never occur to modern, western readers. We are not required to choose between the apparently literal meaning of Exod. 12:40 and the apparently literal meaning of Gal. 3:16–17. Rather, we should be careful about assuming that we know exactly how biblical numbers have been computed and are meant to be used. Either Exodus, or Galatians, or both may compute the 430 years in a way we do not understand.

Umberto Cassuto points out that the Sumerian king lists have the names of kings of various Mesopotamian cities together with the number of years of their reigns. Since these kings ruled over separate cities at the same time, their reigns overlapped. But when the list gives the total number of years of the reigns of the kings, it does not give a total for the region as a whole. It acts as though every king had reigned successively, one after another and in a single sequence, disregarding the fact that many kings reigned as contemporaries.[152] The authors of the list were not stupid; they simply had their own reasons for doing it as they did it.

---

152. Umberto Cassuto, *A Commentary on the Book of Exodus,* trans. Israel Abrahams (Jerusalem: Magnes, 1967), 86–7.

In the Bible, the numbers are correct, but they are correct in asserting what they actually meant, and this is not necessarily the same as what we think they meant. If we do not know how the authors computed their numbers or what, to them, was the significance of the numbers, our interpretations will be wrong, even when we read a text that to us seems obvious and unambiguous in its meaning. And in fact, we probably do not understand the reasoning behind some of the biblical numbers.

A Very Early Date or a Very Late Date?
Thus far, we have focused only on the Early Date of about 1447 and the Late Date of about 1250 as proposed dates for the exodus. The reader should understand, however, that on the basis of biblical and archaeological evidence one could also argue for a "Very Early Date" and a "Very Late Date." An examination of these two positions illustrates, if nothing else, that the evidence can be taken to point in a direction completely different from the two standard positions.

THE VERY EARLY DATE
One could argue for a much earlier date for the exodus, with a conquest of about 1550 B.C. This would harmonize Joshua's invasion with the standard archaeological interpretation of the fall of Jericho and would allow one to read the chronological data of Judges fairly literally, without the need for a compression of the number of years found there. The total number of years explicitly given in the biblical text for this period is 554, but some chronological information is not supplied (we lack clear information for the years of Joshua, Samuel, and Saul). Beginning from the fourth year of Solomon's reign (967) and adding 554 plus a few additional years to make up for missing biblical information, while also allowing for a margin of error in the standard date for the fall of Jericho (1550), one could easily argue that the chronology of Joshua–Judges–Samuel favors a conquest date contemporary with the fall of Jericho and the end of the Middle Bronze Age in Canaan.[153] One the basis of archaeological data alone, no period would seem a better candidate for the time of the biblical conquest. As described

153. Hoffmeier, "Biblical Date," 227–8, estimates a period a 633 years, which is a bit high for my purposes. But where the Bible does not give us any chronological information, filling in the gaps is, after all, guesswork. More importantly, however, I am not arguing that the biblical data must be taken to agree with a 1550 conquest; I am simply observing that they could be reasonably interpreted in that way.

above, Canaan abruptly went from being a heavily populated region with numerous fortified cities to being a fairly ruined civilization, with its walled cities brought down and its population a fraction of what it had been before. The Middle Bronze Age cities of Canaan were indeed "fortified to the heavens" (Deut. 9:1), but this is not true of the cities of the Late Bronze Age I. In addition to Jericho, moreover, Middle Bronze Age Shechem ended in a cataclysmic destruction at this time.[154] This could explain how the Israelites were able to have their covenant renewal ceremony at that site (Josh. 24): Israel had already obliterated the city. Also, Middle Bronze Hazor suffered a massive destruction at the end of the Middle Bronze Age,[155] in agreement with the biblical account of the destruction of Hazor (Josh. 11:10–13).

There are, however, serious problems with this scenario. First, it places the exodus in the latter part of the Hyksos period of Egypt. This is not compatible with the biblical account. One might argue that the pharaoh of the exodus was Egyptian and equate the expulsion of the Hyksos with the Israelite exodus. But the two events were radically different, as described above (see "The Hyksos"). In addition, there is no physical evidence that Israelites began to live in Canaan as early as 1550. Evidence for an Israelite presence does not show up until Iron I (1200–1000 B.C.). If Israel was in Canaan for a period of 350 years prior to the beginning of Iron I, how does one account for their invisibility in the archaeological record for so long a period? Why aren't the Israelites mentioned in the Amarna Letters if in fact Israel controlled a significant amount of the territory in Canaan and had been there for 200 years? Finally, one would have to account for all the biblical data that seems to demand a lower date for the exodus and conquest (Exod. 1:11; 1 Kings 6:1).

The Very Late Date

By contrast, one could argue for a Very Late Date exodus, in the early 12th century, with a conquest at about 1150 B.C. This position has been capably defended by Gary Rendsburg, and it is based upon certain cities in the archaeological record in the mid- to late-12th century and on various other pieces of biblical evidence. For example, Rendsburg states that the "evidence from places such as ʿIzbet Sartah,

154. The evidence for the destruction of Shechem at the end of Middle Bronze Age "displays a calculated ferocity and an intent to cause complete destruction of the city," according to Lawrence Toombs, "Shechem," in Freedman, *ABD* Vol. 5, 1182.

155. Ben-Tor, "Hazor," 2:595.

Giloh, Shiloh, Ai, Khirbet Raddana, and others points to the arrival of the Israelites in this region only in the 12th century."[156] These are all in the central hill country, the area that Israel settled first. He observes that King David is a fifth-generation descendant of Nashon, who was a prominent member of the tribe of Judah during the exodus (Ruth 4:18–22; 1 Chr. 2:5–15; see Exod. 6:23 and Num. 1:7). Allowing for an average of 30 years per generation, Nashon and the exodus generation are placed in the early part of the 12th century.

Rendsburg also argues that the mention of "Israel" in the Merenptah Stele refers to Israel while still enslaved in Egypt. This enables him to resolve a long-standing problem. During the empire period of the New Kingdom of Egypt, Canaan was essentially in vassal status to Egypt, and Egyptian pharaohs (especially Thutmose III and Ramesses II) conducted major military operations throughout the region. But the Egyptians never mention an encounter with Israel (until the Merenptah Stele), and the Bible never mentions an encounter with the Egyptians during the Judges period. Rendsburg claims that his reconstruction explains why Joshua and Judges never mention the campaigns of the great New Kingdom pharaohs in Canaan—he says it is because Israel itself was not yet in Canaan.[157] Rendsburg argues that Ramesses III, the pharaoh who repulsed the Sea Peoples, was the pharaoh of the exodus.[158]

There are, of course, objections to the Very Late Date for the conquest. First, it requires a rather extreme compression of the period from Joshua to David. Second, it, too, has significant problems with the archaeological record. Two cities that are explicitly declared to have been destroyed by Joshua—Jericho and Hazor—do not have destruction levels that correspond with a mid-12th century conquest. Rendsburg argues from the hieroglyphs that the Israel of the Merenptah Stele refers to a people in slavery in Egypt, but to all appearances, the Stele

156. Rendsburg, "Date of the Exodus," 514–5.

157. One should note that this problem is also resolved in the standard Late Date model, since in that model Israel was not in Canaan during the 18th dynasty or the early 19th dynasty. Joshua's conquest only begins after Ramesses II has ceased leading campaigns into Canaan. The standard Late Date only has to get Israel into the land prior to Merenptah's incursion into Canaan.

158. All the arguments for the Very Late Date summarized here, and others, can be found in Rendsburg, "Date of the Exodus." See also Cyrus H. Gordon and Gary Rendsburg, *The Bible and the Ancient Near East* (New York: W. W. Norton, 1997), 149–52.

presents Israel as living in Canaan. In context, it groups Israel with Canaan, Ashkelon, Gezer, Yenoam (south of the Sea of Galilee) and Hurru (Syria).[159] The standard view of the Merenptah Stele is that it identifies Israel as residents of Canaan and not as slaves in Egypt, and this is surely correct.[160]

The Reality of the Exodus

Did the exodus really happen, or is it, as many believe today, a fictional national saga? The case against the historicity of the exodus is primarily negative in nature: there is in Egypt no evidence for a Hebrew sojourn or exodus. That is, no Egyptian text refers to either event,[161] and no physical evidence for an Israelite sojourn has been found. Superficially this appears to be devastating, but in reality it is not even surprising.

There are relatively few texts at all from ancient Egypt. Indeed, it is said that an Egyptologist can, in the course of his or her career, read every surviving text from classical Egypt. The Egyptians wrote on papyrus, an early version of paper, and even in the arid conditions of Egypt almost no papyrus documentation from as early as 1400 B.C. has survived. It has been estimated that at least 99 percent of all papyrus documents from Egypt have completely perished. Many of the written records that we do have are carved into stone or painted on tomb walls. Monuments, by their very nature, celebrate the victories and achievements of a government and leave its failures in obscurity.[162] It is unthinkable that any pharaoh would erect a monument to victory of the Hebrews and their God. And no Egyptian would want his "house of eternity" (his tomb) decorated with information about this episode,

159. Rendsburg, "Date of the Exodus," 517–20. Rendsburg contends that Israel is listed among the Canaanite states because the Egyptians knew that this was where the Israelites came from.

160. Rainey and Notley, *Sacred Bridge*, 99: "One thing is certain: there was a socioethnic group called *'Yasirˀil'* (Israel) in the southern Levant during the final decade of the thirteenth century BCE."

161. Josephus, *Against Apion* 1:228–52, summarizes an account of the exodus written by Manetho (an Egyptian priest who wrote a history of Egypt in Greek, c. 300 B.C.), but this version is so late and so confused as to have little or no weight as evidence. Also, I am not counting the claim that the Speos Artemidos inscription refers to the exodus.

162. We should also observe that a large number of Egypt's monuments have also been lost. Some were deliberately defaced by later pharaohs, and some were dismantled by later generations in order to recycle and use their cut stone.

when Egypt's gods failed. In addition, the Hebrews inhabited mudbrick homes in the soft, wet soil of the Delta. That being the case, it would be remarkable if identifiable and distinctive remains of their presence had survived to be found. The negative evidence, therefore, does not falsify the biblical account.[163]

The evidence in favor of an exodus that one can cite depends in part on whether one supports an early or a late exodus. Some of the evidence that one might use to make the case for an early exodus (such as the accounts of the Habiru in the Amarna Letters) is irrelevant for an exodus from the time of Ramesses II and, similarly, the construction of Pi-Riᶜamsese by Ramesses II is largely irrelevant if one supports an early exodus. The Habiru in the Amarna letters, Akhenaten's reformation, and the Soleb inscription make for an impressive circumstantial case if one is arguing for the Early Date. Similarly, if one supports the Late Date, it is remarkable that the Egyptian capital was in the south, at Thebes or Memphis, for almost all of Egyptian history up until the time of Ramesses II, when it was close by the Hebrew settlement at Goshen. There exists, therefore, a good bit of evidence that one can use to argue for the biblical account, regardless of which date may seem most probable. In my view, this is not an unhappy state of affairs. It is true that we cannot date the exodus precisely, but the inverse of this is that any one of the dates could be valid, and there is substantial evidence for each. The most important point is that the biblical exodus did happen. But some arguments can be made independently, to a degree, of which date one follows. A few examples are given below.

The Store Cities Again

Whether one supports the Early or the Late Date, both agree on the fact that the city Raamses is Pi-Riᶜamsese at Tell el-Dabᶜa. But the most important fact is that the city there disappeared by the end of the 20th dynasty (c. 1069 B.C.). If the exodus is a piece of fiction devised much later in Israelite history, how did its creators know that there had been Semites in the area of the long-lost city of Pi-Riᶜamsese, or indeed that there had ever been such a city? Some scholars, therefore, will insist

163. Of course, many scholars regard the exodus story as nonhistorical. For a good example of a review of the evidence from this perspective, see Propp, *Exodus 19–40*, 735–53. Propp believes that certain pieces of evidence suggest that there are scattered nuggets of historical truth in Exodus, but he argues that no reconstruction that purports to describe the events as they actually happened is persuasive. For him, Exodus is essentially a work of fiction.

that what the Bible calls Raamses was actually the much later city of Tanis. These scholars will claim that the biblical writers were simply confused about the history of the Delta and wrongly placed Israelites at Tanis because that was the only big, Egyptian city that they knew about. But this argument only shows, as Hoffmeier has written, that these scholars "are bent on denying credibility to the biblical narratives at any cost."[164] A more honest reading of the data tells us that the biblical writers knew their history well and were not making things up. By placing the Israelite workers at Raamses (Tell el-Dabʿa) and not at Tanis, the Bible demonstrates firsthand knowledge of Egypt as it was in the latter half of the 2nd millennium B.C.

The Settlement and Conquest of Canaan

The sudden appearance of Israelite settlements at the beginning of the Iron Age—with no convincing explanation except that they came in from outside—also supports the idea that there was an exodus and conquest. This is true even if, on the early exodus model, one has to explain why the Israelites were archaeologically invisible for a long time (a people who arrived in tents and settled into homes that others had built would for a long time leave no archaeological footprint). The story of the Hyksos and their expulsion can be incorporated into either the late or early exodus, since it affords a plausible explanation for the fear and hatred the Egyptians felt toward the Hebrews with either date. Although we don't quite know how all the details work out, it is clear that Hazor was, as the Bible tells us, the dominant city of Upper Galilee in the Late Bronze Age but that it suffered multiple destructions during this time.

The Tent of Meeting

The structure of the Tent of Meeting, as described in Exod. 25–40, is regarded by many scholars as a piece of fiction, a literary creation of the Priestly writer (P) during the postexilic era. It was supposedly meant to legitimate the postexilic temple structure and priestly system. Here, too, Kitchen has demonstrated that this thinking arises from total ignorance of the actual practices of ancient Near Eastern peoples.

Portable shrines of various kinds, made with wooden frameworks that were plated with gold leaf and made to be set into bases (see Exod. 26:19, 29), are known from Archaic and Old Kingdom Egypt. One of the most famous of these is the canopy of Queen Hetepheres from the Old Kingdom. Descriptions and photographs of the reconstructed canopy

---

164. Hoffmeier, *Ancient Israel*, 58.

can be found in numerous textbooks on ancient Egypt.[165] From the early 2nd millennium, we have examples of portable shrines in the Mari texts. Many more parallels are available from the late 2nd millennium, at a time roughly contemporary with Moses. For example, the Ugaritic epic poem of Kirta refers to the making of sacrifice in a tent, and the text uses vocabulary that is cognate to the terms the Hebrew Bible uses for the Tent of Meeting. The tent of Ramesses II has close analogies to the Tent of Meeting (remember that he was regarded as a god). It was rectangular, with an outer room twice as large as the inner room (analogous to the holy place and the most holy place in the Tent of Meeting). When in camp, the four divisions of the army encamped in a square around pharaoh's tent, just as was done for the Tent of Meeting (Num. 2). In some representations, the inner chamber of the pharaoh's tent includes two falcons facing each other, analogous to the two cherubim facing each other above the mercy seat (Exod. 25:18–20). Silver trumpets for ritual use, similar to those described in Num. 10, were found in Tutankhamun's tomb.[166]

These facts render the theory that the Tent of Meeting is the idealized literary creation of the priestly writer not only unnecessary but unlikely. The theory is unnecessary because we know that such shrines existed, and thus there is no reason to consider them idealized. It is unlikely because it is doubtful that a postexilic writer would be able to describe accurately a 2nd millennium-type portable shrine.[167]

The Other Side of the Jordan

The archaeology of Edom, Moab and Ammon is thought by some to argue against the veracity of the biblical account of the conquest. Scholars note that archaeological evidence for the existence of these kingdoms during the Late Bronze Age is scanty. In the 1930s, for example, Nelson Glueck did a surface survey of Moabite territory and found a gap—a period when the territory appears to have been unoccupied—from about 1900 B.C. until sometime in the 13th century, when there was a surge in occupation.[168] Similarly, archaeologists report

165. For example, Christine Hobson, *Exploring the World of the Pharaohs* (London: Thames and Hudson, 1987), 78–9.

166. Kitchen, *Reliability*, 276–80.

167. For a complete survey of ancient parallels to the Tent of Meeting, see Michael H. Homan, *To Your Tents, O Israel! The Terminology, Function, Form and Symbolism of Tents in the Hebrew Bible and the Ancient Near East* (Leiden: Brill, 2002), 89–128.

168. Nelson Glueck eventually allowed that there was some occupation during this time. See Glueck, *The Other Side of the Jordan* (Cambridge, MA:

that Tell Hesban (the location of Heshbon, the city of Sihon, whom the Israelites conquered [Num. 21:21–35]), was not occupied until the 12th century—too late for Moses's troops to have destroyed it even with the late exodus. On the other hand, although Heshbon for the Iron Age and afterward was located at Tell Hesban, it may have been located elsewhere in the area earlier, at Jalul or Umeiri.[169] Kitchen also notes that Ramesses II tells us that he campaigned against Moab in the 13th century and captured five specific forts there, demonstrating that the Moabites were definitely in the area at this time. Finally, Kitchen argues that it is anachronistic to believe that no kingdom exists unless there are fixed settlements with walls, agriculture, and other features of urban life. He observes, for example, that the Assyrian King List opens with 17 kings "who lived in tents."[170]

The Hurrians

The Hurrians were a 2nd millennium people of northern Mesopotamia. Their greatest political entity was the kingdom of Mitanni, which we had occasion to mention in connection with the wars of Egypt's 18th dynasty. They had, in their ascendency, spread across the ancient Near East and especially into the Levant. With the fall of Mitanni, they did not abruptly disappear but remained as an ethnic group identifiable by the personal names they used until around the end of the 2nd millennium. After that, Hurrian culture ceased. It turns out that some of the persons mentioned in the Bible during the conquest period have Hurrian names. These include Hoham of Hebron, Piram of Jarmuth (Josh. 10:3) and two of the Anakim, Sheshai and Talmai (Josh. 15:14).[171] The presence of these Hurrian names speaks to the authenticity of the record; a writer living in the mid-1st millennium, who was essentially making the story up, would not have access to authentic Hurrian names, or indeed have any reason to use them.

American Schools of Oriental Research, 1970). He wrote, "Sometime before the end of the Late Bronze Age, well before the beginning of the thirteenth century B.C. a new agricultural civilization appeared, as we have already noted, belonging to the Edomites, Moabites, Ammonites, and Amorites [and it] became dominant in particular geographical regions in central and southern Transjordan and may have begun to establish permanent settlements" (p. 157).

169. Lawrence T. Geraty, "Heshbon," *NEAEHL* 2:626.

170. Kitchen, *Reliability*, 195–6.

171. Ibid., 176.

Summary and Conclusion

The exodus, we may be sure, did happen as described in the Bible. On the other hand, we must be humble about our ability to assign it to a specific date. We have seen that one can readily argue for four different dates for the exodus, here simply called the Very Early Date, the Early Date, the Late Date, and the Very Late Date. For each one of these there is at least one biblical text that, if interpreted in its normal, literal, and most obvious sense, supports that position. For the Very Early Date, it is the chronology of Joshua–Judges–Samuel. For the Early Date, it is 1 Kings 6:1. For the Late Date, it is Exod. 1:11. For the Very Late Date, it is Ruth 4:18–22. Each of these positions has at least one major archaeological argument it can use to support its case. For the Very Early Date, there is the date of the destruction of Jericho and the collapse of Middle Bronze Age civilization. For the Early Date, there is the possible linkage between the Israelite conquest and the Habiru crisis of the Amarna Age. For the Late Date, there is the destruction of Hazor lower city stratum 1-a and upper city stratum XIII. For the Very Late Date, there is the argument that more specific evidence for an Israelite presence emerges later than even the Late Date suggests. Finally, each position has at least one significant problem. For the Very Early Date, there is the difficulty in correlating the exodus to the Hyksos period. For the Early Date, there is the absence of evidence for a settled Israel in Canaan during the Late Bronze Age and the fact that the archaeology of Shechem, Jericho, and Hazor, as currently understood, do not support the Early Date. Also, neither the Bible nor Egyptian records indicate any contact between Israel and Egypt until Merenptah. For the Late Date, there is sketchy evidence for an Israelite conquest at the end of the Late Bronze Age, except at Hazor. For the Very Late Date, there is the problem of the Merenptah Stele (which strongly suggests that Israel is in Canaan by 1200) and the problems of Jericho and Hazor.

If this causes us to despair, we do well to remember that Exodus never alludes to the Hyksos, or to Ahmose, Hatshepsut, Thutmose III, Amenhotep II, Akhenaten, Ramesses II, Merenptah, Ramesses III, or to any other pharaoh that might be associated with the oppression or the exodus. If we find ourselves vexed at trying to defend, for example, that Thutmose III was the pharaoh of the exodus, we are becoming distraught over defending a claim that the Bible never makes. Not only that, but we cannot be sure that details regarding the chronology of the Egyptian pharaohs or of Canaanite archaeology may not be revised as research continues.

The minister or Bible teacher, therefore, should refrain from specifying that this or that exodus event took place in the reign of this or that pharaoh. We should follow the biblical practice and simply refer to every Egyptian king connected to the story as "Pharaoh." If we had full knowledge of when the exodus and conquest took place and of what the circumstances in Egypt and Canaan were at the time, all the difficulties would melt away. But we have not been given that information.

In addition, the Bible teacher should refrain from adopting any eccentric revision of Egyptian history in order to make a correlation with the biblical account. The Internet is awash in weird theories of who was the pharaoh of the exodus, together with major revisions to biblical chronology that supposedly solve all the problems. Similarly, one should avoid the radical revisions to Egyptian chronology and history carried out by amateurs and by a few unconventional scholars.[172] Egyptology is an enormously complex field. Indeed, those who revise Egyptian chronology in order to sustain some eccentric correlation between the exodus story and Egyptian history end up creating new problems in other areas of biblical chronology. It is not that no revision is possible. But those of us who are amateurs in this field do not help our cause by embracing oddball theories.

It is said that when Europeans rediscovered Egypt after the Renaissance, they looked upon the pyramids of Egypt for the first time and declared them to be the storehouses built by Joseph. These Europeans were not unusually stupid, nor were they necessarily very devout or seeking to verify the Bible. They simply had very limited knowledge about Egypt, and they tried to explain what they observed on the basis of that small base of information. They knew that Joseph had built storehouses, and they saw large, stone buildings, and therefore, applying what little they knew to what little they saw, they assumed that the pyramids were granaries.

Our situation is not really so different. We, too, have limited knowledge of Egyptian history (lists of pharaonic names and the remains of tombs and temples built by these kings does not constitute a history). Indeed, in contrast to what we know of classical Greek and Roman history, Egyptian historiography for the New Kingdom is staggering for its meagerness, for its fragmentary nature, and for how much of it is really scholarly speculation (no disrespect for the intelligence, diligence, and careful scholarship of Egyptologists is implied or intended). The fragments of Manetho for Egyptian history can hardly compare to Thucydides for Greek history or to Polybius for Roman history, and

172. For example, David M. Rohl, *A Test of Time: The Bible from Myth to History* (London: Century, 1995).

these two are but a small piece of the tip of the iceberg of information available on the classical world.[173] Exodus, too, provides only a very narrow window into its historical setting. It is entirely concerned with the theological message of YHWH's deliverance of Israel, and it has no concern whatsoever with contemporary political events—so much so that it does not name a single Egyptian character in the story, to say nothing of not naming the pharaohs involved!

For myself, therefore, I do not think it is wise or right to suppose that we can correct what seems to be a deficiency in the Bible and fix a date for the exodus, describe fully the historical setting, or name the pharaoh of the exodus. At the same time, I see nothing that causes me to distrust the biblical account.[174] An analogous, hypothetical situation might be this: If Israel had encountered Greece during the Greek dark ages, and if the Bible had given us an account of that meeting that was highly theological but that did not name any Greek persons or correlate it to any other events or persons in history (the names of contemporary kings, for example), what could we say about it? Not much. We would very likely find that the biblical story would have echoes in bits and pieces of what we know of Aegean and Anatolian history and geography, but it would be difficult to put it all together. Of course, there would be many theories, and each would have strengths and each would have problems. The limitations of our data, however, would not falsify the biblical account.

In short, we have ample reason to believe that the biblical account is true, but we do not have sufficient information to specify the details of when it all happened and of what pharaohs were present. We should learn as much as we can about Egypt so that we may speak from light and not from darkness, but we should teach the biblical history and not some reconstructed, hypothetical model that tries to make definite what the Bible leaves indefinite. If we desire a bedrock reality that we can absolutely believe in, it is this: At the end of Israel's Egyptian

173. I am here comparing the classical Egyptian period (especially the New Kingdom) to the classical ages of Greece and Rome. I am not speaking of the Mycenaean period or of the Greek dark ages or of the murky time when Rome had kings. For these ages, information on the Egyptian predynastic and early dynastic periods is at least is as good, if not better, than what we know of Greece or Italy.

174. Of course, many will assert that the miracles falsify the exodus story, but this is a genuine presuppositional matter: Does one believe in God or not? I do, and therefore the presence of miracles, such as the plague on the firstborn, does not trouble me.

sojourn, God sent Moses to deliver them from their servitude. God, by the hand of Moses, sent plagues upon an obstinate pharaoh and his nation, until at last he slew their firstborn in a single night and finally drowned their army in the sea. He then brought Israel to Mt. Sinai and gave them his covenant.

THE LOCATION OF THE *YAM SUPH* AND OF MT. SINAI

The Israelites crossed the "Red Sea" or *Yam Suph* (יַם־סוּף [now often translated as "Sea of Reeds"]) on their way out of Egypt. The Bible always presents the "Red Sea" (hereinafter, the *Yam Suph*) as an actual geographical location (a place that can be used as a reference point, as in Exod. 10:19). It is not a mythopoeic setting, like the Island of Ogygia, where Calypso is said to have held Odysseus for seven years. Even references in the Song of the Sea (Exod. 15), although highly poetic, are not mythical in nature.[175] As such, the quest for its actual location is legitimate.

It is also legitimate to search for Mt. Sinai, and for the same reasons: the Bible treats it as a real and specific location, and it asserts that at later times later Israelites could still find it (1 Kings 19:8). Various mountains in the northern, central, and southern regions of the Sinai Peninsula, as well as mountains in Arabia and in ancient Edomite territory, have been proposed as the true Mt. Sinai. Similarly, various bodies of water between the Mediterranean Sea and the Gulf of Suez, as well as the Gulf of Suez itself and the Gulf of Aqaba, have been suggested as candidates for the *Yam Suph*, the sea that the Israelites crossed while fleeing the chariots of Pharaoh. The mountains proposed for Mt. Sinai in the northern or central areas of the Sinai Peninsula can be eliminated, however, on the grounds that they are too close to Kadesh-barnea. This site was located at the southern edge of Canaan (on the northern edge of the Sinai Peninsula) and is now understood to have been at either Ain Qedeis or the nearby Ain Qudeirat, about equidistant between the southern shore of the Dead Sea and the "Brook of Egypt," the Wadi el-Arish.[176] Deuteronomy 1:2 says that it is an eleven-day journey from Horeb (Sinai) to Kadesh-barnea, and these locations are much nearer one another than would require that length of travel time. One could argue that the Hebrews of the exodus, moving with their children, elders, and livestock, would move very slowly, but that argument will not work. The text does not say that it took Israel

175. Against Thomas B. Dozeman, "The *yam-sûp* in the Exodus and the Crossing of the Jordan River," *CBQ* 58, no. 3 (1996): 408–11.

176. Rainey and Notley, *Sacred Bridge*, 121.

eleven days to make the journey; it states that it is "an eleven-day journey," meaning that an ordinary traveler could make it in eleven days. Indeed, the whole point of Deut. 1:2–3 is how absurdly long it took Israel to make the journey—40 years!—in comparison to how quickly one might make the trip. This leaves only the locations in the southern Sinai Peninsula and Arabia. Generally speaking, those who locate Mt. Sinai in the southern Sinai Peninsula advocate a crossing of the sea either at the Gulf of Suez or at one of the small bodies of water between the Suez and the Mediterranean. Those who locate Mt. Sinai in Arabia place the crossing of the sea at the Gulf of Aqaba. We will focus on these two alternative interpretations.

We should say at the outset that one should not be prejudiced by the name "Sinai Peninsula" in seeking to determine where Mt. Sinai was. That name is of fairly recent origin; the earliest tradition for placing Mt. Sinai at Jebel Musa or at one of the mountains in the southern region of the Sinai Peninsula is from the 4th century A.D. We are not certain what the Israelites called the great triangle of land that we call the Sinai Peninsula. (They may have called it the Wilderness of Paran; it may be, however, that the Wilderness of Paran was only the north and central part of the Sinai Peninsula. Paran certainly included Kadesh-barnea.)[177] At any rate, the modern name "Sinai Peninsula" is irrelevant for placing the biblical Mt. Sinai. By the same token, we should be wary of allowing local traditions and names to make the case for which route or mountain is the right one. There are traditions and names that link both the southern Sinai Peninsula and northwestern Arabia to the biblical story, and one can use essentially the same arguments to dismiss either set of traditions.

The Southern Sinai Peninsula

The majority of scholars believe that Mt. Sinai is in the southern Sinai Peninsula, and these same scholars generally place the *Yam Suph* at one of the lakes between the Gulf of Suez and the Mediterranean Sea (or place it at the northern tip of the Gulf of Suez). Many presentations of the "route of the exodus" that one encounters, however, are quite impressionistic and lack precise argumentation. Happily, this situation

177. See Num. 13:26. A number of scholars locate Paran in the northern and central Sinai Peninsula and the Wilderness of Sinai in the southern Sinai Peninsula (e.g., Rainey and Notley, *Sacred Bridge*, 120). Perhaps the name Paran included the whole of the Sinai Peninsula. It may be that the Egyptians called the Sinai Peninsula "Bia" (Egyptian: *bjꜣ*; Hoffmeier, *Ancient Israel*, 39, following a suggestion by Sir Alan Gardiner).

has been remedied by a recent study by James Hoffmeier, a scholar who has done extensive field work in the Sinai Peninsula, who is familiar with the primary and secondary literature, and who is trained in Egyptology. He has given us the most complete treatment of the issue to date from this perspective.[178]

Two interpretations of the data factor into Hoffmeier's understanding of the account. The first is that the Israelites, in leaving Egypt, would need to avoid Egyptian fortifications along Egypt's eastern border, at the northwestern edge of the Sinai Peninsula. The second is the belief that, because the account mentions fewer sites between Succoth (point of departure from Egypt) and the *Yam Suph* than it does for the trek from the *Yam Suph* to Mt. Sinai, the distance from Succoth to the *Yam Suph* was shorter than the distance from the *Yam Suph* to Mt. Sinai.

At the heart of Hoffmeier's presentation are his contention that the *Yam Suph* is the "Sea of Reeds" and his claim to have identified this and the nearby locations of Migdol, Pi-hahiroth, and Baal-zephon. Exodus 13:20 tells us that as the Israelites began their departure from Egypt they first came to Succoth (almost certainly to be identified as generally in the Wadi Tumilat region and perhaps specifically at Tell el-Maskhuta),[179] and that they then moved on to Etham (Exod. 13:20 tells us that it was on the edge of the wilderness, although it is debatable which "edge" and from which direction, is meant). The next three named locations in the itinerary are Pi-hahiroth, Migdol and Baal-zephon (Exod. 14:2). The name "Migdol" appears to be related to Hebrew, "tower," and to refer to a Canaanite style of fortress. Egyptian texts indicate that one of the frontier fortresses guarding access to Egypt from Canaan was Migdol of Menmaatre (Menmaatre = Pharaoh Seti I). After a detailed treatment of the problem, Hoffmeier locates Migdol of Menmaatre at the southern tip of a now vanished lagoon or bay on the Mediterranean Sea (the ancient shoreline was considerably south of the present shoreline). He equates this, his Migdol of Menmaatre, with the biblical Migdol. Southwest of the lagoon on which Migdol of Menmaatre sat was a body of water known as Lake Ballah (no longer extant, but in New Kingdom Egypt a lake [or lakes] at the northeast corner of the Delta, running from south to north and bending northeast to within about 5 km of the then shoreline of the Mediterranean). Migdol, along with several other forts, guarded the "Ways of Horus," or Via Maris, the roadway from Egypt

178. Hoffmeier, *Ancient Israel*.
179. Kitchen, *Reliability*, 257–9.

into Canaan along the Mediterranean, and it marked the frontier of Egypt.[180] This highway, going from Egypt to Canaan, ran northeast along the Mediterranean shore, then turned southeast when it hit the lagoon, and passed between the lagoon and Lake Ballah. After it made its way around the lagoon, it resumed its way along the Mediterranean coastline. Migdol was thus situated to guard the land-bridge between the lagoon and Lake Ballah.

For the identification of Pi-hahiroth and Baal-zephon, Hoffmeier turns to Papyrus Anastasi III, a letter dated to the third year of Merenptah. Line 2.9 is translated by James Allen as, "The Lake of Horus [*pꜣš ḥr*] has salt, the Canal [*pꜣ ḥrw*] has natron. Its ships set out and dock, and the food of sustenance is in it every day."[181] Hoffmeier identifies the Lake of Horus as the aforementioned (but no longer extant) lagoon opening on to the Mediterranean Sea (at the southern end of which he places Migdol), and he identifies the Canal as a no-longer-extant waterway that he says intersected with Migdol and ran toward Lake Ballah. He thus suggests that the Canal (Egyptian *pꜣ ḥrw*) is the origin of the biblical Pi-hahiroth (פִּי הַחִירֹת). He also notes that Papyrus Anastasi III refers to the "waterway [...] of Baal"[182] (part of the text is lost). He concludes, therefore, that the location called Baal-zephon can be reasonably placed in this area.[183]

The *Yam Suph* (יַם־סוּף), Hoffmeier contends, is derived from the Egyptian *pꜣ ṯwfy* ("the reeds or rushes") and can only mean the "Sea of Reeds" and not "Red Sea." In agreement with Manfred Bietak, Hoffmeier argues that the Egyptian *pꜣ ṯwfy* refers to the now-disappeared Ballah

180. Hoffmeier, *Ancient Israel*, 94–105. For a presentation of the archaeology of the Ways of Horus, see Eliezer D. Oren, "The 'Ways of Horus' in North Sinai," in *Egypt, Israel, Sinai: Archaeological and Historical Relationships in the Biblical Period*, ed. Anson F. Rainey (Tel Aviv: Tel Aviv University, 1987), 69–120

181. "Praise Pi-Ramessu," translated by James P. Allen (*COS* 3.3:15).

182. Ibid.

183. Hoffmeier, *Ancient Israel*, 105–8. It is not clear to me from Hoffmeier's discussion precisely where he puts Baal-zephon and Pi-hahiroth. The maps he provides (figures 5 and 10) show an "ancient canal" running east to west and intersecting his Migdol; I assume that this is where he puts Pi-hahiroth. He does not seem to hazard a guess about where or what Baal-zephon was, but only argues on the basis of Papyrus Anastasi III that it was in the area.

Lake.[184] He says that this was a "swampy lake,"[185] and he refutes the efforts of various scholars who argue either that the *pꜣ ṯwfy* was in another location or that it is a general description for a wetland with reeds and not the name of a specific place. He refers to the work of Sarah Groll, who on the basis of a study of Papyrus Anastasi VIII concluded that Egypt underwent an ecological disaster during the middle years of Ramesses II, at which time the *pꜣ ṯwfy* dried up. She suggests that the Hebrew slaves may have departed across the dry lake bed.[186] Hoffmeier further argues that Exod. 10:19 isolates the *Yam Suph* to the northeast Delta, as that verse says that a strong wind blew the locusts into the *Yam Suph*. This makes sense, he indicates, if the "epicenter" of the plagues was at Pi-Riꜥamsese (the store-city Raamses), and the wind blew the locusts from there in a northeastern direction into Lake Ballah.[187] Therefore, the Sea of Reeds that Israel crossed was Lake Ballah in the northeastern Delta.

Hoffmeier also seeks to demonstrate that the southern Sinai could

---

184. Manfred Bietak, "Comments on the Exodus," in *Egypt, Israel, Sinai: Archaeological and Historical Relationships in the Biblical Period*, ed. Anson F. Rainey (Tel Aviv: Tel Aviv University, 1987), 167; Bietak, *Avaris*, locates the Ballah Lakes on a map on page 2. It appears that there were three lakes that seasonally, due to inundation, became one large lake. See also Hoffmeier, *Ancient Israel*, 88.
185. Hoffmeier, *Ancient Israel*, 84.
186. Sarah I. Groll, "The Egyptian Background of the Exodus and the Crossing of the Red Sea: A New Reading of Papyrus Anastasi VIII," in *Jerusalem Studies in Egyptology*, ed. Irene Shirun-Grumach, ÄAT 40 (Wiesbaden: Otto Harrassowitz, 1998), 173–92; Sarah I. Groll, "Historical Background to the Exodus: Papyrus Anastasi VIII," in *Gold of Praise: Studies on Ancient Egypt in Honor of Edward F. Wente*, ed. Emily Teeter and John A. Larson, (Chicago: Oriental Institute, 1999) 159–62; Hoffmeier, *Ancient Israel*, 81–3. Hoffmeier says that Groll's research "may provide information about the ecological conditions in the Delta during the troubled days of the plague and exodus," but that most importantly she, too, believes that *pꜣ ṯwfy* was near Pi-Riꜥamsese. On the whole, however, Groll's arguments do not strike me as particularly strong. For example, she argues that P. Anastasi VIII indicates that there were drought conditions in northeast Delta during the 19th dynasty, and she links this to the crossing of the *Yam Suph* (Groll, "Background," 161). But the Bible never suggests that drought was one of the plagues, and it certainly does not imply that at the *Yam Suph* the Hebrews were able to cross because the waters had dried up due to drought. It goes without saying that the Egyptians would not have drowned on a dried-up lake bed.
187. Hoffmeier, *Ancient Israel*, 82.

have sustained Israel during their 11-month stay there. He observes that although this region is quite arid,[188] what rainfall there is tends to rush down the granite wadis. These wadis can be dammed up and the water collected, however, and there are examples of small orchards belonging to Bedouin that are sustained by these small reservoirs.[189] He notes that Itzhaq Beit-Arieh found more than 40 small settlements in the area from Early Bronze II (2850–2650 B.C.), each one having five to twenty stone huts.[190] In addition, as many scholars do, he seeks to identify various points of Israel's itinerary along the west coast of the Sinai Peninsula.[191]

With this evidence in hand, Hoffmeier argues that the Israelites first went to Succoth on the Wadi Tumilat, and then abruptly turned north (so interpreting Exod. 14:2) and went along the west side of the waterways that were on the eastern border of the Egyptian frontier. They needed to find a way to get past the water barriers and around the Egyptian military facilities to escape the country. Still within these frontier fortifications, however, they encamped on the west side of Lake Ballah (the *Yam Suph*), not far from the Mediterranean Sea. Israel could have gone north and then east, around Lake Ballah, and then on the narrow strip of land between Lake Ballah and the lagoon, and so on the Ways of Horus out of Egypt. But Migdol (an Egyptian fortress) was on the land-bridge between Lake Ballah and the Lake of Horus lagoon, guarding the path that would have taken them out. But at this point in the story, the crossing of the *Yam Suph* took place, allowing the Israelites not only to escape Pharaoh's chariots but also evade Migdol and the other fortifications, since they crossed the sea well to the south of the forts. After that, the Israelites turned directly south, went down the east side of Lake Ballah and the Bitter Lakes and into western Sinai, then followed the west coast of the peninsula

---

188. Hoffmeier, *Ancient Israel*, 45, states that the southern Sinai receives about "50–75 millimeters (1/4–3/8 inch)" of rainfall annually, but this cannot be correct, since 25 mm = approximately 1 inch. According to M. M. Soliman et al, "The Environmental Impact of the Rainfall-Runoff upon Groundwater Quality in Wadi Sudr, South Sinai," in *Environmental and Groundwater Pollution*, eds. M. M. Sherif, V. P. Singh and M. Al-Rashed (Lisse: A. A. Balkema, 2002), 65, southern Sinai gets an average of 15 mm (.6") per year.

189. Hoffmeier, *Ancient Israel*, 142.

190. Itzhaq Beit-Arieh, "Fifteen Years in Sinai," *BAR* 10, no. 4 (1984): 26–54.

191. Hoffmeier, *Ancient Israel*, 148–75.

(the east side of the Gulf of Suez) into the southern Sinai region, where they came to Mt. Sinai.

Difficulties with the Sinai Peninsula
Notwithstanding the fieldwork and scholarship Hoffmeier brings to this question, there are reasons one should hesitate about following his reconstruction of the events.

- As described above, an important presupposition of Hoffmeier's study is that the Hebrews, in exiting Egypt, would need to avoid the major frontier fortifications. This factor plays a major role in his deliberations over the route of the Israelites in the early stages of the exodus (Hoffmeier is by no means alone among scholars in this regard). Thus, for example, he devotes a considerable amount of attention to locating a major Egyptian military installation called Tjaru (Sile).[192] In my view, this concern is misguided for the simple reason that the Israelites had Pharaoh's explicit permission to leave. More than that, the Egyptians were frantic to get the Hebrews out of their country, and they even gave them gifts as a financial incentive to get moving (Exod. 12:30–36). The guards at the fortresses could not have been unaware of this. Exodus 14:8, moreover, says that the Israelites departed Egypt "with a high hand" (בְּיָד רָמָה). This idiom implies a mood of celebration or even of arrogance; it is equivalent to saying that the Israelites thumbed their noses at the Egyptians. It is not compatible with the idea that they were skulking about looking for an exit, determined to avoid the notice of the border guards. Exodus 13:17 is often cited in support of the view that the Israelites needed to avoid Egyptian border fortifications, since it says that God did not lead Israel into Canaan by the direct route, "the way of the land of the Philistines," so that they would not encounter warfare. But the text is not talking about warfare with Egyptians, as though the Israelites would have to fight their way out of the country. They plainly did not have to do this. The text is concerned with the fact that the Hebrew peasants, immediately after stepping out of Egypt, were not ready to march directly into battle with the peoples inhabiting southwest Canaan. Had the Israelites moved directly along the coastal highway into Canaan, they would have gone from

192. Ibid., 90–4.

being a settled body of serfs to being an invading army in a matter of days. This was simply an impossible transition for them to make—but it had nothing to do with any Egyptian fortifications.

- Hoffmeier's equating of the "Canal" (*pꜣ ḥrw*) of Papyrus Anastasi III with Pi-hahiroth (פִּי הַחִירֹת) is open to question. Scholars have long recognized that הַחִירֹת may be related to the Akkadian *hirītu*, "ditch" or "canal,"[193] and thus that Pi-hahiroth (פִּי הַחִירֹת) could mean "the mouth of the canals," although other suggestions have been made. Hoffmeier believes that both *ḥrw* and חִירֹת are from a Semitic word for "canal." To make his case, he says, "Furthermore, if *pꜣ ḥr* is the feature behind Pi-hahiroth, then the Hebrew *pi*, instead of being the construct form of *peh* (mouth), would be the writing of the Egyptian definite article *pꜣ*."[194] But this is not possible; הַחִירֹת by itself already has the definite article. If פִּי were the Hebrew rendition of the Egyptian *pꜣ*, then the author of Exodus handled the name quite oddly, both *translating* and *transliterating* the Egyptian definite article. It would be as though a reader of the Israeli newspaper *Haaretz* ("The Land") said, "I really enjoy reading Ha The Aretz." In short, the similarity between פִּי הַחִירֹת and *pꜣ ḥrw* may be more coincidental than real.

- For a similar reason, the equation of *pꜣ ṯwfy* with *Yam Suph* (יַם־סוּף) is not without its difficulties. Since *pꜣ* is analogous to the definite article, *pꜣ ṯwfy* should be rendered into Hebrew as הַסּוּף ("the Suph") if סוּף is the Hebrew equivalent of *ṯwf*. If the Hebrew author had wanted to make clear that the place was a body of water, he would have called it יַם־הַסּוּף ("the sea of the Suph"), and not simply *Yam Suph*. If the Hebrew author had followed the peculiar translation technique Hoffmeier suggests for Pi-Hahiroth, he would have given *pꜣ ṯwfy* the name "Pi-Hassuph."

- Furthermore, we need to be careful about the meaning of the word סוּף. Hoffmeier is in good scholarly company when he says that it is "certain" that the Hebrew word is derived from the

193. פִּי הַחִירֹת, *HALOT*, 3.925.
194. Hoffmeier, *Ancient Israel*, 107.

Egyptian *ṯwf*,[195] "reed" (often believed to be papyrus). Whether סוּף is a loanword from Egyptian I cannot say, but the translation of "reed" for סוּף is overly precise and thus inaccurate. The Hebrew word is generic for aquatic plants. Outside of occurrences of *Yam Suph*, it appears in Exod. 2:3, 5; Isa. 19:6 and Jonah 2:6. In Isa. 19:6, it is used with קָנֶה and refers to a freshwater plant, possibly reeds. In Jonah 2:6, however, it is a submarine, saltwater plant, and probably refers to kelp. Most instructive is Exod. 2:3, 5, where Moses's mother places him in a papyrus basket and sets it among the סוּף of the Nile. Here, סוּף is some kind of freshwater plant that held the basket in place and prevented it from drifting down the river. But סוּף is not the papyrus reed with which his mother made his basket, since 2:3 uses גֹּמֶא to refer to papyrus (see also the use of גֹּמֶא in Isa. 18:2, where it is used of papyrus boats, and in Job 8:11, where גֹּמֶא is said to grow in a marsh). The use of גֹּמֶא in Exodus to specify papyrus in contrast to סוּף is instructive. Combined with the fact that Jonah 2:6 uses סוּף of kelp, it implies that גֹּמֶא is specific to papyrus reeds whereas סוּף is generic for aquatic plants.

- The above consideration should make us wary of using *pꜣ ṯwfy* to define *Yam Suph* as the "Sea of Reeds." Bernard Batto argues that the Hebrew name for the sea should be vocalized as יַם־סוֹף ("sea of the end")[196] but I do not find this persuasive. The LXX translated the name as τὴν ἐρυθράν θάλασσαν, "the Red Sea," and this was followed by Jerome, himself no inferior Hebraist, who translated it as *mare rubrum* ("Red Sea"). This is routinely dismissed by scholars today, preferring "Sea of Reeds," but one should be careful about this; we do not know why the early translators preferred this rendition. Surely the translators of the Old Greek, as well as Jerome, knew that סוּף can refer to an aquatic plant, yet they ignored that possible meaning. On the other hand, they may have translated *Yam Suph* as "Red Sea" because they thought that they could identify the *Yam Suph* with the Gulf of Suez. But even if the translation "Red Sea" is wrong, this does not mean that "Sea of Reeds" (or equating the *Yam Suph* with the *pꜣ ṯwfy*) is correct.

---

195. Ibid., 81.

196. Bernard F. Batto, "The Reed Sea : Requiescat in Pace," *JBL* 102, no. 1 (1983): 27–35.

- Hoffmeier's placement of Migdol does not agree with the biblical text. Exod. 14:2 states that Israel encamped "between Migdol and the sea," but in Hoffmeier's reconstruction, Israel camped on the west side of Lake Ballah, while Migdol was several kilometers northeast of Lake Ballah. That is, he has the *Yam Suph* between Israel and Migdol instead of having Israel between the *Yam Suph* and Migdol, and he has the latter set some distance off from the *Yam Suph* and situated beside the lagoon he identifies as the Lake of Horus. Hoffmeier may well have identified the site of the Egyptian border fortress Migdol of Menmaatre, but this does not prove that Migdol of Menmaatre is the Migdol of Exod. 14:2. The term מִגְדֹּל is common in Hebrew and it is frequently incorporated into proper nouns (Migdal-eder, Gen. 35:21; Migdal-gad, Josh. 15:37; Migdal-el, Josh. 19:38; Migdal-shechem, Judg. 9:46; Migdal-hananel, Jer. 31:38). From the 7th and 6th centuries, Jeremiah and Ezekiel refer to an Egyptian Migdol which, as Hoffmeier observes, is not the same site as Migdol of Menmaatre.[197]

- The Israelites' perception of their location while at the *Yam Suph* does not agree with Hoffmeier's presentation. In Exod. 14:11 they complain, "Is it because there are no graves in Egypt that you have taken us out to die in the wilderness? What is this you done to us in bringing us out of Egypt?" They say that they are in the wilderness and outside of Egypt. The Egyptian fortresses (such as Tjaru [Sile] and Migdol of Menmaatre) marked the frontier. If the Israelites were on the west side of Lake Ballah, looking for a way out of Egypt that did not involve confronting an Egyptian fortification, they would have described themselves as still within the frontiers and therefore still in Egypt. Their complaint should not have been, "Why have you taken us out of Egypt?" It should have been, "You have put us in great danger and you can't even get us out of Egypt!" Lake Ballah (*pꜣ ṯwfy*) and its environs were within the local network of waterways in the northeastern Delta during the late 2nd millennium. They are celebrated in Papyrus Anastasi III as being in the vicinity of the capital, Pi-Riʿamsese, and as being the source of much of its bounty. I do not think that one can read the Egyptian text and claim that *pꜣ ṯwfy* is not in Egypt. It is difficult, at any rate, to imagine the Hebrews describing

197. Hoffmeier, *Ancient Israel*, 95–6.

this area as out in the wilderness when they were in fact only a few miles from the Egyptian capital city and trying to figure out how to get by the border fortifications.

- Hoffmeier's contention that there is sufficient water in the southern Sinai to have sustained Israel for nearly a year is hard to maintain. Even if one accepts a modified version of the Israelite census of Num. 1–2 (which, taken more literally, implies that the Israel of the exodus had the enormous population of 3 million people), one still is left with a population of at minimum 20,000.[198] Note also that the Bible never hints that there was a miraculous supply of water at Mt. Sinai. Beit-Arieh's discovery of about 40 tiny clusters of stone structures in the Early Bronze Age, if anything, makes the case for a sojourn in the southern Sinai Peninsula weaker rather than stronger. These settlements were scattered throughout the region and did not tax the resources at any one place. Altogether they would have sustained a population far lower than 20,000. Beit-Arieh's

198. A literal reading of Num. 1–3 indicates that Israel had a massive population, some 2,000,000 to 3,000,000 in total. Many scholars claim that such a literal interpretation is not intended by the text. They argue for a smaller figure, about 20,000 to 30,000. See Colin J. Humphreys, *The Miracles of Exodus: A Scientist's Discovery of the Extraordinary Natural Causes of the Biblical Stories* (New York: HarperCollins, 2004), 103–10. Apart from Humphreys's computations, this figure is derived from the belief that אלף in Num. 1–3 is not to be interpreted as a "thousand" but as a military "squad" of about ten men. This reduces the size of the army to about 6,000 and thus the size of the whole population to at most 30,000. For other studies of the difficulties with the numbers, see Eryl W. Davies, "A Mathematical Conundrum: The Problem of the Large Numbers in Numbers I and XXVI," *VT* 45, no. 4 (1995): 449–69; Gary A. Rendsburg, "An Additional Note to Two Recent Articles on the Number of People in the Exodus from Egypt and the Large Numbers in Numbers I and XXVI," *VT* 51, no. 3 (2001): 392–6; and Mark McEntire, "A Response to Colin J. Humphreys's 'The Number of People in the Exodus from Egypt: Decoding Mathematically the Very Large Numbers in Numbers I and XXVI,'" *VT* 49, no. 2 (1999): 262–4. But Hoffmeier, *Ancient Israel*, 159, asserts that the population was "in the thousands, maybe a few tens of thousands." It is not clear to me how Hoffmeier gets the number down to "thousands," if by that he means fewer than 10,000. For example, a total population of 5,000 would mean that there were about 2,000 men of military age, which would in turn mean that each squad (אלף) averaged 3.3 men. This is an impossibly small number.

article itself observes that these settlements were "so small they could not be considered villages or even hamlets."[199] But even a population of 20,000 people is, for the Late Bronze Age, an enormous city. The Israelites were all concentrated in one location, and they would have required ample resources in their immediate vicinity. No such city existed in the southern Sinai for the simple reason that the land could not sustain it. We need to recall, moreover, that the people traveled with all of their livestock, which would greatly increase the amount of water they would need, in addition to needing local pasturage sufficient for a prolonged stay. Exodus 19:14 even indicates that they had so much water available to them at Mt. Sinai that they were able to wash their clothes soon after their arrival. The notion that they could extend their annual water supply of 15 mm of rainfall[200] by damming up wadis is not realistic. That might work for a very small, nomadic group, which could dam up several wadis and move about over a long period of time, waiting for rain to come and relying on oases in the interim. But the Israelites would need a massive amount of water immediately upon their arrival. We can hardly imagine that as soon as they arrived they set about damming up the dry wadis. As former residents of the Egyptian Delta, they would have no knowledge about survival in the severely arid environment of the southern Sinai Peninsula.[201] Stuart suggests that the Israelites could have gone back to Rephidim (where water flowed from the rock) for water,[202] but Rephidim was a full day's

199. Beit-Arieh, *Fifteen Years*, 36.

200. Soliman, et al., "Impact of the Rainfall-Runoff," 65.

201. Ze'ev Meshel, "Wilderness Wanderings: Ethnographic Lessons from Modern Bedouin," *BAR* 34, no. 4 (2008): 32–29, describes various parallels between the biblical account of the exodus and the practices of the Bedouin of the Sinai Peninsula, but these are far from demonstrating that the Israelites sojourned in the Sinai Peninsula. The most telling point is the following statement from Meshel: "We may begin with the very basic characteristic of Bedouin life: They live as nomadic shepherds" (p. 34). But the Israelites of the exodus were not nomadic shepherds. They had lived for generations as a settled people in houses in the Egyptian Delta, and they then congregated en masse as one community at Mt. Sinai for almost a year. Even the wilderness wandering was not a Bedouin lifestyle; it was forced upon them, and they remained encamped together in a single, massive campsite.

202. Stuart, *Exodus*, 428.

march away, an untenable situation for a large encampment with numerous livestock. Furthermore, there is no indication that the water from the rock at Rephidim became a perpetual spring. To the contrary, Exodus 32:20 indicates that the people had a sizable body of water right in the middle of their camp at Mt. Sinai. In short, an encampment in the southern Sinai Peninsula is untenable.

- Hoffmeier's idea that the Israelites moved north from Succoth to Lake Ballah is also difficult to maintain. Exodus 13:17–18 states that God did not lead the people north into Canaan by "the Way of the Philistines" and instead sent them out by the "Way of the Wilderness, [toward the] *Yam Suph*." Hoffmeier (along with all other interpreters) understands that the "Way of the Philistines" corresponds to the Via Maris or "Ways of Horus" along the Mediterranean Coast from Egypt to Canaan, and that the "Way of the Wilderness" is the Darb el-Hagg, the road that leads directly across the Sinai Peninsula from just north of the Gulf of Suez to Ezion Geber, at the north tip of the Gulf of Aqaba. He argues, however, that Exod. 14:2 indicates that the Israelites turned back from entering the Sinai Peninsula by the "Way of the Wilderness" and went north toward the exit from Egypt at the "Way of the Philistines."[203] Approaching this northern exit, he says, they camped at the *Yam Suph* (Lake Ballah) and the crossing of the sea followed. The problem with this is that Exod. 13:18 specifically identifies the Way of the Wilderness as the way toward the *Yam Suph*. Given the dichotomy that Exod. 13:17–18 sets up between "Way of the Philistines" and "Way of the Wilderness, to the *Yam Suph*," Israel cannot possibly have turned away from the Way of the Wilderness, toward the Way of the Philistines, and thereby toward the *Yam Suph*. Again, it is very clear (as Hoffmeier himself states) that the Way of the Wilderness leads directly to Ezion Geber and the Gulf of Aqaba.[204] The only way around this, I suppose, is to contend that the *Yam Suph* of Exod. 13:18 and the *Yam Suph* that Israel crossed (Lake Ballah) are two different bodies of water. This is, I think, quite unreasonable, as it has the same text switching back and forth between two completely different bodies of water while calling both by

203. Hoffmeier, *Ancient Israel*, 71–3.
204. Ibid., 131, 138.

the same name and giving no clarification. Hoffmeier's interpretation of Exod. 14:2 is not possible.

- Exodus 14:5 states that when Pharaoh was informed that Israel had "fled" Egypt he became enraged at having lost their services (he apparently expected them to return after the three-day journey into the wilderness). But Israel encamped on the west side of the Ballah Lakes can hardly be said to have fled the country; they were not even beyond its frontier. Pharaoh's response makes sense only if Israel is already well out into the wilderness, pressing further eastward and obviously not intending to come back.

- Deuteronomy 1:2, in addition to telling us that it is an eleven-day journey from Mt. Sinai to Kadesh-barnea, states that this route is specifically via "the way of Mt. Seir." Mt. Seir is a range of mountains located in Edomite territory; it is east of the Great Rift in the Arabah of Edom and is between Wadi el-Ḥesā in the north and Râs en-Naqb in the south.[205] That is, it is between the Dead Sea and the Gulf of Aqaba and it is on the east side of the gorge. Contrary to some commentators,[206] it is not on the western side of the Arabah.[207] But where is the "way of Mt. Seir"? The phrase occurs only here in the Bible. Hoffmeier does not discuss this in his major treatment of Deut. 1:2,[208] but he does show it on his map (figure 1 in *Ancient Israel at Sinai*) snaking its way up the east coast of the Sinai Peninsula from the southern end of the Gulf of Aqaba to its northern end at Elath. This location for the route strikes me as arbitrary, there being no external evidence placing it here, and I wonder if marking it here is based on the presupposition that Mt. Sinai is in the southern end of the Sinai Peninsula. What makes this location for the "way of Mt. Seir" particularly unlikely is that there was no urban civilization in the southern Sinai. The "way of Mt. Seir" is almost certainly a trade route,

205. See Ernst Axel Knauf, "Seir," in Freedman, *ABD* Vol. 5, 1072–73; and Ronald A. Simkins, "Seir," in Freedman, *Eerdmans Dictionary*,1179. See also the map at Rainey and Notley, *Sacred Bridge*, 38.

206. E.g., Duane L. Christensen, *Deuteronomy 1:1–21:9, revised*, 2nd ed., WBC 6a (Nashville: Thomas Nelson, 2001), 34.

207. Rainey and Notley, *Sacred Bridge*, 85.

208. Hoffmeier, *Ancient Israel*, 121–6.

but a road toward the southern Sinai Peninsula would be in effect a road to nowhere. It is far more likely, I think, that the road connected Edomite territory at Seir to civilizations in Arabia (Midian and, further south, Saba [Sheba]). That is, it probably was a southern extension of the "King's Highway" from Edom to Elath, and continued down a highway known to have existed on the west side of the Arabian Peninsula. If so, then Deut. 1:2 explicitly locates Mt. Sinai south of Edom and in Arabia. Furthermore, there is no reason that the Israelites, if they were going from the southern Sinai Peninsula to Kadesh-barnea, would cross to the east side of the Great Rift (to Mt. Seir) and then cross back again to the west side. One might counter that, if we allow for the possibility that the "way of Mt. Seir" is located in the eastern Sinai Peninsula, Deut. 1:2 does not require that Israel went all the way to Mt. Seir; it only implies that they followed the "way of Mt. Seir" northward and then at some point (perhaps at Elath?) turned west toward Kadesh-barnea. But this argument will not work. Deuteronomy 33:2 says, "YHWH came from Sinai, and dawned from Seir upon us; he shone forth from Mount Paran." Some have used this verse to suggest that Mt. Sinai was actually in Edom, but as Hoffmeier himself observes, this sequence probably describes the progress of the divine presence in the Tent of Meeting with the camp of Israel.[209] That is, YHWH appeared at Sinai, was then resident in the Tent of Meeting, and then moved with Israel to Seir, and finally made his way to Paran, that is, to Kadesh-barnea. This is precisely the same route as the journey described in Deut. 1:2, and it plainly goes through, and not just toward, Seir. But if Mt. Sinai is in the southern Sinai Peninsula, then the Israelites went northeast from Mt. Sinai, crossed the Great Rift to the east and went into the area of Seir, and then doubled back, crossed the Great Rift toward the west, and then made their way to Kadesh-barnea. Such an itinerary would take an extraordinarily rigorous detour for no reason, and it is therefore unlikely.

- The wind that blew away the locusts did not blow them into Lake Ballah. As stated above, Hoffmeier believes that Exod. 10:19 says that a wind blew the locusts into the *Yam Suph* and that this shows that the *Yam Suph* must be in the northeast

209. Ibid., 128–30.

Delta.[210] But in Exod. 10:19, יָמָּה סוּף only means "toward the *Yam Suph*" and effectively means, "toward the east." It hardly requires the interpretation that the locusts were driven into the waters of the *Yam Suph*. More than that, blowing all of the locusts into or even toward Lake Ballah is very difficult to conceive. Exodus 10:14 states that the locusts covered "the whole country of Egypt." Even if this does not require us to believe that locusts filled the whole land from the Mediterranean to the first cataract, it would at least demand that locust filled the entire Delta and some tracts of the upper Nile valley. A highly localized locust plague at Pi-Riʿamsese, as Hoffmeier seems to envision (he calls it the "epicenter"), would hardly be the national calamity that Exodus describes. But if a wind blew locusts from all over the Delta and the Nile valley toward Lake Ballah, that wind would be blowing toward due east from the northern Delta, but blowing toward northeast from the southern Delta and blowing almost due north from the Nile valley. In effect, the wind would be converging from all over the Delta and Upper Egypt upon the very small Lake Ballah area. That, to me, is an odd idea.

- Numbers 33:8–10 indicates that there was a journey of, at minimum, six days after the crossing of the *Yam Suph*, at the end of which the Israelites were again camping beside the *Yam Suph*. They plainly were not going in a circle. The only reasonable conclusion is that the *Yam Suph* is a long body of water, that they crossed it at one end, and that they then travelled parallel to it. This indicates that the only two possible candidates for the *Yam Suph* are the Gulf of Suez and the Gulf of Aqaba. To assert that there was more than one *Yam Suph*, or that the *Yam Suph* includes both the Gulf of Suez and every lake and swamp between it and the Mediterranean Sea, is implausible. Hoffmeier has built his entire case on his belief that the *Yam Suph* is to be identified with a single lake, *pꜣ ṯwfy*, which the New Kingdom literature isolates to one specific place. But he abruptly changes his reasoning at Num. 33:10 and says that the Israelites "applied" the name *Yam Suph* to a completely different water body, the Gulf of Suez (certainly not a marshy lake filled with reeds!) on the grounds that it was "an

210. Ibid., 82.

extension of the sea of crossing."[211] This is, I think, a hopeless argument. The Israelites would have known that *pꜣ ṯwfy* was a specific body of water in the north and that the Gulf of Suez was in every respect a different place. Applying the name of the former to the latter would simply be a bizarre thing to do.

- One cannot get away from the fact that the Bible identifies only one body of water as the *Yam Suph*: the Gulf of Aqaba. 1 Kings 9:26 says that Ezion-geber, the port of Solomon, was on the *Yam Suph*, and Ezion-geber is universally recognized to be at the north end of the Gulf of Aqaba. As indicated above, Exod. 13:18 identifies the Way of the Wilderness, which goes toward Ezion-geber at the north end of the Gulf of Aqaba, as the way from Egypt toward the *Yam Suph*. Exodus 23:31 describes the extent of greater Israel as "from the *Yam Suph* [Gulf of Aqaba, Israel's southeast corner] to the Sea of the Philistines [the bend of the Mediterranean near Gaza, at Israel's southwest corner], and from the wilderness [Negev, south central limit of Israel] to the Euphrates [northern limit of Israel]." One cannot possibly take the *Yam Suph* of Exod. 23:31 to be the Gulf of Suez, the Ballah Lakes, or any other body of water in that vicinity. Deuteronomy 2:1 says that after the failure at Kadesh-barnea, the Israelites went from there toward the *Yam Suph*, and for a long time traveled around Mt. Seir. The mention of Mt. Seir can only mean that the *Yam Suph* was east or southeast of Kadesh-barnea. Also, Jeremiah 49:17–22, an oracle against Edom, refers to various locations associated with Edom (v. 20, Teman; v. 22, Bozrah). In v. 21, it says that the sound of Edom's calamity would be heard at the *Yam Suph*. Being at the southern end of Edomite territory, the Gulf of Aqaba is plainly meant here; it is not a lake on the frontier of Egypt.[212] The evidence is not ambiguous, and the Bible never suggests that more than one body of water is called *Yam Suph*.[213]

---

211. Ibid., 164.

212. For a discussion of the location of Shur and its bearing upon the location of the *Yam Suph*, see the commentary on Exod. 15:22 below.

213. Propp, *Exodus 19–40*, 752, illustrates the confusion of many scholars about the location of the *Yam Suph*. First, he correctly states, "Nevertheless, there is little doubt that in Exod 23:31; Num 14:25; 21:4; Deut 1:40; 2:1; Judg 11:16 [?]; 1 Kgs 9:26; Jer 49:21, the Suph Sea is the Gulf of Aqaba." But then he wrongly states, "In Exod 10:19; 13:18; Num 33:10–11,

- The phenomena associated with the crossing of the *Yam Suph* are important for this discussion. Exodus 14:21 tells us that a strong east wind blew all night, and that as a result of that the waters parted and were heaped up like a wall, allowing the Hebrews to pass through. Exodus 14:26–28 then tells us that the waters came back when the Egyptians were in the *Yam Suph*, and the Egyptians drowned. What can account for this? Certainly Sarah Groll's notion that the *Yam Suph* had simply dried up is no help, as it allows neither the waters to be heaped up nor the Egyptians to have been drowned. Inasmuch as the Bible explicitly asserts that the east wind was responsible for the heaping up of the waters, one cannot even appeal directly to supernatural causation; one must have an interpretation that takes this natural causation into account. But, in fact, no amount of wind will cause the waters of a lake or wetland to behave in the way the Bible describes.[214] In short, the parting of the *Yam Suph* could not have occurred at Lake Ballah or any other of the local lakes.[215]

From the above, it is clear that there are difficulties with Hoffmeier's thesis. Of course, not every scholar who holds to a crossing of the sea near Egypt and to locating Mt. Sinai in the Sinai Peninsula

---

however, the Suph Sea appears to be the Gulf of Suez." As described above, Exod 10:19 does not specify a location for the *Yam Suph* other than that it is to the east of Egypt; that is, it is the direction in which the wind blew the locusts. It in no way suggests that the Gulf of Suez is meant. In Exod. 13:18, we have a retrograde motion around the *Yam Suph*, but there is no reason to suppose it is the Gulf of Suez. In Num. 33:10–11, Israel marches southward near the east shore of the *Yam Suph* and so encounters it a second time. As we have shown, this is consistent with its being the Gulf of Aqaba. But Propp is characteristic of many scholars who take *Yam Suph* to mean virtually all the waters east of Egypt, including what we now call the Gulf of Suez, the Gulf of Aqaba, and the Red Sea. As such, the name becomes essentially useless for locating the sea of crossing.

214. Humphreys, *Miracles*, 249.

215. The only comment I can find on this matter in Hoffmeier, *Ancient Israel*, is on pp. 108–9, where he asserts that no one "is equipped to explain how the event happened or what might be the source behind it." But this is not right. The Bible does give us specific data about how it happened, and we have as much right or duty to investigate that information as we do, say, to investigate the location of Migdol. Furthermore, our explanation must operate within the boundaries of the data we are given.

would agree with all that Hoffmeier has written. John Currid, for example, locates the crossing of the *Yam Suph* at the northern end of the Gulf of Suez and so proposes that the other sites related to the crossing (Pi-hahiroth, etc.) were in the general vicinity. But his treatment of the problem is less rigorous than Hoffmeier's, and it has many problems.[216] Hoffmeier's analysis is by far the most thorough, and it generally avoids the vague guesswork that characterizes many other studies of this issue.

Northwestern Arabia

The most recent and most persuasive argument in favor of locating the *Yam Suph* at the Gulf of Aqaba and Mt. Sinai in Arabia is not by a biblical scholar but a physicist, Colin Humphreys, a professor at Cambridge University.[217] His book, *The Miracles of Exodus*, deals with many aspects of the exodus account, but we are only concerned with the locations of the sea of crossing and of Mt. Sinai, and with essential details about the route of the exodus.

---

216. John D. Currid, *Ancient Egypt and the Old Testament* (Grand Rapids: Baker, 1997), 121–41. Placing the *Yam Suph* at the Gulf of Suez faces a number of the same difficulties mentioned above. For example, the biblical passages that place the *Yam Suph* at the Gulf of Aqaba cannot be reconciled with placing the *Yam Suph* at the Gulf of Suez. Currid's suggestion also suffers from other problems. For example, most interpreters put Shur at the corner of the Mediterranean coastline between Canaan and Egypt. This cannot be reconciled with a crossing at the Gulf of Suez, as it would mean that the Israelites after crossing the Suez immediately headed north along the Egyptian frontier to Shur near the Mediterranean coast, and then presumably doubled back toward the southern Sinai Peninsula, where Currid places Mt. Sinai. This makes no sense. If one locates Shur further south, alongside the Gulf of Suez, then Gen. 25:18 is incomprehensible (it places Shur on the road to Assyria, a very strange thing to say about a location in the barren wilderness of the Sinai Peninsula by the Gulf of Suez). The *Yam Suph* simply cannot be the Gulf of Suez. (For my own view of the location of Shur, see the commentary below on Exod. 15:22–23.)

217. There are, of course, plenty of eccentric and sensationalist theories about the Red Sea and Sinai, some of which place Mt. Sinai in the Arabian Peninsula (most notably among the followers of Ron Wyatt), but we will not concern ourselves with these. We should also note that Humphreys's idea that Mt. Sinai was at Mt. Bedr in Arabia is not new; Roland de Vaux was already seriously interacting with this proposal many years earlier (Vaux, *The Early History of Israel,* trans. David Smith [London: Darton, Longman & Todd, 1978], 433).

The starting point for Humphreys is that Moses fled from Egypt to the land of Midian, where he worked as a shepherd for Reuel. Moses first visited Mt. Sinai when he was grazing his sheep "behind the wilderness" (Exod. 3:1). Midian is in northwestern Arabia. It is in the low coastal area of western Arabia called the Tihama, a region extremely hot in summer. Just east of the Tihama is a desert band called the Shifa, and behind that is the Hisma, terrain of higher elevation with numerous oases. Shepherds keep their sheep in the warmer Tihama during winter, but lead them to the cooler Hisma during summer. But to get to the Hisma they must cross the desert. Humphreys suggests, following Exod. 3:1, that Moses led his sheep from the Tihama, across the desert (the "wilderness") and into the Hisma, where he encountered the burning bush.[218] This, of course, puts Mt. Sinai somewhere in the Hisma of northwestern Arabia.

Another factor for locating Mt. Sinai, for Humphreys, is the description of the mountain at the time of Israel's arrival. Exodus 19:16–19 asserts that on the mountain there were earth tremors, sounds like trumpet blasts, fire, smoke, and lightning strikes. All of these phenomena are associated with a volcanic eruption.[219] Of course, alternative explanations are possible. One could suggest that the action was the direct result of a divine appearance but that the mountain itself was not volcanic, or one could suggest that the language is not to be taken literally, and that this description is simply narrative code for theophany. But the simplest explanation is that the events on Mt. Sinai were as described and that Mt. Sinai was an active volcano. There have been no active volcanoes in the southern Sinai Peninsula within historical times. One may argue, therefore, that if events at Sinai transpired as described, biblical Mt. Sinai was not in the Sinai Peninsula. There have been, however, volcanoes in northwest Arabia. Humphreys fixes on a specific volcano located in the Hisma, Mt. Bedr (Hala'-l-Bedr; it is at 27°15' N and 37°12' E). This volcano sits on a high plateau called the Tadra, which is about 5,000 ft above sea level; the cone of Mt. Bedr is about 500 ft above that. The Tadra itself sits within a fertile basin called al-Ǧaw, and this area is lush with flora and has abundant water. Thus, Humphreys contends, Mt. Bedr meets two essential requirements for being Mt. Sinai: it is volcanic and it is situated in a region with enough water to sustain the population of Israel. In recent times, an Arabian tribe called the Billi (or "Beli") are said to have used the al-Ǧaw as a winter camp. In the years before World

218. Humphreys, *Miracles*, 61–9.
219. Ibid., 82–93.

War I, when they would have been essentially unaffected by modern technology and would have been surviving there in the way that people have for thousands of years, they were said to number in excess of 40,000 people.[220]

As an aspect of his volcano hypothesis, Humphreys believes that the "pillar of fire" and "pillar of cloud" of Exod. 13:21 was a volcanic column: in the day it appeared to be smoke, but in the night it appeared to be fire.[221] Exodus 14:19, where the angel of God and pillar of cloud moves behind the Israelites, in Humphreys's view, means that the Israelites turned around, so that the volcanic column was temporarily behind them.[222]

Not surprisingly, Humphreys places the *Yam Suph* at the Gulf of Aqaba, arguing that it is legitimately called both the "Red Sea" (because of red coral growing in the sea) and the "Sea of Reeds" (because of reeds growing in wadis that fed into the north end of the gulf).[223] Most intriguing is his explanation for the parting of the sea. He notes that the Hebrew has no word for "northeast" or "southwest," but uses only the terms north, east, south and west. Therefore, "east" can mean anything from northeast to southeast. He further notes that there is a phenomenon in nature known as a "wind setdown effect." This occurs when a strong wind blows for a sustained period of time over a relatively long, narrow, and deep body of water. The waters will stand up like a wall, so that the bottom of the sea or lake is exposed. It turns out that of all the bodies of water suggested for being the biblical sea of crossing, only the Gulf of Aqaba has all the necessary criteria for experiencing a wind setdown as described in the Bible. It is long, deep, and narrow, and it runs from northeast to southwest. A wind from the northeast, which the biblical writer could call an "east wind," would blow down the length of the gulf, causing at some point the waters to pile up in the wall formation described in the Bible.

The lakes that would have been in the area east of the Delta, such as the Bitter Lakes and Lake Ballah, could not have had the proper shape or depth for this to occur. Also, a wind across these lakes would not have the funnel effect that it would have had at the Gulf of Aqaba, where mountain ridges on each side of the gulf form a natural channel for the wind. Similarly, the setdown effect could not have occurred in the Gulf of Suez because of its orientation from northwest to southeast;

220. Ibid., 310–24.
221. Ibid., 164–71.
222. Ibid., 240.
223. Ibid., 172–205.

the wind would have to have been out of the northwest. An east or northeast wind would have blown across the Suez and had no effect. A southeast wind would have blown up the Suez and actually created a “wind setup,” in which waters would suddenly be pushed up beyond the northern end of the Gulf of Suez as a dangerously high tide, but producing no wall of water or open path across the sea to the other side. (A wind setup has actually happened there.) Therefore, Humphreys concludes, the miracle at the *Yam Suph* happened just as stated in the Bible, but it could only have happened at the Gulf of Aqaba.[224]

Humphreys therefore believes that the Israelites set out from Succoth as they departed Egypt, went by border fortifications without incident (since they had permission to go), travelled across the Sinai Peninsula along the Way of the Wilderness (the Darb el-Hagg) to Etham, which he identifies as the northern territory of the Gulf of Aqaba. Then, at God’s command, they turned back from simply going around the north end of the Gulf of Aqaba and camped with the sea behind them, to their east, and they were trapped by the Egyptians. At this point, the wind setdown occurred and the Israelites crossed to safety while the Egyptians drowned. The Israelites then proceeded down the western side of the Arabian Peninsula, east of the Gulf of Aqaba, before moving inland toward the al-Ǧaw and Mt. Sinai.

Difficulties With Northwestern Arabia

There are a number of arguments that can be made against Humphreys’s proposal that, as far as I can see, are not very strong. In the text below, the argument is set in italics, and the response is in plain text.

- *Biblical references to Mt. Sinai never mention Midian, and therefore Mt. Sinai was not in Midian.*[225] But the al-Ǧaw basin in which Mt. Bedr sits is some distance removed from the coastal Tihama, the domain of Midian. It may be that Mt. Sinai is never said to be in Midian for the simple reason that Mt. Bedr and its environs were not regarded as within Midianite territory.

- *Groups of Midianites are known to have travelled far and wide; therefore, there is no reason to assume that Moses went to the*

224. Ibid., 244–60.
225. Hoffmeier, *Ancient Israel*, 131–2.

Arabian Peninsula.[226] But when Moses fled Egypt he did not simply find a group of wandering Midianites; Exod. 2:15 specifically states that he went to the "land of Midian," a designation that requires that he went into northwest Arabia. It was there he met and married Zipporah, and her father dwelt in the immediate vicinity (that is, in Midian; Exod. 2:16–21). The only natural interpretation of the text is that Moses lived in Midian and shepherded his father-in-law's sheep with that location as his home base.

- *Several English translations of Exod. 3:1 (RSV, ESV, and NASB) say that Moses took the sheep "west" of the desert. Therefore, Moses could not have taken the sheep from the Tihama on the Arabian coast eastward across the desert Shifa and into the Hisma.* The response to this is simple enough: translating אַחַר in Exod. 3:1 as "west" is not correct (see translation notes to 3:1 in the commentary below). Apart from the fact that going west would have put Moses and his sheep in the Gulf of Aqaba, the word אַחַר means "beyond" or "to the backside of," as in the KJV, NIV, TNIV, and NRSV.

- *The Gulf of Aqaba is oriented more in a north-to-south direction than in a northeast to southwest direction. Therefore, a wind that ran down the length of the Gulf of Aqaba should be called a "north" wind rather than an "east" wind.* But this does not take into account the location and time of year. Since it was some time after Passover, it was some time in the spring, and at the north end of the Gulf of Aqaba, the Israelites were well north of the equator. If we assume a location a few miles south of modern Eilat on the coast of the Gulf of Aqaba, we can postulate a position of 29°40' N and 34°48' E. If we furthermore assume a date corresponding to our April 25 for the date of their arrival there, perhaps two weeks after Passover, we discover that sunrise is at declination 13.21°. An ancient person facing sunrise would call that "east," but because of the declination, he would actually be facing about 13° toward the north and not be facing true east. He would be all the more likely to call a wind out of the northeast an "east" wind.

226. Hoffmeier, *Ancient Israel*, 121–2, makes this argument, as do many others (e.g., George Mendenhall, "Midian," in Freedman, *ABD* Vol. 4, 815–818).

- *The first stop mentioned in Israel's itinerary after leaving Succoth (in Egypt) was at the Yam Suph near Etham, and Humphreys identifies Etham with Mt. Yitm (also called Mt. Etham or Mt. Biggir) just north of the Gulf of Aqaba. But Mt. Yitm is 180 miles (288 km) from Succoth, and obviously the Israelites could not have made this journey in a single day.*[227] This argument depends upon the presupposition that the itinerary for the exodus journey lists each place where the Israelites camped each night of their journey. There are only two reasons why the text might be expected to name a place of encampment: either something significant happened there, or it was a familiar spot with a recognized name. In fact, we know that the text does not name every place where Israel camped. Exodus 12:37–16:1 (also Num. 33:3–11) lists the following places in the first half of their itinerary: Raamses → Succoth → Etham → Pi-hahiroth, Migdol, Baal-zephon, and the *Yam Suph* (four names identifying the location of a single campsite) → Wilderness of Shur ("Etham" in Num.) → Marah → Elim → *Yam Suph* (again; Num. only) → Wilderness of Sin. If we relied on names alone, we would assume that it took Israel eight days after the start of the exodus to get to the Wilderness of Sin. But in fact, it took them a month (Exod. 16:1). Obviously they stopped at a number of unnamed sites. Exodus 15:22 mentions three days of travel within the Wilderness of Shur without naming any sites. Furthermore, if Etham is in fact at the north end of the Gulf of Aqaba, there is no reason for the itinerary to mention any campsites they stayed at in the middle of the Sinai Peninsula along the way. Nothing significant happened there, and the route hardly has important or familiar places. Hoffmeier himself acknowledges that campsites may be omitted from the itinerary.[228] Exodus 13:17–18 had already stated that they took the "Way of the Wilderness," the Darb el-Hagg, and this is known to cut across the wilderness area toward the north of the Gulf of Aqaba. Giving names to places along this route would be superfluous, especially if the reader could be expected to know where Etham was. Furthermore, it appears that the Israelites did not set up camp along the way from Succoth to Etham, but marched day and night (perhaps briefly pausing for rest but without pitching tents) until they reached Etham (see the

227. Hoffmeier, *Ancient Israel*, 137–8.
228. Ibid., 163.

commentary on 13:17–22). That being the case, the text would not give names to places along the Darb el-Hagg where they only stopped for a few hours of rest. Humphreys states that he thinks it took the Israelites "seven or eight days" to get from Succoth to Etham[229] but, given that it took them a month to reach the Wilderness of Sin, they may not have made it across the Sinai Peninsula quite so quickly. Assuming that it took them half of the month, or 15 days, to get to the sea, they would have been travelling about 12 miles (19.3 km) per day. If it took them 20 days, their speed averaged 9 miles (14.5 km) per day. Humphreys notes that spring is the rainy season in this area, and thus there would have been sufficient water for them as they passed through, and pasturage for their livestock.[230] We should note, moreover, that Exod. 13:21 implies that they did travel by both day and night at this stage; as such, they could have made it across the peninsula in a reasonably short time.

- *The Egyptian chariots could not have made it across the Sinai Peninsula*. Hoffmeier makes this argument, stating that the thin wheels of the Egyptian chariots could not have survived the rough terrain of the Darb el-Hagg.[231] This argument, I think, fails to take into account the realities of any military organization, in which there are engineer units charged with the task of seeing to it that the weapon systems get to where they are supposed to go. Roman armies travelled with baggage trains carrying their spare javelins, artillery, and so forth. But one need not postulate an extremely sophisticated corps of engineers for the Egyptian army—certainly nothing like that of the highly skilled Roman army. In effect, all the Egyptians had to do was find a way to get the light combat vehicles to the enemy. If they could not do this, it is hard to see what good a chariot corps would do them, as they often had to travel long distances across varied terrain on military campaigns (e.g., when campaigning against the Mitanni or the Hittites). A. J. Spalinger, in his analysis of logistical and transportation issues that confronted the Egyptian army, suggests that they may have dismantled their chariots and transported them on

229. Humphreys, *Miracles*, 235.
230. Ibid., 231–2.
231. Hoffmeier, *Ancient Israel*, 138.

pack animals.[232] It is, at any rate, gratuitous to say that they simply could not have done it. Armies can be very resourceful. Thutmose III, in his eighth campaign, actually built ships in Byblos and took them across Syria on carts for crossing the Euphrates in order to attack Mitanni.

- *Mt. Bedr is too far from Kadesh-barnea to be the biblical Mt. Sinai.* This argument depends upon Deut. 1:2, with its assertion that it is an eleven-day journey from Kadesh-barnea to Mt. Sinai. Hoffmeier notes that Humphreys alludes to Arab pilgrims covering an amazing 38 miles (60 km) per day.[233] Obviously the nation of Israel, with livestock and children, could not make that kind of speed. But one must be fair. Humphreys explicitly says that he does not think that the people of Israel ever covered the distance from Sinai to Kadesh-barnea in eleven days.[234] In fact, Deut. 1:2 does not say that Israel covered that distance in eleven days; it describes it as an eleven-day journey for the purpose of highlighting how terrible was Israel's failure, that it took them 40 years to get to Kadesh-barnea (v. 3). We should also note that according to 1 Kings 19:3–8, it took Elijah 40 days to get from the vicinity of Beersheba to Mt. Sinai. This suggests that the eleven-day journey mentioned in Deut. 1:2 may be the minimum amount of time a determined traveler might take in making the journey (it might refer to how quickly a mounted traveler could make it). Humphreys states that the trip is called an eleven-day journey as measured by a specific series of eleven way-stations.[235] This is not unreasonable, although it is perhaps debatable.

- *Where are Migdol, Pi-hahiroth, and Baal-zephon? One cannot successfully locate the Yam Suph crossing without locating these places.* I do not think that Humphreys has given us much help here, although that is through no fault of his. First, let us be clear: if the Gulf of Aqaba is the biblical *Yam Suph*, then all we can say about these three places is that they were somewhere close by its northwestern shore. Apparently Israel was about

232. Anthony J. Spalinger, *War in Ancient Egypt: The New Kingdom* (Oxford: Blackwell, 2005), 34.
233. Hoffmeier, *Ancient Israel*, 139–40.
234. Humphreys, *Miracles*, 314.
235. Humphreys, *Miracles*, 333–6.

to round the north end of the gulf, but then turned around and went a short distance south down its western side, and camped with the sea to its east and the three locations of Migdol, Pi-hahiroth, and Baal-zephon in the immediate vicinity. But we do not know where these places were. This may seem hopeless, but one should consider several factors. First, we should be careful with our assumptions. We do not know that the biblical Migdol was indeed an active fortress (it could have been abandoned, or it could have been simply a tower), and we do not know that it was Egyptian. Although it is obviously attractive to identify it with a place like Migdol of Menmaatre, that equation, for reasons described above, is probably altogether wrong. Second, the archaeology of the Gulf of Aqaba is very thin. For example, we know that Ezion-geber was in the area, but it has yet to be located (for a long time, following the work of Nelson Glueck, it was thought to have been at Tell el-Kheleifeh, but that identification is now open to serious doubt).[236] There are many potential archaeological sites in the area, but the coastal area has been subjected to massive construction because of the development of port and resort facilities. A great deal of data is no doubt lost forever. Third, we should take note of how odd it is that one campsite was identified by three different places. What could account for this? A reasonable answer is that even in Moses's day no one site near Israel's crossing of the *Yam Suph* camp was sufficiently large or well-known to be easily recognized, and thus the narration resorts to mentioning three places that happened to be nearby. If even a well-known port city such as Ezion-geber is difficult for us to find and positively identify, it is not surprising that three other small and possibly ephemeral sites should be lost. Therefore, although the inability of this theory to demonstrate where these three sites were constitutes an embarrassment, it is not a fatal weakness.

There is one critique of Humphreys's work that I think is valid: his notion that the pillar of fire and pillar of cloud was a volcano plume off in the distance is not possible. Hoffmeier correctly notes that the pillar of cloud went before Israel when they left Mt. Sinai, something that obviously could not happen if the cloud was a plume of smoke going up

236. Gary Pratico, "Where Is Ezion–Geber? A Reappraisal of the Site Archaeologist Nelson Glueck Identified as King Solomon's Red Sea Port," *BAR* 12, no. 5 (1986): 24–35.

from Sinai (Num. 10:34).[237] Also, Exod. 14:20 says that the pillar came between the Israelites and the Egyptian chariots. This is impossible if it was a plume rising from a distant volcano.

However, Humphreys's opinion about the pillar of cloud and fire has no real bearing on the location of Sinai or the *Yam Suph*. In fact, it is not even important for the question of whether or not Mt. Sinai was volcanic. But if it were not for the fact that there are no volcanoes in the Sinai Peninsula, I think that in light of the biblical description of the theophany it would be a near-universal consensus that Exod. 19 is describing a volcano.[238]

Mt. Sinai Which Is in Arabia

St. Paul flatly states that Mt. Sinai is in Arabia (Gal. 4:25). We might ask ourselves where the "Arabia" was that Paul refers to. There were three regions of Arabia recognized in Roman times. These were Arabia Petra, Arabia Deserta, and Arabia Felix. Arabia Petra was the region of the Arabah south and east of the Dead Sea, corresponding to ancient Edom or to the southern part of modern Jordan (Josephus refers to Arabia Petra quite often, but usually only calls it "Arabia"[239]). Arabia Deserta, sometimes simply called the "Desert," was the arid region south and east of the Euphrates, west of the Levant, and in the northern part the Arabian Peninsula. It was (and is) largely barren, being the great desert of eastern Jordan, northern Saudi Arabia, and southwestern Iraq. In ancient times, it was the domain of a few nomadic, camel-riding Arabs. Arabia Felix was especially the wealthy kingdoms along the southwestern coast of Arabia, but the term could be used to describe a much larger territory, what we would call the whole Arabian Peninsula, as described below. The clearest description of the geography that I have found is in the anonymous *Geographiae Expositio Compendiaria*, section 21.[240] I have translated the text below.

---

237. Hoffmeier, *Ancient Israel*, 137.

238. Cf. Vaux, *Early History*, 438: "It cannot be denied that the Yahwist's account of the theophany on Mount Sinai has many volcanic aspects, but it is possible that they were borrowed." He goes on to speculate that some Israelites may have observed a volcanic eruption in Arabia, perhaps during Solomon's reign, and that this event made such an impression on them that they incorporated volcanic phenomenon into the Sinai narrative. Notwithstanding his speculative comments, Vaux's remarks demonstrate that a casual reading of the text suggests that it is describing a volcano.

239. E.g., Josephus, *War* 1:125 (1.6.2.125).

240. "Geographiae Expositio Compendiaria," in *Geographi Graeci Minores*, Vol. 2, ed. Karl Müller (Parisiis: Firmin Didot et sociis, 1882).

> Again, Armenia lies below Iberia and Albania, being separated from Cappadocia by the Euphrates. Mesopotamia lies below this, having Syria at its most western end. Judea lies below Syria. Arabia Petra lies toward the south of where this is situated, going as far [south] as the enclosed end of the Arabian Gulf. But the region between those aforementioned peoples and the western side of the Persian Gulf is called "Desert." This region contains the Arabian tribes. The mainland enclosed by the most southern parts of Desert and by Arabia Petra and by the Arabian Gulf, by the Gulf of the Red Sea, and by the area of the Persian Gulf is called Arabia Felix, and it is the largest in size.[241]

The above description has Arabia Petra extending south to the "Arabian Gulf." This gulf is apparently the Gulf of Aqaba. The account describes Arabia Felix as bounded by the Persian Gulf on one side and by the Desert to the north, and this confirms that the "Arabian Gulf" is the Gulf of Aqaba. This indicates that its "Arabia Felix" is what we presently call the Arabian Peninsula. When Paul spoke of Arabia in Gal. 4:25, he could have meant either Arabia Petra or Arabia Felix (he certainly did not mean Arabia Deserta), placing Mt. Sinai in either the Arabah of Edom or in the Arabian Peninsula. The term "Arabia" does not appear to include the Sinai Peninsula. On the other hand, the LXX of Gen. 45:10 and 46:34 reflect another usage, describing "Arabia" as extending into Egypt itself.[242] From that evidence, Paul's "Mt. Sinai in Arabia" could actually be in Egypt! But surely he did not mean this. It is not impossible, one may say, that Paul's "Arabia" included the Sinai Peninsula, but it is more likely that, writing during

241. *Πάλιν δὲ τῇ μὲν Ἰβηρίᾳ καὶ μέρει τῆς Ἀλβανίας ὑπόκειται ἡ Ἀρμενία, χωριζομένη τῆς Καππαδοκίας τῷ Εὐφράτῃ. Ταύτῃ δὲ ὑπόκειται ἡ Μεσοποταμία, δυτικωτέραν ἔχουσα τὴν Συρίαν. Συρίᾳ δὲ ὑπόκειται ἡ Ἰουδαία. Ταύτης δὲ κατὰ νότον κειμένης ἀντιπαρεκτείνεται μέχρι τοῦ μυχοῦ τοῦ Ἀραβίου κόλπου ἡ κατὰ τὴν Πέτραν Ἀραβία. Ἡ δὲ μεταξὺ τῶν εἰρημένων ἐθνῶν καὶ τῆς δυτικῆς τοῦ Περσικοῦ κόλπου πλευρᾶς καλεῖται Ἔρημος. ἔχει δὲ καὶ αὕτη ἔθνη Ἀραβικά. Ἡ δὲ περιγραφομένη ἤπειρος ὑπό τε τῶν νοτιωτάτων τῆς Ἐρήμου καὶ τῆς Πετραίας Ἀραβίας καὶ τοῦ Ἀραβίου [καὶ] κόλπου τῆς Ἐρυθρᾶς θαλάσσης καὶ μέρους τοῦ Περσικοῦ κόλπου, καλεῖται Ἀραβία Εὐδαίμων, καὶ ἐστὶ τῷ μεγέθει μεγίστη.*

242. Gen. 45:10 has, *καὶ κατοικήσεις ἐν γῇ Γεσεμ Ἀραβίας* ("and you shall dwell in Goshen of Arabia"). It also identifies Goshen as in the land of Egypt at Gen. 47:27, *κατῴκησεν δὲ Ισραηλ ἐν γῇ Αἰγύπτῳ ἐπὶ τῆς γῆς Γεσεμ* ("And Israel dwelt in the land of Egypt upon the land of Goshen").

the Roman period to a Gentile audience in Galatia, Paul used the standard Roman era meanings for "Arabia" (referring to Arabia Petra or Arabia Felix). This places it either south of the Dead Sea or in the Arabian Peninsula.

Conclusion

It should be clear that there are enormous difficulties with locating the *Yam Suph* at one of the bodies of water adjacent to the Egyptian Delta. Similarly, it is very hard to see how locating Mt. Sinai in the Sinai Peninsula can work. Does this mean that Humphreys is validated? I find his solution very attractive, but as of yet it is impossible to verify. The reason is simple: no one has done meaningful excavation and research in the Mt. Bedr area and in the northwestern part of the Arabian Peninsula. Egypt has been under intensive archaeological and historical research for more than a century. Accomplished scholars such as Flinders Petrie, Alan Gardiner, and Manfred Bietak (and indeed James Hoffmeier) have gone over the eastern Delta with laudable thoroughness looking for the remains of Pithom, Raamses, and other locations related to Exodus. But Saudi Arabia is under a theocratic and xenophobic Islamic regime, and the northwestern Arabian Peninsula remains terra incognita. We can only look at Mt. Bedr and the proposed exodus route from afar (I mean this literally; we can look at it from space with the help of Google™ Earth). Until on-the-ground research can be done by competent scholars, and until these scholars can gain the kind of familiarity with the terrain there that they have with Egypt and the Sinai, it will be impossible to compare fully and fairly the relative merits of each proposed location.

Another factor that makes it difficult to look at the present Gulf of Aqaba and draw conclusions about the crossing of the *Yam Suph* is the geological activity of the region. The Gulf of Aqaba is part of the Great Rift Valley that extends from Syria (between the Lebanon and Anti-Lebanon mountains), through the Jordan Valley and Arabah, down through the Gulf of Aqaba and Red Sea, and finally into eastern Africa. This region is going through significant geological transformation because of plate tectonics, as the Arabian plate moves northeastward into southern Asia. The Great Rift, from its northern edge to the southern end of the Red Sea, forms the western boundary of the Arabian plate. This movement has been highly significant geologically. For example, it has created an Alpine orogenic belt (that is, a region of mountain uplift) extending from eastern Turkey toward the southeast, all along the western border of Iran. The African plate, meanwhile, is moving toward the southwest, so that the Red Sea is widening as Africa and

Arabia separate. For our purposes, it is important to note that the region of the Gulf of Aqaba is, in geologic terms, very active. In addition to the separation of the plates, it appears that there is also a strike-slip fault along the rift in the zone of the Jordan Valley, Arabah, and Gulf of Aqaba, so that there is northward movement on its east side and southward movement on its west side.[243] In geologic time, the roughly 3,300 years since the exodus is very brief. Plates move at about one inch per year, but the speed can vary significantly. But even a movement of only about 200 feet since the time of the exodus, with both spreading and slippage, could be enough to significantly distort the picture of the land and sea topography.

Specific details regarding Humphreys's interpretation remain fuzzy. For example, although I believe that the *Yam Suph* has to have been the Gulf of Aqaba, the precise location of the crossing remains a mystery. Two factors for a Gulf of Aqaba crossing are critical: first, the depth of the water at the point of the crossing, and second, the nature of the submarine terrain. If the water is too deep for an "east wind" to have had an appreciable effect,[244] or if the ground beneath the sea is too rugged or steep for people and animals to walk over, the event could not have happened there. The Gulf does become quite deep, and much of the terrain beneath it is very steep and cragged. The crossing had to have been near the north end of the Gulf, as this is consistent

243. The precise nature of the geology of the Jordan Rift Valley is disputed. See Aharon Horowitz, *The Jordan Rift Valley* (Lisse: A. A. Balkema Publishers, 2001) and in the same volume, Zvi Garfunkel, "The Nature and History of Motion along the Dead Sea Transform (Rift)," 627–651.

244. Glen A. Fritz, *The Lost Sea of the Exodus: A Modern Geographical Analysis* (Ann Arbor: UMI Dissertation Services, 2006), 305, argues that the depth of the water is irrelevant since it was a miraculous crossing. But this disregards the biblical account, which explicitly states that a wind parted the waters. Fritz himself argues for a crossing about halfway down the Gulf of Aqaba, at what he calls the "Nuweiba Route," but he states that the sea here is 15.5 km (9.6 miles) wide and has a maximum depth of a staggering 850 m (2,788')! This is almost twice the height of the Empire State Building (443.2 m). No wind could have parted waters that wide and deep, and such a downhill and then uphill climb over such a distance would be taxing for a man in the prime of his life. Also, the slope up the east side is quite severe. Fritz describes the uphill climb as on average at 13%, but in fact his own data show that at points it is much more severe than that, including a lengthy stretch at 18% (pp. 308–12), a very strenuous climb for a group that included people of all ages and their livestock. Fritz also fails to take into account that the biblical crossing was near Shur.

with the fact that Israel was near Shur and Etham after the crossing, which I believe were at north and east of the Gulf. Presumably the sea was at that time shallow there, and the seabed was terrain that ordinary people could walk over and that chariots could attempt to dash through. It seems to me that Humphreys's solution is the best available.

THE STRUCTURE OF EXODUS

Exodus can be described as having seven major divisions with the following structure:

- I. Until Moses (1:1–2:10)
  - A. People of God (1:1–7)
  - B. Facing Persecution (1:8–22)
  - C. Three Women (2:1–10)
- II. An Unlikely Savior (2:11–7:7)
  - A. Zeal and Folly (2:11–22)
  - B. The Call (2:23–4:17)
  - C. Of Parents and Sons (4:18–26)
  - D. Fragrance of Life, Stench of Death (4:27–5:21)
  - E. I am YHWH (5:22–6:8)
  - F. Unbelief (6:9–13)
  - G. The Commission Renewed (6:14–7:7)
- III. The Twelve Miracles of the Exodus (7:8–15:21)
  - A. One: A Private Showing (7:8–13)
  - B. Two: The Nile (7:14–24)
  - C. Three: The Frogs (7:25–8:15)
  - D. Four: The Mosquitoes (8:16–19)
  - E. Five: The Flies (8:20–32)
  - F. Six: The Livestock (9:1–7)
  - G. Seven: The Skin Ulcers (9:8–12)
  - H. Eight: The Hail (9:13–35)
  - I. Nine: The Locusts (10:1–20)
  - J. Ten: The Darkness (10:21–29)
  - K. Eleven: The Firstborn (11:1–13:16)
  - L. Twelve: The Sea (13:17–14:31)
  - M. The Song of the Sea (15:1–21)
- IV. The Journey to God (15:22–19:25)
  - A. First Stage: A Bitter Disappointment (15:22–27)
  - B. Second Stage: A Great Need (16:1–36)
  - C. Third Stage: An Urgent Crisis (17:1–7)
  - D. Fourth Stage: A Sudden War (17:8–16)

- E. Fifth Stage: A Difficult Encounter (18:1–12)
- F. Sixth Stage: A Heavy Responsibility (18:13–27)
- G. Seventh Stage: Encountering God (19:1–25)

V. The Sinai Covenant (20:1–24:11)
- A. The Ten Commandments (20:1–17)
- B. Respect for God (20:18–26)
- C. Respect for Human Life (21:1–32)
- D. Respect for What Belongs to Another (21:33–22:17)
- E. Respect for Human Dignity (22:18–27)
- F. Respect for Those Toward Whom Honor is Due (22:28–31)
- G. Respect for the Truth (23:1–9)
- H. Respect for Divine Provision (23:10–19)
- I. The Blessings of Obedience (23:20–33)
- J. The Covenant Ceremony Concluded (24:1–11)

VI. The Worship of God (24:12–31:18)
- A. By Revelation (24:12–18b)
- B. With Reverence (24:18c–25:40)
- C. With Awareness of Sin and of Holiness (26:1–27:21)
- D. Under a Priesthood (28:1–29:37)
- E. In Constant Communion (29:38–46)
- F. With Prayer (30:1–10)
- G. With Purity (30:11–31:18)

VII. Sin and Restoration (32:1–40:38)
- A. The Besetting Sin (32:1–8)
- B. The Intercessor (32:9–35)
- C. Repentance and Mercy (33:1–34:9)
- D. Covenant Renewal (34:10–27)
- E. Veiled Glory (34:28–35)
- F. Giving (35:1–36:7)
- G. Obedience: Building the Sanctuary (36:8–39:43)
- H. A Walk after God (40:1–38)

In some cases, the unity of a section is demonstrable from formal considerations. As described in the commentary, subsections of sections III, IV, V, and VI follow formal patterns. That is, the formal structures of all of the subsections of section III are essentially the same, and the same can be said for sections IV, V, and VI. Here, the formal patterns to which the subsections conform help us to distinguish one major section from the next. In other cases, content and other markers indicate major divisions. Section I is plainly a prologue, describing events up to the coming of age of Moses. Section II describes the process whereby Moses is fashioned into a man fit to lead God's people from Egypt.

Section VII describes the restoration of the people after the sin of the golden calf.

THE MESSAGE OF EXODUS

The message of Exodus has many facets, and no summary can do justice to all the areas of life and theology that Exodus touches upon. The following summary only highlights the most salient features of the message of the book. The reader can find more detail by looking to the theological summaries included at the end of every section of this commentary.

The Place of Exodus in Old Testament Theology

Exodus is in some respects more foundational than Genesis for Old Testament theology. According to Deut. 6:20–25, when an Israelite child asked his parents why they were under so many religious rules and regulations, the answer was to be, "We were slaves of Pharaoh in Egypt, but YHWH brought us out of Egypt with a mighty hand..." For the people of Israel, their founding event was not the call of Abraham; it was the exodus. That history, along with the establishment of the Sinai covenant, was their pride, their identity, and their claim to being the people of YHWH.

The prophecy of Amos illustrates the point. When Amos criticizes Israel, he does it on the basis of the traditions that are most important to them. He hardly refers to the patriarchs at all. Instead, he declares, "Hear this word that YHWH speaks against you, Israelites, against the whole family that I brought up out of the land of Egypt: You only have I known of all the families of the earth; therefore I will punish you for all your iniquities" (Amos 3:1–2). Allusion to the exodus is obvious, but there is more here than meets the eye. With "You only have I known," Amos also refers to the promise of the Sinai covenant that Israel would be YHWH's special possession out of all the nations (Exod. 19:5). Amos' next question, "Will two walk with each other without coming together?" (Amos 3:3), alludes to the sojourn in the wilderness, when YHWH walked with Israel and had his dwelling in the Tent of Meeting.[245] Amos closes his indictment of Israel with yet another reference to the exodus (Amos 9:7). And Amos is not unusual. Throughout the prophets, we see that the exodus, the figure of Moses, and above all the statutes of Torah (that is, the stipulations of the Sinai covenant)

---

245. See Duane A. Garrett, *Amos: A Handbook to the Hebrew Text* (Waco: Baylor University Press, 2008), 82–3. The verb for "agreed" in Amos 3:3 is יעד—the root of מֹועֵד in אֹהֶל מוֹעֵד, the "Tent of Meeting."

express what is Israel's true origin and what are the ideals that it must live up to.

By comparison, the patriarchs receive comparatively little attention, even in Torah, outside of the book of Genesis. In the great confession that accompanies the ceremony of First Fruits (Deut. 26:5–10), the Israelite would only briefly allude to the patriarchs, and that without making mention of the promises or of any other event of Genesis except the descent into Egypt: "A wandering Aramean was my father. He went down to Egypt." The worshipper would, however, give a succinct but complete account of the exodus story: "When the Egyptians treated us cruelly. . . . we cried to YHWH, the God of our fathers . . . YHWH brought us out of Egypt with a mighty hand." It is as though history began at Exod. 1:1, with the descent into Egypt.

It is remarkable that the story of the fall (Gen. 3), a text that is critically important in Christian theology, gets almost no attention in the prophets. One might argue that even though Genesis is very important for the theology of the whole Bible, it is not nearly so much a theological fountainhead for the message of the Old Testament as Exodus is. Furthermore, it is not unfair and not disrespectful to say that Deuteronomy, a book that many regard as the theological center of the Old Testament, is essentially a restatement and expansion of the Book of the Covenant found in Exod. 20—24. Exodus is the true heart of the Old Testament.

The Narrative

The Exodus narrative has three major movements. The first is the story of the exodus itself, the departure from Egypt. This includes the introduction and background to the story (1:1–2:10), the account of the development of Moses (2:11–7:7), and the account of the plagues and the departure (7:8–15:21). This movement focuses upon glorifying YHWH for his fidelity and power. He multiplies Israel in captivity, remembers his promises to the patriarchs, hears the cries of the people, raises up Moses and shapes his character even while Moses is yet unwilling to take on the task of leading Israel, and above all else demonstrates his power by humbling Egypt and Pharaoh through the plagues.

The second movement is the journey to Sinai and the creation of the Sinai covenant. This movement has three parts: the journey to Sinai (15:22–19:25), the covenant itself, including its terms and its ceremonial ratification (20:1–24:11), and the instructions for making the Tent of Meeting (24:12–31:18). This movement describes the origin and meaning of Israel's identity as the people of God. As modern readers who from the constant retelling of the story have become perhaps too familiar with its details, we do not readily grasp how important and indeed unexpected this part of the story actually is. There was, in fact, nothing in the promises to the patriarchs that required YHWH to enter into a covenant with Israel. He could well have simply saved them from Egypt and delivered them to the Promised Land. If Israel had taken possession the land, that alone would have constituted the fulfillment of God's essential obligations to the patriarchs. Nothing required that he become their covenant God, and indeed in the initial statements about redeeming Israel from Egypt the focus is always on either God's fidelity to the patriarchs or his compassion on the Israelites for their suffering (e.g., 2:24; 3:7–10). The offer of a covenant in Exod. 19, stipulating that they could become his special possession, was a surprising work of God and act of grace. Israel, of all the nations of the earth, would become YHWH's people and they alone would be bound to him in a covenant. The Sinai covenant means that Israel is not simply the beneficiary of promises YHWH made to Abraham, Isaac, and Jacob. They are his elect nation. The command to build the Tent of Meeting signifies that YHWH, maker of heaven and earth, would sojourn among them.

The third movement of Exodus is in two parts: first, the sin of the golden calf and its aftermath, including Moses's intercession for Israel (32:1–34:35), and second, the account of the building of the Tent of Meeting (35:1–40:38). This movement demonstrates first of all what is Israel's besetting sin: idol worship. The episode sets a pattern of apostasy and idolatry that would persist in Israel until the fall of the Jerusalem temple to the Babylonians in 586 B.C. Second, the story fully demonstrates the greatness of Moses. When YHWH is ready to destroy Israel, or at best to abandon them to make their way to Canaan without his presence, Moses by his intercession secures their full pardon. With Israel having broken the covenant, YHWH by rights could walk away and consider the covenant to be voided. Instead, he reaffirms the covenant, and Israel is allowed to make the Tent of Meeting. As the book ends, Israel is sojourning with YHWH, fulfilling its role as the people of God.

The Nature of YHWH

John, after his telling of the life and events of Jesus, asserts that if everything Jesus said and did were written, the world itself could not find room for the books that would have to be composed (John 21:25). The same is surely true of the account of YHWH in the great act of redemption in the Old Testament, the exodus. We will here only consider certain salient aspects of YHWH as described in Exodus.

- *YHWH, the one and universal God.* From the narrative moment in which YHWH first decides to redeem Israel from slavery (2:23–25), there is never any question about whether he is able to effect their deliverance. That is, the text makes no suggestion that YHWH must strive to overcome Egypt or Egypt's gods. To the contrary, all the powers of Egypt, especially as epitomized in Pharaoh, the divine king, are no more than clay in YHWH's hands. He can direct them (4:21) or destroy them (9:15) as he wills, and the story that follows is not a conflict in any meaningful sense because Pharaoh can no more defeat God than he could overcome gravity by leaping in the air. In this narrative, the gods of Egypt are hardly worth mentioning (and in fact, they are hardly mentioned at all). The plagues are a visible manifestation of YHWH's superior power. They are gradually increased in severity only because YHWH wants the lesson to sink in over time for one and all that he is the one great God and that the powers of the nations are helpless before him. The single most important text on the divine nature of YHWH is of course 3:14–15, where YHWH calls himself "I AM." This title sets him apart from all other so-called gods; YHWH is the only person not bound by any classification, history, or particular identity. He is the only being who truly is, and all other beings (including the gods) depend upon him for their existence. By contrast, the gods of the nations are idols, and thus it is the greatest possible offense to portray YHWH with an idol, as Israel did in Exod. 32. Furthermore, YHWH is maker of heaven and earth (20:11). As creator, only he, the one called "I AM," stands outside of and above the created order.

- *YHWH's wrath.* In light of the plague narrative, it goes without saying that YHWH can be wrathful. It is noteworthy, however, that the first flare-up of divine anger in the Exodus narrative is directed not at Egypt but at Moses (4:14). YHWH is not one to show favoritism; anyone who persists in disobedience will face his fury. YHWH's anger can be truly terrible, as in the slaying of the firstborn. However, the gradual buildup in the intensity of the plagues is also meant to demonstrate that God repeatedly warns before he destroys. He even gives specific advice on how to avoid suffering the worst effects of his plagues (9:18–21). The most terrible expression of divine fury is directed not against Egypt but Israel, when at the provocation of the golden calf he threatens to destroy the entire nation all at once (32:10).

He did not do it, but no Israelite reader can miss the point that their nation came perilously close to obliteration at the very beginning of their existence. Finally, the whole Sinai experience, in which the mountain burns and quakes and roars and flashes with lightning when YHWH descends, is meant to drive home the lesson that their God is holy, righteous, and terrible.

- *YHWH's mercy.* The focus of the great credo of YHWH is that he is "the compassionate and gracious God, slow to anger, abounding in love and faithfulness" (34:6). Wrath is secondary, not primary, in his nature. The mercy of YHWH is demonstrated in several ways. First, he is moved to compassion by human suffering (3:7). Second, as described above, when he shows his wrath, he typically does so gradually and with ample warning. Third, he endures great provocation, as demonstrated by how mildly Israel is rebuked for their constant complaining in the journey to Sinai. Fourth, even when provoked to the uttermost, when with the golden calf incident Israel gave the greatest possible affront to the person and being of YHWH, he could be persuaded to forgive, renew the covenant, and sojourn with Israel.

- *YHWH as wholly other.* God is hardly an absent figure in the book of Exodus. From beginning to end, he is speaking, acting, and directing events. It is remarkable, however, that throughout the narrative and with very few exceptions, YHWH never has direct dealings with any person but Moses.[246] When YHWH has a message for Pharaoh, he delivers it through Moses. When he works a miracle, he works it through Moses (even if Aaron is the one who holds the staff or performs the ritual). When YHWH makes a covenant with Israel at Sinai, Moses is the intermediary between the two parties. At the making of the covenant, a barrier is set about Mt. Sinai, and apart from Moses, any Israelite who presumes to cross it to approach YHWH is to be put to death by stones or arrows. The lesson, plainly enough, is that no person has the right to come near YHWH without having either his explicit permission or an intercessor to serve as mediator. This is not only because YHWH is a high king; it is because he is, above all, holy. His

246. A rare exception is at 4:27, where YHWH tells Aaron to go meet with Moses. This report is extremely brief, and nothing of the nature of the encounter between YHWH and Aaron is recounted.

symbol is a burning bush, and even Moses, when bidden to approach, had to remove his sandals because the very ground around the fire was holy.

- *YHWH's sovereignty.* When Moses complains that his inability to speak well disqualifies him for a leadership role, YHWH, to the astonishment of many readers, answers, "Who has made man's mouth? Who makes him mute, or deaf, or seeing, or blind? Is it not I, YHWH?" As maker of heaven and earth, he does not shy away from accepting responsibility for what happens. He is in charge of all circumstances. YHWH's sovereignty most powerfully shows itself in another matter that troubles readers, the hardening of Pharaoh's heart.[247] In addition, the choice of Moses to bring Israel out of Egypt is entirely YHWH's. Not only did Moses not seek the task, he actively tries to get out of it. Most importantly, YHWH chooses the patriarchs and then the nation of Israel out of all the peoples of earth to be his special possession. This plainly is not brought about by the will of Israel, a people who fail or resist their calling at almost every step along the journey.

- *YHWH, the God of Israel.* In choosing Israel, YHWH gives them a history and identity unlike that of any other people. They owe their existence to divine intervention; he saves them when they are an oppressed, enslaved people. For Israel alone God works great miracles. To Israel alone he gives laws and teachings. Most importantly, out of all the nations of earth, God enters into a covenant agreement with only Israel. He is maker of heaven and earth, and yet he sojourns with Israel in a tent that they made for him.

- *YHWH and moral law.* The essential element of the covenant is that it identifies YHWH, the God of heaven, as Israel's God, and conversely that it marks Israel as YHWH's people. But the covenant stipulations, beginning with the Decalogue, do more than demand fealty to YHWH. They also demand moral behavior from his people. The Decalogue itself, after commands that relate to the service of YHWH (rejection of idols, keeping the Sabbath, and so forth), moves into areas of social ethics

247. See the excursus, "The Hardness of Pharaoh's Heart," in the commentary on 11:1—13:16.

(the prohibitions against murder, adultery, theft, and perjury, for example). The more expanded laws of the Book of the Covenant describe a wide range of rules and principles related to respect for human life, respect for property rights, and the duties of compassion. It is true that anyone who seeks to follow the moral law without first coming to terms with the demand for devotion to God has missed the main point. But it is also true that anyone who claims to be loyal to YHWH but does not obey the moral commands deceives himself. YHWH is not only Israel's God; he is also righteous, and he demands that Israel exhibit righteous behavior.

Moses, the Man of God

Moses is at the heart of Exodus. Although the book, above all, seeks to glorify God, it also seeks to establish the status of Moses as the founder of the nation. From the very beginning, various signs point to his special status. As God saw that the creation was "good," so also Moses's mother sees that he is "good" (see Gen. 1:12 and Exod. 2:2), implying that Moses is a kind of beginning of a new creation. As Noah escaped the flood in an ark, so also Moses survives the river in an ark (Exod. 2:3). Like Jacob, Moses finds a wife by behaving heroically at a well (see Gen. 29:9–10 and Exod. 2:15–22). Moses is a new Adam, a new Noah, and a new Jacob.

But Moses is not perfect or a hero of faith from birth; he must be molded. Although zealous for Israel, he wrongly and foolishly kills an Egyptian foreman, and he flees for his life to Midian. There, he takes on a new role as a shepherd in his wife's clan, apparently wanting to put his Egyptian life behind him forever (Exod. 2:11–25). God meets him at the burning bush and commissions him to lead Israel out of Egypt, but he resists, throwing up objection after objection until God is forced to give him a blunt command to do as he is told (Exod. 3:1–4:17). Back in Egypt he is cursed by his own people for the troubles he seems to have brought upon them, and he reaches his spiritual nadir, crying out to God that the whole exercise is a lost cause (5:21–23). Nevertheless, he accepts divine encouragement (6:1–8) and soldiers on, at last initiating the plagues of Egypt. As the narrative progresses, Moses becomes more and more wise, faithful, persevering, and compassionate.

Two episodes epitomize the greatness of Moses. The first is in Moses's last interview with Pharaoh, just before the plague of the firstborn, when he informs the king of the terrible calamity that is about to befall Egypt. Moses, the text tells us, is furiously angry with Pharaoh (11:8). This anger, it is clear, does not arise because Moses feels personally affronted by Pharaoh, and it really has nothing to do with Israel. Rather, Moses is angry because Pharaoh's stubborn behavior will bring about so many needless deaths in Egypt. Moses has no desire to see Egyptians suffering and dying. He is truly compassionate.

The second episode is his work of intercession for Israel at the golden calf episode, where he saves Israel first from total destruction and then from abandonment by YHWH. Israel owes its existence to Moses. His selflessness and devotion is most powerfully expressed in his cry to YHWH, "Alas! This people has committed a great sin! They made a god of gold for themselves! And now, if you would only forgive their sin—but if it is not to be, erase me from your book that you have written!" (32:31–32). It is not difficult to see Christ in the character of Moses.

Egypt as the Symbol of Worldly Power

Egypt's persecution of Israel is not only a historical fact, it also sets up Egypt as a type for the opposition of the kingdoms of earth to the kingdom of God. Like Babylon and Sodom, Egypt remains in the Bible a standing metaphor for godless society (see Rev. 11:8).

Egypt possesses every aspect of the kingdom of earth that stands opposed to the kingdom of God. First and foremost, Egypt is a land where gods of stone, gold, and wood are worshiped. YHWH's defeat of Egypt is also a defeat of her gods (Exod. 12:12). Second, Egypt is under a tyrannical autocrat, Pharaoh. The concentration of power in the hands of one ruler and the virtual or real deification of that ruler are characteristic of the "beast"—human governmental authority that sets itself up against God. The ideal of the beast is presented in Dan. 7 and Rev. 13, but its first great historical expression in the Bible is in the pharaohs of the oppression and the exodus. Third, Egypt oppresses Israel by murder, enslavement, and irrational hatred. The attempts to kill the Israelite firstborn, the imposition of corvée labor, the pursuit of Israel with a chariot army, and even Pharaoh's irrational outbursts (such as at Exod. 5:17–18) are all indicative of deep-seated hatred for God and his people. Fourth, a fixation on material prosperity, even if it means the cruel exploitation of people, reflects the ideal of the worldly kingdom. In Exodus, this manifests itself in the unwillingness of Egypt to release Israel from the servitude of building "store cities" and from working in Egyptian fields. This worldly ideal of amassing wealth and luxuries while crushing the people of God appears repeatedly in the Bible; its last great expression is the great harlot in Rev. 17–18. Fifth, Egypt has a debased dependence on magicians, sorcerers, and diviners (e.g., Exod. 7:11, 22; 8:7, 18). Revelation 9:21; 18:23; 21:8; 22:15 also stress that this characterizes the worldly kingdom. Sixth, Egypt is subjected to the direct wrath of God in a series of plagues that are poured upon it (Exod. 7–14). This, too, reappears in Revelation—most especially at the seven trumpets and the seven seals (Rev. 8–10; 16). Egypt is the first great expression of the ideals of Antichrist and of the kingdom of earth.

Egypt also represents apostasy for the people of God. The desire to go back to Egypt indicates that Israel has lost faith in YHWH (Exod. 14:11–12; 16:3). Later texts therefore describe going down to Egypt and imitating Egyptian ways as a mark of apostasy (Deut. 17:16; 1 Kings 3:1; 10:28–29; 2 Kings 18:21; Isa. 31:1). Prophets, moreover, threaten Israel with a return to Egypt in captivity and diaspora (Hos. 9:3; 11:5).

Israel as the People of God

Israel is formed to be the people of God on earth. They owe their existence to the faithfulness of God to the patriarchs, and their rapid multiplication fulfills the original creation mandate (see Gen. 1:28 and Exod. 1:7). Their high status does not give them wealth or ease, however. To the contrary, it results in persecution (1:8–22). Their deliverance from Egypt is entirely a work of God; Israel is almost completely passive in the process. In their journeys, they are sustained by manna from heaven and led by the pillars of fire and of cloud. At Sinai, they are wedded to YHWH as his covenant people, becoming "a kingdom of priests and a holy nation" (19:6). This covenant and this identity dominate the rest of the Old Testament. Israel has been chosen by God and is bound to him. In their story, fidelity to the covenant, or the lack of fidelity, will be the only thing that really matters.

PART I

Until Moses (1:1–2:10)

All of 1:1–2:10 is essentially prologue. We are reminded of how Israel came to be in Egypt, we are told of the crisis that developed, and we are shown Moses in his infancy. He will not act independently, as an adult, until 2:11ff. But the prologue lays out key themes. The whole point of the exodus is that God is making a people for himself, Israel, and this theme emerges immediately in 1:1–6. The prologue also introduces the major theological theme and a central motif of the exodus story: the people of God face persecution in this world. Finally, it shows how a series of women showed themselves to be righteous during a time of trouble.

PEOPLE OF GOD (1:1–7)

Exodus resumes the story of Genesis and in the process signals that Israel is a new creation and the people of God.

Translation

1:1–4 And these are the names of the sons of Israel who came to Egypt with Jacob (each one came with his household):[1] Reuben, Simeon, Levi, and Judah, Issachar, Zebulun, and Benjamin, Dan and Naphtali, Gad and Asher.[2]

---

1. "Each one came with his household" (אִישׁ וּבֵיתוֹ בָּאוּ) is a parenthetical clause meant to make the point that this was a full migration and not a temporary visit by the family heads, such as had occurred in Gen. 42.
2. The initial verbless clause (וְאֵלֶּה שְׁמוֹת; "And these are the names…") indicates that this is offline, giving background information for the narrative

1:5a And all the persons, who were direct descendants from Jacob,[3] were[4] seventy[5];
1:5b Joseph was already in Egypt.[6]
1:6 And Joseph and all his brothers and all that generation died.[7]
1:7a But the Israelites were fruitful[8]
1:7b and they became a swarm,[9]
1:7c and they were numerous,
1:7d and they became more and more of a force to be reckoned with,[10]
1:7e and the land was filled with them.

---

that is to follow. The clause continues to the end of the list of names.

3. "Who were direct descendants from Jacob" translates יֹצְאֵי יֶרֶךְ־יַעֲקֹב (lit., "the ones coming out from the genitals of Jacob"). It is parenthetical and in apposition to כָּל־נֶפֶשׁ, "all the persons," indicating that the seventy were the actual descendants of Jacob and that the number does not include slaves or any other persons attached to the household.
4. The *wayyiqtol* with היה here is a simple copulative clause and continues to give background information.
5. Gen. 46:27; Exod. 1:5; Deut. 10:22 all state that the initial immigration into Egypt consisted of seventy persons, but there are different figures given in the textual witnesses. The LXX of Exod. 1:5 and 4QExod[b] have "seventy-five." Acts 7:14, possibly following the LXX, also has "seventy-five." See further discussion in W. H. Propp, *Exodus 1–18* 1999, 121.
6. Another copulative clause with היה gives additional background information.
7. The *wayyiqtol* clause וַיָּמָת ("and he died") carries the story forward within the background framework. That is, the main narrative has not yet begun.
8. The pattern ו + noun + qatal verb (וּבְנֵי יִשְׂרָאֵל פָּרוּ) is here contrastive: "But the Israelites...." Verse 7 is transitional between the proper beginning of the narrative at v. 8 and the prolegomenal material in vv. 1–6. All the *wayyiqtol* clauses of 7b-e are epexegetical of the qatal clause of 7a.
9. "Became a swarm" translates וַיִּשְׁרְצוּ (lit., "and they swarmed"). The idea is that they became so numerous that they were like large swarm of insects or school of fish. The word is used of humans only here and in Gen. 9:7, and its usage here may reflect Egyptian sentiments, that the Israelites were to them a swarm of vermin (W. H. Propp, *Exodus 1–18* 1999, 129–30).
10. "Became more and more of a force to be reckoned with" translates וַיַּעַצְמוּ בִּמְאֹד מְאֹד (lit., "and they were mighty by much, much"). Their numbers were becoming so great that they were looking more and more like a political and military threat. They were becoming powerful by virtue of demographics, the sheer weight of numbers. The idiom בִּמְאֹד מְאֹד is used of something that steadily increases, be it population (Gen. 17:2, 6, 20), wickedness (Ezek. 9:9), or the enhancement of beauty and glory (Ezek. 16:13).

Structure

This text, an introductory summary, resumes the narrative of Genesis and carries it forward. It resumes Genesis in that Exod. 1:1–5 summarizes the genealogical list in Gen. 46:8–27 (the Exodus text is shorter, in that the Genesis text names both the twelve tribal patriarchs and their sons; Exodus lists only the twelve). Both passages mention that seventy persons entered Egypt. Exodus also resumes Genesis in that both Exod. 1:6 and Gen. 50:26 (the last verse in Genesis) mention Joseph's death. Thus, Exod. 1:1–6 summarizes and resumes the whole story of the migration into Egypt described in Gen. 46:8–50:26. But Exod. 1:7 gives us new information: Israel multiplied very fast in Egypt. This sets the stage for the new story to begin. The outline is thus:

I. Old background information: Resumption of Genesis narrative (1:1–6)
II. New background information: the large Israelite population (1:7)

Commentary

1:1. וְאֵלֶּה שְׁמוֹת, "These are the names," serves as the title of the work; in the standard Hebrew Bible the title is shortened to שְׁמוֹת, "Names." The conjunction marks continuity with the previous text, Genesis.

1:2–4. The tribes are grouped in a matrilineal manner, with the wives listed before the concubines: Leah (Reuben, Simeon, Levi, Judah, Issachar, and Zebulun), Rachel (Benjamin, with Joseph listed separately), Rachel's maid Bilhah (Dan and Naphtali), and Leah's maid Zilpah (Gad and Asher). This follows the order given in Gen. 35:23–26. The probable reason for following the order for the tribes used in Gen. 35, rather than the order used in Gen. 46:8–27, is that Gen. 35:11 includes a blessing on the fertility of Israel: "And God said to him, 'I am El Shaddai; be fruitful and increase in number. A nation and a congregation of nations will come from you, and kings will come from your genitals.'"[11] This anticipates the account of the fecundity of Israel in Exod. 1:7.

1:5–6. This portion of the text is superficially pessimistic in nature: there were only seventy "Israelites" to begin with, and they have all died. But this dark beginning to the narrative serves to make a

11. See Sarna 1991, 3.

contrast with the much more positive word in v. 7, that the Israelites multiplied rapidly. The death of Joseph and his brothers also marks the termination of the Genesis story and tells us that an unspecified time has elapsed since the time of Abraham, Isaac, and Jacob, the patriarchs.

1:7. This verse uses five different verbs (פרה, "be fruitful"; שׁרץ "swarm"; רבה, "be numerous"; עצם, "be mighty"; מלא, "fill up") to make the point that the family of Israel grew surprisingly large, even to the point that they became a power to be reckoned with (see notes above). Most significantly, the language echoes the divine command to humanity in Gen. 1:28, "Be fruitful and multiply and fill the earth." The implied meaning is that Israel is fulfilling God's creation mandate.

Theological Summary of Key Points

1. The story of Genesis, and in particular God's covenant with the patriarchs, is continuing even though the patriarchs themselves all died. God had promised to make Abraham's offspring into a mighty nation and had said that all nations would be blessed through him and his offspring (Gen. 12:1–3). Now, in Exodus, this program is going forward. The true agent in the history of salvation is God. His work continues even when the great heroes of the faith, such as Abraham, are dead and gone.

2. The numerical insignificance of the patriarchal clans as they entered Egypt was misleading. Although the patriarchs died without having seen the fulfillment of the promises, the blessings God had pronounced over Jacob and his offspring bore fruit. The unexpectedly rapid population increase recalls Jesus' parables of the mustard seed and leaven (Luke 13:19, 21). The kingdom of God may look very small at a given time and place, but its destiny is to become a great multitude (Rev. 7:9).

3. God is determined to make a people for himself. The original creation of humanity could have fulfilled this purpose, but it failed due to human sin. Rather than abandon the project, however, God resumed the work by means of Israel. They were to be the new people of God, chosen for himself out from the fallen human race. Nothing, not even the sin of Israel itself, will thwart this plan. The whole book of Exodus, after all, is about the creation of the nation of Israel, and the allusion to Gen. 1:28 in Exod. 1:7 demonstrates that this is the focus of this text.

FACING PERSECUTION (1:8–22)

The fact that Israel is the new people of God might lead us to suppose that they would be specially protected and spared every hardship. Surprisingly, the first reality that the people of God face is enslavement and persecution.

Translation

1:8 And a new king, who did not acknowledge[12] Joseph, arose over Egypt.[13]
1:9a And he said to his people,
1:9b "Listen,[14] the Israelite people are too many and too mighty for us.
1:10a Come on, we need to be smart[15] about dealing with them,
1:10b or they will multiply,
1:10c and here is what will happen:[16]
1:10d a series of events will lead[17] to a war,
1:10e and then they, too, will join our enemies,
1:10f and they will fight against us,
1:10g and they will take over the land."[18]

---

12. The meaning of the phrase "who did not know Joseph" (אֲשֶׁר לֹא־יָדַע אֶת־יוֹסֵף) is not entirely clear. It could mean that this pharaoh had actually never heard of him, or it could mean that he had no respect for a standing tradition of honoring the Hebrews for the sake of Joseph. The latter, I think, is more probable. So also in Exod. 5:2, when Pharaoh says, "I do not know (ידע) YHWH," he does not necessarily mean that he has never heard of YHWH. Rather, he does not recognize his authority. In both verses, ידע means "acknowledge" rather than "know."
13. The opening *wayyiqtol* of v. 8, וַיָּקָם, begins the first episode, the persecution of the Israelites.
14. The particle הִנֵּה is notoriously difficult to translate without recourse to the archaic "behold." Here, it merely calls for the hearers to pay attention and so is translated, "Listen."
15. "We need to be smart" translates the cohortative נִתְחַכְּמָה , where the root חכם does not connote "wisdom" in the sense of moral sagacity but only describes the ability to behave astutely in one's own interest.
16. The verb וְהָיָה is formally a protasis; the rest of the sentence is the apodosis. The protasis signals to the audience that a series of predictions is about to begin, and thus it is here translated, "and here is what will happen."
17. The verb תִקְרֶאנָה is here a feminine plural used impersonally; it could be translated fairly literally as, "and (things) will come together." It means that sooner or later a series of events will lead to war, and thus is translated that way here.
18. The phrase וְעָלָה מִן־הָאָרֶץ is usually translated, "and they will escape from the land." But this makes little sense. Israel has not yet been enslaved and there is no reference here to the loss of a labor force. The pharaoh

1:11a And they set corvée bosses over them to afflict them with heavy labors.
1:11b And [the Israelites] built for Pharaoh[19] store cities, Pithom and Raamses.[20]
1:12a But to the degree they afflicted[21] them,
1:12b to that same degree [the Israelites] multiplied
1:12c and to that same degree they expanded.[22]
1:12d And they were in dreadful fear[23] of the Israelites.

---

fears them because they are mighty and may wage war against him (וְנִלְחַם־בָּנוּ, "and they will fight against us"). He is not afraid that they might leave. Literally, the clause וְעָלָה מִן־הָאָרֶץ seems to say, "And (Israel) will go up from the land." Parallel usage suggests that the words mean to take over the land, not to depart from it. Hosea 2:1–2 (English 1:10–11) says that the Israelites will become very numerous and "go up from the land" (וְעָלוּ מִן־הָאָרֶץ). This clearly does not mean that they will depart the land; it is based in a metaphor of plant growth and means that they be like a massive growth that rises from the ground and covers it. They will fill the land and so control it, like weeds that spring up and take over a field. See Stuart 2006, 65–6, and Sarna 1991, 5–6.

19. The term "Pharaoh" (פַּרְעֹה) is a Hebraized form of the word *per-aa*, Egyptian for "great house." The term came to be used in Egypt as a designation for the king during the New Kingdom, in the 18th and 19th dynasties (Shaw and Nicholson, *Dictionary* 1995, 222), and as such the usage here is appropriate. Usage of the term in Genesis, when the patriarchs had interactions with the king of Egypt (e.g., Gen. 12:15), is anachronistic, reflecting usage in the time of composition rather than in the time of the events themselves.
20. The LXX adds *καὶ Ων ἥ ἐςτιν Ἡλίου πόλις* ("and On, which is Heliopolis"). Heliopolis, located at the southern tip of the Delta, was sacred to the sun god Re. It is difficult to say whether this addition reflects the Hebrew Urtext. It is not impossible that Hebrews were scattered across the Delta as far south as Heliopolis. The city is located near Tell el-Yahudiya ("The Mound of the Jews"), but this toponym almost certainly reflects the fact that Ptolemy VI Philometor (r. c. 180–145 B.C.) allowed the exiled Jewish priest Onias to build a temple and town there (Baines and Malek 2000, 174). It has no relationship to the exodus.
21. The *yiqtol* verb יְעַנּוּ here, in a past tense context, refers to repeated or sustained action. Here, with וְכַאֲשֶׁר, it forms a protasis clause.
22. Both יִרְבֶּה in 12b and יִפְרֹץ in 12c are *yiqtol* verbs that describe sustained action. Preceded by כֵּן, they form the apodosis clauses to 12a.
23. The *wayyiqtol* וַיָּקֻצוּ resumes the mainline of the discourse. The protasis-apodosis construction of lines 12a-c is offline and is the background to 12d.

1:13 And they made the people of Israel work[24] as slaves in cruel conditions,
1:14 and they made their lives bitter with hard work in mortar, and in brick, and in all kinds of field work—with all the work at which [the Israelites] slaved away in cruel conditions.[25]
1:15 And the king of Egypt said to the women who served as midwives to the Hebrew women[26]— one of them was named Shiphrah and the other Puah—
1:16a he said,[27]
1:16b "When you assist the Hebrew women in giving birth and look[28] at the baby's bottom,[29]

---

24. The *wayyiqtol* וַיַּעֲבִדוּ is sequential to line 12d and implies that the Egyptians redoubled their efforts to make life as hard as possible for the Hebrews.
25. The words אֵת כָּל־עֲבֹדָתָם אֲשֶׁר־עָבְדוּ בָהֶם בְּפָרֶךְ ("with all the labor in which they worked in cruelty") restate and summarize how the Egyptians treated the Israelites. The words are governed by the previous finite verb וַיְמָרְרוּ ("and they made bitter"). Verse 13, beginning with וַיַּעֲבִדוּ and ending with בְּפָרֶךְ, is echoed in this phrase. Notice that the relative clause begins with אֲשֶׁר־עָבְדוּ and ends with בְּפָרֶךְ. The first part of v. 14 fills in the details, describing what kind of work the Israelites did ("in mortar, and in brick, and in all kinds of field work").
26. The phrase לַמְיַלְּדֹת הָעִבְרִיֹּת could mean "to the Hebrew midwives"; this is the proper translation if הָעִבְרִיֹּת is regarded as adjectival—and this may well be correct. On the other hand, הָעִבְרִיֹּת could be read substantively as the direct object of לַמְיַלְּדֹת (an objective genitive relationship), with the meaning, "to the women who assisted the Hebrew women in childbirth." Thus it is conceivable that the midwives were Egyptian (Houtman 1993, 1:252–2). On the other hand, their names are probably Semitic (see commentary below), implying that they were Hebrew.
27. The *wayyiqtol* וַיֹּאמֶר here is resumptive of the *wayyiqtol* וַיֹּאמֶר in v. 15 and could be omitted in translation.
28. The construction with the infinitive construct בְּיַלֶּדְכֶן and the *weqatal* וּרְאִיתֶן together form a circumstantial clause that is background for the two protasis-apodosis constructions in lines 16c–f. The infinitive construct with ב is semi-clausal and has to be translated with an English finite verb, and it is best here taken as joined to the following *weqatal* as a pair of circumstantial clauses.
29. The word (lit., "the [two] stones") is often taken to refer to the birth stool, since Egyptian women at birth squatted with their feet spread apart on two mudbrick blocks. The midwife would be positioned in front of the mother, and other women would support the mother from behind (Silverman 1997, 84). This birthing position allowed the mother to use gravity as an assist. These blocks would often have magical charms written on

1:16c if it is a boy,[30]
1:16d kill him;
1:16e but if it is a girl,
1:16f she may live."
1:17a But the midwives feared[31] God

---

them (meant to invoke protection on the mother and baby). It is doubtful, however, that הָאָבְנָיִם refers to such a birthing stool. First, it is unlikely that mudbrick blocks would be called "stones." Second, it is hard to imagine how וּרְאִיתֶן עַל־הָאָבְנָיִם, "and you look upon the two stones," can be a description of midwives attending to their duties. A second possibility is that עַל־הָאָבְנָיִם means "on the potter's wheels" (see Jer. 18:3). This could then be an Egyptianism for a baby that was in utero. Egyptians believed that the god Khnum formed a child on a potter's wheel and referred to a child in the womb as being *ḥr nḥp*, "on the potter's wheel" (Morschauser 2003). This would indicate that Pharaoh is referring to prenatal visits, with the provision that if the baby in the womb is a boy, the pregnancy is to be terminated (Morschauser argues that it was within the abilities of Egyptian midwifery both to determine the sex of a child in the womb and to terminate the pregnancy). The problem is that both v. 16 and v. 19 indicate that the procedure in view is childbirth and not a prenatal visit. Also, notwithstanding Morschauser's claims, I am skeptical about the idea that Egyptian midwives could predict a child's gender during a prenatal visit, that they could induce abortion without endangering the mother, and that they could get the mothers to submit to such a procedure. A third possibility is that הָאָבְנָיִם is a euphemism for the baby's genitals. After all, one of the first things one does at the birth of a child is to check to see whether it is a boy or a girl, and that is the principal concern in this verse. הָאָבְנָיִם ("the two stones") could refer specifically to a boy's testicles, or it could refer either to a boy's testicles or to a girl's labia. Both boys and girls have their genitals somewhat swollen at birth due to hormones from the mother, and "the two stones" would be an apt euphemism for either. But the difficulty with this interpretation is that it is purely deductive, with no corroborating evidence. On the other hand, if *ḥr nḥp*, "on the potter's wheel," is the expression behind עַל־הָאָבְנָיִם, it might be a euphemism for sexual organs, male or female, as agents of reproduction, and still be derived from the mythology of Khnum. Thus, whether the basic idea is "two stones" or "potter's wheel," it is probably a euphemism for genitals. It is thus translated here with a corresponding English euphemism, the "baby's bottom."

30. The word "boy" is literally "son" (בֵּן), just as "girl" is literally "daughter" (בַּת). But this only reflects the different conventions of biblical Hebrew and modern English for specifying the gender of a newborn. The words are properly translated into English as "boy" and "girl."
31. The *wayyiqtol* וַתִּירֶאןָ continues the mainline sequence of the narrative.

1:17b and they did not do[32] in accordance with the instructions of the king of Egypt;
1:17c they let the boys live.[33]
1:18a And the king of Egypt summoned the midwives
1:18b and he said to them,
1:18c "Why did you do this thing—
1:18d you let the boys live?"[34]
1:19a And the midwives said to Pharaoh,
1:19b "It's just that[35] the Hebrew women are not like the Egyptian women!
1:19c They are vigorous![36]
1:19d Before the midwife gets[37] to them,
1:19e they give birth!"[38]
1:20a And God was good[39] to the midwives.

---

32. Although it is a debatable notion, it is probably best to regard all negated statements as by nature offline. Thus, וְלֹא עָשׂוּ is offline and explanatory of how the women's fear of God, mentioned in the previous clause, showed itself. Also, offline statements are generally more prominent than mainline clauses. As such, this is a pivotal point in the narrative.
33. The *wayyiqtol* וַתְּחַיֶּיןָ is epexegetical of clause 17b.
34. The clause וַתְּחַיֶּיןָ אֶת־הַיְלָדִים ("and you let the boys live") is epexegetical of הַדָּבָר הַזֶּה ("this thing").
35. The particle כִּי is here explanatory, but unlike the English "because," it does not require that the clause associated with it be subordinated. כִּי לֹא כַנָּשִׁים הַמִּצְרִיֹּת הָעִבְרִיֹּת is an independent clause.
36. The words כִּי־חָיוֹת הֵנָּה form a complete sentence and should not be combined with the previous clause. כִּי has the same function as in clause 19b.
37. בְּטֶרֶם with a *yiqtol* forms a protasis indicating that the action of the *yiqtol* is prior to the action of the other verb. The tense used to translate the *yiqtol* is dependent on context. Here, context describes a routine occurrence and requires a present tense.
38. The *weqatal* וְיָלָדוּ forms the apodosis of the previous clause.
39. From the standpoint of the surface grammar, the *wayyiqtol* וַיֵּיטֶב does not appear to imply any causal relationship between what the midwives did and how God treated them. It seems to be purely a mainline sequence of events—a simple assertion that God treated the women well. Verse 21, however, does describe a causal relationship: because of what the women did, God rewarded them. Why is clause 20a structured as it is? Or why is it included at all? I would suggest that in this context, the understatement of the *wayyiqtol* in this clause is very powerful: The women did what they did, and God treated them well. The reason for this remarkable pattern is, I think, that the reader may wonder whether God would reward them for saving the babies or would punish them for lying. In this subdued manner the text deals with the ethical dilemma that this passage poses:

1:20b And the people multiplied,
1:20c and they became a considerable force.
1:21a And it was the case[40]
1:21b that because the midwives feared God,
1:21c he made their houses [distinguished[41]].
1:22a And Pharaoh commanded all his people,
1:22b "Throw every newborn [Hebrew] boy into the Nile,

God rewarded them, and that is the decisive fact. The issue is further explored in the Theological Summary to this passage.

40. "And it was the case" translates וַיְהִי. It is usually left untranslated in this passage, but the particular pattern used here, וַיְהִי כִּי, occurs just 17 times in the Hebrew Bible and deserves note. The pattern is found in texts that are transitional, either introducing a new narrative or, as is the case here, closing a paragraph (in this case, the paragraph of vv. 15–21). Normally the clause with כִּי is followed by an apodosis clause with a *wayyiqtol* verb (e.g., Gen. 6:1, with apodosis at 6:2; 27:1; 44:24; Exod. 13:15; Josh 17:13). The כִּי may be temporal ("when") or explanatory ("because"). Strong examples of the latter are Exod. 13:15; Judg. 6:7–8, and 2 Kings 17:7–18 (in the latter case, the protasis is extended through v. 17, with the apodosis coming in v. 18). In short, the pattern in Exod. 1:21 is an especially prominent way of pointing out the causal relationship between what the women did and how God rewarded them.

41. The words וַיַּעַשׂ לָהֶם בָּתִּים ("and he made houses for them") are usually taken to mean that God provided families for the midwives. Some speculate that perhaps the midwives previously had no children. But there is no reason to think that the midwives were childless prior to this time and indeed no reason to think that midwives in general should be childless. Also, the Bible is generally explicit when a previously barren woman bears children (as in the cases of Sarah, Rebekah, Rachel, and Hannah). To "make a house" is an odd and roundabout way of describing having children. An alternative, rabbinical interpretation, that the pharaoh put them under state control (Sarna 1991, 8), is quite far-fetched. Rather, for God to "make a house" means that he has established a family in security and honor (1 Kings 2:24). The idiom is used for establishing a royal dynasty, but there is no reason that it could not also describe the giving of high prestige to a non-royal house. Notice that of all the people mentioned in Exod. 1–2 (except for Moses himself), only Shiphrah and Puah are explicitly named, indicating that they are singled out for the prestige of remembrance. This explanation would also account for why the masculine pronoun is used (לָהֶם, "for them") since, in Hebrew and Egyptian thinking, the midwives' households belonged to the midwives' husbands.

1:22c but you can let every girl live."[42]

Structure

The structure of this passage is built around three policies of Pharaoh, and it describes the outcome of the first two policies. No immediate result for the third policy is described in the text. Rather, the third policy leads into the narrative of chapter 2. In effect, the ultimate result of the third policy is that Moses is elevated to the status of the adopted son of Pharaoh's daughter.

I. Pharaoh's First Policy: Slavery (1:8–10)
II. Result (1:11–14)
III. Pharaoh's Second Policy: A Quiet Genocide (1:15–16)
IV. Result (1:17–21)
V. Pharaoh's Third Policy: An Overt Genocide (1:22)

Commentary

1:8–10. As described in the notes above, Pharaoh's action is more a deliberate rejection of precedent than an act of ignorance. It is hard to imagine that he knew nothing of Joseph or of the ancient provision of sanctuary to the Hebrews. There is no indication of how long was the time between the death of Joseph and the ascension of this pharaoh.

When Pharaoh addressed "his people" (v. 9), it does not necessarily mean that he spoke to the entire populace. "People" (עַם) can refer to the army, and here it probably refers to politically powerful people in the state. Although pharaohs were in theory absolute, they had to have the backing of political, military, and religious leaders if they wanted to hold on to power. So also the Israelite "people," which in one sense is the entire population, especially referring to the size of the army they might field and to the power that their demographics would give them. As described in the notes above, Pharaoh's principal concern is that their numbers will be a threat to himself and to the class he represents—that the Hebrews might take over the land. This fear may be a result of the recent experience with the Hyksos (see Introduction). Notice that Pharaoh does not make a specific proposal here; he merely asserts that something needs to be done to control the Hebrews. This indicates that the decision to enslave them was a joint decision arrived at by Pharaoh and his high officers and counselors. Even so,

42. The two clauses of 22b and 22c begin respectively with כָּל־הַבֵּן ("every boy") and וְכָל־הַבַּת ("but every girl"), setting up a construction analogous to the Greek *μεν* ... *δε*.

the enslavement of Israel is implicitly if not explicitly the pharaoh's suggestion.

1:11–14. The results of Pharaoh's alarmist warning to his people were, first, that the Egyptians enslaved the Hebrews; second, that the Hebrews built the supply cities Pithom and Raamses; third, that the Hebrews' lives became bitter; but fourth, to the frustration of the Egyptians, that the Israelite population growth only accelerated. Although it seems counter-intuitive, a people who are economically deprived and in great suffering can reproduce at a faster rate than a population that is quite prosperous (as is illustrated by the population decline in Europe and Canada over against population growth in poorer parts of the world). The Egyptian policy of enslavement was therefore a failure, despite the fact that the Egyptians saw some short-term economic benefits since they suddenly had a supply of cheap labor to work their fields and to build supply depots (see the Introduction for a discussion of the location, history, and significance of Pithom and Raamses).

The imposition of "corvée bosses" (שָׂרֵי מִסִּים) over the Hebrews tells us that they were organized into forced-labor groups, the corvée (מַס), a term that is also used for the Israelite forced-labor that served under Solomon's construction program (1 Kings 9:15). Apparently an Egyptian official was set over each of the Israelite labor gangs. These bosses would be assigned a quota of production from their labor gang, whether it was a matter of number of bricks to be produced, or of the pace of progress in the construction work, or of the number of bushels of harvested grain. The Hebrews probably still lived in their own homes and worked their own fields and flocks to provide for themselves, but their time was divided between labor for Egypt and labor for their own families. And of course, they had to make the quota demanded by the government no matter how little time that left them for providing for themselves. The bosses would have been extremely harsh and demanding both because they despised the Hebrews and because a boss knew that he would pay the price if his particular labor gang did not meet its quota. Harassment, deprivation, and exhaustion would all have contributed to the Hebrews' sense of bitterness.

1:15–16. Frustrated at the failure of forced labor to limit the population of the Hebrews, the pharaoh was prepared to resort to genocide. His first effort in this direction was evidently clandestinely done, as he privately told the two midwives to kill all the boys born to the Hebrews. It may be that he initially feared that such an act, if publicly proclaimed, would result in a Hebrew uprising or that even his own people would recoil at such a monstrous act. Readers wonder why he wanted to kill the boys instead of the girls, since it is obviously the girls who would bear the next generation of Hebrews. First, Pharaoh was primarily concerned with eliminating future warriors who might rise up against him. Second, he probably identified the race of a child with the race of the father, not of the mother. The later Jewish notion that a Jew is someone who has a Jewish mother is irrelevant here. Third, he may have supposed that in the absence of Hebrew boys, Hebrew girls would be sold off to Egyptian families to serve as domestic slaves, and that the Hebrew race would eventually melt away.

The names "Shiphrah" and "Puah" are authentic personal, Semitic, feminine names from the latter part of the 2nd millennium. "Shiphrah" appears in an Egyptian list of Semitic slaves from this time.[43] Her name means "beauty," whereas "Puah" is probably the same name as Ugaritic *pǵt*, the heroine of the Ugaritic myth of Aqhat.[44] There is no reason to doubt that these are two real, individual women, and that their names realistically reflect names that West Semitic women of the New Kingdom/Late Bronze Age would have. As pointed out in the notes, it is possible that the midwives were Egyptian. For this to be the case, however, one would have to assume that some Egyptians used Semitic names (when two cultures are mixed, people of one culture sometimes use names that they like from the other culture). If the midwives were Egyptian, it would explain the pharaoh's apparent astonishment that his commands were not carried out. Also, it would suggest that the pharaoh's command to "all his people" (v. 22) is an extension of the command he first gave to only two of his people. On the available evidence, however, it is more likely that the midwives were indeed Semitic.

Some readers are surprised at the fact that Israel only has two midwives. Some interpreters have therefore argued that these two were the head of a midwife "guild" who would communicate the pharaoh's commands to the rest of the guild. But the biblical text seems quite clear that there were in fact only two midwives, and it is not at all evident that a "midwife guild" existed in ancient Egypt (the whole notion of a "midwife guild" is, I think, an ad hoc solution to a perceived problem, and not based on any ancient evidence). Verse 19 does not imply that there are other midwives besides the two named; it merely asserts that Hebrew women could give birth without benefit of

43. Albright 1954.

44. W. H. Propp, *Exodus 1–18* 1999, 139. For the Aqhat myth, see COS 1.343-56. The name *pǵt* is anglicized as *Paghat* or *Pūgatu*.

a midwife.[45] The honor given to the midwives in vv. 20 and 21 implies that only the two named women are meant. If many other midwives also risked their lives by disobeying the pharaoh, they should have been named as well, or at the very least their existence should have been explicitly acknowledged. If only Shiphrah and Puah out of all the midwives disobeyed the edict, there is little reason for Pharaoh to have noticed this anomaly, since his program of killing Hebrew babies would have been progressing as planned. In short, the text says that there were two midwives, and we should leave it at that.

1:17–21. The results of Pharaoh's second attempt to stop the Hebrew population growth was as great a failure as the first. The midwives quietly disobeyed him, and the Hebrew numbers grew as fast as ever. More than that, the midwives were honored by God himself. As suggested in the notes, it seems that "he made a house for them" (v. 21) implies that God established their households, giving them honor and perhaps longevity in a manner analogous to how he "made a house" for David (2 Sam. 7:11).

The claim of v. 19, that the reason Shiphrah and Puah were not able to exterminate the boys is that the Hebrew women gave birth without benefit of a midwife, is manifestly untrue. Verse 17 plainly indicates that the midwives allowed them to live, showing that the midwives were in fact present when boys were born. We therefore have the moral and theological issue that these women are honored by God, it seems, for an act of deceit. This issue is discussed under the Theological Summary below.

We should also observe that the women's answer is in the literary tradition of the oppressed finding ways to make a mockery of their oppressors. First, they insult Pharaoh's racial pride by claiming, with all apparent innocence and sincerity, that Hebrew women are stronger than Egyptian women. Second, they tell a lie which is really far-fetched—and get away with it. The pharaoh has no understanding of childbirth, and the women, aware of his arrogance and ignorance, treat him as a gullible fool.

1:22. Pharaoh's third attempt to thwart Hebrew population growth is by public decree calling for the murder of the Hebrew boys. They were to be cast into the Nile River.[46] Possibly soldiers made sweeps through

---

45. Against Stuart 2006, 76.
46. It is possible (as W. H. Propp, *Exodus 1–18* 1999, 159, observes) that this detail deliberately echoes the myth of Atrahasis. In this version of the world

Hebrew villages looking for baby boys, and perhaps all Egyptians were expected to notify the authorities whenever they suspected that a Hebrew woman had given birth to a boy. The result that would follow from this was altogether unexpected by Pharaoh: one of the Hebrew boys, who otherwise would have remained in obscurity, was found and adopted by an Egyptian princess, and he would rise up to break the power of Egypt.

We should observe that this draconian measure, the decree to kill the baby boys, does not appear to have been in effect for very long. Aaron, who was three years older than Moses (Exod. 7:7), was apparently not endangered by the decree. When Moses grew up and began to observe the conditions of the Hebrews in Egypt, there were plenty of Hebrew men around and no indication that Israelites were still hiding their newborn boys. To the contrary, what outraged him was their hard labor (2:11; "their burdens" [סִבְלֹתָם] refers to forced labor, as at 1:11). If their babies were still being massacred, forced labor would have been a minor issue. The Egyptian princess, moreover, seems to have disregarded the decree without hesitation. One may argue that this was because the princess would use her position to get what she wanted, but it may also be that she knew that the decree was too outrageous to last, and that it would soon be allowed to quietly expire.

Theological Summary of Key Points

1. The fundamental issue of this passage is that the people of God should expect persecution. In 1:1–7, as described above, we see that God, through Israel, was creating a new people for himself. Our natural supposition is that to be God's people is to enjoy great favor. There is obvious truth in this: "I will bless those who bless you, and whoever curses you I will curse" (Gen. 12:3). But there is another side to it, and that side comes to the forefront in Exodus. In a fallen world, to be God's people is to be hated. "You will be hated by all for my name's sake,"

---

deluge story, the noise created by humans, as their numbers increased through a population boom, so disturbed the gods that Enlil decided to kill them all by a flood. But Ea warned Atrahasis, and he built a boat for his family and some animals, thus saving the world (see COS 1.450-2). If an Israelite audience, while listening to the story of Pharaoh's decree, made a connection to the Atrahasis tale, they would have concluded that Pharaoh, like the pagan deities, tried to limit Israel's population by throwing Israelites into the waters. But of course, Atrahasis is an Akkadian and not an Egyptian myth, and thus we cannot be sure that the audience would have made such a connection.

Jesus says (Matt. 10:22). A Christian congregation should expect and to endure hostility as part of the walk of faith. Many Christians endure severe persecutions today, especially in Islamic or communist countries. All Christians should identify with the persecuted church. Pastors should also preach of the need to pray for and support the persecuted and, as needed, protect them and suffer with them.

2. Persecuting the Jews is also a mark of depravity, and comes from the same motivation of hatred for the church. Anti-Semitism in a Christian is perverse and inexcusable. Hostility toward Israel and the Jews is as old as the Egyptian sojourn and as recent as the Holocaust and the pronouncements by 21st century Islamic leaders to the effect that Israel should be wiped off the map.

3. Evil is frustrated by its inability to stop what is right. The three efforts of Pharaoh to put an end to Israel's population growth all ended in Israel growing more rapidly than ever. In his frustration, Pharaoh resorted to measures that were even more horrible and outrageous. This pattern, too, has been repeated in the persecution of the church. When initial efforts by the ancient Roman government to persuade Christians to submit to emperor worship failed, the government used progressively harsher methods.

4. Those who refuse to go along with efforts to persecute God's people, and who instead shield them at personal risk, are rewarded by God (Matt. 10:42).

5. God rewarded Shiphrah and Puah, two women who deceived the lawful head of state who was over them.[47] Precisely speaking, however, God did not reward them for lying to Pharaoh but for preserving the lives of Hebrew babies. Even so, we must come to terms with the fact that they did lie as part of their efforts to protect these children. The theological lesson to take away from this is not that lying is a "gray area" that is sometimes allowable. The moral requirement of honesty and its converse, not to engage in deception, is an absolute. For that

47. Ryken 2005, 42, tries to excuse the women on the grounds that what they said was so implausible that no one could take it seriously, and thus that it could hardly be called a lie. But in fact Pharaoh was at least taken in to the extent that he did not punish the women. Otherwise, it is hard to see how they kept their heads on their shoulders. Ryken fails to see that the mockery of Pharaoh's arrogance and gullibility is the point of the verse.

matter, there is also a moral requirement to obey the government, since whoever resists governmental authority rebels against God (Rom. 13:2). But the midwives most certainly did not obey the government. But there are higher rules or, as Jesus put it, "weightier matters of the law" (Matt. 23:23). In this case, the weightier matter was that one should not participate in the murder of babies. The requirement to protect innocent life (And what life could be more innocent than that of a newborn?) outweighs the need to tell the truth or to obey the king. But it is completely wrong to conclude that the Bible says that lying is acceptable. Lying is no more acceptable, in biblical thinking, than are killing, stealing, or the wanton destruction of property. But in fact, in time of war, for example, one may have to kill the enemy,[48] or steal from him, or wantonly destroy his supplies. One should no more take lightly the prohibition against lying than one should take acts of violence and theft lightly. If one is put in the position of the midwives, where the choice is between killing babies and disobeying the government, then one should disobey the government. But one should remember that God, for whom all moral absolutes are clear and every commandment important, will bring every act into judgment. That is, one should fear God, just as the midwives did (v. 17).

6. The Christian reader can hardly fail to see a parallel between the effort to slaughter the Hebrew boys in this text and the slaughter of the Jewish boys in Herod's effort to kill Jesus (Matt. 2:16). Jesus, in his own person, recapitulated the experience of Israel. Like Moses, he narrowly escaped a slaughter of the innocents, and the hostility that Pharaoh directed at all the Israelite boys was directed by Herod at Jesus personally. Jesus' experience also parallels that of Israel in that there were several attempts to do away with him. The last attempt to put an end to Jesus, the crucifixion, had an unexpected result in the resurrection, just as the final attempt to kill the Israelite boys had the unexpected result of elevating Moses to prominence.

THREE WOMEN (2:1–10)

Moses, the savior of Israel, is born. But to survive the first years of his

48. We should note that the word for "kill" in the Sixth Commandment (רצח) does not exclusively mean "murder," contrary to recent translations. See commentary below. Licit killing, whether by lawful execution or in a lawful war, is still a horrible thing.

life he had to be protected by three women who, in this narrative, are anonymous.

Translation

2:1 And a man from the house of Levi went and took[49] a Levite woman [as his wife].
2:2a And the woman became pregnant
2:2b and she gave birth to a son,
2:2c and she saw that he was good,
2:2d and she hid him for three months.[50]
2:3a But she could not[51] hide[52] him longer than that,
2:3b and she got him a box made of papyrus
2:3c and she coated it with tarry bitumen.[53]
2:3d And she put the boy in it,
2:3e and put it among the aquatic plants[54] by the bank of the Nile.

---

49. The verb וַיֵּלֶךְ is virtually an auxiliary to the verb וַיִּקַּח; as in the English, "he went and took," it does not imply a specific motion from one place to another and need not be treated as a separate clause (and it need not be emended). וַיֵּלֶךְ does serve, however, to introduce a new narrative analogous to how וַיְהִי often does. The action of these verbs is not necessarily subsequent to the prior narrative. In other words, he probably took his wife prior to the decree to kill the male babies.
50. With four *wayyiqtol* verbs, this verse maintains the mainline narrative.
51. The negated statement is offline, contrastive, and marks a minor transition in the narrative.
52. The form of the Hiphil infinitive construct, הַצְּפִינוֹ, is anomalous. The root is צפן, and it should be written asהַצְפִּינוֹ. It looks as though the scribe confused the hiphil preformative with the definite article (W. H. Propp, *Exodus 1–18* 1999, 143-4).
53. "With tarry bitumen" is literally "with bitumen and with tar" (בַחֵמָר וּבַזָּפֶת), but this is probably a hendiadys in which the two words "bitumen" and "tar" mean essentially the same thing. Some scholars do attempt to find two different substances behind the words; see Houtman 1993, 1:276, but that is probably futile. By itself, the word חֵמָר is somewhat ambiguous since there are four different roots for חמר in the Hebrew Bible and several nouns with these letters. Adding the noun זֶ֫פֶת ("tar") clarifies the meaning, and this probably accounts for the hendiadys.
54. The word סוּף refers to some kind of aquatic plant. In Isa. 19:6 it refers to plants that grow along Egypt's canals and is used in conjunction with קָנֶה, "reeds," and probably refers to a variety of reed or something like water lilies. In Jonah 2:6 (E 5), however, סוּף is clearly a deep-water, oceanic plant, such as kelp. Here in Exod. 2, it no doubt refers to some kind of freshwater plant.

2:4 And his sister stood at a distance to find out what would be done to him.
2:5a And the daughter of Pharaoh[55] came down to bathe in the Nile,
2:5b while her young women went walking[56] along the river,
2:5c and she saw the box among the aquatic plants
2:5d and she sent her servant woman,
2:5e and [the servant] got it.
2:6a And she opened [it]
2:6b and saw him, the baby.[57]
2:6c It was a crying boy![58]
2:6d And she took pity on him,
2:6e and she said,
2:6f "This is one of the Hebrews' baby boys."
2:7a And his sister said to Pharaoh's daughter,
2:7b "Should I go summon[59] a wet-nurse for you from the Hebrew women
2:7c so that she can nurse[60] the baby for you?"
2:8a And Pharaoh's daughter said to her,
2:8b "Go."
2:8c And the girl went
2:8d and she summoned the baby's mother.
2:9a And Pharaoh's daughter said to her,
2:9b "Take this boy home
2:9c and nurse him for me,
2:9d and I will pay you."[61]

---

55. "Pharaoh" is here a title, almost a proper name, and thus the construct chain בַּת־פַּרְעֹה is definite. But the expression, "the daughter of Pharaoh," does not imply that she was Pharaoh's only daughter (pharaohs had sizable harems and typically many children). The definite article points to her status, not that she was the only one of her kind.
56. This participial clause is circumstantial, and it makes the point that the princess and her entourage actually observed a considerable stretch of the river bank, explaining how it was that they found the baby.
57. The pleonastic "she saw him, the child" (וַתִּרְאֵהוּ אֶת־הַיֶּלֶד) is probably the narrator's touch for dramatic effect. It needs no further explanation and no emendation (Durham 1987, 14).
58. The וְהִנֵּה clause (וְהִנֵּה־נַעַר בֹּכֶה) vividly describes the moment of discovery from the perspective of the women on the shore, helping the reader to empathize with the princess' tender feelings for the child.
59. Although formally two clauses, "Should I go summon" (הַאֵלֵךְ וְקָרָאתִי) are functionally a single action, as in the English, "I'll go get…"
60. The *weyiqtol* is here a purpose clause.
61. Lit., "give you your wages."

2:9e And the woman took the boy,
2:9f and she nursed him.
2:10a And the boy got big,[62]
2:10b and she brought him to Pharaoh's daughter,
2:10c and he became her son.
2:10d And she named him Moses,
2:10e and she said,
2:10f "[It's] because I drew him out of the water."

Structure

Apart from a few pieces of reported speech, this text is composed almost entirely of *wayyiqtol* clauses, making it little more than a straightforward sequence of events. Any attempt to break it down structurally, therefore, is somewhat arbitrary, but it clearly follows the actions of various characters (who are all, surprisingly, anonymous). One can also see that, apart from the mention of Moses' father in the opening of the text, three women play decisive roles in the story. The actions of the women, therefore, should be understood to dominate the structure.

I. The father gets a wife (2:1)
II. The mother protects Moses (2:2–3)
III. The sister protects Moses (2:4)
IV. The princess protects Moses (2:5–6)
V. The sister protects Moses (2:7-8)
VI. The princess protects Moses (2:9abcd)
VII. The mother protects Moses (2:9ef–10ab)
VIII. The princess protects Moses (2:10cdef)

Commentary

2:1. The narrator is determined to keep all the characters in this story, up to the naming of Moses, anonymous. There may be two reasons for this. First, by maintaining the anonymity of the other players, Moses, although entirely passive in the story (except for crying!) is made more prominent. In other words, the reader understands that this narrative is really about Moses and not about his parents, his sister, or the princess. Second, the matter of Moses' parentage is somewhat complicated.

62. "And the boy got big" translates וַיִּגְדַּל הַיֶּלֶד. This could be translated as, "and the boy grew up," but this translation might suggest that he reached adulthood, which is not the point. Rather, the meaning is simply that he was big enough to be weaned and be moved into the home of the pharaoh's daughter.

Amram and Jochebed are named as his father and mother in Exod. 6:20, but this creates difficult problems (see the commentary on 6:14–25). It may be that the names of Moses' actual father and mother have been left out in order to avoid confusion with the data given in the official genealogy in Exod. 6. All we know for sure about Moses' father from Exod. 2:1 is that he was a Levite.

2:2–3. The first hero of our tale is Moses' mother who, no doubt at considerable risk to herself, hid the baby for three months. Reading v. 2, one would assume that Moses was her firstborn, but we find out in v. 4 that he had an older sister, and we discover in Exod. 7:7 that Aaron was three years older than him. But the births of the two older siblings are passed over in order not to distract from Moses. The fact that Moses was not the firstborn is significant; he follows in the line of Israel's leaders being chosen from younger sons (Isaac over Ishmael; Jacob over Esau; and later, the choosing of David, the youngest of Jesse's sons).

The note that Moses was "good" may explain how it was that he endeared himself to the women who came in contact with him. "Good" (טוֹב) here connotes healthy and attractive. The LXX translates this as *ἀστεῖον*, "beautiful" (so also Heb. 11:23). On the other hand, line 2c, "and she saw that he was good" (וַתֵּרֶא אֹתוֹ כִּי־טוֹב הוּא), echoes God's repeated evaluation of creation in Gen. 1 (e.g., "and God saw that it was good" [וַיַּרְא אֱלֹהִים כִּי־טוֹב], Gen. 1:12). As Israel is the beginning of God's new creation of a people for himself, so also the evaluation of Moses shows him to be an example and token of the new work of God, the beginning of a new humanity that is "good."

It is not clear why the boy became more difficult to hide at three months. The "three months," however, may refer to a period in which both mother and child would stay secluded for the health of the baby. In traditional Korean culture, for example, a mother and newborn remained in isolation until the 100-day anniversary of the child's birth, at which time the child would be considered viable and could be shown to the world. If the Hebrews had a similar custom, and if the day of the child's coming out were approaching, she would have known that she could not conceal the child and his gender after that. But of course, we do not know what post-natal customs the Hebrews in Egypt observed. Later legislation, in Lev. 12:2–6, mandated that a woman who bore a son was unclean for a week and then had a 33-day purification period (two weeks if the child was a girl, followed by a 66-day purification), but this relates only to ritual purity and does not tell us at what age a baby would be customarily be presented before the community for celebration. Circumcision, of course, was to take place on the eighth day after birth, but we do not know if the circumcision ritual at this time was the public event it became in later Judaism, or if it was done privately in the home. If it were a public event, she may have deferred Moses' circumcision as long as possible (and this could account for why she felt she could no longer hide him). Or, if it were a private affair, she may have done it herself in her home.

The basket that Moses' mother got for him is here called a "box." It may have been something like a basket made of woven papyrus, but the standard word for "basket" is סַל. The word here is תֵּבָה, a word that means "box" but which is also used for the ship that Noah built, the "ark" (Gen. 6:14–16), which was essentially a great box. The choice of the word תֵּבָה is probably deliberate to make the connection to Noah. The likelihood of intentional allusion to the flood narrative is reinforced by the fact that she made the basket waterproof with a tarry bitumen, although the words used here in Exodus (בַחֵמָר וּבַזָּפֶת) are not the same as the word for "pitch" used in Genesis (כֹּפֶר, at Gen. 6:14). Even so, Moses is a new Noah, who goes through water in his ark sealed with tar in order to save the people of God from a wicked generation. We should also note that the details here conform to the Egyptian context, where there was a tradition of making boats for service on the Nile out of papyrus. The papyrus would be bound and tied at both ends to create the characteristically buoyant shape of a boat and then sealed with bitumen.[63] It may be that Moses' "box," despite its name, actually had this boatlike shape.

The text tells us that Moses' mother placed him among the aquatic plants that grew along the banks of the Nile. We sometimes have an image of Moses in his little basket floating down the middle of the broad river. In fact, the last thing Moses' mother would have wanted would be for him to go floating off; not only would she lose track of him, but he would be heading north, toward the open Mediterranean. Also, a small, moving object might draw the attention of dangerous wildlife (crocodiles!). But she put him among the plants by the shore precisely so that he would not drift but stay put, waiting to be found. We should also note that Moses' mother ironically fulfills Pharaoh's decree that the Hebrew babies should be cast into the Nile, except that she did it to save him and not to kill him.

2:4. The second hero is Moses' sister, who watches over him from a distance. The text does not tell us whether she did this on her own

63. David 1998, 263; Houtman 1993, 1:276.

initiative or at her mother's command. But she is obviously portrayed as a quick-witted and spunky girl, as illustrated by how she inserts herself among the princess' attendant women and offers to find a wet-nurse. Thus, the text suggests that she acted on her own. Were it not for her, the mother would not have been reunited with the baby. We know from later texts, of course, that the sister's name was Miriam. She was evidently the oldest of three siblings.

2:5–6. The participial clause וְנַעֲרֹתֶיהָ הֹלְכֹת עַל־יַד הַיְאֹר ("while her young women walked beside the river") is circumstantial, describing what some of her girls were doing while the princess bathed. This implies that they were able to observe a considerable stretch of the river bank, explaining how it was that Moses was found. The following clause ("And she saw the box") does not necessarily mean that the princess herself first saw the basket; as the ranking member of the group, the discovery of the child is attributed to her. Also, of course, the women were drawn to the baby by his crying. The princess sent one of her servant girls to fetch the basket to her. This sets up an implied parallel between Moses' actual mother and the princess, who will be his adoptive mother: as the former sent Moses' sister to watch over him, so the latter sent her servant to bring him safely to shore.[64] This literary pattern implies that the princess accepted the role of mother that was being handed off to her. She immediately recognized that the boy was a Hebrew, no doubt because when they checked his gender, they saw that he was circumcised. In a text that generally shows the Egyptians to have been spiteful to the Hebrews, this passage points out the compassion of an Egyptian aristocrat.

2:7–8. As mentioned above, Moses' sister showed initiative and resourcefulness by putting herself forward and offering to find a wet-nurse.

2:9–11. Although Moses' mother takes him home and nurses him until he is weaned, she is more of a passive player in this part of the narrative, as she is subject to the commands of the pharaoh's daughter. Even so, the happy nature of the outcome, that she is able to continue to nurse her son, and that she does so under the princess' protection (and gets paid for it!) is obvious. Still, it is the princess who is the moving agent here. She determines to save the boy and to adopt him. Her compassion insures the boy a bright future indeed.

There is a problem with the fact that the princess names the boy

64. See W. H. Propp, *Exodus 1–18* 1999, 153.

Moses with the explanation, "Because I drew him out of the water." In this explanation, the name Moses (מֹשֶׁה) is based on a word-play with the Hebrew word משה, "to draw out (from water)." But most scholars believe that the name Moses is from the Egyptian *mśy*, a word that means "born" or "child." This word was often used as part of a compound name, as in the name Har-mose, "Horus is born."[65] The word Mose (anglicized as Moses) could be used by itself as a proper name; other men named Moses are mentioned in Egyptian texts. But if Moses is an Egyptian proper name, then it obviously makes no sense for the Egyptian princess to explain the name by giving a Hebrew etymology—and an etymology which, at any rate, would be wrong.

Kitchen avoids this problem by denying that the name Moses is related to the Egyptian *mśy*. He argues that the Hebrew version of this Egyptian name should be transliterated with a ס (as מסה) instead of with a שׁ (as משה). He contends that Moses is fully a Hebrew name and that the boy was named by his Hebrew mother.[66] But this explanation cannot be correct. First, it is unnatural and forced to read Moses' mother as the speaker in 2:11e, right after the verse has declared, "and he became her son." The princess, who is now his mother, is clearly the one who named him. Second, Moses' birth mother would not have said, "Because I drew him out of water." She put him in the water; it was the princess who drew him out. Since Moses is a common Egyptian name, and since he was named by an Egyptian, it is pointless to contend that the name Moses here is of Hebrew origin. Some would contend, therefore, that having the princess give the Hebrew-based explanation, "because I drew him out of water," is simply a late piece of Israelite folk-etymology concocted by people who did not know that the name was Egyptian (and, therefore, that the explanation is completely fictional). This conclusion is unnecessary, although reconstructing events does require a bit of imagination on our part.

It is certain that the princess maintained some contact with Moses' mother. As his wet-nurse, she would bring the boy around to his adoptive mother fairly frequently. There is no reason to doubt that the women would talk, and that the princess would tell the mother that she had decided to name the boy Moses. The mother would have told the princess that this name is similar to the Hebrew word משה, "to draw out of water." An Egyptian woman would have immediately seen the congruence of the Egyptian name and the Hebrew verb with the manner in which she found the boy, and she would have regarded

65. HALOT, מֹשֶׁה; Houtman 1993, 83.
66. Kitchen, *Reliability* 2003, 296–7.

that as a very good omen. She would have adopted the Hebrew verb as an explanation of how she was led to choose the name Moses. But she was not a philologist and she was not claiming that the Hebrew verb was literally the origin of the Egyptian name. As for the Hebrew transliteration מֹשֶׁה instead of מסה, the spelling with שׁ may have been adopted on the basis of the connection created between the name and the Hebrew verb.[67]

In the literary structure of the book, the circumstances of Moses' discovery on the Nile foreshadow future events. Although Moses' sister and the compassionate princess came to terms with one another in their discussions on the Nile, Moses and the irrational Pharaoh would never come to terms in their negotiations on the Nile. Pharaoh failed to kill the baby Moses, but YHWH through Moses would succeed at killing Egypt's firstborn males. As Moses was saved from the waters, so he would deliver his people through the waters.

Theological Summary of Key Points

1. At the moment when it seems that the situation for the Hebrews could not be worse, God uses those very circumstances to raise up a deliverer. When evil seems to have triumphed, the appearance that God has abandoned his people is altogether wrong. God is not absent, however much he may appear to be.[68]

2. As described above, all the major actors of the events described above are women, and each one of them contributes to Moses' survival and elevation.[69] Notwithstanding that one of the characters is a princess, women clearly had lower status in the ancient world. The obvious point is that God can do a work of salvation through the humble and even anonymous persons.

3. We know nothing about the Egyptian princess except that at this one moment she showed compassion for a child. Although still anonymous, she is today among the more famous members of the ancient Egyptian aristocracy. By comparison, the Bible has no interest at all in

---

67. Other proposed explanations for the origin of the name "Moses," that it is Hurrian, Kassite, or Sumerian, are intrinsically unlikely, as noted in W. H. Propp, *Exodus 1–18* 1999, 152.
68. Gowan 1994, 1–2, notes that acts of God are conspicuously rare in Exod. 1:1–2:23.
69. For a study of the portrayal of heroic women in the early chapters of Exodus, see Exum 1983.

the conquests of Thutmose III or Ramesses II, or in the great buildings constructed under Hatshepsut. In the biblical text, the greatest work ever done by a member of the Egyptian royal family was a singular act of kindness toward an apparently abandoned baby.

4. The language of this narrative at two points calls Genesis to mind in a way that elevates the figure of Moses. First, his mother called him "good" after giving birth to him, in a manner that recalls how God called creation "good." Moses thus represents a new creation and is symbolically a new Adam and a founder of a new humanity. In this, he anticipates Christ, who is fully the second Adam. The analogy of Moses in his little ark to Noah in the ark presents Moses as a second savior of humanity. Like Noah, he will take his people to safety through an outpouring of the wrath of God. The drowning of the Egyptians at the sea recalls the drowning of humanity in the flood narrative.

Excursus: The Sargon Story and the Story of Moses

The birth narrative of Moses has a striking similarity to the story of the birth of Sargon of Akkad (c. 2334–2279 B.C.). The Sargon birth legend was discovered in the Nineveh library of the Neo-Assyrian king Ashurbanipal. It was recovered in excavations conducted in the mid-19th century by Austen Layard and George Smith for the British Museum. The text is in the form of a first-person narrative from Sargon himself, in which the king declares that his mother was a high priestess and that she bore him in secret (apparently the high priestess was not allowed to bear a child). She then placed him in a reed basket, the hatch of which she had sealed with pitch, and set him adrift on the Euphrates. He was discovered by a man named Aqqi, a water-drawer and, therefore, a peasant. Sargon then abruptly tells the reader that he ruled in Akkad for fifty-five years and invites any king to try to match his achievements.[70]

The date of composition of the Sargon birth narrative is unknown, but it is universally regarded to be pseudepigraphal; that is, Sargon I did not write it. Theoretically, it could have been written at any time from soon after the death of Sargon until the reign of Ashurbanipal (r. c. 668–627 B.C.).[71] A commonly held position is that the text was commissioned by Sargon II sometime in the years 721–705 B.C., and that Sargon II's purpose was to bring glory to himself by propagating a text purportedly written by his namesake. Although this is possible,

70. For the text, see COS 1.113.
71. Lewis 1980, 98.

one must be careful; definitive evidence linking Sargon II to this text is lacking. Similarly, we do not know if the story has any basis in fact.

The obvious parallel with the Moses' birth account is that in both cases the hero is placed by his mother in a basket that is sealed with pitch and that is then set upon a river. Later, the boy in the basket rises to become a great leader. One might argue from this that the Moses story was composed in imitation of the Sargon legend. If, moreover, the Sargon birth narrative were not composed until the late 8th century, then the story of Moses being placed in the basket would have to be very late indeed—after the fall of Samaria to Assyria.

Brian Lewis, on formal grounds, seeks to make such a case. He argues that the *Vorlage* of the Moses story had seven elements that parallel the Sargon narrative, as follows: (1) explanation of abandonment, (2) hero of noble birth, (3) preparation for exposure, (4) exposure in water, (5) nursed in an unusual manner [this is absent in Sargon], (6) discovery and adoption, and (7) the accomplishments of hero.[72] This argument fails on two grounds. First, Lewis only succeeds in creating the appearance of a strong parallel between the Moses and Sargon stories by "stripping away" (his term) elements in the story not paralleled in Sargon. These include that (1) genocide is the motivation for hiding Moses, (2) Moses is hidden for three months, (3) Moses' sister watches over him, (4) a person of high rank, Pharaoh's daughter, adopts Moses, and (5) Moses' own mother nurses him.[73] But one cannot simply excise everything in story B that is unlike story A, and then declare stories A and B to be parallel. Unless one has prior knowledge that there is a *Vorlage* to story B that is dependent on story A, one has no basis for recreating this putative *Vorlage*. Otherwise, any time two stories had something in common, one could declare the *Vorlage* of B to be dependent on A simply by excising as a later accretion everything in B that is different from A. Second, the parallels that Lewis claims for Moses and Sargon are for the most part illusory, and there are numerous differences. For example, it is not correct to say that in both cases the hero is born to a mother of high rank. This is true of Sargon, born to a "high priestess," but Moses' mother is simply a "Levite woman" (Exod. 2:1).[74] In addition, Moses is not truly abandoned or even set adrift on the river, as Sargon is. Moses' mother places his basket among the reeds so that he will not drift away (and also Moses' sister watches

72. Lewis 1980, 266.
73. Lewis 1980, 264–5.
74. It is true that Exod. 6 present Jochebed, daughter of Levi, as the mother of Moses, but this cannot be considered part of the birth narrative of Exod. 2.

over him). The Sargon narrative leaps ahead to a retrospective look at Sargon's fifty-five years of rule; the Moses narrative does no such thing. Sargon is raised by a peasant and is set to work in an orchard; Moses is raised in the aristocracy. The Moses story has an account of the hero's naming, and the name reflects the fact that the child was set on a river (Exod. 2:10); the Sargon story does not. The Sargon story is first person; the Moses story is not. There is no formal basis for the argument that the Moses story has a relationship to the Sargon story.

Even the one obvious parallel, setting the baby in a basket, is probably not significant. One can hardly doubt that in the ancient world there were many examples of women who for some reason (poverty, disgrace, danger, etc.) decided that they could not keep their children. These women would, as in the more recent counterpart of putting a baby in a basket on a doorstep, place their children outside either to die of exposure or to be cast upon the charity of others. In a country such as Greece, with many mountains but with no significant rivers, the logical place to do this was on a mountain side (as in the story of Oedipus, whom a shepherd was supposed to abandon on a mountain). In the cases of Mesopotamia and Egypt, two regions dominated by rivers, the logical places to do this was on the Euphrates or the Nile. In short, the setting of a baby in a basket onto a river is simply something that arises from the environment; it is not a motif useful for establishing literary dependence.

PART II

An Unlikely Savior (2:11–7:7)

Exodus 2:11–7:7 follows the life and career of Moses from his time as a young adult in Egypt to his flight to Midian, his call from YHWH to return to Egypt, and his first experiences in dealing with Pharaoh and with the Israelites. In this, we see him first as a fiery vigilante, determined to redress the wrongs done to the Israelites. Next, he is a refugee in Midian, apparently wanting to keep all of his experiences of Egypt firmly locked in the past. Finally, he is a most unwilling and then very discouraged agent of YHWH. This narrative has two centers. These are the two encounters between Moses and YHWH at Exod. 3–4 and 6:1–8, where we learn about YHWH's purposes and about his intent to use Moses to accomplish those purposes. Through these encounters, Moses is transformed into the compassionate and courageous man of God who calls down the plagues and leads his people to safety.

ZEAL AND FOLLY (2:11–22)

Moses displays zeal for Israel, but it is an unwise and immature zeal that almost ends his life and then seemingly ruins it. He loses all position and prestige, and he finds himself no longer a son of privilege in the cultural center of the world. Instead, he is a shepherd on the very fringe of civilization.

Translation

2:11a Now it happened, in the course of time,[1]

1. Literally "in those days," בַּיָּמִים הָהֵם here means, "in the course of time."

2:11b that Moses grew up.[2]
2:11c And he went out to his brothers[3]
2:11d and he saw their heavy labors.
2:11e And he saw[4] an Egyptian man beating a Hebrew man, one of his brothers.
2:12a And he turned this way and that,
2:12b and he saw
2:12c that there was no one [around],[5]
2:12d and he struck[6] the Egyptian
2:12e and he hid him in the sand.
2:13a And he went out the next day,
2:13b and now[7] two Hebrews were fighting!
2:13c And he said to aggressor,[8]
2:13d "Why do you strike your comrade?"
2:14a And [the bully] answered,
2:14b "Who made you our boss man and judge?

---

2. "Now it happened" (וַיְהִי) in 11a is a protasis, to which the apodosis is formally the *wayyiqtol* clause "that Moses grew up." Functionally, the protasis alerts the reader that a new phase of the historical narrative is beginning.
3. Today, אֶחָיו is routinely translated "his people." But the literal "his brothers" should be retained because it conveys more accurately the implied sense of racial solidarity Moses felt toward the Hebrews.
4. On a purely grammatical level, the *wayyiqtol* verbs וַיֵּצֵא ("and he went out" [11c]), וַיַּרְא ("and he saw" [11d, e]) are simple sequential events in a past tense narrative. But the grammar alone does not always bring out the pragmatics of the text; the narrator expects us to read the account intelligently and with empathy. In this case, the first two clauses assert that Moses came to be aware of how cruelly his people were oppressed. The third clause, "And he saw an Egyptian man" initiates a specific episode.
5. "Around" is supplied for clarity in English. Presumably the assault took place after the Egyptian finished beating the Hebrew, when Moses thought he was alone with the Egyptian.
6. The verb נכה in the Hiphil stem ("to strike") does not necessarily imply a fatal blow; the same verb is used in the next verse for a blow that presumably was nonlethal. Clearly, however, the Egyptian did die, as Moses buried him. It may be that Moses struck out in anger without meaning to commit homicide, but that death ensued anyway.
7. וְהִנֵּה presents the episode from the viewpoint of Moses. He is stunned to find two Hebrews going at each other.
8. Literally "to the wicked one," לָרָשָׁע here refers to the one who is the aggressor and is obviously more violent and bullying. He is represented as a vile man, pushing around a fellow Hebrew and sneering scornfully at Moses when rebuked.

2:14c Are you threatening to kill me
2:14d as you killed the Egyptian?"
2:14e Then Moses was afraid,
2:14f and he thought,
2:14g "No doubt the facts are known."
2:15a And Pharaoh did hear about this matter,
2:15b and he began proceedings to kill[9] Moses.
2:15c And Moses fled from Pharaoh,
2:15d and he stayed in the land of Midian.
2:15e And he sat down[10] by a well.
2:16a Now the priest of Midian had seven daughters,[11]
2:16b and they came
2:16c and they drew water
2:16d and they filled the troughs to water their father's flock.

---

9. The Hebrew וַיְבַקֵּשׁ לַהֲרֹג אֶת־מֹשֶׁה (lit. "and he sought to kill Moses") could mean that the pharaoh physically attacked Moses and tried to kill him, but this is extremely unlikely. Kings generally have others do their killing for them. Also, Moses did have relatively high social standing, and thus the pharaoh would have had to be sure of his political and legal ground before having him executed. Thus, it is here translated with, "he began proceedings." Like any capital city, the palace always had rumors circulating. Apparently word was out that the pharaoh was setting forces in motion against Moses. We should note that exile, rather than execution, was sometimes the punishment given when an aristocrat committed a serious crime against a commoner in the ancient world. Thus, by merely letting word out that he was coming after Moses, and having Moses flee the country, the pharaoh probably accomplished his purpose.
10. We have two occurrences of ישׁב ("sit, dwell"), one after another. In the first (15d), וַיֵּשֶׁב בְּאֶרֶץ־מִדְיָן, the verb plainly means that he "dwelt" or "stayed" in the land of Midian. The second (15e), וַיֵּשֶׁב עַל־הַבְּאֵר, is more ambiguous. It could mean that he "sat" on or at a well (as in Gen. 48:2, וַיֵּשֶׁב עַל־הַמִּטָּה ["and he sat on the bed"). This would imply that Moses had just arrived at the well and was only sitting there for a brief rest. Or it could mean that he was for the time being "staying" in the vicinity of this particular well (as in Num. 13:29, וְהַכְּנַעֲנִי יֹשֵׁב עַל־הַיָּם ["and the Canaanites dwell by the sea"]). In a large majority of cases, however, ישׁב על means to "sit upon" and not to "dwell near," and this is followed in the translation. But it is possible that the text means that Moses had been for a few days staying near the well.
11. The opening verbless clause וּלְכֹהֵן מִדְיָן שֶׁבַע בָּנוֹת ("Now the priest of Midian had seven daughters") sets it apart as offline information. This sets up the background for a new episode in the story.

2:17a And some shepherds[12] came
2:17b and began to drive[13] them away,
2:17c and Moses arose
2:17d and he saved them,
2:17e and he watered their[14] flock.
2:18a And [the women] went[15] home to their father Reuel.
2:18b And he said,
2:18c "How is it that you have hurried back today?"
2:19a And they said,
2:19b "An Egyptian saved us from the brutality[16] of the shepherds,
2:19c and he even drew up [all the water][17] for us

12. Literally "the shepherds," the article on הָרֹעִים describes these men as belonging to the occupational class of shepherd, and it is appropriately translated as "some shepherds."
13. These shepherds obviously did not succeed in driving away the women and their flocks, and thus an ingressive translation of the *wayyiqtol* וַיְגָרְשׁוּם is legitimate.
14. There is some difficulty in the gender of the pronominal suffixes. The hostile shepherds were driving away "them" (masculine suffix: וַיְגָרְשׁוּם), but Moses saved "them" (feminine suffix: וַיּוֹשִׁעָן), and then he watered the flocks belonging to "them" (masculine suffix: צֹאנָם). It is true that Hebrew is not consistent in always using a feminine suffix to represent a feminine noun, but since this verse does use a feminine suffix one time, it seems unlikely that the two masculine suffixes are accidental. Probably we are to understand that the female shepherds had some boys working under them, and that their group as a whole was a mixed group of males and females. Such a group would be represented in Hebrew with the masculine pronoun. But when Moses got up to "save" them, he was particularly motivated to help the young women, and thus that verb has a feminine suffix.
15. The feminine verb וַתָּבֹאנָה shows that the women are the subject of this verb, and thus "women" has been supplied.
16. The verb נצל ("snatch, save") is characteristically used with מִיַּד ("from the hand of"). The word "hand" could be omitted in translation, but it connotes the domination of one person or group over another, whether that be by political and military control (Exod. 18:9; Judg. 8:34; 1 Sam. 7:3) or by the threat of personal violence, as when one person bullies or threatens another (Gen. 32:11; 37:21; Deut. 25:11). The latter is the case here, and thus, it is translated as "brutality."
17. The phrase "all the water" is supplied; it is implied by the infinitive absolute in דָּלֹה דָלָה. The verb דלה is rare, it occurs (Qal stem) only in this passage (twice) and in Prov. 20:5, where it means to "draw water" from a well or cistern. It appears one time in the Piel stem (Ps. 30:2[1]), where it means to draw something or someone up from the water.

2:19d and he watered the flock."
2:20a And he said to his daughters,
2:20b "So where is he?
2:20c Why is it that you left the man?
2:20d Invite him to dinner!"[18]
2:21a And Moses willingly stayed[19] with the man,
2:21b and he gave to Moses his daughter Zipporah.
2:22a And she bore a son,
2:22b and he called his name Gershom,
2:22c for he said,
2:22d "I am[20] a sojourner in a foreign land."

Structure

The two major divisions of the section are nicely broken up in the Hebrew text. Both halves begin with Hebrew patterns commonly employed to initiate a new episode. The first, 2:11–15, begins with a וַיְהִי clause. The second, 2:16–22, begins with a conjunction and verbless clause, וּלְכֹהֵן מִדְיָן שֶׁבַע בָּנוֹת, to indicate the circumstances at the beginning of the second episode. In addition, the content of these two sections parallels each other. In the first, Moses intervenes to save a Hebrew who is being beaten by an Egyptian taskmaster, but the result is a murder, and he must leave his people and homeland. In the second, he intervenes to save some women from a group of thugs, but this time comes off as a gallant hero, and he gains a new homeland. Thus, we have the following outline.

I. First Episode (2:11–15)
  A. Israelites Oppressed (2:11)

18. In וְיֹאכַל לָחֶם, the *weyiqtol* serves as a final clause ("to eat"), and the noun לָחֶם ("bread") refers to a meal. From the standpoint of surface grammar, וְיֹאכַל actually begins a separate clause, but it is here a virtual auxiliary to the verb קִרְאֶן, "invite." Thus, the two verbs are translated together as, "invite to dinner."

19. The Hiphil of יאל with an infinitive construct verbal complement means to do something willingly, deliberately, boldly, or with determination. See Gen. 18:27; Deut. 1:5; Josh. 7:7; Judg. 1:35. Here, it means that Moses stayed willingly.

20. The Hebrew הָיִיתִי could be either, "I have been" or "I am." Neither is quite adequate; the verb implies present status, and thus it is like the English present and should not be taken in a past tense, as though it referred to his former status. On the other hand, it does convey something of how his past life has brought him to this point, as in the perfect tense translation.

B. Moses Intervenes (2:12)
C. Report of the Event Spreads (2:13–14)
D. Authority Responds (2:15ab)
E. Moses Flees Egypt (2:15cde)

II. Second Episode (2:16–22)
A. Shepherd Women Oppressed (2:16–17ab)
B. Moses Intervenes (2:17cde)
C. Report of the Event Spreads (2:18–19)
D. Authority Responds (2:20)
E. Moses Settles in Midian (2:21–22)

Commentary

2:11–15. At our first introduction to Moses, we discover certain clear traits of his background and character. First, he knew himself to be Hebrew and not Egyptian. This may be explained first by the fact that he was nursed by his mother, since nursing could go on for several years in the ancient world (three years was about the average, and thus nursing went well beyond the time that a child could walk and talk). An aristocratic child would often form a very close relationship with his or her wet-nurse that would last beyond the time of breast-feeding, to say nothing of the fact that Moses at some point came to realize that she was actually his mother. Also, the fact that his adoptive mother allowed Moses to be nursed in a Hebrew home tells us that she had no desire to hide his Hebrew ethnicity from him. Moses also knew that Miriam and Aaron were his sister and brother, as the subsequent narrative indicates.

Second, Moses was an excitable, young idealist. He could have chosen to hide his Hebrew nationality and become more Egyptian than the Egyptians, and thus cynically sought to have made his fortune among the people of his adoptive mother. Instead, he observed how life was for the Egyptians and how much worse it was for the Hebrews, and he grew increasingly angry about the subjugation of the latter. He plainly had a strong sense of outrage at injustice, as shown both by his attack on the Egyptian taskmaster and by his standing up to fight for some Midianite shepherd girls who were being bullied. On the other hand, his ideals were not tempered with moderation. He could only strike out against the Egyptian taskmaster, and end up himself being a murderer, rather than wait to find a better way to remedy the situation. That is, as a typical young idealist, he was impatient to set things right.

Finally, Moses was physically strong. Neither the Egyptian taskmaster nor the bullying, Midianite shepherds seem to have been much of a match for him.

With this portrait of Moses in mind, we can perhaps better understand Stephen's claim that "Moses supposed that his brothers would realize that God would rescue them through him" (Acts 7:25). The Exodus version says nothing like this, but it is not unreasonable to think that Moses, the passionate, young idealist, thought that the Hebrews should unify under him against their oppressors. For his part, Stephen passes over the impetuous and violent behavior of Moses. Stephen's main point is that the sneering answer of the aggressor (lit. "wicked man" [רָשָׁע] in the Hebrew text; "the one behaving abusively" [ὁ δὲ ἀδικῶν] in the Greek text of Acts 7:27), when Moses tried to stop the fight, was characteristic of the stubborn Israelite resistance to divine leadership through the ages. In short, Stephen was not trying to give a full exposition of Exod. 2:11–13; he merely wanted his audience to understand that the spiteful bully of Exod. 2:13 typifies the attitude that would culminate in the Jewish rejection of Jesus.

Similarly, Heb. 11:27 superficially makes a flat contradiction of Exod. 2:14b–15a. The former says, "By faith he left Egypt, *not fearing the king's anger*"; the latter says, "Then Moses was afraid and thought, 'No doubt the facts are known.' And Pharaoh did hear about it, he began proceedings to kill Moses. But *Moses fled from Pharaoh. . . .*" (emphasis added in both citations). Hebrews is making the point that one misreads Exodus if one takes Moses's flight to be no more than the act of a murderous fugitive in fear for his life. Now, in fact, Moses was a fugitive and a murderer, but he was also, as indicated above, much more than that. He strongly identified with his people and believed that they should be set free. He was willing to reject the relatively easy life of a minor aristocrat[21] and chose to take his place as a Hebrew. In that sense, his decision was an act of faith.

We should finally note that this episode makes it easier to understand why Moses, when called by God at the burning bush, was so resistant to the idea of going back to Egypt. He may have sought to escape the call, we may speculate, not because he feared retribution for

21. There is no reason to suppose that Moses would have ever been more than a minor aristocrat. As the adopted son of a princess (and we have no grounds to think that she was more than a minor princess), and as one who was known to be Hebrew, he had no chance of becoming the pharaoh. The fact that Heb. 11:26 says that he chose Christ over the "treasures of Egypt" does not mean that he personally had access to all the wealth of Egypt. It merely sets the temptations of one world, the Egyptian aristocracy, against what is offered by the other world, the Hebrews and their God.

his crime but because Egypt held terrible memories. He had committed murder there, and no doubt, as he grew older and more reflective, he bitterly regretted it. He had built a life for himself in Midian, had tried to put his past behind him, and probably hoped to grow old and die in peace as a shepherd. The last place he would want to go was back to the scene of the worst moment of his life.

2:16–22. Midian was located in the north Hejaz region, east of the northern half of the Gulf of Aqaba. They were not a Bedouin people; Bedouin culture probably did not exist at this time. To the contrary, they were a sophisticated society which was probably organized as a confederation of city-states. They were Semitic, their language being an ancestor of Arabic. Midian became a significant regional power around the thirteenth century. Excavations show that they had cities with massive walls, irrigation systems, metallurgy and smelting, and a painted pottery analogous to what is seen in the faraway but contemporary Mycenaean pottery. Shepherding was an essential feature of their economy, and shepherds would seasonally lead sheep far afield in search of pasture.[22] Groups of Midianites did from time to time dwell as expatriates in other areas; a number of Midianites of high social standing were living among the Moabites when the Israelites arrived there (Num. 22:4, 7; 25:15). But the place to which Moses fled was Midian itself, their territorial homeland. He was not among a group of Midianite expatriates.

The account of the episode at the well is quite straightforward. While Moses was there, a flock and its shepherds, led by young women, approached the well. Another group of shepherds claimed that this was their well and began to bully the women, seeking to frighten them away, if not worse. Moses interposed himself in favor of the women and, in whatever confrontation followed, forced the bullies to back down or run away. Not content to do that alone, he also filled the watering trough for the women's sheep. He was then invited to the home of the women's father for a meal. One thing led to another, and he soon became a member of the family and took up the shepherding profession. The fact that he did this "willingly" (v. 21) indicates that he had put Egypt and his efforts to free the Hebrews behind him. As far as he was concerned, that life no longer existed.

Moses's wife had the Semitic name Zipporah ("bird"), a not surprising fact since the Midianites were Semitic. His father-in-law is first

---

22. George E. Mendenhall, "Midian," in Freedman, *ABD* Vol. 4, 815–18.

anonymous (v. 16), then called Reuel (v. 18), and then called Jethro (3:1). To make matters more confusing, Moses's father-in-law is called Hobab in Judg. 4:11, and Hobab is said to be Reuel's son in Num. 10:29. We therefore cannot simply say that Reuel, Jethro, and Hobab were all different names for one person. Source critics typically see the confusion of names to be evidence for different sources and traditions behind the text, but this is unnecessary and probably wrong. It appears that Reuel was Zipporah's grandfather;[23] as the living head of the extended family, he could be called "father" of Zipporah and "father-in-law" (חֹתֵן) of Moses. Probably Jethro was Zipporah's biological father; he was the one who had actually sired seven daughters (v. 16). In Exod. 2, Reuel, as the head of the household, speaks as the "father" and authority figure in the clan. Many years later, at the time of Moses's encounter with God and after Reuel's death, Jethro would have taken over as head of household, so that he is named in Exod. 3:1. Then who was Hobab? We do not know, but he may have been another son of Reuel, a younger brother of Jethro and an uncle of Zipporah.[24] The last time we see Jethro is in Exod. 18, and the first time we see Hobab is in Num. 10. Thus, we can suppose that Jethro died in the interval and that Hobab took over as head of the clan (since Jethro apparently had no sons, clan leadership would go to the next male in line). As head of the household, Hobab became Zipporah's protector and the "father-in-law" of Moses.[25]

The title for Zipporah's father, "the priest of Midian," might, but need not, imply that her family was the only priestly family in Midian, analogous to the Aaronic line in Israel. We do not know enough about Midianite religion to make such a claim. In fact, on the analogy of Exod. 2:5, where "the daughter of Pharaoh" is titular and certainly does not mean that she was his only daughter, it would be fair to say that he was probably one of many priests, although he may well have been of high rank. We are also told nothing about the religion in which Reuel and Jethro served, but Num. 25:17–18 condemns the Midianites as pagan followers of a fertility cult. Jethro, however, seems to have been sufficiently impressed by the account of what God had done for Israel to have become devoted to YHWH (Exod. 18:12).

---

23. This is a traditional interpretation of the rabbis, although they believed that Jethro and Hobab were the same person. See Sarna, *Exodus*, 8.

24. It is equally possible that Hobab was a grandson of Reuel, a nephew of Jethro and cousin of Zipporah.

25. For other opinions about the diverse names, see Houtman, *Exodus*, 1:81–2, and Cassuto, *Exodus,* 30. Cassuto's harmonization is not convincing and fails to take into account the additional problem posed by Hobab.

The account of Moses meeting his future wife at a well alludes to Gen. 24:11 (where Abraham's servant finds a wife for Isaac at a well) and Gen. 29:1–10 (where Jacob meets Rachel at a well). The latter parallel is especially close, since Jacob, like Moses, came to the well while fleeing for his life from his homeland. Also, Jacob first talked to some local shepherds and then assisted Rachel in a heroic manner by single-handedly removing a stone that covered the well, an act analogous to the heroism of Moses at the well. The allusion in Exodus to these episodes indicates that Moses is taking the place of Isaac and Jacob to be a new father to the nation.

We learn in this text of the birth of one son to Moses, Gershom. The origin of the name is unknown, but it was somewhat popular among the Levites; one of Levi's sons was called Gershom (see 1 Chron. 6:16; the spelling "Gershon," in Gen. 46:11 and Exod. 6:16, is a variant), and Phinehas the priest had a descendant named Gershom (Ezra 8:2). The explanation Moses gives for the name, "I have been a sojourner (גֵּר) in a foreign land," is wordplay and not a formal etymology. Moses had a second son, Eliezer, by Zipporah, but Eliezer is not mentioned by name until Exod. 18:4.

Theological Summary of Key Points

1. The use of this story in Acts 7 and Heb. 11, as discussed above, illustrates how the New Testament uses the Old. On the one hand, the New Testament is right to point out that Moses renounced the wealth of Egypt and identified himself with his people. On the other hand, the portrayal in Exodus itself is considerably less flattering. Both accounts are true, but the New Testament is using the Moses story to make specific points; it is not at any point seeking to give a full exposition of the Exodus account.

2. Moses is at the same time zealous and foolish. Positively, he identifies with his own (and God's) people rather than with the power and wealth of Egypt. Negatively, he behaves impulsively and commits a terrible and senseless crime. Even if he had not been discovered and if his people had joined him, violence of this kind was not going to be how Israel was delivered. By being exposed and forced to flee, Moses was saved from becoming the first terrorist. Salvation for Israel would be by the direct action of God.

3. At the same time, Moses's decisiveness and sense of justice could be channeled properly and turn out for good, as when he stood up for the young shepherd women who were being bullied. On this occasion, it seems, there were no fatalities! But a wrong was set right, and a group of bullies were put in their place. Moses, who had been rejected by both his own people Israel and his adopted people of Egypt, was received by a family of Midianites.

4. As the structure of the text is presented above, the content of 2:11–15 (where Moses intervenes to stop an Egyptian taskmaster) parallels that of 2:16–22 (where Moses intervenes to stop some shepherd bullies). In this, the text presents the masculine traits of courage and initiative wrongly and then rightly applied. One may compare to this the character of Christ, who was always bold in confronting evil but never reckless. He could turn over the tables of moneychangers in the temple, but he rejected the violence of Peter when the latter cut off a man's ear.

5. Moses would, in the providence of God, spend many years learning leadership by tending sheep. He would mature and spend time reflecting in the wilderness, acquiring a humility that was lacking when he was young. No one is a born leader; everyone must learn.

6. The wordplay Moses makes with his son's name, Gershom, reflects the bitterness of the life of the exile, removed from his family (v. 22). The impetuous action of his earlier life had painful repercussions, and the long pain of separation was only removed by an act of God.

Excursus: Israel and Moses as Prototypes of a New Creation

The first two chapters of Exodus contain several allusions to Genesis that together present Moses and Israel as the pattern for a new work of God in creating a new humanity. These allusions have already been mentioned in the commentary, but it is useful to draw them together to see how they give us insight into the theology of Exodus. This is an example of inner-biblical exegesis, whereby the message of one book (in this case, Exodus) is brought to light by discovering how it cites, reworks, or alludes to prior biblical books (in this case, Genesis). The background to the inner-biblical exegesis in Exod. 1–2 is the story of the fall of humanity into sin (Gen. 2–3), whereby God's original intent to create a people for himself was thwarted by human disobedience and subsequent moral and spiritual decadence. The other important background element is the promises to the patriarchs (Gen. 12:1–3, etc.) and the patriarchal history.

The first allusion to Genesis comes in Exod. 1:1–6, a passage that summarizes Gen. 46:8–27 and 50:26, thereby effectively giving an abbreviated recapitulation of the events of Gen. 46:8–50:26. The point here is that the story unfolding in Exodus is the legitimate sequel to the events of Genesis. In addition, Exod. 1:2–4 follows the tribal order of Gen. 35:23–26, thereby alluding to the promise of many offspring in Gen. 35:11 and linking Israel in Egypt to the patriarchal covenants and in particular to the expectation that the offspring of Abraham, Isaac, and Jacob would become a great nation. This further legitimates Israel, as their rapid population growth is seen to be a fulfillment of that promise.

The second allusion to Genesis is in Exod. 1:7, a text that repeats the language of Gen. 1:28, in which humanity is told to multiply and fill the earth. This indicates that Israel in Egypt is fulfilling the creation mandate, but more particularly it takes us back to the situation prior to the story of the fall in Eden. The implication is that God has not abandoned the project of making a people for himself. But he will not make a people by a new act of creation; he will instead raise up a people for himself out of the wreckage of the old humanity. Israel is that new people of God.

The third allusion is at Exod. 2:2, where it says of Moses's mother: "and she saw that he [Moses] was good" (וַתֵּרֶא אֹתוֹ כִּי־טוֹב הוּא). This recalls the divine evaluations of creation in Gen. 1, such as at Gen. 1:10, "and God saw that it was good" (וַיַּרְא אֱלֹהִים כִּי־טוֹב). This presents Moses as a token of the new creation of God, a kind of "firstfruits" of God's intent to remake humanity in a new creation.

The fourth allusion is seen in comparing Exod. 2:2–3 to 7:7. Reading just 2:2–3, we might suppose that Moses is the firstborn son of the Levite couple, but in 7:7 we discover that he is actually the younger son, his brother Aaron being three years older. This repeats the pattern found in Genesis and elsewhere of the younger son being chosen over the older (Abel over Cain, Isaac over Ishmael, Jacob over Esau, and later David over all his brothers). The implication here is that the pattern of election and redemption that began with the patriarchs, but which seemed to be dormant during the long Egyptian sojourn, is being resumed in the person of Moses.

The fifth allusion is in Exod. 2:3, where Moses's mother sets him in the Nile River. The choice of vocabulary is remarkable in that she puts him not in a "basket" (סַל), as we might expect, but a "box" (תֵּבָה), using the same word as is used for the ark of Noah. She also coats this papyrus box with "pitch" (see Gen. 6:14). Moses is therefore a new Noah, taking his people through the calamity of divine judgment (the Egyptian plagues and especially the crossing of the sea being analogous to the flood) and into a new future and new relationship with God.

The sixth allusion is seen in comparing Gen. 29:9–10 to Exod. 2:15–22. Moses is a new Jacob. Like the patriarch, he flees his homeland for his life, comes to a well, encounters female shepherds in some distress, resolves their problem, and waters their sheep. After that, he is taken to the home of the father of the shepherdess, and he subsequently takes the young woman as his wife. The parallels between Jacob and Moses are numerous and obvious. The significance is that Moses has the status of being a new father to Israel. He will lead them out of Egypt, just as Jacob had led them into Egypt.

In summary, Israel is at the center of God's restoration of humanity, and Moses is the man through whom this work takes place. Exodus asserts that within salvation history, Moses did more than bring about the release of Semitic slaves; through him the eschatological work of redemption began.

THE CALL (2:23–4:17)

Moses encounters YHWH at the burning bush. Moses is commissioned, against his own desires, to return to Egypt and lead the Israelites out of bondage. The encounter begins the transition of Moses's character from being a recluse, hiding in the desert hills from his past life, to becoming the great hero and prophet of Israel.

Translation

2:23a And it happened, during that long period of time,[26]
2:23b that the king of Egypt died.[27]
2:23c And the Israelites moaned because of their slavery
2:23d and they cried out,[28]
2:23e and their plea, [which arose][29] from slavery, went up to God.

26. Lit. "in those many days" (בַיָּמִים הָרַבִּים הָהֵם).

27. The *wayyiqtol* וַיָּמָת is the apodosis to the protasis וַיְהִי in clause 23a.

28. The verb זעק ("to cry out") often implies a call for help. Frequently, it occurs with either אֶל or לְ (both meaning "to") and with God as the addressee (e.g., Judg. 3:9; 10:10; 1 Sam. 12:10; Jer. 11:11; Mic. 3:4). But here, no addressee is indicated. We should not make too much of this, as though it proved that they were not calling on YHWH but were calling on someone else (see 1 Sam. 12:8). Still, the main point here is not that prayers were addressed to YHWH, but that the people were simply crying out. It is a statement about their misery, not a statement about their religious life.

29. Their plea (שַׁוְעָתָם) arose out of their condition of slavery (מִן־הָעֲבֹדָה), and thus the words "which arose" have been supplied. In keeping with clause 23d, the point of this clause is not that YHWH heard prayers that were specifically addressed to him, but that he heard and responded to their

2:24a And God heard their groaning,
2:24b and God remembered his covenant with Abraham, with Isaac, and with Jacob,
2:25a and God saw the Israelites,
2:25b and God knew.[30]
3:1a Now Moses[31] was shepherding the sheep of his father-in-law, Jethro, the priest of Midian,
3:1b and he led the sheep to the back side[32] of the wilderness,

---

general outcries. Notice also that the text here uses the more generic "God" rather than "YHWH," his covenant name. This has nothing to do with sources; it relates to the fact that Israel was crying out as an afflicted people, and that God, as judge of all the earth, heard their cry. The significance of the covenant for this story is introduced in 2:24b.

30. The dramatic close to this section, ending with the verb ידע ("know") but with no direct object, is unusual and should not be made smoother in translation. For the significance, see the commentary below.

31. In the structure of this narrative, all of 2:23–25 is essentially background information. It begins at 2:23a with the temporal protasis וַיְהִי בַיָּמִים הָרַבִּים הָהֵם and then gives, as the apodosis, a series of *wayyiqtol* clauses. These describe both the circumstances for Israel in Egypt at that time and how God looked upon those conditions. Exod. 3:1a, beginning with the pattern וְ + noun + היה + participle (וּמֹשֶׁה הָיָה רֹעֶה), introduces a second piece of background information, describing Moses's circumstances at the beginning of the narrative. This account of Moses's situation is continued in two *wayyiqtol* clauses at 3:1bc. The action of the narrative, the story that brings Moses and Israel together, begins at 3:2.

32. The primary meaning of אַחַר is "after" or "behind." Because of the Israelite orientation toward the east, some argue that אַחַר should be translated as "west" in this verse (see RSV, ESV, NASB). However, when Hebrew means to indicate the western direction unambiguously, it typically orients itself to the Mediterranean Sea (from the perspective of Canaan), using an expression such as "to the sea" (יָמָּה). An example is Josh. 5:1, "the Amorites who were beyond the Jordan toward the sea" (that is, "toward the west"; הָאֱמֹרִי אֲשֶׁר בְּעֵבֶר הַיַּרְדֵּן יָמָּה). This formulation is used even when the Israelites were actually in a position south of the Mediterranean, in Egypt, as in Exod. 10:19, where a west wind is called a רוּחַ־יָם ("sea wind"). In the Pentateuch, it is difficult to find a single example of a clear designation for "west" that does not include the word יָם ("sea"), regardless of where the people are located at the time. See, for example, Gen. 12:8; 28:14; Exod. 10:19; 27:12; 38:12; Num. 2:18; 3:23; 35:5. An alternative term for "west" (used four times in the Hebrew Bible) is מְבוֹא הַשֶּׁמֶשׁ (lit. "sunset"). Joshua 1:4 thus describes the western direction with two expressions, וְעַד־הַיָּם הַגָּדוֹל מְבוֹא הַשָּׁמֶשׁ, "and to the Mediterranean Sea, (to) sunset." Deut. 11:30 has a difficult phrase, אַחֲרֵי דֶּרֶךְ מְבוֹא הַשֶּׁמֶשׁ, which the ESV

3:1c and he came to the mountain of God, to Horeb.

3:2a And the angel of YHWH[33] appeared to him in a fire blazing[34] out of the midst of the sineh.[35]

3:2b And he looked [at it],

---

mistranslates as, "west of the road, toward the going down of the sun." The phrase is a single construct chain, and it is more accurately translated, "behind the Sunset Road," with "Sunset Road" being a proper noun (דֶּרֶךְ מְבוֹא הַשֶּׁמֶשׁ). If the "Sunset Road" actually went from east to west, as the name implies, then "behind the Sunset Road" would actually be toward the north (since the Israelites were in the southern Transjordan). The words מְבוֹא הַשֶּׁמֶשׁ cannot be translated as "towards the going down of the sun" and be separated from אַחֲרֵי דֶּרֶךְ. In fact, setting aside Exod. 3:1, there are 235 occurrences of אַחַר or אַחֲרֵי in the Pentateuch; it does not mean "west" in a single instance. In short, it is incorrect to translate אַחַר הַמִּדְבָּר in Exod. 3:1 as "west of the wilderness." It means, "the back side of the wilderness," as reflected in the KJV, NIV, TNIV and NRSV.

33. Stuart 2006, 110–11, says that the construct מַלְאַךְ יְהוָה is appositional, "the Angel YHWH." But this is not correct; such a use of the construct would be unusual. An appositional construct is most common where there are three nouns: the first construct is in apposition to a phrase made up of the second construct and the absolute. For example, בְּתוּלַת בַּת־צִיּוֹן ("the virgin, the daughter of Zion"; Isa. 37:22), and אֵשֶׁת בַּעֲלַת־אוֹב ("a woman, a possessor of a divining spirit"; 1 Sam. 28:7). See GKC §130e. When just two nouns are in apposition, typically both are absolute, as in נַעֲרָה בְתוּלָה ("a young girl, a virgin"; 1 Kings 1:2) and אִישׁ כֹּהֵן ("a man, a priest"; Lev. 21:9). See *IBHS* §12.3.

34. The word לַבָּה is a *hapax legomenon*, perhaps a byform of לֶהָבָה ("flame") or possibly from a root לבב ("to burn"); see לַבָּה, *HALOT*, 2.516. The construct chain בְּלַבַּת־אֵשׁ is probably descriptive, in a "blazing fire" as opposed to a smoldering fire.

35. The meaning of סְנֶה is uncertain, although it is assumed to be a kind of bush. It may have cognates in Akkadian, Syriac, and Arabic, and there is a post-biblical term סַנְיָא, "thorn" (K. Lawson Younger, Jr., "סְנֶה," *NIDOTTE*, 3.273). Some compare the name to the plant *genus senna*, a word of Arabic origins (סְנֶה, *HALOT*, 2.760). The word סְנֶה is most likely a particular plant, the "sineh," but we know no more about it than that. The word has this meaning only in this passage (Exod. 3:2–4) in the Old Testament. Elsewhere, in Deut. 33:16 and 1 Sam. 14:4, it refers to Sinai (see also Ps. 68:9[8]). It may be that the plant name was the basis for renaming "Mt. Horeb" as "Mt. Sinai."

3:2c and it was clear that[36] the sineh was burning in the fire,
3:2d but the sineh was not being consumed.
3:3a And Moses said,
3:3b "Well, I am going to turn aside[37]
3:3c so that I can have a look[38] at this great sight,
3:3d [to see] why the sineh is not burned."[39]
3:4a And YHWH saw
3:4b that he turned aside to have a look,
3:4c and God called to him out of the sineh.
3:4d He said,[40]
3:4e "Moses, Moses!"
3:4f And [Moses] said,
3:4g "Here I am."
3:5a And he said,
3:5b "Do not approach this area!
3:5c Take your sandals off your feet,
3:5d for the place on which you are standing is holy ground."
3:6a And he said,
3:6b "I am the God of your father—the God of Abraham, the God of Isaac, and the God of Jacob."
3:6c And Moses hid his face,
3:6d for he was afraid to look at God.
3:7a And YHWH[41] said,
3:7b "I most certainly have seen the affliction of my people who are in Egypt,
3:7c and I have heard their pleading before[42] their taskmasters,

---

36. וְהִנֵּה here draws the reader into the perspective Moses had, indicating that, as he looked at the spectacle, the nature of the event was obvious but astonishing.
37. The cohortative אָסֻרָה־נָּא here connotes determination or deliberate intention; it should not (in this case) be translated as "let me" which in English tends to connote a request for permission.
38. The *weyiqtol* וְאֶרְאֶה states the purpose for Moses's "turning aside."
39. Clause 3:3d is an indirect question; it tells the reader Moses's motivation for going to have a look at the sineh.
40. וַיֹּאמֶר here is epexegetical of וַיִּקְרָא in the previous clause.
41. With the verb וַיֹּאמֶר, the subject often is not explicitly named if the speaker's identity is obvious from context or the content of the speech (as in vv. 4–5). The fact that YHWH is explicitly named as the subject here suggests that this should be regarded as a paragraph break.
42. The phrase מִפְּנֵי נֹגְשָׂיו is often translated, "because of their taskmasters" (NIV, ESV). This is not wrong, but the idea of physical proximity implied

3:7d for I know their sufferings.
3:8 And I have come down to deliver them from the power of the Egyptians and to bring them up out of that land to a good and broad land, to a land flowing with milk and honey, to the place of the Canaanites, the Hittites, the Amorites, the Perizzites, the Hivites, and the Jebusites.
3:9a And now, understand that[43] the pleading of the Israelites has reached me,
3:9b and also that I have seen the oppression—
3:9c that[44] the Egyptians are oppressing them.
3:10a And now, come on, I will send[45] you to Pharaoh
3:10b that you may bring my people, the Israelites, out of Egypt."
3:11a And Moses said to God,
3:11b "Who am I,
3:11c that I should go to Pharaoh,
3:11d and that I should bring the Israelites out of Egypt?"[46]

---

by מִפְּנֵי should not be obscured in translation. In Isa. 7:2, trees shake "before the wind" (מִפְּנֵי־רוּחַ) and not simply because of it. In Mic. 1:4, wax melts "in proximity to the fire" (מִפְּנֵי הָאֵשׁ). Again, there is a causal idea, but it is not a logical abstraction but something brought by the immediate presence of the fire. Thus, the Hebrews' pleading is "before" their taskmasters. Whether they are calling out to God or to the taskmasters is not specified. The point is that the taskmasters hear their outcries and are unmoved. God, however, is moved.

43. "And now, understand that" translates וְעַתָּה הִנֵּה. The הִנֵּה calls on Moses to draw the right conclusions from what YHWH has said to him.

44. The use of אֲשֶׁר here is analogous to כִּי and introduces an explanatory rather than a relative clause.

45. The words וְעַתָּה לְכָה וְאֶשְׁלָחֲךָ are literally, "And now, go! And I will send you." But in this case, לְכָה is virtually an interjection, like the English "come on." A similar text is Gen. 37:20, וְעַתָּה לְכוּ וְנַהַרְגֵהוּ ("And now, come on, let's kill him"). Clearly they are not meant to "go" anywhere. In every text that has this pattern (וְעַתָּה + an imperative of לְכוּ + a *weyiqtol* verb), the imperative of הלך is not a literal command to "go" somewhere (see also 2 Kings 7:4, 9; Neh. 6:7). If they are literally supposed to go somewhere, the exhortation to go is in the *weyiqtol* verb, as in 2 Kings 7:9. The primary point of לְכָה here is thus not a directive for Moses to go to Egypt. Rather, YHWH is treating Moses as a partner, encouraging him to join him in the task of saving the Israelites.

46. Moses asks a rhetorical question ("Who am I?") which is explained by two subordinate clauses. The two clauses are often translated in a way that almost merges them ("that I should go to Pharaoh and bring"). But the text presents these as two distinct clauses, using first כִּי and then

3:12a And [God] said,
3:12b "But I will be with you,
3:12c and this will be your sign,
3:12d that I have sent you:
3:12e when you have brought the people out of Egypt, you shall serve God on this mountain."[47]
3:13a Then Moses said to God,
3:13b "Well now, here I am, going[48] to the Israelites,
3:13c and I say to them,
3:13d 'The God of your fathers has sent me to you!'
3:13e And they say to me,
3:13f 'What is his name?'
3:13g What do I say to them?"
3:14a And God said to Moses,

וְכִי. This implies that there are two tasks for which Moses feels inadequate: standing before the pharaoh and leading the nation of Israel.

47. Some scholars treat clause 12e as an independent sentence: "When you have brought the people out of Egypt, you shall serve God on this mountain." They assert that coming to the mountain is not the "sign" indicated in the first part of v. 12 (Sarna 1991, 17). But this leaves God simply saying, "this is the sign" with no indication of what the sign is. In addition, this verse has a clear analogy in 1 Sam. 2:34, where the sign that disaster is going to befall the house of Eli is the disaster itself: "And this will be your sign, which will come to your two sons, to Hophni and Phinehas: on the same day both of them will die." That is, the major, initial fulfillment of the prophecy is itself the sign that verifies the prophecy. The Hebrew of 1 Sam. 2:34, which opens with וְזֶה־לְּךָ הָאוֹת ("And this is the sign to you"), and in which the sign is indicated by a temporal בְּ followed by a *yiqtol* verb (בְּיוֹם אֶחָד יָמוּתוּ שְׁנֵיהֶם), is quite similar to Exod. 3:12. I therefore take clause 3:12e to be the sign. The significance of this is explored in the commentary.

48. All of clauses 13b-e are an extended protasis; the apodosis is 13f. The beginning of the protasis, בָּא הִנֵּה אָנֹכִי (lit. "Look, here I am, going") paints a picture of Moses making his way to the Israelites. The action of the protasis is sustained with the two *weqatal* clauses וְאָמַרְתִּי and וְאָמְרוּ and with the nested, reported speech of 13d and 13f. Clause 13b could be rendered, "Behold, if I go." Such a rendition brings out the pragmatics of the text—that this is a conditional structure—but it loses the vivid language of the original.

3:14b "This is who I am:[49] 'I AM!'"[50]
3:14c And he said,
3:14d "Say this to the Israelites,
3:14e 'I AM has sent me to you.'"
3:15a God also said to Moses,
3:15b "Say this to the Israelites,
3:15c 'YHWH, the God of your fathers, the God of Abraham, the God of Isaac, and the God of Jacob, has sent me to you.'
3:15d This is my name forever,
3:15e and this is my abiding identity[51] throughout all generations.

---

49. The traditional translation, "I am who I am," is not incorrect but it sounds as though God were deliberately being enigmatic, or worse, saying with a shrug of the shoulders: "Well, I am who I am, so take it or leave it!" That is obviously not the point. Scholars often define אֶהְיֶה אֲשֶׁר אֶהְיֶה as an *idem per idem* sentence, in which the second clause substantially repeats the first, as in 2 Sam. 15:20, "I am going where I am going." See the discussion at Cornelis G. den Hertog, "The Prophetic Dimension of the Divine Name: On Exodus 3:14a and its Context," *CBQ* 64, no. 2 (2002): 223–4. In my opinion, however, such proposed analogies to Exod. 3:14 are superficial and do little to illuminate אֶהְיֶה אֲשֶׁר אֶהְיֶה, which is almost by definition a unique statement. In my view, the first אֶהְיֶה functions as a normal predicator. אֲשֶׁר points to the second אֶהְיֶה as the predicate of the clause. It means, "I am 'I AM.'" But this is obviously too jarring a translation; in fact, the אֲשֶׁר had to be inserted because אֶהְיֶה אֶהְיֶה would be as odd and ungrammatical in Hebrew as "I am I am" is in English. Thus, "This is who I am: 'I AM'" best communicates the meaning.
50. For a discussion of the divine name, see the commentary below. The *yiqtol* אֶהְיֶה could be rendered a number of ways, including "I will be," "I should be," or even, "Let me be" (being a III-ה verb, it would not take a paragogic ה for the cohortative). The traditional translation from the LXX, *ἐγώ εἰμι ὁ ὤν*, is "I AM" (see also John 8:58). A potential or subjunctive meaning such as "I will be" is by nature inappropriate for God. For the meaning "I AM," one might expect the *qatal* form הָיִיתִי. But the *yiqtol* אֶהְיֶה is chosen no doubt because it sounded more like the original pronunciation of YHWH, not because of the various grammatical nuances of the *yiqtol* over against the *qatal*. Thus, notwithstanding the use of the *yiqtol*, the traditional translation "I AM" is to be preferred.
51. It is difficult to know how to translate זִכְרִי, which, on the basis of the root זכר, seems to mean something like, "my remembrance." *HALOT* (1.271), זֵכֶר, suggests that it refers to a name by which a god is invoked. But the meaning "remembrance" or "memory" is implied in usage such as Ps 9:7(6), where, in reference to fallen cities, it says, אָבַד זִכְרָם ("the memory of them has perished"). Hence, "memory" and not "invocation" seems to be the idea

3:16a Go
3:16b and gather the elders of Israel
3:16c and say to them,
3:16d ‘YHWH, the God of your fathers, the God of Abraham, of Isaac, and of Jacob, has appeared to me, saying,
3:16e “I have taken note of you and what has been done to you in Egypt,
3:17a and I said,
3:17b ‘I will bring you up out of the affliction of Egypt to the land of the Canaanites, the Hittites, the Amorites, the Perizzites, the Hivites, and the Jebusites, a land flowing with milk and honey.’”’
3:18a And [the elders] will listen to your voice,
3:18b and you and the elders of Israel will go to the king of Egypt,
3:18c and you will say to him,
3:18d ‘YHWH, the God of the Hebrews, has met with us;
3:18e and now, let us go a three days’ journey into the wilderness,
3:18f that we may sacrifice to YHWH our God.’
3:19a But I know
3:19b that the king of Egypt will not let you go unless forced by a strong hand.[52]

---

behind זֵכֶר. But referring to the name YHWH as “my remembrance” is meaningless to modern readers. In the ancient world, and certainly in Egypt, the memory of a name was closely connected to the existence of the being who had that name. Thus, for example, inscriptions with the name Akhenaten were defaced by later pharaohs, not simply to wipe out the memory of him in the modern sense, but so that his eternal soul, conveyed by the Egyptian concepts of *ka* and *ba*, would cease to be. That is, one’s identity and one’s being were closely bound to the memory of one’s name. By analogy, Hos. 2:19(17) says of the Baals, “They will no longer be remembered by their names” (וְלֹא־יִזָּכְרוּ עוֹד בִּשְׁמָם). The idea is that if nobody remembers the names of the Baals, then they have no identity and no longer exist. What, then, does God mean by describing the name he gives himself in this verse as his זֵכֶר through all generations? It is that he has forever bound his being and identity to the name “YHWH, the God of the fathers.” See the commentary for further discussion.

52. The expression וְלֹא בְּיָד חֲזָקָה (“and not by a strong hand”) is here a famous problem since in fact YHWH did bring Israel out of Egypt “by a strong hand” (Exod. 6:1; 13:9; 32:11), but this text seems to deny that. Peter Addinall, “Exodus III 19B and the Interpretation of Biblical Narrative,” *VT* 49, no. 3 (1999): 289–300, reviews the history of the interpretation of the problem and concludes that it should be translated to mean that

3:20a So I will stretch out my hand
3:20b and I will strike Egypt with all the wonders that I will do in it.
3:20c And after that he will send you off.
3:21a And I will make the Egyptians well-disposed to this people;[53]
3:21b and it shall be
3:21c that when you go,
3:21d you shall not go empty-handed.[54]
3:22a But each woman shall ask of her neighbor, and of any woman who lives in her house, for silver and gold jewelry, and for clothing,
3:22b and you shall put them on your sons and on your daughters.
3:22c And you will plunder the Egyptians."
4:1a And Moses answered.
4:1b He said,[55]
4:1c "Now look,[56] they will not believe me
4:1d and they will not listen to my voice,
4:1e for they will say,
4:1f 'YHWH did not appear to you.'"
4:2a And YHWH said to him,
4:2b "What is that in your hand?"
4:2c And he said,
4:2d "A staff."
4:3a And he said,
4:3b "Throw it on the ground."
4:3c And he threw it on the ground,

Pharaoh will not release Israel even if a strong hand tries to force him to do so. He argues that this is the storyteller's rhetoric, preparing the reader for the fact that, in spite of Pharaoh's intent, YHWH would force him to relent "by a strong hand." However, the idiom וְלֹא בְּ + noun can mean "without X," in which the noun X has an instrumental function. An example is in Job 4:21: "they shall die without wisdom." That is, for the lack of wisdom, they shall die. Thus, the idiom here means, "without the use of a strong hand." In other words, he will not act unless forced to do so.

53. Lit. "And I will set the favor of this people in the eyes of the Egyptians."

54. Clause 21b (וְהָיָה) is a protasis, clause 21c (כִּי תֵלֵכוּן) qualifies the protasis with a temporal construction, and clause 21d (לֹא תֵלְכוּ רֵיקָם) is the apodosis.

55. וַיֹּאמֶר is epexegetical of וַיַּעַן.

56. The word וְהֵן could be translated as a conditional ("And if") or it could be translated more forcefully, as is done here: "Now look." Either way, this is a fairly argumentative response. A close parallel is Lev. 25:20, where alarmed Israelites ask what they are supposed to eat during the Sabbath year, and they make the argument: הֵן לֹא נִזְרָע ("Look, we can't sow seed").

4:3d and it became a serpent,
4:3e and Moses fled from it.
4:4a And YHWH said to Moses,
4:4b "Put out your hand and catch it by the tail."
4:4c And he put out his hand
4:4d and he caught it,
4:4e and it became a staff in his hand.
4:5a "[This is] so that they may believe
4:5b that YHWH, the God of their fathers, the God of Abraham, the God of Isaac, and the God of Jacob, has appeared to you."
4:6a And YHWH also said to him,
4:6b "Put your hand in the breast of your tunic."
4:6c And he put his hand in the breast of his tunic,
4:6d and he took it out,
4:6e and there, [before his very eyes,] was[57] his hand, afflicted with skin disease[58] [and white][59] as snow!
4:7a And he said,
4:7b "Return your hand back to the breast of your tunic."
4:7c And he returned his hand in the breast of his tunic,
4:7d and he took it out from the breast of his tunic,
4:7e and it was plainly restored, like his [normal] flesh.
4:8a "And it shall be,
4:8b if they will not believe you,
4:8c and if they will not pay attention to the message[60] of the first sign,
4:8d that they will believe the message of the latter sign.[61]
4:9a And it shall be,

---

57. "And there, [before his very eyes,] was" translates וְהִנֵּה (traditionally, "and behold"). The expression vividly describes what Moses saw, as if from his perspective.
58. The root צרע is often translated as "leprous," but the symptom described, whiteness of color, does not correspond to what we call leprosy (Hansen's disease). It seems clear the affliction called in the Bible צָרַעַת did not include true leprosy. It is likely that צָרַעַת is a generic term for a variety of skin conditions, or it may have been a specific skin condition associated with ritual uncleanness. See David P. Wright and Richard N. Jones, "Leprosy," in Freedman, *ABD* Vol. 4, 277–82.
59. The comparison to snow obviously implies that a whitish color is the point. See Lev. 13:4.
60. Lit. "voice." Cf. the use of קוֹל in Neh. 8:15 and 2 Chr. 30:5. But these and similar uses of קוֹל are very late. It may be that here in Exod. 3 the miracles are personified as having a "voice" that people should listen to.
61. In this verse, the protasis וְהָיָה and its apodosis וְהֶאֱמִינוּ are embedded as the

4:9b if they will not believe even these two signs
4:9c and they will not listen to your voice,
4:9d that you shall take some of the Nile water
4:9e and pour it on the dry ground—
4:9f and it will be the water that you take from the Nile—
4:9g and it will become blood on the dry ground."[62]
4:10a And Moses said to YHWH,
4:10b "Oh please, Lord,[63] I am not a man of words and never have been,[64] and indeed [I have] not [become one] in the time that you have been speaking to your servant,[65]
4:10c for I am of heavy mouth and heavy tongue."[66]
4:11a And YHWH said to him,
4:11b "Who has made man's mouth?
4:11c Who makes him mute, or deaf, or seeing,[67] or blind?
4:11d Is it not I, YHWH?
4:12a And now go!
4:12b And I will be with your mouth,
4:12c and I will teach what you should speak."
4:13a And he said,

---

apodosis to another, double protasis, אִם־לֹא יַאֲמִינוּ and וְלֹא יִשְׁמְעוּ. So also in v. 9.

62. 4:9f and 4:9g are plainly two separate clauses, although they are usually merged in English translation. But clause 9f should be treated separately; it is an aside, making the point that the water must be from the Nile and not from another source, such as from a well dug into the water table of the Egyptian Delta.

63. The expression בִּי אֲדֹנִי (or, when addressing God, בִּי אֲדֹנָי) is an interjection and vocative used in making an appeal to an authority. See Gen. 44:18; Num. 12:11; Judg. 6:13; 1 Kings 3:26.

64. "And never have been" is literally "even yesterday, even the day before" (גַּם מִתְּמוֹל גַּם מִשִּׁלְשֹׁם). This idiom is used frequently in Exodus.

65. Lit. "even from the time that you have been speaking to your servant" (גַּם מֵאָז דַּבֶּרְךָ אֶל־עַבְדֶּךָ). The point is that even his encounter with God did not suddenly change the fact that Moses speaks poorly.

66. "Heavy mouth and heavy tongue" literally translates כְבַד־פֶּה וּכְבַד לָשׁוֹן. The meaning of the term is discussed in the commentary section.

67. It is possible that there is a textual corruption at this point, since "seeing" does not fit in well with mute, deaf, or blind. Samuel T. Lachs, "Exodus IV 11 : Evidence for an Emendation," *VT* 26, no. 2 (1976): 249–50, argues that the text should read פִּסֵּחַ ("lame") instead of פִּקֵּחַ ("seeing").

4:13b "Oh please, Lord, commission[68] whomever you want to commission—[but not me[69]]!"
4:14a And YHWH got angry at Moses,
4:14b and he said,
4:14c "Your brother Aaron is the Levite, isn't he?[70]
4:14d I know that he, at least,[71] can speak.
4:14e Also, he is actually[72] on his way out here[73] to meet you,
4:14f and he will see you
4:14g and will be glad in his heart.
4:15a And you will speak to him
4:15b and you will put the words in his mouth,
4:15c and I will be with your mouth and with his mouth,
4:15d and I will teach you what you should do.
4:16a And he will speak for you to the people.
4:16b And it will be[74]
4:16c that he will be your mouth,
4:16d and you will be his god.

---

68. To send (שׁלח) by the hand (בְּיַד) of someone is to commission that person with a task. See Lev. 16:21; 1 Sam. 16:20; 2 Sam. 11:14.
69. "But not me" is plainly implied but not stated.
70. Both word order and Masoretic accents (הֲלֹא אַהֲרֹן אָחִיךָ הַלֵּוִי) indicate that "your brother Aaron" is the subject and "the Levite" is the predicate. It cannot mean, "Isn't Aaron the Levite your brother?" since that would require הַלֵּוִי to be immediately after אַהֲרֹן. Nor, contrary to how it is usually translated, can this be an existential statement ("Is there not your brother Aaron, the Levite?"), as though God were saying, "Don't you have a Levite brother named Aaron?" This is appealing, but it cannot be right. If that were the meaning, it should be preceded by הַאֵין, not הֲלֹא. In the Hebrew Bible, there are twelve occurrences of הֲלֹא followed by a proper noun. In no case does it mean, "Is there not X?" The question is a simple verbless clause with an explicit subject and predicate. Two similar examples with similar accentuation are in Ruth 3:2 (הֲלֹא בֹעַז מֹדַעְתָּנוּ ["Isn't Boaz our relative?"]) and 1 Chr. 22:18. The significance of this question is explored in the commentary below.
71. "At least," a statement of exasperation, brings out the force of the infinitive absolute in דַּבֵּר יְדַבֵּר here.
72. The expression וְגַם הִנֵּה introduces additional information which will surprise the addressee. It is used here and in Gen. 38:24; 42:28.
73. "On his way out here" represents the action of the participial periphrastic phrase הוּא יֹצֵא, "he is going out."
74. This וְהָיָה clause is a discourse marker, indicating the concluding sentence of the dialogue. Verse 17 reads as a kind of afterthought, as though it said, "And don't forget your staff."

4:17 And take in your hand this staff, by which you shall do the signs."

Structure

This is a lengthy passage and its structure is somewhat complex.

I. Prologue to the Call of Moses (2:23–3:6)
  A. On Earth and in Heaven (2:23–3:1)
    1. The Situation in Egypt (2:23a–d)
    2. The Situation in Heaven (2:23e–25)
    3. The Situation of Moses (3:1)[75]
  B. Between Earth and Heaven at the Burning Bush (3:2–6)
II. The First Commission (3:7–10)
  A. Background: YHWH's Compassion and Purpose (3:7–9)
  B. Commission: An Invitation to Moses (3:10)
III. Moses's First Dialogue with YHWH (3:11–3:15)
  A. First Issue: Moses's Inadequacy (3:11–12)
  B. Second Issue: Israelite Confusion over God's Name (3:13–15)
IV. The Second Commission (3:16–22)
  A. A Mission to the Israelites (3:16–18a)
  B. A Mission to Pharaoh (3:18b–19)
  C. A Happy Outcome Predicted (3:20–22)
V. Moses's Second Dialogue with YHWH (4:1–12)
  A. First Issue: Israelite Unbelief (4:1–9)
  B. Second Issue: Moses's Limitations as a Speaker (4:10–12)
VI. The Third Commission (4:13–17)
  A. Moses's Plea to be Excused (4:13)
  B. YHWH's Anger and Final Command (4:14–17)
    1. Aaron's Role (4:14–16)
    2. The Staff (4:17)

After the prologue (2:23–3:6), the text is almost all reported speech. In part, Moses is raising questions and being answered in dialogue with YHWH, and in part, YHWH makes longer speeches that give Moses his commission to go deliver the Israelites. The reported speeches have an A-B-A-B-A pattern, with two dialogues (3:11–4:13; 4:1–12) set amid three statements of commission (3:7–10; 3:16–22; 4:13–17). There is a progression in the commissions. The first essentially repeats 2:23–25, giving Moses a heavenly perspective on the events transpiring on earth. This is the loftiest call from a spiritual or moral point of view.

75. See the translation notes to 3:1a.

God allows Moses to see the world as he sees it and asks Moses to join him in his work. The second is a lengthy prophecy, meant to encourage Moses by telling him exactly what would happen. From the standpoint of spiritual excellence, it is a step down. Moses seems unwilling to go unless absolutely assured of success. The third is set on the lowest level; it is an angry command. It makes a concession to Moses's excuses but will allow for no further discussion. Moses is simply told to get moving. We should also observe that there is something of a chiastic structure to Moses's four points in his dialogue with YHWH. His first and final objections (3:11; 4:13) both relate to his own sense of inadequacy, whereas his second and third (3:13; 4:1) relate to his suspicion that the Israelites will reject his message.

Commentary

2:23–25. This passage can be described as proto-apocalyptic. It does not use the fantastic imagery of Daniel or Revelation, but it does have the essential element of apocalyptic: it describes an earthly reality in which evil seems triumphant, and then it gives the heavenly perspective, describing God's observation of the events and his intention to intervene. Verse 23 describes the triumph of evil on earth: time has moved on, one pharaoh died and another has arisen, and yet the Israelites have remained enslaved. They cried out (2:23c–d), but they are not specifically said to have prayed. This does not mean that they did not pray, but it is significant that the text lacks any language that might suggest communion with God. It tells us that from the earthly perspective, the people were crying out into empty space; God seems to be absent. Clause 23e is transitional: their outcry makes its way upward, into the heavens. Verses 24–25 then describe the heavenly perspective. God is not absent; he hears their pleas, remembers his obligations to them, and sees their plight.

The ending to this section at v. 25b, "and God knew," is deliberately terse and without an object. It does not primarily mean that God "understood" in the sense of empathizing with their suffering. Rather, at the head of the apocalyptic tradition, it stands as a denial of the opposite possibility, that God neither knew nor cared. This assertion most dramatically sets the earthly appearance—that evil has triumphed and that God is nowhere to be found—against the heavenly reality that God does see, know, and care. The heavenly truth calls both the sufferer and the reader to faith.

Observers have noted that in 2:23e–25 the deity is called "God" (אֱלֹהִים, *elohim*) and not "YHWH" (יהוה). Source critics, of course, take this to be evidence that this is an E (or P) text, but this is neither useful nor valid. The choice of "God" here is deliberate, making the point that he acts first of all in his capacity of the God of all humanity and as the "judge of all the earth" (Gen. 18:25). He is also the covenant God of Israel (as mentioned in clause 24b), but this is only one of two reasons that God must act. The first stated reason is that he cares about the suffering of the oppressed; the second reason is that he has obligated himself to the Israelites' ancestors. Use of the divine name YHWH here would have skewed the perspective, viewing their suffering strictly from the standpoint of his being YHWH, the covenant deity of Israel. Instead, both the oppression and the covenant are viewed from the perspective that he is God, maker of heaven and earth, and the one with whom we have to do, from whose sight no creature is hidden (Heb. 4:13). Also, the use of the more lofty and abstract "*elohim*" instead of the personal name "YHWH," more starkly sets forth the distinction between the heavenly and earthly perspectives. Almost by definition, *elohim* conveys more of the transcendence of God, while YHWH conveys more of his immanence. And the point of the text is that it is precisely the heavenly, transcendent deity, whom all peoples fear as the final judge of all things, who was aware of the earthly suffering.

3:1. See the Introduction for a discussion of the location of Sinai. This verse is obviously circumstantial in the narrative: Moses is in the wilderness near Sinai when the burning bush is manifested. In context with 2:23–25, however, it sets up Moses as the third character, the other two being God and Israel. Israel is in Egypt and Moses is at Sinai, but God will bring them back together.

3:2–6. The second half of the prologue takes us to the burning bush, a place that is high on a mountain and alive with the fire of God. It is, therefore, a place where heaven and earth meet. The burning bush is the first apocalyptic image. As fire, it is a token of the purity and ferocity of God. As a bush that burns but is not consumed, it is part of the natural world, and yet unnatural and even bizarre. This is analogous to the imagery of Revelation, where ordinary things are juxtaposed in extraordinary ways. Jesus is portrayed as a man, but his eyes are blazing fire and he has a sword coming from his mouth (Rev. 1:14–16). Later, he is a slain lamb that stands and lives (Rev. 5:6).

God's demand that Moses take off his sandals (v. 5) reflects the fact that Moses, as a shepherd, spent his days following the flock, and that he would have had the shoes to prove it. Obviously filth should not be tracked into the presence of God. It may be that Midianite custom dictated that one remove one's shoes before entering another's residence; the common custom of washing the feet before entering a house is also instructive. If their sandaled feet were dirty enough to need washing, their sandal bottoms could be extraordinarily foul. When Moses realized before whom he stood, he also hid his face so as not to look directly at God's glory. The act of seeing God is understood to be fatal to the observer (Deut. 5:24; Judg. 6:22; 13:22).

The divine being, who speaks from the bush and is called "the angel of YHWH" (מַלְאַךְ יְהוָה) in 3:2, is called "YHWH" and "God" in 3:4. This does not indicate a plurality of sources; such ambiguity about a theophany is not unusual in the Old Testament. In Gen. 16:7–13, Hagar has an encounter with the "angel of YHWH," but she calls "YHWH who spoke with her" by the name אֵל רֳאִי, (perhaps, "God who sees"). In Gen. 22:11–12, "the angel of YHWH" calls out to Abraham, saying, "now I know that you fear God, since you have not withheld your only son from me" (in context, "me" is plainly God and not a mere angel). In Judg. 13:21–22, Manoah, father of Samson, realizes he has been speaking to the "angel of YHWH" and cries out, "We have seen God!"

On the other hand, the angel of YHWH can be described as subordinate to YHWH, as in Zech. 1:12, where the angel of YHWH prays to YHWH of Hosts (יְהוָה צְבָאוֹת). The angel of YHWH appears to be a local manifestation of YHWH rather than an independent being. In other words, the angel of YHWH usually is not what we mean when we speak of an angel, a supernatural being that is distinct from and less than God, as in Heb. 1. But the angel of YHWH is in some sense local and subordinate to YHWH of the high heavens, יְהוָה צְבָאוֹת. For the significance of this, see the theological discussion below.[76]

76. A radical reinterpretation of the data is Thomas L. Thompson, "How Yahweh Became God: Exodus 3 and 6 and the Heart of the Pentateuch," *JSOT* 68 (1995): 57–74, who believes that all of the relevant biblical texts are from the Persian and Hellenistic periods (450 to 150 B.C.), a time when (he argues) there was a movement among Persians and then Greeks to assimilate all local deities into a single, monotheistic "God." He thinks that a similar assimilation took place in "Palestine" (he believes that "Israel" is a literary invention and not a real, historical nation), where he says an emergent monotheism assimilated and embraced the gods of an earlier polytheism. Thus, YHWH was simply the "Israelite" version of "God" or even the local messenger of "God" to Palestine. This monotheism was inclusive rather than hostile to polytheism. Historically, this reconstruction is problematic, as it is not at all clear that *Ahura-Mazda* (of Persia) should be thought of as an assimilation of polytheistic deities. Also, it is doubtful that any real assimilation of polytheistic deities into a monotheistic deity

In 3:6, God identifies himself as the God of the Israelite patriarchs. This identification is more grounded in the history and ethnicity of the Israelite people than is even the name YHWH. God's first self-disclosure is not as the high God, the maker of heaven and earth. He is the God who is identified with the tribes of Israel.

3:7–10. God's first commission of Moses begins with a recitation that essentially repeats 2:23–25. God draws Moses into the heavenly perspective on Israel's enslavement, allowing Moses to, as it were, sit beside God as he sees the suffering of his people. Moses now knows the truth, that God has not abandoned Israel. The significance of this emerges in v. 10, where God in effect invites Moses to join him in his enterprise of freeing the Hebrews (see the translation note to clause 3:10a). The first commission is therefore a very high calling. Moses is brought alongside God, made privy to God's view of the world and his intentions, and is invited to participate in God's work.

Exodus 3:8 contains the first of 20 occurrences of Canaan being called a "land flowing with milk and honey" (אֶרֶץ זָבַת חָלָב וּדְבָשׁ). The expression always occurs within the divine promise to give the land to the Israelites. It is almost always found in the Pentateuch, and even when it occurs in later books, it is always in a context of citing the pre-conquest promises (Josh. 5:6; Jer. 11:5; 32:22; Ezek. 20:6, 15). That is, this is the language of promise; it is not a term that Israelites customarily used to describe the land. It implies that the land is abundantly productive of foodstuff, with emphasis on foods high in fat content ("milk") or sugar content ("honey"). In other words, it is a place where one can enjoy life and not merely survive. The word for "honey" is not necessarily exclusively bee's honey; it may include jellies or sweetmeats made from fruits such as dates. It is also possible that the language has religious significance. Philip Stern points out that the Ugaritic text *KTU* 1.6 (*CTA* 6), lines 13–14, state, "The heavens rain fat/oil, The wadis flow with honey." In context, this refers to agricultural abundance that flows after the resuscitation of Baal. Therefore,

---

took place in the Hellenistic period (it is unlikely that Plato's notion of the "good" can be equated with monotheism, and Hellenism as a whole remained stoutly polytheistic). The biblical texts firmly reject any kind of inclusive theology (which is more a mark of polytheism than of monotheism). Baal, for example, is never legitimated in the Bible as an authentic, local manifestation of "God."

it may be that Exod. 3:8 is making the point that it is YHWH, not Baal, who actually makes the land fruitful.[77]

The stock list of names ("the Canaanites, the Hittites, the Amorites, the Perizzites, the Hivites, and the Jebusites") appears verbatim here, at Exod. 3:17, and at Judg. 3:5. With minor variations, the list also occurs at Gen. 15:20–21, Exod. 23:23; 33:2; 34:11; Deut. 7:1; 20:17; Josh. 12:8; 1 Kings 9:20; Ezra 9:1; Neh. 9:8; 2 Chron. 8:7. All these peoples lived within Canaan, but their ethnic, linguistic, and geographic boundaries are hard to isolate.

The term "Canaanite" seems to be a fairly broad and generic term; it designates inhabitants of the southern Levant who spoke a northwest Semitic language. Canaan is said to have been a son of Ham (Gen. 10:6), but it is impossible to know whether all the peoples called "Canaanites" were thought to be lineal descendants of Ham and non-Semitic (if by "Semitic" we mean descendants of Shem; the term as used today implies more of a linguistic than an ethnic identity). After Canaan, all the peoples in the list except the Perizzites are said to be descendants of Ham through Canaan (Gen. 10:15–19). Again, however, we should be careful about drawing a conclusion of racial identity from this. Culturally and linguistically, the majority of the inhabitants of Canaan (except for the Philistines) were certainly Semitic.

The Hittites are a special problem. The term "Hittites" today generally refers to the people from Hatti, the central Anatolian kingdom that became the Hittite empire during the Late Bronze Age. These people were Indo-European, spoke a language distantly related to Greek and other western languages, and had the center of their power at Boğazköy, far removed from the Promised Land. They were a great power in the Late Bronze Age, and they became the chief rival to the New Kingdom of Egypt in the contest for control over Syria. Certainly these people had some presence and cultural influence in Canaan. But it is not known whether the people of Canaan whom the Bible calls "Hittites" can be identified with the Hittites of Anatolia; they could be an entirely different people.[78]

Amorites are west Semites of Syria and the Levant ("Amorite" means "westerner"), although they appear in Mesopotamia during the Ur III period (late 3rd millennium). They spoke a west Semitic dialect

---

77. Philip D. Stern, "The Origin and Significance of 'The Land Flowing with Milk and Honey,'" *VT* 42, no. 4 (1992): 554–7.

78. See Harry A. Hoffner, Jr., "Hittites," in *Peoples of the Old Testament World*, eds. Alfred J. Hoerth, Gerald L. Mattingly and Edwin M. Yamauchi, (Grand Rapids: Baker, 1994), 127–55.

and so are distinguished from those who spoke Akkadian, a northeastern Semitic language. The old kingdom of Babylon was under an Amorite dynasty which included the famous Hammurabi. There seems to be broad semantic overlap in the Bible between the terms "Amorite" and "Canaanite" to designate residents of Canaan. Both are general terms. The Amorites of the Levant do not seem to be localized in any region; peoples on both sides of the Jordan were called "Amorites" (Josh. 2:10; 10:5). "Amorite," in fact, includes various subgroups. Joshua 10:5 says that Amorites occupied Jerusalem and Hebron, but the former is associated with the Jebusites and the latter with the Anakim (Josh. 15:63; 11:21).

Perizzites are difficult to identify; some suggest that it is not an ethnic identification but a social classification meaning "rural folk" after פְּרָזוֹת, "open country." No eponymous ancestor is given for the Perizzites. But 1 Kings 9:20 suggests that the Perizzites were an identifiable foreign element in Israel as late as Solomon's time; this implies that they had some kind of cultural, ethnic, or linguistic identity that persisted. Some suggest that they were Hurrian.[79] The Hivites are very hard to identify, being sometimes confused or equated with the Horites[80] or Hurrians. They lived in the north, in the area of Lebanon (Judg. 3:3), but they also lived in the central hill country, at Gibeon (Josh. 11:19). The Jebusites were located in the hill country and were most famous for having controlled Jerusalem up until the time of David. The Jebusites almost always occur last in the lists of Canaanite peoples. A notable absentee people from the lists is the Philistines; this reflects the fact that the Philistine occupation of the southwestern Levant did not occur until sometime after the conquest.[81]

3:11–12. The first dialogue between Moses and YHWH (3:11–3:15) begins with Moses's assertion that he is inadequate for this task. As mentioned in the translation notes, Moses actually speaks of being inadequate for two tasks: putting himself before Pharaoh and leading Israel out of Egypt. We should not be quick to censure these objections. Moses was indeed inadequate for this task, as anyone would be. God's response ("I will be with you") is the only thing that could answer this

79. Stephen A. Reed, "Perizzite," in Freedman, *ABD* Vol. 5, 231.

80. In the LXX of Josh. 9:7, the Hivites are called Horites.

81. The Philistines of Gerar (Gen. 21; 26) are a special problem; they do not appear to be identified with the classic Philistine threat that occupied Samson, Eli, Samuel, Saul and David.

objection. Moses will not need to be adequate or competent; God himself will be there to do the heavy lifting.

But the "sign" that follows is astonishing: the Israelites will worship God at Sinai after Moses has completed his mission! How can it be a sign, that is, a token of divine presence meant to reassure Moses before he heads off toward Egypt, if it will not actually occur until after he gets back to Sinai and has accomplished his primary mission? One would expect the sign to be something that Moses could see or experience immediately, before he goes, such as the turning of his rod into a snake. But, as described in the translation note to clause 3:12e, it is undeniable that Israel's coming to worship on the mountain is itself the sign. What are we to make of this? It is probably that God was initially giving Moses a call to faith. "Faith is the substance of things hoped for, the proof of matters not seen" (Heb. 11:1). God wanted Moses to keep the vision of Israel gathered at Sinai to worship God as the "proof" that would sustain him as he embarked on his difficult mission. That is, the greatest sign one can have is a guiding vision. By keeping in his mind's eye the vision of a free Israel worshipping God at the mountain, Moses should have been able to set out on his task and to endure the setbacks along the way. Unfortunately, Moses did not find this sufficient, and he required other, more tangible signs.

3:13–15. As indicated in the translation of v. 13 above, Moses's second objection is not merely a hypothetical matter; it is a fairly vigorous protest. Again, however, it is not an unfair protest. The Israelites have been living in a pagan context for a long time, and the fathers are a distant memory. Moses has good reason to believe that they will want more identification than what has been provided. The question, "What is his name?" suggests a pagan outlook. In Egypt, every god had a name that identified the deity by gender, cult location, powers, specialized tasks, and rank within the hierarchy of deities. Some gods, such as Osiris and Amun, ranked very high. Others, such as the household deity of childbirth, the dwarf god Bes, were relatively minor. Amun had his great shrine at Thebes; Ptah was the principal creator deity of the Memphis cult. Osiris was lord of the dead; Thoth was the god of scribes, Hathor was a fertility deity, and Mut was the divine mother of the pharaoh. This list could be extended to many names, and similar lists could be compiled for the gods of Canaan and Mesopotamia. Furthermore, different peoples or states closely identified with specific gods; Marduk, for example, was the chief deity of Babylon during the Neo-Babylonian Empire. In short, "What is his name?" implies a specific set of presuppositions about the deity whom Moses will claim to represent. It suggests that he is not unique but one of many gods; that he is geographically limited to his special place or cult; that he has certain areas of specialization, whether it be making babies or ruling over the dead; and it suggests that YHWH is somewhere in the hierarchy of deities, with some gods above and some below him. In short, his "name" is a way to distinguish him from all the other gods in the pantheon.

It is in this light that we must understand the answer in v. 14, "I AM." Although God will accept the name YHWH, the title "I AM," set against the pagan context of the question, rejects the very idea of a name for God. He is not like Amun or Ptah; he cannot be assigned a place and identity in the cosmos as one of the gods. In the most ultimate sense, he has no name; he is simply I AM. Furthermore, the title I AM implies that he is not a contingent being. This is not an insertion of an alien philosophical theology into the text; it is germane to the point that the text makes. His identity is not tied to any shrine, cult, city, people, or title. His powers are not limited to specific activities such as the scribal art or the annual inundation of the Nile. He is not even contingent upon the primeval forces that, in pagan theogony, preceded the births of the gods.[82] He exists independently of all things, and is the only being for whom existence is part of his essence. Everything else is contingent on him. In simplest terms, he is the one, eternal, all-powerful, creator God. To ask his "name" is to miss the point completely, because he is not one of the gods at all.

Saying that "I AM" contradicts the idea of God having a name seems itself to contradict this very passage. Here, and in the rest of the Old Testament, God's name is expressly declared to be "YHWH." It is more correct to say that YHWH in one sense is God's name, but in another sense is not. YHWH is God's name in the sense that it is the covenant identification that binds God to Israel. It is not God's name in the way that Seth, Horus, Thoth, or Bastet identify and define individual Egyptian gods. That is, the name YHWH is the proper designation for Israelites to use for their God, but the name is purely an accident (in the philosophical sense of a nonessential attribute); it is not of the essence of God and it does not define his being. Of himself, he is simply "I AM" or the "unknown God" (Acts 17:23). Or, as the angel of YHWH said to Manoah, "Why do you ask my name? It is too wonderful" (Judg.

82. In Egyptian mythology, these forces were the Ogdoad, eight godlike forces of cosmic chaos that existed prior to the emergence of the gods and the beginning of creation. In Greek mythology, theogony begins with the primordial deities (or forces) Ouranos (heaven) and Gaia (earth).

13:18). Unlike the myth of Isis and Re, where the goddess used the sun god's name to gain power over him, the biblical story does not imply that knowledge of YHWH's name implies any power over him. For a discussion of theories on the meaning and origin of the name "YHWH" itself, see the excursus below.

The translation note above for clause 3:15e suggests that זִכְרִי should be translated as "my abiding identity" on the basis of how ancient people closely tied one's identity and being to one's name. Exodus is not saying, of course, that God's continued existence depends upon whether people remember the name YHWH (such thinking would be akin to the pagan notion of a name). But it is saying that God has, as it were, given Israel a single designation for their God that they are to regard as standard. One cannot meaningfully speak of him apart from the name, and without the name, "God" becomes merely an abstraction. As is well known, YHWH is the "covenant name" of God; what matters is not remembering the pronunciation of YHWH but that this is the God of Israel. We should observe, moreover, that the "name" here is not just YHWH; it is "YHWH, the God of your fathers, the God of Abraham, the God of Isaac, and the God of Jacob." In short, he forever identifies himself with the covenant, with the patriarchs, and with Israel. This has enormous theological implications, and these are explored in the Theological Summary below.

3:16–22. God's second commission of Moses is essentially a predictive text. God first assigns Moses the task of giving the message of hope to the people, and he adds the prediction that they will listen and believe (3:16–18a). His second assignment is for Moses and the elders to confront Pharaoh and demand that the people be released; God predicts that Pharaoh will refuse (3:18b–19). God finally predicts that after he has struck Egypt with plagues, the Egyptians will not only release the Hebrews but enrich them as well (3:20–22). We will discuss the specific events in the appropriate passages; for now, the significant point is that God has encouraged Moses by telling him precisely how events will transpire. The intent is to encourage Moses and to get him moving.

4:1–9. Moses, however, is not encouraged. The divine predictions have made little impact on him, as he is not convinced that the people will believe him (4:1). We should not be too harsh in our censure of Moses even here, however. Subsequent events would indeed show the Israelites to be remarkably obstinate (although God's prediction of the Israelites' initial obedience would be fulfilled; Exod. 4:31). God continues to show patience with Moses, not rebuking him for unbelief, but giving him stronger, even more immediate proofs. The rod becoming a snake foreshadows YHWH's domination of Egypt (see the discussion at 7:8–13), and Moses's diseased hand foreshadows the plagues on Egypt (God also predicts the first plague at v. 9). But the important point here is that God now shows Moses miraculous signs in an effort to convince him to believe and accept the divine commission.

4:10–12. Moses again objects that he cannot go by reason of personal incompetence, this time asserting that his poor speaking ability disqualifies him. The precise nature of his deficiency is uncertain, but three proposals are commonly made. Either he had a speech defect such as a stutter, or he was not eloquent and felt uncomfortable in public speaking, or with the passing of years he had lost his fluency in Egyptian. The latter is unlikely, since Moses insists that he has always had trouble with speaking. This would not be the way to describe a gradual loss of fluency in a particular language. It is true that in Ezek. 3:5–6 כִּבְדֵי לָשׁוֹן ("heavy [expressions] of tongue") is used of foreign languages, but the point there is not individual fluency but that these other languages had sounds that were hard (for a Hebrew speaker) to pronounce. This suggests that Moses actually had a speech defect; either there were certain sounds he could not make (as some Italians have difficulty trilling the 'r' sound of their own language), or he stuttered, or lisped, or had some other speech disability. Of course, this would also make it hard for him to speak in public or before people of high authority, since nervousness probably exacerbated his condition. God's response in v. 11 also suggests that Moses had a speech defect, since the conditions of being deaf, mute, or blind are actual disabilities and not simply matters of having or not having an acquired skill, such as refined powers of elocution. God implies that he knows all about Moses's problems, inasmuch as he is Moses's maker, but that he has chosen Moses as his agent anyway. Theologically, however, God's answer is significant for how it confronts the issue of theodicy; this is explored in the theology section below.

4:13. At this point, Moses does not make any excuses or raise any questions—he simply begs to be released from this assignment. His previous queries all had some degree of legitimacy, but now he plainly shows that he just doesn't want to do it.

4:14–16. God, for his part, is equally weary of dealing with side issues, and he is equally direct. He sets aside Moses's concern about his speaking ability by appointing Aaron as the spokesman. His rhetorical question ("Your brother Aaron is the Levite, isn't he?") points to Aaron's status as "the Levite" as somehow relevant to the present issue. God cannot mean simply, "Your brother is a member of the tribe of Levi, right?" After all, Moses is a member of the tribe as well, as are many other people, and it has no bearing on Moses's limitations as a speaker. It appears that the term "the Levite" is used here in reference to his sacerdotal function and not to his tribal membership. This is similar to the usage for "the Levite" (הַלֵּוִי) we see elsewhere, as in Deut. 14:27, "Also you must not neglect the Levite who is within your gates." See also Deut. 18:6–7; 26:11; Judg. 17:10–13. This suggests that the Levites already had a kind of clerical or sacerdotal status in Israel, even before the exodus.[83] Furthermore, to call Aaron "the Levite" suggests that he is, among the Hebrews, the Levite par excellence, or the first among equals. Four factors in Exodus support this. First, at 4:27 Aaron receives a direct communication from God. Second, the genealogy for Aaron and Moses in Exod. 6:14–25 (with Aaron listed first) establishes them as having the best possible genealogical credentials for priestly leadership in Israel.[84] Third, when Moses is absent on Mt. Sinai and the Israelites demand the making of the golden calf, they automatically go to Aaron (Exod. 32:1). This cannot be because of respect for the fact that Aaron is Moses's brother, for they are turning their backs on Moses and dismissing him as no longer relevant. And yet they seem to assume without question that Aaron must take the lead in building an image for worship. Fourth, God himself seems to have the same attitude toward Aaron. He never announces that he has "chosen" Aaron for the priesthood; he simply tells Moses what steps he should take to ordain Aaron and what vestments he should provide for him (Exod. 28; contrast Exod. 31:2–11, where God announces that he has chosen Bezalel son of Uri and Oholiab son of Ahisamak to take the lead in constructing the priestly equipment). In other words, the fact that Aaron is Israel's priest is taken by everyone to be a given that needs no explanation.

In short, Aaron is the foremost Levite of Israel, and he is accustomed to standing before people. Therefore, God says, he obviously knows how to speak in public, and he will take on that role. Apparently anticipating that Moses would claim that his speech defect disqualified him from leadership, God had already directed Aaron to make his way to Moses (4:27), and he was coming as they spoke. The assertion of v. 16, "he will be your mouth and you will be his god," is the classic

83. On Exod. 24:5, see the discussion below.

84. See the discussion of 6:14–25 below.

definition of a prophet. He is one who gives a message in behalf of God. The fact that Aaron would be "glad in his heart" to see Moses (v. 14) seems to be a touching but perhaps irrelevant detail. But it may mean more than just that Aaron will be happy to see his brother again; perhaps Aaron will be glad to hear of God's commissioning of Moses to deliver the people from Egypt. As far as we know, Aaron never voiced objections to the mission in the way that his younger brother did.

4:17. The command to take the staff seems almost like a parting shot shouted out by God to Moses as he grudgingly walks away to take up his task, rather like a mother saying, "And don't forget to take your books!" to her unhappy child as he heads off to school. Be that as it may, the staff was important as the sign of divine commissioning and the means by which Moses would work his miracles.

Theological Summary of Key Points

1. The people of God often find themselves in situations where evil appears triumphant and God appears to be absent. Words of encouragement can fail, and prayer can seem to be a dead exercise. God himself appears to be an abstraction, more of a cosmic postulate than a living being who knows and cares for us. But this is misguided. God knows all about the sufferings of people on earth. We are expected to continue to bear the cross even in the face of apparently having been abandoned by God because, in reality, we never are.

2. The angel of YHWH is at once a local manifestation of God and at the same time subordinate to God (see the commentary on 3:1–6). This seems irrational, but it is analogous to the Christian doctrine of the Trinity, whereby God can be one being in three persons. God is the Father in heaven at the same time that he is incarnate in Jesus of Nazareth, praying to the Father. The traditional idea that the angel of YHWH is the Logos, the second person of the Trinity, is not a pious projection of post-New Testament Christian teaching on to the Old Testament. It is in fact the only way to make sense of the seemingly contradictory portrayal of the angel of YHWH in the Old Testament itself.

3. The title "I AM" implies that God is the only self-existent being. That is, above everything else, "I AM" implies absolute existence[85] without

85. The verb היה means "to be." Although it might include a greater semantic range than the English "to be," it certainly does not exclude that meaning.

limitation either in time or contingency. He is not contingent upon anything, and everything is contingent upon him.[86]

4. I have argued from 3:15 that God's "name forever" and his "abiding identity" is "YHWH, the God of your fathers, the God of Abraham, the God of Isaac, and the God of Jacob." This is significant for theology in five areas:

a. *The Essence and Identity of God*. We are accustomed to thinking of God in Aristotelian terms, that is, as entirely removed from contingency and the human condition. This indeed is the natural conclusion if one thinks of God only as I AM. But the immanence of God is most vigorously expressed in the claim that God's eternal identity is as "God of Abraham, Isaac, and Jacob." God refuses to be identified simply as "the supreme being," "the unmoved mover," or "the uncaused first cause." It is not that these designations are wrong; they are simply not how God relates to humans. He has involved himself in a human family and story, and makes himself known through their names. We can relate to this in the west, where a woman in marriage is traditionally called by her husband's name. In ancient Israel, a son or daughter would have the father's name as part of his or her identity. But God condescends to the human condition in this: he allows himself to be identified by the names of the patriarchs! The text could hardly be more emphatic in the point that God is present among us.

b. *The Incarnation*. God's willingness to tie his identity to a human family and story is given a much more radical expression in the New

---

Cf. Hertog, "Prophetic Dimension," 225: "The verb *hyh* in itself does not differentiate a stative sense ('being') from mutative sense (e.g., 'becoming'). . . . In this respect *hyh* is not more concrete than the verb 'be' and other Indo-Germanic equivalents, though it is often thought to be, presumably from a nineteenth-century evolutionary understanding; on the contrary, it is even more abstract." In short, there is no lexical basis for denying that the idea of "being" is fundamental to היה. As such, there is no basis for denying that it can be used for an ontological statement.

86. Contrary to Charles R. Gianotti, "The Meaning of the Divine Name YHWH," *BSac* 142, no. 565 (1985): 41–3, who rejects any ontological explanation. He exaggerates the difference between "Hebrew thought" and "Greek thought" (as though the Israelites were incapable of thinking in ontological categories), and he incorrectly argues that אֶהְיֶה must be regarded as "future tense" (he does not see that the *yiqtol* form is used for the sake of making a paronomasia; it is not used for reasons of tense—Hebrew does not inflect for tense). The verb does not point to any future activity on God's part; it is a statement of identity.

Testament. In Exodus, God says that he is forever linked in his identity to the patriarchs. In Jesus Christ, God is forever bound to humanity and to Israel in his being in the body and person of the Jew, Jesus of Nazareth. The incarnation is the ultimate conclusion to the great condescension whereby God links himself to the particularity of the human condition.

c. *Knowing God and Finding Salvation*. The promise that all nations would be blessed in Abraham (Gen. 12:3) is the beginning of salvation history, but the declaration of Exod. 3:15 is a major milestone along the way. God is identified forever with Abraham, Isaac, and Jacob. For us, therefore, it is not enough to be pious, or even to be a monotheist, as the pharaoh Akhenaten was. The Samaritan woman whom Jesus met at the well was wrong to identify her religious tradition as an alternative version of the covenant faith. "Salvation is from the Jews" (John 4:22) and from no other source. Islam is said to be one of the "great Abrahamic faiths," but God has identified himself not with Abraham alone, but with Abraham, Isaac, and Jacob. The Allah of the Koran is not the God of Jacob. Rather, as described above, the God of the patriarchs has completed the process of identifying himself with Israel in the incarnation of Jesus Christ. For this reason Peter is justified in his claim that there is "no other name" whereby people can be saved but that of Jesus the Messiah (Acts 4:12).

d. *Eternal Life and the Resurrection*. When a group of Sadducees tried what they hoped would be a knock-down argument demonstrating the illogic of the resurrection, Jesus answered their reasoning and also confronted them with a profound but enigmatic proof text from Exod. 3 for the resurrection: YHWH is "the God of Abraham, Isaac, and Jacob" (Luke 20:27–37). How does this text, which says nothing about a resurrection, make Jesus's point? The answer is surely that when God took their names to himself, he eternally bound himself to them. He knows Abraham, Isaac, and Jacob, and they know him. "This is eternal life, that they should know you, the only true God, and him whom you have sent, Jesus Christ" (John 17:3). Understanding the resurrection is not fundamentally about comprehending how relationships among former spouses will be worked out (as in the Sadducees' question), nor is it a matter of being able to describe heaven or how the resurrection body will rise and function (1 Cor. 15:35–44), nor is it based in the ability to demonstrate that one has an "eternal soul." It is a matter of knowing God. If God has bound himself to human particularity in his identification with the patriarchs and especially in the incarnation, then the only hope of escaping mortality is in being joined to God's chosen people and to the God-man.

e. *Anti-Semitism and the Survival of the Jews*. Although we who are Christians believe that Jesus is the final and ultimate expression of God identifying himself with human particularity and with a human name, this does not mean that we can set aside God's eternal identification with Abraham, Isaac, and Jacob. YHWH can no more forget Zion than a woman can forget the child she bore and nursed (Isa. 49:14–15). It is perverse for someone both to confess the Christian faith and to hate the Jew. Apart from the fact that the one "eternal Jew" is none other than Jesus himself, the incarnation itself is based in God's eternal identification with Abraham, Isaac, and Jacob. If the Jews had perished, then God's commitment to the human race would have perished with them.

5. At the same time, the name YHWH is not truly essential to God but is an "accident" in the philosophical sense. In the Bible, "forever" is often relative to context. YHWH was God's name "forever" as long as Israel continued under the Sinai covenant. With the passing of that covenant and the inauguration of the new covenant, no one anymore calls God "YHWH", and rightly so. God is now the "God and Father of our Lord Jesus Christ." We are now directed to address God as "Father" (Luke 11:2).

6. The problem of theodicy arises in Exod. 4:11. Theodicy concerns the fact that, on the one hand, we confess that God is almighty, good, and compassionate, and on the other hand, we see evil and suffering everywhere. The two ideas seem incompatible. Some argue that, the world being what it is, God is either too weak to overcome evil, or too malevolent to care, or simply nonexistent. This problem is particularly acute when we see suffering inflicted on someone who has done no wrong, as when a child is born with a condition such as blindness or spina bifida. We should bear in mind, moreover, that ancient societies were not concerned to make facilities "accessible," and there were no educational programs or technologies to assist persons with debilitating problems. They simply had to get along as well as they could, at best having whatever help family members could give, and at worst being left on the street. Christians, confronted not only with these but with all the other evils that fill the world, have developed various arguments to justify the rule of God.

a. One strategy is to attribute all calamity and all wickedness to Adam's sin. If Adam had not sinned, there would be no destructive earthquakes, famines, murders, adulteries, or children born with heart defects. This explanation has value; Gen. 3:16–24 does attribute various troubles to Adam's sin, making especially the point that his expulsion from the garden has cut him off from the tree of life. The New Testament also attributes human woe to the fall (Rom. 5:12). On the other hand, the Old Testament never attributes any specific disaster, natural or man-made, to Adam's sin. Joel's locust plague, for example, is never said to be a result of the fall. In contrast to contemporary evangelical thinking, where Adam's sin has become the default apologetic to every crisis, calamity, and issue of theodicy, the Old Testament very seldom—and then only obliquely—refers to Adam (significantly, the Old Testament book that is most concerned with theodicy, Job, never invokes Gen. 3).

b. Another approach is to claim that every human sorrow is the direct result of specific human sins (not just Adam's sin). That is, suffering is divine judgment on human misdeeds. To be sure, the Old Testament does often assert that God will punish people who do not repent, and it sometimes attributes specific disasters to specific sins (as when the fall of Jerusalem to Babylon is attributed to Judah's idolatry). But this approach stumbles at various points; it has difficulty explaining the suffering inflicted on small children (and thus the disciples' question regarding the man born blind in John 9:2). It also fails in the book of Job, where Job's three friends, Eliphaz, Bildad and Zophar, three stout advocates of the "suffering is punishment for specific sins" school, are repudiated by God himself.

c. Some Christians, hoping apparently to limit God's liability, effectively absolve God of responsibility for what goes on in the world. If a child is born blind, it is a result of a prenatal infection or genetic defect; God had nothing to do with it. If religious zealots bring down buildings and kill thousands, God was not involved. The problem with this is that it effectively limits God's power and sovereignty. What if an infection was the proximate cause of a baby's being born blind? Couldn't God have saved the child if he had wanted to? Couldn't God have stopped the mass-murderers? God cannot be almighty and all-knowing and also be absolved of responsibility for what happens in the world.

d. God's response in Exod. 4:11 is striking: he takes full responsibility for the suffering that people experience. He makes some blind, some deaf, and some mute. The text does not deny that there are proximate causes to such things (injuries, infections, etc.; the ancients knew nothing about viruses and bacteria, but they certainly knew that accidents and injuries could make a person blind or lame). Furthermore, the issue of human sin is never raised in God's response. This passage is not at all concerned with proximate causes—and human sin, like disease or injury, is really just another proximate cause. This text is focused on the ultimate cause, God, and does not shrink from affirming that God is in control of all that happens. Of course, the issue of theodicy is very large, and merely asserting that God takes responsibility for all that happens in the world does not resolve all the issues. This topic is explored much more fully in Job. We can say, however, that this text tells us that divine sovereignty is meant to give us comfort. Moses was supposed to understand that God knew what he was doing when he made Moses as he did and then chose to use him to redeem Israel. God's sovereignty should encourage us to remain patient and hopeful in times of darkness.

Excursus: Theories on the Origin and Meaning of "YHWH"

How does the term "I AM" (אֶהְיֶה) relate to YHWH (יהוה)?[87] Where does the name "I AM" come from, and why is it used here? One answer is that God's original answer to Moses was v. 15, that he was YHWH, the god of the fathers, and that v. 14, with the name "I AM," is a later interpolation. This follows the documentary hypothesis, which argues that this text is where E places the original revelation of the name YHWH.[88] This, of course, leaves unanswered the question of where "I AM" came from, or what its purpose is. But following this line of reasoning, Anthony and Lucy Phillips argue that "I AM" is actually derived from Hos. 1:9. That is, Hosea created a pun on the divine name YHWH to signify that Israel had lost its elect status, but the pun is reversed here at Exod. 3:14, where a proto-Deuteronomic revision inserts אֶהְיֶה to signify that YHWH remains committed to Judah.[89] There are several reasons that this is wrong. First, apart from the existence of Exod. 3:14, no one could possibly see the name "I AM" (אֶהְיֶה) within Hos. 1:9, nor would they know what to make of it if they did see it. As this supposed meaning of Hos. 1:9 depends upon Exod. 3:14, it cannot explain the existence of Exod. 3:14. Second, in my opinion, Hos. 1:9 does not refer to the "I AM" at all; this notion is merely the conceit of modern exegesis and is not supported by the Hebrew text at all.[90] If so, Hos. 1:9 certainly is not the origin of the "I AM." Third, v. 14 is what

87. For a survey of different proposals on the origin and meaning of the divine name, see Dennis J. McCarthy, "Exod 3:14: History, Philology and Theology," *CBQ* 40, no. 3 (1978): 311–22.

88. See Childs, *Exodus*, 52–62, who describes the history of such source-critical interpretation, but himself declares that a solution to the problem is not to be found in source criticism.

89. Anthony C. J. and Lucy Phillips, "The Origin of 'I AM' in Exodus 3.14," *JSOT* 78 (1998): 81–4.

90. See Duane A. Garrett, *Hosea, Joel,* NAC (Nashville: Broadman, 1997), 70 n.93. If Hosea had meant, "And I will not be I AM to you," he would have written וְאָנֹכִי לֹא־אֶהְיֶה לָכֶם אֶהְיֶה; the actual text (וְאָנֹכִי לֹא־אֶהְיֶה לָכֶם) simply does not have that meaning. It only means, "but I will not be yours."

gives Exod. 3:13–16 its narrative power. With v. 15 as the only answer to Moses's question, the text is oddly anticlimactic. If vv. 13 and 15 (minus v. 14) were E's account of the revelation of the name YHWH, an event E would surely regard as momentous, it is odd that Moses's accepts this new name for God, a name he had never heard of, without surprise, amazed reverence, or comment (and that later, all Israel does the same).

The word "I am" (אֶהְיֶה) looks like and no doubt sounded like the name YHWH (although precisely how the verb and the name were pronounced in archaic Hebrew is unknown to us). At the very least, יהוה has consonance with אֶהְיֶה. Of course, the verb אֶהְיֶה is an inflection of the verbal root היה, "to be." This being the case, many interpreters assume that יהוה, too, is an inflection of היה, as though God were telling Moses that היה is the etymology of יהוה. Accepting this premise, scholars have long debated whether יהוה is in the Qal stem of היה (thus, "he is") or the Hiphil stem (thus, "he causes to be" or in effect, "he creates").

On this basis, interpreters claim that the name YHWH itself is the key to understanding how the earliest Israelites defined the nature of their God. Taking YHWH to be from a Qal stem of היה, one could claim that "he exists" is the main idea. Taking it to be a Hiphil stem, one could argue that the name means "he makes (things) exist," that is, "he creates." Other interpretations are possible. William Propp, on the grounds that היה means "fall" in Job 37:6 and that it is a Hiphil stem in the divine name, understands YHWH to mean "he makes (someone) fall." So understood, and taking יְהוָה אִישׁ מִלְחָמָה in Exod. 15:3 to be an earlier and more complete form of the divine name, Propp argues that YHWH is but a shortened form of the name *YHWH ish milchama*: "He *throws down* the man of war." Similarly, he suggests, יְהוָה צְבָאוֹת means, "He casts down armies."[91]

The popular pronunciation "Yahweh" looks just like what a Hiphil

91. Propp, *Exodus 19-40*, 758. Against this interpretation of Exod. 15:3 (יְהוָה אִישׁ מִלְחָמָה יְהוָה שְׁמוֹ), one may make three points. (1) Since the words of the second line are a nominal (verbless) clause, probably the parallel first line is the same. That is, the verse means, "YHWH [is] a man of war; / YHWH [is] his name." Propp would need to render it something like, "He brings down a man of war; / 'He brings down' [is] his name." That rendition would not be the translator's first or best choice. (2) Since the second line expressly states "YHWH is his name," it is unlikely the text means for us to understand that YHWH is actually a shortened form of יְהוָה אִישׁ מִלְחָמָה, God's full name. (3) The meaning "to fall" for היה is at best very rare and is in fact debatable. It seems to be a peculiar choice for the name of Israel's God.

of היה ought to look like—if such a form existed in biblical Hebrew. But in fact, that is the important point: there is no Hiphil of היה. As such, claiming that "Yahweh" is just such an inflection is highly dubious (it is a circular argument to say that the Hiphil of היה is not used elsewhere because of reverence for the divine name). In fact, a causative form of this verb is not attested in any Semitic language.[92] Also, it is not at all certain (to me, at least) that "Yahweh" is the correct pronunciation.[93]

Does this mean that יהוה is a Qal stem, and that it perhaps should be vocalized as יִהְיֶה (yihweh ["he is"])? I think not. This interpretation in effect has God saying, "My name, HE IS (יִהְיֶה), is I AM (אֶהְיֶה)." This is a tautology and, frankly, it is not a very impressive thing to say. If the name YHWH is no more than a third-person inflection of היה, "he is," it is pointless for God to rename himself by simply shifting to the first person. After all, the name would already be making the point that God "is." Changing to first person is not grammatically necessary since God could have answered Moses's question with, "My name is HE IS." In fact, God frequently in the Old Testament says אֲנִי יְהוָה ("I am YHWH"). But if יהוה is simply the third person singular of היה, we would have to translate this as "I (am) HE IS." This is, to say the least, a very strange thing to say.

There is another serious objection to taking YHWH to be either a Qal or a Hiphil inflection: in both cases, it puts the name into the *yiqtol* conjugation. The *yiqtol* (imperfect), in contrast to the *qatal* (perfect), inflects a verb's aspect as potential, desired, or in process of completion. Its default translation is the future tense, although other translations are appropriate in various contexts (jussive, past imperfective, etc.). Examples in translation would be "he will be," "let him be," "he used to be," and so forth. The *qatal* is perfective, and it is normally

92. Barry J. Beitzel, "Exodus 3:14 and the Divine Name: A Case of Biblical Paronomasia," *TJ* 1 (1980): 18.

93. Against Stuart, *Exodus*, 121. If יהוה is a true four-letter root (see Beitzel "Exodus 3:14," 18–9), then the medial ה must be fully consonantal and cannot function inflectionally, simply closing the first syllable of a *yiqtol* type verb. One would suspect that the early pronunciation was something like *yeho-wehu*, or perhaps *yeho-weh* (with voiced final ה if there were no case ending). This would seem to be verified by the appearance of the divine name in theophoric names such as יְהוֹשָׁפָט (Jehoshaphat) and זְכַרְיָה (Zechariah), and especially the former, where the vocalization of the first half of the name, יה, is evidently preserved and the u-class vowel after the ה cannot be regarded as a mere anaptyctic vowel. But the pronunciation of יהוה is a side issue. Even if it were pronounced "Yahweh," this would not establish that it was a Hiphil of היה.

translated as an English perfect, past, or present tense (for example, "he has been," he was," or "he is"). It is very difficult to explain why the Israelites would use a *yiqtol* form as the name of their God if the name is in fact an inflected verb. The *yiqtol* would seem to imply that there is something potential or incomplete about YHWH. The reason for the use of the *yiqtol* אֶהְיֶה is described below.

Let us be clear: יהוה is not an inflection of היה, and it means neither "he causes to be" nor "he is." It is a proper name; its origin and meaning (if it has any meaning) are both unknown,[94] and in Exod. 3:14 God is not giving the etymology of the name. God is making a paronomasia (a wordplay).[95] In the Bible, a paronomasia is never a "pun," that is, a silly joke based on verbal ambiguity or multivalence. Paronomasia in the Old Testament is always a serious matter, God himself often being the speaker. For example, in Jer. 1:11–12 we read of God asking, "What do you see, Jeremiah?" To this Jeremiah replies, "I see the branch of an almond tree (שָׁקֵד)," and God explains, "You have seen correctly, for I am watching (שֹׁקֵד) to see that my word is fulfilled." This is plainly paronomasia; God is not saying that שקד ("to watch") is the origin or meaning of the plant name שָׁקֵד, "almond." The dreadful seriousness of the matter is apparent; God is announcing destruction on Jerusalem; he is not making a joke. In a similar agricultural wordplay, Amos in a vision sees a basket of "summer fruit" (קָיִץ) as a sign that the "end" (קֵץ) has come for Israel (Amos 8:2). Micah 1:10 has the famous wordplay, "Tell it not in Gath" (בְּגַת אַל־תַּגִּידוּ), in which the letters גַת ("Gath") are reversed as תַג (from the word for "tell"). Therefore, when God declares "This is who I am: 'I AM'," he is using a wordplay that links יהוה and אֶהְיֶה to make the point that he is the God who truly is. The only predication that is appropriate for God cannot apply to any of the "gods," because he is categorically different. For an ancient person, the fact that יהוה and אֶהְיֶה sound alike would have made the point quite effectively. As an aside, we should note that the use of a paronomasia on יהוה indicates that, contrary to the documentary hypothesis, this text implies

94. Beitzel, "Exodus 3:14," 18–9, gives examples of divine names similar to YHWH from Ugarit, Egyptian inscriptions, Byblos, and Cassite Babylon, but Beitzel's only point is that this demonstrates that YHWH is a true proper name, not that we know its origin or meaning. He observes that היוה is a true "*quadriliteral* divine name in which the initial *yod* is lexically intrinsic." In other words, it cannot be an inflectional prefix on a verbal root.

95. Ibid., 5–12, gives numerous examples of different kinds of paronomasia employed in the Bible and the ancient Near East.

the name was already known in Israel. One cannot make a paronomasia on the basis of a word that the audience has never heard of.

This also explains why the *yiqtol* form is used in the paronomasia: it works with YHWH, but the *qatal* does not. As stated above, the *yiqtol* form אֶהְיֶה sounded and looked like יהוה. The *qatal* form, הָיִיתִי, does not. That is, the choice of the *yiqtol* אֶהְיֶה over the *qatal* is driven by the sound of the word and the need for a paronomasia on the name YHWH. In this context, the aspect of אֶהְיֶה is not significant.

God commissions Moses with two parallel messages for the Israelites: "I AM has sent me to you" (clause 3:14e) and "YHWH, the God of your fathers, the God of Abraham, the God of Isaac, and the God of Jacob, has sent me to you" (clause 3:15c). I AM, the eternal God who cannot be compared to any of the gods, is the same being who spoke to the fathers. The parallel statements also point to the fact, in case anyone has missed it, that I AM is a paronomasia based on YHWH. The origin of YHWH is unknown, and all supposed descriptions of the etymology and of its original meaning are speculations, many of them based on misinterpretations of Exod. 3:14–15.

OF PARENTS AND SONS (4:18–26)

Three episodes that revolve around the theme of how parents care for their sons are juxtaposed in this text. In addition to illustrating the nature of God's love for Israel, it anticipates the death of the firstborn and the importance of circumcision and Passover.

Translation

4:18a And Moses went [from Horeb],[96]
4:18b and he returned to Jethro his father-in-law,
4:18c and he said to him,
4:18d "Let me go away
4:18e so that I may return to my brothers in Egypt
4:18f and that I may see whether they are still alive."
4:18g And Jethro said to Moses,

96. While a number of translations understandably render וַיֵּלֶךְ מֹשֶׁה וַיָּשָׁב as a single clause (such as, "Then Moses went back" [TNIV]), the first Hebrew clause וַיֵּלֶךְ מֹשֶׁה seems to refer to a departure from the bush, while the second, beginning with וַיָּשָׁב, refers specifically to his return to Jethro. Contrast Gen. 22:19, which begins, וַיָּשָׁב אַבְרָהָם ("and Abraham returned"), referring only to going back to his servants, without leaving the vicinity of Moriah. Then the whole group actually leaves Moriah, using the expression וַיָּקֻמוּ וַיֵּלְכוּ ("and they got up and went away").

4:18h “Go in peace.”
4:19a And YHWH said to Moses in Midian,
4:19b “Go!
4:19c Return to Egypt!
4:19d For all the men who were seeking your life have died.”
4:20a So Moses took his wife and his sons
4:20b and had them ride on a donkey,
4:20c and he returned to the land of Egypt.
4:20d And Moses took the staff of God in his hand.
4:21a And YHWH said to Moses,
4:21b “When you go off to return to Egypt, don’t forget[97] about the miraculous powers[98] that I have put in your hand,
4:21c and perform them before Pharaoh.
4:21d But I will make his heart implacable,
4:21e so that he will not release the people.
4:22a And you shall say to Pharaoh,
4:22b ‘Thus says YHWH,
4:22c Israel is my firstborn son,
4:23a and I said to you,
4:23b “Release my son
4:23c that he may serve me.”
4:23d And you refused[99] to release him.

---

97. A number of versions translate רְאֵה with וַעֲשִׂיתָם subordinated to it, such as “see that you perform before Pharaoh” (TNIV; ESV is similar). But there are no examples of the imperative of ראה used with a *weqatal* to mean, “See that you do” (i.e., “Be sure to do”). But ראה can mean to pay close attention to a certain detail prior to fulfilling a secondary command. In 1 Sam. 16:17 we have, רְאוּ־נָא לִי אִישׁ מֵיטִיב לְנַגֵּן וַהֲבִיאוֹתֶם אֵלָי (“Look for a man for me who plays the lyre well, and bring him to me”). In 2 Sam 13:28, Absalom tells his men to “watch closely” (רְאוּ) for the time when Amnon is drunk, and “then kill him” (וַהֲמִתֶּם אֹתוֹ). So here, God tells Moses to “watch” or “pay attention to” the miracle-working powers God has bestowed upon him. In this context, I think it is equivalent to the English, “don’t forget about.”

98. מוֹפֵת means “wonder” or “miracle.” Here, it refers to the ability to work wonders, inasmuch as God has put הַמֹּפְתִים (“the wonders”) in Moses’s hand. The power to do miracles is quite literally in Moses’s hand, in the form of his staff.

99. The ESV wrongly translates וַתְּמָאֵן as a conditional (“If you refuse to let him go”). It is a simple past tense; v. 21 has set this in a context of Pharaoh having already refused to release the people.

4:23e Now, watch![100] I am going to kill your firstborn son.'"
4:24a Now it happened along the way at a lodging place
4:24b that YHWH encountered him
4:24c and sought to put him to death.
4:25a And Zipporah took a flint,
4:25b and she cut off her son's foreskin,
4:25c and she touched[101] his feet,[102]
4:25d and she said,

---

100. הִנֵּה here does two things: it indicates that Pharaoh's treatment of YHWH's son is the basis for the plague on the firstborn, and it calls on Pharaoh to observe and draw that conclusion.

101. There are three possible ways to read וַתַּגַּע לְרַגְלָיו ("and she touched his feet"). 1) One can understand עָרְלָה ("foreskin") to be the implied direct object and the feet to be the indirect object, with וַתַּגַּע taken in a causal sense: "She made the foreskin touch his feet." Thus, most English versions supply the words "with it," as in, "She touched his feet with it." The purpose of touching the feet with the foreskin is left unclear. 2) One can understand the "touching" to be a violent act and meant to show her disgust, as in the NASB, "[she] threw it at Moses's feet." This interpretation also takes עָרְלָה to be the implied direct object. 3) One can understand the feet to be the direct object, but עָרְלָה is not supplied as an understood instrumental and וַתַּגַּע is not taken to be causative. That is, she simply touched his feet (perhaps a euphemism for "genitals"), and not with the foreskin (probably she touched the "feet" with her hand). There is no case elsewhere of נגע (Hiphil stem) being used with לְ to mean "cause A to touch B," as in the first and second interpretations. Exodus 12:22, however, using אֶל instead of לְ, does have bearing on this issue. See the commentary. Interpretation 2 has some support in Isa. 25:12 and Lam. 2:2, but in both those cases we have fortifications being brought to the ground in what appears to be a specific idiom with לָאָרֶץ, "to the earth," and with fortifications being the explicit direct object. All in all, "she threw (the foreskin) at his feet" is an unlikely if not impossible interpretation. The third interpretation is supported in 2 Chron. 3:11–12, where one of the cherub's wings was touching the wall of the house (מַגַּעַת לְקִיר הַבַּיִת) and the other wing was touching another cherub's wing. Here, the Hiphil of נגע is not causative. As it is the simplest interpretation, the third is followed here.

102. The word "feet" (רֶגֶל) is sometimes used euphemistically for the private parts in the region of the genitals and buttocks in Hebrew (Deut. 28:57; Judg. 3:24; Ezek. 16:25). It is possible to take the word in this way here; we should remember that this is a passage that concerns circumcision, which of course takes place at the genitals and not the feet. Someone performing a circumcision would of necessity touch the genitals. On the other hand, it may be that touching the feet is a ritual act analogous to applying blood to the big toe of the right foot in Lev. 8:23.

4:25e "You are my *hatan damim* (kinsman by the blood of circumcision)[103]!"
4:26a And he let him alone.
4:26b In that episode[104] she said *hatan damim* with reference to the circumcision ritual.[105]

Structure

This text appears to contain a series of separate episodes, but on close inspection, the material does not seem to be a simple sequence of events.[106] In 4:27 God tells Aaron to go meet Moses, and yet already in 4:14 God had said that Aaron was on his way to meet Moses. Furthermore, the prediction God makes concerning Pharaoh's refusal to listen to Moses and the subsequent plague upon the firstborn (4:21–23) seems to belong with the extended prediction in 3:16–22. Set where it is, 4:21–23 does not fit in with the narrative sequence but appears somewhat obtrusive. This suggests that the episodes are organized logically or thematically rather than by strict chronology. The chronological sequence may have been something like: (1) God tells Aaron to go meet Moses;

103. The phrase חֲתַן־דָּמִים is almost always translated as "bridegroom of blood," applying the default meaning of "bridegroom" to חָתָן. But if חָתָן here means "bridegroom," then חֲתַן־דָּמִים has to mean, "murderous bridegroom." For further discussion of the common meaning of חָתָן, see T. C. Mitchell, "The Meaning of the Noun *ḤTN* in the Old Testament," *VT* 19, no. 1 (1969): 93–112. The word דָּמִים, as an absolute noun at the end of a construct chain, normally refers to lawless violence. Thus, in Nah. 3:1 עִיר דָּמִים is a "violent city." In Ps. 5:7(6), God abhors the אִישׁ־דָּמִים ("murderous man"). In Ps. 26:9, the psalmist asks that his life not be swept away with אַנְשֵׁי דָמִים, "murderous men." Such examples (where דָּמִים comes after a construct noun referring to persons, and where it has the meaning "violence" or "bloodguilt") are so numerous that one can hardly translate it simply as "bridegroom of blood" here. However, דָּמִים can be used of menstrual blood or the blood of childbirth (Lev. 12:7) in a religious setting, where it has no connotation of bloodguilt. If חֲתַן does not mean "bridegroom" here but is used as ritual expression, then דָּמִים need not mean "murderous." For further discussion, see commentary.

104. The word אָז here refers to the just narrated episode. It does not mean "then" in the sense of "right after that."

105. The use of the plural מוּלֹת suggests that this refers not just to the physical act of circumcision but to the whole ritual process.

106. Athena E. Gorospe, *Narrative and Identity: An Ethical Reading of Exodus 4* (Leiden: Brill, 2007) also reads 4:18–26 as a single unit, but her interpretation is in my view eccentric, as she follows Ricoeur's hermeneutics and in particular reads the text from the standpoint of a Filipino migrant worker.

(2) Moses hears God's word at the bush, including all the predictions; (3) Moses and Aaron meet; (4) Moses returns to Jethro; (5) Moses says goodbye to Jethro and sets out for Egypt with his wife and children; (6) the episode with Zipporah along the way takes place. I would suggest that the material is organized thematically. Exodus 4:18–26 revolves around issues of family and kinship. We see, first, Moses's dealings with his father-in-law, wife, and sons (4:18–20). Then we have God's prophecy, a text that sets Israel, God's firstborn, as the counterpart to an Egyptian prince, Pharaoh's firstborn (4:21–23). Finally, Zipporah circumcises her son (4:24–26). The structure is thus as follows.

I. Moses and His Family (4:18–20)
II. YHWH and His Firstborn Son; Pharaoh and His Firstborn Son (4:21–23)
III. Zipporah and Her Son (4:24–26)

Commentary

4:18–20. The most striking thing about this text is that it shows Moses to be a dutiful son and father. To his father-in-law, he is a good son. He respectfully asks to be relieved of his shepherding duty so that he may go back to his people in Egypt. For his wife and sons, he is a good father. He provided the best means of transportation available in the form of a donkey (Moses himself apparently walked). In his request to Jethro, "My brothers" refers to the Israelite people in general and perhaps especially to his relatives and acquaintances; it does not refer just to Moses's immediate family (Exodus implies that he only had one brother in that it mentions no other). Moses does not give the full reason for his going—to redeem the Israelite people from slavery—as he himself seems to have hardly believed in the mission at this point. When he says he is going to see if they are alive, Moses obviously does not mean that he fears that all the Israelites may be dead; he wants to see what their condition is. It is analogous to Gen. 45:3. When Joseph asks, "Is my father still living?" he was really asking for more information about his father, since he already knew that he was alive (Gen. 44:30–31).[107] Moses's concern for his kindred people is genuine, and this, too, shows him to be dutiful to his family.

The message in 4:19, that those who wanted to kill Moses are now dead, is somewhat surprising. Nothing else in context suggests that Moses was dawdling in Midian, hesitating to return to Egypt out of fear of retribution for his homicide. But this assurance from God may

107.Cassuto, *Exodus*, 53.

tell us one of the real reasons Moses did not want to go back: because he hated to be again in the place where he had done such a dreadful deed. God's words do more than assure Moses of his physical safety. They mean, in effect, that God has forgiven Moses and that Moses should no longer fear his own past or retribution for his deeds.

4:21–23. This brief prediction, that Pharaoh will refuse to let the Hebrews go and that God will slay the firstborn of Egypt, has at its core an analogy of two pairs of fathers and sons. On the one side is YHWH and Israel, and on the other is Pharaoh and his son (and all the firstborn sons of Egypt). YHWH is a dutiful father, willing to do all that is necessary to protect his children. Pharaoh suffers a penalty appropriate to his sin and, more particularly, shows himself to be a poor father, needlessly putting his son at risk by opposing God.

4:24–26. This text is very difficult.[108] What would probably pass for the standard interpretation among evangelical Protestants is as follows.[109] Moses had two sons, but he had not yet circumcised one of them.[110] On the way to Egypt he was suddenly incapacitated (by a se-

108. Numerous interpretations have been proposed. See, for example, Henry P. Smith, "Ethnological Parallels to Exodus iv.24–26," *JBL* 25, no. 1 (1906): 14–24; Pieter Middelkoop, "The Significance of the Story of the 'Bloody Husband' (Exodus 4:24–26)," *SEAJT* 8, no. 4 (1967): 34–8; Benjamin E. Scolnic, "From Bloody Bridegroom to Covenant Rite: *Brit Milah*—The Perspective of Modern Biblical Scholarship," *Conservative Judaism* 42, no. 4 (1990): 12–20; Pamela T. Reis, "The Bridegroom of Blood: A New Reading," *Judaism* 40, no. 159 (1991): 324–31; William H. C. Propp, "That Bloody Bridegroom (Exodus IV 24–6)," *VT* 43, no. 4 (1993): 495–518; G. W. Ashby, "The Bloody Bridegroom: The Interpretation of Exodus 4:24–26," *ExpTim* 106, no. 7 (1995): 203–5; Serge Frolov, "The Hero as Bloody Bridegroom: On the Meaning and Origin of Exodus 4,26," *Bib* 77 (1996): 520–23; Seth D. Kunin, "The Bridegroom of Blood: A Structuralist Analysis," *JSOT* 70 (1996): 3–16; Ronald B. Allen, "The 'Bloody Bridegroom' in Exodus 4:24–26," *BSac* 153 (1996): 259–69; Joseph A. Walters, "Moses at the Lodging Place: The Devil is in the Ambiguities," *Encounter* 63, no. 4 (2002): 407–25; Jeffrey M. Cohen, "*Hatan Damim*: The Bridegroom of Blood," *JBQ* 33, no. 2 (2005): 120–6; Christopher Hays, "'Lest Ye Perish in the Way': Ritual and Kinship in Exodus 4:24–26," *HS* 48 (2007): 39–54.

109. This interpretation is most plainly in evidence in the NIV, which inserts Moses's name in vv. 24–25.

110. Alternatively, both Moses and his son had not been circumcised, but Zipporah circumcised the son as a surrogate for the father (Durham,

vere illness) as a punishment from God for this neglect. Moses, calling from his sickbed, told Zipporah what the problem was and that she had to circumcise the boy, and she performed the circumcision. By doing this, she averted the wrath of God against Moses. But she found the whole process disgusting and blamed Moses for putting her through the ordeal, so she threw the boy's foreskin at Moses's feet and called him a "bloody bridegroom" (that is, a husband who had her do something bloody and disgusting). Her revulsion toward what had happened was so great that she went back to her father at that time; we do not see her again until Exod. 18:2.

Every aspect of the above interpretation, except that Zipporah circumcised her son, is almost certainly wrong. We should pay attention to the following.

- The text does not say that YHWH met and tried to kill Moses, who is in fact never mentioned in the story. The antecedent to the pronoun "him" in v. 24 is not specified. We therefore should not assume that Moses is the implied victim of YHWH's wrath. In fact, there is no indication that he is involved in this story at all. Within the confines of this brief episode, there are only three explicit persons: YHWH, Zipporah, and her son. The pronoun "him" would most likely be read as a prolepsis, pointing forward to Zipporah's son.[111] The peculiar narrative style of vv. 24–26, which begins with undefined pronouns for the object of YHWH's hostility, ought to be preserved in translation. The account looks like it is an abbreviation of an original, longer narrative. Or, this could be a narrative technique, whereby the reader is meant to ask, "What's going on? Who is YHWH trying to kill?" The answer, given in v. 25, is that it was Zipporah's son. But a translation should not preempt the narrative by inserting "Moses" into the text as the object of YHWH's hostility.

- Genesis 17:14 indicates that an uncircumcised male should be "cut off" from his people. There is no indication that the father of an uncircumcised male should be punished, and thus no basis for thinking that God attacked Moses because his son was uncircumcised.

Exodus, 56–9). But the idea of surrogate circumcision is quite alien to the Old Testament.

111. Stuart, *Exodus*, 153 n.114.

- The text says that Zipporah circumcised "her son" rather than "his son."[112] If God were attacking Moses because he had not circumcised his son, wouldn't the text say that she circumcised "his son"? In the standard interpretation, the son's lack of circumcision had dire implications for Moses, not for Zipporah, and thus one would expect the boy to be identified as Moses's son.

- We have no grounds for thinking that Moses told her to perform the circumcision. From what we see in the text, she did it on her own.[113] Therefore, there is no reason to think that Zipporah was angry that Moses made her do the circumcision.

- Many translations state that Zipporah touched Moses's feet with the circumcised foreskin (ESV, NIV, and NRSV). More dramatically, the NASB says that Zipporah "threw" the foreskin at Moses's feet. But, as described in the translation notes above, this interpretation is improbable. The Hebrew only indicates that she touched the "feet" (possibly the genitals; see translation notes). It does not say or imply that she touched the "feet" with the foreskin (she probably touched the "feet" with her hand or with the flint, the tool of circumcision).

- We have no reason to think that the "feet" she touched belonged to Moses. The most logical antecedent to "his" (in "his feet") is "her son" and not Moses, who is never mentioned. Recall that the text actually says, "And she cut off her son's foreskin, and she touched his feet." It is quite a leap to claim that this refers to Moses's feet.

---

112. Exodus 2:22 tells us that Zipporah bore Gershom to Moses, but says nothing about her bearing another son to him prior to the exodus. But in 4:20, we read that Moses put his wife and "sons" on a donkey upon setting out for Egypt. Exodus 18:3–4 tells us that Zipporah had two sons with her when she came to meet Moses after the exodus, and that Gershom's brother was named Eliezer.

113. We do not know when and where the practice of circumcision developed, but it was known in both Syria and Egypt from the early 3rd millennium. See Jack M. Sasson, "Circumcision in the Ancient Near East," *JBL* 85, no. 4 (1966): 473–76.

- Furthermore, the use of the word "touch"[114] in Exod. 12:22, where blood is applied to the doorframe in the Passover ritual, suggests that her touching of the "feet" is a ritual act, not an outburst of anger. As such, it would have been done to her son, the object of the ritual, and not to Moses. Touching the "feet" completed the act of consecrating the boy.

- If the "feet" are not Moses's feet, and if she did not "throw" the foreskin at his feet, we have no reason to think that when she spoke, she addressed Moses. And there is no basis to the idea that her statement is an angry outburst.

- This brings us to the phrase usually translated as, "a bloody bridegroom." As described in the translation notes, if חָתָן means "bridegroom" here, then חֲתַן־דָּמִים has to mean "murderous bridegroom." But this makes no sense. The word חָתָן only means "bridegroom" in the context of a wedding ceremony (Isa. 61:10; 62:5; Jer. 7:34; 16:9; Joel 2:16; Ps. 19:6[5]). A married woman with children would not call her husband, the father of her children, חָתָן. After marriage, and as a term for a family member, the word חָתָן means "son-in-law" (Gen. 19:12, 14; Judg. 15:6; 19:5; 1 Sam. 22:14). Had Zipporah called Moses her חָתָן, she would have been calling him her son-in-law. Also, there is no reason for Zipporah to speak of Moses as "murderous," even if she did detest the circumcision ritual. A "murderous חָתָן" would be, one would think, a man who murdered his bride or his in-laws.

- Most importantly, v. 26 says that she spoke the words חֲתַן־דָּמִים in reference to the circumcision, not in reference to Moses. We should also observe that, since the text has to explain that the words חֲתַן־דָּמִים refer to circumcision, it seems clear that native Hebrew readers found the expression obscure and hard to understand. It turns out that there is an Arabic word, *hatana*, which means "to circumcise." We should recall three things about Zipporah: first, she was a Midianite—that is, she was from Arabia. Thus, her language was probably a southeastern Semitic dialect and closer to Arabic than to biblical Hebrew. Second, she was the daughter of a priest, Jethro, and she probably had a good understanding of ritual

114. The Hiphil of נגע.

procedures. Third, she was a shepherd, and thus she would have been very familiar with aspects of animal husbandry (the birthing of the young, dealing with the sick and injured, castration techniques, and so forth). Combining her priestly background with her profession as a shepherd, it is very unlikely that she was squeamish about ritual or biological matters. Circumcision among Semites was common, and it would not be at all strange if Zipporah's tribe practiced it. There is no reason to think that she was offended at the practice or thought of it as alien and bizarre. In fact, she apparently knew exactly how to do it. Therefore, it seems likely that חָתָן in חֲתַן־דָּמִים refers to circumcision.

- In addition, since the Hebrew חָתָן can mean "son-in-law," the term as used here may refer to making someone become a relative by a covenantal bond.[115] If so, then חָתָן may describe bringing someone into the community by the ritual of circumcision. Everyone, even those who were born into the community, had to be ritually brought into it by circumcision.

- What, then, do we make of the term דָּמִים? It is almost certainly used here as a ritual reference to blood and has nothing to do with murder, its more common Hebrew meaning. It was probably a liturgical expression to be used at the end of the circumcision as practiced in Midian. It survives here in Exodus as a "linguistic fossil,"[116] and does not follow normal Hebrew meaning of דָּמִים. Saying "You are *hatan damim* to me" is therefore part of an ancient Midianite circumcision liturgy.[117] The

115. For discussions of the lexical significance of חֲתַן־דָּמִים, see Hans Kosmala, "Bloody Husband," *VT* 12, no. 1 (1962): 14–28; Julian Morganstern, "The 'Bloody Husband' (?) (Exod 4:24–26) Once Again," *HUCA* 34 (1963): 35–70; William J. Dumbrell, "Exodus 4:24–26: A Textual Re–Examination," *HTR* 65, no. 2 (1972): 285–90; Bernard P. Robinson, "Zipporah to the Rescue: A Contextual Study of Exodus IV 24–6," *VT* 36, no. 4 (1986): 457–8.

116. Sarna, *Exodus*, 26. One might suggest that "You are *hatan damim* to me" is a partial calque, being a Midianite expression that is partially translated and partially made of imported loanwords or of words used in a way that is not standard for biblical Hebrew.

117. Several ancient versions indicate that Zipporah's words are to be understood as ritualistic. For example, the Ethiopic can be translated, "May the blood of the circumcision of my son be in his place." See Géza Vermès, "Baptism and Jewish Exegesis: New Light from Ancient Sources," *NTS* 4,

fact that it is formulaic is indicated in the last line of the story, "At that time she said 'hatan damim' with reference to the circumcision ritual." The Hebrew readers would not recognize this Midianite-based expression, and the concluding annotation serves to tell the reader the significance of the phrase.

- The text does not state or imply that Zipporah returned to Jethro immediately after this episode, or that the episode prompted her departure, whenever that took place. If she did leave soon after this, it was not necessarily out of anger at Moses. We know nothing of the domestic life of Moses and Zipporah.

We might, therefore, suggest the following reconstruction of the story behind this text. Moses and Zipporah set out for Egypt. Along the way, their son suddenly became deathly ill. Zipporah recognized that the boy needed to be circumcised, and she did the act with a flint knife (flint can be more finely sharpened than can bronze and is therefore better for performing surgery). After the removal of the foreskin, she ritually touched the boy's feet (or genitals) with her hand or the flint while saying, "You are *hatan damim* to me" (a member of my community by virtue of the blood of circumcision). These formulaic words concluded the circumcision ceremony. The act formalized the inclusion of the boy in the community. After that, the boy recovered. Zipporah had turned aside the wrath of God.[118]

---

no. 4 (1958): 309–19. The LXX is difficult (*ἔστη τὸ αἷμα τῆς περιτομῆς τοῦ παιδίου μου*; "The blood of my son's circumcision stood"), but it, too, is most likely meant to be understood as ritual language.

118. Bruce Wells, "Exodus," in *Zondervan Illustrated Bible Backgrounds Commentary*, ed. John H. Walton (Grand Rapids: Zondervan, 2009), 1.177–9, proposes an alternative interpretation: YHWH attacks Moses because he is contaminated with the blood-guilt of the murdered Egyptian, but Zipporah circumcises their son and touches Moses's penis with the boy's foreskin, symbolically recircumcising Moses in order to expiate the guilt (Zipporah could not circumcise Moses because he had already been circumcised). This interpretation fails for many reasons, some of them already mentioned. (1) The text does not say that YHWH attacked Moses, who is never mentioned in the story. (2) YHWH evidently had forgiven Moses's past crimes and did not regard him as defiled, since Moses had been allowed to stand before him on "holy ground" at the burning bush; see also 4:19. (3) The text does not imply that Zipporah touched anything with the boy's foreskin; she only touched the boy's—and not Moses's—"feet" while

Which son was it? We do not know, but since there is no birth report for Eliezer during their time in Midian, it is possible that he was born right about the time Moses set out for Egypt.[119] This would explain Moses's desire to get a donkey for the woman and the children. Why was one son not circumcised? Again, we do not know, but if the above conjecture is correct, it may be that they thought it dangerous to circumcise the boy right as they set out on a journey across the wilderness. On the other hand, it may be that the uncircumcised son was Gershom, the firstborn, as some Jewish interpreters have maintained.[120] Why is the boy called "her son" and not "Moses's son"? Probably because Moses plays no role in the story; this is about what Zipporah did.

An important feature of the text, however, is how it is linked to its context. In v. 20, Moses provides for "his sons," while v. 23 speaks of "my son" and "your son," and v. 25 speaks of "her son." Thus, the issue of how parents treat their sons dominates this passage. In addition, as Sarna points out, 4:22–23 is focused on the life and death of the "firstborn," while 4:24–26 indicates that the son must be circumcised in order to live. Similarly, 12:43–49 teaches that one must be circumcised in order to be a member of Israel and eat of the Passover,[121] while 13:1, 11–15 describe the consecration of the Israelite firstborn and death of the Egyptian firstborn.[122] This parallel further suggests that it was the son, not Moses, whose life was in danger. By being circumcised, he is

---

saying, "You are *hatan damim* to me." (4) The whole idea of recircumcision by proxy is bizarre and has no analogy. (5) Circumcision is never said to have expiatory power.

119. An obvious problem is that if Moses entered Midian at age forty, married Zipporah soon thereafter, and returned to Egypt at age eighty, one would expect his sons to be grown by now. There is no simple answer for this; several aspects of Moses's personal life are confusing. But the sons do seem to be small children, and not grown men who would have wives and families of their own. Two pieces of evidence support this. First, Moses's wife and sons can all ride on one donkey in Exod. 4:20. Second, when the sons see Moses in Exod. 18:3–6, they appear to be young. They have no families of their own, and they are trailing behind their mother.

120. Scolnic, "Bloody Bridegroom," 16.

121. For scholarly speculations on the origin and significance of circumcision, see William H. C. Propp, "The Origins of Infant Circumcision in Israel," *Hebrew Annual Review* 11 (1987): 355–70; John Goldingay, "The Significance of Circumcision," *JSOT* 88 (2000): 3–18; Kimberly D. Russaw, "Zipporah and Circumcision as a Form of Preparation: Cutting Away at the Comfort Zone," *JITC* 31, no. 1–2 (2003–4): 103–12.

122. Sarna, *Exodus*, 25.

now counted as part of Israel, the firstborn of God. Prior to the circumcision, the son was counted as the son of Moses, earlier identified by Zipporah as "an Egyptian man" (Exod. 2:19). In the broader context of Exodus, the portrayal of Zipporah turning aside God's wrath from her son is paralleled in Moses's doing the same for all of Israel in Exod. 32:9–14.

Theological Summary of Key Points

1. Moses, in his actions, demonstrates the pattern of the dutiful son and caring father. This indicates the kind of respect Israel ought to have for God and shows how God cares for Israel.

2. The speech that Moses is to give to Pharaoh in YHWH's name (4:22–23) is the theological center of this passage. Israel is God's firstborn son, and God will defend his son. The implication is that God will ultimately defend and vindicate his people against all who attack them.

3. The circumcision of Zipporah's son makes the point that one cannot be considered to be part of Israel, and so to be YHWH's son, unless one is circumcised. For the Israelites, the warning was that they could only escape the great wrath of God directed against Egypt's sons by being sure that their own sons were circumcised. By analogy, one is not one of God's people by mere association.

4. Zipporah, in her actions, demonstrates spiritual insight applied to the protection of her children. Spiritual wisdom and intervention is necessary in order to save one's children from destruction.

5. Christ is the supreme example of the obedient son. He is also the true firstborn of God, and he provided for us the circumcision that removes the defilement of the flesh and allows us to join the people of God (Eph. 2:11–13; Col. 2:11).

FRAGRANCE OF LIFE, STENCH OF DEATH (4:27—5:21)

Moses brings life and hope to Israel, but he provokes hatred and harsh reprisal in Pharaoh. This, in turn, converts the Israelites' initial enthusiasm into bitter resentment.

Translation

4:27a And YHWH said to Aaron,
4:27b "Go to meet Moses in the wilderness."
4:27c And he went,

4:27d and he encountered him at the mountain of God,
4:27e and he kissed him.
4:28 And Moses related to Aaron all the words of YHWH, by which he had commissioned him, and all the signs, with which[123] he had charged him.
4:29a And Moses and Aaron went [to Egypt],
4:29b and they gathered all the elders of the Israelites.
4:30 And Aaron spoke all the words that YHWH had spoken to Moses, and he performed the signs before the eyes of the people.
4:31a And the people believed:
4:31b they heard[124]
4:31c that YHWH had paid attention to the Israelites
4:31d and that he had seen their affliction.[125]
4:31e And they knelt down[126]
4:31f and they worshiped.
5:1a And after that,[127] Moses and Aaron came
5:1b and they said to Pharaoh,
5:1c "Thus says YHWH, the God of Israel,
5:1d 'Release my people
5:1e so that they may celebrate a festival to me in the wilderness!'"
5:2a And Pharaoh said,
5:2b "Who is YHWH, whose voice I am supposed to obey by releasing Israel?

123. A number of versions supply the words "to do" or the like, and take this relative clause to mean, "all the signs that he had commanded him to do." See ESV, NASB, TNIV. But the two relative clauses in this verse closely parallel each other, and it appears that the signs are primarily those that Moses had experienced on the mountain, by which God had compelled him to obey. Secondarily, they are the signs he will do in the future. The translation "with which he had charged him" (NRSV) captures this double meaning nicely.

124. The *wayyiqtol* וַיִּשְׁמְעוּ is epexegetical of וַיַּאֲמֵן, explaining what they believed. The following two *wayyiqtol* clauses, וַיִּקְּדוּ and וַיִּשְׁתַּחֲוּוּ, are dependent on וַיִּשְׁמְעוּ. There are thus three clauses that give exposition to "they believed": they heard, knelt down, and worshiped.

125. "That YHWH had paid attention . . . affliction" is made up of two indirect statements.

126. The verb קדד is often accompanied by the words אַפַּיִם אַרְצָה, "with face to the ground" (e.g., 1 Sam. 24:9). The verb therefore implies falling to one's knees, as one could not do that from a standing bow.

127. וְאַחַר בָּאוּ, instead of the normal *wayyiqtol* pattern, marks a minor episode break.

5:2c I do not know YHWH,
5:2d and as for Israel, I will not grant a release."[128]
5:3a And they said,
5:3b "The God of the Hebrews has met with us.
5:3c We must go[129] a three days' journey into the wilderness
5:3d that we may sacrifice to YHWH our God,
5:3e or he will fall upon us with pestilence or with the sword."
5:4a And the king of Egypt said to them,
5:4b "Why, Moses and Aaron, do you draw the people away from their work?
5:4c Go to your heavy labors!"
5:5a And Pharaoh said,
5:5b "Look, the people of the land[130] are now many,
5:5c and you are keeping[131] them from their heavy labors!"
5:6 And on that day Pharaoh commanded the taskmasters of the people and their liaison officers,[132] saying,
5:7a "No longer give straw to the people to make bricks, as previously.
5:7b They can go[133] and gather[134] straw for themselves.

---

128. Clauses 5:2c–d have a chiastic structure: negated verb + object // וְגַם + object + negated verb. The pharaoh properly presents his rejection of YHWH and his maltreatment of Israel as events that are bound together.

129. This could be translated as "Let us go." But the *yiqtol* with paragogic ה followed by a *yiqtol* clause with פֶּן sets out the necessity of performing an action in order to avoid the consequence of failing to perform it. See Exod. 1:10. The particle נָא does not mean "please," as it is often translated, as it can be used by a superior, or even by God. My own opinion is that נָא is used for more formal speech, which is appropriate here.

130. The use of the phrase עַם הָאָרֶץ ("people of the land") in reference to Israel is surprising. It is often used for the native population of a land. See Gen. 23:7; 42:6; Num. 14:9. The Israelites were of course aliens in Egypt. In this case, however, the expression refers to peasants, as in 2 Kings 24:14.

131. The *weqatal* וְהִשְׁבַּתֶּם of 5:5c, after the nominal clause of 5:5b, is imperfective and progressive.

132. From 5:14, it is clear that the שֹׁטְרֵי are Hebrews who serve as officers of the corvée. They apparently served as liaison officers between the Egyptians and the Hebrews and as foremen over Hebrew work crews. They probably had scribal training; the word שטר is probably related to the Akkadian *šaṭâru*, "to write" (Houtman, *Exodus*, 1.469).

133. A *yiqtol* used as a volitive normally fronts its clause. Thus, "Let them go" is probably not the best rendition. I think the English "They can go" captures the mood of the expression here.

134. The *weqatal* here is, in effect, an auxiliary to the preceding יֵלְכוּ.

5:8a But as for the quota of bricks, you must impose on them what they had been making previously.
5:8b You are not to reduce any of it,
5:8c for they are lazy.
5:8d That is why they cry out,
5:8e 'Let us go and sacrifice to our God.'
5:9a Let the work be heavy on the men,[135]
5:9b so that they may be kept working at it
5:9c and not look hopefully[136] toward false words."
5:10a And the taskmasters of the people and their liaison officers went out,
5:10b and they said to the people,
5:10c "Thus says Pharaoh,
5:10d 'I am not going to give you straw.
5:11a You go get straw for yourselves wherever you can find [it],
5:11b but no item of your labor will be reduced.'"
5:12 And the people scattered through all the land of Egypt to gather stubble for straw.
5:13a The taskmasters were in a great hurry,[137] saying,
5:13b "Complete your daily work assignment on time,[138]
5:13c just as [you did] when you had straw!"
5:14a And the liaison officers of the Israelites, whom Pharaoh's taskmasters had set over them, were beaten to the sound of the words,[139]
5:14b "Why have you not completed your stipulated amount of brick production, as [you did] previously?

---

135. The NASB has, "Let the labor be heavier on the men," suggesting that the Hebrew women should be given lighter labor than the men. This is almost certainly not correct; תִּכְבַּד should not be read as having comparative force. Archaeological evidence indicates that conscripted labor of the sort done by the Hebrews was done exclusively by men. The women probably worked the fields and herds belonging to the Hebrews while their men were away in the corvée.
136. The verb שׁעה means to "gaze" at something and here means to look off toward something as toward a distant hope. See 2 Sam. 22:42, יִשְׁעוּ וְאֵין מֹשִׁיעַ ("they looked hopefully, but there was no savior").
137. Although it is conceivable that אָצִים is here used transitively, as "they made them hurry," the Qal of אוץ is elsewhere intransitive.
138. Lit. "Complete your work, the amount of a day in its day."
139. "To the sound of the words" translates לֵאמֹר, lit. "to say." The word simply indicates that a direct quote follows. Since the Israelite liaison officers obviously did not speak these words but heard them, the translation is appropriate.

5:14c Yesterday's [quota is still required] today!"[140]
5:15a And the liaison officers of the Israelites came
5:15b and they cried out to Pharaoh,
5:15c "Why do you do this to your servants?
5:16a Straw! There is none given to your servants!
5:16b And bricks! They keep saying to us, 'Make [bricks]!'[141]
5:16c And, look here, your servants are beaten!
5:16d And your people are to blame!"
5:17a And he said,
5:17b "Lazy! You are lazy!
5:17c That is why you keep saying,
5:17d 'Let us go!
5:17e Let us sacrifice to YHWH!'
5:18a And now, go!
5:18b Work!
5:18c And straw will not be provided for you,
5:18d But you will provide the full amount of bricks!"
5:19a And the liaison officers of the Israelites could see that they were in trouble from the words,
5:19b "You must not have a shortfall from your daily quota of bricks under any circumstances."[142]
5:20 And they encountered Moses and Aaron standing [outside] to meet them when they came out from [their session] with Pharaoh.
5:21a And they said to [Moses and Aaron],

First Poem: A Bitter Curse

5:21b "May YHWH look upon you and may he judge
יֵרֶא יְהוָה עֲלֵיכֶם וְיִשְׁפֹּט 2-4-4

5:21c You, who have made us a stench
אֲשֶׁר הִבְאַשְׁתֶּם אֶת־רֵיחֵנוּ 1-3-3

5:21d In the eyes of Pharaoh and in the eyes of his servants,
בְּעֵינֵי פַרְעֹה וּבְעֵינֵי עֲבָדָיו 0-2-4

140. Lit. "also yesterday, also today."
141. This is actually one clause (אֹמְרִים לָנוּ) embedded in another clause (וּלְבֵנִים עֲשׂוּ). It cannot be laid out as two separate clauses without destroying the Hebrew structure.
142. Lit. "You will not make reduction from your bricks in the matter of a day in its day." In other words, on any given day, that day's number of bricks must be met no matter what the situation.

5:21e By putting[143] a sword in their hand to kill us."
לָתֶת־חֶרֶב בְּיָדָם לְהָרְגֵנוּ 0-4-4

Structure
This passage gives an account of seven meetings and of the discussions that took place at those meetings.

I. Aaron Meets Moses (4:27–28)
II. Aaron and Moses Meet the Israelites (4:29–31)
III. Aaron and Moses Meet Pharaoh (5:1–5)
IV. Pharaoh Meets the Taskmasters and Hebrew Liaison Officers (5:6–9)
V. The Taskmasters and Hebrew Liaison Officers Meet the Israelites (5:10–14)
VI. The Hebrew Liaison Officers Meet Pharaoh (5:15–19)
VII. The Hebrew Liaison Officers Meet Aaron and Moses (5:20–21)

The first two meetings are positive in nature. First, Aaron joyfully meets Moses and apparently accepts without a murmur of doubt Moses's account of his encounter with God. Second, the Israelites believe in the message and miracles that Moses and Aaron bring to them. The last five meetings are negative. Pharaoh rejects Moses's message, and then he tells the taskmasters, in brutal terms, to force the Hebrews to find straw for themselves. The taskmasters then convey the message and the brutality to the Israelites. The Israelite liaison officers have a blunt but futile meeting with Pharaoh, at which the latter explodes in rage. Finally, as the climax of the text, the Israelite liaison officers pronounce on Moses and Aaron a formal curse which is, as is normal, poetic. The curse, because of its content and its poetic form, serves as a boundary marker for the narrative. It also, with 4:27–28, serves as an inclusio for the whole passage. It begins with joy and optimism for Aaron and Moses (4:27–28) and ends with them under a curse (5:20–21).

Commentary
4:27–28. This passage begins prior to Moses's Sinai experience, with God telling Aaron to go meet Moses at the "mountain of God" (see 4:14, where Aaron is already en route to Moses). The means by which God communicated to Aaron are not disclosed, but the fact that Aaron was

143. The Hebrew infinitive construct with ל often serves the function of the English gerund. This is the case with לָתֶת־חֶרֶב here.

able to receive such a message suggests that he already had some kind of priestly or prophetic function. The scene quickly shifts to the meeting of Aaron and Moses, after the theophany. Aaron's response to Moses's words is not recorded, but subsequent events imply that he accepted Moses's story completely. The detail of Aaron's kiss opens the story on a very positive note, with joy and love. This contrasts with the end of the passage, where Moses and Aaron are put under a curse.

4:29–31. With equal abruptness, the scene shifts to Egypt, where Moses and Aaron tell the story and do the miracles before the Israelite elders. The initial response of faith and worship by the Israelites is passed over quickly, but it is of critical importance. It is hard to imagine how the exodus could have ever happened had the Israelites refused to believe. Notably, they did not ask what God's name was, as far as we can tell (see 3:13). If they had any doubts about Moses, these were allayed when they saw the miracles. Subsequent events would show that the Hebrews were semi-paganized, but they were not thoroughly paganized. They still remembered the God of their fathers. Whatever else the narrative tells us about the Israelites, it tells us that they began the pilgrimage of the exodus in faith.

5:1–5. If the Israelites did not claim ignorance about who was the God of Israel, Pharaoh did (5:2). Pharaoh's question, "Who is YHWH?" does not necessarily mean that he had never heard the name. It is a rejection of the authority of YHWH. The language is dismissive, implying that even if the pharaoh had heard of YHWH, he did not think much of him.

One may wonder why Moses and Aaron only asked for permission to take a brief holiday in order to hold a festival to YHWH, instead of asking outright to be released from slavery. Is it that God had instructed them to request only this (3:18)? Possibly, but the relevant clause in 3:18, "you will say to [Pharaoh]," could be read as a simple prediction and not as a directive. If that is the meaning, God was only saying what they would do, not what they ought to do. This is a forced interpretation, however. Can it be that Moses and Aaron were too intimidated to make a request for an outright release?[144] This is possible, but the text never suggests that YHWH had allowed Moses and Aaron to make the more modest request as a concession to their weakness, or that they made the more modest request because of a lack of nerve.

144. Durham, *Exodus*, 64.

All in all, it seems more likely that the three-day request should be construed from 3:18 to be a directive from YHWH.

This still leaves us wondering why such a request would be made. Stuart argues that a "three-day journey" actually suggests a fairly lengthy trip, and that the purpose, to worship YHWH, is an indirect but transparent way of stating that they in fact would be leaving for good.[145] I do not find this persuasive. A three-day journey for a large body of people would be a fairly modest distance, and the text never suggests, for example, that they wanted to go all the way to Mt. Sinai for their sacrifice. More than that, in 8:25–27 Moses asserts that he simply wants to worship outside of Egypt proper to avoid giving offense to the Egyptians, and Pharaoh indicates that he understands the request to be for a temporary leave of absence in the near vicinity of Egypt, not for permission to leave permanently. If the "three-day trip" petition was in fact a thinly veiled request to be allowed to depart Egypt permanently, Pharaoh clearly did not get it, and Moses did not clarify the nature of the request.

A major theme of the exodus narrative is that Israel was released solely because of the power of God, and not because of any generosity on the Egyptians' part or because of any heroics on the Hebrews' part. The relatively modest request and Pharaoh's peremptory rejection of the same make the point that the Egyptian king was intractably opposed to making any kind of concession to his captive people. Ancient Egypt had an enormous number of religious festivals that served as major public holidays (a text from the time of Ramesses II lists 46 festivals). Each of the three Egyptian seasons (inundation, sowing, and summer), had a whole series of associated holy days. Many of the gods had special days and associated rituals. Some were large public spectacles, in which the god (that is, the image) would be brought out of a temple and taken on a procession; sometimes it would be placed on a special boat and sailed up the Nile to be adored by throngs of ordinary people. Each of the five intercalary days was regarded as the birthday of a god (for Osiris, Horus, Seth, Isis, and Nephthys). The Egyptians understood the importance of allowing people to get off from work, attend sacrifices and festivities, and perform their religious duties. In Egyptian society, many festivals included a ritual known as the "reversion of offerings," in which large amounts of the food offerings to the gods were redistributed to the masses.[146] The holy days of Egyptian gods might be observed with solemnity or with raucous celebration, but they

145. Stuart, *Exodus*, 124–5.
146. Shaw and Nicholson, *Dictionary*, 99

would not be ignored. In addition, an ancient person—and certainly an Egyptian—would normally take very seriously the concern expressed in Exod. 5:3, that a deity had made a demand of his people, and that the deity would be vengeful if the demand were not met. In short, this was a request that, in the context of that culture, would ordinarily at least receive thoughtful consideration and would probably be granted outright after certain details had been negotiated. But Pharaoh only reacted with fury, going so far as to increase the Hebrews' workload. This shows that he was completely and irrationally implacable. This, I think, is the real point of the "three-day" request.

Pharaoh's statement that the "people of the land" are "now many" is not an indication of fear on his part, along the lines of the xenophobic sentiments of 1:9. If this pharaoh shared the anxieties of his predecessor, he would not have spoken of his fears before Moses. He uses the term "people of the land" to mean "peasants" (see translation notes), and he is looking at the situation from an economic perspective. He has a large and very cheap labor pool, but thanks to Moses, this labor pool is somewhat restive. He is irritated by that; he wants to squeeze out of the people all the work he can get.

5:6–9. The pharaoh maliciously added to the Hebrews' workload by ordering that straw not be supplied to them anymore. This does not mean that they were to make bricks without straw, but that they would have to gather the straw themselves, as 5:12 indicates. The straw was not used for firing the brick, which was sun-dried. Straw was added to the mud and clay to act as a binding agent; it helped to prevent shrinkage and cracking. Chaff or animal dung could also be used. The first brick mold (essentially an open wooden frame, like a box with neither top nor bottom but only the four sides) appeared in Egypt around 3400 B.C. A scene from the tomb of the 18th dynasty vizier Rekhmire at Thebes illustrates the brickmaking process. The procedure was as follows: first, mud was broken up with a hoe, and then the binding agent and water was mixed in. This was kneaded with the feet until it had the right consistency, and then it was pressed into the brick mold. Bricks were then pushed out of the mold and arranged in rows in order to be dried by the sun. Since they were formed in molds, they had consistent size and could be easily employed in construction. Kiln-fired bricks did not come into use in Egypt on any large scale until the Roman period.[147] The English word "adobe" comes from the Middle Egyptian word *ḏbt*, "mud brick."

147. David, *Handbook*, 284-6.

The picture of brickmaking in Egypt found here is in complete accord with what we know from Egyptian records. K. A. Kitchen has assembled extant Egyptian texts related to the subject, and he points out that the details described in Exodus, including the government management of brickmaking, the assigning of quotas to individual work groups, the keeping of meticulous records of production, and the need for a source of straw are all reflected in the Egyptian records. And just as in the Bible, where work crews are under two layers of administration (in Exodus, it is the Egyptian taskmasters and, under them, the Hebrew liaison officers), so also in the Egyptian records one finds a two-tier system of oversight. Egyptian records also make the point that workmen were given days off to perform religious duties, making it clear that Pharaoh's refusal to give in to the request of Moses was unreasonable.[148]

Pharaoh's act of refusing to provide straw was apparently meant as a punishment for their having had the impudence to ask for a few days' off. More than that, he thought that if he worked them incessantly, they would not have time even to dream of escape. His policy was meant to break their spirits. He recognized that the faith they were putting in Moses and in their God gave them hope. These ideas, which he called "lies," were a threat to his authority over them. He wanted them to sink into despair.

5:10–14. The orders of Pharaoh worked their way down the bureaucratic chain from the Egyptian officials to the Hebrew liaison officers and finally to the Hebrew work crews. The people fanned out across the Delta looking for straw, but obviously they could not find it and transport it back, and then still have time to make as many bricks as they had before. The Egyptian officers may have been by nature brutal men, but even if they were not, they would themselves face Pharaoh's wrath if the quotas were not met. Thus, they rushed about demanding that the people work faster. They would also, in turn, hold the Hebrew liaison officers directly responsible if the people did not produce enough brick. The liaison officers were truly caught in the middle. If they tried to force their people to work faster, they would be met with bitter reproaches from working-class men who were doing all they could. When they tried to explain the situation to their Egyptian superiors, they were beaten. The beatings would of course be painful, but because the Hebrew liaison officers were of a scribal class, such treatment was a great affront

148. Kenneth A. Kitchen,"From the Brickfields of Egypt," *TynBul* 27 (1976): 137–47.

to their dignity. Unable to mollify their immediate superiors, they could only go over their heads and appeal directly to Pharaoh.

5:15–19. The Hebrews' complaint in v. 16 is quite direct, but it also contains unusual word structure, such as one would hear from men who were distraught and exasperated (the translation above seeks to reproduce this). The pharaoh responded in kind, repeating that the Hebrews are "lazy," and using the terse language one would expect from someone who was shouting. But this was a shouting match that the Hebrew officers could not possibly win. More than that, Pharaoh made it plain to them that their request to go sacrifice to their God was at the root of all their troubles. The implication, which he communicated to them very well, was that Moses and Aaron had brought all this trouble upon the people, and that things were just fine before these two men showed up. Furthermore, Pharaoh's callous policy of not delivering straw but demanding the same quota of bricks made the Hebrew officers realize that their situation was impossible: they could not meet the quota under any circumstances, and they saw nothing ahead for themselves but more beatings (v. 19).

5:20–21. Moses and Aaron knew about the deputation to Pharaoh, and they waited outside in order to find out how it went. They caught the full fury of the liaison officers, whose emotions had been cleverly managed by Pharaoh in order to drive a wedge between them and the men who had given them hope. The Hebrew officers knew that there were many in Egypt who hated them and who were looking for the right excuse to destroy them. They believed that Moses and Aaron had provided just such an excuse—the "sword" that they had put into their enemies' hands. Their fear and frustration was understandable but wrong. Moses and Aaron were not the cause of their troubles, and they had done nothing that could have justified the pharaoh's response. But the officers voiced their anger toward Moses and Aaron in the most forceful way possible, by uttering a formal curse, an appeal for divine judgment against the two brothers in the form of a poetic imprecation. This was extremely powerful language. As the following text (5:22–23) illustrates, it left Moses badly shaken.

Theological Summary of Key Points

1. There are two fundamental responses to the message and messengers of God. The one is to believe, serve, and worship, as illustrated by the response of Aaron and then the initial response of the Hebrews. The other is to disbelieve and hate not only the message but the messenger, and to strike out against it. This is the response of Pharaoh. Like Paul, Moses was the fragrance of life to some and the stench of death to others.

2. Many people, distraught and intimidated by the fury that they see the word of God provokes, tend to join in the fury or to blame the messengers. We see this on the one hand from the Egyptian overseers, who frantically drove on the Hebrews, and we see it also among the Hebrew leaders, whose hopes were dashed and who turned against Moses. This is analogous to what we see today in the contemporary persecution of the church by Muslims in the Islamic world. Many ordinary Muslims may themselves be disinclined to participate in persecution but, whether actively or passively, out of conviction or out of fear, they feel they must go along with it. But many Christians, too, are angry whenever a Christian leader does something to "provoke" the Muslims, such as denying that the Koran is the word of God. A similar analogy could be drawn with the response of ordinary Germans prior to the holocaust. Many did not share in the Nazis' maniacal hatred of the Jews, but they went along with the persecution rather than oppose the power of the state. Similarly, there were Jews in the early years of the Third Reich who thought they could avoid trouble by not giving offense. Sooner or later, however, both the Egyptian overseers and the Hebrew officers had to decide whether they were with Moses or with Pharaoh. In short, someone who speaks the truth cannot be blamed when evil people respond to the truth with violence.

3. The Israelites began the exodus experience in faith. In Christian sermons, we commonly dwell upon the failings of the Israelites in the narrative, pointing out their lack of faith as illustrated by their anger at Moses in 5:21, or at the *Yam Suph*, or when short of water. But we should recognize that they began in faith and worship. This should make us a little less harsh toward the Israelites and a little more fearful for ourselves. Paul points out that the Israelites were all "baptized" into Moses and yet fell into disobedience, and he stresses that this is a warning and example for us (1 Cor. 10:1–12).

I AM YHWH (5:22—6:8)

God reassures Moses with an oracular poem on YHWH's identity and purpose. This oracle compares what YHWH did in the past to what he is about to do, making the point that YHWH is consistent and faithful. This poetic nature of the divine oracle in this text has not been recognized, and the standard translation is quite confusing, as it indicates that the patriarchs did not know the name YHWH at all. As such, it is a linchpin for the documentary hypothesis, as it is taken to be a P text that makes the claim that the divine name YHWH was not revealed until the time of the exodus. By contrast, J, which routinely uses YHWH in the patriarchal period, believed that the name was revealed much earlier, during the antediluvian era (Gen. 4:26). The following exposition seeks to do the following:

1. To demonstrate that the divine oracle is a poem and that its poetic features, particularly its parallelism, must be taken into account in its translation and interpretation;
2. To show the text does not support the documentary hypothesis;
3. To describe the function of the oracle in context.

Translation

5:22a And Moses returned to YHWH
5:22b and he said,
5:22c "Lord, why have you done harm to this people?
5:22d Why did you send me here?
5:23a From the time that I came to Pharaoh to speak in your name,
5:23b he has done harm to this people,
5:23c and you have certainly not delivered your people."
6:1a And YHWH said to Moses,
6:1b "Now you will see what I will do to Pharaoh;
6:1c by a strong hand he will release them,
6:1d and by a strong hand he will expel them from his land."
6:2a And God spoke to Moses,
6:2b and he said,

Second Poem: I am YHWH

Refrain

6:2c I am YHWH.
אֲנִי יְהוָה 0-2-2

Stanza 1.1

6:3a And I appeared to Abraham, to Isaac, and to Jacob.
וָאֵרָא אֶל־אַבְרָהָם אֶל־יִצְחָק וְאֶל־יַעֲקֹב 1-4-4[149]

149. Although 6:3ab is a single clause, it has too many units to be a single line.

6:3b	As El Shaddai. בְּאֵ֣ל שַׁדָּ֑י	0-1-2
6:3c	But my name is YHWH.[150] וּשְׁמִ֣י יְהוָ֔ה	0-2-2
6:3d	Did I not make myself known to them?[151] לֹ֥א נוֹדַ֖עְתִּי לָהֶֽם	1-2-2

150. Lines 6:3cd are routinely translated as "But by my name YHWH I did not make myself known to them." Several arguments may be advanced against this rendition. First, this is a poetic strophe and, as translated above, it demonstrates the A-B-B-A parallelism that Hebrew poetry often employs. The standard translation ("But by my name") has no such parallelism. Second, וּשְׁמִ֣י יְהוָ֔ה does not mean, "*by* my name YHWH." It means, "And my name is YHWH." One might argue that the preposition בְּ on בְּאֵ֣ל is doing double-duty, but (1) בְּאֵ֣ל שַׁדָּ֑י ("as El Shaddai") is not truly parallel to the supposed counterpart phrase ושמי יהוה, "and by my name YHWH." A true parallel would be וביהוה, "but as YHWH." A word used for double-duty should have parallel functions in both phrases. (2) One would normally expect to see a double-duty preposition governing two nouns in the same clause rather than nouns in two separate clauses; it is especially odd to have a double-duty preposition first in a positive clause and then in a negated clause. (3) This poem does not elsewhere use double-duty prepositions; see 6:3a; 6:6e-f; 6:8d. Third, it is not unreasonable to take line 6:3d as a rhetorical question instead of as a negative statement. The interrogative particle ה is not necessary, particularly since context, in line 6:3a, makes it plain that God did reveal himself to the patriarchs. Fourth, if the text had meant to say that God did not reveal the name "YHWH" to the patriarchs, a clear and unambiguous way of doing so would be ולא הודעתי שמי יהוה, "But I did not make known my name YHWH to them."

151. W. Randall Garr, "The Grammar and Interpretation of Exodus 6:3," *JBL* 111, no. 3 (1992): 385, argues for the translation, "I, my name YHWH, was not known to them." As is common, he considers this a P text, and he believes that for P, El Shaddai "is the postdiluvian manifestation of God, whose activity is restricted to the patriarchal period" (p. 400). His argument is that 6:3cd is a "possessor=subject" construction in which וּשְׁמִ֣י יְהוָ֔ה is a second-level designation, while the principal grammatical topic is the "possessor," that is, God (the "I" of נוֹדַ֖עְתִּי). Garr produces a number of texts that he considers to be analogies. An example (p. 393) is Ps. 44:3(2), אַתָּה יָדְךָ גּוֹיִם הוֹרַשְׁתָּ ("You [by] your hand dispossessed nations"). Here, as

Stanza 1.2

6:4a And also I set up my covenant with them,
וְגַ֨ם הֲקִמֹ֤תִי אֶת־בְּרִיתִי֙ אִתָּ֔ם 1-3-4

6:4b To give to them the land of Canaan,
לָתֵ֥ת לָהֶ֖ם אֶת־אֶ֣רֶץ כְּנָ֑עַן 0-3-4

6:4c The land of their sojourning,
אֵ֛ת אֶ֥רֶץ מְגֻרֵיהֶ֖ם[152] 0-1-2

6:4d In which they sojourned.
אֲשֶׁר־גָּ֥רוּ בָֽהּ 1-2-3

Stanza 1.3

6:5a And also I heard the groaning of the Israelites,
וְגַ֣ם ׀ אֲנִ֣י שָׁמַ֗עְתִּי אֶֽת־נַאֲקַת֙ בְּנֵ֣י יִשְׂרָאֵ֔ל 1-4-5

6:5b Whom the Egyptians were enslaving,
אֲשֶׁ֥ר מִצְרַ֖יִם מַעֲבִדִ֣ים אֹתָ֑ם 1-3-4

---

is common in the Psalter, an instrumental preposition is omitted, but this is not truly parallel to Exod. 6:3, nor does it make the case for the elaborate "possessor=subject" construction theory Garr is propounding. Most significantly, none of Garr's examples is negated, as is the case with Exod. 6:3. Apart from the fact that his whole argument is undermined by this deficiency, his interpretation also leads to unintended consequences. Garr states, "'Yahweh' is identical with the subject (= possessor) of Exod 6:3c. In the whole-part relationship of the verse, 'Yahweh' (= 'I'/'my') is the whole. His 'name' itself, as an undefined representational entity, is the part. Thus for Exod 6:3c, the name 'Yahweh' represents the whole God" (397). But following this interpretation, Exod. 6:3cd can only mean that the patriarchs did not know God at all! This could hardly be the perspective of Exodus, which predicates all of YHWH's actions on his oaths to the fathers (e.g., 2:24). On p. 407, Garr tries to claw back the implications of his own analysis by inserting the word "fully" ("But I, my name Yahweh, was not [fully] known to them"). This has no legitimacy. To use his own analogy, if Ps. 44:3 said, אַתָּה יָדְךָ גּוֹיִם לֹא הוֹרַשְׁתָּ, it could only mean that YHWH did not dispossess nations at all. It could not mean that he did not fully dispossess them, nor could it mean that although he dispossessed them, he did not use his hand.

152. The *tifha* sometimes comes at a line break. From the standpoint of the constituents, 6:4c–d could be read as a single line, but the content is parallel ("The land of their sojourning / in which they sojourned") suggesting that it is two lines.

6:5c And I remembered my covenant.
וָֽאֶזְכֹּ֖ר אֶת־בְּרִיתִֽי 1-2-2

6:6a Therefore, say to the Israelites:
לָכֵ֞ן אֱמֹ֣ר לִבְנֵֽי־יִשְׂרָאֵ֘ל[153] 1-3-4

Refrain

6:6b I am YHWH.
אֲנִ֣י יְהוָ֒ה[154] 0-2-2

Stanza 2.1

6:6c And I will bring you out from under the heavy labor of the Egyptians,
וְהוֹצֵאתִ֣י אֶתְכֶ֗ם מִתַּ֙חַת֙ סִבְלֹ֣ת מִצְרַ֔יִם 1-3-5

6:6d And I will deliver you from their service
וְהִצַּלְתִּ֥י אֶתְכֶ֖ם מֵעֲבֹדָתָ֑ם 1-3-3

6:6e And I will redeem you with an outstretched arm,
וְגָאַלְתִּ֤י אֶתְכֶם֙ בִּזְר֣וֹעַ נְטוּיָ֔ה 1-3-4

6:6f And with great judgments.
וּבִשְׁפָטִ֖ים גְּדֹלִֽים 0-1-2

Stanza 2.2

6:7a And I will take you as my people
וְלָקַחְתִּ֨י אֶתְכֶ֥ם לִי֙ לְעָ֔ם 1-4-4

6:7b And I will be your God.
וְהָיִ֥יתִי לָכֶ֖ם לֵאלֹהִ֑ים 1-3-3

6:7c And you will know that I am YHWH your God,
וִֽידַעְתֶּ֗ם כִּ֣י אֲנִ֤י יְהוָה֙ אֱלֹ֣הֵיכֶ֔ם 1-3-4

---

153. Although *pashta* is not one of the stronger disjunctives, it does occasionally mark a line break. If there were no break here, the combined line would have too many constituents. Also, 6:6b begins the long, direct speech of YHWH and so ought to be preceded by a break.

154. If there were no line break here, the combined 6:6b-c would have too many units and constituents. Thus the *segolta* in יְהוָ֒ה marks a break.

6:7d Who brings you out from under the heavy labor of the Egyptians.
הַמּוֹצִ֣יא אֶתְכֶ֔ם מִתַּ֖חַת סִבְל֥וֹת מִצְרָֽיִם 0-3-5

Stanza 2.3

6:8a And I will bring you to the land
וְהֵבֵאתִ֤י אֶתְכֶם֙ אֶל־הָאָ֔רֶץ 1-3-3

6:8b That I lifted my hand [in an oath]
אֲשֶׁ֤ר נָשָׂ֙אתִי֙ אֶת־יָדִ֔י 1-3-3

6:8c To give to Abraham, to Isaac, and to Jacob,
לָתֵ֣ת אֹתָ֔הּ[155] לְאַבְרָהָ֥ם לְיִצְחָ֖ק וּֽלְיַעֲקֹ֑ב[156] 0-3-5

6:8d And I will give it to you as a possession.
וְנָתַתִּ֨י אֹתָ֥הּ לָכֶ֛ם מוֹרָשָׁ֖ה[157] 1-4-4

Refrain

6:8e I am YHWH.
אֲנִ֥י יְהוָֽה 0-2-2

Structure

The previous text consisted of a series of meetings among various men, ending with a poetic curse and imprecation against Moses and Aaron as delivered by afflicted Hebrews. This text begins with a meeting between YHWH and Moses and concludes with a poetic oracle, a promise from YHWH that he will vindicate Moses and save the Hebrews from their afflictions. Its structure is as follows:

I. Moses's Complaint (5:22–23)
II. YHWH's Reassurance (6:1–8)
  A. Prose Reassurance (6:1)
  B. Oracle: Poetic Reassurance (6:2–8)

---

155. Although לְאַבְרָהָ֥ם לְיִצְחָ֖ק וּֽלְיַעֲקֹ֑ב could be read as three constituents, the fact that the three are indicating the patriarchs as a single group and that formally all three are the same justifies reading it as one constituent.

156. This *zaqeph qaton* has no subordinate disjunctive within its domain, and therefore is probably not marking a line break.

157. The *tifha* here marks a line break. If there were no break between 6:8d and 6:8e, the combined line would have too many units. Also, the *tifha* has a subordinate disjunctive (*tevir*) within its domain.

The oracle is a poem of two stanzas, and it contains a number of recurring patterns. In the above presentation of the poem, the strophes are numbered by stanza and strophe, so that 1.1 refers to the first stanza and first strophe. The first stanza has three strophes, each a quatrain (four lines). The second stanza also has three quatrains. At the beginning of the poem, between the two stanzas, and at the end of the poem, there appears a refrain that is a monocolon (a one-line strophe) having only the two words אֲנִי יְהוָה ("I am YHWH"). This short clause also begins the poem at 6:2c and ends it at 6:8e, placing the entire text in an inclusio; "I am YHWH" dominates the poem. Another inclusive element is that both 6:3a, at the beginning of the poem, and 6:8c, at its end, refer to Abraham, Isaac, and Jacob.

Numerous structural parallels give balance to this poem.

- The first stanza is historical, explaining why God would save the Israelites, and the second stanza is predictive, indicating what God is about to do. Also, the first stanza is first person narrative, while the second stanza is a quotation—the speech that Moses is to give to the Israelites.

- In the first stanza, the second and third quatrain (strophes 1.2 and 1.3) both begin with וְגַם, "and also," but the first quatrain (strophe one) is different. In the second stanza, all three strophes (2.1, 2.2, and 2.3) begin with the *weqatal* lines.

- In both stanzas, the second line of the third quatrain begins with אֲשֶׁר, the relative pronoun.

- In describing the land, the first stanza speaks of it as "The land of their sojourning, / In which they sojourned," employing a redundancy with the root גור ("sojourn"; lines 6:4cd). The second stanza similarly speaks of the land in two lines with "To give to Abraham, to Isaac, and to Jacob, / And I will give it to you as a possession," repeating the root נתן ("give"; lines 6:8cd).[158]

Commentary

5:22–23. What immediately strikes the reader about Moses's

158. One can thus see elements of chiasmus in the poem. See the analysis in Jonathan Magonet, "The Rhetoric of God: Exodus 6.2–8," *JSOT* 27 (1983): 56–67, and Pierre Auffret, "The Literary Structure of Exodus 6.2–8," *JSOT* 27 (1983): 46–54.

complaint to God is that he is as vehement with God as the Hebrew liaison officers had been with him. The way things have turned out, including the curse that was laid upon him, has obviously unsettled Moses badly. He also implies that the charges laid against him have been deserved; his act of approaching Pharaoh has only made things much worse for the Israelites. What is worse, God seems to be doing nothing.

6:1. YHWH does not rebuke Moses for his lack of faith. Instead he assures him that things are just as they should be. "Now" in clause 6:1b implies that things have taken their proper course. God's intention has always been to display his power by saving his people from an Egypt that stood against him; there was never any intent to depart Egypt by virtue of Pharaoh's generosity. God will save the people "by a strong hand" (בְּיָד חֲזָקָה). In the Hebrew Bible, this expression is almost always formulaic for the miraculous deeds by which YHWH brought his people out of Egypt (an exception is the usage in Num. 20:20). Here in Exod. 6:1, however, the phrase occurs in an ambiguous context. Normally, one would take "and by a strong hand he will expel them from his land" to mean that the subject of the verb, "Pharaoh," would use all the power at his disposal to get the Hebrews out of Egypt. The ambiguity may be deliberate; because God would use his mighty hand against Egypt, in its turn Egypt would eventually use its power to be free of the Hebrews rather than to hold on to them, as illustrated by how the Egyptians enriched the Hebrews in order to hurry them out of the country. Even so, the primary meaning is that Egypt would only release Israel because it was forced to do so by God's mighty hand.

6:2c–8. As described in the translation notes, 6:3cd are generally translated, "But by my name YHWH I did not make myself known to them." This is a cornerstone of the documentary hypothesis; it is regarded as a P text, and it is understood to mean that P believed that the name YHWH was not revealed until the time of the exodus. Thus, advocates of the documentary hypothesis believe that the preference for using אלהים (God) over יהוה (YHWH) as a term for the deity is a key indicator of P in Genesis and Exod. 1–5. This view, I think, is entirely based on a mistranslation of the text (see translation and translation notes above).

In the oracular poem, God emphatically identifies himself as YHWH, the covenant God of Israel. He declares: 1) that he revealed himself to the fathers, 2) that he made a covenant, promising to give Canaan to their descendants, and 3) that he has heard and cares about their current troubles (first stanza; 6:2c–6:6a). Having given the background to his actions in the three quatrains of stanza 1, he tells what he is about to do in stanza 2. In the three quatrains of stanza 2, he says that he will: 1) deliver the people from their current slavery, 2) become their God, and 3) give them the land of Canaan.

The meaning of Shaddai (שַׁדָּי) is much debated. Propp catalogues the astounding array of suggested etymologies and interpretations attached to the name. These include "the pourer," "the hurler," "the violent," "the mountain," "the mountain-dweller," "the mountain wind, east wind, easterner," "the breast-fed," "the breasted," "the tent-dweller," "the savior," "the field-dweller," and "the spirit." But Propp is probably correct that the most convincing interpretation is that Shaddai is the "mighty one" or the "almighty," following the Arabic root *šdd*. This is in agreement with the traditional translation "Almighty," which is based on the Greek translation *παντοκράτωρ* and the Syriac *ḥsynʾ*.[159] One could argue for the meaning "breasted" on the basis of Gen. 49:25, where the blessings of Shaddai (שַׁדַּי) are described as including the blessings of the breasts (שָׁדַיִם). This would suggest that Shaddai was associated with abundance and fertility, like the Egyptian god of inundation, Haapy, who is routinely depicted with large breasts. But it is more likely that the connection between שַׁדַּי and שָׁדַיִם in Gen. 49:25 is wordplay; it is neither an etymology nor a description of the theological significance of the name.

In Genesis, God twice names himself Shaddai to the patriarchs (17:1; 35:11). Four times a patriarch gives a blessing using the name Shaddai (28:3 [the speaker is Isaac]; 43:14; 48:3; 49:25 [in each case the speaker is Jacob]). These are the only occurrences of Shaddai in Genesis; the narrator never uses the word except in reported speech. In every case in Genesis, the name is associated with God's care for and blessing of the patriarchs. This is not incompatible with the idea that Shaddai essentially connotes "power," and it does not imply that the "breasted" interpretation of Shaddai is correct. Elsewhere in the Bible, Shaddai can use his power for much darker purposes. Isa. 13:6 and Joel 1:15 speak of "destruction" (שֹׁד) coming from Shaddai (שַׁדַּי). This is obviously more wordplay, but it makes the point that Shaddai is not exclusively associated with abundance or fertility. In Ezek. 1:24, similarly, the sound of Shaddai is "like the sound of an army," and Ps. 68:15(14) speaks of Shaddai scattering kings. In Job, Shaddai is almost the standard word for "God" in the dialogues, appearing 31 times and with all kinds of connotations. In Job 6:4, the hero endures the "arrows" of Shaddai. In Job 8:5, he is advised to "plead with Shaddai

159. Propp, *Exodus 19–40*, 760–1.

for mercy." In 21:15, a distraught Job asks, "What is Shaddai, that we should serve him?"

It seems clear that the Israelites regarded Shaddai as an archaic name that essentially connoted power. As such, it was not surprising that the men of old, such as the patriarchs or the characters of the Job speeches, would employ it in blessings or in debates over divine justice. Israelites could still use the name in the later period, as in Joel or Ezekiel, but when they did it was for poetic effect and it would not have been regarded as a current or common designation for God.

The repetition of "I am YHWH" in Exod. 6 is certainly not meant to be a revelation of a name that no one had ever heard of before. It is not even, as some suggest, filling out the name YHWH with new meaning and content. The main point is not novelty but continuity. He made promises to Abraham, Isaac, and Jacob regarding their offspring and the land of Canaan, and now he is fulfilling those promises. Furthermore, just as he was the fathers' God, and in covenant with them, now he is the God of all of Israel, entering into covenant with them (6:7, anticipating Exod. 19–24). In fact, one could hardly more badly misread the text than to claim that Exod. 6 is the revelation of something new. It is the completion of something very old. It was no new God that was going to save Israel from Egypt; it was the God the fathers had known. If he had come in a different name, he would have been a different god, or he would have been the kind of pagan god that the Egyptians knew so well, one that could easily merge identities and traits with another god. But such a god would not have been the "I AM" of Exodus.

There is one element of the oracle poem that is somewhat new. In keeping with Exod. 3:15, the poem reinforces the demand that henceforth the standard name for the God of Israel is YHWH. That is, Israelites are to routinely use YHWH when referring to their God. This does not mean that the use of any other name from that time forward was absolutely forbidden, and it does not mean that they had never heard of YHWH before. But God would not be described under a chaotic multitude of names. This is different from Egypt, where different gods might be thought of at times as separate beings and at times as merged. Thus Bastet (a protective, domestic cat), might or might not be thought of as a variant of Sekhmet, a ferocious lioness. And indeed, Sekhmet could be thought of as the alter-ego of Hathor, the cow-goddess of fertility. Re was the ancient sun god, but he could be thought of as merged into Horus, son of Osiris and Isis, as the eye of Horus or as Horus, the sun on the horizon. True devotion to one God, in fact, would be difficult for Israel to achieve if Israel's God went by numerous names. Thus, while understanding that the occasional use of Shaddai or some other name was not forbidden, the regular name they were to use for God was YHWH. For that reason, when the narrator speaks in Job (as opposed to the reported speeches of the ancient protagonist and his opponents), God is routinely called YHWH (Job 1:6, 7, 8, 9; 2:1, 2, 3; 38:1, etc.). For this reason also, we should note, it is entirely wrong to think that a "P" or "E" would avoid using YHWH in the Genesis narrative; they would have thought it their duty to use YHWH to make the point that YHWH was the God who led the patriarchs, even if they thought that the patriarchs themselves did not know the name.

The whole oracle of Exod. 6 is predicated on the proposition that he will be the same God to Israel that he was to the patriarchs—that he remains YHWH. Beyond that, we should note that the whole purpose of this oracle is to vindicate Moses, to reassure him, and to reassure the nation. In contrast to the poetic imprecation laid upon Moses in YHWH's name, YHWH himself vindicates Moses. But in terms of actual content, there is nothing at all here that is new. In fact, the oracle does little more than repeat what YHWH had already told Moses on Mt. Sinai (see 3:6–10, 12, 15–22). And this is the whole point; Moses did not need some new information about God, he needed reassurance. The reassurance was a repetition of the words of faith he had already heard. Moses was fairly skeptical after his interview at the bush in Exod. 3–4. One might hope that he was now ready to accept the message, but this was not yet the case.

Theological Summary of Key Points

1. In times of great discouragement, the servant of God needs a word from God. The oracle of God came to Moses at the very blackest time, when the people of Israel and Moses himself were all but in despair. The long expected victory of God comes when all seems lost, and no one can save the situation but God himself.

2. The word of encouragement need not be new information; in fact, it seldom is. The reading of a familiar text of Scripture or the recitation of the words of a psalm can each reassure the believer about the promises of God. For this reason also churches will repeat the same gospel message week after week. A congregation may recite the Apostles' Creed or Nicene Creed every Sunday, or they may say the Lord's Prayer in unison. The same words are spoken over the Eucharist again and again, and the same biblical texts are recited seasonally, at Christmas or at Easter. This is not done because people can't find something new to say. In hearing the message repeated, faith is made stronger, and fortitude and perseverance are deepened. The poetic form of YHWH's oracle in Exod. 6, moreover, is appropriate for a message that would be recited many times over.

3. Our hope in God depends upon the belief that he is consistent and faithful, the "same yesterday and today and forever" (Heb. 13:8). The YHWH who made promises to the fathers was the same YHWH who encountered their children in Egypt. The God we worship is the same one who made promises to the patriarchs, brought about the exodus, gave the Decalogue, and raised Christ from the dead. Our whole faith is based on joining ourselves to that God, to that story, and to those people. And we also depend upon the consistency of God. The God who raised Christ from the grave will not abandon us to corruption. Even on a personal level, the God who has guided us and helped us individually in the past can be counted on to do it in the future.

4. Theological clarity is often achieved by very simple means. Israel was told that YHWH was the same God whom the patriarchs knew and whom they had sometimes called Shaddai. Furthermore, Israel was informed that YHWH is the name by which they should routinely call upon their God. They thus understood that there was continuity from the past to the present and that there was but one God. Keeping these basic but important facts straight was made much easier by making it a matter of standard practice to call their God YHWH. "YHWH is our God, YHWH is one" (Deut. 6:4) encapsulates this truth. It is very simple, and it is the first catechism.

UNBELIEF (6:9–13)

Moses is at the nadir of his experience, in which he no longer believes in his mission. Only the persistent command of God keeps him in his task. Were it not for that persistence of God, the whole task would have failed before it really had gotten started.

Translation

6:9a And Moses gave this message to the Israelites,

6:9b but they did not listen to Moses because [they were a people] of small spirit[160] and because of the harsh slavery.

160. The phrase מִקֹּצֶר רוּחַ is lit. "from shortness of spirit." It is often taken to mean "because of discouragement," and no doubt some discouragement is implied. However, the idiom does not exclusively mean that. A cognate

6:10 And YHWH spoke to Moses, as follows:
6:11a "Go!
6:11b Tell Pharaoh, king of Egypt,
6:11c that he should release the Israelites from his land!"
6:12a And Moses spoke before YHWH, as follows:
6:12b "Now look, the Israelites don't listen to me!
6:12c So how is it that Pharaoh will listen to me?
6:12d And my articulation is disgusting!"[161]
6:13a And YHWH spoke to Moses and to Aaron,
6:13b and he commanded them [to take the message] to the Israelites and to Pharaoh,[162] king of Egypt, that he would remove the Israelites from the land of Egypt.

---

pattern using the verb appears in Job 21:4, where it implies impatience: וְאִם־מַדּוּעַ לֹא־תִקְצַר רוּחִי ("And so why should I not be impatient?"). In Mic. 2:7 a "short spirit" is a flaw that cannot be attributed to YHWH. In Prov. 14:29 having this condition is contrasted with being slow to anger. The literal meaning, "short spirit," should not be washed out in translation. The expression implies not just a condition imposed on a person from without, but an internal character weakness. In other words, it is the opposite of what English implies when one says that a person has a "great spirit" or a "great soul." It is a smallness of soul that cannot endure setbacks, but falls either into despair or angry impatience.

161. The phrase וַאֲנִי עֲרַל שְׂפָתָיִם is lit. "and I am uncircumcised of lips." This relates again to the matter of Moses's speaking ability and to the question of whether he had a speech defect or simply lacked eloquence. See the commentary for 4:10–12. It appears that he actually had a speech defect but, regardless, the expression he uses here is very strong. It is first of all somewhat vulgar, in that "uncircumcised" alludes to the male genitals. But more than that, it needs to be understood against Israelite culture, in which the condition of being uncircumcised was regarded as vile and savage. Thus, David, a man who was no stranger to coarse speech, routinely derided the Philistines as "uncircumcised" (1 Sam. 17:26; 2 Sam. 1:20), implying that they were thereby shown to be barbarians. A sinful and depraved heart was likewise "uncircumcised" (Jer. 9:26). Moses's language implies that he thought his articulation was truly horrible and he was deeply embarrassed about it.

162. The clause וַיְצַוֵּם אֶל־בְּנֵי יִשְׂרָאֵל וְאֶל־פַּרְעֹה is lit. "and he commanded them to the sons of Israel and to Pharaoh." This probably means to command someone to take a message to someone else, as in Exod. 25:22, אֵת כָּל־אֲשֶׁר אֲצַוֶּה אוֹתְךָ אֶל־בְּנֵי יִשְׂרָאֵל ("all that I will command you [to relay] to the Israelites"). See also Esth. 4:10, וַתֹּאמֶר אֶסְתֵּר לַהֲתָךְ וַתְּצַוֵּהוּ אֶל־מָרְדֳּכָי ("and Esther spoke to Hathach and she commanded him [to carry the message] to Mordecai").

Structure

This text is perhaps the low point of Exodus. There will be other terrible moments in the story, such as the Golden Calf episode, but at this point Moses himself, having encountered God at Sinai and then having gotten a second word from God in the form of the preceding oracle, very nearly falls into outright rebellion. He and the Israelites together are people "of small spirit." They turn a deaf ear toward God's message of hope and reassurance. The structure of the text is as follows.

I. The Response to the Oracle (6:9–12)
  A. Israel Does Not Believe (6:9)
  B. Moses Does Not Believe (6:10–12)
II. YHWH's Command (6:13)

Commentary

6:9. The unbelief of the Israelites is attributed to two factors: their "small spirit" (see translation notes) and the intensity of their suffering under slavery. This indicates that their unbelief came about because of both internal and external factors. Their small spirit (weakness of character, impatience, lack of courage, and so forth) can be compared to what Luke says about the Bereans and, by comparison, about the Thessalonicans: "They had more nobility than those in Thessalonica" (Acts 17:11). The Israelites did not have noble spirits. But they were also under intense suffering. These two factors remind us that our failings and sins are often brought about by two causes, our own weak characters and the corrupting effect of the evil that is done to us.

6:10–12. The unbelief of Moses is set up as a contrast to the word of God by the use of parallel structure. YHWH's message to Moses is introduced with "And YHWH spoke to Moses, as follows" (וַיְדַבֵּר יְהוָה אֶל־מֹשֶׁה לֵּאמֹר), and this is followed by three clauses. Moses's response is introduced with "And Moses spoke before YHWH, as follows" (וַיְדַבֵּר מֹשֶׁה לִפְנֵי יְהוָה לֵאמֹר), and three clauses follow. It is as though the two were having a head-to-head confrontation. Two other factors are worthy of note. First, only Moses is addressed here, and only he is charged with unbelief. We generally think of Aaron as a much weaker character than Moses (primarily because of his role in the Golden Calf episode), but he escapes all censure in this part of the narrative. Second, because YHWH has given Moses such a strong oracle of assurance, he is now ready to commission Moses to go to Pharaoh and demand outright release for Israel (with no more talk about a three-day trip to a festival). Moses rejects this command immediately, making two arguments: (1) if even the Israelites don't believe me, it is certain that Pharaoh won't, and (2) my speaking is so incredibly bad that I am mortified to go back into Pharaoh's presence and make any kind of demand.

Moses's unbelief also tells us two things about the nature of faithlessness. First, it comes about because one forgets that one is supposed to have faith in God and not in oneself. Moses was not supposed to persuade Pharaoh to let the people go, so the fact that Pharaoh would not be persuaded is irrelevant. Moses was simply to announce what God commanded Pharaoh to do and allow God to enforce the command. Second, faithlessness often comes about from giving undue attention to one's own weakness, unworthiness, and inability. Moses was too concerned about how he would look, making an announcement for God with his horrible speech. But apparently his speaking ability was good enough for God.

6:13. Once again, YHWH's direct speech is introduced with very formal language: וַיְדַבֵּר יְהוָה אֶל־מֹשֶׁה וְאֶל־אַהֲרֹן ("And YHWH spoke to Moses and Aaron"). The language may convey iciness in the relationship between YHWH and his servant. As in 4:14–17, YHWH responds to Moses's unbelief and resistance with a blunt command. No further argumentation would be allowed.

Theological Summary of Key Points

1. Unbelief, disobedience and despair can arise from several causes.

a. A weak character or "short spirit." This manifests itself in discouragement, impatience, and an argumentative attitude toward anyone who calls us to duty and faith.

b. A soul that has been damaged by evil done to it by others. This could include suffering physical abuse, sexual abuse, or verbal abuse. On a larger scale, it could come about from living under an oppressive system, such as a theocratic or secular totalitarianism.

c. Taking upon ourselves the entire burden of success or failure. It is not our responsibility to prove that God is faithful; that is his responsibility. We are often profoundly disturbed when the evidence seems to go against us or when things are going impossibly wrong, and we feel that the whole weight of a ministry, an enterprise, or the vindication of the Christian faith is on our shoulders.

d. Giving too much attention to ourselves—in particular to our deficiencies and failures. We tend to be excessively conscious of ourselves. Sometimes this leads to arrogance about our strengths, but just as damaging, it can be a false humility about our weaknesses, sins, and shortcomings.

2. No matter how unhappy we are with the situation or how greatly we are aware of our limitations, there comes a point that we simply have to obey. That, ultimately, is what God expects.

THE COMMISSION RENEWED (6:14—7:7)

A genealogy reassures the reader of Moses's place as the leader and human founder of Israel. Then Moses resumes his mission.

Translation

6:14a These are the heads of their paternal households.
6:14b The sons of Reuben, the firstborn of Israel: Hanoch and Pallu, Hezron and Carmi;
6:14c these are the families of Reuben.
6:15a The sons of Simeon: Jemuel and Jamin and Ohad and Jachin and Zohar and Shaul the son of a Canaanite woman;
6:15b these are the families of Simeon.
6:16a These are the names of the sons of Levi according to their genealogical records: Gershon and Kohath and Merari;
6:16b and the length of Levi's life was one hundred and thirty-seven years.
6:17 The sons of Gershon: Libni and Shimei, according to their families.
6:18a The sons of Kohath: Amram and Izhar and Hebron and Uzziel;
6:18b and the length of Kohath's life was one hundred and thirty-three years.
6:19a The sons of Merari: Mahli and Mushi.
6:19b These are the families of the Levites according to their genealogical records.
6:20a Amram took his aunt Jochebed as his wife,
6:20b and she bore him Aaron and Moses.
6:20c And the length of Amram's life was one hundred and thirty-seven years.
6:21 And the sons of Izhar: Korah and Nepheg and Zichri.
6:22 And the sons of Uzziel: Mishael and Elzaphan and Sithri.
6:23a And Aaron took Elisheba, the daughter of Amminadab, the sister of Nahshon, as his wife,
6:23b and she bore him Nadab and Abihu, Eleazar and Ithamar.
6:24a And the sons of Korah: Assir and Elkanah and Abiasaph;
6:24b these are the families of the Korahites.
6:25a And Eleazar son of Aaron took one of the daughters of Putiel as his wife,

6:25b and she bore him Phinehas.
6:25c These are the patriarchs[163] of the Levites according to their families.
6:26a It was Aaron and Moses to whom YHWH said,
6:26b "Bring out the Israelites from the land of Egypt division by division."[164]
6:27a They were the ones telling Pharaoh, king of Egypt, to send the Israelites out from Egypt;
6:27b it was Moses and Aaron.
6:28 Now it happened on the day that YHWH spoke to Moses in the land of Egypt,
6:29a that YHWH spoke to Moses, as follows:
6:29b "I am YHWH!
6:29c Speak to Pharaoh, king of Egypt, all that I say to you."
6:30a And Moses said before YHWH,
6:30b "Look, my articulation is disgusting![165]
6:30c So how is it possible that Pharaoh will listen to me?"
7:1a And YHWH said to Moses,
7:1b "See, I have set you in the position of God before Pharaoh,
7:1c and your brother Aaron shall be your prophet.
7:2a You shall speak all that I command you,
7:2b and your brother Aaron shall tell Pharaoh
7:2c that he must release the Israelites from his land.
7:3a But I will harden Pharaoh's heart
7:3b so that I may bring about in great number my signs and my wonders in the land of Egypt.
7:4a But Pharaoh will not listen to you,
7:4b and I will lay my hand on Egypt
7:4c and I will bring out my divisions,[166] my people the Israelites, from the land of Egypt by great judgments.

---

163. The noun phrase רָאשֵׁי אֲבוֹת ("heads of fathers") is analogous to the word "patriarch" (from *πατήρ*, "father," and *ἀρχή*, "source"), meaning "originating father."

164. The phrase עַל־צִבְאֹתָם is lit. "upon their hosts," but צָבָא here describes the mass of Israelite men as divided into military companies. In Deut. 20:9, military commanders are called שָׂרֵי צְבָאוֹת, and the usage here is analogous.

165. See note to 6:12d.

166. It seems remarkable that YHWH should refer to Israel as צִבְאֹתַי, a word that could be rendered, "my hosts." God does acknowledge Israel as his people here, but one should not read the title "YHWH of Hosts" (יְהוָה צְבָאוֹת) back into this text. That term is never used in the Pentateuch.

7:5a And the Egyptians will know, when I stretch out my hand on Egypt and bring[167] out the Israelites from among them,
7:5b that I am YHWH."[168]
7:6a And Moses and Aaron did [it].
7:6b Just as YHWH commanded them,
7:6c so they did.
7:7a And Moses was eighty years old
7:7b and Aaron was eighty-three years old when they spoke to Pharaoh.

Structure

The reader is surprised to encounter a genealogical text in the middle of the story of the exodus. As described below, moreover, this is plainly only a partial genealogy, with material extracted from a larger set of records. One must determine, therefore, why genealogical material is inserted here, and how it relates to the rest of the context. After the genealogy, the text returns to narrative with a brief resumptive passage that recapitulates prior material, and this is followed by a renewal of the commission to Moses. The structure is as follows.

I. Excerpt from a Genealogy (6:14–25)
II. Resumption of Story (6:26–27)
III. The Renewal of the Commission (6:28–7:7)

Commentary

6:14–25. The insertion of genealogical information at this point is unusual on several counts. First, it only contains information on the first three of Jacob's sons—Reuben, Simeon, and Levi—and says nothing about the other sons. Second, for Reuben and Simeon, it lists only the names of their immediate sons, members of the second generation, who were the eponymous clans of the tribes. But for Levi it lists several generations of descendants; in the case of Phinehas, it goes down to the sixth generation (Levi > Kohath > Amram > Aaron > Eleazar > Phinehas). Third, it includes extra information about the births of the priestly and Levitical leaders (first of Aaron and Moses, then of Nadab, Abihu, Eleazar, and Ithamar, and then of Phinehas). It names their maternal grandfathers and, in every case except for Phinehas, their mothers. Fourth, it is odd that it goes down to Phinehas at 6:25; he

167. The *weqatal* וְהוֹצֵאתִי could be read as a separate clause, but it is probably subordinate to the temporal semi-clause בִּנְטֹתִי, "when I stretch out."
168. This is indirect speech. In the above translation, it has been moved to the end of the sentence to separate it from the main clause.

alone is mentioned of such a late generation, although he plays no role in Exodus at all (he is not mentioned again until Num. 25:7, at the end of the wilderness wandering period).

These facts indicate that this information has been extracted from a much larger set of genealogical data, one that would have included the names of all twelve sons of Jacob along with several generations of descendants. The fact that it includes Phinehas indicates that the genealogical records date to a time after Phinehas gained renown in Israel (see Num. 25:7–13, where YHWH gives him and his sons the covenant of a perpetual priesthood). Phinehas was evidently a fairly young man at the time of the Num. 25 episode, since in Num. 31 he went out with his father to lead a priestly contingent that accompanied the army in a war against Midian (v. 6). Furthermore, he was still alive at the time of the civil war against Benjamin in the judges period (Judg. 20:28). Thus, Phinehas almost certainly was not yet born at the time of the exodus. All of this indicates that this part of the passage is derived from material written sometime after Phinehas attained his high status among the priests, and no earlier than the Baal of Peor episode of Num. 25.

Another curious fact about this genealogy is that it tells us that Moses's father, Amram, married his own aunt, Jochebed (such an act would be forbidden in Lev. 18:12). This indicates that Levi was grandfather of Moses on Jochebed's side and great-grandfather of Moses on Amram's side. Apart from the unusual family relations, this creates a significant problem. Even allowing for the possibility that Levi fathered Jochebed near the very end of his life (he died at age 137 according to v. 16), Jochebed could not have given birth to Moses 80 years before the exodus if there were 430 years between Levi's entrance into Egypt and the exodus (see Exod. 7:7; 12:41).[169] To do so, Jochebed would have been about 350 years old when she gave birth to Moses.[170] Surely such an astonishing feat would have merited some notice in the Bible!

In addition, Kohath, father of Amram and paternal grandfather of

169. The assumption of a 430 year period follows a literal reading of these verses. It is possible that we are not meant to understand the numbers in this way. See "Chronological Conundrums" in the introduction.

170. It is of course impossible to know when Jochebed was born, but obviously she was born either before Levi entered Egypt, or afterward. The most neutral date for her birth, therefore, is the year of the entrance into Egypt. She apparently gave birth to Moses 80 years prior to the exodus (he was in Egypt for 40 years and then in Midian for 40 years). Thus, if she bore Moses 80 years prior to the exodus, and if she was born in the year of

Moses, was among the seventy who entered Egypt (Gen. 46:11). This means that when estimating the number of years from the entrance of the seventy into Egypt until Moses's birth, one must begin with Kohath; one cannot include Levi's years. Kohath is said to have lived 133 years, and Amram 137 years (Exod. 6:16, 18). Thus, even allowing for the absurd notion that each man fathered his son in the very last year of his life, in addition to the 80 years of Moses's life before the exodus, there is not enough time for a 430-year period between the entrance to Egypt and the exodus (133 + 137 + 80 = 350).[171] Furthermore, according to 1 Chron. 7:20–27, Moses's assistant Joshua was in the tenth generation after Ephraim. It is, of course, strange that Moses should be the maternal grandson of Levi while Joshua was eleven generations removed from Joseph.

This is not the only text that describes Moses and Aaron as the sons of Amram, son of Kohath, and of Jochebed, daughter of Levi and sister of Kohath (see also Num 26:57–59). One might suggest that the genealogy has simply skipped some generations, but the problem is not so easily solved as that. If the text simply said that Moses was the "son" of Amram, we could easily take "son" to mean "descendent" of Amram. Or, we could argue that Amram was himself a distant descendant of Kohath (we cannot resolve things by making Kohath a distant descendant of Levi, because Kohath was both a clan head and one of the seventy who entered Egypt). But, in reality, we cannot easily make Moses out to be a distant descendant of Amram, or make Amram out to be a distant descendant of Kohath. The reason is that Amram married Jochebed, and she was the sister of Kohath. As such she cannot possibly be regarded as a later descendent of Levi—she has to be Levi's actual daughter. Also, the text says that she "bore" Moses and Aaron to Amram (Exod. 6:20). This expression is only used of a woman who is the immediate mother of a person.[172] It is never used of a woman

---

entering Egypt, and if Israel was in Egypt for 430 years, then she was 350 years old when she bore him.

171. Against Stuart, *Exodus*, 76, who wrongly includes Levi in his calculations.

172. I have found 144 instances in the Hebrew Bible of ילד in the Qal stem with a feminine singular subject. Also, I have found 44 texts in which a woman bore (ילד) a child to a man; in every case it refers to the immediate parents of the child and never to more distant ancestors. See Gen. 3:16; 4:1, 17, 25; 16:11, 15; 17:17; 21:2, 3, 9; 29:32; 35:17; 41:50; Exod. 2:2, 22; 21:4; Lev. 12:2, 5; Deut. 25:6; Judg. 8:31; 13:3, 24; 1 Sam. 1:20; 2:21; 4:20; 2 Sam. 12:15; Isa. 8:3; etc. A woman who is an ancestor of a people may be described as their "mother" (or they may be described as her "children"),

who is a distant ancestor. It is difficult to imagine how the Bible could be clearer in its assertion that Amram and Jochebed, grandson and daughter of Levi, were the immediate parents of Moses and Aaron.

We must therefore ask several questions. Why is this genealogical information inserted here? Why does the genealogy extend to Phinehas? Why are the mothers or maternal grandfathers of the Levitical leaders mentioned? How can the short pedigree of Moses and Aaron be reconciled with other data regarding the length of the Egyptian sojourn?

The answer to all these questions may be that the text is reaffirming the legitimacy of Moses and Aaron as Levitical and priestly leaders of Israel. First, as indicated above, it seems certain that this material has been extracted from a larger body of genealogical data and inserted here. Probably the brief statements about the descendants of Reuben and Simeon are simply there because protocol demands it, these brothers being older than Levi (for the same reason in v. 20 Aaron is, contrary to normal usage, placed before Moses; Aaron was the older brother according to 7:7). But the main interest of the genealogy is clearly the line of Levi; after him, the genealogy abruptly breaks off without mention of Judah and the rest of the tribes.

Second, this genealogy is inserted after Exod. 6:10–13, in which Moses, in the face of hostility from Pharaoh and unbelief from the Israelites, comes near to flatly refusing to carry God's message to the pharaoh. That is, Moses's lapse might raise questions about whether he and Aaron have a legitimate claim to leadership. The genealogy, with its focus on the purity of their lineage from Levi, helps to establish their bona fides.

Third, the inclusion of Phinehas may be meant to further assert the legitimacy of their leadership credentials. The reader is expected to be biblically literate and to recall Phinehas's heroism and especially the bestowal on him of an everlasting covenant (Num. 25:7–13). Retrospectively, Phinehas legitimates the Aaronic line. In the end, and whatever the failings of the priestly and Levitical lines (of Nadab and Abihu in Num. 3:4; of Korah in Num. 16), ultimately the line of Aaron would be vindicated and get a promise of continuity because of the zeal of Phinehas.

Fourth, the text mentions the mothers and maternal grandfathers of the Levitical leaders in order to doubly establish the genealogical purity of these men. First, in saying that Moses and Aaron are not only of the clan of Kohath but, on their mother's side, grandsons of

---

as in Ezek. 16:45 and Jer. 31:15, but these texts do not speak of a woman bearing (ילד) children to a man.

Levi himself, it shows that the purity of their Levitical claim is unimpeachable. It is analogous to what we see in Genesis, where first Abraham and then Isaac desire their sons to maintain the purity of the line by taking a wife from their family in Haran (Gen. 24:1–9; 28:1–2). Similarly, Aaron's wife is "Elisheba, the daughter of Amminadab and the sister of Nahshon" (Exod. 6:23). Amminadab is a descendent of Judah through Perez (Ruth 4:18–19). Nahshon, Elisheba's brother, was נְשִׂיא בְּנֵי יְהוּדָה, a "leader of the men of Judah" (1 Chron. 2:10), and is prominently mentioned in that role (Num. 1:7; 2:3; 7:12, 17; 10:14). Aaron's four sons thus had Israelite aristocracy on both side of the family.[173] Phinehas's mother is not named, but his maternal grandfather is said to have been a certain Putiel (Exod. 6:25). This man is not mentioned in any other text, so we know nothing about him.[174] All in all, however, it seems clear that the text wants us to recognize that Aaron and Moses are of high and noble lineage within the tribe of Levi..

This interpretation also helps us to make sense of the fact that Moses and Aaron are said to be only two generations removed from Levi. In the text, as described above, Amram and Jochebed are made out to be Moses and Aaron's parents. But the chronology is difficult. Either the Egyptian sojourn was much shorter than 430 years or Amram and Jochebed were not literally the parents of Moses and Aaron.

Umberto Cassuto argues that the number 430 is artificial. He takes the total lifespans of Levi, Kohath, Amram and Aaron (137 + 133 + 137 + 83), deducts 60 for the years of Levi in Canaan, and thus comes up with 430 years.[175] Taken literally, this is absurd on three counts. First, it assumes that Levi, Kohath, and Amram each in the year of his death, fathered his respective son. Second, it fails to reckon with the fact that Kohath was born prior to the Egyptian sojourn; as such, Levi's years should not be counted. Third, it disregards the shorter genealogy through Jochebed. But Cassuto does not mean for the figures to be taken literally; he is merely describing what may have been an ancient way of reckoning the numbers. He notes that in the Sumerian King

173. By comparison, the status of a certain Saul son of Simeon (v. 15) is debased by virtue of his being a son of a Canaanite woman.

174. It is noteworthy, however, that his name is a composite Egyptian-Semitic word meaning, "the one whom El has given" (see Edwin C. Hostetter, "Puti-el," in Freedman, *ABD* Vol. 5, 561). This does not tell us anything about the social rank of Putiel, but it does reflect an Egyptian provenance for the name, which in turn helps to affirm its antiquity and authenticity. That is, the name is what one may expect of Semites who lived in Egypt.

175. Cassuto, *Exodus*, 86–7.

List, contemporary kings (one reigning in one city and one at the same time in another city) are tallied artificially, as though they all reigned successively. That is, all the years of their reigns are added together as though it were a single sequence.

Cassuto's interpretation allows one to claim that Moses was literally the son of Amram and Jochebed and that the period of the Egyptian sojourn was a great deal shorter than 430 years. Cassuto observes that Gen. 15:16 states that the Israelites would return in the "fourth generation." Since both Jacob and Levi entered Egypt, Moses was in the fourth generation from Levi on his father's side and in the fourth generation from Jacob on his mother's side. Against Cassuto's interpretation is the aforementioned fact that Joshua is in the eleventh generation from Joseph. This suggests a much longer Egyptian sojourn. On the other hand, we recall that Paul in Gal. 3:16–17 says that there were 430 years between the "promises to Abraham" (Gen. 12:1–3) and the Sinai covenant (Exod. 19). This suggests an Egyptian sojourn much shorter than 430 years. Thus, we must not be too dogmatic about chronological matters, as there is clearly something here we do not fully understand.

We cannot avoid the fact that Amram and Jochebed are presented as Moses and Aaron's immediate parents here and everywhere else in the Bible where his parents are named (Num. 26:59; 1 Chron. 6:3; 23:13). On the other hand, there is one place where his parents are anonymous—in the actual birth narrative of Moses (Exod. 2). Retrospectively, it seems astonishing that of all texts the birth narrative would not name Moses's parents. This suggests that the actual names of his parents have been withheld, and that Exod. 6:20 and its parallels give a legal genealogy. That is, for legal purposes, Amram and Jochebed are treated as the immediate parents of Moses and Aaron. In this manner, Moses and Aaron are placed on a level almost equal with the clans of Levi (Gershon, Kohath, and Merari). This gives Moses, as leader of the people, the highest possible status, and it makes the priestly line of Aaron equal in prestige to that of these three Levitical clans.

We must realize that we are reading an ancient book, in which things are described according to the standards of ancient people. The text is not trying to deceive us; even the most casual reader can see that Moses cannot literally be the grandson of Levi if the sojourn lasted 430 years. We should not read the text incorrectly, applying standards that are inappropriate and anachronistic. For the ancient reader, if this interpretation is correct, Amram and Jochebed are effectively "adopted" as the parents of Moses and Aaron. We do know from Exod. 2:1 that Moses and Aaron were Levites on both sides of their family. Thus, although it is probably correct to say that Moses and Aaron were distant descendants of Amram and Jochebed, we should not make this claim lightly, saying that the text has simply "skipped" some generations. It has not skipped generations at all; it has by a legal "adoption" made Amram and Jochebed the parents of Moses and Aaron.

6:26–27. The narrative resumes by repeating previous details, that God had commissioned Moses and Aaron to bring Israel out of Egypt and that these two men were the ones who spoke to Pharaoh. It is curious that the text speaks as though we need to be told which persons named "Moses and Aaron" are under discussion, as though wanting to avoid any confusion about some other "Moses and Aaron." There is no other Moses or Aaron in the Bible. Probably the intent of these verses is not to clear up any confusion about the identity of Moses and Aaron; rather, it is to emphasize that God commissioned specifically these two men. Once again, the best explanation for this is that the text is asserting that, despite their failings, these were the men God chose.

6:28–7:7. Once again we read of Moses's protest that he cannot speak well and once again God says that Aaron will be his spokesman. This is the third time that Exodus mentions this issue (see 4:10; 6:12). Probably, however, this text is a recapitulation of Moses's complaint in 6:12; it is not a third episode. God's explanation of the roles of Moses and Aaron is essentially the same as in 4:16, although the language is slightly different. In the former text, Moses would be as God to Aaron; in this text, Moses is as God to Pharaoh. In both cases, however, Moses plays the role of God, in that he gives the message, and Aaron plays the role of the prophet, in that he delivers it. Pharaoh is the recipient.

In Egypt, the pharaoh was the ex-officio high priest for every shrine and the chief representative of the gods. Before YHWH, he was in an unaccustomed role of layman and subordinate. In 7:3–4, God again predicts that Pharaoh will refuse to listen to them and that God himself will bring the Israelites out by means of miraculous works. The repetition is not pointless, however. This time, it ends with Moses and Aaron obeying his commands, and the story of the plagues on the Egyptians is set to begin. The significance is that Moses has finally accepted the commission of God fully, and that he is now ready to stand before Pharaoh with courage. As the story progresses, Aaron's role as the spokesman will diminish.

Theological Summary of Key Points

1. Despite their failings, Moses and Aaron were the legitimate leaders of Israel and God's representatives. The Israelites would discover, in a very painful lesson, that it was not their place to question Moses's and Aaron's position or to choose other leaders for themselves (Num. 16). Leaders are to be respected by virtue of the offices they hold.

2. The priestly privileges of the Levites and of the house of Aaron depended on genealogical descent. By contrast, Jesus's priestly claims are based on divine election alone, after the order of Melchizedek (Heb. 7).

3. The above exposition makes the case that one must either shorten the time of the Egyptian sojourn to considerably less than 430 years, or one must treat the assertion that Moses and Aaron were the sons of Amram and Jochebed as a kind of legal adoption, whereby distant ancestors are for legal purposes treated as their immediate parents. Taking the latter to be correct, one can regard this as an act of grace on God's part, comparable to God's adoption of believers to be joint heirs with Christ. Moses, by his stubborn excuse-making, showed that he was not worthy of this adoption, an act that gave him enormous authority and prestige. Nevertheless, he received it, and ultimately his faith and behavior vindicated it.

4. Exodus gives much more attention to Moses's unbelief and resistance to God than it does to the sins of his youth, even though his youthful sins included killing a man. It is not that the importance of the earlier failings is minimized, but that Moses's lack of faith and unwillingness to obey a direct commission is, in God's eyes, a serious act of disobedience. The lesson of Moses here is that we should allow neither doubts about ourselves nor doubts about God to prevent us from obeying God's commands.

5. The great miracles of the exodus did not begin until after Moses stopped pulling back and gave himself to the task God had appointed him to.

PART III

The Twelve Miracles of the Exodus (7:8–15:21)

One normally hears of the "ten" plagues on the Egyptians, but in fact 7:8–14:31 describes a series of twelve miraculous events. Formally, all twelve miracles follow the same basic pattern.

I. YHWH commissions Moses and Aaron to appear before Pharaoh. This may include:
   A. Background information
   B. A demand that Pharaoh release Israel
   C. A warning about a coming judgment
   D. Specific instructions for Aaron
II. YHWH commands Moses to begin the plague
III. Moses and Aaron carry out the commission. This may include:
   A. A ritual act performed by Moses and Aaron initiate the plague
   B. The miracle or plague begins and its effects are described
IV. Pharaoh's advisors and magicians respond. This may include:
   A. A duplication of YHWH's miracle
   B. Counsel given by the advisors and magicians to Pharaoh
V. Pharaoh interviews Moses in the course of the plague. This may include:
   A. A request that Moses intercede for Egypt to stop the plague

B. A promise to release the people to go into the wilderness and sacrifice
C. An answer from Moses to Pharaoh

VI. Moses intercedes for Egypt, and the plague stops
VII. Pharaoh/YHWH hardens Pharaoh's heart, and he refuses to listen/to release Israel
VIII. Affirmation that YHWH's word was fulfilled
IX. Other information

Not every plague has every one of the formal elements, but they all have this pattern. Sometimes the order of the events will vary slightly from the above pattern. The first miracle, for example, does not involve a plague, but it follows the standard pattern and it prefigures the course of the plagues. By observing what elements are present or absent in each episode, we can better understand the progress of the plagues and the interaction of Moses and Pharaoh. The sequence of twelve miracles is followed by the Song of the Sea (15:1–21), a paean to YHWH's victory over Egypt.

In addition, the twelve miracles of 7:8–15:21 display clear progression both in the intensity of suffering brought on by the plagues and in the intensity of the folly or madness indicated by Pharaoh's response. That is, things get worse and worse as the story moves forward. These levels of intensification break down into four discreet levels, as described in Table 5.

The first two events are highly symbolic. The turning of the rod into a snake does not harm Egypt, but its swallowing of the magicians' snakes warns of trouble to come. Even the turning of the Nile to blood is, as described below, more a warning than a crisis. Fish die, as often happens when toxins enter a body of water, and the presence of dead fish all along the Nile prefigures much greater death in Egypt. But the people apparently did not suffer unduly, as they needed only to dig temporary wells along the river to obtain filtered, potable water, and no loss of life for livestock or people is described. In both cases, the Egyptian response, indicated in Pharaoh's actions, is to rationalize the event as not particularly meaningful, since even the magicians could do similar things. Real suffering begins with the plagues of frogs, mosquitoes, and flies, although still there is no direct threat to the lives of people or livestock. But the agony of being tormented by pests is real, and it is compounded by the realization that some people, the Israelites, have been exempted from suffering (in the case of the flies). On these occasions, Pharaoh either feigned a willingness to release the people or simply remained stubborn. The suffering is much more

TABLE 5. THE PROGRESS OF THE TWELVE MIRACLES			
Intensity	**Event**	**Meaning**	**Response**
Warning	Staff to Snake (7:8–13)	Token of future disaster; no harm to anyone	Magicians imitate miracle; Pharaoh shrugs off event
	Nile (7:14–24)	Real but limited and transitory ecological disturbance; symbolic of future disaster	Magicians imitate miracle; Pharaoh shrugs off event
Misery	Frogs (7:25–8:15)	Emotional disgust for Egyptians	Magicians imitate; Pharaoh disturbed and lies to get relief
	Mosquitoes (8:16–19)	Emotional and physical discomfort for Egyptians	Magicians fail to imitate miracle; Pharaoh refuses to listen to advice
	Flies (8:20–32)	Emotional and physical discomfort for Egyptians	Pharaoh deceitfully negotiates
Economic Loss and Physical Affliction	Livestock (9:1–7)	Wealth and livelihood damaged in loss of livestock	Pharaoh hardens heart but wants to see if Hebrews really were unscathed
	Skin Ulcers (9:8–12)	Physical discomfort and disfigurement	Pharaoh's magicians afflicted, but Pharaoh is unyielding
	Hail (9:13–35)	Massive loss in labor force, crops and remaining livestock	Some officials heed warning; Pharaoh makes pseudo-repentance
	Locusts (10:1–20)	Remaining crops wiped out	At pleading of officials, Pharaoh negotiates but loses temper and breaks off talks
Death	Darkness (10:21–29)	Token of death	Pharaoh makes concession but then refuses to yield; furiously dismisses Moses
	Firstborn (11:1–13:16)	Real death; symbolic of battle	Pharaoh, out of despair, lets Israel go
	Yam Suph (13:17–14:31)	Real death in real battle	Pharaoh's madness: after all the calamities, he pursues Israel to re-enslave them

tangible in the plague that strikes down livestock and in the boils. By comparison, the earlier events were mere annoyances. Pharaoh's response is more irrational, as he knows that Israel has been exempted from the suffering; his heart is hard. Absolute economic catastrophe strikes the land in the plagues of hail and locusts. Pharaoh's response is an exaggeration of his previous responses, including an extravagant but temporary contrition (9:27), and his behavior displays a complete loss of sound judgment (10:7). The last three events deal in death. The darkness, like the first miracles, is symbolic; it does not actually hurt anyone. But it is a token of the darkness of death. The death of the firstborn involves real death and is like a defeat in battle: the flower of Egypt's youth perishes and the victors plunder the losers (12:36). The event at the *Yam Suph* is a military defeat: a pursuing army is caught in a trap and annihilated. In these events, Pharaoh and Egypt are consumed first by anger (10:28–29), then by despair (12:29–33), and finally by madness (14:5, 23–24).

ONE: A PRIVATE SHOWING (7:8–13)

The first miracle is a token of the disaster that is facing Pharaoh and Egypt. It is highly symbolic, but it is only a warning.

Translation

7:8 And YHWH spoke to Moses and to Aaron, as follows:
7:9a "When Pharaoh speaks to you, saying,
7:9b 'So show me a miracle,'[1]
7:9c then you shall say to Aaron,
7:9d 'Take your staff
7:9e and throw [it] before Pharaoh!
7:9f Let it become[2] a cobra!'"[3]

---

1. The so-called "ethical dative" לָכֶם in תְּנוּ לָכֶם מוֹפֵת (lit. "give for yourselves a miracle") probably implies that Moses and Aaron should prove themselves to Pharaoh by doing a miracle.
2. This is often translated with a purpose clause, "so that it may become." But one would expect the *weyiqtol* form for this (that is, it ought to have a conjunction). It is more likely that יְהִי לְתַנִּין is a simple jussive.
3. The translation "cobra" is not certain, but it seems to be the best choice. Contrary to some (Cassuto, *Exodus*, 94), the word תַּנִּין does not refer to a crocodile; in Exod. 7:15, the rod is said to have turned into a נָחָשׁ, which is certainly a snake and not a crocodile. Egypt has both venomous and nonvenomous snakes. A beneficial nonvenomous snake is the sand boa, which consumes large numbers of rodents. But תַּנִּין almost certainly refers to a venomous snake. The word תַּנִּין usually refers to a sea monster

7:10a And Moses and Aaron came to Pharaoh,
7:10b and they did those things,[4]
7:10c just as YHWH had commanded:
7:10d Aaron threw[5] his staff down before Pharaoh and his servants,
7:10e and it became a cobra.
7:11a And Pharaoh also called for the wise men and the sorcerers,
7:11b and they, too, the magicians of Egypt, did the same with their secret tricks:[6]
7:12a Each one threw down his staff[7]
7:12b and they became cobras.

(Isa. 27:1; Jer. 51:34; Ps. 74:13; Job 7:12), suggesting that as a snake it is deadly rather than harmless. This is confirmed by Ps. 91:13, where the תַּנִּין is parallel to the lion. A particularly aggressive snake with a powerful hemotoxic venom and indigenous to the area is the Echis or "saw-scaled viper." When agitated, it rubs its serrated scales together to produce a sizzling sound, similar to how the rattlesnake will shake its rattle in a threatening manner. But the Echis is relatively small (never larger than about 90 cm). It is unlikely that Moses' rod, which may have been 2 m long, was transformed into a smaller snake. Another viper found in Egypt is the Pseudocerastes, but it, too, is relatively small. Several factors suggest that the snake here is the cobra. First, several varieties of cobra are found in Egypt (the Egyptian cobra or Naja haje; the Mozambique spitting cobra; the black-necked spitting cobra; the desert cobra). See John Coborn, *The Atlas of Snakes of the World* (Neptune City: T.F.H. Publications, 1991), 445-61, 484-88; Keith A. Harding and Kenneth R. G. Welch, *Venomous Snakes of the World: A Checklist* (New York: Pergamon Press, 1980), 110, for further discussion of Egyptian snakes. Second, the cobra was important in Egyptian culture; it was frequently depicted in Egyptian art, and there were several goddesses that were in cobra form (the most famous being Wadjyt). Third, cobras are large enough to correspond to Moses's rod; they average a length of 1.2–2.5 meters (the Egyptian cobra, or asp, averages about 2 meters). Fourth, some cobras are known to be ophiophagous (snake-eaters), although the Egyptian cobra usually eats birds and toads. But the eating of the other snakes by Moses's snake would not be unnatural behavior.

4. Lit. "and they did thus" (וַיַּעֲשׂוּ כֵן).
5. The *wayyiqtol* here is epexegetical of the previous clause.
6. The word לַהֲטֵיהֶם, a by-form of לָט, implies secrecy or deceit. It does not imply supernatural power. See Judg. 4:21; 1 Sam. 18:22; Ruth 3:7.
7. The *wayyiqtol* (וַיַּשְׁלִיכוּ; "and they threw") is epexegetical of the previous clause.

7:12c And Aaron's staff swallowed their staffs.[8]
7:13a And Pharaoh's heart was implacable:
7:13b he would not listen to them.[9]
7:13c [It was] just as YHWH had said.

Structure

I. YHWH Commissions Moses and Aaron to Appear Before Pharaoh (7:8–9)
   A. Background Information
   B. Specific Instructions to Give to Aaron
II. Moses and Aaron Carry Out the Commission (7:10)
III. Pharaoh's Advisors and Counselors Respond (7:11–12)
IV. Pharaoh Hardens his Heart (7:13ab)
V. Affirmation that YHWH's Word Was Fulfilled (7:13c)

This episode has no demand that Pharaoh release Israel, no plague, and thus no request from Pharaoh for relief from the plague. The only question is whether Moses can authenticate his claim to be an emissary from God by working a miracle.

Commentary

7:8–9. The business that Moses and Aaron have with Pharaoh, that they are agents of God sent to demand that the Israelites be released to go out and worship YHWH, is already known (Exod. 5:1–4). What is yet to be established is Moses's bona fides, that his claim to be God's spokesman is valid. YHWH anticipates that Pharaoh will demand a miracle as proof of that claim, and he commissions Moses and Aaron to go before Pharaoh and work the miracle of the rod becoming a snake. God told Moses to command Aaron, in Pharaoh's presence, to throw down the staff in order that it would be clear to Pharaoh that Moses, not Aaron, was the one to whom God had given the miracle-working power.

7:10. Of itself, this miracle is not an attack upon Pharaoh or Egypt; the text does not imply that the snake behaved aggressively toward

8. This is often translated as, "but Aaron's staff swallowed" to mark a contrast. But the *wayyiqtol* (וַיִּבְלַע, "and he swallowed") is not prominent in the narrative.

9. The negated clause (וְלֹא שָׁמַע; "and he would not listen") is offline; it is epexegetical of the previous clause, but is also prominent. It is, in fact, the main point of this entire text.

Pharaoh. The transformation simply proves that God has given Moses the ability to work miracles, and so it serves as his credentials. But the fact that the miracle involved a snake, probably a cobra, is significant. First, a cobra is by nature dangerous, and one does not want to provoke it. The implied warning to Pharaoh is that he should not provoke YHWH. Second, Egyptians understandably feared snakes, both real and mythical. They had magical incantations and amulets to ward off snakes or cure snakebite. In the mythological arena, Spell 33 in the Book of the Dead was meant to protect the deceased from the snake of the underworld. Also, the god Seth had to fight a great serpent to protect the sun as it made its nightly voyage through the underworld. Third, the cobra also had positive connotations to the Egyptians; it was a potent religious and national symbol. Several deities had snake form, including Renenutet, a cobra-goddess who was the guardian of the pharaoh, and Edjo (Wadjyt), a cobra-goddess who was the patron deity of Lower Egypt (where the Israelites lived). Usually depicted as a rearing cobra, the uraeus, Edjo famously appears on the pharaonic crown alongside Nekhbet, the vulture goddess and patron deity of Upper Egypt.[10] YHWH has therefore co-opted a major symbol of the power of Egypt and of the pharaoh personally. The spiritual guardians that Pharaoh thinks he can depend upon are actually under the direct control of YHWH.[11]

7:11–12. As stated in the translation notes above, the Hebrew does not imply that the Egyptian magicians had supernatural powers; translations such as "by their occult practices" (HCSB) are misleading. Throughout the ancient world, pagan priests regularly used trickery to fool the gullible. For example, some large idols actually contained hollow compartments in which a priest would hide and speak for the god. The "magic" done by the Egyptian magicians was probably analogous to tricks with animals performed by modern stage magicians. Also, snake charming is an ancient art in Egypt. The Brooklyn Museum of Art contains a papyrus from the 30th dynasty that is a kind of manual for snake charming; it lists some 30 species of snakes, describing their appearance, their bites, and the gods they were associated with.[12] It

10. See Shaw and Nicholson, *Dictionary*, 262–3.
11. To make an analogy, one might suggest that if Pharaoh had been Chinese, the miracle would have involved a Chinese dragon; or if American, it would have involved a bald eagle.
12. Patrick Houlihan, "Spellbound: Charming the Snake & the Scorpion," *Ancient Egypt* 3, no. 6 (2003).

appears that the Egyptians practiced a method of snake charming that allowed them to put a snake into a kind of catalepsy, whereby it remained as stiff as a rod until awakened.

The surprising turn of events was the swallowing of the magicians' snakes by Moses's snake. It should be read as a warning to Pharaoh. Moses's snake, representing YHWH, was more powerful than the magicians' snakes, representing Egypt. In addition, this turn of events showed that YHWH was the true God and that Moses was no trickster. Moses could have used a trick to make it appear that his rod had become a snake, but he could not have caused his snake to swallow theirs. The magic of the magicians, however, was as phony as were their gods. Pharaoh should humble himself, the event implies, lest YHWH devour Egypt itself.

7:13. Pharaoh turned away in contempt, apparently believing that Moses was as much a con artist as his own magicians were. The Bible does not dwell on the issue of how the magicians turned their rods to snakes because its purpose is not to debunk the Egyptians' magic. The message is that YHWH had given Pharaoh a supernatural warning, but Pharaoh had found a way to rationalize the event and disregard the warning.

Theological Summary of Key Points

The main point of this text is that God credentialed Moses by enabling him to work a miracle, and that Pharaoh dismissed the miracle as insignificant.

1. It is a dangerous thing to resist or dismiss a work of God. The New Testament parallel is Matt. 12:22–32, where the Pharisees claim that Jesus casts out demons by the power of Beelzebul. In this, they treated a work of God with contempt, and Jesus warned them that there could be no escape for those who blaspheme the Holy Spirit.

2. Pseudo-miracles and false religion subvert the true worship of God. To the gullible, such tricks are the evidence that validates a false faith. To the skeptical, they are proof that all religion is meaningless hocus-pocus and that only fools allow themselves to be taken in.

TWO: THE NILE (7:14–24)

YHWH sends a much more terrible token of death to come. Little actual damage is done to Egypt in this miracle, however, and Pharaoh remains unimpressed.

Translation

7:14a And YHWH said to Moses,
7:14b “Pharaoh’s heart is leaden;[13]
7:14c he refuses to release the people.[14]
7:15a Go to Pharaoh in the morning—
7:15b [you will find him[15]] going out to the water—
7:15c and station yourself to meet him on the bank of the Nile.
7:15d And the staff that turned into a serpent—you must take [it with you] in your hand.[16]
7:16a And you shall say to him,
7:16b ‘YHWH, the God of the Hebrews, sent me to say to you,
7:16c “Release my people,
7:16d that they may serve me in the wilderness.”
7:16e But, in fact, thus far you have not listened.
7:17a Thus says YHWH:
7:17b “By this you shall know
7:17c that I am YHWH:[17]
7:17d [You see that] I strike[18] the water that is in the Nile with the staff that is in my hand,
7:17e and it will be turned to blood.

---

13. This is a nominal clause; it is offline (taking כָּבֵד to be an adjective; although the clause is still offline even if it is regarded as a *qatal* stative). It both initiates YHWH’s discourse and gives background for the command that follows in 7:15a. On the translation “leaden,” see translation note at 8:15c.
14. This clause is asyndetic, beginning with a *qatal* form (מֵאֵן). Asyndeton is often used to restate or clarify a prior clause. In this case, it clarifies how Pharaoh’s hardness of heart is manifesting itself.
15. The clause is offline, giving background information. The particle הִנֵּה sometimes describes what someone may find or see in a given situation or place, particularly when bound to a nominal or periphrastic clause. See Gen. 16:14, where הִנֵּה בֵין־קָדֵשׁ וּבֵין בָּרֶד in effect means, “You can still find it between Kadesh and Bered.”
16. The fronting of this clause with וְהַמַּטֶּה indicates that it is offline; it is a secondary, procedural command. The mainline commands are לֵךְ (7:15a), וְנִצַּבְתָּ (7:15c), and וְאָמַרְתָּ (7:16a). Also, the fronting of וְהַמַּטֶּה marks the staff as the topic of this sentence.
17. This clause is an indirect statement.
18. Another use of הִנֵּה with a periphrastic clause indicating what one may find or see.

7:18a And so,[19] the fish that are in the Nile will die,
7:18b and the Nile will stink,
7:18c and the Egyptians will have a wearisome task[20] in getting water to drink from the Nile.'""
7:19a And YHWH said to Moses,
7:19b "Say to Aaron,
7:19c 'Take your staff
7:19d and stretch out your hand over the waters of Egypt, over their rivers,[21] over their tributaries, and over their ponds, and over all their bodies of water,
7:19e and then they will become blood;[22]
7:19f and there will be blood throughout all the land of Egypt, even [where the Nile flows] among trees and among stones.'"[23]
7:20a And Moses and Aaron did so,
7:20b just as YHWH commanded:

---

19. The pattern ו + noun phrase + *yiqtol* (וְהַדָּגָה אֲשֶׁר־בַּיְאֹר תָּמוּת) is offline, suggesting that the clauses of v. 18 are not a mere sequence of events but separate consequences of the Nile turning to blood. This makes the clauses of this verse more prominent.
20. The verb לאה (Niphal stem) does not mean, as is often translated, to be "unable" or "unwilling" to drink. It means "to be wearied." The point is that getting water will involve a lot more work than simply going to the Nile and scooping out water. This is fulfilled when the Egyptians must dig small holes along the river to use the sand to filter the water.
21. Moses is in the Delta, where the Nile has split into several major branches.
22. The *weyiqtol* clause וְיִהְיוּ־דָם is telic or final, indicating the purpose or outcome of Aaron's action.
23. The standard translation for וּבָעֵצִים וּבָאֲבָנִים is "in vessels of wood and in vessels of stone," even though the literal translation is simply "in trees and in stones." It is doubtful that the term עֵצִים ("trees" or "wood") by itself would mean "wooden vessels" or that אֲבָנִים ("stones") would mean "stone vessels." Also, wood in ancient Egypt was too precious for use in household buckets, and stone buckets would be difficult to make in quantity. Almost certainly water containers in Egypt were of pottery. See Cornelis Houtman, "On the Meaning of *Ûbā'ēṣîm Ûbā'ăbānîm* in Exodus VII 19," *VT* 36, no. 3 (1986): 347–52, for various proposals for the translation of the phrase. In light of the fact that the sentence is speaking of the entire Nile as it goes through the entire land of Egypt, probably "trees and rocks" refers to patches of trees or rocky terrain through which the Nile travels, and this would be in contrast to the alluvial plain with its cultivated fields that straddled most of the Nile within Egypt. In other words, "trees and stones" refers to wilderness areas; the Nile would be turned to blood even in areas where humans were not active.

7:20c he lifted up[24] the staff,
7:20d and he struck the water that was in the Nile, before the eyes of Pharaoh and before the eyes of his officials,
7:20e and all the water that was in the Nile turned to blood.
7:21a And so,[25] the fish that were in the Nile died,
7:21b and the Nile stank,
7:21c and the Egyptians were not able to drink water from the Nile,
7:21d and there was blood in all the land of Egypt.[26]
7:22a And the magicians of Egypt did[27] the same with their secret tricks;
7:22b and Pharaoh's heart was implacable:
7:22c he would not listen to them.[28]
7:22d [It was] just as YHWH had said.
7:23a And Pharaoh turned,
7:23b and he went into his house.
7:23c And he did not give much thought even to this.[29]
7:24a And all the Egyptians dug around the Nile for water to drink,
7:24b for they were not able to drink from the water of the Nile.

Structure

The structure of the Nile-turned-to-blood narrative follows the standard form quite closely, but lacks three elements: a command from YHWH to initiate the plague, an interview with Pharaoh in the course of the plague, and an intercession by Moses. Pharaoh was not sufficiently shocked by the event to seek an interview with Moses or to ask for his help.

I. YHWH Commissions Moses and Aaron to Appear Before Pharaoh (7:14–19)
   A. Background Information
   B. A Warning About a Coming Judgment

---

24. The *wayyiqtol* וַיָּרֶם is epexegetical of 7:20a.
25. Here in the narrative, וְהַדָּגָה + *qatal* has the same function as וְהַדָּגָה + *yiqtol* in the predictive text at 7:18a.
26. All the *wayyiqtol* forms of 7:21 are syntactically subordinate to 7:21a and thus are not mainline clauses.
27. The mainline narrative resumes with the *wayyiqtol* וַיַּעֲשׂוּ.
28. See translation note to 7:13b.
29. As a general rule, negated clauses are by nature offline, but this does not mean that they are unimportant. Often the negated clause in a sentence is the most prominent or important. It is of little significance that Pharaoh turned and went into his house, but 7:23c gives meaning to that action. It is a deliberate ignoring of the display of YHWH's power.

C. Specific Instructions for Aaron
II. Moses and Aaron Carry Out the Commission (7:20–21)
A. Moses and Aaron Perform a Ritual Act to Initiate the Miracle
B. The Miracle Begins and its Effects Are Described
III. Pharaoh's Advisors and Magicians Respond with a Duplication of YHWH's Miracle (7:22a)
IV. Pharaoh's Heart Hardened, and he Refuses to Listen (7:22bc)
V. Affirmation that YHWH's Word Was Fulfilled (7:22d)
VI. Other Information (7:23–24)

Commentary

7:14–19. As prophets such as Amos and Hosea did when confronting Israel, Moses and Aaron are first to confront Pharaoh with a message that accuses him of disobedience (v. 16) and then to announce judgment (vv. 17–18). The structure of the narrative also makes the analogy to prophecy: YHWH first gives his message to his prophet, who then takes it to its recipients. Pharaoh's going out to the Nile in the morning presumably had a ritual purpose, since the Egyptian pharaoh had many priestly duties. Probably the morning ritual related in some way to Egypt's two great sustainers of life, the sun and the Nile. It was thus appropriate that Moses, bringing a message of death, should confront Pharaoh there. It is also noteworthy that the plagues begin with the Nile being turned to blood and end (just prior to the climactic death of the firstborn) with the land shrouded in darkness. Both events are visual symbols of death.

7:20–21. The carrying out of YHWH's entire commission, including both the message for Pharaoh and the ritual initiation of the plague, is implied. In the description of the fulfillment, much of the language of vv. 17–18 is repeated almost verbatim. This is a feature of the narrative technique of Exodus, emphasizing that a word has been fulfilled by describing the fulfillment in a way that fulsomely repeats the words of the prediction.

7:22a. As with the turning of the rods to snakes, the word לָט ("secret trick") does not imply supernatural power. It may just be more a stage magician's trickery, but the text does not tell us anything about the setting or nature of what the magicians did. We do not know, for example, how much water they turned to blood. Their actions did, however, reinforce Pharaoh's resolve to ignore YHWH's miracle, and this is the main point. He may have rationalized either that his magicians were as powerful as Moses and Aaron, or perhaps that Moses and Aaron were as fraudulent as he knew his court magicians to be. Some readers wonder: If all the water in Egypt had already turned to blood, where did the magicians get the water to transform into blood in imitation of YHWH's act? One could argue that they pulled water up from one of the side wells described in vv. 23–24, but that is, I think, unnecessary. It is more likely that the word "all" is used rhetorically rather than literally (a case of hyperbole). We have the same thing in Exod. 9:6, which says that "all" the livestock in Egypt died by a disease. This cannot be taken literally, since there were still plenty of livestock around when the plague of hail came (Exod. 9:19).

7:22bc. The rather nonchalant manner in which Pharaoh shrugged off this event is astonishing if the whole Nile River literally turned to blood. His reaction suggests that the event was not altogether new to him. This may well have been the case if the redness of the river was not literal blood but due to an unusually high amount of red clay ("*Roterde*") mixed in with the water due to a very high annual inundation (see excursus below: Did the Nile Turn to Literal Blood?). This, in conjunction with a higher than usual quantity of flagellates in the water would cause the oxygen levels to fluctuate and kill fish. If the reddening of the Nile and the death of fish was a natural and therefore not unprecedented event, it is not so surprising that Pharaoh showed little surprise or concern, even if the event that took place under Moses's direction were far more severe than usual. If the entire river had actually turned to (literal) blood, one might expect Pharaoh to have been bowled over with fear and astonishment by the event.

7:23–24. The text indicates that the Egyptians dug shallow wells in the vicinity of the Nile so that they might retrieve water filtered by the sand and made potable. It turns out that, contrary to what one might think of a people who got their water from the Nile River, the Egyptians of this time were adept at well construction. In the 1940s, an Egyptian Egyptologist, Labib Habachi, discovered a well in the vicinity of the 19th dynasty capital city Qantir (Pi-Riʿamsese). The well was examined again in 2000–2001 by a team from the Roemer-Pelizaeus Museum (Hildesheim, Germany). The well made use of cut stones from the Amarna period, which demonstrated that it dated to the 19th dynasty. The stones were skillfully cut to allow them to form the circular shape necessary for lining the shaft of the well. The present depth of the well is about 8 meters, and the ancient excavators faced a difficult task, as they had to find a way to deal with the rapid inflow of water as they dug out the last meter or two of the well (they may have driven timber into the bottom of the shaft to temporarily block off the water flow). They used impermeable clay to seal off the sides and surface around the well, protecting it from a seepage of contaminated surface water (also, the top of the well was on an elevated mound, lessening the chance of seepage into the well). Potsherds formed a filtration level at the bottom of the well; dirt and sand would settle under the potsherds, and the water above it remained relatively clean. The well may have served a temple or military installation.[30] The elaborate and sophisticated construction of this well indicates that it was not one of the temporary, ad hoc wells dug in the midst of the Nile River crisis described in this passage. Even so, its location and the date of its construction place it near the time and place of the exodus, and it illustrates the point that the Egyptians had an advanced understanding of well technology.

Theological Summary of Key Points

1. The turning of the Nile to blood is best understood as an apocalyptic sign analogous to the moon turning to blood as a token of the day of YHWH (Joel 2:31 [Hebrew: 3:4]; Rev. 6:12). That which ought to be the source of life, the Nile, is here symbolically a bleeding wound and filled with tokens of death in the dead fish. It serves to warn Egypt that God is coming in judgment. The point is that for those who are willing to see them, there are portents of terrible things to come. Jesus makes a similar point in Matt. 16:3, observing that just as a red sky at morning is a portent of a great storm, so also there are signs of judgment for those who can discern them. Regardless of what one makes of the meaning of it turning to "blood," it is clear that there was little significant damage to the nation in this event. Thus, one should not dwell on the transformation of the Nile, as though "the Nile turned to blood" were of itself the meaning of the text. God gives warnings to people, but people disregard the warnings, preferring explanations that see only surface facts while ignoring deeper significance.

2. Pharaoh and the Egyptians disregarded the sign. If our understanding of the events is correct, they were able to scoff at Moses, explaining that the redness of the Nile was not unprecedented even if it was unusually severe. But the fact that an event has a rational,

30. Henning Franzmeier, "Sherds, Clay and Clean Water," *Ancient Egypt* 8, no 6 (2008): 45–49.

natural explanation does not mean that it is not also a sign from God. To return to Jesus's warnings to the Pharisees in Matt. 16:1–3, we can see that Jesus upbraided them for demanding an extraordinary, unnatural or spectacular sign from God while ignoring the signs that were right before their eyes. The problem with them and with the Egyptians was not that no sufficient sign had been given to them, but that their hearts were evil and hostile to God (Matt. 16:4). In a similar manner, Amos rebuked Israel for ignoring the many "natural" signs of judgment that God had sent their way (Amos 4:6–12).

3. God spoke to the Egyptians in a way that was relevant to their culture. Their whole existence depended on the Nile, and thus the event had obvious symbolic implications. More than that, their own literature, as illustrated by the "Admonitions of Ipuwer," testifies that they looked upon the condition of the Nile as a reflection of the moral health of the nation and that they saw it as a sign of calamity when, as they put it, the Nile turned to blood. By their own standards, they should have realized that something was terribly wrong and that they faced disaster if they did not change their ways.

4. The turning of the Nile to blood was essentially a token in that no Egyptians died and none of their property was destroyed. The death of the fish would entail some economic loss, but the fish did not really belong to anyone. By contrast, the death of the cattle and the destruction of the crops in later plagues were direct attacks on the property of Egyptians. The point is that God begins his judgment with a warning. He does not strike with deadly plagues without first giving the people a chance to repent and obey.

Excursus: Did the Nile Turn to Literal Blood?

Readers naturally ask if the word "blood" here should be taken literally. In favor of doing so, it is the normal word for blood (דָּם). Against taking it literally, several factors are important.

First, the Egyptians themselves could speak of the Nile becoming blood, but not mean it literally. It was a way of describing catastrophe in the land. The "Admonitions of Ipuwer" describes the chaos of the first intermediate period, when Egypt lacked central authority, and lawlessness and deprivation prevailed. According to this text, thieves and robbers became wealthy, routine maintenance of facilities in the land was neglected, and prosperity disappeared. Wild animals such as crocodiles were out of control, unemployment was rife, and people despaired of life. In the midst of this, Ipuwer 2.10 says, "Indeed, the river is blood, yet one drinks from it."[31] Clearly this is not meant to be taken literally; it suggests that the waters are befouled. It perhaps also alludes to the fact that there were dead bodies in the Nile (Ipuwer 2.6–7) and that an ecological crisis had beset Egypt (Ipuwer 3.1).

Second, the Bible uses the term "blood" in a nonliteral manner. Most significant here is the eschatological sign that the moon turns to blood (Joel 2:31 [Hebrew: 3:4]; Rev. 6:12).[32] We are not meant to suppose from such language that the moon is to become a great ball of literal blood; the language is a sign of judgment. The same is true here. Similarly, and notwithstanding the notion of transubstantiation, Jesus did not mean for his disciples to understand that the wine in the cup of the Eucharist was literally his blood (Mark 14:24).

Third, in Exod. 7:24 the liquid in the Nile during this plague is actually called "water" and not "blood." The verse reads, "And all the Egyptians dug around the Nile for water to drink, for they were not able to drink from the water of the Nile."[33] This should not be construed as a slip on the narrator's part.

Fourth, the Egyptians dug wells along the sides of the Nile, using the sand to filter the water and make it potable. This implies that the water was not literal blood, as one cannot obtain potable water from blood in this manner.

Fifth, the plague seems to have been rather mild in its effects. The water was for a time toxic so that many fish died, and the frogs came up from the banks. Episodes of pollutants striking bodies of water and killing off large numbers of fish are not uncommon, and most of us have seen masses of dead fish washed up on a beach or riverbank due to manmade or natural toxins, such as a "red tide" or an algal bloom. But such events are typically transitory and are rarely horrendous calamities. The narrative in fact implies that the Egyptians came off relatively unscathed, being able to obtain water and continue with their lives. But had the whole river turned to literal blood, it would have been a catastrophe of unimaginable proportions. The Nile in Egypt

---

31. "The Admonitions of an Egyptian Sage: The Admonitions of Ipuwer," translated by Nili Shupak (COS 1.42.93)
32. C. F. Keil and F. Delitzsch, *Commentary on the Old Testament,* Electronic Edition from Oaktree Software (Edinburgh: T. & T. Clark, 1866–1891), comments to Exod. 7:14-25.
33. The text of 7:24b (כִּי לֹא יָכְלוּ לִשְׁתֹּת מִמֵּימֵי הַיְאֹר) plainly does not mean that there was no water in the Nile but only blood. The phrase מִמֵּימֵי הַיְאֹר ("from the waters of the Nile") indicates that the liquid that made up the Nile was water.

is almost 600 miles long. If it had all become literal blood under the Egyptian sun, the whole river would have become a thick, decaying sludge of biological waste. No potable water would have been available for the entire population for months or even years. It is difficult to calculate how long it would have taken waters from the sources of the Nile far to the south in Ethiopia to wash away the tens of millions of gallons of blood as well as the coagulated and decomposing remains of that blood. Meanwhile, those who did not die of thirst would probably have succumbed to disease brought on by the overwhelming amount of decay that would have taken place in the staggering amount of biological waste (almost all Egyptians lived within five miles of the Nile, and many lived right beside it). It is more likely that the waters looked like blood and were a token of the death and judgment on Egypt that was to come.[34]

It is important to take note of Pharaoh's response. For the entire Nile to turn to literal blood would have been, as mentioned above, unimaginably horrible and deadly, as well as unprecedented. But Pharaoh regards the event with complete indifference. By contrast, he hastens to come to terms with Moses when there are too many frogs in the land, and that despite the fact that his magicians could imitate the event by producing a few frogs of their own! Pharaoh was not astonished by the Nile event, and he did not regard it as a threat.

THREE: THE FROGS (7:25—8:15 [Hebrew 7:25—8:11])

For the first time, Egypt experiences severe discomfort. An alarmed Pharaoh promises to accede to Moses's demands in return for relief, but he reneges.

Translation

7:25 Seven days passed after YHWH struck the Nile,
8:1a and YHWH said to Moses,
8:1b "Go to Pharaoh

34. Currid, *Ancient Egypt*, 106, confusedly states, "In no way does the Book of Exodus present that plague as having been metaphorical in nature; rather, it relates the disaster as direct historical narrative." But the claim here is not that the plague was merely a metaphor; the transformation of the Nile really did occur. The point is that the term "blood" relates to the color of the Nile, not its chemical composition. And even if one believes that the Nile literally became blood, it is still, in the narrative, symbolic of worse things to come and only a token of death. In the Nile event itself, according to the text, no Egyptians died; they were merely inconvenienced.

8:1c and say to him,
8:1d 'Thus says YHWH,
8:1e "Release my people,
8:1f that they may serve me.
8:2a But if you persist in refusing[35] to grant a release,
8:2b then watch as I plague[36] all your territory with frogs.
8:3a The Nile will swarm with frogs,
8:3b and they will emerge[37]
8:3c and they will go into your house and into your bedroom and on your bed, and into the houses of your officials[38] and upon your people, and into your ovens and into your kneading bowls.
8:4 And against you and your people and all your officials will the frogs arise."'"[39]
8:5a Then YHWH said to Moses,
8:5b "Say to Aaron,
8:5c 'Stretch out your hand with your staff over the streams, over the rivers and over the pools,
8:5d and raise up frogs on the land of Egypt.'"
8:6a And Aaron stretched out his hand over the waters of Egypt,
8:6b and the frogs arose
8:6c and they covered the land of Egypt.
8:7a The magicians did the same with their secret tricks:

---

35. The Piel participle of מאן is routinely written without the preformative מְ. See Exod. 9:2; 10:4; Jer. 13:10; 38:21. The participle implies persistence in refusing to yield.
36. The pattern הִנֵּה אָנֹכִי serves as the apodosis, but it is particularly vivid, calling on Pharaoh to observe (הִנֵּה) and giving focus to the process of God bringing about an infestation, using the participle (נֹגֵף).
37. This short clause describes the frogs rising up out of the Nile and invading the countryside and towns.
38. Here and throughout the plague narratives, Pharaoh's "servants" (עֲבָדֶיךָ) are his officials, not his slaves or the common people. The common people are his עַם.
39. The idiom here is comparable to 2 Chron. 21:17, וַיַּעֲלוּ בִיהוּדָה ("and they went up against Judah"). The inversion of the normal word order to an order of object–verb–subject indicates that the sentence is offline. It serves several functions. First, the change in pattern signals the end of the discourse. Second, this sentence is a comment on the previous sentence. Third, the fronting of the direct object makes that the focus. In other words, the frogs will seem to be attacking the pharaoh, his officials and his people personally, and will not seem to be merely present as a nuisance.

8:7b they raised[40] frogs up on the land of Egypt.
8:8a And Pharaoh called for Moses and for Aaron,
8:8b and he said,
8:8c "Make supplication to YHWH
8:8d that he remove the frogs from me and from my people;[41]
8:8e and then I will release[42] the people
8:8f so that they may sacrifice to YHWH."
8:9a And Moses said to Pharaoh,
8:9b "Exalt yourself above me![43]
8:9c When[44] shall I make supplication for you and your servants and your people, that the frogs be exterminated from you and your houses?
8:9d Only in the Nile will any remain!"
8:10a And he said,

---

40. The *wayyiqtol* is epexegetical.
41. This clause is an indirect statement.
42. The *weyiqtol* with paragogic ה marks this clause as an apodosis; the protasis is 8:8cd. That is, Pharaoh is proposing terms; if Moses will get rid of the frogs, Pharaoh will let the people go.
43. The root פאר (II) essentially relates to the idea of glory. In the Piel, it means to "glorify," as in Isa. 55:5 פֵּאֲרָךְ ("he has glorified you"). In the Hithpael it means to glorify oneself or to display glory, as in Isa. 61:3, where Israel is a מַטַּע יְהוָה לְהִתְפָּאֵר ("planting of YHWH to display [his] glory"). Two interpretations of Moses's words here (הִתְפָּאֵר עָלַי) are possible. It could be a polite and even enthusiastic response, perhaps in formal court language, meant to show how pleased Moses is that Pharaoh is willing to release the Hebrews. Thus the TNIV translates it, "I leave to you the honor of setting the time." But Rashi (11th century Rabbi Solomon ben Isaac) and Rashbam (12th century Rabbi Samuel ben Meir) both take the phrase in a negative sense, suggesting that Pharaoh was presumptively assuming that he could demand that Moses intercede for him (Martin L. Lockshin, ed., trans., *Rashbam's Commentary on Exodus: An Annotated Translation* (Atlanta: Scholar's Press, 1997), 77). The two other uses of פאר (Hithpael) with על (Judg. 7:2; Isa. 10:15) support the latter interpretation, as both imply a boasting in oneself over against another party. On the other hand, context suggests that Moses really does believe Pharaoh at this point and is excited that Israel is to be released. Moses's disappointment and disillusion are reflected in his words at 8:29(25). As such, Moses's words here should not be taken as a sarcastic rebuke.
44. Only here does the interrogative particle מָתַי ("when?") have the preposition לְ. It does not seem to change the meaning, but it is perhaps more formal than מָתַי by itself. It is followed by a *yiqtol*, and by analogy עַד־מָתַי with a *yiqtol* can also mean "when" (e.g., Amos 8:5).

8:10b “Tomorrow.”
8:10c And he said,
8:10d “[It will be] as you say[45]
8:10e so that you may know
8:10f that there is no [god] like YHWH our God.[46]
8:11a The frogs will depart[47] from you and your houses and your officials and your people;
8:11b only in the Nile will any remain.”
8:12a And Moses and Aaron went out from Pharaoh,
8:12b and Moses cried to YHWH concerning the matter of the frogs that he had inflicted upon Pharaoh.
8:13a And YHWH did as Moses said,[48]
8:13b and the frogs that had been[49] in the houses, the courts, and the fields died.
8:14a So they piled them in heaps all over the place,[50]
8:14b and the land reeked.
8:15a And Pharaoh saw
8:15b that there was relief,
8:15c and he made his heart leaden,[51]

---

45. Lit. “like your word” (כִּדְבָרְךָ).
46. This is an indirect statement.
47. The *weqatal* וְסָרוּ is epexegetical of כִּדְבָרְךָ in clause 8:10d.
48. Lit. “according to the word of Moses” (כִּדְבַר מֹשֶׁה).
49. “That had been” is literally “from,” as in מִן־הַבָּתִּים, “from the houses.” The preposition establishes where the frogs were at the time they died out.
50. The phrase חֳמָרִם חֳמָרִם (“heaps, heaps”) means that there were heaps of dead frogs everywhere.
51. The use of כבד (whether in the Qal, the Hiphil or as an adjective) with לֵב to describe the heart as being resistant, or making the heart resistant, to prudent counsel and to the word of God appears in Exod. 7:14; 8:11(15), 28(32); 9:7, 34; 10:1; 1 Sam. 6:6. In every case it refers to the heart of Pharaoh and of the Egyptians. The root כבד literally means to be “heavy.” This should not be lost in translation, but the phrase “a heavy heart” would be misleading since in English that phrase implies a heart that is sorrowful. Here, it plainly means that the heart is stubborn in persisting in evil behavior and is impervious to good advice. I have used the translation “leaden” as that connotes not only heaviness but also being unresponsive and sealed shut. Dorian G. Cox, “The Hardening of Pharaoh’s Heart in Its Literary and Cultural Contexts,” *BSac* 163, no. 3 (2006): 304-5, notes that כבד is used elsewhere of organs of speech or perception with the meaning that they are not functioning properly (Gen. 48:10; Exod. 4:10; Isa. 6:10; 59:1). This suggests that Pharaoh’s heart is not functioning properly; that is, he is being irrational. It is possible that the metaphor of a “heavy” or “leaden” heart

8:15d and he would not listen to them.
8:15e [It was] just as YHWH had said.

Structure

The narrative of the frogs contains every formal element for a plague narrative.

I. YHWH Commissions Moses and Aaron to Appear Before Pharaoh (7:25—8:4)
  A. Background Information
  B. A Demand that Pharaoh Release Israel
  C. A Warning About a Coming Judgment
  D. Specific Instructions for Aaron
II. YHWH Commands Moses to Begin the Plague (8:5)
III. Moses and Aaron Carry Out the Commission (8:6)
  A. Moses and Aaron Perform a Ritual Act to Initiate the Plague
  B. The Miracle or Plague Begins and its Effects Are Described
IV. Pharaoh's Advisors and Magicians Respond with a Duplication of YHWH's Miracle (8:7)
V. Pharaoh Interviews Moses in the Course of the Plague (8:8–11)
  A. A Request that Moses Intercede for Egypt to Stop the Plague
  B. A Promise to Release the People to Go into the Wilderness and Sacrifice
  C. Moses Answers Pharaoh
VI. Moses Intercedes for Egypt, and the Plague Stops (8:12–13)
VII. Other Information (8:14)
VIII. Pharaoh Hardens his Heart, and he Refuses to Listen (8:15abcd)
IX. Affirmation that YHWH's Word Was Fulfilled (8:15e)

Commentary

7:25–8:4. The commission to Moses and Aaron is dominated by a

---

had some significance in Egyptian culture. In the standard treatment of the judgment of the soul in Egyptian religion, a person's heart was weighed in a balance against a feather of Maat, goddess of truth and order. It may be that the idea was that a heart that was heavy with evil would cause the scale to tilt, putting the scales out of balance (this image was widely used in New Kingdom tombs). If so, this would explain why this idiom is used in this context.

direct warning to Pharaoh. This is appropriate, since the first two miracles were essentially symbolic. Genuine suffering for the Egyptians begins with this plague. The language is blunt (8:2b) and the nature of the troubles to come is described in detail (8:3). The frogs are even described as an enemy of Egypt (8:5; see translation note). In short, this is a clear warning.

8:5. At this stage of the story, Aaron is still the public face of the delegation, with Moses staying in the background. Thus, the directive is for Moses to tell Aaron what to do. As the events progress, Moses will be more and more in the foreground.

8:6. The fulfillment of the directive is the point here; Moses and Aaron did their part, and God did his. That is, the verse is testimony both to the faithfulness of Moses and Aaron and to the power of God.

8:7. Egyptian magicians are somehow able to produce frogs. While some would see this as evidence of demonic power, it was more likely the equivalent of a stage magician pulling a rabbit out of a hat. It certainly had no effect on Pharaoh who, though he had dismissed the Nile turning to blood as insignificant, was thoroughly alarmed at the frogs overrunning his land. This suggests that Pharaoh himself knew that the magicians' trick was phony and therefore meaningless, but that the volume of frogs swarming up from the Nile was new and very disturbing to him.

8:8–11. Moses appears to be thrilled by Pharaoh's quick capitulation. His words, "Exalt yourself above me," may be a way of saying, "Don't feel humiliated by this episode; I have no desire to boast of how I forced you to submit." In other words, it is meant to allow Pharaoh to save face. Granting Pharaoh the right to set the time when the plague would end shows respect, but it also makes the point that only Moses, as God's prophet, has the power to bring this calamity to an end. Pharaoh, the divine king, does not have the power, even if Moses does show him deference. It is possible to be critical of Moses for being gullible here (God had told him that Pharaoh would not let the people go, and thus he should not have believed that Pharaoh's change of heart was real). But I think we should be more sympathetic toward Moses. This is the first time Pharaoh feigned repentance; in subsequent episodes, Moses would be more skeptical. Meanwhile, it was to Moses's credit that he gave Pharaoh the benefit of the doubt (1 Cor. 13:7) and that he hoped to end this business without inflicting great suffering on Egypt.

8:12–13. The power of God and authority of Moses are displayed as clearly in the abrupt termination of the plague as they were displayed in its commencement.

8:14. The extra information that the frogs were piled in heaps enables the reader to comprehend how massive the infestation was.

8:15. Here, the stubbornness of Pharaoh is attributed not to God but to Pharaoh himself. Pharaoh is portrayed as at the point where his will is on a knife's edge; he can either yield or stiffen his resolve to fight against God. In making his heart impervious to what is right and to good sense, he set himself on a path whereby change would be impossible. God, in this passage, is portrayed as merely foreknowing what Pharaoh would do, not as causing it.

Theological Summary of Key Points

Every plague narrative in Exodus makes the same basic points: 1) The calamities show that YHWH is powerful, 2) Pharaoh was stubborn, and 3) Israel's deliverance from slavery is due entirely to the faithfulness of YHWH to his covenant with the patriarchs. Beyond that, this narrative gives us insight on the two principal human characters, Moses and Pharaoh. The former is respectful, willing to take Pharaoh at his word, eager to see this business end, and no more happy about the suffering of the Egyptians than he is about the suffering of the Hebrews. The latter is weak (looking for deliverance from an affliction no more serious than frogs), deceitful (or at best unreliable), and willing to risk greater calamities for his people rather than swallow his pride and let the Hebrew slaves go.

Excursus: The Plagues as a Battle with the Gods of Egypt

A number of scholars contend that the biblical plagues should be regarded as a battle between YHWH and the gods of Egypt, in which each plague represents a triumph by Israel's God over a specific, individual Egyptian deity. The biblical justification for this view is Exod. 12:12, which speaks of YHWH executing justice against all the gods of Egypt. In essence, this interpretation assigns at least one Egyptian god to each of the plagues and then describes how that plague displays the power of YHWH over that deity. This interpretation is enthusiastically championed by Currid,[52] although it finds other advocates as

52. Currid, *Ancient Egypt*, 108–13. On p. 108, n.13, Currid seems perplexed that anyone should question this interpretation.

well.[53] Egyptian gods supposedly attacked in the Exodus miracles are given in Table 6.[54]

Numerous scholars connect the turning of the Nile to blood with the god Hapy.[55] This deity is portrayed in the Egyptian iconography as a somewhat androgynous man, with folds of belly fat and enlarged breasts. The breasts symbolize the abundance provided by Hapy, as the Nile inundation deposited the fertile, alluvial soil into which crops were sown. Interpreters who contend that this plague is an attack on Hapy argue that the plague showed that he was no true deity and that he could not provide food for the people. A significant problem here is that Hapy was not a "river god" or the personification of the Nile, he was the god of the inundation itself. As R. David states, "Although the Nile was a bringer of life to Egypt, the Egyptians do not appear to have deified the river at any time in their history. The god Hapy was a personification of the inundation and not of the Nile."[56] This is not an insignificant distinction; an attack upon Hapy should have been a failed inundation, not the turning of the Nile blood-red. Since Hapy was thought to bring about abundant harvests (he was a kind of horn-of-plenty god), a defeat of Hapy should have meant failed crops, but as the subsequent plagues of hail and locusts show, the plants for that year grew reasonably well. As the Egyptians did not think of the river itself

53. E.g., Sarna, *Exodus*, 40; Peter Enns, *Inspiration and Incarnation: Evangelicals and the Problem of the Old Testament* (Grand Rapids: Baker, 2005), 100-1.
54. Currid, *Ancient Egypt*, 108-13.
55. E.g., Sarna, *Exodus*, 39; Enns, *Exodus*, 200.
56. Rosalie David, *Religion and Magic in Ancient Egypt* (London: Penguin, 2002), 9. It is also noteworthy that the main cult center of Hapy was at Aswan and Gebel el-Silsila, on the southern boundary of pharaonic Egypt and therefore as far from Moses and the Israelites as it could possibly have been (Lorna Oakes and Lucia Gahlin, *Ancient Egypt: An Illustrated Reference to the Myths, Religions, Pyramids and Temples of the Land of the Pharaohs* (New York: Hermes House, 2002), 275). See also Shaw and Nicholson, *Dictionary*, 118. This further challenges the idea that the Egyptians would have regarded the events as directed against Hapy. Egyptians in the Delta may not have worshipped him at all.

as a god, it is difficult to see how they would have regarded this event as directed against Hapi or any other specific deity.[57]

TABLE 6. GODS SUPPOSEDLY ASSOCIATED WITH THE PLAGUES		
Plague	**Egyptian God**	**Alleged Significance of Plague**
Nile to Blood	Hapy	River god, defeated by YHWH, cannot provide food for Egypt
Frogs	Heket	The goddess was unable to prevent YHWH from multiplying the frogs
Mosquitoes and Flies	Khepri	Plagues directed against this god because he is depicted as a "flying beetle"[59]
Livestock	Apis, Ptah, or Hathor	YHWH more powerful than any Egyptian bovine god
Skin Ulcers	Sekhmet, Amen-Re	YHWH more powerful than Egyptian gods who could send or cure plagues
Hail	Nut, Shu, and Tefnut, or Seth	Plague mocks Egyptian sky deities, or it defeats Seth the bringer of storms
Locusts	Senehem	Plague defeats Egyptian god who protects against locusts
Darkness	Amen-Re	Attack on chief Egyptian god, a solar deity
Firstborn	Pharaoh or Osiris	Attack upon dynastic succession of Pharaoh, or upon the god of the underworld

Heket, supposedly the goddess who was attacked in the frog plague, was a goddess of childbirth. She is sometimes said to have been the wife of the god Khnum, a ram-headed god whose cult center was far to the south, near Elephantine. Khnum is a creator god who is said to have made humans at a pottery wheel. As such, it is not surprising that

---

57. Osiris was also associated with the fertility of the Nile, but he was not a river god. Kitchen, *Reliability*, 253, makes the far-fetched claim that the redness of the river would have been symbolic of Seth, murderer of Osiris. But this would have been only to exalt one Egyptian god at the expense of another, something Moses was not keen to do, and there is really no reason to think that the Egyptians connected the color of the river to Seth. The red color of Seth is associated with the desert, not with the Nile. Otherwise, except for making a limited connection between the first plague and Hapy, and between the ninth plague and Amen-Re, Kitchen dismisses other linkage between individual gods and the plagues as "unjustified subjectivity."

58. Currid, *Ancient Egypt*, 111.

he should have been associated with a goddess of childbirth.[59] Currid asserts that Heket was "one of the main goddesses of Egypt,"[60] but this is difficult to affirm. She is scarcely seen the iconography of Egypt (except for amulets used in magic to assist women in childbirth[61]) and does not figure prominently in the myths. Handbooks on Egyptian religion hardly mention her at all.[62] The remains of a temple to her can be found at Qus, just north of Luxor, but this is very late, from the Ptolemaic period.[63] Heket is associated with the frog, probably because the abundance of frogs that emerged from the river symbolized new life for the Egyptians. It is therefore very difficult to see how an unusually large number of frogs from the Nile could be regarded as an attack on Heket. Currid argues that Heket "also had the responsibility to control the multiplication of frogs in ancient Egypt by protecting the frog-eating crocodiles," but that YHWH "overwhelmed" her.[64] This claim strikes me as far-fetched, and Currid's only evidence is a citation of G. A. F. Knight, who himself provides no evidence at all.[65] An assertion of this sort needs documentation: Is it based on an inscription or papyrus, or based on a later Greco-Roman source, or is it simply an exegetical legend? There being no real evidence that New Kingdom Egyptians believed that Heket controlled the frog population, it is hard to see how this plague could be a polemic against her.

The notion that the plagues of mosquitoes and flies may have been

---

59. On the other hand, a Greco-Roman era temple to Khnum at Esna, south of Luxor, links him to the goddess Neith (Shaw and Nicholson, *Dictionary*, 151).
60. Currid, *Ancient Egypt*, 110.
61. Also, frog amulets used as symbols of life and rebirth were very common in Egypt, but these were not necessarily associated with Heket. See Shaw and Nicholson, *Dictionary*, 103–4. Heket is portrayed in a limestone relief at Deir el-Bahri (Thebes) in Hatshepsut's temple, where she is assisting Khnum as he fashions Hatshepsut and her *ka*. See Watterson, *Gods*, 184.
62. Passing descriptions of her appear, for example, in Barbara Lesko, *The Great Goddesses of Egypt* (Norman: University of Oklahoma Press, 1999), 180 and 267-8, and Robert A. Armour, *Gods and Myths of Ancient Egypt* (Cairo: American University in Cairo Press, 2001), 46, 126, 165.
63. Baines and Málek, *Cultural Atlas*, 111. She may have also had a temple at Hur in Middle Egypt. Watterson, *Gods*, 185, claims that after Heket lost prominence in Aswan her cult center moved to the Faiyum Oasis.
64. Currid, *Ancient Egypt*, 110.
65. George A. Knight, *Theology as Narration: A Commentary on the Book of Exodus* (Grand Rapids: Eerdmans, 1976), 62.

directed against Khepri[66] is altogether unpersuasive. The god Khepri is represented by the scarab, or dung beetle. He is sometimes equated with Atum, the self-created god who emerged from the waters and then created the primordial gods. Because the dung beetle appears to emerge spontaneously from balls of dung, Khepri, as the self-created Atum, is associated with that beetle. In addition, since the dung beetle pushes a little ball of dung across the ground, the Egyptians connected it to the progress of the sun across the sky, and Khepri is also identified with the sun-god, Re. Even if the scarab beetle could fly, this plays no role in Egyptian mythology. There is no reason to associate mosquitoes and flies with the dung beetle, and Currid provides no explanation of how the plagues represent a polemic against Khepri. I do not believe that Egyptians, seeing a swarm of flies, would take that as evidence that Khepri had been defeated, or indeed would connect them to Khepri at all.

This brings us to the plague on the livestock. The Apis was a sacred bull kept near the temple of the god Ptah at Memphis; the bull was thought to be a living manifestation of the god. When the Apis died, there was a period of national mourning and the dead bull was embalmed and buried at Saqqara. A search for a new bull was made, and it was identified by having a diamond-shaped pattern of white hair on its forehead, a scarab mark under its tongue, and the image of a vulture on its back. The Apis cult is thus linked to the god Ptah, but the deity himself is generally portrayed as a semi-mummified man (although a creator-god, he was also an earth deity and associated with funerary rites).[67] Hathor, the fertility goddess, is associated with the cow and in iconography is often portrayed as a woman with cow's ears; she sometimes appears simply as a cow or simply as a woman.

One thus might suppose that, there being ample association between cattle and Egyptian gods, the death of cattle by plague was an assault on those gods. But this is wrong. The fact that Egyptians associated their gods with various animals does not mean that they regarded the ordinary animals themselves as sacred. The existence of the sacred Apis bull is especially misleading to westerners and Christians; it by no means implied that Egyptians worshipped cattle or regarded them all as manifestations of Ptah. "Only one bull at a time was regarded as Apis rather than the whole species."[68] For the Egyptians, ordinary cattle were exactly what they were to other

66. Currid, *Ancient Egypt*, 111.
67. Watterson, *Gods*, 161.
68. Ibid., 165.

peoples: dumb animals that were a source of milk, labor, food, and leather. They would slaughter their cattle, just as any other people would.[69] By analogy, the manifestation of the goddess Ta-weret was the hippopotamus, but this does not mean that Egyptians revered ordinary hippopotami. To the contrary, they regarded the beasts as a great nuisance and organized hippopotamus hunts.[70] The Egyptians would have regarded the death of large numbers of cattle as an economic disaster, not as an attack on Ptah or Hathor. We should also bear in mind that the Bible never says that the Apis died in this plague; it surely would not have omitted this if that had been the whole point of the narrative.

Sekhmet, the lion-headed goddess, was regarded as a bringer of plagues but also was said to have the ability to cure people of disease.[71] Her chief sanctuary was at Memphis. She came to be identified with Mut, goddess of Thebes and wife of Amun. Amenhotep III set up an enormous number of statues of a seated Sekhmet/Mut at Karnak.[72] Amun, whose central shrine was at Thebes and who, in the New Kingdom, was as close to being a universal deity as Egypt ever had (excepting the eccentric and short-lived cult of Aten), was also said to have healing powers.[73] Currid therefore argues that the plague of boils was directed against these gods.[74]

This claim is not as strong as it may at first appear. First, Sekhmet as a bringer of plagues bears no resemblance to the skin affliction, something like boils, described in the Bible. The plagues attributed in the myths to Sekhmet are true pestilences that wipe out masses of people. Mythology associated with Sekhmet is probably the Egyptians' way of accounting for bubonic plague and other catastrophic pandemics that killed tens of thousands. The biblical affliction of "boils," by contrast, does not kill anyone at all. It is most doubtful that Egyptians would see any relationship between the lesions on their skin and the stories of Sekhmet killing whole populations.

On the other hand, as described above, Sekhmet is associated with healing. Of course Egypt had healing gods—every ancient culture did, since a primary function of magic and ritual was to cure people. The

69. David, *Handbook*, 326.

70. Shaw and Nicholson, *Dictionary*, 129-30.

71. Lesko, *Great Goddesses*, 273.

72. Watterson, *Gods*, 171. Over 600 of these statues are extant.

73. "The God Amon as Healer and Magician," translated by John A. Wilson (*ANET* 369).

74. Currid, *Ancient Egypt*, 111.

fact that this or that god was thought to be a healer is not of itself meaningful. More significantly, the power of a god in the ancient world was connected to ritual and cult life. When Elijah wanted to demonstrate that YHWH was more powerful than Baal, he did so in a cultic setting, with both him and the priests of Baal meeting on Mt. Carmel and calling upon their deities after their own fashions (1 Kings 18). For an Egyptian to see the plague of boils as a triumph of YHWH over Sekhmet, they would need to see some kind of ritual contest between Aaron and the priests of Sekhmet analogous to what we see in the confrontation on Mt. Carmel. Yet the Bible describes no such episode. Obviously the biblical writer was not unaware of the activity of the Egyptian priests (as indicated by the report that they could change their rods to snakes), but it never suggests that there was any failed effort by the priests of Sekhmet or Amen-Re to counteract the "magic" of Moses and Aaron in this plague with magic of their own. Because of the ritualized way in which Moses and Aaron began the plague (Exod. 9:10), the Egyptians would have connected their suffering to the power of YHWH. But they would not have necessarily supposed that the event had anything to do with Sekhmet or Amen-Re unless there were an explicit ritual confrontation between Moses and the priests of those gods.

Currid calls the plague of hail "a mockery of the Egyptian heavenly deities" (Nut, Shu, and Tefnut).[75] This claim, too, goes far beyond the evidence. Nut, Shu, and Tefnut are primeval deities of a standard version of the Egyptian ennead (the nine gods). In the Heliopolitan creation theology, the self-generated Atum emerged from the primeval mound in the primeval waters, and by some means[76] he brought forth Shu, god of the air, and Tefnut, goddess of moisture. Shu and Tefnut then produced two children, Nut, goddess of the sky, and Geb, god of the earth. Geb impregnated Nut, who gave birth to the sun, stars, and planets. But Shu decided to separate them, so he interposed himself between the two, the air (Shu) separating the earth (Geb) from the sky (Nut).[77] This is one of the most familiar images of Egyptian religious art, with Shu portrayed as a man standing up. Beneath him lies a nude man on the ground (Geb), and above him is nude woman (Nut). The woman's body is arched to represent the vault of heaven, and she

75. Ibid., 112.

76. Sometimes he is said to have spat, but the more likely original version of the myth has this procreation to be by masturbation (presumably because he had no consort).

77. The myth, in its various versions, is much more complex than indicated here. See Watterson, *Gods*, 45–58.

looks down, touching the ground with only her toes and the tips of her fingers. Sometimes Nut is shown with the sun and stars in her body. In another myth, Nut is the mother of the sun; she swallows the sun every evening and gives birth to him every morning, and thus the sun makes its daily circuit along her body, the vault of heaven. Because of this myth of rebirth, and because she is the deified sky, Nut is prominent in funerary ritual, with paintings of her adorning tombs and coffins. Nut thus became the mother of the dead, as she had the power to revivify them.[78] Tefnut, as a primeval goddess, represented order, and in another myth she was one of the eyes of Re who roamed about as a lioness doing terrible destruction. Shu, besides his role in the creation myth, has various mythological associations (as sunlight, as the moon, and even as a torturer of the dead in the underworld).[79] All of this indicates that it is very difficult to make a link between Nut, Shu, or Tefnut and the hailstorm of Exodus. The myths do not portray them as protectors against storms, and the mere fact that they are cosmic deities has no bearing on this episode. Exodus does not allude to them in any way. They and their cults play no role in the story. This is not to say that the hailstorm would not have provoked a religious terror in the Egyptians; certainly it would have.[80] The fact that Moses had summoned the storm by calling on his God would have filled the Egyptians with dread of YHWH, but we have no grounds for making any claims beyond that.

An alternative, proposed by Enns, associates the hail with the god Seth.[81] This god is most prominent in the Osiris myth (as the brother and murderer of Osiris); he appears in iconography as a peculiar dog-like animal, although he sometimes appears as other detested animals, such as the hippopotamus. He generally represented disorder, and for this reason perhaps is thought to have been a bringer of storms. Many Egyptians may have feared him as a kind of devil-figure, but others revered him. He was especially popular with the Hyksos of the 2nd Intermediate Period (he was sometimes regarded as a god of foreigners[82]), although Seti I of the 19th dynasty was named for him. Thus, although it is true that Seth was associated with storms, it is not clear how YHWH's sending of a hailstorm would be a "defeat" of

78. Lesko, *Great Goddesses*, 38-44.
79. Shaw and Nicholson, *Dictionary*, 270.
80. See Hoffmeier, *Israel in Egypt*, 150–1.
81. Enns, *Inspiration*, 101.
82. Veronica Ions, *Egyptian Mythology* (New York: Peter Bedrick Books, 1968), 64.

Seth unless the storm were placed in the context of a contest between Moses and the priests of Seth—which is plainly not the case. Although the Egyptians might try to placate Seth in order to restrain his chaotic nature so that he would not send storms,[83] he was not a protector of Egypt from storms.

For the specified deity of the locust plague, Currid asserts that the Egyptians worshipped "Senehem," a "protector against ravages from pests," but he also says that this Senehem was a minor deity, and so suggests that perhaps the gods "in general" were supposed to protect Egypt from locusts.[84] There is in fact no evidence that the Egyptians had a deity named Senehem. The Egyptian word *snḥm* means "locust."[85] But this does not mean that there was a god, "Senehem," who protected people from locusts. If one is going to claim that the plague was directed against this "god," one has the duty to show evidence that the Egyptians worshiped a being of this name. Was "Senehem" a god or a goddess? How is "Senehem" depicted in Egyptian religious art? What texts or inscriptions refer to this deity? Where is a temple or cult center dedicated to "Senehem"? Are there any extant prayers or liturgies that call on "Senehem" to save people from locusts? Unless one can satisfactorily answer such questions, one should not claim that YHWH directed his power against a god of this name. At the same time, it is hardly surprising that Egyptians might invoke the gods for protection against locusts, as Egypt from time to time did suffer from locust migrations. But the biblical text says nothing about "Senehem" or any other god, and the claim that this plague was meant as a polemic against Egyptian religion rings hollow. The plague was not an attack on their religion but on their crops.

The darkness seems to suggest a polemic against the sun god. Egypt, in fact, had many gods associated with the sun. One normally speaks of Re (or "Ra") as the sun god, but other gods could be merged with Re by syncretism and thus be regarded as solar deities: Amun became Amen-Re, Montu (the war god) became Mont-Re, and Horus, son of Isis and Osiris, became Re-Horakhty, the sun at the horizon. Atum, the Heliopolitan creator god, is also Re. Other gods are in some way associated with the sun: Aten is the sun disk, and Shu, god of the air, is associated with sunlight. The god Seth was supposed to sail

83. Shaw and Nicholson, *Dictionary*, 264.

84. Currid, *Ancient Egypt*, 112. His evidence for the claim that many gods protected against grasshoppers is a line from the 25th dynasty Tanis Stele.

85. Raymond O. Faulkner, *A Concise Dictionary of Middle Egyptian* (Oxford: Griffith Institute, 1999), 233.

into the underworld with the sun (Re) in the solar ship (the Barque of Re) during the night; he would defend the sun against the serpent Apophis (although the role of Seth is sometimes taken by Thoth). In another myth, the sky goddess Nut gave birth to the sun every morning. Egyptian veneration of the sun being what it was, we might suppose that the darkness was meant as a refutation of Egyptian religion. Even here, however, we should be careful; the Bible never describes the darkness as a defeat of Egyptian gods, or specifically as a defeat of Re.[86] To do so would be to deny a fundamental tenet of biblical creation theology, that the sun is not a deity at all, but an object created by God.[87] YHWH would no more set out to "defeat" the sun than he would set out to defeat any other inanimate object. Although we might speculate that the Egyptians, in the darkness, would fear that their gods had failed, this is not a point that the biblical text explicitly makes or concerns itself with.

A more likely Egyptian interpretation of the darkness is provided by the religious inscriptions from Deir el-Medina. This was the workers' village on the west bank of the Nile, at the Valley of the Kings, near Thebes. Because these workers were literate (they built the tombs of the kings and inscribed the walls with hieroglyphs), they were able to record their prayers and religious sentiments, and thus we have a window into the religious lives of ordinary Egyptians. Two such inscriptions speak of an affliction of darkness. One, of Nebre, son of Pay, entreats the god Horus, "Let mine eyes behold the way to go."[88] In another, the scribe Nekhtamun prays to the cobra-goddess Mertseger,[89] whose domain was a nearby mountain peak, "Thou causest me to see darkness by day."[90] It may be that the workmen were literally going blind as a result of their many hours working in dimly lit tombs, or it may be that "darkness" in these texts is at least sometimes metaphorical for depression and sorrow. Regardless, the important point for

86. In fact, Exod. 10:21–29, the account of the darkness, never mentions the sun at all. Cassuto, *Exodus*, 126, suggests that there may be a pun on "evil" (רָעָה) in 10:10 and the name of the god Re, but that is at best a (heavily) veiled swipe at Re and is not the main burden of the text.

87. For this reason Gen. 1:16 does not name the sun at all, but simply calls it "the big light" (הַמָּאוֹר הַגָּדֹל). Had the text used the normal word for sun, שֶׁמֶשׁ, one might take it to be a reference to Shamash, the sun god.

88. David, *Religion and Magic*, 279.

89. As a spitting cobra, this goddess in particular may have been supposed to punish people with blindness (Shaw and Nicholson, *Dictionary*, 184).

90. David, *Religion and Magic*, 279.

our purposes is that these Egyptians associated blindness or darkness with the wrath of a god, and thus they thought their inability to see the light was not a sign that Re or some other god had failed, but a sign that they were being punished by an angry deity. And that is precisely how Exodus portrays it: the great God YHWH was indeed angry with Egypt and punishing the people with darkness by day.

There is no reason to regard the death of the firstborn as a polemic against the notion that the pharaoh was a god. The Egyptians knew that their pharaohs and their pharaohs' sons died. More importantly, the text itself portrays the event as directed against all Egyptians, from Pharaoh on his throne to the slave girl at the handmill (Exod. 11:5). That being the case, this is not an attack on the royal mythology. Similarly, against Enns,[91] it is difficult to see how the death of the firstborn could be directed against Osiris. He was the god of the underworld, the realm of the dead. Although Egyptians hoped to pass the tribunal of Osiris and so enter the blessed realm after death, Osiris did not protect their sons from death.

We are then left with the question of why Exod. 12:12 says that YHWH was executing justice against all the gods of Egypt by the plagues. The point is not that each plague is directed against a specific god. Rather, Egypt was closely associated with her gods, so that a defeat of Egypt was in effect a defeat of her gods. This understanding of the close tie between a nation and its gods is in keeping with what we see elsewhere in the Bible and the ancient Near East (1 Kings 20:23; 2 Kings 18:33–35).[92] When a nation is defeated, its gods are defeated.

But we must be clear that Exodus does not concern itself with a polemic against any specific Egyptian god. The contrast with the strong polemic against Baal in later biblical texts is striking. The preacher or teacher of Exodus should avoid this mode of interpretation both because it is not the point of the biblical story and because it has no meaning for the modern audience.

---

91. Enns, *Inspiration*, 101.

92. James K. Hoffmeier ("Egypt, Plagues in," in Freedman, *ABD* Vol. 2, 374–78) suggests that the plagues were a refutation of Pharaoh in his role of maintainer of *maʿat* (justice, order) and of prosperity in Egypt. This is no doubt true in the same broad, general sense that the plagues are a refutation of Egyptian religion. But one should not speculate too specifically about the relationship between this or that plague and this or that role of Pharaoh (Hoffmeier makes no such speculations).

FOUR: THE MOSQUITOES (8:16–19 [Hebrew 12–15])

Severe discomfort continues to plague Egypt, but Pharaoh endures and refuses to budge in spite of warning from his own people.

Translation

8:16a And YHWH said to Moses,
8:16b “Say to Aaron,
8:16c ‘Stretch out your staff
8:16d and strike the dust of the earth,
8:16e and it will become mosquitoes[93] through all the land of Egypt.’”
8:17a And they did it:
8:17b Aaron stretched out[94] his hand with his staff,
8:17c and he struck the dust of the earth,
8:17d and it became mosquitoes[95] on man and beast.
8:17e All the dust of the earth became mosquitoes in all the land of Egypt.
8:18a And the magicians did the same thing[96] to bring forth mosquitoes with their secret arts,

---

93. The identity of this insect is uncertain, being identified as “gnat,” “mosquito,” or “louse.” But “louse” seems unlikely since the word appears to be onomatopoetic for buzzing (כֵּן [V], *HALOT*, 2.483, suggests that the word is cognate with Arabic *junna*, to “buzz”). The word appears in Exod. 8:12(16), 13(17), 14(18); Ps. 105:31 and possibly in Isa. 51:6. Numbers 13:33 is sometimes cited as having the word כֵּן [V] “gnat, mosquito” (as in *HALOT* and in Eugene Carpenter/Michael A. Grisanti, “כֵּן [VI],” *NIDOTTE*, 2.665), but this is in error; the word there is כֵּן (II), “thus.” Both gnats and mosquitoes occur in abundance in Egypt, but the latter, because of its painful bite, is much more of a torment to humans, and thus seems to be the more likely of the two to be the agent of a “plague.” Deserts are not conducive to large numbers of mosquitoes, but they do breed rapidly in Egypt wherever there is standing water (see Ralph E. Harbach, et al., “Records and Notes on Mosquitoes [Diptera: Culicidae] Collected in Egypt,” *Mosquito Systematics* 20 [1988]: 317–342, a report on a survey that collected 17 species of mosquito in Egypt; an older but more thorough work is T. W. Kirkpatrick, *The Mosquitoes of Egypt* [Cairo: Government Press, 1925]). As will be argued below, there likely was a great deal of standing water prior to this plague.
94. The *wayyiqtol* is epexegetical.
95. Assuming that the pointing of the MT is correct, the form כִּנָּם must be accounted for. Either the final ם is a suffix of some kind, as Rashbam suggested (Lockshin, *Rashbam*, 78–9), or it is a radical, and the word is a by-form of כֵּן. See GKC §85t. In either case, it would seem to have little bearing on the translation.
96. So translating כֵּן. Cassuto, *Exodus*, 105–6, sees a major problem here, with וַיַּעֲשׂוּ־כֵן (“and they did so”) implying that the magicians actually could

8:18b but they could not.
8:18c And there were mosquitoes on man and beast.
8:19a And the magicians said to Pharaoh,
8:19b "This is the finger of God."
8:19c And[97] Pharaoh's heart was implacable,
8:19d and he would not listen to them.
8:19e [It was] just as YHWH had said.

Structure

This plague account is quite short, having only the following elements:

I. YHWH Commands Moses to Begin the Plague, with Special Instructions for Aaron (8:16)
II. Moses and Aaron Carry Out the Commission (8:17)
  A. Moses and Aaron Perform a Ritual Act to Initiate the Plague
  B. The Miracle or Plague Begins and its Effects Are Described
III. Pharaoh's Advisors and Magicians Respond (8:18–19ab)
  A. A Failed Duplication of YHWH's Miracle
  B. Counsel Given by the Advisors and Magicians to Pharaoh
IV. Pharaoh's Heart Hardened, and he Refuses to Listen (8:19cd)
V. Affirmation that YHWH's Word Was Fulfilled (8:19e)

No background information is given; it is implied from the previous account. Pharaoh had gone back on his word to release Israel. YHWH therefore commanded Moses and Aaron to initiate the plague without giving any warning to Pharaoh.

---

produce mosquitoes, only to be contradicted in the next clause, which says that they could not. He resolves the problem by saying that the magicians faithfully tried to do their work but failed. It is more likely that the parallel between וַיַּעֲשׂוּ־כֵן in v. 13 (17) and v. 14 (18) implies that the magicians imitated Moses and Aaron. They may have tried to stir up a cloud of mosquitoes by hitting the ground with a rod, as they had seen Aaron do. There is also an apparent wordplay on the meanings of כֵּן. The magicians did the same thing (כֵּן) to bring forth mosquitoes (לְהוֹצִיא אֶת־הַכִּנִּים), but they were not able to.

97. The common translation of the conjunction of the *wayyiqtol* וַיֶּחֱזַק as here as "but" may subtly mistranslate the text. If the purpose were to show contrast one would expect an offline statement (such as ו + X + *qatal*). But the *wayyiqtol* suggests continuity; the idea is that Pharaoh kept right on with his purpose and paid little heed to what was happening. Rather than open refusal, he simply ignored the facts and his advisers.

Commentary

8:16. We should not take the assertion that the "dust" of the earth became mosquitoes (or gnats) literally, as though the dust were magically transformed apart from normal insect reproduction. Such an excessively literal hermeneutic would also imply that "all" the dust became mosquitoes (v. 17)—that is, that there was no dust left in Egypt, for it had all become mosquitoes. This is simply inconceivable. But the land of Egypt apparently had a large number of stagnant pools upon the ground after the excessive flooding of the Nile (see Excursus: The Plague Sequence in Natural History). In this sense, the dust of the earth became mosquitoes.

8:17. The use of the rod was critical in this event, since it was the ritual object that communicated to all observers that what followed was by the will of YHWH. The rod was not magical, but apart from it, an ancient observer would have no reason to connect the insect infestation to the wrath of Israel's God. The massive mosquito infestation was brought about by the will of God and not by the rod, but we should not ask why God "needed" to use the rod; for the sake of the audience, both Egyptian and Hebrew, it was an essential token of divine power.

8:18–19. The magicians are unable to duplicate the miracle, undoubtedly because they had no experience using slight-of-hand with such insects. Stuart aptly comments, "But what magician has ever done a trick with trained mosquitoes?"[98] It appears that they actually tried to raise up a cloud of mosquitoes by hitting the ground with a rod, since that was what they had seen Aaron do (see the translation note to 8:18a). In the phrase "finger of God," the word "finger" is a synecdoche for "hand," which in turn represents a deed or the exercise of power. In short, the magicians are confessing that this is no trick, but that some divine power is at work, and that they cannot imitate it. Against various interpreters, the Egyptian magicians are not trying to defend themselves by claiming that this event was brought about by astral deities (as opposed to it being a work of YHWH),[99] nor are they saying that this was merely a natural event and not brought about by Moses and Aaron,[100] nor are they making a pious statement (to the effect that God is so strong that he could do this using his finger only, and need not use his whole hand). They are simply admitting that Moses

---

98. Stuart, *Exodus*, 211.
99. See the discussion in Houtman, *Exodus*, 2:57.
100. Against Rashbam; see Lockshin, *Rashbam*, 79.

is truly able to invoke God's power. Pharaoh does not exactly take a stand against their advice; he simply ignores them (see the translation note to 8:19c). Also, he makes no effort to persuade Moses to remove the plague. Either he was convinced that it would run its course and be done or, having just broken a promise to release the Israelites, he felt that going back to Moses to ask for relief would entail too great a loss of face for himself. That is, he did not want to admit that he was a liar.

Theological Summary of Key Points

In looking at a series of texts that are formally very similar, it is often what is different that demands attention. This is certainly the case with the plagues. Here, the distinctive element is the failure of the magicians to replicate the miracle of Moses and their admission that what was happening was a work of God. The point made, within the flow of the narrative, is that Pharaoh had no excuse. If he earlier could have claimed that Moses's miracles were fraudulent, he lost that defense when his magicians admitted defeat. To the reader, moreover, this narrative more clearly demonstrates that the exodus is a work of God. The essential theological lesson, therefore, is that one may for a while deny the evidence for the working of God in the world, but eventually it becomes so strong that continued denial is irrational.

FIVE: THE FLIES (8:20–32 [Hebrew 16–28])

More discomfort forces Pharaoh back into negotiations with Moses, but again Pharaoh shows himself to be untrustworthy.

Translation

8:20a And YHWH said to Moses,
8:20b "Rise early in the morning
8:20c and position yourself before Pharaoh—
8:20d you will find him[101] coming out to the water—
8:20e and say to him,
8:20f 'Thus says YHWH,
8:20g "Release my people,
8:20h that they may serve me.
8:21a For if you persist in not releasing[102] my people

101. The word הִנֵּה here vividly describes the circumstances in which Moses will find Pharaoh. The clause is offline and explanatory, giving background information.

102. The words אִם־אֵינְךָ מְשַׁלֵּחַ imply a persistent refusal to release the people. It is stronger than a simple negated *yiqtol*.

8:21b you will see[103] me releasing[104] flies[105] on you and on your officials and on your people and into your houses;
8:21c and the houses of Egypt will be full of flies, as will also the ground on which the people dwell.[106]
8:22d And I will on that day give special treatment[107] to the land of Goshen, on which my people are standing,[108] by there being no flies there,
8:22e in order that you may know
8:22f that I, YHWH, am in the midst of the land.[109]
8:23a I will put a division[110] between my people and your people.
8:23b Tomorrow this sign will take place.'"'"
8:24a And YHWH did that:

---

103. Another use of הִנֵּה for vivid description; it allows the reader to perceive the event through Pharaoh's eyes.
104. The Hiphil participle מַשְׁלִיחַ implies a dispatching of the insects to do harm to Egypt, as opposed to the Piel מְשַׁלֵּחַ, which is used for granting the people their freedom. But there is plainly a wordplay with מַשְׁלִיחַ and מְשַׁלֵּחַ.
105. The word עָרֹב is used in the Bible only with reference to the pest that appears in this plague, but *HALOT* (עָרֹב, 2.879) suggests that it is here a subgroup of זְבוּב, the generic word for "fly," and may be something like the horsefly.
106. Lit. "the ground on which they are" (הָאֲדָמָה אֲשֶׁר־הֵם עָלֶיהָ).
107. Except for Ps. 4:4 (3), the verb פלה (Hiphil) only appears in Exodus (here; 9:4; 11:7; 33:16). It means to set someone apart for special, favorable treatment.
108. The use of עמד, "to stand," to describe where the Israelites live (instead of the more ordinary ישב) may reflect Israel's status as resident aliens as opposed to permanent inhabitants.
109. This clause is an indirect statement.
110. The MT has פְּדֻת, "redemption," but this makes little sense, as it is hard to see how one can set redemption between one people and another. The LXX has *διαστολὴν* and the Vulg. has *divisionem*, both of which mean "distinction" or "division." A. A. Macintosh, "Exodus 8:19, Distinct Redemption and the Hebrew Roots פדה and פדד," *VT* 21, no. 5 (1971): 548–55, suggests a root פדד with the meaning "separate" on the basis of Arabic. Other options are that the original was either פְּלֻת (root: פלה, "to treat specially") or פרדת (root: פרד, "to separate"), although neither noun is attested elsewhere in the Hebrew Old Testament. Graham I. Davies, "Hebrew text of Exodus 8:19 (Evv 23): An Emendation," *VT* 24, no. 4 (1974): 489–92, supports emending the text to פרדת, contending that there are too many objections to Macintosh's theory for it to be persuasive and that פְּלֻת involves too severe an emendation. See also Lockshin, *Rashbam*, 81, for rabbinical interpretation.

8:24b a dense cloud of flies came into the house of Pharaoh and the houses of his officials and in all the land of Egypt.[111]
8:24c The land was being brought to ruin because of the flies.[112]
8:25a And Pharaoh called for Moses and Aaron,
8:25b and he said,
8:25c "Go ahead,[113] sacrifice to your God in the land."
8:26a And Moses said,
8:26b "It is not safe[114] to do so,
8:26c for our sacrifices to YHWH our God are abhorrent to the Egyptians.[115]
8:26d If we should make a sacrifice that is abhorrent to the Egyptians right before their eyes,
8:26e will they not stone us?
8:27a We must go a three days' journey into the wilderness
8:27b and sacrifice to YHWH our God in the manner he tells us."
8:28a And Pharaoh said,
8:28b "I will let you go,
8:28c and you may sacrifice to YHWH your God in the wilderness;
8:28d Only you must not travel a far distance.
8:28e Make supplication for me!"
8:29a And Moses said,
8:29b "I hereby make my departure from you,[116]

---

111. This interpretation places a major break after וּבְכָל־אֶרֶץ מִצְרַיִם, contrary to the Masoretic cantillation, which places the athnach at וּבֵית עֲבָדָיו. The MT interpretation is overly redundant: "and in all the land of Egypt the land was being devastated."
112. Asyndeton implies that this clause is offline, providing additional information in a summarizing fashion. The *yiqtol* תִּשָּׁחֵת is imperfective, implying here a progressive action.
113. The word לְכוּ is plainly more of an interjection than a separate imperative, as Pharaoh does not intend for them to "go" anywhere, as he wants them to stay "in the land."
114. Literally "fixed" or "established," נָכוֹן here does not mean "right," as in many translations, but "safe." Something that is "fixed" is reliable and therefore safe. For example, the refrain that "the world is fixed and shall never be moved" (תִּכּוֹן תֵּבֵל בַּל־תִּמּוֹט) means that it is in YHWH's power and therefore not dangerously out of control (e.g., 1 Chron. 16:30; Ps. 93:1).
115. Lit. "for we sacrifice to YHWH our God [what is] an abomination to the Egyptians."
116. The precise nature of this הִנֵּה clause seems to be that Moses is solemnly declaring what he is about to do in response to Pharaoh's pleas. This serves as the prelude to Moses's warning to Pharaoh not to go back on his word again.

8:29c and I will make supplication to YHWH
8:29d and the flies will turn away from Pharaoh, from his officials, and from his people tomorrow;
8:29e only Pharaoh must not again behave deceitfully by not releasing the people to sacrifice to YHWH."
8:30a And Moses departed from Pharaoh,
8:30b and he made supplication to YHWH.
8:31a And YHWH did as Moses said:
8:31b the flies turned away[117] from Pharaoh, from his officials and from his people;
8:31c not one remained.[118]
8:32a And Pharaoh made his heart leaden this time also:
8:32b he did not release[119] the people.

Structure

While this section follows the basic formal pattern of a plague narrative, it gives particular emphasis to YHWH's message to Pharaoh and then to Pharaoh's interview with Moses in the course of the plague.

I. YHWH Commissions Moses and Aaron to Appear Before Pharaoh (8:20–23)
   A. A Demand that Pharaoh Allow Israel to Go Make a Sacrifice
   B. A Warning About a Coming Judgment
II. The Plague Begins and Its Effects Are Described (8:24)
III. Pharaoh Interviews Moses in the Course of the Plague (8:25–29)
   A. A Request that Moses Intercede for Egypt to Stop the Plague
   B. A Promise to Release the People to Go into the Wilderness and Sacrifice
   C. Moses Answers Pharaoh
IV. Moses Intercedes for Egypt, and the Plague Stops (8:30–31)
V. Pharaoh Hardens his Heart, and he Refuses to Release Israel (8:32)

117. The *wayyiqtol* is epexegetical.
118. The asyndeton marks an offline comment that gives further detail on the previous clause.
119. Another epexegetical *wayyiqtol*.

Commentary

8:20–23. We do not have enough information to know why Moses was sent to Pharaoh early in the morning; perhaps it had symbolic significance, or perhaps it was for a purely practical reason, that it was easier for Moses to get an audience with Pharaoh at this time of day. The "water" where Pharaoh could be found was presumably the banks of the Nile. Pharaoh may have gone there for his daily lustration, an essential activity in light of the fact that Pharaoh was in effect Egypt's high priest, or it may have been that he conducted a morning ritual to the sun at the river. But if there is any significance to Moses confronting Pharaoh in YHWH's name while the latter was fulfilling priestly duties, the Bible does not dwell on it.

Moses's message is essentially unchanged, except that for the first time Goshen, where the Hebrews lived, is exempted from the effects of the plague. Such a move was necessary in order to make the point that the disaster really was specifically directed against Egypt for Pharaoh's refusal to release Israel. The purpose of the plague is said to be that Pharaoh might understand that YHWH was "in the land." The message here is that YHWH had, as it were, invaded Egypt and was really present there. Pharaoh must come to terms with God, and he could do that only by yielding.

8:24. It seems surprising that the text says that the land was "brought to ruin" because of the flies. The verb שׁחת is quite strong, and can mean to "destroy," as in Gen. 18:28 (in reference to God's destruction of Sodom by fire). Flies, one would think, cannot destroy a country, however irritating they may be. But here, unlike in Genesis 18, the verb does not imply blasting something out of existence. Rather, it means that the flies made life unbearable, and the people were hardly able to function. The usage is analogous to Gen. 6:12, where the earth was said to be "corrupt" (שׁחת). The point there is not that the antediluvian people had physically destroyed the world, but that they had ruined it, so that it was no longer good. In the same way, the flies made life agonizing. One may also compare Eccl. 10:1, where the point is not that dead flies obliterate a perfumed ointment, but that they make it disgusting to people.

8:25–29. For the first time, Pharaoh tries to negotiate with Moses, trying to see if he can get Moses to agree to terms more to his liking. His first tack is to try to have the Hebrews conduct their worship within Egypt, or if not that, to at least demand that the Hebrews not go very far away. Ultimately, however, he will simply break his word and not allow them to leave at all, so that the whole negotiation process turns out to have been in bad faith.

In the negotiations, Moses says that the Hebrews cannot carry out their worship within Egypt because their sacrifices are abhorrent (תּוֹעֲבַת) to the Egyptians. Why would this be the case? An old, rabbinic interpretation is that תּוֹעֲבַת is a dysphemism for "pagan deity." In other words, the Hebrews could not sacrifice sheep because the sheep was a god to the Egyptians.[120] Evidence supporting this interpretation is ambiguous. It is true that the god Khnum was portrayed as a ram, but his cult was far to the south, near Elephantine. But there was another ram-god, Ba-neb-djedet, whose cult center was in the Delta town of Mendes.[121] The god Amun, in the New Kingdom, began to take on the role of a ram-god. However, the mere fact that a god was associated with a particular animal does not mean that the Egyptians would not sacrifice that animal. To the contrary, for example, Egyptians sacrificed cats to the cat-goddess Bastet. Herodotus (2.42) claims that Egyptians sacrificed sheep at Mendes, but that at Thebes they did not, except for a sacrifice of one ram per year to Amun. Egyptians did keep sheep and goats for meat, milk, and wool. It is also true that in 410 B.C. rioting Egyptians, led by the priests of Khnum, destroyed the temple of the Jewish colony at Elephantine, but it is not clear that their animosity was aroused specifically because of Khnum's association with the ram. It is more likely that they were angry because an alien cult had invaded the sacred territory of their god.

Exodus does not claim that it is specifically the sacrifice of sheep that the Egyptians objected to. There may have been many points at which the worship carried out by the Hebrews was strange or offensive to Egyptians, the frequent sacrifice of sheep and goats perhaps among them. Possibly Moses is contending that the Egyptians tolerated small expressions of Israelite religion in their midst (obviously the Hebrews had some kind of local religious practices), but that they would have rioted at the sight of a large and public display of Hebrew sacrifice and worship within their borders. There are many examples of societies that tolerate an alien religion in their midst as long as it stays relatively quiet. The larger community, however, may go on a rampage at the sight of a major festival publicly observed by the minority religion. At the end of the negotiations (v. 29), Moses shows that he no longer trusts Pharaoh, who has lied to him before.

120. Lockshin, *Rashbam*, 82.
121. Shaw and Nicholson, *Dictionary*, 240.

8:30–31. Pharaoh could not have reasonably doubted that Moses's God had brought on this disaster, as Moses had the power both to summon the flies and to terminate the plague. On the sudden disappearance of the flies, see Excursus: The Plague Sequence in Natural History.

8:32. The hardening of Pharaoh's heart is here attributed to Pharaoh himself. It was not forced upon him by God or circumstances.

Theological Summary of Key Points

Apart from the main point of all the plagues, that God brought Israel out of Egypt with a mighty hand, several points in this narrative are notable, and most center on the biblical concept of sin (hamartiology).

1. Pharaoh is obstinate and duplicitous. He first tries to negotiate down YHWH's demands by suggesting that the Israelites have their worship service inside of Egypt. When that fails, he simply breaks his word, despite plain evidence that God is at work against him. The point, simply enough, is that the human heart can be irrationally stubborn. The Jewish leaders of Jesus's day, similarly, irrationally disregarded the evidence that he was the Messiah.

2. Religious sensibilities can be seriously misguided. Moses says that the Egyptians would be offended and even violent towards Hebrew worship. No doubt the Egyptians would think that in doing so they would be demonstrating their religious devotion. One cannot but think of Jesus's warning in John 16:2 and of the jihadist mentality of Islam.

3. It is true that Christian charity demands that we look for the best in others and give them the benefit of the doubt. On the other hand, we are within our rights to consider their former behavior to be indicative of how they will behave in the future. Moses, having been cheated by Pharaoh, rightly distrusts him (8:29).

4. The flies "ruined" the land of Egypt; that is, they made life there unbearable. The lesson is that an unrepentant life, abiding under the wrath of God, is ultimately miserable.

SIX: THE LIVESTOCK (9:1–7)

For the first time Egypt experiences major economic disaster in the plagues—but the Hebrews are unscathed. Pharaoh broods and remains adamant.

Translation

9:1a And YHWH said to Moses,

9:1b "Go to Pharaoh

9:1c and speak to him [as follows]:[122]

9:1d 'Thus says YHWH, the God of the Hebrews,

9:1e "Let my people go,

9:1f that they may serve me.

9:2a For if you persist in refusing[123] to grant a release

9:2b and continue to hold them,

9:3 you will find that[124] the hand of YHWH is set[125] against[126] your livestock which are in the field: against the horses, against the donkeys, against the camels, against the herds, and against the flocks—a very severe plague—

9:4a and that[127] YHWH will make a distinction between the livestock of Israel and the livestock of Egypt;

9:4b and not a single thing that belongs to the Israelites will die."'"

9:5a And YHWH fixed a time, saying,

9:5b "Tomorrow YHWH will do this thing in the land."

9:6a And YHWH did this thing on the next day:

9:6b all the livestock of Egypt died,

9:6c but out of the livestock of the Israelites, not a single one died![128]

---

122. This clause has an implied לֵאמֹר.

123. The word מָאֵן is evidently a Piel participle, although one would expect the form מְמָאֵן. The point of the participle is that Pharaoh is persisting in refusing, not that he currently refuses. The same is implied by the Hiphil participle מַחֲזִיק in the next clause (9:2b), as indicated by the use of עוֹד.

124. הִנֵּה with a participle here represents the events that Pharaoh will observe or experience.

125. The participle here (הוֹיָה) is in answer to the participle in clause 9:2a (מָאֵן), implying that if Pharaoh persists in his actions, "holding" on to the Israelites with his implied hand, YHWH's hand will remain fixed against the cattle of the Egyptians.

126. The idiom יָד + היה + בְּ frequently implies hostile action, and the בְּ should be translated "against." See Gen. 37:27; Deut. 2:15; 13:10(9); 17:7; Josh. 2:19; 1 Sam. 24:13–14.

127. The *weqatal* clause וְהִפְלָה יְהוָה is not particularly prominent; it would be more prominent or at least more clearly contrastive if it were a וְ + X + *yiqtol* pattern, or if the exceptional treatment given for the Hebrews was introduced with a וְהָיָה clause ("and it shall be that"). It is likely that this clause continues the הִנֵּה clause from 9:3a.

128. This clause is prominent, as indicated by its placement of וְ + the

9:7a Pharaoh sent [an enquiry],[129]
9:7b and [he was informed that][130] not so much as one of the livestock of Israel died.
9:7c And the heart of Pharaoh was leaden,
9:7d and he did not release the people.

Structure

This is a brief narrative with only a few elements of the standard form of the miracle report pattern used in Exodus.

I. YHWH Commissions Moses and Aaron to Appear Before Pharaoh (9:1–4)
   A. A Demand that Pharaoh Release Israel or Allow them to Go Make a Sacrifice
   B. A Warning About a Coming Judgment
II. Additional Information (9:5)
III. The Plague Begins and its Effects Are Described (9:6)
IV. Pharaoh's Advisors Respond (9:7ab)
V. Pharaoh's Heart Hardened, and he Refuses to Release Israel (9:7cd)

Commentary

9:1–4. The most prominent element in YHWH's speech to Pharaoh is the listing of all the kinds of livestock that would die in the coming plague. Nothing would escape or be exempted. For all these animals, it would be a pitiful death from which there would be no escape. For the Egyptians, it would be an economic catastrophe in which every kind of livestock would be lost. The fact that Israel's livestock would be exempted, something that one might expect to be treated as very significant, is not made grammatically prominent at all (see translation notes to 9:4a). This is important: the main point of YHWH's message

---

prepositional phrase before the negated *qatal*, and by the final placement of אֶחָד ("one").

129. To "send" (שׁלח) implies an official enquiry through the offices of his administrative staff and counselors. Although not explicitly mentioned, this verse alludes to the role played by the officials who are often mentioned in the plague narrative: they informed him that Moses's claims about the exemption of Israel from the effects of the plague were true.

130. The point of הִנֵּה is to describe the reception of the information from Pharaoh's point of view. In this case, he received the information via what we would call an official report.

to Pharaoh is that Egypt will suffer terribly. It is not that the Hebrews will not suffer. The exemption of the Israelites from the plague simply makes the point that this is an act of YHWH directed against Egypt.

9:5. The fixing of the time when the plague would commence validates the claim that it is from YHWH and by the hand of Moses.

9:6. At this point in the narrative, the fact that no livestock belonging to the Hebrews died is made grammatically prominent. Why is there here a change from the non-prominent description of the event in 9:4? In 9:4, the main point is to warn Pharaoh of the calamity that will soon befall Egypt if he does not release Israel. Telling him that Israel will not suffer is secondary; it only makes the point that Egypt is indeed facing the anger of God. Here in 9:6, the event is given more from Israel's point of view. God struck the nation that enslaved them while remarkably leaving their cattle untouched. While 9:4 is a grim warning, this verse is a celebration.

9:7. The fact that Pharaoh ascertained the truth, that YHWH really did spare the Hebrews, should have made him realize that continued refusal to release them was madness. But his heart was closed and insensitive.

Theological Summary of Key Points

Two factors stand out in this miracle.

1. God's wrath toward a nation increases gradually, moving from relatively small irritants (as illustrated by the flies) to true calamity. Economic catastrophe may precede something even more terrible, such as military disaster (the eleventh and twelfth miracles of the Exodus sequence).

2. God is able to preserve his people from the effects of a calamity. For the Christian, the ultimate fulfillment of this is in their redemption, through Christ, from final condemnation at the last judgment. But it should not lead us to think that we are exempted from suffering in this world; this is a gross misapplication of the lessons of Exodus. The fact that a nation is undergoing an economic reversal may be divine punishment, but unless one has the prophetic gift, one should be hesitant about speaking too precisely for God. It is enough to call people to repentance during hard times without claiming to know exactly what sins God is punishing. Too often, in speaking for God, we give ourselves the presumption of innocence and give to others a presumption of guilt, especially when we associate them with sins that we do not ourselves commit. Similarly, we can give the church a false assurance, telling people that if they believe rightly or come to (our) church, God will protect them from poverty while everyone else languishes. This may be a prosperity gospel, or it may be a theological claim that the "true" church is exempted from such suffering by the blood of Christ. In fact, the exemption for Israel only pertains to the exodus narrative; it makes no claim of establishing a universal principle that God's people are exempted from the punishment that God pours out on the nations in which they live. Ultimately, faithful believers will be saved, but one should be careful not to claim that believers are always exempted from the troubles that swirl around them.

SEVEN: THE SKIN ULCERS (9:8–12)

For the first time Egyptians face a plague that strikes their persons, as skin ailments break out on everyone. But Pharaoh continues to hold out, not even summoning Moses.

Translation

9:8a And YHWH said to Moses and Aaron,
9:8b "Get some kiln soot, as much as you can hold in your hands,[131]
9:8c and Moses shall toss it toward the sky before the eyes of Pharaoh.
9:9a And it will become dust over all the land of Egypt,
9:9b and on man and beast it will become sores[132] that break out[133] with blisters[134] throughout the whole land of Egypt."
9:10a And they got the kiln soot,
9:10b and they stood before Pharaoh,
9:10c and Moses tossed it toward the sky,

131. Lit. "the fullness of your hands."

132. The precise meaning of שְׁחִין is uncertain, but it seems to be related to a Semitic root meaning "heat" and to refer to an inflammation or skin ailment of some kind (שְׁחִין, *HALOT*, 4.1460). It is often translated as "boil," but cattle do not get boils of the kind that afflict humans, and so it must be something else that is common to both.

133. פרח essentially means to "emerge." It is most commonly used of plants, whether of the sprouting of grass (Isa. 66:14) or of the blossoming of flowers (Song 6:11). From this usage, it often means to "flourish." It is, however, used for the breaking out of a skin affliction, as in Lev. 13:12.

134. The word אֲבַעְבֻּעֹת appears related to a word that describes bubbles in wet clay (as in the process of making pottery), and therefore probably is some kind of blister (אֲבַעְבֻּעֹת, *HALOT*, 1.9).

9:10d and it became blistering sores that broke out on man and beast.
9:11a And the magicians could not stand before Moses because of the sores,
9:11b for the sores were on the magicians and on all the Egyptians.
9:12a And YHWH made Pharaoh's heart implacable,
9:12b and he did not listen to them.
9:12c [It was] just as YHWH had spoken to Moses.

Structure

This text has a fairly minimal outline for a plague narrative. The one element that stands out is the response of the magicians in 9:11.

I. YHWH Commissions Moses and Aaron to Appear Before Pharaoh (9:8–9)
II. Moses and Aaron Carry Out the Commission (9:10)
  A. Moses and Aaron Perform a Ritual Act to Initiate the Plague
  B. The Plague Begins and its Effects Are Described
III. Pharaoh's Advisors and Magicians Respond (9:11)
IV. YHWH Hardens Pharaoh's Heart, and he Refuses to Listen (9:12)
V. Affirmation that YHWH's Word Was Fulfilled (9:12)

Commentary

9:8–9. The tossing of soot into the air is a ritual act meant to serve as the symbolic catalyst for the plague that follows. The action conveys to the audience the message that the subsequent sufferings are not coincidental but are divine actions that Moses has the power to invoke. To the Egyptians, this would have been a work of magic. It is not magic, however, since magic is supposed to always be successful after one has used the appropriate words, actions, and manipulation of objects. That is, this ritual is for this one episode. There is no suggestion that anyone, even Moses himself, could at another time cause boils to break out on people by throwing soot in the air.

9:10. Enns, following Cassuto, argues that the "soot" was taken from kilns used in brickmaking, and thus argues that this was an appropriate punishment for the Egyptians, who forced the Hebrews to bake bricks in kilns.[135] This is wrong; the Egyptians did not use kiln-baked bricks in construction (even for constructing their royal palaces); they used sun-dried bricks. The kilns mentioned here would be pottery kilns;

135. Enns, *Exodus*, 218; Cassuto, *Exodus*, 112–3.

as the Hebrews were not engaged in pottery-making for the Egyptians, there is no indication of a symbolic punishment here.

9:11. The most striking feature of this narrative is the statement that the magicians could not stand before Moses. That is, it appears that they could not present themselves publicly. Egyptian religion had strict standards of ritual purity for priests. An outbreak of skin lesions would have surely meant that they could not appear before the pharaoh, since a skin disease would have been defiling (the same is true for Israelite priests). They possibly needed to stay secluded because of their impure condition. But the text states that they could not stand "before Moses." The expression לא יכל לעמד לפני, meaning "(he was) not able to stand before (someone)," is used three times in the Bible: here, in Judg. 2:14, and in 1 Sam. 6:20. In Judges, it states that the Israelites, under God's punishment, could not stand before their enemies in battle. In 1 Samuel, some of the men of Beth-shemesh are struck down by plague for looking into the ark of the covenant, and they are terrified, realizing that they cannot "stand before" God (that is, resist his power). Thus, the inability of the magicians to stand before Moses is a statement of their defeat by the power he represented. Their ritual defilement is symbolically indicative of their weakness before Moses and his God.

9:12. Pharaoh remained stubborn, as YHWH had said he would. He ought to have seen in the humbling of his magicians the fact that he was dealing with a power he could not resist.

Theological Summary of Key Points

1. The skin affliction represents the first event that is centered upon the persons of the Egyptians. Heretofore, their suffering had been limited to the irritation and annoyance caused by the frogs, mosquitoes, and flies, and to the economic loss represented by the cattle plague. Here, the actual locus of the event is the very bodies of the Egyptians. Similarly, Job first loses his property and possessions and then suffers with a skin affliction. Boils and sores in the skin are also listed among the curses for apostasy at Deut. 28:27, 35. In Revelation, the final series of seven judgments—the seven bowls—begins with a skin affliction (Rev. 16:2). It is probably going too far if one draws a broad theological principle from these examples, but at least sometimes the Bible portrays economic attacks as a lower form of punishment, and portrays loss of health as a more intense and more direct form of punishment (but this is not to suggest that every economic loss or health-related affliction is a punishment from God). The idea seems to be that people can view external troubles as simply bad circumstances that they are caught up in, but must view afflictions in their own bodies as directed against themselves. It is clear, at any rate, that the passage is indicating that God is gradually increasing the severity of the afflictions. This is an act of grace, meant to provoke repentance before the situation becomes catastrophic.

2. The inability of the magicians of Egypt to "stand before" Moses reflects the failure of every form of superstition, magic, and paganism before the word of God. The resurgence of paganism and magic in our day via the use of amulets, witchcraft and Wicca, horoscopes, and so forth reflects a general turning away from God and biblical revelation. This text shows that such ritualized attempts to gain access to supernatural power are futile. God can demonstrate magic-like power when he chooses, and by doing so he demonstrates that human acts of ritualized magic are fraudulent, but the power is in God himself and is not in the ritual. In the New Testament, the weakness of demons in the presence of Jesus (e.g., Matt. 8:31) and the stories of Simon Magus and of the sons of Sceva (Acts 8:9–24; 19:13–16) illustrate the folly of trying to harness supernatural power by dark arts.

Excursus: The Plague Sequence in Natural History

A common explanation of the ten afflictions of the plague narrative (from the turning of the Nile to blood to the death of the firstborn, excluding the transformation of the rod into a serpent and the crossing of the *Yam Suph*) is that the sequence of natural disasters is not arbitrary, as though there were no reason for them to be in the order in which they occur except for divine fiat. Furthermore, it is urged, the plagues cannot be dismissed as religious fiction or myth. Rather, they are events that are in accord with the natural history of Egypt,[136] even if this particular sequence of events was far more severe than Egypt ever experienced before or after the exodus. In evaluating this approach to the plagues, we must take into account several factors, including whether the individual plagues struck all of Egypt or exempted Goshen (where Israel lived), whether the plagues ended abruptly, whether the text gives us information on the timing of the event, and whether the plagues are explicitly attributed to some natural cause. Regarding the latter, only one plague is obviously linked with a natural

136. Thus Greta Hort, "The Plagues of Egypt," *ZAW* 69, no. 1–4 (1957): 84–103 and *ZAW* 70, no. 1 (1958): 48–59, whose study is among the most cited and respected to make this case.

cause: the locusts are said to have been brought into Egypt by an east wind (10:13).

On the other hand, the fact that no natural causality is explicitly mentioned for other plagues does not mean that they were all purely supernatural in origin. That is, the Bible does not assert that the frogs, mosquitoes, flies and locusts that swarmed over Egypt were specially created *ex nihilo*, or that the hail fell from a blue sky. It is reasonable to assume that the frogs and insects were spawned in the normal manner and that the hail fell from heavy storm clouds. Furthermore, to assert that these events do fit within the facts of natural history is not to deny their miraculous nature. The intensity of the plagues, together with the fact that they begin and often end at Moses's word, is proof enough that they were a work of God. By analogy, no one can doubt that earthquakes are part of the natural history of the earth and caused by geologic faults. But if a man repeatedly demonstrated that he could, by raising his staff, summon an earthquake, one would have to say that he had access to some kind of special power. Also, if Egypt were never troubled by mosquitoes or locusts, we might well see those plagues as altogether outside of any natural causality. But in fact, pre-modern Egypt was rife with mosquitoes and gnats,[137] and serious locust invasions occur there to this day.[138] An initial survey of the data appears in Table 7.

If the Nile turned to literal blood, then obviously no explanation is possible. Above, however, I have argued that it is more likely that the Nile turned blood-red in color. This is supported by the fact that the event did not have a sudden ending; apparently the coloration gradually washed out of the river. As described above, if the river had turned to literal blood, it quickly would have turned to a sludge and begun to decompose, and it is hard to imagine how long it would have taken for waters from the Nile sources to make it downstream and wash out the remains (unless it were miraculously transformed back into water, which in fact did not occur). Assuming, as 7:24 indicates, that the liquid in the Nile was still water, we must determine what would make it become blood-red. Following the analysis done by Greta

137. Napoleon's invasion of Egypt provides an excellent window into pre-modern Egypt. For an account of the mosquitoes and gnats that tormented the French troops, see Nina Burleigh, *Mirage: Napoleon's Scientists and the Unveiling of Egypt* (New York: HarperCollins, 2007), 44.

138. A major locust invasion of Egypt occurred in Nov., 2004. See, for example, "Egypt swarms with locusts," USA Today, accessed 4/23/14, http://www.usatoday.com/news/world/2004-11-17-locusts_x.htm.

TABLE 7. THE NATURAL HISTORY OF THE PLAGUES: PRELIMINARY DATA			
Plague	**Chronological Data?**	**Plague in All Egypt?**	**Abrupt End?**
Nile (7:14–24)	No	All Egypt	No
Frogs (7:25—8:15)	Seven days after Nile event (7:25)	All Egypt	Yes
Mosquitoes (8:16–19)	No	All Egypt	No
Flies (8:20–32)	No	Goshen Exempted	Yes
Livestock (9:1–7)	No	Goshen Exempted	No
Skin Ulcers (9:8–12)	No	Goshen Exempted	No
Hail (9:13–35)	Barley ripening, flax in bloom, wheat and spelt not yet ripening (9:31–32)	Goshen Exempted	Yes
Locusts (10:1–20)	Plants in field, fruit on trees (10:15)	All Egypt	Yes
Darkness (10:21–29)	Lasted three days (10:22)	Goshen Exempted	Yes
Firstborn (11:1—12:51)	At Passover (12:1–11)	Passover Homes Spared	Yes

Hort,[139] it appears that the best solution is that when there is an exceptionally large amount of rainfall at the sources of the Nile, especially at the Blue Nile and the Atbara River, these rivers overflow their channels and pick up an enormous amount of *Roterde* ("red earth"). The Atbara, for example, flows through badlands and is especially likely to pick up such sediments when in flood stage. Once picked up, the waters carry these sediments through the whole course of the Nile. This implies that the Nile had a very high flood in conjunction with the event. This is corroborated by the fact that "all the Egyptians" had to dig wells along the river to get water. Normally, those who lived a few miles back from the river would get water from permanent wells, such as the one described above in the commentary on 7:23–24. However, heavy flooding and the expansion of the river overwhelmed even those permanent wells, as indeed always happened when the flood was too

139. Hort, *Plagues*, 1957, 87–98.

high.[140] Therefore, even those who lived further back had to dig along the edges of the expanded river to get potable water.

Reddish soil alone does not account for the biblical description, however, since these sediments would only turn the water pinkish, would not cause a massive fish kill, and would not make the water smelly and undrinkable. From the mountains at the Blue Nile, however, various flagellates would also wash into the waters as a result of the severe precipitation. Chief among these is the deep-red *Euglena sanguinea*,[141] which would turn the waters already colored by the *Roterde* into a blood-red color and would also make it foul and undrinkable. This flagellate, when present in massive numbers, would also spike the amount of oxygen in the water and result in a large number of dead fish.

The Nile flood begins in midsummer and reaches its maximum in September. One may therefore suggest that the waters were visibly polluted during the rise of the Nile, probably during August. Since the Bible does not record an immediate disappearance of this plague, we conclude that the waters receded and that the pollutants were washed away gradually over the course of the following weeks.

Every year, large numbers of small frogs would be seen along the banks of the Nile as the flood waters receded and the frogs' mating season began. This was in early October and was a phenomenon that the Egyptians knew well. The Bible, however, says that frogs emerged in massive numbers one week after the onset of the defiling of the Nile, suggesting that this event took place in August–September—before the mating season and possibly even before the waters had crested. In addition, these frogs behaved most oddly, going into human habitations and taking refuge in all kinds of containers, including kneading bowls and (presumably cold) ovens (8:3). After that, the frogs died abruptly and in great numbers (8:13–14). The timing of the event, a week after YHWH struck the Nile, is important. During that week, large numbers of fish died, were washed up beside the habitations of the frogs, and began to decay. Apparently the putridity became too much for the frogs, which fled their natural, watery habitats, but not before they had become infected by the cesspools they had formerly inhabited. The infection that most likely struck the frogs was anthrax (*bacillus*

140. Hort, *Plagues*, 1957, 93.

141. *Euglena sanguinea* is described as "haematochrome" (blood-colored) in "Protist Images: Euglena sanguinea," Protist Information Server, accessed 4/23/2014, http://protist.i.hosei.ac.jp/PDB/images/Mastigophora/Euglena/sanguinea/index.html, where one can also see an enlarged microscopic photograph that plainly shows its blood-red coloration.

anthracis); either the frogs breathed in the spores from the dead fish, or they ate insects that had been eating the fish. Having fled the river, however, and incapable of surviving long in the Egyptian heat while removed from the river, the frogs sought out whatever cool places they could find—particularly the homes and vessels made by people. Very abruptly, however, the diseased frogs died, both from disease and their displacement from their natural environment. The anthrax may also have contributed to the strong stench made by the dead frogs.[142]

After the cresting of the Nile, numerous pools of standing water would naturally be left behind. Mosquitoes and gnats were always a problem in Egypt, but this year, with so many more breeding grounds, they would have become horribly abundant. Since this event would have happened shortly after the subsidence of the Nile flood, its date can be fixed at October–November. The Bible gives no indication that the Israelites were exempted from either this event or the previous two events, and indeed it is hard to see how they could have been.[143]

The next three plagues (the flies, the sudden death of cattle, and the outbreak of skin infections) need to be considered together. It is noteworthy that Goshen, where the Hebrews lived, was spared all three events. If we continue with the hypothesis that the disease that killed the frogs was anthrax, we have a scenario that is coherent in the subsequent three events. First, the flies that in the Hebrew text are called עָרֹב, a subgroup of the זְבוּב, were probably a kind of horsefly, the *Stomoxys calcitrans*. This fly breeds especially rapidly when large amounts of decaying vegetation or dung are present (such as in a stable). In Egypt in the aftermath of the unusually high Nile flood there would have been decomposing vegetation in abundance. Also, the *Stomoxys calcitrans* breeds best in a hot environment. This would have been the case in arid Upper Egypt, but in Lower Egypt, near the Mediterranean, conditions would have been much cooler as December approached (the waters of the annual inundation recede significantly during October and November, suggesting that by the time of the plague of flies, it was already December or January). What this means is that even though Lower Egypt would have experienced the pollution of the Nile, the excessive flood waters, the frogs, and the mosquitoes, by the time the waters had receded enough for *Stomoxys calcitrans* to be a significant problem, weather conditions in the northern Delta would not have been right for the breeding of these flies.

In addition, *Stomoxys calcitrans* is a major transmitter of anthrax

142. Hort, *Plagues*, 1957, 95–8.
143. Ibid., 98–9.

via its bites.[144] Specifically, if the fly has been in contact with anthrax, and it bites a person or animal, its victim will develop cutaneous (skin) anthrax. This develops as a boil-like lesion that forms an ulcer with a black center, eventually becoming blistered, itchy, and resembling a dark bread mold. It affects both humans and animals. This suggests that the skin lesions, which afflicted both people and cattle (9:9), were a result of being bitten by the horseflies. It also helps to explain why the Hebrews were not afflicted; being in a place where the flies did not breed, they were not bitten. But how did the flies become transmitters of the disease?

If the frogs had anthrax, their dead bodies, littered across the ground and subsequently piled up in heaps, would have transmitted the anthrax to the grass and soil all around them. Cattle that ate infected vegetation would have ingested the anthrax and contracted gastrointestinal anthrax, a terrible and fatal affliction. It turns out that the Egyptians tended to keep their animals inside during the inundation, but as the waters receded, they would take them out to pasture. It was the cattle that were out in the fields that died in this plague (9:3). Indeed, when 9:6 says that "all" of the Egyptian cattle died, it means all of the cattle that had been in the field, not absolutely all their cattle (thus there were still other cattle alive when the subsequent plagues arrived). In Goshen, however, the low-lying Delta would have stayed inundated much longer than the Nile valley of Upper Egypt, and thus the Hebrews there would have kept their cattle confined long after the Egyptians of the south had taken theirs out to pasture. In addition, the winter rains that come to the Mediterranean regions of Lower Egypt are likely to have washed off a good part of the anthrax from the vegetation. As such, the Hebrews would have been spared this affliction as well. But if the Egyptian cattle died from intestinal anthrax, we can also understand how the *Stomoxys calcitrans* fly could have come into contact with it. The flies would have bitten the infected animals,[145] picked up the infection, and transmitted it as cutaneous anthrax to the animals and people they bit.

Finally, we should say a word about the abrupt disappearance of the flies that the Bible describes. This may be in part because the

144. Michael J. Turell and Gregory B. Knudson, "Mechanical Transmission of Bacillus anthracis by Stable Flies (*Stomoxys calcitrans*) and Mosquitoes (*Aedes aegypti* and *Aedes taeniorhynchus*)," *Infection and Immunity* 55, no. 8 (1987): 1859–1861.

145. Ibid., 1860, for the ability of *Stomoxys calcitrans* to become carriers of anthrax by biting infected animals.

hot sun of Upper Egypt dried the decaying vegetation to a powder, depriving the flies of their breeding area. On the other hand, it may be that the flies were themselves killed by the anthrax that they carried.[146]

For the hailstorm, we do have a fairly specific chronological marker in Exodus: the flax was in bloom, the barley kernels were ripening, but the wheat and spelt were unharmed because they were not yet ripening (9:31–32). Hort indicates that flax was normally sown in early January and flowered about three weeks later, while barley was sown in August and harvested in February. Hort speculates that the severe flooding may have delayed things by a few weeks, but we are probably on safe ground to say that this event took place in the first half of February.[147] It is doubtful, however, that this is much help to us in understanding the hailstorm, as it was an exceptional event. Lower Egypt gets a little rain each year (Alexandria gets about 100-200 mm of precipitation annually), and Upper Egypt gets much less. Any part of Egypt might get the occasional severe storm with driving rain. Such rain as Egypt normally has generally occurs in the winter months, but an event such as the Bible describes would be highly unusual. It may be that the storm gathered and swept in from the north, but was concentrated as it rushed down the narrow Nile valley. Severe weather of this kind is by nature capricious; one house may be totally demolished while the one next to it is untouched. Thus, the fact that Goshen was spared needs no special explanation.[148]

We are on much firmer ground with the locust plague. The locusts in question are Desert Locusts. These particular Desert Locusts breed in the Sudan. The same heavy rains at the source of the Nile that brought about the severe inundation and fouling of the Nile would have also provided excellent breeding conditions for locusts. The website of the Desert Locust Information Service of the Food and Agriculture Organization (FAO) of the United Nations states, "For the Desert Locust, favourable conditions for breeding are (1) moist sandy or sand/clay soil to depths of 10–15 cm below the surface, (2) some bare areas for

---

146. I cannot say with certainty that anthrax kills *Stomoxys calcitrans*. However, a UCSD study found that anthrax toxins "cause cellular damage and death in the fruit fly *Drosophila melanogaster*." See "UCSD study finds anthrax toxins also harmful to fruit flies," Biology News Net, accessed 4/23/2014, http://www.biologynews.net/archives/2006/01/31/ucsd_study_finds_anthrax_toxins_also_harmful_to_fruit_flies.html.

147. Hort, *Plagues,* 1958, 49.

148. For a discussion of the "fire" associated with this hailstorm, see the discussion below at the commentary on 9:23–26.

egg-laying, and (3) green vegetation for hopper development."[149] Thus, the rains that caused the original Nile flooding in the biblical account provided also the moisture and greenery to produce a catastrophically large number of locusts.

When there is abundant vegetation for the young locusts (hoppers), moreover, the physical contact among the insects provokes a chemical and behavioral change that transforms the locusts from the "solitary" form to the "gregarious" form, giving off a pheromone that causes them to reproduce more rapidly. Gregarious locusts, moreover, eventually swarm and migrate (they have longer wings than do solitary locusts). Furthermore, according to the Desert Locust Information Service, "A Desert Locust lives a total of about three to five months although this is extremely variable and depends mostly on weather and ecological conditions. The life cycle comprises three stages: egg, hopper and adult. Eggs hatch in about two weeks (the range is 10–65 days), hoppers develop in five to six stages over a period of about 30–40 days, and adults mature in about three weeks to nine months but more frequently from two to four months."[150] There thus could have been a period of some months during which the ground in Sudan became sufficiently lush, the locusts began to lay eggs, and finally a critical mass of locust adults was reached in order to become gregarious and finally to swarm and migrate (a swarming migration is a response to the population density of the locusts). In addition, locusts need vegetation in order to grow wings for migration; locusts in very dry conditions may never grow into winged adults and thus never migrate. The moist conditions in Sudan during this year of unusually heavy rains, therefore, both enabled the locusts of the Exodus plague to multiply wildly and also to develop into the adult, gregarious and migratory state.

The swarms from Sudan normally move northward from their breeding area. They can move directly into Egypt, but their more ordinary migration track is to cross the Red Sea, cross into the Arabian Peninsula, and from there sweep northward toward modern Jordan or Israel. Locust migration, however, is strongly influenced by the wind.[151]

---

149. "Desert Locust Information Service of FAO: Locust FAQs," Food and Agriculture Organization of the United Nations, accessed 4/23/14, http://www.fao.org/ag/locusts/oldsite/LOCFAQ.htm.

150. Ibid.

151. J. S. Kennedy, "The Migration of the Desert Locust (Schistocerca gregaria Forsk.). I. The Behaviour of Swarms. II. A Theory of Long-Range Migrations," *Philosophical Transactions of the Royal Society of London.* Series B, Biological Sciences 235, no. 625 (1951): 163–290.

On this occasion, there was an "east wind" (10:13) that caught the locusts as they were moving northward across the Red Sea and moved them toward the west, into Egypt, where they naturally alighted in the green Nile valley. After Moses interceded for Egypt, a west wind blew the locusts eastward, in the direction of the *Yam Suph*.[152] The Bible does not indicate that Goshen was spared this plague; considering the northward movement of the Desert Locust, it is not likely that Lower Egypt would be spared. The text gives us little indication of when the locust plague took place. It speaks of plants and fruit trees (10:15), but is not specific enough for us to assign a date to the event. Apart from the grains, Egyptian farmers produced a variety of garden crops (beans, onions, lettuce, leeks, radishes, garlic, and cucumbers, for example). Grapes and dates were common fruits. But not knowing precisely what plants were affected, or in what stage of growth they were, we cannot tell anything about the date of the plague. In connection with the sequence of the other plagues, however, it appears that the locust invasion was in February or March.

The almost universal assumption of interpreters is that the plague of darkness is some version of the khamsin, a severe dust- and sandstorm to which Egypt is subject. The event is from the Arabic word for "fifty," and it is so-called because it is most likely to occur within a period of about 50 days from late March to early May (corresponding to the time from Coptic Easter to Pentecost). It is brought about by a depression in the Sudan, causing the khamsin to move northward into Egypt. In a year of very severe weather, therefore, conditions similar to those that brought about the hail may have brought on an unusually severe low pressure center and thus a very bad khamsin. The khamsin can be quite debilitating; Nina Burleigh describes how badly the French troops of Napoleon were shaken by their encounter with such an event.[153] The khamsin of Exodus, if that is what it was, may have been especially severe not only because of the extreme weather but also because the excessive flooding of the Nile had deposited especially large amounts of black, alluvial soil, along with *Roterde*, during the summer inundation. This, combined with the fact that the locusts had denuded the soil, would have allowed far more sand, soil, and dust to be thrown up into the air than was usual. But how is it that Goshen was spared? Hort observes that Exod. 10:23 actually says that the

152. I do not agree with Hort, *Plagues*, 1958, 51–2, who argues that the רוח ים was a "sea wind" blowing from the north and that it drove the locusts to the south (she emends ים סוף to ימין).

153. Burleigh, *Mirage*, 135.

TABLE 8. THE PLAGUES AND THE NATURAL HISTORY OF EGYPT		
Plague	**Description of Event**	**Approx. Time**
Nile (7:14–24)	Heavy rain at Nile source pollutes river with *Roterde* and flagellates; water is blood-red and smelly; fish die; people dig along swollen river to obtain potable water.	August
Frogs (7:25–8:15)	Frog habitat fouled by dead fish; frogs flee, but only after infected with anthrax; they take refuge in man-made places but suddenly die.	One week after onset of Nile event; late Aug. or early Sept.
Mosquitoes (8:16–19)	Subsidence of Nile leaves behind many stagnant pools; mosquitoes proliferate wildly.	September–October
Flies (8:20–32)	*Stomoxys calcitrans* flies breed rapidly in decaying vegetation left behind by inundation. But in north, where cooler weather prevails, flies do not breed. Flies suddenly die, perhaps because of anthrax.	December–January
Livestock (9:1–7)	Cattle go to pasture as flood recedes; eat grass infected by dead frogs, and contract gastrointestinal anthrax. But cattle in Delta not put out to pasture because flood waters prevail longer there; by the time cattle go out in the Delta winter rains have washed anthrax from vegetation.	December–January
Skin Ulcers (9:8–12)	*Stomoxys calcitrans* flies pick up anthrax spores from cattle; when biting people and animals, flies infect them with cutaneous anthrax.	January
Hail (9:13–35)	A severe storm such as Egypt may sometimes experience; the rains may have swept down the Nile valley from the north.	Early February
Locusts (10:1–20)	Rains in Sudan create conditions for massive multiplication of the Desert Locust; it migrates northward, but is blown by an east wind into Egypt.	February or March
Darkness (10:21–29)	A severe khamsin stirs up abundant alluvial soil and *Roterde*, as well as soil exposed in denuded agricultural fields, to darken the sky.	March or April
Firstborn (11:1—12:51)	A direct act of God, although possibly with a disease such as plague or influenza.	April

Hebrews had light "in their dwellings." This suggests that the Hebrew "ghetto" may have been in an isolated spot near the Wadi Tumilat. The high ground of the Eastern Desert south of the Wadi Tumilat may have shielded the Hebrew settlement from the worst of the khamsin.[154]

154.Hort, *Plagues*, 1958, 54.

The death of the firstborn cannot be explained by any natural means.[155] This does not mean that the firstborn did not die of a normal disease; some diseases, such as plague or influenza, can strike down apparently healthy people in an amazingly short space of time. But nothing can account for the selectivity of the disease: it struck only firstborn males and avoided homes that had the blood of the Passover lamb on the door frame. Nor can anything account for the fact that, as far as we know, the pandemic struck and was over in a single night. We do not call this plague an "inexplicable act of God" as a last resort, but because that is where the data, both biblical and natural, lead us. From the fact that this plague came at Passover, we know that it occurred in or near April.

EIGHT: THE HAIL (9:13–35)

Egypt faces another and more catastrophic assault upon its economy. Pharaoh becomes desperate and pleads for mercy, but then reneges on a promise to release Israel.

Translation

9:13 And YHWH said to Moses,
"Rise up early in the morning
and stand before Pharaoh
and say to him,
'Thus says YHWH, the God of the Hebrews,
"Release my people,
that they may serve me.
9:14a Although during this time I have been sending[156] all my plagues on your person[157] and your officials and your people[158]
9:14b (so that you may know

155. I do not accept the suggestion of Hort, *Plagues*, 1958, 55, that בכר, "firstborn," should be read as בכרים, "firstfruit."

156. The participle here is retrospective, describing what has been happening up until now. It is not future, contrary to a number of English versions (ESV, NASB, etc.). Compare Exod. 10:11, כִּי אֹתָהּ אַתֶּם מְבַקְשִׁים ("because you have been asking for it"; *IBHS*, §37.6b). There is plainly a contrast between כִּ בַּפַּעַם הַזֹּאת אֲנִי שֹׁלֵחַ in 9:14a and כִּי עַתָּה שָׁלַחְתִּי in 9:15a. For this reason, כִּי בַּפַּעַם הַזֹּאת אֲנִי שֹׁלֵחַ in 9:14a must be regarded as a progressive past and not a future verbal construction.

157. Lit. "your heart." In Egyptian anthropology, as in Hebrew, the heart was the center of the self and the seat of thought, personality and will.

158. Verse 9:14a is concessive and gives the background for the conditional sentence in 9:15. It is a verbless (participial) clause and is therefore offline.

9:14c that there is no one like me in all the earth),[159]
9:15a if I were now to give free rein to[160] my power[161]
9:15b and strike you and your people with the pestilence,
9:15c you would be obliterated from the earth.[162]
9:16 But, in fact, I have allowed you to remain standing for this reason, for you to display my power and in order for [people] to tell of my name through all the earth.
9:17 Still you vaunt yourself[163] toward my people by not letting them go.
9:18 About this time tomorrow, [you will see][164] me raining down a very heavy hail, which has had no equal in Egypt from the day it was founded until now.
9:19a And now dispatch [messengers]!
9:19b Bring under shelter your livestock and whatever you have in the field.
9:19c [If there be][165] any man or beast that is found in the field and not brought inside,
9:19d then the hail will come down upon them,
9:19e and they will die.'""

---

159. Verse 9:14bc is parenthetical; the main flow of the sentence is from 9:14a to 9:15.

160. The verb שׁלח (Qal stem) is literally "send," but here it implies a letting go of power that heretofore had been restrained. Cf. Ps. 50:19, פִּיךָ שָׁלַחְתָּ בְרָעָה ("You give your mouth free rein for evil"; NRSV).

161. Lit. "my hand."

162. The three clauses of this verse are כִּי עַתָּה + *qatal* (9:15a), *wayyiqtol* (9:15b), and *wayyiqtol* (9:15c). Clause 9:15a uses כִּי conditionally and sets up a protasis. Clause 9:15b continues the protasis. An analogy for extending the protasis to a second clause in this manner is at Jer. 12:5 (כִּי אֶת־רַגְלִים רַצְתָּה וַיַּלְאוּךָ; "if you have run with footmen and they have wearied you"). Clause 9:15c is the apodosis. The whole conditional sentence is a contrary-to-fact condition, but translators, apparently influenced by the presence of the *wayyiqtol* forms, have supposed it to be past contrary-to-fact. This is incorrect; the presence of עַתָּה ("now") indicates that it is present contrary-to-fact.

163. The root סלל essentially means to build something up, like the raising of ground to build a road (Isa. 57:14), and from this it comes to mean to "exalt" (Ps. 68:4[5]), with the Hithpolel meaning "exalt oneself."

164. The phrase הִנְנִי מַמְטִיר, lit. "behold me sending rain," here vividly presents the event from Pharaoh's perspective.

165. The *weyiqtol* verb וְיָרַד in 9:19d implies that 9:19c is the protasis of a conditional clause.

9:20 Any of the Pharaoh's officials who feared the word of YHWH had his servants and his livestock flee into the houses;
9:21a but if[166] anyone had no regard to the word of YHWH,
9:21b he left his servants and his livestock in the field.
9:22a And YHWH said to Moses,
9:22b "Stretch out your hand toward the sky,
9:22c that there may be hail on all the land of Egypt, on man and on beast and on every plant of the field, throughout the land of Egypt."
9:23a And Moses stretched out his staff toward the sky,
9:23b and YHWH did [indeed] cause thunder and hail:[167]
9:23c fire came earthward,
9:23d and YHWH rained hail on the land of Egypt;
9:24a there was hail,
9:24b and fire was mixed in with the hail.
9:24c [It was] a very severe hail, the like of which had not occurred in all the land of Egypt from the time it became a nation.
9:25a And the hail struck, throughout the whole land of Egypt, everything that was in the field—man or beast—
9:25b and the hail struck every plant of the field[168]
9:25c and it shattered every tree of the field.
9:26 Only in the land of Goshen, where the Israelites [were], was there no hail.
9:27a And Pharaoh sent [messengers]
9:27b and he summoned Moses and Aaron,
9:27c and he said to them,
9:27d "I have sinned this time;
9:27e YHWH is in the right,
9:27f and I and my people are in the wrong.
9:28a Make supplication to YHWH—

166. The relative אֲשֶׁר is here used for introducing a conditional statement, as in Lev. 4:22 (אֲשֶׁר נָשִׂיא יֶחֱטָא; "if a leader sins").

167. This clause is offline, having the pattern וְ + noun + *qatal* instead of the *wayyiqtol*. Clearly the clause is sequential to the prior clause (9:23a) and one would normally expect a *wayyiqtol* here. Its offline pattern makes it more prominent, and it sets up a matching statement with the prior clause (Moses did this and then YHWH responded by doing that). It also serves as a summarizing statement about the storm; the subsequent *wayyiqtol* clauses (9:23c–25a) are epexegetical of 9:23b.

168. Clauses 9:25bc both have an offline pattern (וְ + object + *qatal* verb) because they form a counterpart to 9:25a: as the hail struck man and beast, so also it struck plants and trees.

9:28b the divine thunder and hail is terribly severe—[169]
9:28c and I will let you go,[170]
9:28d and you shall stay no longer."
9:29a And Moses said to him,
9:29b "As soon as I leave the city, I will spread out my hands to YHWH;
9:29c the thunder will cease
9:29d and the hail shall be no more,
9:29e that you may know that the earth is YHWH's.
9:30a But you and your officials!
9:30b I know
9:30c that you do not yet fear YHWH God."
9:31a Now the flax and the barley were struck down,[171]
9:31b for the barley was in the ear
9:31c and the flax was in bud.
9:32a But the wheat and the emmer were not struck down,
9:32b for they are later.
9:33a And Moses went out of the city, from Pharaoh's presence,
9:33b and he spread out his hands to YHWH,
9:33c and the thunder and the hail stopped,
9:33d and rain no longer poured on the earth.
9:34a And Pharaoh saw
9:34b that the rain and the hail and the thunder had ceased,
9:34c and he repeated his sin:
9:34d he and his officials made their hearts leaden,[172]
9:35a and Pharaoh's heart was implacable,
9:35b and he did not let the Israelites go.

169. This clause is usually translated as something like, "for there has been enough of God's thunder and hail" (ESV), but the clause וְרַב מִהְיֹת קֹלֹת אֱלֹהִים וּבָרָד is quite difficult. The word רַב seems to be the predicate, with מִהְיֹת having comparative force after רַב. The subject is קֹלֹת אֱלֹהִים וּבָרָד. It could thus be translated literally, "The divine thunders and hail are more than to be." The infinitive could be read in a historical sense (infinitives of themselves lack tense). Interpreted this way, it means that the hail is "more than ever was." But probably רַב מִהְיֹת means "too much to be." This could mean that the hail is too much for people to be, i.e., too severe for life to continue. In addition, רַב מִהְיֹת as "too much to be" may be idiomatic for "terribly severe" or "an incredibly large amount."

170. This clause serves as an apodosis to 9:28a; 9:28b is parenthetical.

171. Vv. 9:31–32 are offline, describing the situation in the aftermath of the hail.

172. The *wayyiqtol* is epexegetical of 9:34c.

9:35c [It was] just as YHWH had spoken through the agency[173] of Moses.

Structure

This is a lengthy plague narrative, and it contains all the main formal elements.

I. YHWH Commissions Moses and Aaron to Appear Before Pharaoh (9:13–19)
II. A Warning to Pharaoh About his Refusal to Release Israel (9:13–17)
III. A Warning About a Coming Judgment (9:18–19)
IV. Pharaoh's Advisors Respond (9:20–21)
V. YHWH Commands Moses to Begin the Plague (9:22)
VI. Moses and Aaron Carry Out the Commission (9:23–26)
  A. Moses and Aaron Perform a Ritual Act to Initiate the Plague (9:23a)
  B. The Plague Begins and its Effects Are Described (9:23b–26)
VII. Pharaoh Interviews Moses in the Course of the Plague (9:27–30)
  A. Pharaoh's Plea (9:27–28)
  B. Moses's Answer (9:29–30)
VIII. Other Information (9:31–32)
IX. Moses Intercedes for Egypt, and the Plague Stops (9:33)
X. Pharaoh's Heart Hardened (9:34–35ab)
XI. Affirmation that YHWH's Word Was Fulfilled (9:35c)

Commentary

9:13–17. YHWH opens his speech to Pharaoh with a statement of four facts about the plagues that he has been sending upon Egypt. First, he has done it to instruct the Egyptians, that they may understand that YHWH is the true God. Second, he could obliterate Egyptian power. If his only objective were to get Israel out of Egypt, he would have already so shattered Egyptian power that the Israelite departure would have been no issue at all. Third, he has restrained his power and left Egypt standing in order to make an example of Egypt. Had YHWH simply destroyed Egypt in one blow, no one would know what to make of it. But the successive pummeling of an obstinate Egypt gave everyone time to see that YHWH's power and patience were both very great. All of this has the effect of thoroughly demoting Egyptian power. Egypt is not really YHWH's adversary—it is too weak to be in that

173. Lit. "hand."

role. Pharaoh would be wise to understand that he is simply a tool in God's hands, and abandon all pretense of power. But the fourth point is that Pharaoh has been blind to the truth and has been ridiculously arrogant, supposing that he can resist God to the end.

9:18–19. Against the recent history of YHWH's dealings with Egypt, this warning is a matter of pure mercy. God is about to deal a terrible blow against their agricultural economy, but it need not be a crippling blow. The Egyptians can save both personnel and livestock by bringing everyone under shelter. Verses 14–17 serve as a prologue to this warning and make the point that despite everything, YHWH is willing to show Egypt mercy by telling them how to avoid the worst of the coming destruction. Also, the review of previous events should force Pharaoh to realize that YHWH's warnings should be taken seriously.

9:20–21. Some of the Egyptian officials supported and imitated Pharaoh in his folly, but others recognized the futility of their position and the power of God by hurrying their people and animals inside. Those who heed the warning are of course to be applauded for their prudence, but they also make for a stark contrast with the earlier response of Pharaoh's officials. Any thought of mimicking YHWH's miracles is long forgotten now!

9:22. The hand is metaphorical for the power that a person possesses (Num. 20:20; Deut. 8:17; Isa. 59:1). Moses is told to extend his hand, and not the rod, toward heaven. This does not mean Moses was not to use the rod (see 9:23a), but the language, portraying Moses as extending his hand toward heaven and calling down a terrible hailstorm, implies that Moses has been invested with enormous authority.

9:23–26. The statement that "fire" came down with the hailstorm may mean that lightning (perhaps ball lightning) struck and ignited inflammable objects on the ground. All other aspects of the description suggest that this was a normal, albeit very severe, storm. Stuart observes that the destructive power of this hailstorm has analogies in recent history.[174] There may be an alternative explanation for the "fire" in the hail, however. The exodus may have occurred during a time of volcanic activity; Mt. Sinai appears to have been volcanic, and numerous scholars have speculated on the relationship of the plagues

174. Stuart, *Exodus*, 237.

to eruptions such as Santorini (probably late 17th century B.C.) and Yali (in the eastern Aegean, and probably dated to the mid-15th century B.C.[175]). Ash particles from an eruption can travel great distances and be the "seed" for precipitation of rain or hail. According to geologist Barbara Sivertsen, the "icy ashballs" from a volcanic eruption could be electrically charged and perceived as "hail shot through with lightning."[176] Hail and rain with a high concentration of volcanic ash might also cause chemical burns on the skin. The sparing of the land of Goshen, where Israel resided, needs no real explanation. Severe storms are outrageously unpredictable, annihilating one community and leaving a neighboring community untouched. This storm, directed by God, was selective.

9:27–28. While it is impossible to know what went on in Pharaoh's heart, in this account it appears that his remorse is genuine and not a pretense. This does not mean, however, that his remorse was effective in the sense that it actually brought about a change in his behavior and attitude. At the moment of his grief-stricken meeting with Moses, he may have been absolutely sincere in his willingness to allow Israel to depart. His repentance would remain in a kind of provisional status until he actually acted on his promise to let the people depart. As it turned out, his willingness to do this was ephemeral; it vanished as rapidly as did the hailstorms.

9:29–30. Moses does not call Pharaoh a liar, but he is not persuaded that his repentance has any lasting value. He knows that Pharaoh's greed for the free labor is far too deep, and that his understanding of YHWH is far too shallow, for this change of heart to be lasting. Even so, he agrees to call on YHWH to stop the storm. The cessation of the storm evidently took place in a sudden and dramatic manner, immediately after Moses spread his hands in prayer to God, so that Pharaoh could not deny that the storm's termination was a direct result of Moses's intercession.

9:31–32. The flax and barley were most vulnerable, as both were large enough to be struck and damaged by the hail. But neither was at a stage that anything was ready to be harvested. As such, there was nothing to salvage after the hailstorm. The fiber of flax was used for making linen, while the grain of barley was used for making bread and

175. Sivertsen, *Parting of the Sea*, 134-5.
176. Ibid., 41.

beer. The fact that the barley was just showing young ears and that the flax was in bud suggests that the hailstorm took place in early February. The wheat and emmer (a kind of grain with a "bearded ear" and a double grain in the spikelets) were not harvested until late spring or early summer.

9:33. Moses, as God's agent, had power both to destroy and to heal. This should have moved Pharaoh to a lasting respect for Moses and fear of YHWH.

9:34–35. Pharaoh's fear of YHWH lasted only so long as conditions demanded it. Ironically, Jesus would portray this kind of ephemeral repentance with an agricultural metaphor, comparing it to grain plants planted either among weeds or in shallow soil (Matt. 13:3–9).

Theological Summary of Key Points

1. Even when God afflicts a people, he does it in order to teach them truths. The most fundamental lesson of all is that God is powerful and the human pretension of strength is madness.

2. God's purposes in history are manifold and complex. While it is true that God afflicted the Egyptians in order to force them to release Israel, there is more to it than that. He also did it in order to make Egypt an object lesson for all time, to prove that YHWH, the God of Israel, is the true God. But he also acted for the sake of Egypt, seeking to make that nation understand the truth about God.

3. In the plague of hail, God both afflicted Egypt and provided the Egyptians with a means of minimizing that affliction by telling them in advance to take shelter. Even in punishing, God may give people the means of reducing their suffering, so long as they believe and act upon that belief.

4. Sincere remorse may not be genuine repentance. The ultimate test of the reality of one's claim to faith and repentance may be in perseverance. Pharaoh failed to follow through in his promise to release the Hebrews. Those who promise to act and do not do it, or who for a time change their behavior and then return to their former ways, are not truly repentant, however sincere they may have been in their professed awareness of their sin.

5. In this particular plague narrative, the distinctive feature is the three responses described among the Egyptians: outright unbelief, shown by those who left their people and animals in the fields; genuine fear of God, shown by those who brought their people and animals inside; and pseudo-faith, shown in the remorseful promise but subsequent reversal of that promise by Pharaoh.

NINE: THE LOCUSTS (10:1–20)

Desperate Egyptians beg Pharaoh to give in to Moses's request, and he again enters into negotiations. But he loses all rationality when it is clear that he must yield entirely, and he angrily casts Moses out of his palace. Another and yet worse economic calamity befalls the country of Egypt.

Translation

10:1a And YHWH said to Moses,
10:1b "Go to Pharaoh,
10:1c for I have made his heart and the hearts of his officials leaden,
10:1d so that I may set these signs of mine[177] among them,
10:2a and so that you may tell in the hearing of your children and of your grandchildren [the fact] that[178] I made fools[179] of the Egyptians and about my signs that I set among them,
10:2b that you may know
10:2c that I am YHWH."
10:3a And Moses and Aaron went to Pharaoh
10:3b and they said to him,
10:3c "Thus says YHWH, the God of the Hebrews,

177. The general rule is that the demonstrative אֵלֶּה has the definite article when serving as a determiner for a definite plural noun. Thus we have הַדְּבָרִים הָאֵלֶּה ("these things") in Gen. 15:1. This rule is not followed, however, if the noun is definite by virtue of having a pronominal suffix. In this case, the article is not used with אֵלֶּה. Examples include וְשַׂמְתֶּם אֶת־דְּבָרַי אֵלֶּה ("and you shall set these words of mine"; Deut. 11:18) and אַשְׁרֵי עֲבָדֶיךָ אֵלֶּה ("happy are these your servants"; 1 Kings 10:8).

178. The words אֵת אֲשֶׁר הִתְעַלַּלְתִּי בְּמִצְרַיִם are a relative clause serving as a direct object and thus, despite the presence of the finite verb, do not form an independent clause. The same is true for אֲשֶׁר־שַׂמְתִּי בָם.

179. The verb עלל in the Hithpael stem means either to make a fool of someone (Num. 22:29) or to abuse someone (Judg. 19:25). The word implies complete disregard for the dignity of Egypt, and it is very strong language.

10:3d 'How long will you refuse to be brought down into subjection[180] before me?
10:3e Release my people,
10:3f that they may serve me.
10:4a For if you continue in refusing to release my people,
10:4b then guess what![181] Tomorrow I will be bringing locusts into your territory.
10:5a And they will cover the features of the land,[182]
10:5b so that no one will be able to see the land.
10:5c And they will consume the rest of what has survived—what is still left to you from the hail—
10:5d and they will consume every tree belonging to you that sprouts from the field.
10:6a And your houses and the houses of all your officials and the houses of all the Egyptians will be full [of them].
10:6b [This is a thing] that neither your fathers nor your grandfathers have seen, from the day that they came upon the earth until this day.'"
10:6c And he turned
10:6d and he went out from Pharaoh's presence.
10:7a And Pharaoh's officials said to him,
10:7b "How long will this man be a snare to us?
10:7c Release the men
10:7d so that they may serve YHWH their God.
10:7e Do you not yet comprehend
10:7f that Egypt perishes?"[183]
10:8a And Moses and Aaron[184] were brought back to Pharaoh,
10:8b and he said to them,

---

180. The Niphal of ענה (II) is strong language. It is not just a matter of showing due humility, but of being brought low by severe affliction and violence (Isa. 53:7). In this case, it describes someone who, in effect, cringes in the dust from the beating he has taken. For the infinitive construct, we would expect to see לְהֵעָנוֹת, but the ה has disappeared.

181. The word הִנְנִי is here part of a blunt and harsh rebuke, calling on Pharaoh to listen up. The traditional translation "behold" gives it a misleading dignity.

182. The phrase אֶת־עֵין הָאָרֶץ is literally "the eye of the land." The eye is that with which one sees, but here it refers to that which is seen, the surface of the land. See Num. 22:5.

183. This clause is an indirect statement.

184. The subject of a passive verb sometimes has the object particle אֵת. See *IBHS*, §10.3.2b.

10:8c “Go!

10:8d Serve YHWH your God!

10:8e Who exactly will be going?”

10:9a And Moses said,

10:9b “We will go with our young and with our old.

10:9c We will go with our sons and with our daughters, with our flocks and our herds.

10:9d For ours is a feast of YHWH.”

10:10a And he said to them,

10:10b “May it be so!

10:10c May YHWH be with you!

10:10d As if I would release you and your toddlers![185]

10:10e See?[186] Your treachery is obvious![187]

10:11a No way!

10:11b Let the men go[188]

10:11c and serve YHWH,

10:11d for that is what you have been seeking.”

10:11e And he drove them out[189] from Pharaoh’s presence.

10:12a And YHWH said to Moses,

10:12b “Stretch out your hand over the land of Egypt for the locusts,

10:12c that they may arise over the land of Egypt

10:12d and eat every plant of the land—everything that the hail has left.”

10:13a So Moses stretched out his staff over the land of Egypt,

10:13b and YHWH drove[190] an east wind on the land all that day and all that night.

---

185. The word טַף is traditionally taken to refer to small children. It is from the root טפף, “to take little steps,” and thus may be an exact equivalent to the English “toddler.” It is possible, however, that the word טַף also includes other people who walk gingerly or with difficulty, such as the elderly (see טַף, *HALOT*, 2.378).

186. רְאוּ is here used as an interjection.

187. Lit. “evil is before your face.” The phrase נֶגֶד פְּנֵיכֶם occurs in 1 Sam. 26:20; Isa. 5:21; Hos. 7:2; Lam. 3:35, but none of these is fully analogous to this text.

188. The imperative (לְכוּ־נָא) has a third-person subject (הַגְּבָרִים); it is, in effect, a third-person imperative.

189. The verb וַיְגָרֶשׁ could be translated as a virtual passive (“and they were driven out”), but the text presents Pharaoh as irrationally sarcastic and frantic, and it probably implies that Pharaoh personally shoved them out the door.

190. The use of the וְ + X + *qatal* pattern (וַיהוָה נִהַג רוּחַ) as opposed to the *wayyiqtol* may be used to emphasize that although Moses did the ritual act of

10:13c Morning arrived,[191]

10:13d and the east wind had brought[192] the locusts;

10:14a and the locusts arose over all the land of Egypt

10:14b and they settled throughout the territory of Egypt.

10:14c [The swarm was] very dense:

10:14d prior to this, there had been no locust plague like it,

10:14e and after this, no [locust plague] will [ever] be like it.

10:15a And they covered the features of the whole land,

10:15b and the land was black,

10:15c and they ate every plant of the land and all the fruit of the trees that the hail had left.

10:15d And nothing green was left on the trees or the plants of the field through the whole land of Egypt.

10:16a And Pharaoh hurried to summon Moses and Aaron,

10:16b and he said,

10:16c "I have sinned against YHWH your God and against you.

10:17a And now forgive my sin only this [one, final] time,[193]

10:17b and make supplication to YHWH your God,

10:17c that he would just remove this death from me."

10:18a And [Moses] went out from Pharaoh's presence,

10:18b and he made supplication to YHWH.

10:19a And YHWH turned it into a very strong west wind,

10:19b and it picked up the locusts

10:19c and it blew them toward the *Yam Suph*.

10:19d Not a single locust remained in all the territory of Egypt.

10:20a But YHWH made Pharaoh's heart implacable,

---

lifting the staff, it was actually YHWH who performed the miracle.

191. Literally "the morning was" (הַבֹּקֶר הָיָה), this asyndetic clause is particularly dramatic, and it marks the start of a small narrative describing the arrival and destruction brought about by the locusts within the larger narrative of the plague. The structure of this mini-narrative is: 1. Initial clause of mini-narrative (10:13c). 2. Initial situation with offline וְ + X + *qatal* (10:13d). 3. Sequence of arrival of locusts with mainline *wayyiqtol* clauses (10:14ab). 4. Offline summary of devastation (10:14cde). 5. Sequence of locust plague resumed with mainline *wayyiqtol* clauses (10:15abc). 6. Offline concluding summary of after-effects (10:15d).

192. The verb נשׂא (Qal stem) can mean to "bring" something, as in 1 Kings 10:11; Ps. 96:8. The offline status of this clause here justifies translating it as a pluperfect.

193. The phrase אַךְ הַפַּעַם ("only the time") appears to mean "only on this final occasion." That is, he is promising that he has learned his lesson and that his previous offence of resisting YHWH won't happen again.

10:20b and he did not release the Israelites.

Structure

This is a lengthy plague sequence, and it contains almost all of the standard formal elements.

I. YHWH Commissions Moses and Aaron to Appear Before Pharaoh (10:1–2)
   A. Commission (10:1ab)
   B. Background Information (10:1c)
   C. The Glory of the Exodus Story Predicted (10:1d–2)
II. Moses and Aaron Carry Out the Commission (10:3–6)
   A. A Demand that Pharaoh Release Israel (10:3)
   B. A Warning About a Coming Judgment (10:4–6)
III. Pharaoh's Advisors and Magicians Respond with Counsel to Pharaoh (10:7)
IV. Pharaoh Interviews Moses Before the Plague (10:8–11)
   A. Pharaoh's Conditional Promise to Release the People (10:8)
   B. Moses's Answer (10:9)
   C. Pharaoh's Limited Release of the People (10:10–11)
V. YHWH Commands Moses to Begin the Plague (10:12)
VI. Moses Obeys (10:13–15)
   A. Moses Performs a Ritual Act to Initiate the Plague (10:13ab)
   B. The Plague and its Effects Are Described (13cd–15)
VII. Pharaoh Requests that Moses Intercede for Egypt to Stop the Plague (10:16–17)
VIII. Moses Intercedes for Egypt, and the Plague Stops (10:18–19)
IX. YHWH Hardens Pharaoh's Heart, and he Refuses to Release Israel (10:20)

Commentary

10:1–2. YHWH's statement that he has made Pharaoh's heart "leaden" is matched at the end of the narrative by the statement that YHWH made Pharaoh's heart "implacable" (10:20a). These two statements thus form an inclusio for the narrative, but they also set its theological tone. YHWH is giving Pharaoh over to a bitterness that is unyielding to the point of madness. Furthermore, the text tells us that YHWH intended the Egyptians to remain implacable about releasing the Hebrews in order that God might unleash a full range of plagues upon Egypt (10:1d). This is a hard truth—that God would provoke the wicked to remain in their wickedness so that he might show his power in punishing them. This is Rom. 9:11–22 made vivid. Israel, in turn, will celebrate how their oppressor was knocked to the ground and made to look hapless.[194]

10:3–6. The language of 10:3–4a suggests that Pharaoh's continued stubbornness is tiresome to God, as though God himself cannot believe how obstinate Pharaoh is acting in the face of one catastrophe after another. This should not be set against God's prior statement to Moses that God himself hardened Pharaoh's heart, as though God were here pretending exasperation with Pharaoh's refusal to release the people. It is a paradoxical truth that both aspects of the events are fully correct: God both hardened Pharaoh's heart and genuinely appealed to him to relent and so spare himself and his nation further grief. God offers to end the plagues, here and now, on condition of Israel's release, and this is an offer made in good faith. The threat, on the other hand, is very grave. With the locust plague, the agricultural wealth of Egypt will be wiped out. Their livestock and crops were already sorely damaged in the prior episodes; the locusts will leave them with nothing but the cattle that escaped the previous plagues (but with no pasturage available). Humans and animals alike will face the threat of starvation.

10:7. The officials' description of Moses as a "snare" implies that he is a problem from which they cannot extricate themselves. They have had enough, and they simply want this nightmare to end. They only urge Pharaoh to let the "men" go and say nothing about letting the whole nation depart, and this suggests that they may have been in sympathy with Pharaoh's determination to allow only the adult males to go worship YHWH. Even so, they are plainly pressuring Pharaoh to bring this to an end.

10:8–11. Pharaoh begins by telling Moses that Israel is free to go and only afterward asks who specifically would be going. Furthermore, he begins with a terse imperative ("Go!"). He could have spoken more rationally and in a manner befitting negotiations, beginning with a condition (along the lines of, "If you limit the people who will go out to the men alone") and then offering release. But he is yielding to pressure and necessity and so blurts out that the people can leave and only then tries to claw them back with his questions and conditions. Moses will have none of this, and will accept nothing but a full release. Pharaoh, outraged at this effrontery and frustrated that he cannot find a way to

---

194. This is suggested in the Hithpael of עלל in 10:2a.

end the plagues without releasing all the people, responds with invective and sarcasm, spewed out in a manner that is scarcely coherent. He ended the interview by giving Moses the bum's rush out the front door!

10:12–15. Moses does the ritual of summoning the locusts, but it is YHWH who actually brings them. The natural history of locusts in the area is described above in Excursus: The Plague Sequence in Natural History.

10:16–17. Pharaoh pleads again for forgiveness even as he indicates that his prior offense will not be repeated (see translation note to 10:17a). His tone is almost that of a broken man. He calls the locusts "this death" in reference to the famine that comes in their wake.

10:18–20. Moses does not even answer Pharaoh in this narrative; he is so far from being persuaded that Pharaoh is capable of genuine repentance that he does not even warn him that he must keep his word. This is far different from how Moses received Pharaoh's first promise of letting the people go (Exod. 8:9). But he responds to the words of Pharaoh even if not convinced of the genuineness of his heart. He goes out, intercedes for Egypt, and lifts the plague. As he probably expected, Pharaoh quickly reverted to his former stubbornness.

Theological Summary of Key Points

The language of this episode is considerably more charged with hostility and tragedy than the previous episodes. YHWH begins by telling Moses that he has made the hearts of the Egyptians "leaden," and he describes the plagues in very harsh language, stating that he has "abused" or "made fools" of the Egyptians (10:2a, using the Hithpael of עלל). Pharaoh is told that he must be "abased" or "brought down into subjection" before YHWH (10:3d, using the Niphal of ענה). The Egyptian officials tell Pharaoh that Egypt "perishes" (or, "has died"; 10:7f, using the Qal *qatal* of אבד). In his interview with Moses, Pharaoh's anger and bitterness are far more evident and pronounced than was seen in earlier encounters. His speech has the staccato pattern of a man who, being so angry he can barely speak, splutters out his invective. It is also laced with sarcasm (10:10bc). As described in the translation note to 10:11e, it even appears that Pharaoh personally manhandled Moses, rushing him out the door. The plague is said to be worse than anything in Egypt's history, and it veiled the whole country in black (10:14–15). Pharaoh calls the locusts "this death" (10:17c). After the onslaught of the plague, Pharaoh makes another speech of remorse and repentance, but Moses does not even answer him, suggesting that he is so cynical about Pharaoh's character by this point that he judges it not worth his breath to exhort or rebuke him. Finally, after the locusts are removed, Pharaoh's continued stubbornness is actually described as an act of YHWH: "But YHWH made Pharaoh's heart implacable" (10:20a). Therefore, although this narrative is in form and content like the others, it is distinctively ominous in its portrayal of the events. The series of judgments is nearing its finale, and the mad stubbornness of Pharaoh is likewise coming to a crescendo. Theologically, this text portrays how a divine judgment concludes: God gives the people over to their evil, the suffering is increased, and any hope for a true repentance fades. It is a tragic episode for any people, and Egypt here serves as a paradigm for all peoples who become hardened in their sin and are simultaneously both punished by God and given over by him to it (Rom.1:24).

1. They refuse to change even when the consequences of such stubbornness are exceedingly painful.

2. They have furious and irrational anger toward God's messengers.

3. The sufferings inflicted upon them are intense, but not yet fatal (compare the account of the locust-like creatures in Rev. 9:5). Final destruction is imminent.

4. Any small signs of change for the good are quickly dropped when the pressure upon them diminishes.

TEN: THE DARKNESS (10:21–29)

Darkness enshrouds Egypt as a token of the death and ultimate calamity that is about to strike. Pharaoh again tries to negotiate his way out of the dilemma, but he will not face reality, and only becomes more irrational in his dealings with Moses.

Translation

10:21a And YHWH said to Moses,
10:21b "Stretch out your hand toward the sky,
10:21c so that there may be darkness over the land of Egypt,
10:21d and so that darkness will cause [people] to grope about."[195]

195. The precise meaning of וְיָמֵשׁ חֹשֶׁךְ is debatable. The word חֹשֶׁךְ could be the direct object; in this case it would mean, "so that [people] may feel the

10:22a And Moses stretched out his hand toward the sky,
10:22b and there was pitch darkness in all the land of Egypt for three days.
10:23a No man could see his brother,
10:23b and no man could get up from his position[196] for three days,
10:23c but for all the Israelites,[197] there was light in the region where they lived.[198]
10:24a And Pharaoh called to Moses,
10:24b and he said,
10:24c "Go!
10:24d Serve YHWH!
10:24e Only your flocks and your herds must stay put.
10:24f Even your toddlers[199] may go with you."
10:25a And Moses said,

---

darkness." The idea would seem to be that the darkness is so great that one can (metaphorically) feel it. This is followed in most English translations. Alternatively, חֹשֶׁךְ could be the subject, meaning, "so that darkness may touch [the people]," although this seems unlikely and would in any case mean essentially the same thing as the first interpretation. Both of these interpretations, however, proceed from the understanding that משׁשׁ here conveys the idea of being tangible. But the root does not mean to be "touchable." It always conveys the notion of "groping"—that is, of searching for something by the sense of touch. In Gen. 27:12, 22 (Qal), it describes Isaac searching for information (the identity of the person with him) by feeling along his arm. In Gen. 31:34, 37 (Piel), it describes Laban groping through the household goods of Jacob, looking for his idols. In Deut. 28:29 and Job 5:14; 12:25 (all Piel), it describes the groping about of people who are blind or in darkness. Probably it has that sense here, except that the Hiphil is causative. Thus, the darkness forces people to grope about in order to find their way.

196. This follows the standard translation, as found in the NRSV, "and for three days they could not move from where they were," taking תַּחַת to mean "place" instead of the usual "under." This interpretation finds support in 2 Sam. 2:23; Job 40:12; and especially Exod. 16:29. It is conceivable that the antecedent of the 3rd masc. sing. suffix (in מִתַּחְתָּיו) is חֹשֶׁךְ ("darkness," a masculine noun), and that the meaning is, "and no one rose up from under the darkness for three days." The point would be not that the people were immobilized, but that the darkness was everywhere. This, in turn, would set up a good contrast to clause 10:23c. But the standard interpretation is probably correct.

197. All three clauses of 10:23 are offline, but 10:23ab are descriptive of the conditions, while 10:23c, fronted by וּלְכָל־בְּנֵי יִשְׂרָאֵל, is in contrast to 10:23ab.

198. Lit. "in their dwelling-place" (בְּמוֹשְׁבֹתָם).

199. See the translation note at 10:10d.

10:25b "And you will provide us with sacrifices and whole burnt offerings,[200]
10:25c that we may sacrifice [them] to YHWH our God?
10:26a Either that, or[201] our livestock must also go with us:
10:26b not a hoof shall be left behind,
10:26c for we will take some of them for the sacrifice to YHWH our God.
10:26d But we will not know
10:26e what sacrifice we will make to YHWH until we get there."[202]
10:27a And YHWH made Pharaoh's heart implacable,
10:27b and he was not willing to release them.
10:28a And Pharaoh said to him,
10:28b "Depart from me!
10:28c Beware of ever seeing my face again![203]
10:28d For on the day that you see my face you will die!"
10:29a And Moses said,
10:29b "As you have spoken:
10:29c I will never see your face again."

Structure

This is a very short plague narrative and omits a number of formal

---

200. This is usually translated as something like, "You must also let us have sacrifices and burnt offerings" (ESV), which appears to mean simply that Pharaoh must allow the Israelites to take their own animals with them to make sacrifice. However, to "give" (נתן) something into someone's "hand" (בְּיָד) cannot possibly mean to allow someone to make use of his own property, as this interpretation of נתן implies. It must mean that one party (in this case, Pharaoh) is giving or providing something for another party (in this case, Israel). Also, the standard interpretation of this clause does not take into account the unusual pattern setting גַּם־אַתָּה ("also you") against וְגַם־מִקְנֵנוּ ("also our livestock") in clause 10:26a. The point is that either Pharaoh must provide the sacrifices or the Hebrews' herds must provide them. Finally, we should note that Moses's reply is clearly sarcastic; I have tried to show that by presenting it as a question.
201. The pattern in vv. 25–26, גַּם followed by וְגַם, in effect means "on the one hand. . . on the other hand." See the usage of וְגַם (used twice) in Gen. 21:26.
202. This clause is an indirect question.
203. It is possible to follow a number of Hebrew MMS and emend הִשָּׁמֶר לְךָ אֶל־תֹּסֶף רְאוֹת פָּנַי to have אַל instead of אֶל. As emended, it is, "Be careful! Do not see my face again!" However, אֶל is used with שמר as that about which one takes care, as in 1 Sam. 26:15, וְלָמָּה לֹא שָׁמַרְתָּ אֶל־אֲדֹנֶיךָ הַמֶּלֶךְ, "And why do you not give protection to your lord, the king?" Thus the unemended text means, "Be careful with respect to [whether] you again see my face." That is, "Beware of seeing my face again."

elements, including most notably any giving of advance warning to Pharaoh. Moses is told to initiate the plague at the very beginning of this text.

I. YHWH Commands Moses to Begin the Plague (10:21)
II. Moses Carries Out the Commission (10:22–23)
   A. Moses Performs a Ritual Act to Initiate the Plague (10:22a)
   B. The Plague Begins and its Effects Are Described (10:22b–23)
III. Pharaoh Interviews Moses in the Course of the Plague (10:24–26)
   A. A Conditional Promise to Release the People (10:24)
   B. Moses Answers Pharaoh (10:25–26)
IV. YHWH Hardens Pharaoh's Heart, and he Refuses to Release Israel (10:27)
V. Other Information (10:28–29)

Commentary

10:21–23. The plague begins abruptly and without forewarning. This may be in part because the plague of darkness does not itself do any damage. Being in the dark is inconvenient, but it does not harm people or livestock or otherwise damage the economy. This could be interpreted, therefore, as an exception to the general trend of plagues becoming increasingly severe. On the other hand, the symbolic value of the plague is very great. Darkness suggests death. From the biblical perspective, it implies a reversion into pre-creation chaos, the lifeless and void state that existed before God said, "Let there be light." From the Egyptian standpoint as well, darkness is symbolically an end of the world. Many Egyptian myths focus on the rising of the sun as the daily renewal of the earth and all the life that it contains, and many Egyptian gods have some connection to the sun. Engulfing the world in darkness would in terms of Egyptian mythology be a victory for Apopis or Seth, gods of chaos, over the order and harmony that Egypt idealized under the motif of the light of the sun. This is particularly true if the darkness were associated with a massive sandstorm, a phenomenon associated with Seth. But this is not YHWH fighting against or in alliance with any Egyptian deities. It is simply YHWH making use of an event of natural history that, in terms of Egyptian culture and religion, would be charged with dreadful meaning. Later in biblical literature, the coming of darkness would be a standard apocalyptic motif, representing death and the end of all things (Rev. 16:10).

10:24–26. Pharaoh continues to seek a way to win this struggle, this time suggesting that all the Israelites could go worship but that their animals would remain behind. This way, he could be sure either that the Hebrews would return to his service or that he would be amply paid for letting them go, as he could seize all of their abandoned livestock for himself. Moses, in response, is as sarcastic to Pharaoh as Pharaoh had been to Moses in the previous episode (Exod. 10:10). The notion that Israel should go out to perform a religious festival to YHWH without taking their livestock was absurd, Moses argues, as they would need a considerable number of animals for the sacrifice and they could not be sure beforehand which animals would be most needed. It is striking to us that even at this late stage, the struggle between Moses and Pharaoh is still centered on the request to allow Israel to go out on a short journey to make a sacrifice, as opposed to Israel being allowed to abandon Egypt entirely.

10:27. Once again, the text states that YHWH made Pharaoh's heart unyielding. As we do not comprehend the power or the mind of God, there is no need for us to ask how God may be said to have done this without violating Pharaoh's free will. The important point is that God had determined that Pharaoh would not release the Hebrews until the plagues had run their course.

10:28–29. The only unusual bit of information in the plague of darkness narrative is here, where Pharaoh tells Moses never to come before him again. Its inclusion here seems particularly odd since Moses is in fact summoned back into Pharaoh's presence fairly soon (Exod. 12:31). But the purpose of including 10:28–29 is not to make light of the fact that Pharaoh had to reverse himself and call Moses back; it is rather a signal to the reader that the negotiations were at an end. Pharaoh was not willing to deal with Moses anymore, and no further attempts to persuade him to let the people go were possible. Therefore, there was nothing left to be done but hit Egypt with the most terrible of the plagues, the death of all the firstborn males. Any further prolonging of the process was pointless.

Theological Summary of Key Points

Light is a powerful theological metaphor in the Bible. Its creation is the beginning of all things (Gen. 1:3). It is symbolically life and the source of life (John 1:4); to see the light of day is to be alive (Eccl. 11:7; 12:2). It represents truth, and especially the truths revealed by and about God (Isa. 2:5; Dan. 2:22; Rom. 2:19). It is associated with justice and right behavior, as opposed to evil deeds (Zeph. 3:5; John 3:20). A joyful and wholesome life that comes from heeding wisdom is equated with walking in light (Prov. 6:23). God himself is the light, and as such the source of life (Ps 36:9; John 8:12; 1 John 1:5). Hell, by contrast, is the "outer darkness" (Matt. 8:12). The elimination of light is a sign of the end of all things and of death (Isa. 13:10; Ezek. 32:7; Matt. 24:29). For the Egyptians, the darkness was a sign that the final calamity was about to fall upon them. The abiding lesson, for which Egypt stands as a type, is that when a people have lost all light (in terms of spiritual blindness), destruction is at the gates.

ELEVEN: THE FIRSTBORN (11:1—13:16)

The firstborn of Egypt are slain, Israel is released, and the Passover is instituted.

Translation

11:1a And YHWH said to Moses,
11:1b "One more plague I will bring on Pharaoh and on Egypt;
11:1c after that he will release you from this place.
11:1d When he releases you, he will completely expel you from this place.
11:2a Give an address directly to the [Israelite] people[204]
11:2b [instructing] that each man ask from his neighbor and each woman from her neighbor for items of silver and items of gold."
11:3a And YHWH caused the Egyptians to be favorably inclined toward the people.[205]
11:3b Also, in the land of Egypt Moses himself[206] was regarded as a great man by[207] Pharaoh's officials and by the people.
11:4a And Moses said [to Pharaoh],[208]
11:4b "Thus says YHWH,
11:4c 'At midnight I am going out into the midst of Egypt,
11:5 and all the firstborn in the land of Egypt shall die, from the first-born of the pharaoh who sits on his throne, even to the firstborn

204. The idiom דַּבֶּר־נָא בְּאָזְנֵי הָעָם (lit. "Speak in the ears of the people") means to directly address the people with the purpose of being sure that they get the message. See Deut. 5:1; Josh. 20:4; Judg. 9:2; 1 Sam. 11:4.
205. Lit. "And YHWH provided the favor of the people in the eyes of Egypt" (וַיִּתֵּן יְהוָה אֶת־חֵן הָעָם בְּעֵינֵי מִצְרָיִם).
206. "Moses himself" is lit. "the man Moses."
207. "Was regarded as a great man by Pharaoh's officials" is lit. "was great in the eyes of Pharaoh's servants."
208. From v. 8 it is clear that Pharaoh is the addressee.

of the slave girl who is behind the millstones, and [including] all the firstborn of the livestock.

11:6 And there shall be a great outcry through all the land of Egypt, the like of which has never occurred and the like of which shall never be repeated.

11:7a But against any of the Israelites, whether man or beast, not [even] a dog will growl,[209]

11:7b that you may know

11:7c that YHWH makes a distinction between Egypt and Israel.'

11:8a And all of these officials of yours will come down to me

11:8b and they will bow before me, saying,

11:8c 'Go out, you and all the people who follow you,'[210]

11:8d and after that I will go out."

11:8e And he went out from Pharaoh in a furious anger.

11:9a (And YHWH had[211] said to Moses,

11:9b "Pharaoh will not listen to you, [my purpose being][212] that my wonders should be many in the land of Egypt."

11:10a Although Moses and Aaron had performed all these wonders before Pharaoh,

11:10b YHWH had made Pharaoh's heart implacable,

11:10c and he had not released the Israelites from his land.)

12:1 And YHWH said to Moses and Aaron in the land of Egypt,

12:2a "This month shall be the first of the months for you;

---

209. The meaning of יֶחֱרַץ־כֶּלֶב לְשֹׁנוֹ is somewhat obscure. Its literal meaning seems to be "to fix/cut (with the) tongue." Since the subject is a dog, one supposes that it means to bark or growl. Fensham 1966 argues that it means that the dogs will not eat the flesh or lick the blood of the Israelites. This is an interesting but not compelling possibility. The verb חרץ is elsewhere used of some kind of negative speech, whether a curse (Josh. 10:21), a sentence of death (1 Kings 20:40), or a decree of destruction (Isa. 10:23; 28:22; Dan. 9:26–27). Thus, it seems that this is the growling of a dog.

210. "Who follow you" is literally "who are at your feet."

211. Two factors suggest that the *wayyiqtol* here is not representing the normal mainline narrative sequence but is retrospective and should be translated as a pluperfect. First, the reference to "all these wonders" is more likely to be all the plagues that had already taken place, and not the one final plague. Second, the pattern of 11:10ab (ו + X + *qatal* pattern followed by *wayyiqtol*) suggests that 11:10a is the setting or background to 11:10b. This further suggests that 11:9–10 is parenthetical and not part of the mainline sequence.

212. Of itself, לְמַעַן could be taken to mean that it was Pharaoh's purpose to have many miracles in Egypt, but in context it is plainly YHWH's purpose.

12:2b it is to be the beginning of the months of the year to you.

12:3a Speak to all the congregation of Israel, saying,

12:3b 'On the tenth of this month they shall take for themselves, individually, a lamb for the paternal households—a lamb per household.

12:4a And if the household is too small for a lamb,

12:4b then he and his neighbor nearest to his house are to take one according to the number of persons;

12:4c you must allocate the lamb in proportion to what each one will eat.

12:5a Your lamb shall be a flawless male yearling;

12:5b you may take it from the sheep or from the goats.

12:6a And it shall be [held] for safekeeping until the fourteenth day of the same month,

12:6b then the whole assembly of the congregation of Israel is to slaughter it at twilight.

12:7a And they shall take some of the blood

12:7b and put it on the two doorposts and on the lintels[213] of the houses in which they eat it.

12:8a And they shall eat the meat that very night, roasted with fire,

12:8b and they shall eat it [with] unleavened bread over bitter herbs.

12:9a Do not eat any of it raw or boiled in water;

12:9b Rather, [it is to be] roasted with fire, [including] its head with its legs and its entrails.

12:10a And do not allow any of it to remain until morning,

12:10b but what remains of it until morning, you must burn with fire.

12:11a And this is how you shall eat it: your loins girded, your sandals on your feet, and your staff in your hand;

12:11b and you shall eat it in haste.

12:11c It is YHWH's Passover.

12:12a And I will go through the land of Egypt that very night,

12:12b and I will strike all the firstborn in the land of Egypt, both man and beast;

12:12c and against all the gods of Egypt I will execute judgments.[214]

12:12d I am YHWH.

---

213. It is not clear whether the מַשְׁקוֹף is the lintel (at the top of the door) or threshold (at the bottom).

214. The verb עשׂה with שְׁפָטִים means to "execute judgments," and the recipient of the judgments is generally marked with the preposition בְּ (Ezek. 5:10, 15; 11:9; 30:14), as is done here.

12:13a	And for you, the blood will serve as[215] a sign on the houses where[216] you are.
12:13b	And I will see the blood
12:13c	and I will pass over you,
12:13d	and there shall not be a plague of destruction upon you when I strike the land of Egypt.
12:14a	And this day will be for you a memorial,
12:14b	and you shall celebrate it as a festival to YHWH;
12:14c	throughout your generations you are to celebrate it as a perpetual ordinance.
12:15a	For seven days you shall eat unleavened bread.
12:15b	Indeed, on the first day you shall remove leaven from your houses.
12:15c	If [there is] anyone who eats leavened food [in the period] from the first day until the seventh day,[217]
12:15d	that person shall be cut off from Israel.
12:16a	And you shall have a holy convocation on the first day and a holy convocation on the seventh day.
12:16b	No kind of work shall be done on them, except what shall be eaten by each person;
12:16c	that alone may be done among you.
12:17a	And you shall keep the [Feast of] Unleavened Bread,
12:17b	for on this very day I brought your multitudes out of the land of Egypt.
12:17c	And you shall observe this day throughout your generations as a perpetual ordinance.
12:18	In the first [month], on the fourteenth day of the month, at evening, until the twenty-first day of the month, at evening, you shall eat unleavened bread.
12:19a	For seven days no leaven shall be found in your houses;
12:19b	for [if there is] anyone who eats what is leavened,
12:19c	then that person, whether [he is] one of the aliens or one of the

215. The idiom הָיָה followed by לְ often means "become," but here it indicates "serve as."

216. The relative pronoun אֲשֶׁר has הַבָּתִּים as its antecedent and with שָׁם means "there."

217. The phrase מִיּוֹם הָרִאשֹׁן עַד־יוֹם הַשְּׁבִעִי has to be transposed from 12:15d to 12:15c for clarity.

natives[218] of the land, shall be cut off from the congregation of Israel.

12:20a You shall eat nothing that is leavened [during this time];[219]
12:20b wherever you live[220] you shall eat unleavened bread.'"
12:21a And Moses called for all the elders of Israel
12:21b and he said to them,
12:21c "Pick out[221] and take for yourselves lambs for your families,
12:21d and slay the Passover lamb.
12:22a And you shall take a bunch of hyssop
12:22b and you shall dip it in the blood which is in the basin,
12:22c and you shall apply some of the blood that is in the basin to the lintel and the two doorposts.
12:22d But you must not go out, any one of you, from the door of your[222] house until morning.
12:23a And YHWH will pass through to slay the Egyptians;
12:23b and he will see the blood on the lintel and on the two doorposts,
12:23c and YHWH will pass over the door and will not permit the Destroyer[223] to enter your houses to slay.

---

218. The preposition בְּ in בַּגֵּר and וּבְאֶזְרַח has a partitive function. In both cases, the nouns represent a class or group.

219. In context, this rule applies only to the Week of Unleavened Bread. It is not a complete prohibition of the use of leaven.

220. Lit. "in all your habitations" (בְּכֹל מוֹשְׁבֹתֵיכֶם). But this does not mean, "in all your houses" but "in whatever place you happen to reside."

221. The verb מָשַׁךְ is almost always translated here as "go," but proposed examples of the verb (Qal stem) having that meaning are highly dubious (*HALOT* [2.646] suggests Judg. 4:6; 20:37; Job 21:33, but none of these examples is convincing). The verb literally means to "draw out," and in this case it means to separate or select one lamb from the flock. It is probably used here in hendiadys with לקח. For that reason, the two verbs are considered here to be constituents of a single clause.

222. Lit. "his," the pronoun here is third person by attraction to אִישׁ.

223. It is difficult to know what to make of the word הַמַּשְׁחִית. It could be the abstract noun "destruction," as in Ezek. 25:15, בְּנֶפֶשׁ לְמַשְׁחִית ("with an appetite for destruction"). Or it could be the Hiphil participle of שׁחת, "destroyer," as in 2 Sam. 24:16, וַיֹּאמֶר לַמַּלְאָךְ הַמַּשְׁחִית ("and [YHWH] said to the destroying angel"). The analogy of the latter text speaks in favor of it being understood concretely, as there seems to be an underlying theology of God using angels to bring judgment upon a people, as at Gen. 19:1–25 and Ezek. 9:1–2.

12:24 And you shall maintain this story and custom[224] as an ordinance for you and your children forever.
12:25a And it shall happen,
12:25b when you enter the land that YHWH will give you,
12:25c just as he promised,
12:25d you shall maintain this rite.
12:26a And it shall be,
12:26b when your children say to you,
12:26c 'What does this rite mean to you?'
12:27a then you shall say,
12:27b 'It is a Passover sacrifice to YHWH, who passed over the houses of the Israelites in Egypt when he slew the Egyptians,
12:27c and he spared our houses.'"
12:27d And the people bowed
12:27e and worshiped.
12:28a And the Israelites went [to their homes]
12:28b and they performed [the work of Passover];
12:28c just as YHWH had commanded Moses and Aaron,
12:28d so they did.
12:29a And it happened, in the middle of the night,
12:29b that YHWH struck all the firstborn in the land of Egypt, from the firstborn of the pharaoh who sits on his throne to the firstborn of the captive who is in the dungeon,[225] and all the firstborn of the livestock.
12:30a And Pharaoh rose in the night, he and all his officials and all the Egyptians,
12:30b and there was a great outcry in Egypt,
12:30c for there was no house where there was not someone dead.
12:31a And he called for Moses and for Aaron at night
12:31b and he said,
12:31c "Rise up!
12:31d Get out from among my people, both you and the Israelites!
12:31e And go!
12:31f Worship YHWH as you said!

---

224. The word דָּבָר is particularly difficult to translate here. On the one hand it is the "account" or "story" of the Passover night that the Israelites are to preserve. On the other hand, it is the rules for the Passover celebration that they are to observe.

225. Hebrew uses various terms for "prison," including בֵּית מִשְׁמַר ("house of guarding"; Gen. 42:19) and בֵּית הָאֲסוּרִים ("house of [men] in bondage"; Judg. 16:21 Qere). Here, however, בֵּית הַבּוֹר ("house of the cistern") suggests keeping prisoners in a dank, underground chamber.

12:32a Take both your flocks and your herds,
12:32b just as you have said,
12:32c and go!
12:32d And bless me also."
12:33a And the Egyptians encouraged the people to hurry, to get them out of the country,[226]
12:33b for they said,
12:33c "All of us will be dead."
12:34a So the people carried off their dough before it was leavened.
12:34b Their kneading troughs were on their shoulders wrapped in their clothes.
12:35a And the Israelites did what Moses had instructed:[227]
12:35b they requested[228] from the Egyptians articles of silver and articles of gold, and clothing;
12:36a and YHWH caused the Egyptians to be favorably inclined toward the people;
12:36b they yielded to their request.
12:36c And they plundered the Egyptians.
12:37 And the Israelites journeyed from Raamses to Succoth, about six hundred thousand[229] foot-soldiers (the warriors, not counting the noncombatants[230]).
12:38 And also a mixed multitude went up with them, in addition to flocks and herds—a huge quantity of livestock.
12:39a And they baked the dough that they brought out of Egypt into loaves of unleavened bread.
12:39b For it was not leavened,
12:39c since they were driven out of Egypt
12:39d and they could not wait,
12:39e and they had not made for themselves any travelling provisions [in advance].
12:40 And the time that the Israelites lived in Egypt was four hundred and thirty years.
12:41a And it came about, at the end of four hundred and thirty years—

226. The infinitive לְמַהֵר ("to hurry") is a complement to וַתֶּחֱזַק ("and [they] encouraged"), but the infinitive לְשַׁלְּחָם ("to get them out") indicates purpose.
227. Lit. "according to the word of Moses."
228. Epexegetical *wayyiqtol*.
229. Or, if אֶלֶף is taken to be "squad," it could be "600 squads of infantry."
230. The meaning of טַף is debatable; it could mean "infants" or it could refer to anyone, young or old, who lacks the ability to walk well. See the note at 10:10d.

12:41b it came about on this very day [of Passover[231]]—
12:41c all the multitudes of YHWH came out from the land of Egypt.
12:42a It is a night of vigilance[232] for YHWH, for having brought them out from the land of Egypt;
12:42b this night is for YHWH, a vigilance maintained by all the Israelites throughout their generations.
12:43a And YHWH said to Moses and Aaron,
12:43b "This is the rule of Passover: no foreigner may eat of it;
12:44a but in the case of any man's slave, [if he is] purchased with money,
12:44b and you circumcise him,
12:44c then he may eat of it.
12:45 A sojourner or a hired [foreign] worker shall not eat of it.
12:46a It must be eaten in a single house;
12:46b you are not to bring any of the meat outside of the house,
12:46c and you must not break a bone of it.
12:47 The whole congregation of Israel is to observe this.
12:48a And if a stranger sojourns with you,
12:48b and he would observe the Passover of YHWH,
12:48c then every male belonging to him is to be circumcised,
12:48d and then let him come near to observe it;
12:48e and he shall be regarded as a native of the land.
12:48f But no uncircumcised person may eat of it.
12:49 There shall be one law for the native and for the stranger who sojourns among you."
12:50a And all the Israelites did [it];
12:50b just as YHWH commanded Moses and Aaron,
12:50c so they did.
12:51a And it happened that on that very day [of Passover]:
12:51b YHWH brought the Israelites out of the land of Egypt with their multitudes.
13:1 And YHWH spoke to Moses, saying,
13:2a "Sanctify for me every firstborn, the first offspring of every womb among the Israelites, both of man and beast;

231. The phrase וַיְהִי בְּעֶצֶם הַיּוֹם הַזֶּה does not mean that it was 430 years to the day after their entrance into Egypt that they departed it. It means that their departure was on "this very day," i.e., Passover. See the analogous usage in Exod. 12:17.

232. The word שִׁמֻּרִים occurs only here in the Old Testament. It is rooted in the meaning "keep" or "guard" (שׁמר), and indicates that Passover is an event to be remembered and observed. It also implies vigilance, alluding to the fact that families are up late that night observing the ceremony.

13:2b it belongs to me.”

13:3a And Moses said to the people,

13:3b “Remember this day, when you came out from Egypt, from the house of slavery;

13:3c for by a powerful hand YHWH brought you out from this place.

13:3d And nothing leavened is to be eaten.

13:4 On this day in the month of Abib, you are departing [Egypt].

13:5a And it shall be,

13:5b when YHWH brings you to the land of the Canaanite, the Hittite, the Amorite, the Hivite and the Jebusite, which he swore to your fathers to give you, a land flowing with milk and honey,

13:5c that you shall conduct this rite in this month.

13:6a For seven days you shall eat unleavened bread,

13:6b and on the seventh day there shall be a festival to YHWH.

13:7a Unleavened bread shall be eaten throughout the seven days;

13:7b and no leavened [food] shall be seen among you,

13:7c and no leaven shall be seen among you in all your territory.

13:8a And on that day you shall tell your son the following:

13:8b ‘This is on account of what YHWH did for me when I came out of Egypt.’

13:9a And it shall become for you a sign on your hand and a reminder between your eyes,

13:9b so that the law of YHWH may be in your mouth.

13:9c For with a strong hand YHWH brought you out of Egypt.

13:10 And you shall keep this rule at its appointed time from year to year.[233]

13:11a And it shall be,

13:11b when YHWH brings you to the land of the Canaanite,

13:11c just as he swore to you and to your fathers,

13:11d and he gives it to you,

13:12a you shall sacrifice[234] to YHWH the first offspring of every womb,

13:12b and the first offspring of every beast[235] that you own—the males—will belong to YHWH.

---

233. “From year to year” is literally “from days to days” (מִיָּמִים יָמִימָה).

234. Although the Hiphil of עבר could mean to “transfer” ownership, it here appears to mean to sacrifice, analogous to its usage for making child sacrifice (Lev. 18:21; Jer. 32:35).

235. Sarna, *Exodus*, 67, points out that שֶׁגֶר elsewhere in the Torah always appears in the phrase שְׁגַר־אֲלָפֶיךָ (“offspring of your cattle”) and in parallel with וְעַשְׁתְּרֹת צֹאנֶךָ (“and the young of your sheep”); see Deut. 7:13; 28:4, 18, 51. Ashterot is the Canaanite fertility goddess, and a deity named *shgr* also

13:13a But every first offspring of a donkey you must redeem with a lamb,
13:13b but if you do not redeem [it],
13:13c you must break its neck.
13:13d But every human firstborn—from your sons—you must redeem.
13:14a And it shall be,
13:14b when your son in the future asks you,
13:14c 'What is this?'
13:14d then you shall say to him,
13:14e 'With a strong hand YHWH brought us out of Egypt, from the house of slavery.
13:15a And it came about,
13:15b since Pharaoh was determined not to release us,[236]
13:15c that YHWH killed every firstborn in the country of Egypt, both the firstborn of man and the firstborn of beast.
13:15d That is why I sacrifice to YHWH every first offspring of every womb—the males—
13:15e but every firstborn of my sons I redeem.'
13:16a And it shall become a sign on your hand and as phylacteries between your eyes;
13:16b for with a strong hand YHWH brought us out of Egypt."

Structure

The above text is lengthy and complex, but it is a variation on the standard pattern for the plagues. The contrasts with the accounts of the earlier plagues, however, are instructive.

I. YHWH Commissions Moses and Aaron to Appear Before the Israelites (11:1–2)
   A. Background Information (11:1)
   B. A Command that Israel Demand Payment (11:2)
II. Other Information: Egyptians Prepared to Give Silver to Israelites (11:3)
III. Moses and Aaron Carry a Message to Pharaoh (11:4–8)
IV. Pharaoh's Stubbornness (11:9–10)

---

appears in Punic inscriptions and in the Deir ʿAlla "Balaam" inscription in parallel with Ishtar. It therefore appears that both the Hebrew terms שׁגר and עשׁתרת have their origin in the names of fertility goddesses, but that in Hebrew vocabulary the terms have come to represent the outcome of fertility, lambs and calves.

236. Lit. "since Pharaoh was harsh about releasing us."

V. YHWH Commissions Moses with the Institution of Passover (12:1–20)
VI. Moses Carries the Passover Message to Israel (12:21–27)
VII. Israel's Obedience (12:28)
VIII. YHWH Begins the Plague (12:29–30)
IX. Pharaoh Interviews Moses in the Course of the Plague (12:31–33)
X. Other Information: Israel's Departure and Related Legislation (12:34–13:16)
   A. Unleavened Bread (12:34)
   B. Plundering Egypt (12:35–36)
   C. The Number of People (12:37–38)
   D. Unleavened Bread (12:39)
   E. The Number of Years (12:40–41)
   F. Legislation Related to Passover (12:42–49)
   G. Israel's Obedience (12:50–51)
   H. More Legislation Related to Passover (13:1–16)
      1. Sanctify Firstborn (13:1–2)
      2. Feast of Unleavened Bread (13:3–7)
      3. Didactic Function of Feast of Unleavened Bread (13:8–10)
      4. Rules for Sanctifying Firstborn (13:11–13)
      5. Didactic Function of Sanctifying Firstborn (13:14–16)

In analyzing the form of the passage, one should make note of the following variations and transformations.

1. The text begins with a commission to carry a message to Israel, not to Pharaoh. Moses does go to Pharaoh as well (11:4–8), but if there was a divine command for him to do so, it is left unstated. The people of Israel, not the pharaoh, have become the primary focus of the story and the recipients of a message from YHWH.

2. The response of the Egyptian people, and not the counsel of the officials, is described. The Egyptians have a higher regard for Moses and a deeper fear of YHWH than do their leaders.

3. The prediction to Pharaoh (11:4–8) contains no explicit demand to release the Israelites and no offer of a way to escape the predicted disaster. The plague is simply coming; Pharaoh's attitude is more or less incidental.

4. Pharaoh is stubborn and refuses to listen (11:9–10), but in this narrative his attitude is set in contrast to the obedience of Israel (12:27–28).

5. YHWH initiates the plague without any involvement from Moses and Aaron. There is no ritual act involving the rod, for example.

6. The ritual that YHWH commands is not a ritual that Moses is to carry out to initiate the plague (such as raising his staff); it is a ritual for Israel to enact, and it has two aspects (12:1–27).

a. The one aspect is the Passover ritual for the night of the exodus. Unlike the rituals carried out by Moses, this does not initiate the plague. Rather, it is a means of escaping the plague.

b. The other aspect is a retrospective Passover that is to be observed in subsequent years to commemorate the plague and the salvation of Israel.

7. Israel can avoid the plague that afflicts the Egyptians, as it had done previously, but this time they must carry out the Passover ritual to do so. Otherwise, Israelite homes would also be struck by the plague.

8. Pharaoh unconditionally releases Israel without seeking any concessions.

9. The narrative of the plague and of Israel's departure is accompanied by legislation meant to commemorate the event: Passover and the Feast of Unleavened Bread, as well as the consecration of the firstborn males. No other plague has a festival or legislation associated with it.

Commentary

11:1–2. The formal pattern of the miracle pattern is maintained, but instead of Moses being commissioned to go speak to Pharaoh, he is commissioned to go speak to the people. This is an appropriate response to Pharaoh's demand that Moses never come near him again (10:28). The promise that Pharaoh would "completely expel" Israel means that Pharaoh won't make any effort to see that they come back after a three-day journey in the wilderness. He will, at least at the moment of his sending them away, want them out of his kingdom forever (he will, of course, have a change of heart afterward).

11:3. The primary point of this verse is that the Egyptians were so disposed toward the Israelites that they were willing to yield to the request for gold and silver instead of doing what people would normally do if asked to hand over their wealth: slam their doors in the Israelites' faces. The brief summary of the Egyptian attitude here is not meant to be read as a survey of all the attitudes of all the Egyptians toward Israel. No doubt there were Egyptians who bitterly hated Moses and the Israelites and who blamed them for all their troubles. But many others no doubt felt that the Hebrews had been treated unjustly and felt a national guilt over the whole affair—a guilt made all the more real by the plagues that had been released upon them. And certainly many considered Moses an impressive figure and believed that the plagues had vindicated him as a prophet. If a political poll had been taken at the time, Pharaoh's popularity probably would have been very low. Finally, there were doubtless not a few Egyptians who, even if they hated the Hebrews, were also terrified of them, believing that if they remained in Egypt much longer the whole land would be utterly ruined (12:33). One can imagine these Egyptians rushing out to give the Hebrews their jewelry and telling them to just take it and go!

11:4–8. The narrative shifts abruptly, without any real transition, to a speech Moses gave to Pharaoh in anticipation of the plague on the firstborn. Two facts about this speech are noteworthy. First, the text never says that YHWH sent Moses to give this message to Pharaoh. It does say that YHWH gave Moses an oracle to the effect that the plague would come and that afterward the Egyptians would beg the Hebrews to leave, but it never says that YHWH told Moses to convey it to Pharaoh. The text only tells us that YHWH commanded Moses to address the Israelites. This suggests that Moses went to Pharaoh on his own accord. But whether he went to Pharaoh on his own or by divine command, he did it at risk to his own life, since Pharaoh had warned him that if he approached the royal court again, he would be put to death. The second notable fact is that Moses was deeply angered at the time he gave the speech and evidently stormed out of the court in something of a rage. The only reasonable object of his anger is Pharaoh, and the best explanation for Moses's anger is that he considered the deaths of so many Egyptian men and boys to be a needless tragedy. He took no pleasure in seeing so many Egyptians struck down or in hearing the wailing of their families. Far from it; his anger is explicable in that he believed that all of this could have been avoided had Pharaoh not been so arrogant.

11:9–10. As indicated in the translation above, these two verses are a retrospective and parenthetic review of the purpose for the plagues from God's perspective. It sets up a surprising but important contrast with Moses's angry speech to Pharaoh in the previous verses. Here, YHWH declares that it was his purpose and intention that Pharaoh not yield to Moses's plea to release the Hebrews in order that YHWH might perform many miraculous works—that is, so that he could strike Egypt with many plagues. This text reaffirms that YHWH himself made Pharaoh implacable. These two passages, 11:4–8 and 11:9–10, should be understood to be complementary and equally valid.

It is true that Pharaoh was culpable for his cruel stubbornness and that Moses was right to be angry at him for the needless Egyptian deaths that followed. It is also correct to say that all of this was within the plan of God and was the outcome of God's direct action in guiding Pharaoh's heart.

12:1–20. To signify its importance, the month of Passover is designated the first month of the calendar year for Israel (12:2). Exodus 13:4 indicates that the month was Abib (also called Nisan), a lunar month that fell within the period of March and April. Today, the Jewish New Year (Rosh Hashanah) occurs in Autumn, on the first and second days of the seventh month, Tishri (September/October). This is perhaps because the Feast of Trumpets, signifying the end of the agricultural year, began on the first day of Tishri (Num. 29:1). The Israelite official calendar year was from Abib to Abib, but their agricultural year was from Tishri to Tishri. By analogy, we have a calendar year that begins on January 1 and an academic year that begins around the end of August. As the agricultural cycle was what actually governed daily life, Tishri 1 ultimately became the Jewish New Year.

The preparations for Passover were to begin on the tenth of the month, four days before Passover on the fourteenth. This gave people time both to select an animal for sacrifice and to determine with whom their family would eat the Passover, in the event that a household was too small to afford or to consume an entire lamb themselves (12:4). The sacrifice had to be an unblemished one-year-old male lamb from the sheep or the goats (12:5). Unlike other sacrifices, no substitution (using doves or calves) was allowed.

Passover was originally a home-based rather than a temple-based ceremony. Israel had no temple at the first Passover, but the instructions made no allowance for a temple: families were to gather in their homes and every family was to make its sacrifice at the same time (12:6). It would never be possible for every family to sacrifice its lamb simultaneously on the one altar at one temple. However, Deut. 16:2 states that Passover was to be sacrificed "in the place where YHWH chooses to have his name dwell" (this is generally taken to be the central sanctuary), and v. 5 indicates that the Passover is not to be sacrificed in any of the other towns of Israel. This could be taken as a radical revision of the earlier observance regulations for Passover; critical scholars routinely argue that it reflects Josiah's centralization of cultic practices. On the other hand, Gordon McConville interprets the text in Deut. 16 to mean that the whole land and its people are to be holy before YHWH. He argues that Deuteronomy is fundamentally opposed to the centralization of authority.[237] So understood, the whole land is "the place where YHWH chooses to have his name dwell." It is possible that there was to be an official, national celebration of Passover at the temple in addition to (not instead of) the local celebrations. 2 Chronicles 30:1–18 describes a national celebration of Passover conducted at the temple. For practical reasons, this probably took place later than the normal Passover time.

This may explain a problem in the New Testament, that Mark 14:12-16 says that the first Eucharist in the upper room was a Passover meal, in contrast to John 18:28, which asserts that Passover had not yet occurred (John says that the Pharisees had not yet eaten Passover on the morning of Jesus's crucifixion). Possibly the Last Supper was a home-based Passover seder, while the Pharisees were preparing for the national, temple-based service that took place on the next day.

Exodus 12:7-11 give us five specific commands regarding the Passover ceremony. First, people were to dab the blood of the lambs on the doorposts and lintels (or thresholds) of the front doors of their homes (v. 7). Second, they were to have their meal during the night and not in daytime (v. 8). Third, the whole lamb was to be roasted; it was not to be boiled or eaten raw (vv. 8-9). Fourth, there were to be no leftovers; if the people assembled within a home could not eat all of it, they had to burn up the remainder (v. 10). Fifth, they were to be dressed for travel while eating (v. 11). To this point in the text, no explanation relating to the tenth plague is given. These are permanent rules for observation of Passover and are not only for the night of the slaying of the firstborn.

Only in 12:12-13 is an explanation for the daubing of blood on the doorposts and lintels that relates to the plague: YHWH was about pass through the land of Egypt and strike every firstborn male, and the blood on the houses would mark those that would not be struck with the plague. YHWH would "pass over" (פסח) them. From this, the Passover celebration is called the "Pesach" in Judaism.

There may be an additional bit of symbolism in putting the blood of the lamb on the doorposts and lintels of their houses. Excavations at Amarna have revealed that during the New Kingdom aristocrats advertised their ownership of their houses by having their names painted in brightly colored hieroglyphs on the doorposts and lintels of

237. J. Gordon McConville, "Deuteronomy's Unification of Passover and Maṣṣôt: A Response to Bernard M. Levinson," *JBL* 119, no. 1 (2000): 47–58.

their homes.[238] Thus, the placing of the blood of the Passover lamb on the same locations on the houses of the Hebrews may have signified YHWH's ownership of those homes.

The statement that YHWH was about to judge the gods of Egypt (12:12) does not justify assigning an Egyptian god to be the object of each of the plagues, as is often done (see Excursus: The Plagues as a Battle with the Gods of Egypt). The statement in v. 12 relates only to the plague upon the firstborn, not to the entire sequence of plagues, and it is tied to the ancient Near Eastern idea that the defeat of a nation was a defeat of its gods. The slaying of the firstborn is, in effect, a military victory, with the finest young men of the defeated nation left dead upon the battlefield. Any ancient people would have seen this as a defeat of the gods of Egypt.

The Israelites were also to eat the Passover dressed for travel and in haste (12:11). This is obviously because they would be leaving Egypt immediately after the plague upon the firstborn, and it also accounts for why they were to eat unleavened bread: the process of baking leavened bread is very time consuming.

From the very beginning, Passover and the Feast of Unleavened Bread (12:15-20) are linked. The Passover lamb was eaten with bitter herbs and unleavened bread on the evening at the end of the fourteenth day, and after that from the fifteenth to the twenty-first day the people not only refrained from eating leavened bread but also kept all leaven outside of their homes. According to 12:16, subsequent celebrations of the Feast of Unleavened Bread were to include sacred assemblies on the first and seventh days of the feast (that is, on the fifteenth and twenty-first days of the month). These rules are plainly designed for subsequent celebrations of the festival; the Hebrews on their way out of Egypt could hardly have paused for a sacred assembly.

12:21–27. The instructions here presuppose the instructions given in 12:1–20, as indicated by the fact that the elders are told to have the people select the Passover lambs (v. 21) but none of the details concerning what lambs may be selected are laid out. Furthermore, 12:21–23 specifically addresses the generation of the first Passover as they prepared for the night of the slaying of the firstborn. According to the instructions, the blood of the lamb was to be applied to the doorframe using hyssop (marjoram). This plant is associated with priestly rituals of cleansing (see Lev. 14:2-6, 49-51; Num. 19:4-18). In Psalm

238. Barry Kemp, "The Amarna Project: What Kind of City was Amarna?" *Ancient Egypt* 8, no. 6 (2008): 34.

51:7, David, in his pleas for forgiveness, asks to be purified with hyssop. By contrast, 12:1–20 addresses all generations, laying out the essential rules for subsequent celebrations of Passover and Unleavened Bread. But vv. 24–27 also describes future celebrations of Passover, telling the Israelites how they are to explain this ritual to coming generations. The important point here is that the Passover celebration dominates the text; it, rather than the historical events of the slaying of the firstborn, is the primary focus. As is the case with all biblical rituals, the ceremony itself serves as a teaching aid, designed to prompt the curiosity of children, who will ask why they are going through this ritual. This would give the parents an annual opportunity to recite the narrative of how God delivered them from slavery in Egypt.

12:28. This verse states twice over that the Israelites performed the ceremony of Passover as they were instructed by Moses. This affirms to the reader that Israel will be safe from the coming plague, and it also establishes a precedent, telling the reader that every generation that celebrates Passover is reenacting what the first celebrants did. In observing Passover, they are in continuity with their ancestors.

12:29–30. The actual event of the deaths of the firstborn males is told succinctly and with minimal elaboration. Only two points are made: first, every family at every level of society was hit; second, people were aware of the plague having struck in the middle of the night, for they were awake and mourning during the night. The text tells us nothing of the nature of the plague (what the symptoms were before onset of death, how long it took for victims to die, or whether there was any visible or tangible evidence of the entry of the "Destroyer" into homes before the firstborn were struck down). From the fact that everyone knew when the plague struck (that is, they did not go to bed and wake up next morning to find that the firstborn were dead, but were up wailing over the deaths in the night), we can surmise that the passing of the firstborn was no quiet or peaceful affair. Possibly the entry of the "Destroyer" awakened and terrified entire households. It is more likely, I think, that the "Destroyer" was unseen and unheard, but that the firstborn males became violently ill, so that everyone else was awakened and was trying to help in any way possible until the firstborn males died. It was, at any rate, a horrible and convulsive night for Egypt.

12:31–33. Formally, this interview between Moses and Pharaoh is similar to the others; the difference is in content, in that Pharaoh makes no attempt to get concessions from Moses. Also, he does not promise to release them, he actually does so (although he still seems to be thinking of a short-term trip to the wilderness in order to conduct a religious festival). His plea that Moses "bless" him is rather pathetic, speaking as it does of Pharaoh's gross inconsistency, at one moment defiant of YHWH and at the next cowering before him. Finally, earlier interview accounts described only the negotiations of Pharaoh and Moses, with perhaps the advice of the Egyptian counselors for Pharaoh included as background information. In this text, the voices of the Egyptian people are heard (12:33). They were desperate to be rid of the Hebrews.

12:34. The historical background for the feast of Unleavened Bread, plainly enough, is that the departing Israelites did not have time to let the dough rise, so they put dough in their kneading bowls and carried it out with them unleavened. Along the way for the first days of the journey, they would bake the dough as it was, unleavened, not having any other travelling provisions (12:39). Thus, they would in later years celebrate a seven-day festival of Unleavened Bread.

12:35–36. The text says little about how the Israelites went about "plundering" the Egyptians. They could not have gone up and down the whole length of the country; they only had time to demand payment from people in their immediate vicinity at Raamses and perhaps along the way to Succoth. However, if the exodus took place in the Raameside period, when the capital was at Raamses, an enormous amount of Egyptian wealth would have been concentrated in their immediate vicinity. The important point, however, is not how much wealth they got but that "plundering" is something a victorious army does to a defeated army. With the death of the firstborn males, we have an image of Israel, under YHWH, triumphantly leaving the field of battle.

12:37–41. Interpreters have debated at length the issue of whether the departing nation had 600,000 men or whether the term means something like "600 squads," suggesting a smaller population.[239] But what is frequently overlooked is that the departing populace is called a "mixed multitude," meaning that it had a fair number of people who were not descendants of the twelve tribes of Israel. Some could have

239. See also Colin J. Humphreys, "The Number of People in the Exodus from Egypt: Decoding Mathematically the Very Large Numbers in Numbers I and XXVI," *VT* 48, no. 2 (1998): 196–213.

been of other Semitic races, and others could have been non-Egyptian expatriates living in Egypt. Some could have actually been Egyptian or of mixed parentage (Lev. 24:10). The Bible does not claim that all "Israelites" are direct descendants of Jacob. From the very beginning, in fact, Abraham had circumcised foreigners in his entourage (Gen. 17:27). The number of years that Israel was in Egypt is given as 430 (12:41). As described in the translation note to 12:41b, this verse does not mean that they left Egypt 430 years to the day after they entered it; it means that they left 430 years after entering Egypt and on the very day of Passover. On the other hand, we should not assume that we fully understand how the Bible uses numbers. Paul, in Gal. 3:16–17, states that it was 430 years from the time of Abraham to the time of the giving of the law at Sinai. This obviously requires an Egyptian sojourn of far less than 430 years (see "A Caveat on Early Biblical Chronology" in the Introduction).

12:42–49. The legislation contained here is plainly oriented toward future celebrations of Passover in the land of Israel and not toward the initial Passover meal in Egypt. Passover is to be kept through all generations (v. 42), and foreign, temporary laborers living among the Israelites could not eat of it (v. 45). But slaves bought from foreigners could partake of it, so long as they were circumcised (v. 44). Resident aliens who wanted to partake of Passover had to be circumcised and so, in effect, become proselytes (v. 48). These rules describe circumstances relevant to Israel in their own land; they do not reflect the lives of the Israelites when they themselves were resident aliens and slaves in Egypt. It is noteworthy that the most important qualification for partaking of Passover was circumcision (obviously this applied only to males; women were either qualified or disqualified on the basis of the status of the males to whom they were attached). But neither racial purity (being a bona fide descendant of Israel) nor length of residence in the land qualified one to partake of Passover; one had to be circumcised (v. 48–9). Circumcision is here understood to be the outward sign of an inward commitment to YHWH and Israel. The importance of circumcision for the Passover ritual is anticipated in Exod. 4:24–26, the episode in which Zipporah saved her son from the wrath of YHWH by circumcising him (see commentary above).

12:50. The simple assertion that Israel observed all the Passover rules that Moses proclaimed again has two purposes. It makes the point that the firstborn of Israel were spared because they observed Passover, and it also reaffirms that Israel's ongoing observance of Passover is in imitation of the first Passover. One should also note that this text belies the sometimes-heard assertion that God always gave Israel laws and rules in response to their acts of disobedience. Here, the assertion that Israel obeyed God comes in the midst of a lengthy text of legislation (12:42–49 and 13:1–16).

13:1–2. Neither the means of "sanctifying" the firstborn nor the significance of the act is immediately apparent. It is, however, a more ominous act than is readily apparent to the modern reader. It could imply not that the firstborn is specially favored but that the firstborn is to be put to death, as in the act of consecrating persons and property to God in the חֵרֶם, the "ban." In the context of the ban, consecrated persons and things are destroyed (Lev. 27:28–29). The provisions of vv. 11–13 make clear, however, that no firstborn human is ever to be sacrificed, and that even the firstborn of non-sacrificial animals can be redeemed so that they need not be killed. It is perhaps significant that this legislation concerns events surrounding Passover, in the spring of the year, when livestock generally bear their young.[240] The most important connection, however, is not to the season but to the events of the first Passover in Egypt. Israel's firstborn, both man and beast, all belong to God because he slew the firstborn of Egypt, both man and beast, in order to redeem Israel.

13:3–7. The month Abib, corresponding to late March and early April, derives its name from אָבִיב, a young, ripened ear of grain. This is because the grain harvest began this month. In later Judaism, the month would be called Nisan (Esth. 3:7), after the Babylonian name for the month. This text repeats many but not all of the stipulations of 12:14–20. It is somewhat surprising that the text gives such prominence to the Feast of Unleavened Bread, and it is not clear why this is so. Perhaps the concern is that the Passover meal, with its sacrificial lamb and precise ritual, was so dramatic and prominent that people might treat the seven days of Unleavened Bread as relatively unimportant and so neglect it.

13:8–10. The rituals of Unleavened Bread and Passover have a pedagogical and symbolic function, reminding the people that they were redeemed from slavery by YHWH and providing a device for passing the tradition on to subsequent generations. The expression "a sign on your hand and a reminder between your eyes" (v. 9) is probably just a metaphor describing a mnemonic device. The festivals are analogous

240.Stuart, *Exodus*, 311.

to putting a mark on your hand or having a reminder right in front of your face, telling you to keep the laws of God. It would not seem that literal phylacteries are in view here, since the Feast of Unleavened Bread is itself the sign and reminder.

13:11–13. The firstborn of every clean animal was to be redeemed by sacrificing it to YHWH at the sanctuary. According to Num. 18:14–19, these animals belonged to the priests and their families. On the other hand, Deut. 15:19–23 indicates that the lay people could partake of the food provided by sacrificing the firstborn of the herd and flock. The donkey is the one unclean animal that an Israelite peasant was likely to own (very few would have horses or camels). To deliberately kill a healthy donkey foal would be extraordinary; the animal represented great value. Probably the cases in which people would actually do this would be quite rare; the legislation makes the point that the donkey must be redeemed, not that breaking its neck is the preferred action to take. In giving a lamb to redeem the animal, the farmer was providing for the upkeep of the priests and the sanctuary, and thus it was a donation to YHWH and not an outright loss. Also, on the basis of Deut. 15, it appears that when a donkey was redeemed by the sacrifice of a lamb, the family that donated the lamb could share in the sacrificial meal.

13:14–16. There is absolutely no suggestion that firstborn sons, although they belong to God, were ever to be sacrificed or put to death. They had to be redeemed, but the means for redeeming them is not stipulated here. Numbers 18:16 sets the redemption price for priestly families at five sanctuary shekels. This price could refer to the price for redeeming an unclean animal, or a son, or either one. At Lev. 27:6, we read that a boy between one month and five years of age who is dedicated by his parents to YHWH was to be redeemed for five shekels, and thus it seems that the five shekel price of Num. 18:16 also applied to the redemption of sons from non-priestly families. The amount was probably paid into the sanctuary treasury.

Theological Summary of Key Points

This is a lengthy text, and it covers both a dramatic event in the narrative, the death of the Egyptian firstborn, and one of the central rituals of Israelite religious life, the Feast of Passover and Unleavened Bread. As such, it contains theological lessons in four broad areas.

1. Hardness of heart and the path to destruction. The death of the Egyptian firstborn, in the context of the whole narrative of the plagues, demonstrates that resistance to God and stubbornly clinging to a selfish, evil path leads to ruin. This is, of course, Pharaoh's story, but it is also the story of many others who have allowed pride and stubbornness to trump doing what is right. More than that, it also illustrates the point that when we choose an evil path, God can give us over to our own evil, so that we carry it out to the bitter end (see Excursus: The Hardness of Pharaoh's Heart, below).

2. Salvation from the wrath of God. The blood of the Passover lamb served as a shield for Israel, protecting them from the "Destroyer" that made its way through Egypt. With good reason, Christians see here a picture of Christ, the Passover lamb who brought about our redemption (1 Cor. 5:7). One cannot escape the wrath of God without taking shelter behind the blood. In addition, one cannot find salvation apart from the means of salvation that God has offered. This was true for the Passover lamb at the plague of the firstborn, and it is true of the name of Christ today (Acts 4:12).

3. The strength of compassion in the face of folly and evil. In no place does the humanity and goodness of Moses shine more clearly than in the fierce anger with which he confronts Pharaoh in 11:4–8. The most reasonable explanation for Moses's anger is his disgust at the fact that so many Egyptians need to die because of the cruelty and stubbornness of Pharaoh. That is, Moses evidently takes no pleasure in being vindicated by the plague that brings ruin and death upon Egypt. From his perspective, none of this needed to happen, and his attitude shows great compassion for the people he could have regarded as his enemy, the Egyptians.

4. The importance of ritual law in Israel. It is striking to the modern reader that an enormous quantity of the narrative of the plague of the firstborn is taken up with description of the Passover celebration and of other laws relating to the redemption of the firstborn in Israel. To many of us, such ritual laws are entirely secondary, the account of the plague being the essential and climactic element in the narrative. In the text, however, the actual deaths of the Egyptian firstborn almost seem to serve as a backdrop for laying out Passover regulations; the primary thing is that Israel understand how and why it is to observe the Passover ritual and the special rules pertaining to the redemption of the firstborn men and domestic animals. For some of us—especially in the Reformed Protestant tradition—the theology of the word is so dominant that the simple recitation of the narrative is thought to be sufficient, with any ritualized commemoration being of much lesser importance and almost a distraction. In Israel's life, however, such ceremonial events were at the heart of their maintaining the memory of the event from generation to generation, of their coherence as a community, and of their worship of God. Furthermore, these laws are given in the context of a great work of redemption and of Israel's obedience to injunctions about how the first Passover was to be carried out. Contrary to some modern evangelical opinion, the laws are not given as a kind of punishment for Israel's disobedience.

Excursus: The Hardness of Pharaoh's Heart

Among the more vexing and heavily discussed theological problems of Exodus is the issue of the hardness of Pharaoh's heart. Specifically, readers wonder how Pharaoh can be blamed for his refusal to release Israel if in fact God himself hardened his heart. How can a person be censured for doing what God compels him to do?[241] More than that, it seems to make the whole narrative of Pharaoh's stubbornness in the face of increasingly severe plagues into something of a sham if in fact Pharaoh was only acting out under divine compulsion his preassigned role. It makes Moses's appeals to Pharaoh seem pointless and even cruel. If God had ordained that Pharaoh would not release Israel and even intervened at critical moments to harden his heart and avert any premature release of Israel, then rebuking Pharaoh for his actions might be considered comparable to rebuking a blind man for not seeing. In order to unravel this difficulty, we might begin by examining the pattern of the relevant passages within Exodus, as in Table 9.

In Table 9, the significance of most of the columns is self-explanatory. Most refer to the verb that is used, to its stem and its function, and to the subject of that verb and its object. The column "possessor" refers to whose heart is being described (almost always Pharaoh's). Because this chart follows the Hebrew text, the verse numbers refer to the Hebrew Bible (English verse equivalents, where different, are in parenthesis). The "episode" column succinctly locates the event within the plague narrative.

241. Brian P. Irwin, "Yahweh's Suspension of Free Will in the Old Testament: Divine Immortality or Sign-Act?" *TynBul* 54, no. 2 (2003): 56–9, attempts to resolve the problem by asserting that YHWH is demonstrating his own divinity and Pharaoh's mortality by taking away Pharaoh's free will. To me, this solution is neither persuasive nor helpful. The text never makes an issue of the fact that Pharaoh is human (and not a god).

TABLE 9. THE HARD HEART IN EXODUS							
Text	**Verb**	**Stem**	**Function**	**Subject**	**Object**	**Possessor**	**Episode**
4:21	חזק	Piel	Factitive	YHWH	heart	Pharaoh	Predictive
7:3	קשה	Hiphil	Factitive	YHWH	heart	Pharaoh	Predictive
7:13	חזק	Qal	Stative	heart	n/a	Pharaoh	After snakes
7:14	כבד	Qal	Stative	heart	n/a	Pharaoh	Prior to Nile
7:22	חזק	Qal	Stative	heart	n/a	Pharaoh	After Nile
7:23	שׁית	Qal	Negated	Pharaoh	heart	Pharaoh	After Nile
8:11 (15)	כבד	Hiphil	Factitive	Pharaoh	heart	Pharaoh	Frogs; after relief
8:15 (19)	חזק	Qal	Stative	heart	n/a	Pharaoh	After mosquitoes
8:28 (32)	כבד	Hiphil	Factitive	Pharaoh	heart	Pharaoh	Flies; after relief
9:7	כבד	Qal	Stative	heart	n/a	Pharaoh	After livestock
9:12	חזק	Piel	Factitive	YHWH	heart	Pharaoh	After skin disease
9:21	שׂים	Qal	Negated	officials	heart	officials	Prior to hail
9:34	כבד	Hiphil	Factitive	Pharaoh w/ officials	heart	Pharaoh w/ officials	Hail; after relief
9:35	חזק	Qal	Stative	heart	n/a	Pharaoh	Hail; after relief
10:1	כבד	Hiphil	Factitive	YHWH	heart	Pharaoh w/ officials	Summary
10:20	חזק	Piel	Factitive	YHWH	heart	Pharaoh	Locusts; after relief
10:27	חזק	Piel	Factitive	YHWH	heart	Pharaoh	Before firstborn
11:10	חזק	Piel	Factitive	YHWH	heart	Pharaoh	Before firstborn
14:4	חזק	Piel	Factitive	YHWH	heart	Pharaoh	Before *Yam Suph*
14:5	הפך	Niphal	Middle	heart	n/a	Pharaoh	Before *Yam Suph*
14:8	חזק	Piel	Factitive	YHWH	heart	Pharaoh	Before *Yam Suph*
14:17	חזק	Piel	Factitive	YHWH	heart	Pharaoh	Before *Yam Suph*

The Qal stem of חזק means to be "strong" and, used of the heart, means that it is "unyielding." In the Piel, it has the factitive meaning, to "make (the heart) unyielding." The verb קָשָׁה, in the Hiphil, is also factitive and means to "make (the heart) hard" in the sense of "stubborn." Interestingly, although English translations regularly render many or all of these Exodus texts with either "hard" or "harden," this verb, that has this specific meaning, occurs only a single time. The verb כבד has the stative meaning "be heavy" (Qal) and the factitive meaning "make heavy" (Hiphil). Used of the heart, it means to be "insensitive, unmovable, or dense" (it does not mean "sad," as in the English idiom of a "heavy heart"). In this commentary, I have rendered it as "leaden," as I think this captures the idea of heaviness while implying "unmovable" and "insensitive." The verbs שִׁית and שִׂים both mean to "place" or "set." Used with "heart" (as in, "He set his heart upon [something]"), both mean to "pay attention" or "have regard" for something. In both occurrences in Exodus (7:23 and 9:21), the verbs are negated and mean the Pharaoh and his officials paid no attention to warnings from God. The Niphal of הפך means to "be changed" and, with "heart" as the subject, it means that someone had a change of mind about something. In Exod. 14:5, it means that Pharaoh changed his mind about his prior decision to release the Israelites.

Looking at Table 9, a clear progression appears. First, there are two predictions that YHWH will make Pharaoh's heart stubborn (4:21 and 7:3). Second, in the early plagues, in every case through 9:35 (an exception is at 9:12), Pharaoh either makes his heart stubborn or his heart is simply described as being stubborn. Sometimes Pharaoh makes his heart stubborn in response to a relief from a plague, and sometimes he is unyielding either before or in the process of a plague. Third, in the latter plagues, YHWH makes Pharaoh's heart unyielding (always using the Piel of חזק). Even the one exception, the Niphal of הפך at 14:5, could be read as a "divine passive" and thus as implying that God had brought about a change of mind in Pharaoh. Regardless, it is clear that in the latter, more severe plagues, YHWH is represented as strengthening Pharaoh's resolve, making him hold on in the face of catastrophe so that he continues his fight against God to the bitter end. As we seek to make sense of these three sets of texts, we must also recognize that the interpreter can look at the issue of Pharaoh's stubborn heart from two different perspectives.

The first is from the perspective of salvation history. Here, the lesson is that God acted in such a way that no one could ever say that Israel escaped slavery either because Pharaoh was generous or because Israel had been valiant. God made Pharaoh's heart stubborn precisely for the purpose of having him hold out until the end, so that God could demonstrate his power to overcome Egypt and save Israel. Viewed in this manner, the text asserts that God alone should receive credit for bringing Israel out of Egypt. Neither kindness nor weakness on Pharaoh's part enabled the Israelites to leave Egypt, and the Israelites themselves did not break out by brave or cunning actions.

The second perspective on Pharaoh's heart is in what it says about God's dealings with the individual person and about personal accountability. If God made Pharaoh's heart stubborn, what does this say about free will? What does it say about human responsibility and accountability? Although this is the theological issue that most modern readers focus upon, Exodus itself shows no real interest in such questions. In Exodus, the main point is that the miracles show YHWH to be a mighty redeemer; all credit for Israel's escape from Egypt belongs to God.[242]

If we accept that Exodus is primarily concerned to show that Israel's release from captivity was entirely a work of God, and that the hardness of Pharaoh's heart was part of this demonstration of YHWH's power, we can proceed on to the latter issue, personal accountability. The two predictive texts (4:21 and 7:3) and the one summary text (10:1) do not come into play here. They do not really imply that Pharaoh does not act of his own accord. Rather, they are broad and general statements that give the divine perspective on the whole history. God sees all things as ultimately determined by himself, but this does not mean that human decisions are not free and genuine. In other words, 4:21 and 7:3 could read as they do, speaking of YHWH hardening Pharaoh's heart, even if every text in the actual plague narrative spoke only of Pharaoh hardening his own heart. YHWH never sees an event as outside of his control or plan, even when the decisions of other persons obviously come into play. To come to terms with the issue of human accountability, we need to look at specific episodes in the narrative.

For this, the initial reception of Moses by Pharaoh in Exod. 5 is critically important. In that text, Moses makes a request that, to an Egyptian, should be received as entirely reasonable: their God, YHWH, has demanded that they come out into the wilderness for a religious celebration, an event that would require a three-day leave from their

242. Childs, *Exodus*, 174, argues that the hardness of heart also explains why Pharaoh did not respond as he should have to YHWH's signs. This is true, but it is subordinate to the explicit purpose described in the text, that YHWH intended to display his power through an extended series of miracles to demonstrate before Israel and the nations that he is God.

duties in Egypt. The Egyptian calendar included many religious holidays and festivals that involved cessation from work (the five intercalary days of the Egyptian calendar were religious holidays, and there were numerous other religious festivals that would release the people from their ordinary routine in order to honor a god). The threatened hostility of YHWH should Israel fail to comply was also something that the Egyptians, an exceedingly religious people, would take seriously. Pharaoh, however, responds with indignity, sarcasm, and cruelty. He denies knowing anything about YHWH, claims that the only reason the Israelites are making this request is so that they can shirk their duties, because they are lazy. He maliciously increases their work load beyond what they are able to bear. They now must gather straw for making bricks on top of all their other tasks. Pharaoh's tone, in speaking to Moses and to the other Israelites, is malicious and spiteful (5:2, 4, 17–18). This is not something that God caused by hardening Pharaoh's heart; this is a glimpse into the man's character and into his attitude toward YHWH and Israel. In short, apart from anything that God might do, Pharaoh is mean-spirited, obstinate, and implacably hateful toward Israel.

This initial portrait of Pharaoh is in keeping with what we see of his behavior in the early plagues. As noted above, from Exod. 7:13 to 9:35, in every occasion but one (9:12) either Pharaoh hardens his own heart or, using a stative verb, his heart is simply said to be implacable. In these occasions, Pharaoh is indifferent or resolute in the midst of a plague, or he renews his resolve when there is relief from a plague. This again suggests that, without any influence from God, Pharaoh is of his own accord determined to resist YHWH and hold on to the service of the Israelites.

In the latter, more severe plagues, however (10:20 to 14:17, with a possible exception at 14:5), Pharaoh is almost a shattered man, and in every case God is said to stiffen Pharaoh's resolve. The Piel of חזק implies that in some manner (that we cannot really understand) God renewed Pharaoh's implacability at a moment when Pharaoh was perhaps about to break under the pressure. From the standpoint of the history of the narrative, therefore, we see that on the one hand Pharaoh was of himself cruel and stubborn, but that on the other hand God somehow replenished Pharaoh's flagging spirits when Pharaoh was ready, somewhat prematurely from the standpoint of the divine purpose, to give up.

Interpreting the hardness of Pharaoh's heart, therefore, we should not deny God's power to bend and move the human heart, but neither should we imply that Pharaoh was coerced into doing something that he did not really want to do. God stiffened Pharaoh's resolve, but the will to oppress Israel and resist God was his own. Perhaps the best analogy is in Paul's description of pagan immorality in Rom. 1, where on the one hand the Gentiles resist God and give themselves over to sensuality, but that on the other hand God gives them over to their own debauchery, so that their desires turn toward homosexuality. It would be a mistake to say that God forced them to become homosexuals, but it would also be a mistake to say that the hand of God had nothing to do with turning and shaping their desires. As God gave those Gentiles over to the full expression of the licentious path they had chosen, so also God gave Pharaoh over to the full expression of hostility to the Hebrews and to YHWH.

TWELVE: THE SEA (13:17—14:31)

Israel drives as hard as possible to get away from Egypt. Pharaoh, informed of this, suddenly sets off with his armies after them. He regrets the loss of their labor and is bitter in his humiliation. YHWH leads Israel into an apparent trap with their back to the sea, but then opens the way for them to cross through the waters. Pharaoh's chariots pursue and are drowned.

Translation

13:17a And it came about that when Pharaoh released the people,
13:17b God did not lead them by the way of the land of the Philistines,
13:17c although it was near;
13:17d for God said,
13:17e "The people might[243] change their minds when they see warfare,
13:17f and return to Egypt."
13:18a And God had the people go in a roundabout[244] way: the way of the wilderness—[that is,] the *Yam Suph* [route];[245]

243. The word פֶּן is traditionally translated "lest," but that translation requires a protasis, which is missing here. פֶּן essentially refers to something that might happen but that the speaker would prefer not to happen. Usage found in Exod. 34:15 and Deut. 29:17(18) is similar to this text.

244. See סבב, *HALOT*, 2.738–40.

245. The phrase דֶּרֶךְ הַמִּדְבָּר identifies the roundabout route they took as "the way of the wilderness." יַם־סוּף is in apposition to this and further identifies the route as the road to the *Yam Suph*. It is "roundabout" since the direct route into Canaan would obviously have been by the Via Maris into southwestern Canaan.

13:18b and the Israelites went up in military formation[246] from the land of Egypt.
13:19a And Moses took the bones of Joseph with him,
13:19b for he had made the Israelites solemnly swear the following:
13:19c “God most certainly will visit you,
13:19d and you shall carry away my bones from here with you.”
13:20a And they set out from Succoth.
13:20b And they camped in Etham on the edge of the wilderness.
13:21 And YHWH was going[247] before them: by day in a pillar of cloud to lead them on the way, and by night in a pillar of fire to give them light so that they could travel[248] by day and by night.
13:22 He did not remove the pillar of cloud by day or the pillar of fire by night from before the people.
14:1 And YHWH spoke to Moses, as follows:
14:2a “Tell the Israelites
14:2b that they should turn back
14:2c and that they should camp in front of Pi-hahiroth, between Migdol and the sea;
14:2d you shall camp in front of Baal-zephon, just opposite it, by the sea.
14:3a And Pharaoh will say concerning the Israelites,
14:3b ‘They are lost[249] in the land;
14:3c the wilderness has shut them in.’
14:4a And I will make Pharaoh’s heart implacable,
14:4b and he will go down after them;
14:4c and I will gain glory through Pharaoh and through all his army,
14:4d and the Egyptians will know
14:4e that I am YHWH.”
14:4f And [the Israelites] did so.
14:5a And the king of Egypt was informed

246. The word חֲמֻשִׁים is sometimes translated “armed,” but there is nothing in the word that connotes weaponry. It is apparently from the root חמשׁ, “five,” and it has a Qal passive participle pattern, suggesting a meaning of “divided into five parts.” Usage elsewhere plainly indicates that it has a military meaning (Josh. 1:14; 4:12; Judg. 7:11). The “five parts” are perhaps the vanguard, rearguard, main body, and two flank guards of a marching army (חמשׁ [I], *HALOT*, 1.331). Thus, the term means they marched in good order, prepared for whatever trouble they might encounter.

247. The participial וַיהוָה הֹלֵךְ is durative and gives offline information.

248. The two infinitives לְהָאִיר and לָלֶכֶת both indicate purpose.

249. The root בוךְ (Niphal) appears three times in the Old Testament (here, Joel 1:18; Esth. 3:15). It implies wandering (Joel 1:18) and being bewildered (Esth. 3:15).

14:5b that the people had fled,
14:5c and the hearts of Pharaoh and his officials [abruptly] changed[250] with regard to the people,
14:5d and they said,
14:5e "What is this we have done,
14:5f that we have released Israel from serving us?"
14:6a And he harnessed his chariot
14:6b and he took his army[251] with him:
14:7 he took[252] six hundred elite chariots, and all the chariots of Egypt,[253] with officers over all of them.
14:8a And YHWH made the heart of Pharaoh, king of Egypt, implacable,
14:8b and he pursued the Israelites.
14:8c But the Israelites were moving out[254] in a carefree, celebratory mood.[255]
14:9a And the Egyptians pursued them
14:9b and they overtook them camping by the sea.[256]
14:9c All the horse-drawn chariots of Pharaoh, with his mounted troops and his infantry, [arrived] at Pi-hahiroth, in front of Baal-zephon.
14:10a But as Pharaoh got closer,[257]
14:10b the Israelites lifted their eyes,

---

250. The Niphal of הָפַךְ means to "be overturned," suggesting a fairly abrupt and complete change of attitude.
251. Lit. "his people."
252. This is an epexegetical *wayyiqtol*.
253. It is not clear whether וְכֹל רֶכֶב מִצְרָיִם is in apposition to the 600 elite chariots, being one and the same group, or is in addition to the 600. It probably means he took 600 chariots that constituted his personal bodyguard and an elite strike force in addition to whatever other chariot troops he had at his immediate disposal.
254. The pattern ו + subject + participle is background information. It implies that there was a process in which the Israelites were following the route of the exodus blissfully unaware that the Egyptians were in pursuit. It suggests that the pursuit went on for some time, consistent with the idea that they were following the Darb el-Hagg across the Sinai for several days while the Egyptian forces were slowly catching up.
255. Lit. "with a high hand." The implication is an attitude of defiance. See Num. 15:30.
256. Against the cantillation marks, this reading places the major break after עַל־הַיָּם instead of after וְחֵילוֹ.
257. Verse 10, beginning with a ו + subject + *qatal* clause, is background information, describing how it was that Israel discovered they were being pursued. By contrast, the mainline narrative of v. 9ab carries the reader forward to the end of the process, when the Egyptians arrived at the camp of Israel.

14:10c and [they saw that][258] the Egyptians were right there on the move behind them,
14:10d and they were very afraid.
14:10e And the Israelites cried out to YHWH.
14:11a And they said to Moses,
14:11b "Is it because there were absolutely no[259] graves in Egypt that you took us to die in the wilderness?
14:11c What is this you have done to us, bringing us out of Egypt?
14:12a Wasn't this precisely what we told[260] you in Egypt:
14:12b 'Leave us alone that we may serve the Egyptians'?
14:12c For it would have been better for us to serve the Egyptians than to die in the wilderness."
14:13a And Moses said to the people,
14:13b "Do not fear!
14:13c Stand still
14:13d and see YHWH's salvation, that he will bring about for you today!
14:13e For those whom you see today—the Egyptians—you will never, ever see them again.
14:14a YHWH will fight for you,
14:14b But you must keep quiet!"[261]
14:15a And YHWH said to Moses,
14:15b "There is no need for you to cry out to me.[262]
14:15c Tell the Israelites
14:15d that they should move out.
14:16a But you, lift up your staff
14:16b and stretch out your hand over the sea
14:16c and divide it,
14:16d so that the Israelites may go through the middle of the sea on dry ground.

---

258. The particle הִנֵּה vividly presents the situation from Israel's perspective.
259. The double negative הַמִבְּלִי אֵין creates an emphatic negative, here used rhetorically with the interrogative ה.
260. The cognate formation הַדָּבָר אֲשֶׁר דִּבַּרְנוּ is forceful, suggesting here that the speaker claims to have anticipated the outcome precisely and specifically.
261. In וְאַתֶּם תַּחֲרִישׁוּן, the pronoun is fronted for contrast with יהוה, and the *yiqtol* form is modal and, in effect, imperatival.
262. The clause מַה־תִּצְעַק אֵלָי is literally, "Why are you crying out to me?" But that translation is misleading, as it seems to indicate that YHWH is irritated with Moses or that he has no intention of heeding Moses (note that the verb is singular, referring to Moses and not to all Israel). But the rhetorical "why" here simply indicates that what Moses is doing is unnecessary, not that YHWH is rebuffing him.

14:17a But I[263]—get this[264]—I will make the hearts of the Egyptians so implacable
14:17b that they will go in after them;
14:17c and I will gain glory through Pharaoh and through all his army, through his chariots and his mounted troops.
14:18a And the Egyptians will know
14:18b that I am YHWH when I gain glory through Pharaoh, through his chariots and his mounted troops."
14:19a And the angel of God, who had been going before the camp of Israel, moved out
14:19b and he went behind them;
14:19c and the pillar of cloud moved out from before them
14:19d and it stood behind them.
14:20a And it went between the camp of Egypt and the camp of Israel;
14:20b and it was cloud and darkness [by day],
14:20c and it lit up the night.[265]
14:20d And the one side did not approach the other side during the night.
14:21a And Moses stretched out his hand over the sea;
14:21b and YHWH moved the sea with a strong east wind [that blew] all night
14:21c and it turned the sea into dry land,
14:21d and the waters were parted.
14:22a And the Israelites went through the middle of the sea on the dry ground,
14:22b and the waters were from their perspective a wall on their right hand and on their left.
14:23a And the Egyptians made pursuit,
14:23b and all Pharaoh's horses, his chariots and his mounted troops went in after them into the middle of the sea.
14:24a And it happened at the morning watch

263. YHWH assigns a task to each of three parties: the Israelites, Moses, and himself. This is signaled first by the construction דַּבֵּר אֶל־בְּנֵי־יִשְׂרָאֵל וְיִסָּעוּ ("tell the Israelites that they should move out") in 14:15cd and then by וְאַתָּה ("but you") in 14:16a and finally by וַאֲנִי ("but I") in 14:17a.

264. Apart from being archaic, we artificially invest הִנְּה with dignity and solemnity when we translate it as "behold."

265. The clauses of 14:20bc seem to contradict each other, but probably "by day" is implied for 14:20b.

14:24b that YHWH looked down[266] on the army of the Egyptians from the pillar of fire and cloud
14:24c and he brought the Egyptian army into confusion;
14:25a he caused their chariots wheels to swerve [out of formation].[267]
14:25b And they drove[268] with difficulty.
14:25c And Egypt[269] said,
14:25d "Let me escape from Israel!
14:25e For YHWH is fighting for them against Egypt!"
14:26a And YHWH said to Moses,
14:26b "Stretch out your hand over the sea
14:26c so that the waters may come back over Egypt—over its chariots and its mounted troops."
14:27a And Moses stretched out his hand over the sea,
14:27b and at daybreak the sea returned to its ordinary state,
14:27c but the Egyptians were fleeing[270] right into it;
14:27d and YHWH tossed about[271] the Egyptians in the middle of the sea.
14:28a And the waters returned

---

266. It may seem a little odd that the text would here speak of YHWH "looking down" (Hiphil of שׁקף) on the Egyptians, but probably the best parallel for this is at Gen. 18:16, where the angels "look down" upon Sodom and Gomorrah in preparation for judging the cities. An analogous text is Gen. 26:8, where Abimelech looks down on Isaac and Rebekah and discerns that they are married. Deuteronomy 26:15 calls on God to look down on his land to bless it. Thus, שׁקף can imply looking down on a situation and making a judgment prior to acting.
267. An army of charging chariots, especially when confined to a narrow space, would need to maintain good order and a tight formation to avoid calamitous confusion. The point of וַיָּסַר אֵת אֹפַן מַרְכְּבֹתָיו is that the chariots began to swerve into one another.
268. The verb וַיְנַהֲגֵהוּ may have as its subject YHWH, in which case it would mean that he caused the chariots to move "with heaviness" (i.e., poorly). But probably the subject is the 3ms suffix on מַרְכְּבֹתָיו (referring to the charioteers). Thus, they drove poorly.
269. While מִצְרַיִם could be translated as "the Egyptians," the use of the singular verb (וַיֹּאמֶר) suggests that it should be translated as "Egypt." Symbolically, the Egyptian army is Egypt. The idea is not just that the individual Egyptian soldiers were terrified, but that Egypt as a whole was thrown into panic.
270. The participial וּמִצְרַיִם נָסִים is background information. Notice also that the participle is plural, indicating that וּמִצְרַיִם here means, "and the Egyptians."
271. The root נער (Piel) means to shake up or toss. It refers to the Egyptians being driven about in the violence of the returning waters.

14:28b and they covered the chariots and the mounted troops that belonged to the whole army[272] of Pharaoh that had gone after them into the sea;
14:28c not a single one remained.
14:29a But the Israelites went on dry ground through the middle of the sea,
14:29b and the waters were for them a wall on their right hand and on their left.
14:30a On that day YHWH saved[273] Israel from the power[274] of Egypt,
14:30b and Israel saw Egypt dead[275] on the shore of the sea.
14:31a And Israel saw the great power[276] that YHWH had used against Egypt,
14:31b and the people feared YHWH,
14:31c and they believed in YHWH and in his servant Moses.

Structure

There are differences between this and the other eleven miracles, the most obvious being that Israel has already left Egypt, and thus there is no request to release the people and no direct confrontation between Pharaoh and Moses. But there are formal parallels. As in other miracle stories of Exodus, the event is initiated with a ritual act, and the Egyptians try to duplicate what Israel does. Instead of a commission from YHWH to Moses that he should go confront Pharaoh, he is commissioned to deceive Pharaoh with a maneuver. And instead of having to listen to Pharaoh's harangue, Moses gets an earful from the Israelites.

I. Background Information: Transitional and Summarizing Material (13:17–22)
II. YHWH Commissions Moses Regarding Pharaoh (14:1–4)
III. The Response to the Commission (14:5–14)
  A. Pharaoh and Officials Respond (14:5–9)

---

272. The phrase לְכֹל חֵיל פַּרְעֹה could mean "including the whole army of Pharaoh" and mean that the infantry died in the sea as well. But 14:23 indicates that only chariots and mounted troops went into the sea. Possibly the infantry was travelling much more slowly and had not arrived at the sea. If so, the לְ of לְכֹל חֵיל is probably possessive and means that the entire chariot corps of his army went into the sea.
273. The *wayyiqtol* וַיּוֹשַׁע is epexegetical and summarizing.
274. Lit. "hand."
275. The phrase אֶת־מִצְרַיִם מֵת should be translated with the singular "Egypt dead" rather than the plural "the Egyptians dead." This is not just because of the singular מֵת. Here, the Egyptian army by synecdoche represents the whole nation.
276. Lit. "hand."

B. Israel Responds (14:10–14)

IV. YHWH Commands Moses and Aaron to Use the Staff (14:15–18)

V. Other Information: The Angel Delays the Egyptians (14:19–20)

VI. Moses Lifts Staff (14:21–22)

VII. Egyptians Seek to Duplicate Miraculous Crossing (14:23–25)

VIII. Moses Lifts Staff Again; Egypt Drowned and Israel Saved (14:26–29)

IX. Affirmation that YHWH's Word Was Fulfilled (14:30–31)

Commentary

13:17–22. The text begins with a quick summary of the journey from Egypt to Etham, giving the following details about the journey. The first detail is that they departed taking the "Way of the Wilderness" (the Darb el-Hagg), which leads directly across the northern edge of the Sinai Peninsula from Egypt to the *Yam Suph*, the Gulf of Aqaba. (For further discussion, see The Location of the *Yam Suph* and of Mt. Sinai in the Introduction.) The stated reason for doing this is that if they took the direct and shortest route from Egypt into Canaan, the "Way of the Philistines" ("the "Way of Horus" or the Via Maris, following the southeast coastline of the Mediterranean Sea), they would be invading Canaan in a matter of days. That is, they would have to go from being brickmaking slaves to being warriors involved in a campaign of invasion with no time for transition or training. This was plainly impossible, and the longer route would allow them time to organize themselves as a migrant people ready to fight an aggressive campaign against a settled population.

The second detail is that the people went up in a military-type formation (13:18b). This by no means implies that they had military training and, contrary to many translations, it does not state that they were all armed. It means that Moses did not permit them to move across the wilderness in a disorderly manner. Insomuch as it was in his power, he had them move out in an array that gave them protection against a surprise attack by desert raiders and that also allowed them to proceed in a rapid manner, not in confusion and not getting in each other's way.

The third detail the text brings out is that they took Joseph's remains with them. The explicit point made here is that this fulfilled Joseph's charge to the Israelites that they should not leave his remains in Egypt when God came to take them from that land. This act also serves as a repudiation of Egyptian religion, which held that a person's chance at attaining an afterlife was greatly diminished if his body was removed from his "house of eternity," his tomb. Egyptian religion would never countenance removing a person's body from the sacred land of Egypt.

The fourth detail of the narrative is the appearance of the pillar of fire and cloud, which are mentioned here for the first time. Old Testament scholarship has primarily concerned itself with the origin of the concept, assuming it to be not historical but essentially myth. Thomas Mann surveys previous suggestions and argues that, on the one hand, the concept of a pillar of cloud idea is analogous to descriptions of the storm theophany of Baal in Ugaritic literature, and on the other hand, that it has connections to cultic language involving the Ark of the Covenant in procession before the Israelites as a war palladium.[277] One may well dismiss such speculations (the connection between the pillar of cloud and the Baal theophany is quite thin) and argue that in fact the story about the pillar of cloud and of fire came out of the actual experiences of the Israelites. But making sense of the narrative is no easy task. Many of us have etched in our imagination the image of the giant, flaming tornado of Cecil B. DeMille's *The Ten Commandments*. Such a phenomenon in real life (as opposed to DeMille's cartoonish special effects) would be spectacular beyond description and absolutely terrifying. Certain details in the narrative do lend themselves to an interpretation similar to DeMille's. The pillar of fire was able to provide illumination as Israel trekked through the wilderness by night (13:21), and it stood between Israel and the Egyptians during the night at the sea, and the Egyptians could not get around it (14:19–20). On the other hand, the characters in the story hardly notice it. The Egyptians are held back by it but otherwise they seem altogether unfazed by its presence. How could that be? One would expect that, having just come through the plagues, Egyptians would be in a panic at the sight of a great pillar of fire in front of them, and that they would break away in terror. Later, the Egyptians actually are terrified when they realize that "YHWH is fighting for them" (14:25), but prior to that the pillar of fire was for them little more than a nuisance that temporarily kept them from their prey. Surely seeing a great fiery column that burned of itself all night would have been enough to convince them that YHWH was with Israel. For that matter, the Israelites also give little heed to the pillar. They panic at the sight of the Egyptian army even though they have a visible manifestation of YHWH right in front of them. One might think that, no matter how puny their faith, they could have easily believed that a great column of fire would be more

277. Thomas W. Mann, "The Pillar of Cloud in the Reed Sea Narrative," *JBL* 90, no. 1 (1971): 15–30.

than a match for Egyptian soldiers. And in fact no one, neither Moses nor the people, seems to consider the idea that the pillar of fire might simply drive away or destroy the Egyptians. We can only surmise that there was something about its appearance that was far more subtle and less threatening than we might imagine. It was able to block the Egyptian advance, but apparently it did not appear awesome or even supernatural.

The fifth detail of the narrative is that the first major leg of their journey took the Israelites from Succoth (Tell el-Maskhuta in the area of the Wadi Tumilat) to Etham. The location of Etham is disputed; many place it somewhere near Succoth on the eastern edge of Egypt; I believe that it is more likely that it is at the northern tip of the Gulf of Aqaba and is perhaps to be identified with the region around the El Yitm peak, at the northeast corner of the gulf (the name "Yitm" may preserve the name "Etham").[278] This suggests that "they camped" in 13:20b means that they came to a full stop at Etham; they may have temporarily ceased travelling for a few hours along the way between Succoth and Etham, but they never stopped long enough to set up a full encampment until they arrived at Etham. This interpretation is supported by the fifth detail of the travel narrative, that the angel of YHWH went before them as a pillar of fire by night so that they could march both day and night (13:21b). Apparently they made very good progress across the Sinai Peninsula, only stopping briefly and without pitching their tents until they arrived at Etham.

14:1–4. If Etham is at the northeast corner of the Gulf of Aqaba, the logical thing for Israel to have done (if they were heading toward Mt. Sinai in the Arabian Peninsula) was to round the northern shore of the gulf and head south into the Arabian Peninsula. Instead, they are told to turn back and encamp on the west side of the gulf with the gulf itself to their backs. This was a doubly strange thing to do. First, it took them in the wrong direction, and second, it placed them in a terrible tactical situation, entrapped against the sea and easily pinned down by a military force. But this, the text tells us, is precisely what YHWH intended, as the plan was to entice the Egyptians to abandon all caution and to press their military advantage against Israel. Tactically, Israel's situation was terrible, but God would fight for them and save them.

14:5–9. Verse 5 is retrospective, describing how a message was brought to Pharaoh several days after Israel departed to the effect that Israel was

278. Humphreys, *Miracles*, 212-4.

rapidly moving away from Egyptian territory. Apparently, even after everything that had happened, Pharaoh still entertained the notion that Israel would come back after a three-day journey into the wilderness and go back to work. The data also suggest that he had mounted troops shadowing Israel as they moved out. Therefore, it seems that approximately four or five days after Israel's departure, Pharaoh was informed that the Israelites plainly were not coming back. In a rage at having lost so many slaves, he immediately began preparations for pursuing the Israelites, who perhaps had a six-day lead by the time he set out with his troops. Pharaoh's forces, however, unencumbered by pregnant and nursing women, old people, children, and livestock, could move much more quickly than the Israelites, and he began to gain ground immediately. For their part, the Israelites, although not making camp as they went along the Way of the Wilderness, were not moving a breakneck speed. To the contrary, they were celebratory, carefree, and even a little cocky (travelling "with a high hand" as 14:8c literally states). Thus, when Israel made their retrograde movement and encamped with their backs to the sea, the stage was set for Egypt to trap them. Verse 9 carries the pursuit narrative to its conclusion, that Egypt caught Israel and pressed them against the western shore of the *Yam Suph*.

14:10–14. Verse 10 is retrospective, describing how Israel first perceived the arrival of the Egyptian forces. They apparently saw the Egyptian troops in the distance, but it was already too late to turn again and try to make around the tip of the Gulf of Aqaba. As such, the Israelites knew that they were already trapped and bitterly protested against Moses's apparently crazy leadership, turning back and placing the nation in such a snare. They claim that he couldn't have done a worse job if he had been intending to get everybody killed, something they sarcastically accuse him of. Moses, however, having been informed of YHWH's intention, simply demanded that the people stop panicking and wait quietly for YHWH's deliverance.

14:15–18. YHWH indicates to Moses that he will proceed with the plan to lure the Egyptians into the sea and that Moses need only get the Israelites moving toward the sea. He also commissions Moses, as before, to inaugurate the miracle with his staff. Perhaps the most remarkable feature of this text is that YHWH says that Egypt would recognize that YHWH is God through this miracle. One might have expected that the miracle was for the benefit of Israel. But the point here is not that Egypt will be converted and have faith. Rather, it is that they will have to bow in defeat and admit to YHWH's supremacy.

14:19–20. The pillar of cloud and fire moved from before Israel to a spot between Israel and the Egyptians, blocking the way and keeping Israel safe until the waters were parted and the Hebrews could make their escape. As described above, it was enough of a physical presence that the Egyptians could not pass through it. On the other hand, it did not greatly disturb the Egyptians and perhaps looked like a natural phenomenon. The Israelites, too, pay no regard to the pillar, always treating Moses (and not the angel of YHWH in the pillar) as the leader of the community. Thus, the pillar was visibly present, but there was something about it that seemed natural enough that it never became the focus of attention for either the Egyptians or Israelites.

14:21–22. As described in The Location of the *Yam Suph* and of Mt. Sinai in the Introduction, the event at the *Yam Suph* appears to have been a wind setdown event caused by a sustained northeast wind blowing down the length of the Gulf of Aqaba. This caused the waters to stand up as if in a wall, as described in the text here.

14:23–29. The destruction of the Egyptian army is described as occurring in the following phases. First, the wind blew all night while the pillar kept the Israelites and Egyptians separated. Just before dawn broke, with the waters now fully parted, Israel began its crossing. The Egyptians, meanwhile, were frustrated by their inability to get at the Israelites and, in their haste to join battle, were ready to throw caution to the wind. Second, the pillar of YHWH moved out of the way and the Egyptian forces began their pursuit. The text indicates that only chariots and mounted forces went into the chasm even though 14:6b implies that Pharaoh took some infantry along with him. It may be that the foot soldiers could not keep up with the mounted troops and were some distance back, still crossing the desert along the Way of the Wilderness. Or, it may be that Pharaoh simply wanted to throw his shock forces, the chariots, immediately into the battle. The Hebrew people were evidently almost through the *Yam Suph* by the time the Egyptian chariots began to enter it. Third, YHWH "looked down" on the Egyptians and threw them into confusion. The divine presence somehow, and very suddenly, panicked the Egyptians. It is as if they only just noticed the sign of God's presence. Fourth, in their panic, the Egyptians began to turn about their chariots in a disorganized manner, so that chaos ensued. It may be that they were close enough to the western shore that they could have made it safely out of the sea bottom had they maneuvered in good order. Being in confusion, however, they only got in each other's way. Fifth, YHWH commanded Moses to use his staff again, and the sea closed upon the chariot forces. But it is important to recognize that the Egyptians were not simply killed by the sea; they died because they fell into panic and disorder at the crucial moment, when escape was still possible. The point here is that the sea need not have been of enormous width at the point at which Israel crossed it. The safety of the shore was not so far away that flight was impossible, but thrashing horses and terrified drivers could not make their way to it.

14:30–31. This is the last great battle between YHWH and Egypt, and the latter floats dead upon the sea. YHWH has shown himself for the final time to be greater than Egypt, and the people saw and believed. And they realized, at least for now, that Moses was the man of God.

Theological Summary of Key Points

1. The sea is in biblical and Israelite thinking an apocalyptic figure representing destruction and death. It is the abyss, a watery hell from which evil things emerge and into which the wicked finally descend. It is the domain of Leviathan (Job 41:1; Ps. 104:26; Isa. 27:1). In Rev. 13:1, the beast rises out of the sea. The sea is also filled with the dead (Rev. 20:13). Jonah goes down into the heart of the sea and becomes a portrait of Christ's descent into death (Matt. 12:40). For Egypt, the event at the *Yam Suph* was the end of an apocalyptic series of judgments that ended with the nation symbolically swallowed by death. To be sure, the historical nation of Egypt did not come to an end here, but Egypt represents human powers set against God and his people. But if apocalypse means final destruction for God's enemies, it is final salvation for all who belong to him. At the very darkest moment, when all hope seems lost and following the path of God appears to have been hopeless folly, the power of God breaks through from heaven, destroys his enemies, and brings his own people safely to a new shore.

2. From the standpoint of what happened to Egypt, we see what happens to a people who resist and reject God. They abandon both wisdom and morality. Egypt should have learned the folly of opposing YHWH from all the prior plagues. But the folly of their stubbornness is compounded by an even greater sin, that they desire to capture and enslave a people who only want to get away and form their own nation. Egyptian greed led to recklessness in the headlong rush into the sea. This was followed by panic and finally destruction. Any people who turn from God may go through similar steps: a foolish disregard for the justice of God, an increase in sin, a loss of all common sense, a time of terror, and then ruin.

3. For the people of God, Israel affords a lesson in obedience (even though the Israelites themselves did not model it very well). Israel is redeemed and led by God, but then they are taken in a direction that seems to make no sense and can apparently only end in their destruction. When YHWH took Israel back to the west side of the *Yam Suph*, it must have seemed that he and Moses did not know what they were doing. And yet God always had events under control, and things turned out as he intended. The point is that the path of obedience can itself seem like a kind of folly, but it is the folly of the cross, in which the weakness and stupidity of God is stronger and wiser than earthly power or common sense (1 Cor. 1:19–30).

4. The peculiar nature of the pillar of fire and cloud may also have a lesson for us. The angel of God was there in great power and did great things for Israel, but Egypt and Israel hardly noticed it and paid it no heed. Perhaps we, too, can have a great work of God in our midst and not recognize it.

Excursus: The Egyptian Army during the New Kingdom

The New Kingdom (18th, 19th, and 20th dynasties; 1550–1069 B.C.), the period in which the exodus occurred, was Egypt's golden age of imperial and military glory. Egypt waged war in every direction: to the west (Libya), to the south (Nubia), to the north (the Mitanni Empire of Syria during the 18th dynasty and the Hittite Empire of Anatolia during the 19th dynasty). And as Egyptian power waned in the 20th dynasty, it still was able to repel an invasion of "Sea Peoples" from across the Mediterranean Sea.

The Egyptian military machine of the New Kingdom grew out of the wars against the Hyksos, when the Theban 17th dynasty created a military class that over the course of several generations honed its technology and its tactics (the Thebans probably learned a great deal about warfare from the Hyksos military aristocracy). When the Hyksos were expelled, the new Egyptian army was in no mood to lay down its arms and go back to the plow. They were a thoroughly militarized society, and they had certainly come to believe that an aggressive foreign policy was the best defense against any future humiliation at the hands of outsiders.

Sources of Information

A primary source of information is the accounts of military successes left by Thutmose III (18th dynasty; reigned 1479–1425), Ramesses II (19th dynasty; reigned 1279–1213), and Ramesses III (20th dynasty;

reigned 1184–1153). The inscriptions and the accompanying artwork tell us a great deal about their weapons, tactics, and standard procedures.[279]

Thutmose III left behind accounts of his many campaigns into the Levant. His most daring exploit was the conquest of the Canaanite city of Megiddo, which had revolted against Egyptian domination with the encouragement of the Syrian city of Kadesh (and probably with the support of Mitanni). Thutmose III, approaching Megiddo from the southwest, famously took his army through a narrow Aruna pass rather than swing around the hills that stood between him and the city. This maneuver forced him to string out his forces, and it could have led to a catastrophic defeat. But his enemies were not expecting him to take the narrow pass and made no effort to block it. He surprised them by emerging from the pass and arraying his army for battle before the very gates of the city. Perhaps parts of the Syrian and Canaanite army were away at the other passes and did not make it back to the city in time to participate in the battle. At any rate, the forces that did confront Thutmose III were defeated outside the walls and had to be hauled up the walls into the city by the inhabitants. Eventually, Megiddo capitulated. In a later campaign, Thutmose III carried boats on oxcarts from Byblos to the Euphrates. Able to move troops up and down the upper part of the river, where it bisected the Mitanni kingdom, he was able to campaign at will in the western half of Mitanni and wage war against its allies in Syria and Canaan.

The most famous battle of ancient Egyptian history is that between Ramesses II and his Hittite counterpart, Muwatalli, at Kadesh on the Orontes River in Syria in about 1274. Driving his army into Syria for an encounter with the Hittites, Ramesses II had foolishly believed a report from two captured men that the Hittites were still far away (they were in fact concealed behind the city of Kadesh). The Egyptian army was attacked while the lead elements, including the pharaoh himself, were making camp, and while the bulk of the army was still on the march. But the pharaoh's forces in the vanguard managed to hold off the enemy until the rest of his army arrived, and disaster was averted. The battle ended as something of a Hittite victory (Ramesses II failed to take Kadesh, and Egyptian power was confined to the area of Canaan, having been driven from Syria). Even so, the pharaoh claimed to have won a great victory through his personal prowess in battle.[280]

---

279. For discussions of the Egyptian military in modern scholarship, see especially Spalinger, *War* and David, *Handbook*, 225-54.

280. See Joyce Tyldesley, *Hatchepsut: The Female Pharaoh* (London: Penguin Books, 1998), 68-73.

Ramesses III, in the eighth year of his reign, had his greatest victory in a battle fought on the northern frontier of Egypt itself. He repulsed the Sea Peoples, who attacked Egypt with a combined sea and land invasion. He thus saved Egypt from foreign domination. Although he also fought off land-based invasions of Egypt (from Libyans as well as from Sea Peoples), his great victory includes a rare example of a sea battle fought by the ancient Egyptians. They did routinely use boats as rapid transports for their troops, but these were mostly river craft, used on the Nile for the deployment of forces against the Nubians in the south. But Ramesses III had to fight ship-to-ship battles against the Sea Peoples.

We do have other sources of information about Egyptian warfare. Haremhab, last pharaoh of the 18th dynasty, issued a decree which tells us something about Egyptian military administration. Also, officers in the Egyptian army sometimes had their tombs inscribed with accounts of their bravery in battle. Finally, Egyptian artwork and artifacts, principally from tombs, gives us a better understanding of the Egyptian military. Several chariots, for example, have been found in tombs.

Organization

The pharaoh was the supreme commander of the armed forces and, if he was a vigorous ruler, would personally lead his army into battle. The vizier (the pharaoh's highest ranking administrator) was, in effect, his chief of staff, and he might command the army in the field as the pharaoh's representative. Officers were chiefly drawn from the aristocracy; the lowest ranking officer, perhaps analogous to a lieutenant, was a "commander of fifty." Common soldiers were conscripted from the peasant classes (about one man in ten might serve time in the army). Foreigners might also serve in Egypt's army. The army of Ramesses II was organized into four divisions of 5,000 men, with each division named for a god (Ptah, Re, Seth, and Amun), with a fifth division being the troops under the pharaoh's direct command.[281] Divisions were subdivided into smaller units, down to the fifty-man platoon. Chariots were organized into squadrons of twenty-five.

Weaponry

Prior to the New Kingdom, Egyptian foot-soldiers were all light

281. The figure of 5,000 men per division is based on a comment in Papyrus Anastasi I, but whether that represents the standard size for an Egyptian division at the time is open to question. It may have been smaller. See Spalinger, *War*, 149-50.

infantry, having no armor except for rawhide shields and using short spears as their offensive weapons. Archers had simple, primitive longbows. By the time of the New Kingdom, leather body armor (with some metal attached), helmets, and short, bronze, scimitar-like swords were in use. The archers, now armed with more powerful composite bows, were a military force to be reckoned with. Still, they were not heavy infantry such as would be found in the later Greek phalanx or Roman legion. The Egyptian army was a rapid strike force that relied upon its chariots and archers.

The Egyptian war chariot first came into use during the New Kingdom; other great powers, such as the Hittite Empire, also employed massed chariots at this time. The war chariot had two wheels, was drawn by two horses, and had a crew of two, a driver and a shield-bearer. The driver approached the enemy and then fired arrows; he might use a javelin or sword at closer quarters. The chariot was of light wicker-work and designed for speed; it was not armored. The massed chariot attack was meant to terrify the lightly armed foot soldiers who opposed it (centuries later, when infantry was more heavily armored and was disciplined to hold its ranks, the chariot became obsolete).

Egyptians did not use cavalry, but did employ mounted troops as scouts. Exodus 14:5 suggests that such scouts were shadowing the Israelites. The Bible also indicates that Egyptian infantry set out with the chariot corps in pursuit of the Hebrews (Exod. 14:6), but no infantry appear to have been present when the chariots were destroyed at the sea (Exod. 14:23). Perhaps they were trailing behind the mounted forces and only arrived after the debacle.

Tactics

We know little about Egyptian military tactics other than that they typically arrayed themselves for battle as a main body with a wing on each side. Such battlefield maneuvering, however, would not have been employed while pursuing a large body of refugees, such as the Israelites.

It appears that the Egyptians' preferred tactic during the New Kingdom was to make a rapid strike with their chariot forces. They never developed the slow and methodical art of siege warfare, and evidence from the battles at Megiddo and Kadesh suggests that they could be bold to the point of recklessness. This is consonant with what we see in Exod. 14, where they rush into the sea without pausing to ask whether this was a sound idea. We need to realize that under normal circumstances the Israelites would have been no match for the

Egyptian chariots. Untrained peasants who only days before had been working as slaves, the Hebrews would have scattered like fallen leaves in a storm before a properly executed Egyptian attack.

Valor and Morale

The Egyptians highly valued personal courage. A soldier who showed valor in battle would be awarded the "Golden Flies," sometimes translated as the "Gold of Valor," a military decoration analogous to modern medals for bravery. More than that, he would receive wealth and slaves as his share of the booty, and could advance through the ranks. A certain Ahmose son of Abana, on the wall of a rock-cut tomb, left an account of his deeds of valor and of the honors he received while under the service of early 18th dynasty pharaohs. Another soldier, named Amenemhab, told of his many battles while campaigning with Thutmose III, and he especially made a point of describing how often he was in hand-to-hand combat.[282]

Egyptian commanders bolstered the morale of their men by speaking of how their gods fought for them. They might call upon Montu, the Egyptian war-god, but during the New Kingdom they especially extolled the all-conquering power of Amun.

Most importantly, the pharaohs of the New Kingdom boosted the morale of the troops under them and of the nation as a whole by assuming the role of military hero. Thutmose III, in the Megiddo narrative, is bold and resolute where his general staff is timid and conventional. Ramesses II, in the accounts he has given of his action at Kadesh, is positively Herculean, single-handedly slaying the enemy hoards while his confused soldiers seek to recover and reorganize themselves. The iconography of the time, portraying the pharaoh as a gigantic figure striding in to vanquish his Lilliputian enemies, is the ultimate piece of morale-building propaganda: Egypt is invincible because Pharaoh is invincible.

Egyptian Élan at the Yam Suph

From the above discussion, one may suggest that a central feature of the New Kingdom Egyptian army, and especially of its chariot corps, was the high value it placed upon élan. This is a particular kind of courage that enables someone to charge headlong into the thick of battle. It is also a tactic designed to force the outcome of battle by overwhelming the enemy with the sheer audacity of one's attack, and

---

282. For the inscriptions of Ahmose son of Abana and of Amenemhab, see Breasted, *Ancient Records*, 2:3-18 and 2:227-34, respectively.

it was employed successfully by such great captains as Alexander the Great and Napoleon. But it is more than a tactic; it is also for certain armies their central creed. Numerous elements described above place the New Kingdom Egyptian army in this class. The officially cultivated faith in Amun and his pharaoh, the examples set by Thutmose III at Megiddo and by Ramesses II at Kadesh, the recognition Egyptians gave to the valor of individual soldiers, and the very nature of the war chariot as a weapon of shock attack all suggest that devotion to élan was part of their military culture. But as a military philosophy élan has a major drawback, as the Romans under Caesar demonstrated when they were attacked by Gallic warriors rushing madly upon them, screaming and swinging their broadswords. When the legions held their lines in the face of these onslaughts, the élan of the Gauls was quickly transformed into terror and chaotic flight, and Caesar rapidly conquered all of Gaul. Considering all that, the Bible credibly describes both the Egyptians' furious rush into the sea and their subsequent panic when they realized that God was fighting for Israel (Ex. 14:25).

THE SONG OF THE SEA (15:1–21)

As a climactic finale to the twelve miracles of the exodus, Moses gave the Israelites a song celebrating the victory of YHWH and looking forward to attaining rest, after their days of slavery, in the Promised Land.

Translation

15:1a At that time[283] Moses and the Israelites began to sing[284] this song to YHWH;

15:1b they said:[285]

283. The word אָז could mean that Moses sang this song immediately after the sea closed on the Egyptians. It probably, however, means that the song dates from that general time and event; it does not preclude the idea that the Israelites took time to get organized after the crossing and to take in the full significance of the event before they began to sing. Also, the Israelites obviously had to learn the words from Moses.

284. The *yiqtol* יָשִׁיר is ingressive.

285. The *wayyiqtol* is epexegetical.

PART III

Third Poem: The Song of the Sea

Stanza 1.1[286]

15:1c I will sing to YHWH for he is thoroughly majestic!
אָשִׁירָה לַיהוָה כִּי־גָאֹה גָּאָה 2-3-4

15:1d [The] horse and its rider he has hurled into the sea!
סוּס וְרֹכְבוֹ רָמָה בַיָּם 1-4-4

Stanza 1.2

15:2a Yah is my strength and protection,
עָזִּי וְזִמְרָת יָהּ [287] 0-3-3

15:2b And he has become my salvation.
וַיְהִי־לִי לִישׁוּעָה 1-3-3

---

286. The first stanza is in four bicola. The first and fourth strophes form an inclusio using יְהוָה (it begins אָשִׁירָה לַיהוָה and concludes יְהוָה שְׁמוֹ, having consonance with the name יְהוָה and the letter שׁ). The first strophe also serves as the title of the poem. It refers to the two themes of the poem: praising God in general terms because of his majesty (15:1c) and more specifically for the acts at the *Yam Suph* (15:1d).

287. The translation of זִמְרָת is debated. Many consider it to be זִמְרָה (I), "song" or "music." This is from the root זמר (I), "to sing" or "to make music." זִמְרָה (I) is found in Isa. 51:3; Amos 5:23; Ps. 81:3(2); 98:5. This gives the traditional translation, "The Lord is my strength and my song." But the root זמר (III), "to protect" or "to be strong," although not attested as a verb in biblical Hebrew, is attested in Ugaritic, Old South Arabian, and Arabic (זמר [III], *HALOT*, 1.274). This suggests a meaning of "strength" for זִמְרָה (II). Two factors favor taking זִמְרָת here to be derived from זמר (III), with the meaning "protection." First, זִמְרָה (I), "song," never appears in the absolute as זִמְרָת. In fact, contrary to the lexicons, זִמְרָת should probably not be listed as זִמְרָה (II), since it always appears as זִמְרָת (Exod. 15:2; Isa. 12:2; Ps. 118:14; see also Gen. 43:11, which is also from זמר [III] unless it is from the root זמר [II], "to prune"). In short, there are no grounds for thinking that זִמְרָת is an older or alternative form of זִמְרָה (I), "song." Second, although one needs to use this lexicographic device with caution, the parallelism with עָזִּי suggests that זִמְרָת means "protection" or "might" and not "song." In addition, and most decisively, cognates strongly favor a meaning of "strength" or "protection" (see Michael L. Barré, "'My Strength and My Song' in Exodus 15:2," *CBQ* 54, no. 4 (1992): 623–37). See also Simon B. Parker, "Exodus XV 2 Again," *VT* 21, no. 3 (1971): 373–9, against Samuel E. Loewenstamm, "The Lord is my Strength and my Glory," *VT* 19, no. 4 (1969): 464–70, and against Edwin Marshall Good, "Exodus XV 2," *VT* 20, no. 3 (1970): 358–9.

Stanza 1.3[288]

15:2c	This is my God, and I will praise him! זֶה אֵלִי וְאַנְוֵהוּ[289]	 1-3-3
15:2d	[This is] the God of my father, and I will exalt him! אֱלֹהֵי אָבִי[290] וַאֲרֹמְמֶנְהוּ	 1-2-3

Stanza 1.4[291]

15:3a	YHWH is a man of war! יְהוָה אִישׁ מִלְחָמָה	 0-2-3
15:3b	YHWH is his name! יְהוָה שְׁמוֹ	 0-2-2

Stanza 2.1[292]

15:4a	He cast Pharaoh's chariots and his army into the sea! מַרְכְּבֹת פַּרְעֹה וְחֵילוֹ יָרָה בַיָּם	 1-4-5
15:4b	The best of his officers[293] were plunged into the *Yam Suph*. וּמִבְחַר שָׁלִשָׁיו טֻבְּעוּ בְיַם־סוּף	 1-3-5

288. Both lines of this strophe end with a first singular *weyiqtol* verb, and both refer to "God" (אֵל and אֱלֹהֵי).

289. נוה (II) (Hiphil) is *hapax legomenon*. Its meaning is inferred from context and from the Arabic cognate *nawwaha*, "to cry aloud." See *HALOT*, 2.678.

290. There is gapping of זֶה from 15:2c.

291. Both lines of this bicolon begin with יְהוָה.

292. The second stanza speaks specifically of the *Yam Suph* miracle, with the first line (15:4a) picking up the theme of the overthrow of Pharaoh's chariot corps from the second line of the title (15:1d). This links the two stanzas. This stanza is made of two bicola. The two lines of the first bicolon begin with consonance (מַרְכְּבֹת and וּמִבְחַר) and end with the parallel terms בַיָּם and בְיַם־סוּף.

293. Peter C. Craigie, "An Egyptian Expression in the Song of the Sea (Exodus XV 4)," *VT* 20, no. 1 (1970): 83–6, argues that the Hebrew שׁלשׁ may be an Egyptianism, based on the Egyptian *srs*, a "commander." Furthermore, he notes that the expression "the best of" in reference to men is an authentic Egyptian expression, with the Hebrew מִבְחַר being the translation equivalent of the Egyptian *śtp.w*.

Stanza 2.2[294]

15:5a [The] deeps began to cover them;
תְּהֹמֹת יְכַסְיֻמוּ[295] 1-2-2

15:5b They sank down to the depths like a stone!
יָרְדוּ בִמְצוֹלֹת כְּמוֹ־אָבֶן 1-3-3

Stanza 3.1[296]

15:6a Your right hand, YHWH, is magnificent in power!
יְמִינְךָ יְהוָה נֶאְדָּרִי בַּכֹּחַ 1-4-4[297]

15:6b Your right hand, YHWH, vanquishes enemies;
יְמִינְךָ יְהוָה תִּרְעַץ[298] אוֹיֵב 2-4-4

Stanza 3.2

15:7a By the abundance of your majesty you bring those who rise against you to ruin.
וּבְרֹב גְּאוֹנְךָ[299] תַּהֲרֹס קָמֶיךָ 1-3-4

15:7b You release your fury; it consumes them like straw.
תְּשַׁלַּח חֲרֹנְךָ יֹאכְלֵמוֹ כַּקַּשׁ 2-4-4

Stanza 4.1[300]

15:8a And by the blast of your nostrils waters were stacked up;
וּבְרוּחַ אַפֶּיךָ נֶעֶרְמוּ מַיִם 1-3-4

15:8b Flowing [waters] stood up in a heap;
נִצְּבוּ כְמוֹ־נֵד נֹזְלִים 1-3-3

---

294. This bicolon has semantic parallelism, with both lines speaking of sinking down into the deeps/depths.
295. The *yiqtol* here is ingressive.
296. This stanza gives general praise to God. It has four strophes. The first, a bicolon, starts both lines with יְמִינְךָ יְהוָה.
297. A vocative counts as a predicator in O'Connor's system.
298. The verb רעץ is hapax legomenon; according to *HALOT* (3.1271), it is cognate (with metathesis) to Arabic *ṣr'*. The *yiqtol* here is probably gnomic.
299. The use of גָּאוֹן links this line to the opening general praise of YHWH, who is גָּאָה (15:1c).
300. This stanza shifts to dominance by *qatal* forms (except in the reported speech of strophes 2 and 3) and speaks of the events at the *Yam Suph*. There is linkage to the previous stanza in line 15:8a, which begins with the conjunction and has as its second word אַפֶּיךָ, parallel to חֲרֹנְךָ in 15:7b.

15:8c [The murky] depths at the heart of the sea were churned up.[301]
קָֽפְא֥וּ תְהֹמֹ֖ת בְּלֶב־יָֽם 1-3-4

Stanza 4.2

15:9a [The] enemy said, "I will pursue; I will overtake;
אָמַ֥ר אוֹיֵ֛ב אֶרְדֹּ֥ף אַשִּׂ֖יג 3-4-4[302]

15:9b I will divide plunder; my appetite will be filled with them;
אֲחַלֵּ֣ק שָׁלָ֑ל תִּמְלָאֵ֣מוֹ[303] נַפְשִׁ֔י 2-4-4

15:9c I will draw my sword; my hand will dispossess them."
אָרִ֣יק חַרְבִּ֔י תּוֹרִישֵׁ֖מוֹ יָדִֽי 2-4-4

Stanza 4.3[304]

15:10a You blew with your wind; sea covered them!
נָשַׁ֥פְתָּ בְרוּחֲךָ֖ כִּסָּ֣מוֹ יָ֑ם 2-4-4

---

301. The verb קפא is often taken to mean "congealed," a meaning that arises from its usage in Job 10:10 (the curdling of cheese) and Zeph. 1:12 (the settling of wine). But in post-biblical Hebrew and in Aramaic the root means to "rise up" and is used of scum forming on the surface of a liquid or of froth rising to the top of a liquid. See Al Wolters, "Not Rescue but Destruction: Rereading Exodus 15:8," *CBQ* 52, no. 2 (1990): 235-8. This suggests that 15:8c is talking about the lower parts of the sea being churned up and brought to the top, not a congealing of the waters.
302. It is impossible to scan v. 9 without violating the poetic constraints, or the cantillation marks, or both. But neither should be considered inviolable. Two factors favor the colometry offered here. First, at 15:9a there is consonance, in that every word begins with the consonant א. Second, 15:9b and 15:9c have strong syntactic matching: a *yiqtol* 1cs + direct object + *yiqtol* 3fs with 3mp suffix ֵמוֹ + direct object with 1cs suffix. The two clauses of 15:9b begin with verbs starting with first א and then ח, and the same is true of 15:9c. Also, the two clauses of 15:9b, as given above, logically go together: the dividing of the plunder will satisfy his appetite for booty. Similarly, the two clauses of 15:9c both concern actions with the hand.
303. The verb מלא is intransitive and is in effect a middle voice (Qal stem, "to be full or filled"), and the suffix מוֹ indicates with what the appetite will be filled.
304. This bicolon (strophe 4.3) has semantic parallelism, with both lines describing the drowning of the Egyptians. Also, these two lines form with lines 15:8ab an inclusio for stanza 4. The phrase וּבְר֤וּחַ אַפֶּ֙יךָ֙ in line 15:8a is echoed by בְּרוּחֲךָ in 15:10a. Line 15:8b has the simile כְּמוֹ־נֵד and refers to the water as נֹזְלִים; line 15:10b has the simile כַּעוֹפֶרֶת and refers to the water as אַדִּירִים.

15:10b They vanished like lead in [the] magnificent waters!
צָֽלֲלוּ[305] כַּעוֹפֶ֫רֶת בְּמַ֫יִם אַדִּירִים 1-3-4

Stanza 5.1[306]

15:11a Who is like you among the gods, YHWH?
מִֽי־כָמֹ֤כָה בָּֽאֵלִם֙ יְהוָ֔ה 1-4-4

15:11b Who is like you, magnificent in holiness?
מִ֥י כָּמֹ֖כָה נֶאְדָּ֣ר בַּקֹּ֑דֶשׁ 0-4-4

15:11c Feared [in the midst of the] praises [given to you]! A worker of wonders!
נוֹרָ֥א תְהִלֹּ֖ת[307] עֹ֥שֵׂה פֶֽלֶא[308] 0-2-4

Stanza 6.1[309]

15:12 You stretch out your right hand; earth swallows them!
נָטִ֙יתָ֙ יְמִ֣ינְךָ֔ תִּבְלָעֵ֖מוֹ[310] אָֽרֶץ 2-4-4

---

305. צלל (II) is hapax legomenon. Various cognates have been suggested (see *HALOT* 3.1027). Perhaps the most convincing is *ḍalla*, from Arabic and meaning, "disappear."

306. This stanza is a single tricolon and praises God in general terms. Each of the first two lines begins with מִי כָמֹכָה. This is similar to the first two lines at strophe 3.1 (15:6), where יְמִינְךָ יְהוָה is used twice. Similarly, the first strophe of stanza 7 repeats the phrase עַד־יַעֲבֹר עַם at 15:16cd. Thus, the phenomenon of repeating a phrase at the beginning of two successive lines is a marker for the major divisions of the poem.

307. Lit. "feared of praises." The word "praises" here refers to the setting in which YHWH is feared. The line is paradoxical; YHWH's works inspire both terror and praise.

308. In this line, two hemistichoi are each made of a two-word construct chain, with the construct word being a participle.

309. This strophe is a tricolon like 5.1. Each line begins with a 2ms verb (with נ as the first letter) + a noun with a 2ms suffix. The fact that it is a tricolon, combined with the fact that each line begins with נ (as does 15:11c), links the end of stanza 5 to the beginning of stanza 6.

310. Both the *qatal* (נָטִיתָ) and the *yiqtol* (תִּבְלָעֵמוֹ) can describe typical or common actions, and this is the case here. This is not a reference to the *Yam Suph* event (note that the earth, not the sea, swallows the enemies) and as such is not historical (past tense) in outlook. It asserts the general truth that God need only stretch forth his hand to destroy his enemies.

15:13a You lead[311] by your grace a people whom you have redeemed.
נָחִיתָ בְחַסְדְּךָ עַם־זוּ גָּאָלְתָּ 2-4-5

15:13b You guide [them] by your strength to your holy pastureland.
נֵהַלְתָּ בְעָזְּךָ אֶל־נְוֵה קָדְשֶׁךָ 1-3-4

Stanza 6.2[312]

15:14a [The] peoples hear; they tremble!
שָׁמְעוּ עַמִּים יִרְגָּזוּן 2-3-3

15:14b Agony grips the inhabitants of Philistia!
חִיל אָחַז יֹשְׁבֵי פְּלָשֶׁת 1-3-4

15:15a Next, the chiefs of Edom are terrified;
אָז נִבְהֲלוּ אַלּוּפֵי אֱדוֹם 1-3-4

15:15b [and] as for the leaders of Moab—trembling starts to seize them!
אֵילֵי מוֹאָב יֹאחֲזֵמוֹ[313] רָעַד 1-3-4

15:15c All[314] melt away—the inhabitants of Canaan!
נָמֹגוּ כֹּל יֹשְׁבֵי כְנָעַן 1-3-4

---

311. Robert Shreckhise, "The Problem of Finite Verb Translation in Exodus 15.1–18," *JSOT* 32, no. 3 (2008): 287–310, considers the *qatal* verbs of this section to be problematic and develops three possible solutions under a complex linguistic theory. In my view, the verbs are not particularly difficult or atypical. All refer to present time and may be translated with an English present tense.

312. This strophe has five lines; after the introductory line (15:14a) three lines refer successively to Philistia, Edom and Moab, and the final line refers to "all the inhabitants of Canaan." The five lines have an A-B-A-B-A pattern, in that the first, third and fifth lines each have verbs in which the peoples are the subjects (שָׁמְעוּ עַמִּים יִרְגָּזוּן ["peoples heard; they begin to tremble"]; נִבְהֲלוּ ["they are terrified"]; נָמֹגוּ ["they melt"]). By contrast, the second and fourth lines have אחז ("seize") as the verb and "agony" or "trembling" as the subject.

313. This *yiqtol*, from the root אחז, should be regarded as ingressive.

314. The word כֹּל could be (and usually is) regarded a construct, giving us "all of the inhabitants of Canaan." However, the construct usually appears as כָּל־, and this suggests that "the inhabitants of Canaan" may be appositional to כֹּל. Furthermore, this sets up a kind of chiasmus, with the appositional יֹשְׁבֵי כְנָעַן ending line 15c while the *casus pendens* noun phrase אֵילֵי מוֹאָב begins line 15b.

Stanza 7.1[315]

15:16a Let terror and dread fall upon them!
תִּפֹּ֨ל[316] עֲלֵיהֶ֜ם אֵימָ֗תָה וָפַ֙חַד֙ 1-3-4

15:16b At the great [power] of your arm, let them be dumb as stone!
בִּגְדֹ֥ל זְרוֹעֲךָ֖ יִדְּמ֣וּ כָּאָ֑בֶן 1-3-4

15:16c Until your people cross over, YHWH!
עַד־יַעֲבֹ֤ר עַמְּךָ֙ יְהוָ֔ה 2-3-3

15:16d Until this people whom you redeemed cross over!
עַד־יַעֲבֹ֖ר עַם־ז֥וּ קָנִֽיתָ 1-3-4

Stanza 7.2[317]

15:17a May you bring them and plant them on the mountain of your inheritance:
תְּבִאֵ֗מוֹ[318] וְתִטָּעֵ֙מוֹ֙ בְּהַ֣ר נַחֲלָֽתְךָ֔ 2-3-4

15:17b A specific place[319] [that] you made for you to inhabit, YHWH;
מָכ֧וֹן לְשִׁבְתְּךָ֛ פָּעַ֖לְתָּ יְהוָ֑ה 2-4-4

315. The poem shifts to a jussive mode, appealing to God to establish Israel as his habitation in the Promised Land. Thus, this should be considered a new stanza. But it is linked to the previous stanza by אֵימָתָה וָפַחַד, words that describe the dread felt by the Canaanites in the previous stanza. There is some semantic parallelism in the first two lines of the first strophe (15:16ab), with both lines referring to the enemies as paralyzed by fear. Both of the second pair of lines (15:16cd) begin with עַד־יַעֲבֹר עַם. But the four lines should probably be considered a quatrain, and not two bicola, because the second two lines depend on the first pair.

316. This *yiqtol*, being in the first position, should be considered jussive in force. It is not indicative; it is, in effect, a request. This suggests that יִדְּמוּ in 15:16b is jussive as well. At the same time, the similarity of this strophe to the previous strophe (6.2) links the two closely together. Moses prays that the demoralized state of the Canaanites will continue until Israel has taken possession of the land.

317. The three lines of this tricolon each refer to the place, mountain, or sanctuary where YHWH will dwell.

318. This *yiqtol* should be considered jussive.

319. The root כון essentially refers to making something "fixed" or "prepared." In this context, it means that a specific site has been chosen in advance.

15:17c A sanctuary, Lord, which your hand has specified.
מִקְּדָשׁ אֲדֹנָי כּוֹנְנוּ יָדֶיךָ 2-4-4

Stanza 7.3

15:18 May YHWH reign[320] forever and ever![321]
יְהוָה ׀ יִמְלֹךְ לְעֹלָם וָעֶד 1-3-4

15:19a For the horses of Pharaoh with his chariots and his horsemen went into the sea;
15:19b and YHWH brought the waters of the sea back on them,
15:19c but the Israelites walked on dry land through the middle of the sea.
15:20a Miriam the prophetess, sister of Aaron, took the tambourine in her hand,
15:20b and all the women went out after her with tambourines and with dancing.
15:21a And Miriam responded to the men[322] [in the song entitled]:[323]
15:21b "I will sing to YHWH for he is thoroughly majestic!
15:21c [The] horse and its rider he has hurled into the sea!"[324]

Structure

This passage is in four parts, as follows:

I. Introduction to the Song of the Sea (15:1ab)
II. The Song of the Sea (15:1c–18)
III. Explanation of the Background of the Song of the Sea (15:19)
IV. Miriam and the Women Sing the Song of the Sea (15:20–21)

The song itself is in four major divisions with seven stanzas. Each of the first three divisions contains two stanzas, and the fourth division

---

320. As a general rule, jussives are indicated by placing a *yiqtol* (in the apocopated form if the morphology of the root allows it) in the first position in a clause. However, in laudatory statements about God, a *yiqtol* often has jussive force even when not in the first position.

321. As 15:1cd serves also as the title and summarizing opening to the poem, so also 15:18 serves also as the summarizing conclusion to the poem.

322. The masculine plural suffix on לָהֶם suggests that Miriam and the women were singing in a responsive manner with the men.

323. What follows is not the whole content of Miriam's song. The words of 15:21bc are identical to the first two lines of the Song of Moses at 15:1cd, and should be regarded as a colophon serving as the song title.

324. See 15:1cd for poetic constraints.

contains only the seventh stanza, as described in Table 10. There is also a summarizing title (15:1cd) and summarizing conclusion (15:18).[325]

Each of the first three divisions begins with general praise for YHWH (Stanzas 1, 3, and 5) and is followed by specific historical examples from the *Yam Suph* and its effect on the nations (2, 4, and 6). The seventh stanza is a prayer for God to establish Israel and his own habitation in the land. This sevenfold structure is therefore analogous to the structure of the creation narrative. As is well-known, the six days are divided into two parallel sets of three each (with the light of day one parallel to the light-bearers of day four, the sky and sea of day two parallel to the fish and birds of day five, and the emergence of land and plants on day three parallel to the creation of land creatures and humanity on day six). The seventh day, the day of God's rest, typifies the Sabbath. The Song of the Sea also has three pairs of stanzas (although the arrangement of the pairs is not the same as in Gen. 1) with a seventh stanza describing the settling of God in his sanctuary in the land, giving Israel an abode of peace in the presence of God. The point here is not that the specific events of the creation week have parallels in the Song of the Sea. However, both begin with six stages in three pairs and, especially importantly, both end with a seventh that envisions a Sabbath rest of God. We should also note that both begin with a summarizing titular text (Gen. 1:1 in the creation narrative, analogous to 15:1cd in the Song of the Sea).

TABLE 10. THE STRUCTURE OF THE SONG OF THE SEA

Divisions of Song	Stanzas
I. (15:1cd–5)	1 (15:1cd–3) YHWH, the mighty God 2 (15:4–5) Victory over Egypt
II. (15:6–10)	3 (15:6–7) YHWH, the mighty God 4 (15:8–10) Victory over Egypt
III. (15:11–15)	5 (15:11) YHWH, the mighty God 6 (15:12–15) Israel moving; Canaan in terror
IV. (15:16–18)	7 (15:16–18) Rest in Canaan

325. For a very different analysis of the stichometry, using different criteria, see Frank Moore Cross, Jr. and David Noel Freedman, *Studies in Ancient Yahwistic Poetry* (Grand Rapids: Eerdmans, 1975), 31-45. For a more extensive analysis from Freedman, see David Noel Freedman, *Pottery, Poetry, and Prophecy: Studies in Early Hebrew Poetry* (Winona Lake: Eisenbrauns, 1980), 179-227.

Commentary

15:1ab. As suggested in the translation notes above, 15:1a probably means that the song dates from around the time of the *Yam Suph* event, not that they sang the song immediately after the drowning of the Egyptians.[326]

15:1c–5. Stanza 1 praises YHWH in general terms and stanza 2 praises him specifically for the acts at the *Yam Suph*. This first division of the song has three foci. First, it praises YHWH by name for being exalted (15:1a), powerful (15:2a), gracious to his own (15:2b), and a ferocious warrior (15:3a). Second, in the second stanza, it specifically speaks of the destruction of Pharaoh's army in the sea (15:4–5). Third, it is strongly personal, as strophes 1.2 and 1.3 (15:2) are dominated by first person nouns ("my strength and protection," "my salvation," "my God," "God of my father") and verbs ("I will praise him," "I will exalt him"). This third feature is the most striking and perhaps unexpected feature. God's victory over the enemies is "my salvation." God is not only great in himself, he is also great and good toward "me." The point of stanzas 1 and 2, in short, is that God's power manifests itself toward his people as salvation.

15:6–10. The second division of the song has two foci: the furious power that God directs toward his enemies, and the arrogant violence practiced by the enemies themselves. Stanza 3, with its general praise of God, speaks of the splendid displays of God's "power," how he shatters his enemies, and how his fury consumes them as a wildfire consumes stubble (15:6–7ab). These are again general statements and not specific to the *Yam Suph*. But stanza 4, in strophes 1 and 3, describes how these qualities have shown themselves specifically at the *Yam Suph*, with God first raising up the waters (strophe 4.1; 15:8) and then drowning the Egyptians (strophe 4.3; 15:10). Between these two, the enemy is presented in a series of first-person boasts as violent, greedy, and arrogant (strophe 4.2; 15:9 ["I will pursue; I will overtake"]). These first-person pretentions are the counterpart to the first-person celebration of God's salvation in strophes 1.2–1.3 (15:2). The point of stanzas 3 and 4 is that God's power manifests itself toward the wicked as destruction.

326. There is fairly strong agreement that The Song of the Sea is ancient. A major, recent study dates it to c. 1150 (Brian D. Russell, *The Song of the Sea: The Date of Composition and Influence of Exodus 15:1–21,* Studies in Biblical Literature 101 [New York: Peter Lang, 2007], 149).

15:11–15. Stanza 5 gives God general praise: he is greater than all other gods, awesome, and a worker of miracles. Stanza 6 is specific to the situation: God causes the earth to swallow the enemy's army, leads his people to their land, and fills the Canaanites with dread. There is thus a transition from the past and the defeated enemy, Egypt, to the present and the yet to be encountered enemy, Canaan. It would be a mistake, however, to regard stanza 6 as prophetic in nature. The point of strophe 6.2 (15:14–15) is not that the peoples of greater Canaan will be in fear, it is that they are afraid now. The three specific regions mentioned are all in the southern border regions of Canaan—Philistia[327] in the southwest, Edom in the southeast, and Moab in the southern territory east of the Dead Sea and the Jordan. These are all regions that Israel might first approach as it invades Canaan. As it turns out,

327. A historical problem is that the classical Philistines—Israel's great enemy during the time of Samson, Saul, and David—do not appear to have taken control of Philistia until Iron I, after their failed attempt to invade Egypt during the reign of Ramesses III (1184–1153). There are "Philistines" in southwestern Canaan in the book of Genesis (e.g., Gen. 26), but these Philistines appear to be Semitic rather than the Indo-European stock that confronted Saul and David (note that Isaac's nemesis Abimelech has a purely Semitic name, whereas the name of the Philistine with whom David dealt, Achish [1 Sam. 27:9], is not Semitic). Also, the "Philistines" of Genesis inhabit Gerar, southeast of the pentapolis of the classical Philistines of 1 Samuel. We cannot resolve this problem by claiming that Moses is speaking prophetically in the song since, as described in the comments above, Exod. 15:14–15 speaks of present inhabitants of the land and not of some future people. We should note, however, that the text speaks of the "inhabitants of Philistia" and not necessarily of the Indo-European Philistines. That is, it speaks of the current residents of that region and not of any ethnic identity. Furthermore, there may well have been pockets of Indo-European Philistines already in Philistia well before the war with Ramesses III; Judg. 3:31 tells how Shamgar killed a small number of Philistines early in the Judges period. Also, we cannot be sure when or how the name "Philistia" entered the language; the Old Testament simply refers to southwestern Canaan as "Philistia" regardless of the ethnic makeup of its inhabitants at any given time. It is possible that this usage of "Philistia" reflects an anachronistic updating of earlier toponyms, given that the term appears to be non-Semitic (see H. J. Katzenstein, "Philistines," in Freedman, *ABD* Vol. 5, 326–28). Be that as it may, the Song of the Sea is referring to a region, southeastern Canaan, which at that time may or may not have already had some Indo-European Philistines as inhabitants. But from the standpoint of regional nomenclature, whoever lived there was a "Philistine."

of course, the region that bore the brunt of Israel's initial assault on Canaan was Moab. At the same time, the text does speak of a broader fear that goes throughout the whole region, and not just the southern territories, at line 15:15c. Strophe 6.2 (15:14–15) also corresponds to strophes 1.2–3 (15:2) and strophe 4.2 (15:9), which describe the inner thoughts and attitudes of various persons. Strophes 1.2–3 have first-person celebrations of Israel (God is "my salvation"), and strophe 4.2 has the first-person boasting of Egypt ("I will overtake"). Strophe 6.2 has no first-person forms, but it is entirely focused on the inner attitudes of the peoples of Canaan—they are in terror. They seem to be too panic-stricken to think, and they cannot use the first person either to praise or to boast. They simply melt.

15:16–18. The final stanza of the poem begins with a jussive (see translation note to 15:16a), initiating a prayer that the Canaanites will continue to be paralyzed with fear until the Israelites have taken possession of the land. The future conquest of Canaan, in this prayer, will see a repetition of God's actions. As the Egyptians sank to the bottom of the sea "like a stone" (15:5b), the prayer is that the Canaanites will be as immobile as a stone (15:16b) until Israel has "crossed over" into Canaan. The crossing over (עבר) into the Promised Land is a mirror of Israel's crossing of the *Yam Suph*; both are works of God (see also the description of Israel's crossing [עבר] of the Jordan in Josh. 3). The prayer continues in strophe 7.2 (15:17) with its anticipation of Israel's settlement in the land. What is distinctive, however, is that it is God's residence in the land, rather than Israel's, that is the focus here. The land is YHWH's "inheritance" (נַחֲלָה). This term refers to a parcel of land that is a family's possession through all its generations. Even if the family should sell the land to pay a debt, they are to get the land back in the year of Jubilee (Lev. 25:13). Applied to God, the term "inheritance" means that this place is holy to him forever and the place of his sanctuary. Israel will be planted in *his* land; he does not come along with them into *their* land. The summarizing conclusion to the song (v. 18) indicates that God's great Sabbath, his "rest," goes on forever.

15:19–21. The prose conclusion to this text needs little exposition. Verse 19 tells us that the song is based in the events at the *Yam Suph*. Verse 20 tells us that Miriam was regarded as a prophetess and that she led the women of the camp in song. As mentioned in the translation notes to v. 21, Miriam and the women probably sang the entire Song of the Sea and not just the first two lines; the opening lines serve as a title. The men and women may have sung the song separately from one another, or together in something like harmony, or antiphonally.

Theological Summary of Key Points

1. The Song of the Sea is easily misread as pure triumphalism: "God is on our side, he hates our enemies, and he destroys them!" But to think in this way is to miss the theocentric outlook of the entire song. It is from the beginning praise to God for his power. The enemies he destroys are his enemies, not ours. The salvation he offers to his people is a gift; their virtue, and indeed even their faithfulness, never enters the song. The pride, violence and greed of the Egyptians are reasons for him to destroy them, but it is the evil of these men, not the goodness of their intended victims, that provokes God. The Canaanites, similarly, tremble because of God, and not because of Israel. At the end, God will lead Israel into his land, where they will dwell around his sanctuary. The election of Israel is not a matter of God choosing sides, so that he supports Israel in their wars against Egypt or Canaan. It is instead a matter of God, having chosen Israel, allowing them to enter his kingdom.

2. For the Christian, there is a theological link between the sea and baptism, as Paul mentions in 1 Cor. 10:2. As the Israelites were pursued by Egypt into the place of death and yet Israel emerged alive while Egypt perished, so also we have gone down into death with Christ and yet by his power we emerge alive, while death itself is swallowed in victory (1 Cor. 15:54).

3. The sevenfold structure suggested above for the song, with its finale at the sanctuary of God in his kingdom, has a strong parallel in the creation narrative and suggests that entering the land is understood to be entering God's great Sabbath. We should note, moreover, that Ps. 95:11 describes the entry into Canaan after the exodus as entering his "rest." Sadly, the generation that sang the Song of the Sea alongside Moses did not enter his rest, but died in the wilderness ("I swore in my anger, they will not enter into my rest"). That should give us great pause, should we be tempted to think of the song in triumphalist terms (1 Cor. 10:5–6). The Christian should not read the song with any smugness. Rather, we should have a holy fear, lest we, too, fail to enter his rest (Heb. 3:9–4:9).

4. The portrayal of the human participants in this song (Israelites, Egyptians, and Canaanites) is instructive.

a. The first group, from the first division, may be called the elect, the saved, or simply the grateful. These are those who are thankful for God's salvation. Their focus is entirely upon the power and goodness of God. Beside the fact that they have received God's grace, they are hardly aware of themselves at all. God is their strength and salvation.

b. The second group, from the second division, are the evil. They are intensely focused upon themselves, as in stanza 4.2 ("I will . . . I will . . ."). Destruction comes upon them suddenly and inescapably.

c. The third group is the fearful; these are the Canaanites of the third division who are "petrified"—like stone—with terror. Their fear is not a proper fear of God but a fear of losing what they possess—their homes, their pleasures, their land, and their lives.

The coming of the kingdom of God is an occasion for celebration and for dread. For some it is "my salvation," and for others it is "my death."

PART IV

The Journey to God (15:22–19:25)

This stage of the narrative describes the journey from the *Yam Suph* to Mt. Sinai. It is laid out as a pilgrimage or journey in six stages, followed by a seventh, at which they arrive at the mountain. At each of the six stages along the way there is problem or crisis, and each of these six episodes formally contains all or some of the following elements:

I. Setting (the initial problem of the narrative, often with a geographical marker)
II. Speech (one or more persons makes a speech relative to the situation)
III. Deliverance (YHWH averts the crisis through Moses)[1]
IV. Lesson (an explicit statement of the significance of the event)
V. Journey or Memorial (the first and last episodes end with a journey account [respectively, "Israel goes to Elim" and "Jethro goes home"] but the other four episodes all end with a memorial act involving the naming of a place or some ritual act, such as a sacrifice)

The seventh stage breaks the pattern of the six. The structure corresponds to the structure of the creation week and to the structure of the Song of the Sea as described above—six elements followed by a seventh that is different. This suggests that the journey to Sinai is deliberately structured to represent the pattern of entering into God's "rest." That is, Israel is on a journey to God, and they have come to the

1. There is no explicit deliverance in the fifth episode, and in the sixth episode the deliverance is actually brought about by Jethro.

place of rest when they arrive at Sinai. In addition, there is an inclusio structure to the seven stages; both the first and seventh stage include an oracular poem from YHWH (15:25e–15:26g and 19:3c–6d).

FIRST STAGE: A BITTER DISAPPOINTMENT (15:22–27)

Israel becomes embittered when the springs they come to yield only bitter water. YHWH shows Moses how to make the water potable and warns the people that they should have confidence in YHWH's leadership.

Translation

15:22a Then Moses led Israel from the *Yam Suph*,
15:22b and they went out into the wilderness of Shur;
15:22c and they travelled for three days in the wilderness,
15:22d and they did not find water.
15:23a And they came to Marah,
15:23b but they could not drink the water of Marah,
15:23c for it was bitter;
15:23d therefore, they called its name "Marah."
15:24a And the people complained about Moses, saying,
15:24b "What are we supposed to drink?"
15:25a And he cried out to YHWH,
15:25b and YHWH instructed[2] him [about] a tree;
15:25c and he threw [it] into the water,
15:25d and the water became sweet.

Fourth Poem: YHWH Your Healer

Strophe 1

15:25e There he made for them a statute and ruling,
שָׁם שָׂם לוֹ חֹק וּמִשְׁפָּט 1-4-5

15:25f And there he tested them and said,
וְשָׁם נִסָּהוּ׃[3] וַיֹּאמַר[4] 2-3-3

Strophe 2

2. This verb (ירה [III], Hiphil stem) is usually translated here as "showed," but it plainly means "instructed" or "taught." The normal Hebrew verb for "show" is the Hiphil of ראה.

3. The colometry proposed here goes against the cantillation, which has silluq at this point.

4. This strophe is held together by the consonance of שם שם . . . ושם

15:26a "If you will listen carefully to the voice of YHWH your God,
אִם־שָׁמ֨וֹעַ תִּשְׁמַ֜ע לְק֣וֹל ׀ יְהוָ֣ה אֱלֹהֶ֗יךָ 1-2-5

15:26b And do what is right in his eyes,
וְהַיָּשָׁ֤ר בְּעֵינָיו֙ תַּעֲשֶׂ֔ה 1-3-3

15:26c And pay attention to his commands,
וְהַאֲזַנְתָּ֙ לְמִצְוֺתָ֔יו 1-2-2

15:26d And keep all his statutes,
וְשָׁמַרְתָּ֖ כָּל־חֻקָּ֑יו 1-2-2

Strophe 3

15:26e [Then] all of the disease that I set upon Egypt
כָּֽל־הַמַּחֲלָ֞ה אֲשֶׁר־שַׂ֤מְתִּי בְמִצְרַ֙יִם֙ 1-4-4

15:26f I will not set upon you;
לֹא־אָשִׂ֣ים עָלֶ֔יךָ[5] 1-2-2

15:26g For I, YHWH, am your healer."[6]
כִּ֛י אֲנִ֥י יְהוָ֖ה רֹפְאֶֽךָ 0-3-3

15:27a And they came to Elim.
15:27b And twelve springs of water and seventy date palms were there,
15:27c and they camped there beside the water.

Structure

The first episode sets forth the structure that will govern episodes 1 through 6. In addition, it has an oracular poem from YHWH, something that will happen again in the seventh episode, at Sinai.

I. Setting: No Potable Water in Shur (15:22–23)
II. Speech: The People Complain (15:24)
III. Deliverance: YHWH Shows Moses the Tree (15:25abcd)
IV. Lesson: The Test of Faithfulness (15:25e–26)
V. Journey: Israel Goes to Elim (15:27)

---

5. The use of שׂים in the third strophe forms an inclusio with the use of the same verb in the first strophe.
6. The cantillation suggests this translation rather than, "For I am YHWH who heals you."

The song of vv. 25e–26 is in three strophes. The first, a bicolon, introduces the oracle of YHWH (v. 25ef; וַיֹּאמֶר from v. 26 belongs with 25f as it is part of the introduction of the divine speech). The second strophe, a quatrain, is the first part of YHWH's speech and is the protasis of a conditional statement (v. 26abcd). The third strophe, a tricolon, gives the apodosis of YHWH's speech (v. 26efg). The song contains various examples of matching and repetition. For example, the verb שׂים ("to set") brackets the poem, being in the first strophe (v. 25e) and twice in the third strophe (v. 26ef). The final line, v. 26g, serves as colophon and motto for the poem; it describes YHWH as "your healer" and also has the familiar אֲנִי יְהוָה ("I am YHWH") from the poem of Exod. 6:2–8. In the first strophe, the word שָׁם ("there") opens both lines of the bicolon, and the two lines have syntactic parallelism. The four lines of the second strophe have an A-B-A-B parallelism (listen [תִּשְׁמַע], do [תַּעֲשֶׂה], pay attention [וְהַאֲזַנְתָּ], keep [וְשָׁמַרְתָּ]).

Commentary

15:22–23. After the crossing of the *Yam Suph*, the people made their way to Shur. Most interpreters locate this area in the northwestern part of the Sinai Peninsula, but this is almost certainly wrong. For further discussion, see Excursus: The Location of Shur, below. Unfortunately for the Israelites, there was no potable water in the immediate vicinity, and their supplies began to run low. When they finally found water, it was not potable because it was "bitter" (that is, it had a high level of salt). They called the waters there "Marah" (מָרָה, Hebrew for "bitter" and the same name by which Naomi calls herself in Ruth 1:20). They complained to Moses, and he turned to God.

15:24. It is easy to read every failure of the Israelites into their complaining here, but one should resist doing that. Running low on water in the desert is a serious and urgent problem, and people with their families and livestock can hardly be expected to be casual about such a thing. Nevertheless, the text plainly does present their behavior as a spiritual failure. But their primary failure was not so much that they "grumbled" as it was that, rather than taking their complaints to God, they instinctively directed their anger at Moses. They did not understand that God was their true leader and that Moses was only his agent.

15:25abcd. Moses, unlike the people, goes immediately to God for help. There are two ways to interpret the sweetening of the water by means of putting a "tree" in it. One is that this was simply a miraculous changing of the water, and that the use of the tree was a ritual act. There are, after all, analogous water miracles in the Bible, such as Jesus's turning water into wine. Two factors speak against a miraculous interpretation, however. First, Moses almost always used his rod for the ritual initiation of an act of God. There are exceptions to this; e.g., he threw soot in the air to initiate the plague of boils (Exod. 9:9–10). But even that was a clear ritual act; the soot evidently symbolized a malignancy spreading through the air to settle on all the people and livestock. It is not clear, however, what would be the symbolic link between a tree and the sweetening of water, and one would think that the rod would have been used had the work been strictly a miracle. More significantly, the text says that God "instructed" Moses (15:25b; see translation note). This suggests not a command to carry out a ritual act but a lesson in how to purify such waters. The verb "teach" or "instruct" normally implies telling someone how to do something that they may repeat, doing it as many times as desired or necessary. One may "teach" a person how to build a campfire or how to ride a bicycle. By contrast, YHWH did not "teach" Moses how to part the waters of the sea with his staff; he simply commanded him to do it. After the one occasion, the parting of the waters of the *Yam Suph*, Moses could have lifted his rod all he wanted, and the waters there would not have parted. If the action of purifying the waters was replicable, then it either had to involve practical wisdom (similar to the knowledge of how to build a campfire), or it was a matter of magic. In contrast to a biblical miracle, magic is (supposedly) replicable. If one knows the right words to say, or has the right object (an amulet, a potion, or some magical tool such as a divining cup), then one may go through the proper routine and repeat the magic as often as desired. But the Bible deals in divine miracles, not in magic. A miracle is an act of God and it cannot be coerced by any words, objects, or rituals. Even if there is ritual involved (such as the lifting of a rod), the ritual is a speech-act, a kind of acted out prayer; it is not the manipulation of an object that has control over God or supernatural powers. God will do what he chooses to do. If "teach" does imply a repeatable act, the throwing of the "tree" into the water had to be a matter of practical wisdom, since magic is by definition illicit in the Bible.

The second interpretation, therefore, is that God instructed Moses practically in how to deal with the situation. The word "tree" (עֵץ), we should note, has a wide range of meaning in the Bible. It can be a tree, brambles, or cut pieces of wood. It need not have been an entire tree. It turns out that wood charcoal, especially charcoal from the Acacia trees that are common in that part of Arabia, are useful for desalinating water.[7] Thus, it may be that God instructed Moses to place charred Acacia wood[8] in the water and thereby make it fit for drinking. Against this interpretation, the text does not specify that the wood should be charred. It may be, however, that the text simply means to emphasize that deliverance came by a word from God and therefore does not go into specifics about how the actual purification came about. Either interpretation is possible, but the use of "instructed" favors the second view.

15:25e–26. The lesson of the episode is given in a poem of three strophes. God "tested" Israel to see how they would respond to a difficulty, and he used this episode to reinforce the point that they were under his care and he would not bring them to ruin, as he did to the Egyptians. The words "commands" and "statutes" anticipate the arrival at Sinai, where Israel would receive the Law. A threat is also implied here, that if Israel disobeys, they will suffer from all the afflictions of Egypt. Amos 4:10 asserts that this threat was fulfilled.

15:27. For now, however, God does not curse Israel with the afflictions of Egypt. Instead, they leave Marah behind and arrive at Elim, an oasis with palm trees and abundant water. This is a token of the good things they can expect from God if they are obedient.

Theological Summary of Key Points

1. God tests his people to see if they look to him in time of need. There are also seasons of prosperity, as indicated by the oasis at Elim, that God gives his people in order to induce them to do right by positive encouragement.

2. As a general rule, a life of obedience to God leads to well-being and disobedience leads to woe. There are exceptions to this, as when God is testing someone who fears him. Prosperity is not necessarily a sign of God's approval and hardship is not necessarily a sign of one's guilt. But the general rule, as described in the oracular poem of vv. 25–26, is still true.

3. The Marah episode is an apt metaphor for the believer's pilgrimage, as everyone goes through experiences both of the Marah variety and of

---

7. Humphreys, *Miracles*, 267–73.
8. The word עֵץ can mean "log" and need not refer to an entire tree (Sarna, *Exodus*, 84).

the Elim variety. This echoes 1 Pet. 1:6–7, that we rejoice in our election even though now we endure various trials, knowing that these trials refine faith as fire refines gold.

4. It would have been better for Israel to have cried out vigorously and with some protesting to God than to mumble against Moses. At least then they would have been clear about who was responsible for their well-being. The prayers of the Psalms can be extraordinarily direct (e.g., Ps. 42:9; 44:23), but the important point is that the psalmist, even when distraught, is looking to God for help. The fact that the Israelites were distressed was no great offense; being low on water for themselves, their children and their livestock was very hard, and finding water that turned out to be impossible to drink would be bitter indeed. Their offense was their complete reliance upon, and subsequent hostility toward, Moses. Their focus should have been on God.

5. If, as suggested above, YHWH taught Moses how to desalinate water by means of charred wood, it illustrates the fact that God desires us to become more competent at dealing with difficult situations through practical wisdom. This is especially important for leaders.

6. The song of vv. 25–26 anticipates the Sinai covenant and Deuteronomic theology, with its emphasis on finding life by obeying God or finding death by defying him (see Deut. 5:33; 6:2; 30:15–16). This is apparent both in the heavy emphasis on obeying God's commands and in the contrast between the diseases that afflicted Egypt and YHWH serving as the "healer" of Israel.

Excursus: The Location of Shur

The land of Shur is mentioned in Gen. 16:7; 20:1; 25:18; 1 Sam. 15:7; 27:8; and this passage. Scholars typically claim it to be in the area just southwest of Philistia and east of the Egyptian frontier, in the northwestern Sinai Peninsula,[9] primarily on the grounds that Gen. 25:18 and 1 Sam. 15:7 (in most translations) describe it as "east of Egypt." If Shur is directly adjacent to and east of the Egyptian frontier, the *Yam Suph* needs to be situated in the region of the Ballah Lakes or Bitter Lakes, as many contend. But this is certainly wrong. The Hebrew term translated as "east" in both verses is עַל־פְּנֵי, which more literally means

9. E.g., Rainey and Notley, *Sacred Bridge*, 113.

"opposite" or "facing."[10] But whether one translates it as "opposite" or as "east of," the expression עַל־פְּנֵי מִצְרָיִם is a slim basis for locating either Shur or the *Yam Suph*. The phrase does not require one to think that Shur abutted Egypt; it means that it was somewhere east of, or opposite, Egypt.

Both Gen. 25:18 and 1 Sam. 15:7 connect Shur to Havilah. Havilah is near the Garden of Eden according to Gen. 2:11; it is probably in southwestern Arabia, although the Havilah of 1 Sam. 15:7 could be in northwestern Arabia.[11] At any rate, Havilah is in western Arabia. Shur, therefore, needs to be in the same general region.

1 Samuel 27:8 states that the Geshurites, Girzites, and Amalekites "dwell in the land [that they have dwelt in] from antiquity, as you travel toward Shur, and up to the land of Egypt."[12] The ESV translation of this verse ("as far as Shur, to the land of Egypt") treats the two phrases "as you travel toward Shur, and up to the land of Egypt" as in apposition to one another and, in effect, as a single region. This is incorrect, and it proceeds from the assumption that Shur is on the edge of Egypt. If Shur were itself between Canaan and the frontier of Egypt, this would give the Geshurites, Girzites, and Amalekites a very small domain (just the area southwest of Israel, between Gaza and the Egyptian frontier), and at any rate the statement would be historically inaccurate. The Amalekites ranged all the way across the southern Levant and into Arabia; they were not confined to territory adjacent to the eastern Egyptian Delta. 1 Samuel 27:8 is given from the perspective of someone standing in southern Israel. He would see that the domain of the Amalekites extends (toward the southeast) to Shur and (toward the southwest) to the frontier of Egypt.

1 Samuel 15:7 states, "And Saul defeated the Amalekites from Havilah, [the place] on your way to Shur that is opposite Egypt." The phrases "from Havilah . . . Egypt" probably describe not the places where Saul fought (it is unlikely that Saul ventured either into Arabia or to the frontier of Egypt) but the domain of the Amalekites. That is, the verse means, "And Saul struck the Amalekites, [who come] from Havilah." It is known that the Amalekites ranged across the southern territory from Edom and the Arabah to the Negev and the area south

10. One might argue that it means "east" on the grounds that the Israelites were oriented toward the east, and thus that עַל־פְּנֵי would mean, "on the east side of." However, *HALOT* (פָּנֶה, 3.943) declares the meaning "east" for עַל־פְּנֵי to be "doubtful."
11. W. W. Müller, "Havilah (Place)," In Freedman, *ABD* Vol. 3, 82.
12. So translating הִנֵּה יֹשְׁבוֹת הָאָרֶץ אֲשֶׁר מֵעוֹלָם בּוֹאֲךָ שׁוּרָה וְעַד־אֶרֶץ מִצְרָיִם.

of Philistia (1 Sam. 30). On the other hand, Shur, which is "opposite Egypt" does not locate Shur beyond stating the fact that it is somehow "opposite" Egypt. This does not mean that it abuts Egypt, as is made clear in the following text.

Genesis 25:18 is more complete in its presentation of geographical data. Referring to the Ishmaelites, it says: "They settled from Havilah to Shur, which is opposite Egypt as one goes toward Assyria." Here, Shur is "opposite Egypt as one goes toward Assyria." While it is true that one could take the Via Maris through Philistia, into Canaan, and (if one veered east) past Damascus, and eventually arrive at Assyria, it seems highly doubtful that one would refer to the territory of the northwestern Sinai Peninsula as being "on the way to Assyria." The verse should be taken to mean that Shur is "opposite Egypt as one goes [from Havilah] to Assyria." This sets Shur north of western Arabia (or Havilah) and astride the highway connecting Arabia to the King's Highway, which skirts Canaan east of the Jordan River and bends northeastward toward Assyria. In other words, it places Shur in the Great Rift region of the Arabah. In this interpretation, it is not surprising that the text mentions Assyria, since the King's Highway bypasses the more populated territory west of the Jordan as it heads into Mesopotamia. Shur is no more adjacent to Egypt than it is adjacent either to Assyria or to Havilah in western Arabia, but these three regions triangulate the location of Shur. "Opposite Egypt," that is, opposite the Delta, should therefore be understood to provide what we would call an approximate latitude for Shur. That is, it was along the corridor from Havilah in western Arabia to Assyria in northern Mesopotamia, and it was "opposite Egypt," i.e., on roughly the same latitude as the Egyptian Delta. The homeland of the Ishmaelites was in the area of the Arabah and northwestern Arabia, and not right up against Egypt.

Locating Shur in the Great Rift region of the Arabah is further indicated by the fact that the name "Shur" (שׁוּר) means "wall," and this is an apt description for the sheer cliff face that dominates this part of the Arabah. In short, therefore, "Shur" is not located near the Ballah Lakes or the frontier of Egypt. It was the area in the immediate vicinity of the northern edge of the Gulf of Aqaba, which is where the *Yam Suph* needs to be located. If the Gulf of Aqaba is the *Yam Suph*, and if the Israelites crossed it at its northern tip, then Shur is properly located in this area.

SECOND STAGE: A GREAT NEED (16:1–36)

Israel runs short of food and complains, and they are given the manna as provision. At the same time, the Sabbath is instituted. Although this text is obviously similar to Num. 11, it should not be regarded as a doublet of that story. The function of the Numbers text is to demonstrate the extent of discontent within Israel and the severity of the punishment they faced. The Exodus text has no real focus on punishment and serves to explain the beginning of Sabbath observance.[13]

Translation

16:1a And they set out from Elim,
16:1b and the whole congregation of the Israelites came to the wilderness of Sin, which is between Elim and Sinai, on the fifteenth day of the second month of [the year of][14] their departure from the land of Egypt.
16:2 And the whole congregation of the Israelites complained against Moses and Aaron in the wilderness.
16:3a The Israelites said[15] to them,
16:3b "If only we had died by the hand of YHWH in the land of Egypt, when we sat by the kettles of meat, when we ate bread until we were full!
16:3c But you brought us out to this wilderness to kill this whole assembly with hunger."
16:4a And YHWH said to Moses,
16:4b "Well then![16] I will rain bread from heaven for you.
16:4c And the people shall go out[17]
16:4d and they will gather a day's portion on its day,
16:4e that I may test them [to determine this]:
16:4f 'Will they walk in accord with my instruction or not?'
16:5a It will happen on the sixth day
16:5b that when they prepare what they are going to bring in,
16:5c it will be double of what they gather from day to day."

---

13. For another comparison of Exod. 16 to Num. 11, see Paul W. Ferris, Jr., "The Manna Narrative of Exodus 16:1–10," *JETS* 18, no. 3 (1975): 197.
14. A number of translations render בַּחֲמִשָּׁה עָשָׂר יוֹם לַחֹדֶשׁ הַשֵּׁנִי לְצֵאתָם מֵאֶרֶץ מִצְרָיִם as "on the 15th day of the 2nd month after their departure from Egypt." This would make the calendar date approximately the first day of the third month. But on the basis of Num. 1:1 and 9:1, it is more likely that לְצֵאתָם is short for "(the year of) their departure" and that בַּחֲמִשָּׁה עָשָׂר יוֹם לַחֹדֶשׁ הַשֵּׁנִי is a calendar reference, not a reckoning of time since their departure.
15. This is an epexegetical *wayyiqtol*.
16. The particle הִנֵּה here suggests that what follows is both a response to the complaining of the Israelites and a surprising act. YHWH will do something that neither Moses nor the people could have expected.
17. The *weqatal* וְיָצָא is directive, serving as a third person imperative.

16:6a And Moses and Aaron said to all the Israelites,
16:6b "At evening—then you will know[18]
16:6c that YHWH has brought you out of the land of Egypt;
16:7a and at morning—then you will see the glory of YHWH, in his response[19] to your complaints against YHWH.
16:7b But what are we,
16:7c that you complain against us?"
16:8a And Moses said,
16:8b "When YHWH gives you meat in the evening to eat, and bread in the morning to satiate [your hunger], when YHWH responds to your complaints that you have been making against him—
16:8c but what are we?[20]
16:8d Your complaints are not against us but against YHWH."
16:9a And Moses said to Aaron,
16:9b "Say to all the congregation of the Israelites,
16:9c 'Gather before YHWH,
16:9d for he has heard your complaints.'"
16:10a And it came about, as soon as Aaron spoke[21] to the whole congregation of the Israelites,
16:10b that they looked toward the wilderness,
16:10c and there it was, the glory of YHWH appeared in the cloud!

18. It appears that this clause (עֶ֫רֶב וִֽידַעְתֶּם) is a protasis-apodosis structure that has been cut short. The full form perhaps would have been וְהָיָה בְּעֶרֶב וִֽידַעְתֶּם, but Moses uses clipped speech out of exasperation.
19. בְּשָׁמְעוֹ אֶת־תְּלֻנֹּתֵיכֶם is more literally, "when he hears your complaints," but in context, to "hear" means to give evidence that he has heard; i.e., when he responds to their complaints.
20. The sentence in 16:8bc is an anacoluthon (a sentence in which one grammatical construction is abandoned midway through a sentence, so that the resulting sentence is not fully coherent). Its use here reflects Moses's exasperation, and it should not be smoothed out in translation.
21. The words וַיְהִי כְּדַבֵּר here mark the termination of a subnarrative within the larger narrative of 16:1–36. This subnarrative of 16:1–10 introduces the story and has the conflict between Moses and the people as its focus. The second subnarrative begins at 16:11 and focuses on the miraculous provision. The two narratives cover some of the same material. In 16:11–12, the second narrative refers back to Moses's interview with YHWH after the people complained, an event described also at 16:4–5 in the first narrative. In other words, 16:11–12 is not a new word from YHWH, spoken from within the glory at 16:10. It is retrospective to the previous encounter.

16:11 And YHWH had spoken[22] to Moses the following:
16:12a "I have heard the complaints of the Israelites.
16:12b Speak to them, as follows:
16:12c 'At twilight you shall eat meat,
16:12d and in the morning you shall be sated with bread;
16:12e so that you may know
16:12f that I am YHWH your God.'"
16:13a And it came about at evening
16:13b that the quails came up
16:13c and they covered the camp,
16:13d and in the morning the layer of dew was[23] around the camp.
16:14a And the layer of dew evaporated,
16:14b and—how about this![24]—on the surface of the wilderness there was a thin, crunchy substance[25]—thin like the frost on the ground.
16:15a And the Israelites looked,
16:15b and they said to each other,
16:15c "What is that?"
16:15d For they did not know what it was.
16:15e And Moses said to them,
16:15f "That is the bread that YHWH gives to you for food.
16:16a This is the command that YHWH has given,
16:16b 'Let each one gather from it what he needs to eat.
16:16c You can take an omer[26] per head, based on the number of persons each has in his tent.'"[27]

---

22. Use of the pluperfect in translation reflects the fact that 16:11–12 refers to the dialogue in 16:4-5. See the note to 16:10a.
23. In 16:13ab the pattern is וַיְהִי בָעֶרֶב וַתַּעַל (using the *wayyiqtol*), whereas in 16:13d the pattern is הָיְתָה (using the *qatal*). The point is that conceptually the two events are one miraculous provision of food, even though they did not occur at the same time. A series of *wayyiqtol* verbs would have emphasized the sequential nature of the events.
24. הִנֵּה here connotes something surprising, as in "What do you think about this?" This is the vivid language of the storyteller, not solemn, "religious" language.
25. The hapax legomenon מְחֻסְפָּס is apparently related to Arabic *hasafa*, "to crackle," a word that is used of snow (חספס, *HALOT*, 1.338).
26. The dry measure "omer" (עֹמֶר) is mentioned only here in Exod. 16, although v. 36 does specify that it is one tenth of an ephah, a more frequently mentioned unit of measure. Estimates vary, but the omer seems to have been equal to about 2 liters.
27. The idea is not that every person necessarily ate one omer per day, but that the total amount each household got was based on the number of

16:17a The Israelites did so,
16:17b and one person gathered much and another person gathered little.
16:18a And they measured it with an omer,
16:18b he who had gathered much had no excess,
16:18c and he who had gathered little had no lack;
16:18d each one had gathered what he needed to eat.
16:19a And Moses said to them,
16:19b "No one should keep any leftover until morning."
16:20a But they did not listen to Moses,
16:20b and some people kept leftovers for morning,
16:20c and it bred worms
16:20d and it became nasty.
16:20e And Moses became frustrated with them.
16:21a Each one gathered what he needed to eat morning by morning,
16:21b but then the sun would get hot,[28]
16:21c and it would melt.
16:22a And it turned out that on the sixth day[29]
16:22b they gathered twice as much bread, two omers per person.
16:22c And all the leaders of the congregation came
16:22d and they told Moses [about it],
16:23a and he said to them,
16:23b "That is what YHWH indicated.
16:23c Tomorrow is a sabbatical day, a holy Sabbath to YHWH.
16:23d Bake what you want to bake
16:23e and boil what you want to boil,
16:23f and set aside whatever is left over to be preserved until morning."
16:24a And they put it aside until morning,
16:24b just as Moses commanded,
16:24c and it did not become nasty
16:24d and no worm appeared in it.
16:25a And Moses said,
16:25b "Eat it today,
16:25c for today is a Sabbath to YHWH.
16:25d Today you will not find it in the field.

---

persons in the household. Thus, a household of five would get five omers, but some members (such as small children) may have eaten less, while others may have eaten more, from that total.

28. The *weqatal* (וְחַם) in a past tense context typically describes recurrent events.

29. The clause וַיְהִי בַּיּוֹם הַשִּׁשִּׁי marks a minor structural break; see the parallel in 16:27a.

16:26a Six days you shall gather it,
16:26b but on the seventh day, [the] Sabbath, there will not be any of it."
16:27a And it turned out on the seventh day[30]
16:27b [that] some of the people went out to gather,
16:27c but they did not find any.
16:28a And YHWH said to Moses,
16:28b "How long will you [people][31] refuse to keep my commands and my instructions?
16:29a Observe
16:29b that YHWH has given you the Sabbath.[32]
16:29c That is why he gives you bread for two days on the sixth day.
16:29d Each person must stay where he is;
16:29e no one is to go out of his place on the seventh day."
16:30 And the people rested on the seventh day.
16:31a And the Israelite community called its name "manna."
16:31b And it was white like coriander seed,
16:31c and its taste was like wafers with honey.
16:32a And Moses said,
16:32b "This is the command that YHWH has given,
16:32c 'An omer [is to be set aside] for safekeeping throughout your generations,
16:32d so that they may see the bread that I fed you in the wilderness, when I brought you out of the land of Egypt.'"
16:33a And Moses said to Aaron,
16:33b "Take a jar
16:33c and put a full omer of manna in it,
16:33d and deposit it before YHWH for safekeeping throughout your generations."
16:34a Just as YHWH commanded Moses,
16:34b Aaron placed it before the Testimony for safekeeping.
16:35a And the Israelites ate the manna for forty years, until their arrival at a habitable land;
16:35b they ate the manna until their arrival at the border of the land of Canaan.
16:36 An omer is a tenth of an ephah.

---

30. The clause וַיְהִי בַּיּוֹם הַשְּׁבִיעִי marks a minor structural break; see the parallel in 16:22a.
31. The verb is plural; the complaint is not against Moses personally.
32. This is an indirect statement.

Structure

The structure of this narrative is much more complex than the other texts of the journey narrative because it includes not only an account of a crisis along the way but also an account of the beginning of the observance of the Sabbath. It is thus analogous to the report of the plague on the firstborn in 11:1—12:15, where we have both the miracle account and a series of directives that relate to Passover. Here, the miracle serves to introduce the Sabbath. In addition, it has a lengthy description of the manna itself.

I. Setting: In the Wilderness of Sin (16:1)
II. Speech: The People Complain of No Food (16:2–3)
III. Deliverance: YHWH Sends Quail and Manna (16:4–26)
  A. First Subnarrative: Moses Vindicated Before the People
    1. God's Response to Moses (16:4–5)
    2. Moses Answers the People (16:6–8)
    3. A Theophany (16:9–10)
  B. Second Subnarrative: The Nature of the Manna (16:11–21)
    1. YHWH's Directive Repeated (16:11–12)
    2. Quail (16:13abc)
    3. Manna (16:13d–21)
IV. Lesson: The Beginning of the Sabbath (16:22–30)
  A. Gathering on the Sixth Day (16:22)
  B. Moses's Response (16:23–26)
  C. Gathering on the Seventh Day (16:27)
  D. God's Response (16:28–29)
  E. Sabbath Observance Begun (16:30)
V. Memorial: The Preserved Manna (16:31–36)
  A. Manna Described (16:31)
  B. Manna Memorial (16:32–35)
  C. Note about the Omer (16:36)

Commentary

16:1. The Wilderness of Sin is said to be located somewhere between Elim and Sinai, and we have no basis for being more specific than that. Obviously the text has skipped over travel days of no narrative significance. The date of Israel's arrival at Sin is debatable. It could be one and one-half months after their departure from Egypt (which took place on the fifteenth day of the first month, at Passover).[33] This would place their arrival at Sin on about the first day of the third month of

33. Durham, *Exodus*, 218.

their calendar year. It is more likely, however, that "on the fifteenth day of the second month" is intended as a calendar reference (see translation note at 16:1b). Thus, they arrived at the Wilderness of Sin one month after the exodus. Having been on the move for one month, the Israelites were low on food.

16:2–3. The narrative proceeds directly to the people's complaint without giving any particulars concerning how much food they had in their supplies. One should probably not make too much of their saying that they wish that they had died "by the hand of YHWH." It is an expression of frustration and anger, as when one says, "I wish to God I had died." It is not a literal statement of their desires. But it is significant that they had fallen into a habit of complaining, and that they were at least being loose with God's name, if not actually taking it in vain.

16:4–5. YHWH's response does not show any anger, although he does indicate that the provision of food, besides being an act of grace, will also serve to test their loyalty to him. The nature of the test is in their willingness to obey his instructions that they should not keep any leftovers from one day to the next, and that they should not try to gather on the seventh day. Both commands test their willingness to trust YHWH for daily provision.

16:6–8. Moses's response indicates considerable agitation on his part. This is to be expected and realistic; the strain of leading all the people through a wilderness and of being responsible for their safety would be enormous. His contention that the people are complaining not against him but against YHWH is based on the fact that YHWH, not Moses, is the true leader of the people. This helps us to understand his otherwise confusing claim, "then you will know that YHWH has brought you out of the land of Egypt." From all the signs and wonders that had already taken place, the people surely already knew that they had been brought out of Egypt by YHWH. But Moses is not concerned with their cognitive recognition of the fact that YHWH delivered them; his point is that they need to start regarding God and not Moses as the commander of the expedition.

16:9–10. We cannot know what the "glory of YHWH" in the cloud looked like, only that it was something that the people recognized as a sign of the presence of God. "The cloud" is possibly the pillar of cloud that led the people, but if so, something new in its appearance made it obvious that God was present in it. This visible presence of God's glory in the cloud confirmed Moses's contentions that YHWH and not Moses had guided the nation and that their complaints were really directed to God. This closes the first subnarrative, having made its points that when the Israelites find themselves in difficult straits it is because God has taken them there—not because of any failing on Moses's part—and that they must trust God implicitly and stop blaming Moses.

16:11–12. This text restates God's word to Moses from 16:4–5. It begins the second subnarrative and should not be regarded as a new word from God to Moses. The text does not indicate that God spoke from the glory that the people observed in 16:10. Rather, the narrative backtracks to God's earlier commands.

16:13abc. This is the only mention of quail in this chapter; clearly the narrative focus is on the manna. Here, unlike Num. 11, there is no indication that the people were punished while eating the quail. In an annual spring migration, quail travel from Africa northward towards eastern Europe and western Asia via the Nile valley, the Sinai Peninsula, or northwest Arabia. This would have brought quail into the vicinity of the Israelites.

16:13d–21. The account of the manna is straightforward but remarkable. A number of interpreters suggest that manna was the secretion of the tamarisk plant, but the properties of manna defy natural explanation. Manna appeared in the early morning hours, like dew, and continued to appear for the Israelites wherever they were in their wilderness wanderings. That is, it kept coming regardless of the season and regardless of the local terrain, indicating that manna was not related to local vegetation. It ceased coming at the end of the wilderness wanderings. The fact that it had to be described for posterity tells us that later generations could not find it by venturing into the wilderness. If kept for more than a day, it would spoil and breed worms (16:20). But on the Sabbath it did not become foul and could be safely stored (16:24). Manna that was not gathered but left on the ground melted away in the heat of the day (16:21). In appearance it was delicate, like hoarfrost (16:14). Nevertheless, it could be ground and used as a meal for baking, and it could be boiled, possibly like noodles in a soup (16:23). Therefore, although it could not withstand the heat of the sun, it retained its qualities when baked or boiled. Finally, as people ate their allotted share, it always satisfied their hunger. It was never more than they could eat and it never left them hungry (16:17-18). The text may even imply that try as they might, the people had difficulty gathering more than an omer per person per day, except on the day before Sabbath, when they easily gathered two omers per person (16:22). We can only conclude that, as the text says, it was of heavenly origin.

16:22. Apparently some of the leaders of the people were sensitive to the problem of people trying to hoard manna, and so reported it to Moses. They were not yet used to the idea of a Sabbath day; this is the beginning of the observation of the Sabbath. Thus, leaders in the community who did not yet grasp the concept of the Sabbath thought that people who took in a double portion on the sixth day were violating God's command, when in fact they were not.

16:23–26. Moses reassured his assistants that there was no problem with the people taking a double portion on the sixth day since the following day would be a Sabbath. Furthermore, he instructed them to do their main meal preparation, the baking or cooking of the manna, on the sixth day so that it would not have to be prepared on the Sabbath. The instructions given here do not repeat the fact that on the sixth day they would get a double portion of manna, allowing them an excess to be kept over for the seventh. But that point has already been made in v. 5 and v. 22.[34] Beyond the command that they not engage in labor, the Israelites were not required to do anything special for the Sabbath. It is noteworthy that Israel's introduction to the Sabbath principle comes at a time when their food came directly from God and they did not have to engage in normal agricultural labor, such as planting, harvesting, and threshing grain. The lesson of the Sabbath is total dependence on God.

16:27. The negative counterpart to the extra gathering on the sixth day is the attempt by some to gather on the seventh day. The Sabbath was a new concept to these people, and they were slow to realize the seriousness of the injunction.

16:28–29. The counterpart to Moses's response in vv. 23–26 is YHWH's response here. He shows exasperation with their slowness to

34. Some source critics exaggerate supposed differences between vv. 5 and 23, allowing them to allege that they come from different sources. This is needless. See W. A. M. Beuken, "Exodus 16:5, 23: A Rule Regarding the Keeping of the Sabbath?" *JSOT* 32 (1985): 3–14.

learn and obey, but he does not punish them. Verse 29 succinctly states what the Sabbath was all about: they were to rest, stay at home, and enjoy the provision that God offered.

16:30. This verse describes not a single event, but the end result of a process. Israel finally got used to the idea of the Sabbath and began to practice it as God directed.

16:31–36. This episode concludes with a summary of the nature of manna. These verses appear to have come from a later period, since they could not have put an omer of manna "before YHWH" (that is, in the Tent of Meeting) until after they had come to Mt. Sinai and made the tent and its furnishings (the term "the Testimony" [הָעֵדֻת] in 16:34b is shorthand for the "Ark of the Testimony" [אֲרֹן הָעֵדֻת] that sat inside the Holy of Holies). Also, the description of the manna is clearly meant for people who had never seen or tasted manna firsthand. It may be that manna was put into the tent just prior to the invasion of Canaan, when the gift of manna was about to end (see Josh. 5:12). It was named by the Israelites "manna" after the Hebrew מָן, "what," because they said, "What is that?" (מָן הוּא) when they first encountered it (16:15).

Theological Summary of Key Points

The primary lesson of this text is that one must learn to depend upon God. That is the essence of both the idea of the Sabbath and of the command that the Israelites not hoard manna. The petition "Give us today our daily bread" (Matt. 6:11) expresses the principle of daily dependence on God and is rooted in the manna experience. Other lessons are as follows.

1. We are quick to complain when things start to go badly. Of course, often things go badly because of our own missteps, but sometimes, as in this narrative, God's people come into hardship by God's own leading and for his purposes. An important purpose in the pilgrimage that God leads his people through is that they must learn to trust him, and the only way to teach this lesson is through testing and hardship.

2. The people of God must recognize the sovereignty of God in all things. This is not fatalism, nor does it absolve anyone of personal responsibility, but it does mean that we must recognize that all things are ultimately in God's power. Having such an attitude ought to diminish our tendency to complain and increase our capacity for faith and inner strength when in the midst of troubles.

3. The works of God ought to be remembered, as implied by both the description for later generations of what the manna was like, and by the storage of an omer of manna in the Tent of Meeting. In the New Testament, the great memorial of the work of Christ is the Eucharist, in which the body of Christ is portrayed, manna-like, as bread.

THIRD STAGE: AN URGENT CRISIS (17:1-7)

Israel is desperately short of water and is at the point of rioting. YHWH shows Moses how to get water from a rock by striking it.

Translation

17:1a	And all the congregation of the Israelites set out from the wilderness of Sin in the course of their journeys at the command of YHWH,
17:1b	And they camped at Rephidim,
17:1c	and there was no water for the people to drink.[35]
17:2a	And the people quarreled with Moses:
17:2b	they said,[36]
17:2c	"Give us water
17:2d	that we may drink!"[37]
17:2e	And Moses said to them,
17:2f	"Why do you quarrel with me?
17:2g	Why do you test YHWH?"
17:3a	And the people thirsted there for water,
17:3b	and they complained against Moses,
17:3c	and they said,
17:3d	"Why is it that you have brought us up from Egypt—to kill me[38] and my children and my livestock with thirst?"
17:4a	And Moses cried out to YHWH, saying,
17:4b	"What can I do with this people?

35. This offline clause with וְאֵין gives background information.
36. Epexegetical *wayyiqtol*.
37. The imperative in 17:2c (תְּנוּ) establishes this reported speech as directive. The *weyiqtol* in 17:2d (וְנִשְׁתֶּה) is offline and serves as a purpose clause.
38. The change from the first plural suffix in הֶעֱלִיתָנוּ to the first singular suffixes in אֹתִי וְאֶת־בָּנַי וְאֶת־מִקְנַי is striking. It is perhaps meant to convey the agitation of the people, who are shouting to Moses not simply as a mass but also as individuals.

17:4c A little more and they will stone me."
17:5a And YHWH said to Moses,
17:5b "Pass in front of the people
17:5c and take with you some of the elders of Israel
17:5d and your staff, with which you struck the Nile—take [that] in your hand,[39]
17:5e and proceed.
17:6a Get this: I will be standing[40] before you there on the rock at Horeb![41]
17:6b And you are to strike the rock,
17:6c and [then] water will come out of it,
17:6d so that the people can drink."[42]
17:6e And Moses did that right in front of the eyes of the elders of Israel.
17:7a And he called the name of the place Massah and Meribah on account of the Israelites' quarreling and on account of their testing of YHWH by saying,
17:7b "Is YHWH among us, or not?"

Structure

The essential structure of this section follows the basic outline of crisis narratives seen throughout 15:22—18:27.

I. Setting and Crisis: No Water (17:1)
II. Speeches: The People Dispute with Moses (17:2–4)
III. Deliverance: Water from the Rock (17:5–6)
IV. Memorial: The Names Massah and Meribah (17:7)

What is distinctive here is the prominence given to the speeches of

39. The fronting of וּמַטְּךָ in this clause makes it the focus of the clause.
40. This clause is offline, being a periphrastic participle within a series of commands. It is explanatory, telling Moses why he is to do all the things commanded. In this context, הִנֵּה marks the clause as decisive and prominent. It is YHWH's presence that guarantees that Moses's actions will have the desired effect.
41. "Horeb" is here evidently the region in which Mt. Horeb (Mt. Sinai) was found, and not the mountain itself, since they had not yet arrived there. Humphreys, *Miracles*, 321, suggests that "the rock in Horeb" is the Tadra, the table mountain on which Mt. Sinai sits. He observes that the Tadra is sandstone and so would have held an enormous quantity of water.
42. The three *weqatal* clauses of 17:6bcd illustrate three uses of the *weqatal*. וְהִכִּיתָ from 17:6b is imperatival, following the mainline of the previous commands found in 17:5. וְיָצְאוּ of 17:6c marks the apodosis to the implied protasis of 17:6b. In 17:6d, וְשָׁתָה is a purpose clause.

the principal characters (the people, Moses, and YHWH). The flowing of the water in response to Moses's striking of the rock is not even described in the narrative; the reader is expected to understand that everything happened as YHWH said it would. The speeches therefore dominate the text.

Commentary

17:1. The location of Rephidim is unknown; where one places it depends entirely on where one locates Mt. Sinai. As indicated in the Introduction to the commentary (see The Location of the *Yam Suph* and Mt. Sinai), I consider an Arabian location for Mt. Sinai to be most likely. If this is correct, Rephidim is somewhere close to the Tadra region of western Arabia.

17:2–4. As described above, speeches dominate this text. The speeches of the people and Moses have a parallel pattern, as follows:

- First cycle (17:1–2)
  - Problem: no water (17: 1)
  - People's demand (17:2abcd)
  - Moses's response to the people (17:2efg)
- Second cycle (17:3–4)
  - Problem: people thirsty (17:3a)
  - People's anger (17:3bd)
  - Moses's response to God (17:4)

The anger and danger of violence spirals upward in these two cycles. In the first cycle, the people are merely without water, but in the second cycle, they are experiencing serious thirst. They went from recognizing that they were running out of water to experiencing parched throats and exhausted bodies. Realizing that their situation was becoming desperate, they began to panic. The people in the first cycle merely demanded water (17:2cd), but in the second round, they bitterly and sarcastically accused Moses of indifference to their deaths (17:3d). Moses had first tried simply to rebuke them at 17:2efg, but in the second round at 17:4c, he understood that they were ready to stone him and so he turned to God. God's speech at 17:5–6 terminates the escalating spiral of reproach and resolves the problem. One should note that Moses almost lets the situation get out of hand in 17:2efg. His rebuke, that they should not test YHWH, is true enough, but not adequate for the situation. His outburst in 17:2f seems especially weak ("Why do you quarrel with me?"). He should have realized that the people quarreled with him because he was the leader. That is, he bore responsibility for the well-being of those he was over. He needed to take charge. We should also observe that in the Marah episode (15:22–27) he did not try to argue with them but immediately cried out to God for help, and the situation never reached the boiling point that it does here.

17:5–6. God commands Moses to strike the rock with his rod. Before that, however, he must assemble the people and, in the presence of the elders, do everything in as public a manner possible. This is to display Moses's leadership in resolving the crisis. That is, no one is to have any doubt that it was Moses's decisive action that solved the problem. This enhances Moses's status and helps avert their anger toward him. In short, God not only saved the people, he saved Moses's leadership. Regarding the water from the rock, it is now well-known that porous desert rocks, particularly sandstone, can hold a good deal of water,[43] and that Bedouin shepherds exploit this by striking the rock walls with their staffs to cause them to release their water.[44] Thus, the water that came from the rock at Rephidim may not have been created *ex nihilo* on the spot but may have been present there by natural means; this is especially more likely if Rephidim was just below the water-laden Tadra area of Arabia. That is, the "rock at Horeb" was the sandstone mountain on which the Tadra sits.[45] God led Moses to the right spot and told him what to do. The people, who were not desert shepherds but had, for generations, lived in the Delta of Egypt, taking water at their ease from the Nile, knew nothing of desert survival.

This episode helps us better to understand the sin of Moses at Num. 20:11–12, where Moses instead of simply speaking to the rock struck it with his staff and so lost the privilege of entering Canaan with Israel. Interpreters have spilt a great deal of ink trying to explain the nature of Moses's sin. In fact, the text plainly states that it was unbelief (Num. 20:12 ["because you did not believe in me"]). Inducing a rock to give water by just speaking to it would indeed involve a purely supernatural work of God, but Moses apparently lacked faith and so stuck with the tried-and-true method of hitting the rock. Thus, the

---

43. Sandstone is the best of all natural aquifers, having both high porosity and high permeability.
44. Hoffmeier, *Ancient Israel*, 170-1.
45. Humphreys, *Miracles*, 321. The description suggests that the Tadra is a perched water table.

somewhat more natural process of the Exod. 17 event explains how greater faith was demanded in Num. 20.

17:7. The memorial act here is the two names signifying Israel's rebellious attitude toward God and Moses. The way stations of this pilgrimage thus are as likely to mark failures as they are to mark successes.

Theological Summary of Key Points

1. God is compassionate to the people. He does not rebuke the people for their attitude. Their bitter words perhaps came out of their severe thirst and not from rational thought. God's patience in such circumstances is described in Ps. 103:14: ("For he knows our frame; he is mindful that we are but dust").

2. The thirst at Rephidim was an emergency. The people were not simply disappointed at the poor quality of the water, as at Marah; they had no water at all. People cannot survive without water, and their plight was made the more urgent by the suffering of their children and the threat to their livestock. Thus, they were on the brink of open rioting and violence. Such a situation calls for leadership and calm. When Moses's leadership was wavering, he regained it by calling on God. Ultimately, no leader is truly competent for all the troubles that can befall a people. Leadership fails without God.

3. The lesson in leadership has special application to the Christian minister. No one is adequate to lead God's people apart from God's help. Paul actually boasted of his weakness so that the power of Christ would be more readily evident in his life (2 Cor. 11:30).

4. Notwithstanding the terrible situation they were in, the people had seen mighty works of God that had brought them out of Egypt and had kept them alive in their journey. Thus, their defiance of God was still wrong, as it always is. The memorial names to this incident bear testimony to their lack of faith and obedience. Similarly, the seven churches of Rev. 2—3 are each memorialized in the text of Scripture for either faithfulness or the lack of it.

5. The inability of the people to restrain themselves from vocal and angry protests made their later, more catastrophic failures all the more likely. A submissive and patient spirit is stronger than a vocal, self-centered one. The strength of a patient spirit is most evident in the life of Christ. He withstood hunger in the wilderness in patient submission to God. He was thus able to withstand satanic temptations and finally to endure Calvary and the cross.

FOURTH STAGE: A SUDDEN WAR (17:8–16)

The next crisis is open warfare. The placement of this text here indicates that the battle took place at Rephidim, just before Israel arrived at Sinai. This was the second crisis at Rephidim, since they also suffered from having exhausted their water supply here. The two events may be related; the Amalekites may have attacked Israel because they perceived them to be weakened by thirst.

Translation

17:8a And Amalek came
17:8b and fought against Israel at Rephidim.
17:9a And Moses said to Joshua,
17:9b "Choose men for us
17:9c and go out;
17:9d fight against Amalek tomorrow.[46]
17:9e I will stand[47] at the top of the hill
17:9f and the staff of God will be in my hand."
17:10a And Joshua did as Moses told him, giving battle[48] against Amalek.
17:10b But Moses, Aaron, and Hur went up[49] to the top of the hill.
17:11a It was turning out that[50]

---

46. Against the clause division implied by the cantillation marks, it makes more sense for "tomorrow" to be with 17:9d rather than 17:9e.
47. The participle clause אָנֹכִי נִצָּב is offline, indicated what Moses will be doing while Joshua goes out to fight. It is also explanatory, reassuring Joshua that Moses will be making use of the rod in Joshua's behalf during the battle.
48. The infinitive construct לְהִלָּחֵם is here explanatory, describing how or in what respect Joshua did as Moses said. This usage is analogous to the epexegetical *wayyiqtol*.
49. This clause, using the ו + X + *qatal* pattern, is contrastive and prominent (it would be neither, had the text used a *wayyiqtol* pattern). Their act of going up the hill, seemingly contributing nothing to the battle, is the decisive event.
50. וְהָיָה sets out the major protasis and employs the *weqatal* (as opposed to the *wayyiqtol*) to indicate that what happened was a process that was developing or repeated a number of times.

17:11b whenever Moses would raise up his hand,[51]
17:11c Israel would prevail,[52]
17:11d but whenever he would set his hand down,
17:11e Amalek would prevail.
17:12a But Moses's hands were heavy;[53]
17:12b and they took a stone
17:12c and they put it under him
17:12d and he sat on it,
17:12e but Aaron and Hur supported his hands,[54] one on this side and one on the other.
17:12f And his hands were steady until the sun set.
17:13 And Joshua routed Amalek and his people with the edge of the sword.
17:14a And YHWH said to Moses,
17:14b "Write this as a memorial in the book—
17:14c and be sure that Joshua hears[55] it—
17:14d that I will completely obliterate the memory of Amalek from under heaven."
17:15a And Moses built an altar
17:15b and he called its name "YHWH My Standard."
17:16a He said,
17:16b "[It has this name] because[56] 'A hand [is] on the standard of Yah!'[57]

51. The *yiqtol* כַּאֲשֶׁר יָרִים both serves as a protasis and indicates repeated events.
52. The *weqatal* וְגָבַר both serves as an apodosis and indicates repeated events.
53. The offline verbless clause וִידֵי מֹשֶׁה כְּבֵדִים is background information, explaining why Aaron and Hur had to get a rock for Moses to sit upon.
54. The shift to the ו + X + *qatal* pattern here makes Aaron and Hur more prominent than would be the case had a *wayyiqtol* pattern been used.
55. Lit. "and set it in the ears of Joshua." The idea appears to be that Joshua, who fought a long battle against Amalek, particularly deserves to hear God's promise.
56. The word כִּי is explanatory, giving the reason for Moses's choice of a name for the altar.
57. The phrase יָד עַל־כֵּס יָהּ could mean "a hand on the throne of Yah," if one may take כֵּס as equivalent to כִּסֵּא. A number of translators believe that the hand on the throne signifies swearing an oath. Understanding the hand to be YHWH's hand, some translate the line as "The Lord has sworn" (KJV; NASB). Others understand the hand to be Moses's; they take it to mean that Moses is raising his hand and swearing an oath. Thus, the HCSB has, "Indeed, my hand is lifted up toward the Lord's throne." In no other text, however, is the swearing of an oath indicated by raising a hand (יָד) to a

17:16c YHWH is at war against Amalek from generation to generation!"

Structure

The structure here follows the normal pattern for the pilgrimage to Sinai narratives, as follows.[58]

I. Setting: War with Amalek at Rephidim (17:8)
II. Speech: Moses Gives Marching Orders to Joshua (17:9)
III. Deliverance: Holding Up the Staff (17:10–13)
IV. Lesson: YHWH Forever Against Amalek (17:14)
V. Memorial: The Altar (17:15–16)

Commentary

17:8. While Israel was encamped at Rephidim, on the outskirts of the territory around Mt. Sinai, they were suddenly attacked by Amalekites. But who were the Amalekites? There was an Amalek, son of Eliphaz and grandson of Esau (Gen. 36:9-12), suggesting that they were a clan of the Edomites. But the Amalekites already appear much earlier, in the lifetime of Abraham and well before the birth of Esau (Gen. 14:7). Balaam, in an oracle, says that the Amalekites were one of the earliest

throne (with כִּסֵּא or כֵּס). Thus, the whole idea that an oath is in view here is dubious. The TNIV takes it in an entirely different direction, understanding the hand to be lifted in hostility and so translating it, "Because hands were lifted up against the throne of the LORD." This is conceivable but not compelling. Moses's words are to be taken as an explanation for his name of the altar, and there is no reason for him to mention a throne. The LXX has, "For the Lord fights against Amalek with a secret hand" (*ὅτι ἐν χειρὶ κρυφαίᾳ πολεμεῖ κύριος ἐπὶ Αμαληκ*), apparently reading כְּסִיָּה for כֵּס יָהּ and lacking עַל. It is likely that the MT does contain a scribal error, but not as represented in the LXX. It seems that the text should read נס ("standard") rather than the anomalous כס. Thus emended, יד על נס יה ("a hand on Yah's standard") is probably a war cry, and the point is that the name of the altar, "YHWH My Standard," solemnizes the perpetual state of war that now exists between Israel and Amalek. This solution is adopted in the RSV and NRSV. The fact that כס is not elsewhere attested as an equivalent for כִּסֵּא supports emending the text.

58. Bernard P. Robinson, "Israel and Amalek: The Context of Exodus 17:8–16," *JSOT* 32 (1985): 15, sees a chiastic structure here with the raising of Moses's arms at the center of the structure. This is not objectionable, as Moses's lifting of his arms is obviously at the center of the narrative, and it is not incompatible with the structure described here.

of the nations (Num. 24:20), something that could not be said of an Edomite clan.

Amalekites lived in the Negev, south of Israel (Num. 13:29), and in Ishmaelite territory in western Arabia, between Havilah and Shur (1 Sam. 15:7). In Judg. 6:33 and 7:12, they are linked to tribes from the deserts of the east and of Arabia, the Midianites and Qedemites (or, "easterners"). Saul fought with Amalekites near the village of Carmel in the Judean hill country (1 Sam. 15:12). In David's lifetime the Amalekites appeared in the Negev, and they carried out a raid on Ziklag in the lowlands of western Judah (1 Sam 30:1). 1 Chronicles 4:42-43 mentions an attack on a small group of Amalekites living near Mt. Seir, in Edomite territory. According to Judg. 6:5, they characteristically rode camels when making raids; this is in keeping with the picture of them as outlaws in the desert. It may be that "Amalekite" was simply a term applied to a loose confederation of desert raiders from the Arabah regions south and east of Israel, and from Arabia. Possibly the name "Amalekite" in biblical narrative is derived from Amalek, grandson of Esau, and he serves as their eponymous, albeit not actual, patriarch. If so, the name has been affixed to desert pirates who fit this description, regardless of the actual tribal origin of any particular group of "Amalekites," and even if they lived prior to the time of Amalek himself.

17:9. In his instructions to Joshua, Moses does not specify why he is going to the top of the hill with the rod in his hand. From the historical context of the plagues of Egypt and the crossing of the *Yam Suph*, however, both Joshua and the reader understand that Moses, by means of the rod, will invoke divine power against the Amalekites as he watches the battle.

17:10–13. Apparently the battle went on for some time, and observers on the hill could readily see when an advantage was gained by one side or the other. The text is altogether uninterested in conveying information about the size of the armies, the tactics they used, their armaments, and whether either side was mounted. The only information about the terrain is that there was a hill near the battlefield. It is the impact of Moses's raising or lowering of the rod, and no other consideration, that determines the outcome.

17:14. The long-term outcome of the battle is that Israel is eternally at war with Amalek. YHWH will obliterate Amalek, but this is not merely a prediction about divine activity. It is a charge that Israel must give no quarter to the Amalekites. This conflict will reappear throughout the early history of Israel, as in Gideon's war with Midianites and Amalekites and in the battles against the Amalekites waged by Saul and David. Most importantly, however, the mandate to exterminate Amalek comes from God himself. It is not just a matter of ancient feuds between two rival peoples. It was for failure to keep this charge fully that Saul lost his crown (1 Sam. 15:20–26). God gives Moses an injunction to read this charge to Joshua because he, as Moses's successor, will have the task of continuing the war against Amalek and of passing on the charge to his successors.

17:15–16. Moses builds an altar to solemnify Israel's acceptance of the charge to destroy Amalek. The making of an altar implies the offering of sacrifices, and these imply a sacred bond between Israel and God, analogous to a covenant, to the effect that neither will show mercy to Amalek. In other words, the altar and its implied sacrifices formalizes the state of perpetual warfare between Israel and Amalek. Moses explains the name of the altar, "YHWH My Standard," by saying it refers to a battle cry, "A hand on the standard of Yah!" (see translation note to 17:16b) that is to be raised up against the Amalekites.

Theological Summary of Key Points

1. The most prominent feature of this narrative is Moses' upholding of the staff. Victory, for Israel, is from God. It is not a matter of having the stronger army.

2. The assistance given by Aaron and Hur to Moses implies that even in spiritual conflict, one needs the assistance of others. Obviously what made Moses's arms heavy was gravity, and the only thing that Aaron and Hur actually did was hold up his arms. But the image is an apt metaphor for one man, in a spiritual conflict, being supported by others. Christian readers properly see Moses's lifting of the rod as an analogy to prayer. Moses does not work alone, but has others to help him (by analogy, he has others to pray with him). Paul, in 2 Thess. 3:1–2 urges the Thessalonian Christians to pray for him in his ministry "because not everyone has faith." Prayer for those enduring persecution, as well as prayer for those in literal military service, also fulfill the principles of this text.

3. For the ancient Israelite, the enduring animosity between Israel and Amalek is a primary message of this text. They are not to make peace with Amalek, or indeed to give them any quarter in battle. The hostility between the two is absolute.

4. Amalek's attack upon Israel was reckless folly. They become Israel's eternal enemies and placed themselves and all their offspring under God's curse. Acts of evil can have terrible and long-term repercussions. Jesus, answering those who claimed that his miracles were of satanic origin, warned that blasphemy against the Holy Spirit would not be forgiven (Matt. 12:31). He also spoke to the people of Jerusalem who drove him to the cross, warning them of the calamity that would soon befall them all (Luke 23:28–31).

FIFTH STAGE: A DIFFICULT ENCOUNTER (18:1–12)

This episode seems to have actually taken place at Mt. Sinai during Israel's encampment there. The text explicitly says as much at 18:5. The account of Moses's receiving the Torah from God and passing it on to Israel (18:20) also implies that this episode is from a later period, after Israel had accepted the terms of the Sinai covenant. In addition, Deuteronomy 1:11–18 indicates that the appointment of a hierarchy of subordinates under Moses and the organization of Israel into thousands, hundreds, fifties, and tens (see Exod. 18:24–27) took place just before Israel's departure from Sinai, not before they arrived at the mountain. We must account, therefore, for the transposition of this episode to this point in the narrative. The most reasonable interpretation is that Jethro's status as a Midianite (culturally and perhaps racially close to the Amalekites) explains the current arrangement of the text. That is, the warfare with the desert people in 17:8–16 contrasts with the friendship with the desert people here. This is explored further below, but we should note that there are two aspects of Jethro's encounter with Moses that are awkward. First, Jethro is a pagan priest, and second, as a Midianite he is closely associated with the now-hated Amalekites. On both scores, being Moses's father-in-law, he could be a source of embarrassment to Moses.

Translation

18:1a And Jethro, the priest of Midian, the father-in-law of Moses, heard about everything that God had done for Moses and for Israel his people,

18:1b [specifically,] that YHWH had brought Israel out of Egypt.[59]

59. This line is an indirect statement.

18:2–3a And Jethro, the father-in-law of Moses, took Zipporah, the wife of
Moses, after his dismissal[60] of her, and her two sons,
of whom one was named Gershom,[61]
18:3b (for Moses said,
18:3c "I am an alien in a foreign land")
18:4a and the other was named Eliezer,
18:4b (for [Moses said],
18:4c "The God of my father was my help,
18:4d and he delivered me from the sword of Pharaoh.")
18:5 So[62] Jethro, the father-in-law of Moses, and [Moses's] sons and his
wife came to Moses in the wilderness where he was making his
camp, at the mountain of God.
18:6a And he said to Moses,

---

60. It is difficult to determine whether the noun שִׁלּוּחֶיהָ here signifies a divorce or simply a sending away of Zipporah for her own safety. In post-biblical Hebrew the word means "divorce." In biblical Hebrew it only occurs three times: here, in 1 Kings 9:16, and in Micah 1:14. Stuart, *Exodus*, 405, argues that the latter two occurrences are in a "neutral" or "positive" context, and that it is therefore unlikely that the word here has the "negative" meaning, "divorce." But this is not persuasive. שִׁלּוּחִים in 1 Kings 9:16 is used for the dowry of the pharaoh's daughter. While this might be regarded as a "positive" usage, it may equally be regarded as signaling the legal and permanent departure of the bride from her parents' home and thus as analogous to divorce. Micah 1:14 is certainly not "positive" in meaning; תִּתְּנִי שִׁלּוּחִים עַל מוֹרֶשֶׁת גַּת ("give parting gifts to Moresheth Gath") effectively means, "Say your goodbyes to Moresheth Gath," a town which is about to be destroyed. This, too, implies the permanent rupture of a relationship. In addition, the noun שִׁלּוּחִים is a formation of the Piel stem of שׁלח, which, as a verb, regularly means to "divorce" when used in the context of a man's relationship to his wife (Deut. 24:1; 21:14; Isa. 50:1; Jer. 3:1, 8). Also, Stuart, *Exodus*, 405, states that the Hebrew word for "divorce" is כְּרִתֻת, and that since this word is not used here, this is not a divorce. But this is not quite accurate; the phrase סֵפֶר כְּרִיתֻת refers to documentation, the "certificate of divorce" (Deut. 24:1, 3). But the action of divorcing a woman is signified by שׁלח, for which the noun form could be שִׁלּוּחִים. Thus, on linguistic grounds alone, there is justification for translating שִׁלּוּחִים as "divorce." I have rendered with the more neutral "dismissal," however, since the matter of whether this is a divorce is not resolved on lexicographic grounds alone. See the commentary for further discussion.
61. The sentence is made of three clauses (2–3ab and 4a) that are interrupted by two sets of parenthetical clauses (3cd and 4bcd).
62. The *wayyiqtol* here is resumptive of the narrative after the asides describing the significance of the names of Moses's sons. It does not carry the mainline narrative forward.

18:6b “I, your father-in-law Jethro, am coming to you,
18:6c [and I have] your wife and her two sons with her.”
18:7a And Moses went out to meet his father-in-law,
18:7b and he bowed down
18:7c and he kissed him.
18:7d And they enquired after one another’s welfare
18:7e and they went into the tent.
18:8a And Moses recounted to his father-in-law about all that YHWH had done to Pharaoh and to the Egyptians for the sake of Israel, about all the hardship that had befallen them on the journey,
18:8b and [that] YHWH delivered them.
18:9 And Jethro rejoiced over all the good that YHWH did for Israel, that he delivered them from the hand of the Egyptians.
18:10a And Jethro said,
18:10b “Blessed be YHWH, who snatched[63] you from the hand of the Egyptians and from the hand of Pharaoh, [and] who snatched the people from beneath the hand of the Egyptians!
18:11a Now I know[64]
18:11b that YHWH is greater than all the gods
18:11c because of the story of how [the Egyptians] seethed against [the Israelites].”[65]
18:12a And Jethro, the father-in-law of Moses, took a burnt offering and sacrifices for God,
18:12b and Aaron and all the elders of Israel came to eat a meal with the father-in-law of Moses before God.

---

63. The Hiphil of נצל frequently means to “deliver” someone from trouble, but here the literal meaning of “snatch” seems more appropriate, as the idea seems to be that YHWH pulled Israel out of the Egyptians’ grasp.

64. The phrase עַתָּה יָדַעְתִּי is often used when someone comes to realize that a person or group has a special relationship to God. See Judg. 17:13; 1 Sam. 24:21(20); 1 Kings 17:24; Ps. 20:7(6). In Gen. 22:12 God uses the phrase of Abraham. Here, Jethro recognizes the elect status of Israel before God.

65. Exodus 18:11c, כִּי בַדָּבָר אֲשֶׁר זָדוּ עֲלֵיהֶם, is difficult, and translations vary greatly. Some help is given by Neh. 9:10, which appears to cite this verse. From Nehemiah, it is clear that the subject of זָדוּ is the Egyptians and that the antecedent of the suffix on עֲלֵיהֶם is the Israelites. This leaves כִּי בַדָּבָר אֲשֶׁר to be interpreted. The simplest understanding of דָּבָר is that it is the story that Moses had been telling. Jethro summarizes the gist of the story by describing the rage of the Egyptians against Israel, the implication being that Israel could have survived this only by divine help.

Structure

This passage is a straightforward narrative of events, in which there is a direct sequence going from Jethro's hearing about Moses's exploits, to his bringing Moses's wife and children to the camp, and to the encounter between Moses and Jethro, and finally to Jethro's sacrifice to YHWH. Apart from the reported speech, there is little here beside a simple sequence of *wayyiqtol* verbs. The climactic moment in the narrative thus comes in the reported speech itself and particularly in the exclamation of Jethro: "Now I know that YHWH is greater than all the gods." This is in response to Moses's recounting all the hardship Israel endured and how YHWH had delivered them (18:8). But Moses's actual words are not given; Jethro's are.

Unfortunately, our eyes are distracted to the question of the relationship between Moses and Zipporah. We should recognize that, however fascinating it is to us, that issue is not the main point of this narrative. It is rather that Jethro confesses that YHWH is God, that he sacrifices to YHWH, and that even Aaron, high priest of Israel, attends a sacrifice in which the priest of Midian officiates. This passage follows, in an abbreviated manner, the same formal structure that dominates all the pericopes of 15:22—18:27. The "crisis" is that Moses, the leader of Israel, is publicly confronted with the fact that he is closely linked to a pagan, Midianite priest. The "deliverance" is in the confession that YHWH is the one, true God.

I. Setting and Crisis: Jethro the Midianite Father-in-Law of Moses (18:1–6)
II. Speech and Deliverance: Moses's Testimony Jethro's Response (18:7–11)
III. Memorial: Jethro Sacrifices to YHWH (18:12)

Commentary

18:1–6. It comes as quite a surprise to the reader to discover that Moses's wife and sons have not been with him all along. We were never told that they had left. The last time we saw them (Exod. 4), they were heading to Egypt with Moses, and the text never says that the wife and children separated from him or turned back. More surprising yet is the phrase "after his dismissal of her" in 18:2. This language could be taken to refer to a divorce (see translation notes to 18:2). Were Moses and Zipporah divorced or separated?

An obvious argument against believing that Moses and Zipporah were divorced is the fact that the text calls Zipporah Moses's "wife" and calls Jethro his "father-in-law." On the other hand, Hebrew does not seem to have had a term for "ex-wife." By analogy, Abigail, whom David married after the death of her husband Nabal, is consistently called the "wife of Nabal" even after Nabal had died and she had become David's wife (1 Sam. 27:3; 30:5; 2 Sam. 2:2; 3:3). A peculiar feature of the narrative is how often it reminds us that Jethro was Moses's father-in-law; the term חֹתֵן ("father-in-law") occurs no less than seven times in 18:1–12! This is not merely using "father-in-law" as an alternative designation to the name "Jethro," since he is three times called "Jethro, the father-in-law of Moses." The text is determined to point to this relationship as much as possible. This could be taken as proof that Moses and Zipporah were not divorced. But it seems to be overkill, like "protesting too much," and it is difficult to know what to make of all this repetition. It may be, in fact, that the frequent reference to Jethro's status as Moses's father-in-law has no bearing on the divorce question at all, as discussed below. Thus, although the use of the words "father-in-law" and "wife" on balance favor the interpretation that they were not divorced, it is not decisive.

We should not try to get behind the text and describe Jethro's motive for announcing that he was coming with Moses's wife and sons (18:6). The language could be taken to be either a joyful announcement of the reunion of the family (there was no divorce) or a plea for reconciliation (there was a divorce or separation). Nor do we have any basis for getting at the details of Moses's domestic life. If there was a divorce, it may have been Zipporah who initiated it (the fact that a divorce is legally described as a man giving a bill of divorce to a woman does not mean that a woman could not initiate divorce; we know that in Egypt, for example, a woman could divorce her husband). We do not know when and why she went back to her father Jethro. It is doubtful that the episode of Exod. 4:24–26 had anything to do with it. Apart from the fact that the traditional interpretation of that passage has serious problems (see commentary above), if that episode caused Zipporah to part from Moses and go back to her father, we might have expected the text to mention it. In fact, Exod. 4 says nothing about Zipporah going back to her father at that time.

We can make two observations about this family reunion. The first is that the text gives great attention to Moses's affectionate welcome of Jethro but says nothing about how Moses received Zipporah or with what attitude she encountered him (Zipporah never appears in the narrative again). But we should resist the temptation to read between the lines in order to discover details about Moses's domestic life. The proper conclusion to draw from this first observation is actually that the real focus of the text is on Jethro, and not on Zipporah. Second, the text refers to Gershom and Eliezer as "her (Zipporah's) sons," but it also parenthetically gives the interpretations of their names, indicating that Moses named them (contrast Gen. 29:32–35; 30:6, 8 etc.). Exodus 2:22 had already explained the significance of Gershom's name, but the meaning of Eliezer's name appears here for the first time. If nothing else, the text makes the point that the children belonged to both Zipporah and Moses. In short, the text asserts that Moses had children by this Midianite woman.

There is, however, one other important factor, and it makes the point that all of this talk in the text about Jethro being Moses's father-in-law and about Moses and Zipporah being parents of two sons really has nothing to do with any divorce question. This text gives prominence to Jethro "the priest of Midian" (18:1). This is important because the text is set immediately after an account of warfare with the Amalekites, and in particular after the declaration that Israel is in a permanent state of war with the Amalekites (17:14–16). Against this, Exod. 18 repeatedly reminds the reader that Jethro the Midianite was Moses's father-in-law, that he was also a Midianite priest, and that Moses had half-Midianite sons. It presents Moses as showing deep respect for Jethro, and it has Aaron, the high priest of Israel, attending a sacrificial meal at which Jethro officiates (18:12). This is significant because of how Midianites are portrayed elsewhere.

In the Old Testament, there is some mixture of the usage of the terms Amalekite, Midianite, Moabite, and Ishmaelite, or else a mixture of the peoples themselves. In Gen. 37:28–36, the traders who purchased Joseph are called both "Midianites" and "Ishmaelites." In Judg. 6—8, the enemy that Gideon fought was composed of "the Midianites and the Amalekites and the sons of the east" (Judg. 6:33); they are also said to have been "Ishmaelites" (Judg. 8:24). Midianites figure prominently as enemies of Israel in the narrative of the invasion of Canaan: they join with Moab in war councils against Israel (Num. 22:4); Moabites and Midianites are involved in the Baal of Peor episode, enticing Israelites into a fertility cult (Num. 25:1, 6); and the Midianites fight a great battle against Israel during the Moabite campaign, and they suffer near extermination (Num. 31). Later, Eglon of Moab has Amalekites in his army (Judg. 3:13), suggesting a close connection between the Midianites and Amalekites who dwell in Moab. The important point is that various texts link the Midianites to various enemies of Israel from the deserts of the Arabah, the Negev, and Arabia. But this passage, Exod. 18:1–12, shows Midian in the most positive light possible, with both Moses and Aaron showing deference to the priest of Midian! Moses's sons are said to be the sons of Zipporah of Midian. That is, in the very family of Moses, Midian and Israel are merged. One can only conclude that the placement of this episode immediately after the narrative of the war with Amalek at Rephidim is no accident.

The two texts are telling us that some of these desert peoples, especially those designated "Amalekite," are Israel's eternal enemies and are to be given no quarter. Others, however, are worthy of high respect. In later narratives, we see the positive side of the Israelite-Midianite relationship in the treatment given to Hobab the Midianite, who serves as a guide for Israel (Num. 10:29–31). Heber the Kenite is a descendant of Hobab (Judg. 4:11), and his household figures prominently in the narrative about the war with Sisera (Judg. 4—5). In Judg. 1:16, Moses's father-in-law is designated "the Kenite." Saul shows kindness to some Kenites during his war with the Amalekites (1 Sam. 15:6) on account of the kindness done to Israel during the exodus. All of this may seem arcane or irrelevant to us, but to the Israelites it was of vital importance. Some Midianites were hated enemies to be slaughtered, as were the Amalekites. Others were honored, especially those designated as "Kenites." The Exodus account, in two adjacent narratives, gives us the roots of both relationships.

18:7–11. Moses greets Jethro with enormous respect. For the Israelite reader, it was perhaps astonishing that Moses, the man of God and the greatest of the Israelites, was bowing before this Midianite priest. Furthermore, he shows him great affection. Beyond that, this story tells of Jethro's conversion experience. He comes to realize that the God of Israel is the great God. The formula "Now I know" is regularly used to describe recognition of the validity of the work of God. The best parallel is in 1 Kings 17:24, where in response to Elijah's miracle the widow of Zarephath, a Phoenician, says, "Now I know that you are a man of God." Jethro, a pagan priest of Midian, similarly acknowledges Israel's God.

18:12. Jethro solemnizes his recognition of YHWH by offering him sacrifice. The remarkable fact here is that Aaron, the high priest of Israel, attends a sacrifice where he does not officiate. The priest of Midian does.

Theological Summary of Key Points

1. In one text, the Amalekites are treacherous enemies. In the next, the Midianite family of Moses, who are ethnically and culturally closely linked to the Amalekites, are beloved and give praise to YHWH. For us, the abiding moral truth is that there is a time for war and a time for peace (Eccl. 3:8). Each is right in its time, and each is wrong when misapplied. There are genuine and legitimate cases of enmity and warfare, but there are also reasons to seek reconciliation. The greatest basis for reconciliation is when both parties submit to God and worship him.

2. The particulars of Moses's domestic life are obscure, perhaps deliberately so, and we should leave it that way. Speculations about the relationship between Moses and Zipporah and about the circumstances of his marriage to the Cushite woman of Num. 12:1 are based on extremely thin evidence. There clearly is a background story to Jethro's bringing back Zipporah and her sons to Moses, but we do not know what it is, and it is not the point of this narrative.

3. The name Eliezer foreshadows Moses's testimony to Jethro, that God has been a helper to Israel. The mighty acts of the exodus were meant to convince people that YHWH of Israel was also God of all the earth. In Jethro's case, they clearly had that effect.

4. In telling Jethro the story of all that God had done for Israel, Moses brought Jethro to faith in YHWH the God of Israel. The testimony of God's mighty works has great power to bring about conversion. In the New Testament we see, for example, a brief account of the Apostle Peter rehearsing the entire gospel story in his evangelistic work (Acts 10:34–43). Stories of what God has done, both from the Bible and from the testimonies of living Christians, are powerful inducements to faith.

5. One may look upon this text as paradigmatic for dealing with an unconverted family member. Moses treats Jethro with great warmth and respect before he tells him the story of what God had done for Israel. Moses does not browbeat him for his paganism. Jethro came as a pagan priest of Midian and left with the confession that YHWH is higher than all the gods. Peter gives analogous advice to Christian wives in 1 Peter 3:1. Jesus used the sudden and perhaps awkward arrival of his mother and brothers as an occasion to teach people how one truly has kinship with Christ (Luke 8:19–21). In doing so, he gently appealed to his family to come to terms with who he really was.

6. The subordinate place of Aaron at Jethro's sacrifice implies that Aaron's priesthood is not the ultimate priesthood. That is, it is not necessarily the one that automatically outranks all others. The Christian reader recalls the messianic priestly oracle of Ps. 110:4, "You are a priest forever after the order of Melchizedek," together with the interpretation in Heb. 7 to the effect that the subordination of the house of Levi to Melchizedek typifies the subordination of the Aaronic priesthood to Christ. This episode in Exod. 18 also suggests that the Aaronic priesthood can be superseded. Note that this does not mean that Jethro himself is a "type" of Christ. It means that the subordination of Aaron to Jethro shows that no human religious authority, including that of the house of Aaron, is final.

SIXTH STAGE: A HEAVY RESPONSIBILITY (18:13–27)

A dilemma for both Moses and Israel is that he bears the entire burden of leadership alone. This time, deliverance comes in the form of advice from his father-in-law.

Translation

18:13a And it happened[66] on the next day
18:13b that Moses sat to issue judgments for the people,
18:13c and the people stood around Moses from the morning until the evening.
18:14a And the father-in-law of Moses saw everything he was doing for the people,
18:14b and he said,
18:14c "What is this business that you are handling for the people?
18:14d Why are you sitting by yourself with all the people standing around you from morning until evening?"
18:15a And Moses said to his father-in-law,
18:15b "[It is] because[67] the people come to me to inquire of God.
18:16a If[68] they have an issue[69] to bring[70] to me,
18:16b then I judge[71] between a man and his adversary.

---

66. An initial וַיְהִי clause initiates a new discourse here.
67. The particle כִּי is here explanatory.
68. The particle כִּי is here conditional, meaning "if." Contrast the usage in the previous clause, 18:15b. In both cases, the particle indicates that its clause is in some way subordinated.
69. Some versions render דָּבָר as "dispute" throughout this passage; it includes that meaning, as indicated in 18:16b, but it is not limited to that. It includes all matters of halakah, that is, of rules governing daily life, as in 18:16c.
70. The participle בָּא is often translated as the apodosis, as in the ESV and TNIV, but actually it is a modifier of דָּבָר. Lit. "an issue coming to me," it means "an issue to bring to me."
71. This *weqatal* is the apodosis of 18:15b.

18:16c And I explain[72] God's rules and his instructions."
18:17a And the father-in-law of Moses said to him,
18:17b "The procedure that you are following is not good.
18:18a Both you and these people who are with you are just going to get worn out,
18:18b for the procedure is too burdensome for you.
18:18c You cannot do it by yourself.
18:19a Now listen to what I am saying;
18:19b let me give you advice,
18:19c and may God be with you.
18:19d You[73] must be [the one who stands] before God for the people,
18:19e and you bring the issues [that arise] to God,
18:20a and you warn them about the rules and the instructions,
18:20b and you explain to them the way in which they should walk and the behavior that they should practice.
18:21a But you[74] must select out of all the people capable men—God-fearers, men of integrity, haters of graft—
18:21b and place [these men] over [the populace as] chiefs over a thousand, [as] chiefs over a hundred, [as] chiefs over fifty, and [as] chiefs over ten.
18:22a They should judge the people under ordinary circumstances.[75]
18:22b And let this be [the policy]:[76]
18:22c they will bring to you every significant matter,
18:22d but they themselves will adjudicate in every minor matter.
18:22e And make [the burden] lighter for you,[77]
18:22f and let them bear [it] with you!
18:23a If you carry out this procedure—
18:23b and may God direct you—
18:23c then you will be able to stand,

72. This *weqatal* continues the prior apodosis and is also reflecting habitual action.
73. The pleonastic use of אַתָּה brings focus on Moses's role in this and the following clauses, as opposed to the role of the lower officials under him.
74. The fronted position of וְאַתָּה here marks it as contrastive. This is another role for Moses, but it is different from all his other roles in that it involves delegating power.
75. The phrase "under ordinary circumstances" (בְּכָל־עֵת) is lit. "at every time."
76. וְהָיָה is the protasis and by itself forms 18:22b; the apodosis is 18:22cd.
77. 18:22ef is a summarizing exhortation; it is not part of the protasis-apodosis structure of 18:22bcd.

18:23d and all these people also will go about their business in peace."[78]
18:24a And Moses listened to his father-in-law's voice
18:24b and he did all that he had said:
18:25a Moses chose[79] capable men out of all Israel
18:25b and he made them heads over the people: chiefs over a thousand, chiefs over a hundred, chiefs over fifty, and chiefs over ten.
18:26a And they began to issue[80] judgments [for] the people under ordinary circumstances:
18:26b they would bring[81] the difficult matter to Moses,
18:26c but they themselves would adjudicate in every minor matter.
18:27a And Moses sent off his father-in-law,
18:27b and he went to his own country.

Structure

In the prior text, Moses provided a kind of deliverance for Jethro by a speech-act, bearing testimony to the mighty works of YHWH, so that Jethro came to acknowledge that YHWH was the true God. Here, Jethro provides deliverance for Moses by a speech-act, the giving of advice.

I. Setting and Crisis: Jethro Observes Moses at Work (18:13–16)
II. Speech: Jethro Advises Moses (18:17–23)
III. Deliverance: The Advice Works (18:24–26)
IV. Aftermath: Jethro Goes Home (18:27)

As with 18:1–12, the setting here is Israel at Sinai; this story has been transposed to its present setting in the book. The Israelites were in a routine of living near one another and, as is inevitable, personal and legal disputes arose. Also, Moses is giving the people the rules (חֹק) and instructions (תּוֹרָה) of God. This terminology describes the legal requirements of the Sinai covenant, and therefore must come from after

78. The expression עַל־מְקֹמוֹ יָבֹא (lit. "he will go upon his place"), signifying perhaps that the people could go home (rather than crowd around Moses), implies more specifically that they go back to their personal business and ordinary activity.
79. This is an epexegetical *wayyiqtol*.
80. The *weqatal* וְשָׁפְטוּ is here ingressive.
81. The *yiqtol* יְבִיאוּן here signifies customary activity. Used after the previous *weqatal* of 18:26a, this X + *yiqtol* pattern is epexegetical. The וְ + X + *yiqtol* of 18:26c is parallel to 18:26b. That is, the two clauses of 18:26bc explain the standard procedure followed by the lower judges in the normal adjudication of cases that is mentioned in 18:26a.

the arrival at Sinai. This episode is mentioned in Deut. 1:9–18 except that Jethro's role is not mentioned there.

Commentary

18:13–16. In the ancient world, leadership was direct and personal. Kings were expected to lead their armies into war and not to send proxy commanders, as modern heads of state do (note the implied censure at 2 Sam. 11:1). Judicial, priestly, and diplomatic tasks also fell directly to the king; Solomon's adjudication of a custody case involving two local prostitutes (1 Kings 3:16–28) illustrates how extensive the judicial duties of a ruler could be. Even in Egypt, which had the closest thing to a bureaucracy that one might find in the ancient Near East, the pharaoh personally directed important activities, such as leading the army into battle. Therefore, it is not surprising that Moses felt compelled to manage Israelite affairs in person. We should also note that much of Moses's prior "leadership" experience consisted in overseeing sheep. While he no doubt learned many important lessons doing this, one cannot delegate to sheep!

18:17–23. Jethro recognized that this level of personal involvement in settling the affairs of the Israelites was untenable and doing harm to both Moses and the people, and Jethro had the personal stature with Moses to advise him directly. His solution is analogous to what we would call a system of lower and appellate courts, with Moses himself sitting as the sole judge in Israel's highest court. The arrangement of judicial authority over groups of ten, fifty, one hundred and one thousand may have been based in the structure of Israel's military. This system would only function while Israel was in the wilderness; after the settlement, court cases would be resolved by village elders at the city gates throughout Israel, although the "judges" would also have a judicial function over the regions where they served as a circuit court. With the establishment of the monarchy, the king would probably constitute the high court of the land, with decisions by elders in the gates of the cities still handling the majority of cases (the two prostitutes of 1 Kings 3 apparently resided in Jerusalem and so came directly under Solomon's jurisdiction). The moral and spiritual qualifications Jethro proposes for the lower judges are reasonable and prudent. Jethro's description of the outcome of the model he proposes, that people will be able to live with one another in peace (18:23d), is the goal of every good judicial system.

18:24–27. The appellate system Jethro proposed was put into effect and was a great success. He went home in peace, having rendered Moses and Israel an important service.

Theological Summary of Key Points

1. Delegating tasks seems to be just a prudent approach to dealing with organizational leadership, but there is an important theological principle. Failure to delegate comes from a false sense of self-importance (the idea that if I don't do it, then it will never get done or will not be done properly). One does not need to argue that Moses personally suffered from such a delusion in order to understand that this is a valid principle. No person is indispensable, and neither the person himself nor the organization should think of any one in that manner.

2. The people of God should think of themselves as a community in which every member plays his or her part. The delegation of authority recognizes the legitimacy of the various roles different people fulfill.

3. It is striking that the sound advice that comes to Moses on the matter of delegation is not from God but from Jethro. The implication is that God does not always directly tell us what to do but also speaks to us through the sound advice of others, especially of elders. On the other hand, one could argue that because this solution did not come from God but from human counsel, it was illegitimate. Later, when Moses was apparently again feeling overwrought by the burdens of his office, he took his complaint directly to YHWH. He was at that time told to bring seventy elders to the Tent of Meeting; YHWH gave his Spirit to these men, and they assisted Moses in carrying out his duties (Num. 11:14–17, 25). The seventy elders of Num. 11 are not set in administrative hierarchy; they are simply given the Spirit. On the other hand, the seventy were already officers over the people (Num. 11:16). Many of the seventy may have been men who were already serving in the administrative hierarchy worked out at Sinai and described here in Exod. 18 and in Deut. 1. Thus, Jethro's advice was strictly administrative. YHWH's solution involved giving leaders the power of the Spirit. My own view is that we should not regard Jethro's solution as wrong, but that we should understand that it, like all administrative solutions, was not a work of God. Good administrative structure and empowerment by God's Spirit can be complementary. They need not be opposed to one another.

4. The above principles bring us to the issue of humility. This includes the humility of realizing that my contribution to an organization is not invaluable and that I am not irreplaceable. It also shows itself in the humility of the people, who must submit their concerns and problems to lower officials before they can approach Moses. Humility also shows itself in willingness to take on a task for the good of a community, even though the task can at times be onerous (as it must have been for Israelites designated to resolve their neighbors' disputes). Finally, it shows itself in the willingness to take sound advice, as Moses did when counseled by Jethro. We should note that all of these examples of humility have counterparts in the New Testament, as illustrated by members of the church each taking on their particular labors (Rom. 12:3–8) and by submitting to the church authorities set over them (Heb. 13:17). Paul, moreover, gives his readers sage advice, asserting that although what he says comes from himself and not directly from Christ, "I too have the Spirit of God" (1 Cor. 7:40).

5. In any community made up of human beings and not of angels, there will be conflict and the need for resolution. Policies, laws, and rules for any organization must take into account the human proclivity for self-centered behavior. If an organization is wisely governed and resolution is quickly and fairly achieved, the likelihood of conflict diminishes. In short, governing rules may be a reflection of the sinful condition of humanity, but they are necessary.

SEVENTH STAGE: ENCOUNTERING GOD (19:1–25)

Israel arrives at the mountain of God and is offered a covenant with YHWH, which they accept.

Translation

19:1 In the third month of [the year of] the Israelites' departure from
the land of Egypt, on this day, [the very same day of the month[82]

82. The language here (בַּיּוֹם הַזֶּה) is somewhat ambiguous with regard to the date of their arrival. It could be taken to mean (1) three months after their departure, that is, on the fifteenth day of the fourth calendar month; (2) on the first day of the third calendar month, as in the ESV, NRSV, TNIV and others; or (3) as in the third calendar month but on the same date of the month as the date of their departure from Egypt, that is, on the fifteenth day of the third month. Against option 1, "In the third month" is not the same as "after three months." Against interpretation 2, there is no basis for assuming that this is the beginning of the third month. Probably לְצֵאת בְּנֵי־יִשְׂרָאֵל מֵאֶרֶץ (lit. "of the sons of Israel's departure from Egypt") refers to the year of their departure, and the "third month" is the third calendar month (see 16:1b). This indicates that "on this day" must refer to the date of the month, that is, the fifteenth. Thus, they appear to have arrived on the fifteenth day of the third month, or exactly two months after they departed Egypt.

as their departure date], they came to the wilderness of Sinai.[83]
19:2a They had set out[84] from Rephidim,
19:2b and they came to the wilderness of Sinai,
19:2c and they camped in the wilderness;
19:2d Israel camped[85] there before the mountain.
19:3a And Moses went up to God.
19:3b and YHWH called to him from the mountain, saying,

Fifth Poem: The Song of the Covenant

Stanza 1

19:3c Thus you shall say to the house of Jacob
כֹּה תֹאמַר֙ לְבֵ֣ית יַעֲקֹ֔ב 1-2-3

19:3d And tell the Israelites:
וְתַגֵּ֖יד לִבְנֵ֥י יִשְׂרָאֵֽל׃[86] 1-2-3

Stanza 2

19:4a You have seen what I did to Egypt!
אַתֶּ֣ם רְאִיתֶ֔ם אֲשֶׁ֥ר עָשִׂ֖יתִי לְמִצְרָ֑יִם 2-5-5[87]

19:4b I carried[88] you on eagles' wings
וָאֶשָּׂ֤א אֶתְכֶם֙ עַל־כַּנְפֵ֣י נְשָׁרִ֔ים 1-4-3

19:4c And I brought you to me.

---

83. Here, as is common, asyndeton (that is, a sentence not beginning with a conjunction) initiates a new narrative. This verse both summarizes the account of the Israelites' arrival at Sinai and introduces the narrative of what happened at Sinai.
84. The *wayyiqtol* is epexegetical, giving details about Israel's movement from Rephidim to Sinai.
85. Another epexegetical *wayyiqtol*; this one provides additional information about where Israel camped.
86. The first and last bicola (19:3cd and 19:6cd) parallel one another (both concern speech) and form an inclusio for the poem. The first bicolon ends with לִבְנֵ֥י יִשְׂרָאֵֽל and the second ends with אֶל־בְּנֵ֥י יִשְׂרָאֵֽל.
87. This is more than the normal number of constituents, but the cantillation marks suggest breaking up the line as done here (the zaqeph qaton in רְאִיתֶ֔ם probably does not indicate a line break as it has no subordinate disjunctive).
88. The *wayyiqtol* is epexegetical.

וָאָבִא אֶתְכֶם אֵלָי׃[89] 1-3-3

Stanza 3

19:5a And now, if you will genuinely listen to my voice,
וְעַתָּה אִם־שָׁמוֹעַ תִּשְׁמְעוּ בְּקֹלִי[90] 1-3-4

19:5b And keep my covenant,
וּשְׁמַרְתֶּם[91] אֶת־בְּרִיתִי 1-2-2

Stanza 4

19:5c Then you will be my possession [chosen[92]] from all peoples,
וִהְיִיתֶם[93] לִי סְגֻלָּה מִכָּל־הָעַמִּים[94] 1-4-5

19:5d Although all the earth is mine.
כִּי־לִי כָּל־הָאָרֶץ׃ 0-2-3

19:6a But you will be to me as a kingdom of priests
וְאַתֶּם[95] תִּהְיוּ־לִי מַמְלֶכֶת כֹּהֲנִים 1-4-5

---

89. There is consonance in the three lines of this strophe (19:4) in that each line begins with א (once without the conjunction and then twice with the conjunction). In addition, each line ends with a prepositional phrase. Lines 19:4b and 19:4c are in fact fully parallel, both semantically and syntactically. This strophe is a prologue, giving the basis for God's covenantal offer to the Israelites: he has already shown himself to be mighty to save.

90. Both lines of this bicolon end with a 1cs suffix. There is also assonance between בְּקֹלִי and בְּרִיתִי.

91. The third strophe initiates the actual covenant offer. וְעַתָּה transitions from the prologue to the divine offer, which is composed of a protasis (19:5ab) and an apodosis (19:5cd–6ab). The protasis is also bound by consonance and seconding, with שׁמע paralleled by שׁמר.

92. The preposition מִן here is partitive in the sense of selecting one from a larger group. In this case, Israel is chosen from all the peoples. A good parallel to this use of מִן is in 2 Kings 10:3.

93. Note that morphologically וּשְׁמַרְתֶּם in 19:5b and וִהְיִיתֶם in 19:5c are exactly the same, but that pragmatically they have different functions. The first is part of the protasis, parallel to 19:5a, and the second marks the apodosis.

94. The first three lines of this strophe all have לִי (the fourth line is dependent on the third). There is also a parallel structure between 19:5c (וִהְיִיתֶם לִי) and 19:6a (וְאַתֶּם תִּהְיוּ־לִי). Finally, the general fact that the whole world belongs to God (19:5d) is set against the fact that Israel will be a "holy nation" (19:6b).

95. The pattern here is וְ + X + *qatal*, having וְאַתֶּם תִּהְיוּ instead of וִהְיִיתֶם. The word וְאַתֶּם is contrastive with "all the earth" (כָּל־הָאָרֶץ) from the previous line.

19:6b And a holy nation.
וְגוֹי קָדוֹשׁ[96] 0-1-2

Stanza 5

19:6c These are the words
אֵלֶּה הַדְּבָרִים 0-2-2

19:6d That you shall speak to the Israelites.
אֲשֶׁר תְּדַבֵּר אֶל־בְּנֵי יִשְׂרָאֵל׃ 1-3-4

19:7a And Moses came
19:7b and he called the elders of the people,
19:7c and set before them all these terms that YHWH had commanded him [to relay].
19:8a And all the people answered together
19:8b and they said,
19:8c "Everything[97] that YHWH has said we will do!"
19:8d And Moses brought the words of the people to YHWH.
19:9a And YHWH said to Moses,
19:9b "All right then![98] I am about to come upon you, [Moses,[99]] in the fog of the cloud,
19:9c so that the people may [only[100]] hear when I speak with you
19:9d and that they may always believe in you, also."
19:9e And Moses had told the words of the people to YHWH.[101]
19:10a And YHWH said to Moses,

This demonstrates that כִּי in 19:5d must be translated as a concessive ("although") and not as explanatory ("because") as is often done (as in the ESV).

96. The words עַמִּים ("peoples"), אֶרֶץ ("earth"), מַמְלָכָה ("kingdom"), and גּוֹי ("nation") add unity to the apodosis, as all the terms relate to people-groups and their domains.

97. The fronting of כֹּל ("everything") makes it the focus of the people's answer.

98. הִנֵּה here indicates a dramatic announcement, and it is also a response to the message Moses brings.

99. The singular suffix on אֵלֶיךָ indicates that the thick cloud will overshadow Moses alone (not the whole people).

100. There does not seem to be a clear connection between YHWH coming over Moses in a dark cloud and the purpose that the people may hear. There is no reason to think that the thick cloud enhanced their ability to hear. Thus, it appears that the purpose is that they may only hear and not see the descent of YHWH.

101. The clause in 19:9e effectively repeats 19:8d. It appears that 19:9e is resumptive, restating the fact that Moses conveyed the people's acceptance

19:10b “Go to the people
19:10c and sanctify them today and tomorrow.
19:10d They must wash[102] their clothes
19:11a and they must be prepared for the third day
19:11b (for on the third day YHWH will descend upon Mount Sinai before the eyes of all the people),
19:12a and you must set a boundary all around [the mountain] for the people, saying,
19:12b ‘Be careful[103] about going up on the mountain or touching the edge of it!
19:12c Anyone who touches the mountain will most definitely be put to death.
19:13a No hand shall touch him;
19:13b rather, he shall be [put to death] purely by stoning[104]
19:13c or he shall be [put to death] purely by being shot [with arrows];
19:13d whether beast or man, he shall not live.’
19:13e When the ram’s horn sounds a long blast, they are to approach the mountain.”[105]

---

of God’s terms to make the point that God’s words in 19:9 and in 19:10–12 are both responses to the people’s words.

102. The *weqatal* verbs וְכִבְּסוּ (19:10d) and וְהָיוּ (19:11a) and וְהִגְבַּלְתָּ (19:12a) are all epexegetical of וְקִדַּשְׁתָּם (19:10c), indicating how the people are to be sanctified.

103. The Niphal imperative of שׁמר means to be careful about doing something, whether one must never do it (Exod. 10:28) or one must be sure to do it (Josh. 23:11). Context determines which meaning is intended; by analogy, “Be careful about that wire!” can mean either, “Don’t touch it!” or “Be sure to attach it properly!” In context here, the idiom plainly means that they are to be careful not to get too close to the mountain.

104. The infinitive absolute and finite verb combination in some way always focuses attention on the action of the verb itself. In this case, the point is exclusivity; they are to execute violators only by means of projectiles and not by any other means.

105. Superficially, the clause הֵמָּה יַעֲלוּ בָהָר (lit. “they shall go up on the mountain”) appears to contradict the injunction in 19:12b that the people are not to go up on the mountain. One might therefore argue that the people were actually supposed to ascend the mountain on the third day, after YHWH had descended, but this would be incorrect. In 19:21–24, after the descent of YHWH, both YHWH and Moses emphatically assert that the prohibition against coming up the mountain is still in place. Biblical Hebrew often has language that is superficially ambiguous, but the writers expect us to have the intelligence to make sense of it. In this case, the people are clearly not to ascend into the mountain heights with Moses;

19:14a And Moses descended from the mountain to the people,
19:14b and he sanctified the people,
19:14c and they washed their clothes.
19:15a And he said to the people,
19:15b "Be prepared for the third day!
19:15c Do not approach a woman [sexually[106]]!"
19:16a And it happened on the third day, when it was morning,
19:16b that there were noises and flashes[107] and a heavy cloud upon the mountain and a very powerful shofar sound,
19:16c and all the people who [were] in the camp trembled.
19:17a And Moses brought the people out of the camp to encounter God,
19:17b and they stood at the foot of the mountain.
19:18a Now Mount Sinai [was] all in smoke,
19:18b because YHWH had descended upon it in fire.
19:18c And its smoke ascended like the smoke of a kiln,
19:18d and all of the mountain trembled mightily,
19:19a and the shofar sound was getting very much stronger.
19:19b Moses was speaking[108]
19:19c and God would answer him audibly.[109]

---

they are only to ascend the slopes leading up to the mountain until they reach the limits that Moses has set.

106. Although this is the only place where נגשׁ is used with אֶל־אִשָּׁה to describe sexual relations, that is plainly the meaning here. It is not a prohibition against being in physical proximity to a female. A related and more common euphemism for sexual intercourse is בּוֹא, sometimes with אֶל־אִשָּׁה, as in Gen. 38:8.

107. The words קֹלֹת וּבְרָקִים include but are not limited to the meanings, "thunder and lightning." קוֹל basically means "sound" or "voice," and while בָּרָק most commonly refers to lightning, it can refer to a bright flash coming out of a fire, as at Ezek. 1:13. The probable meaning is that there were flashes and loud noises that included, among other phenomena, thunder and lightning.

108. The two *yiqtol* verbs here (יְדַבֵּר and יַעֲנֶנּוּ) are past imperfects, describing repeated action.

109. Lit. "in a voice" (בְקוֹל). The word קוֹל does not mean "thunder" here, as though Moses were decoding some kind of Morse code by thunderclap. Rather, God answered Moses "with sound" or "with a voice," i.e., audibly (see also the translation note to 19:16b). This was not an inner, spiritual dialogue. Moses and all the people could hear God answer. The point was to show the people that God was really speaking from the mountain and that it was with Moses that he communicated.

19:20a And [so] YHWH descended[110] upon Mount Sinai, to the top of the mountain.
19:20b And YHWH called Moses to the top of the mountain,
19:20c and Moses went up.
19:21a And YHWH said to Moses,
19:21b "Go down,
19:21c warn the people
19:21d that they must not break through to YHWH to have a look,
19:21e which would result in many of them perishing.
19:22a And also the priests, who [ritually] approach[111] YHWH, must sanctify themselves.
19:22b Otherwise, YHWH will break out against them."
19:23a And Moses said to YHWH,
19:23b "The people cannot come up to Mount Sinai,
19:23c because you warned us, saying,
19:23d 'Set a boundary about the mountain
19:23e and sanctify it.'"
19:24a And YHWH said to him,
19:24b "Make your way down
19:24c then you come up, you and Aaron with you;
19:24d but the priests and the people must not break down [the boundary markers] to come up to YHWH,
19:24e or he will break forth against them."
19:25a And Moses went down to the people
19:25b and he told them.

Structure

This section completes the story of the movement toward God at Sinai, but it breaks the pattern of the previous six episodes in that it is formally different. In this, Exod. 15:22–19:25 has the 6 + 1 pattern observed in Gen 1:1–2:3, in that it has six episodes that have a single pattern followed by a seventh episode that breaks the pattern. Structurally, therefore, it suggests that the arrival at Sinai is a kind of Sabbath experience. Before this, they went through various dangers to make their way to God; now they have arrived and can enter his

110. The *wayyiqtol* וַיֵּרֶד is here summarizing the episode, saying that YHWH descended onto Mt. Sinai. This clause is a kind of epexegetical *wayyiqtol*; it does not advance the narrative and is not sequential to the previous clause.

111. נגשׁ here refers to ritual service in the cult (see Exod. 28:43; 30:20); it does not mean that these men are to go up the mountain with Moses.

"rest." They are now with God and at his mountain sanctuary. On the other hand, there is a surprising twist. In the prior six episodes, there was some external danger or difficulty and often God was the source of deliverance. Now, God himself is the source of danger, as indicated by putting a boundary around the mountain. God can be for them a source of joy and rest—if they keep the covenant. Otherwise, God is a source of death. From the very beginning, therefore, Sinai is both blessings and curses.

I. The Arrival at Sinai (19:1–2)
II. The Covenant Offer and Response (19:3–8c)
  A. Moses Approaches God (19:3ab)
  B. The Oracle of the Covenant Offer (19:3cd–6)
  C. Moses Approaches the People (19:7)
  D. The Response (19:8abc)
III. The Theophany on the Mountain (19:8d–20a)
  A. The First Instruction (19:8d–9)
  B. The Second Instruction (19:10–13)
  C. The Exhortation to the People (19:14–15)
  D. The Theophany Arrives (19:16–20a)
IV. The Preparation for the Giving of the Law (19:20bc–25)
  A. Moses Summoned (19:20bc)
  B. The First Instruction (19:21–23)
  C. The Second Instruction (19:24–25)

The structure of the oracular poem is described in the commentary to 19:3cd–6, below.

Commentary

19:1–2. As described in the translation note to 19:1, there is some confusion about when Israel arrived at Sinai. The most reasonable interpretation is that they arrived on the fifteenth day of the third calendar month, that is, two months to the day after their departure from Egypt. The essential chronology is that they left Egypt on the morning after the Passover meal (the 14th day of the 1st month; 12:41), arrived at the Wilderness of Sin on the 15th day of the 2nd month (16:1), and arrived at Mt. Sinai on the 15th day of the 3rd month.

19:3ab. The arrival of the theophany, with all of its terrifying sights and sounds, would establish Moses in the role of intercessor between YHWH and Israel. But here, even before the spectacular events of the theophany, Moses is in the role of going up to God as Israel's representative.

19:3cd–6. As presented in the translation, the poetic oracle from YHWH has 5 strophes. These have a chiastic pattern, as follows:

A: The command to speak to Israel (19:3cd)
  B: YHWH's past grace toward Israel (19:4abc)
    C: Condition of obedience to the covenant (19:5ab)
  B': YHWH's future grace toward Israel (19:5cd–6ab)
A': The command to speak to Israel (19:6cd)

Often, the central element in a chiastic structure is pivotal, and that is surely the case here. The conditional clause of obedience is the hinge on which the future turns. Israel can continue to experience God's special favor, but only by being obedient to God. The repetition of the command to speak to Israel (19:3cd; 6cd) both gives boundaries to the poem and emphasizes that this message with the offer it contains is of the utmost importance. God's offer to Israel of a covenant relationship with himself is perhaps the most important single event in the history of the nation.

19:4. The two lines of 19:4bc fully parallel one another in the Hebrew and together constitute a counterpart to 19:4a. The contrast is between what YHWH did to Egypt and what he did to Israel. The memorable metaphor of being carried to YHWH "on eagle's wings" is theologically significant precisely because of its contrast with the painful experiences of chapters 15—18. Israel did not fly to Mt. Sinai: they walked. It was a hard journey through a harsh land, and they experienced severe thirst, hunger, and warfare along the way. From this perspective, the claim that they made it to Sinai on eagle's wings sounds propagandistic and might well have been met with bitter scoffs from the tired people. But the claim is entirely true: God broke the power of Egypt and delivered the people from troubles all along the way. The very claim to carrying Israel on eagle's wings is itself a test of faith. If they can see how this claim is true, they have faith; if they scoff, they do not.

19:5ab. The conditional clauses describe Israel's obedience in both internal and external terms. These two lines are obviously similar (both imply obedience) but they are not equivalent. On the one hand, it is a matter of paying close attention to God (19:5a); that is, it is internal obedience from the heart. On the other, it is keeping the stipulations laid down in the forthcoming covenant agreement (19:5b); that is, it is external and observable. The two go together. The claim to heed God in a personal and relational manner is hollow if it is not accompanied by explicit obedience to the Law, and the practice of observing the Law is dead if one does not obey from the heart.

19:5cd–6ab. As 19:4abc contrasts God's actions towards Israel with his actions toward Egypt, so this strophe, looking toward the future, contrasts God's relationship to Israel with his relationship to all the other nations of the world. It is in this context that we must understand "kingdom of priests" and "holy nation." The language does not imply a "universal priesthood," as though there would be no need for an Aaronic, specialized priesthood.[112] It does not suggest that anyone could officiate at the sanctuary. Rather, it indicates that Israel would, in contrast to the nations, enjoy a special relationship to God, a status that could rightly be called a national priesthood. In the ancient world, a priest knew things about the god he served that were withheld from outsiders. These included details about the god's myth, the god's secret names, and the rituals of the god's cult. In addition, a priest had special access to the god and could make intercession to him. Israelites, in contrast to all other peoples of earth, would have knowledge of God in the Torah. They alone could participate in worship at the sanctuary in which he dwelt, and they alone could partake of Passover. They also could call upon him by his chosen name, YHWH, and he would answer them. These were the things that marked them as a holy nation and a kingdom of priests. All peoples of earth belonged to God (19:5d),[113] but Israel's relationship to him was special. They knew God.

---

112. This appears to be the position of John Sailhamer, *An Introduction to Old Testament Theology: A Canonical Approach* (Grand Rapids: Zondervan, 1995), 288, who wrongly believes that Israel would have become a universal priesthood had they not pulled back from going up Sinai, and that they were given a specialized priesthood instead. The concern of the text is hardly that the people would run away rather than ascending the mountain. Rather, it is that they would not be able to resist coming up the mountain. At any rate, the "royal priesthood" of Exod. 19:5–6 does not contradict the the presence of a specialized priesthood, and the specialized priesthood does not cancel Israel's status as a kingdom of priests. As John A. Davies, *A Royal Priesthood: Literary and Intertextual Perspectives on an Image of Israel in Exodus 19.6,* JSOTSup 395 (London: T & T Clark, 2004), 240, states, "The Levitical priesthood as portrayed in Exodus is not seen as diminishing or supplanting the collective royal priesthood, but as providing a visual model of that vocation, and secondly as facilitating it."
113. Stuart, *Exodus*, 422, properly observes that the claim that all the world belongs to YHWH is implicitly monotheistic.

19:7. Moses conveyed YHWH's offer to the "elders" (the leaders of the community) as a matter of efficient communication. He gave the message to the elders, and they carried it to their respective tribes, clans, and family units.

19:8abc. The elders did not answer for the people; this verse indicates that the response was effectively democratic. This does not mean that they held a formal vote. Still, the elders evidently had some means of accurately determining the will of the people in this matter. The people's acceptance of YHWH's offer is, together with the offer itself, the decisive moment in the history of Israel. By this act, Israel became the bearers of the covenant. All of Israel's subsequent history would be grounded in the fact that they were bound to God as no other people were. Israel's subsequent failures do not invalidate the glory of this moment. And one should not criticize the Israelites' claim ("Everything that YHWH has said we will do") as morally presumptuous or legalistic. They were not claiming to be morally perfect; they were obligating themselves to complete obedience to God. Yahweh gave them a specific offer, and they accepted it according to the terms he gave them. There is nothing censurable in that.

19:8d–9. The next stage in the narrative begins with Moses's return to God, taking Israel's response with him. God only then tells Moses to prepare the people for the theophany on Sinai. This is an important matter; Israel did not accept the covenant offer after having seen Mt. Sinai blazing with fire, but beforehand, when apparently all was quiet. On the one hand, Israel was not frightened into accepting the covenant; they were able to enter into the covenant after careful and rational consideration and not while stricken with terror. On the other hand, the immediate display of awesome and dangerous power upon their acceptance of the covenant was meant to convey a lesson: the God with whom they dealt was not to be taken lightly, nor did covenant status imply exemption from punishment. The first lesson the covenant people were to learn was that God ought to be feared.

More specifically, the fear of God that the people would learn began with learning respect for Moses! The first reason God gave for bringing a terrifying display down upon the mountain was so the people might understand Moses's special status. He was the lawgiver, and by submitting to him and his laws, the people submitted to God. The dense cloud on the mountain was part of the process of exalting Moses before the people. Being within the cloud, he could see something of the presence of God that they could not. This is further indication, we should note, that Israel's status as a "kingdom of priests" was never meant to imply that all people had equal access to the divine presence.

19:10–15. The second set of instructions describe how Israel was to learn respect for God by preparing themselves. First, they were to wash their clothes, bodily cleanliness being representative of the moral purity God demanded. Second, they were to set a boundary all around the mountain with the stipulation that any living thing that crossed it was to be killed while treated as utterly untouchable. They would be stoned or shot with arrows so that no one would have to come into contact with them. The mountain upon which God descended was holy, and no one could ascend it without express invitation from God. The boundary was the absolute limit for how far up the mountain the people could go, but until the ram's horn sounded, they were not to approach the mountain at all (see the translation note to 19:13e). But at no time were they allowed to ascend to the heights of the mountain with Moses.[114] Third, the people were to abstain from sexual activity. The prohibition against sexual activity does not appear until 19:15c and is not included in God's commands at vv. 10–13. We should not assume, however, that Moses's prohibition against having sexual intercourse wrongly made God's command more onerous than God himself intended. The idea, plainly enough, is that it is simply improper for people to have sexual relations just before a direct encounter with God, and this is in keeping with God's demands that the people be ritually clean prior to the theophany. Ahimelech the priest at Nob was similarly concerned that no bread from the sanctuary should be given to men who had recently had sexual relations with women (1 Sam. 21:4[5]). The people seem to have done all that was asked of them; there are, again, no grounds for finding fault with their behavior.

19:16–20a. The terrifying sounds and sights of the theophany on the mountain began before the people came near the mountain; possibly they awoke to the thundering, trumpeting sounds and looked up to see that it was enveloped in smoke and lightning. Instead of doing what is natural (running away), they had to make their way toward the mountain. All of the phenomena described here (billowing smoke, fire, trumpet-like sounds, thundering or explosive sounds, lightning flashes, and earthquake) are associated with volcanic eruptions. The people are learning

114. Sailhamer's interpretation, that the people were originally supposed to go up the mountain to meet God but pulled back because of a lack of faith (Sailhamer, *Old Testament Theology*, 284-5), is impossible.

their first lesson about their covenant God—that he is powerful and not to be treated lightly. At the same time, Moses's standing was raised dramatically in the encounter. As he went before the people, leading them to the mountain, he was apparently calling out to God, and the voice of God was answering from the mountain for all to hear (v. 19). In such a situation, the special status of Moses could hardly be greater.

19:20bc–23. God called upon Moses to come separately up to the mountain, and reiterated the instructions that the mountain should have a boundary set about it to restrain the people from approaching, and that the people must sanctify themselves. This time, the warning against crossing the boundary does not contain a stipulation that a transgressor should be executed by the people; rather, God himself will strike out against that person. A notable fact about the command that the people sanctify themselves is that even the priests, who normally had special access to God in the ritual life of Israel, had to be very careful not to give offense to God through some kind of ritual impurity. The significant point here is that Israel already had priests (against the common notion that the priesthood did not begin in Israel until after the consecration of Aaron and his sons in Exod. 40). In fact, the consecration of Aaron was specifically a consecration to minister in the Tent of Meeting; it was not an act that transformed him from a lay person into a priest. From other texts, one may conclude that Aaron was already of priestly status in Israel prior to this time.[115]

19:24–25. Moses is then told to go back down and bring Aaron back up with him. YHWH is about to give Israel the Book of the Covenant, the terms of the agreement into which they have entered. Moses, as the lawgiver, would of course be present. But Aaron, as the priest of Israel, must also be there to represent the people at this most sacred moment, when the essential terms of the covenant governing the relationship between Israel and YHWH will be laid down. Everyone else, however, including the other priests, is excluded.

115. The designation of Aaron as "the Levite" in Exod. 4:14 is not a passing reference to his tribal membership; it marks him as having priestly status already. In fact, there never appears to be any doubt that Aaron is the priestly leader of the people. The people go to him for the making and consecration of the golden calf, and God never has to tell Moses that Aaron is to be the high priest. It appears to be common knowledge. 1 Samuel 2:27 indicates that the priestly duties of the Levites were already in place while Israel was in Egypt.

Theological Summary of Key Points

The essential lesson of this text is that it is right and proper for the covenant people to fear God. An obvious danger to being the "chosen people" is that members of that group may feel that ultimately they have no reason to fear God since, after all, the covenant relationship guarantees that in the end nothing bad will happen to them. On the other hand, there is a fear of God that is without covenant relationship that manifests itself in running from God. Israel at Sinai is offered the opportunity to become the people of God, and they wisely accept the gift rather than run away. But at the very moment of receiving it, they are given a dramatic object lesson in what that status means. They are God's special possession and a kingdom of priests, but if any one of them crosses the boundary that is set between them and God, that person will die. The God to whom they have bound themselves does not take transgression lightly. They all belong to God, but only those whom God calls out from among them may approach him. Common membership in the covenant community does not mean equal privileges. Historically, this episode is a critical moment, the initiation of the Sinai covenant. It is not the covenant of promise, as given to Abraham, but a covenant in the form of a law code, with specific obligations and specific repercussions for obedience or disobedience.

The Christian minister who teaches this passage must balance three factors: the significance of the Sinai covenant in the story of Israel, the moral lessons about obedience to God, and the significance of the Sinai covenant over against the new covenant. The third point is especially explored in Heb. 12:18–24. But the proclamation of the glories of Zion, the new covenant, in contrast to Sinai, requires wisdom and care. On the one hand, the preacher must make clear that the new covenant is not like the old and that in Christ we have died to the law. On the other hand, one must not preach a triumphalist and antinomian theology, neglecting the proper lesson of this text that we who are in Christ ought to fear God and not presume upon our status. In summary, Exodus 19 teaches the following.

1. At Sinai, Israel became the covenant people. Henceforth, their whole history would be determined by their special relationship to God. Some decisions truly are momentous.

2. The holiness of God is not a thing to be trifled with. It is so great that even a member of his covenant people may not approach him unbidden.

3. Whether Israel lives or dies depends upon their fidelity to the covenant, and the entire subsequent history of Israel as described in the biblical narrative follows this as the guiding principle. Israel's narrative history, and the prophets' interpretation of it, have almost no interest in any matter beyond this one. Apart from the matter of fidelity to God and his commands, nothing else in life is really of great importance.

4. God chose representatives for Israel, most especially Moses, and disobedience to Moses was tantamount to disobedience to God. Today, no mortal man in the church is in a position comparable to that held by Moses. Nevertheless, the principle that one should show proper deference to leaders in the church remains valid (Heb. 13:17).

5. Israel has arrived at the place of God and may therefore enter his rest, but they may not do this until they understand the nature of the God with whom they have to do. Merely coming to God is only the first step. We must understand who God is, who we are, and how our lives have to be reshaped accordingly.

Excursus: The Sequence of Events in and after Exodus 19

Reading through Exodus 19, it is somewhat difficult to judge how many times Moses went up and down the mountain. A yet more difficult task is to determine when the golden calf sin occurred. One might get the impression that the golden calf was made while Moses was receiving the Book of the Covenant, but this is not possible. Aaron was with Moses at the giving of the Decalogue and Book of the Covenant (19:24), but Aaron was with the people when they made the calf (32:1). The movements in Exod. 19, however, seem to be as follows:

1. Israel arrives at Sinai and Moses goes up the mountain alone, where he receives the oracle offering the covenant to Israel (vv. 1–6).

2. Moses comes down and conveys God's offer to the people, who accept the terms (vv. 7–8c).

3. Moses goes back to God with their acceptance, and is instructed to set boundaries around the mountain and prepare the people for the theophany (vv. 8d–13).

4. Moses returns to the people and conveys God's instructions (vv. 14–15).

5. On the third day, in the morning, the mountain theophany begins. Moses and the people approach the mountain, and they hear God responding audibly to Moses (vv. 16–20a).

6. Moses is called back up the mountain and receives further instruction about consecrating the people (vv. 20b–24).

7) Moses goes back down to inform the people of the situation and to bring Aaron back up with him to receive the Book of the Covenant from God.

The narrative then proceeds to give the contents of the entire Book of the Covenant (20:1—23:33). It follows this with the covenant ratification ceremony (24:1–8). In the ceremony, Moses, Aaron, Nadab, Abihu, and seventy elders go up to the lower parts of the mountain, and the people approach but stay somewhat further back (24:1–3). The actual covenant ratification ceremony takes place in front of the mountain, where the people are (24:5–8). The narrative sequence indicates that the covenant ceremony took place after the Book of the Covenant was finished. This obviously must be the case (otherwise, the covenant would have been ratified before its stipulations were set forth). Equally in keeping with the narrative sequence and equally obviously, the ceremony of 24:3–8 took place prior to the golden calf episode in Exod. 32 and the subsequent covenant renewal in Exod. 34:10–27 (Israel would not have been in violation of the covenant, and there would have been no covenant for YHWH to renew, had Israel not already ratified it).

Immediately after the covenant ceremony of 24:3–8, and before the golden calf episode, YHWH called Moses, Aaron, Nadab, Abihu, and seventy elders back up to the lower part of the mountain for a vision of the glory of God (24:9–11). Sometime after this, YHWH called Moses alone (except for his assistant, Joshua) into the higher parts of the mountain for further revelations. Aaron explicitly did not go up with him (24:12–18). Moses waited before God for seven days (24:16), and then he was with YHWH for forty days (24:18; it is possible that the forty days included the initial seven of 24:16). It was during this period that YHWH gave Moses the requirements for the making of the great Tent of Meeting (24:9–31:18).

Two other factors complicate things. First, in the context of the golden calf narrative, we are told that there was a small tent of meeting outside of the camp to which Moses would go to consult with God while the people stood outside their tents (33:7–8). Presumably the tent was on the mountain; it was outside of the camp, and it would have made no sense to put it anywhere else, since the mountain was where Moses would meet God. The fact that there was a tent where Moses would converse with YHWH and the fact that there was a standard ritual Israel would follow at such a time suggest that some time had passed since the initial days on Mt. Sinai, when Israel arrived and made its covenant with YHWH (Exod. 19:1–24:8). That is, a routine for getting guidance from God at the small tent of meeting had been established.[116] It appears that there was an unspecified gap of time between the covenant ratification (24:3–8) and the forty days of revelation regarding the great Tent of Meeting (24:9–31:18). In other words, this period of Moses's forty days on the mountain , during which time the golden calf was made, could have occurred months after the covenant ratification.

Second, Exod. 32:15–19 indicates that Moses had the two tablets of the law in his hands when he came down to confront the people over the golden calf. This could cause readers to suppose that the golden calf incident took place while YHWH was giving Moses the Decalogue in Exod. 20, but that would be a mistake. The first mention of the two tablets is in fact at 24:12. God had told Moses that he would give him the tablets in the course of the forty-day period of revelation (24:12), and he did so (31:18). Therefore, it is clear that the initial revelation of the Decalogue and the Book of the Covenant did not involve the making of stone tablets. We should also note that the details about the tablets given in 32:15–19 are meant to indicate what precious objects they were and therefore how great was Moses's anger and frustration, that he would throw them down and break them. In short, Moses received the stone tablets only after the covenant ratification and well after the initial revelation of the Decalogue.

Therefore, we can suggest the following sequence of events after chapter 19:

1. Moses receives the Book of the Covenant, including the Decalogue (20:1–23:33).

2. The covenant ratification ceremony takes place (24:1–8).

3. Moses, Aaron, Nadab, Abihu and seventy of the elders of Israel see the glory of YHWH (24:9–11).

---

116. For further discussion of the small tent of meeting, see the commentary at 33:7–11.

4. There is a gap of some time, during which Moses was communing with YHWH at the little tent of meeting (33:7–8).

5. Moses goes up the mountain, is there for forty days, and receives both instructions on building the great Tent of Meeting and the two stone tablets (24:12–31:18). Meanwhile, the people under Aaron's leadership make the golden calf (32:1–6).

6. Moses begins a series of intercessions for Israel, including another forty-day stay on the mountain. As a result of his efforts, YHWH neither destroys nor abandons Israel. He reaffirms the covenant and authorizes a second set of stone tablets (32:7–34:28).

7. Moses, with glowing face, informs Israel of YHWH's decision (34:29–35).

8. Israel then builds the great Tent of Meeting and begins the sojourn with YHWH (35:1–40:38).

PART V

The Sinai Covenant (20:1—24:11)

The Sinai covenant is at the center of Israel's faith and national existence. It is the governing document that sets the terms of the relationship between YHWH and Israel. The first and most succinct form of the covenant is the "Book of the Covenant." This is widely understood to include 21:1–24:8, but in my view the Ten Commandments should be reckoned as part of this document. The Book of the Covenant was expanded through the inclusion of other laws in Leviticus and Numbers; Deuteronomy is essentially a sermonic and exhortatory restatement of the Book of the Covenant. But just as the Ten Commandments are part of the statement of the covenant in Deuteronomy (at 5:6–21), so, too, can they be considered to be part of the Book of the Covenant. Here in Exod. 20:1–24:8, we have a succinct, yet global, statement of what God expects of the nation. All the essential areas of life—devotion to God, commitment to personal integrity and morality, family responsibilities, judicial principles, and national days of worship—are included.

THE TEN COMMANDMENTS (20:1–17)

At the core of the covenant agreement between YHWH and Israel is the document known as the "Ten Words," a concise statement of God's expectations of Israel.

Translation

20:1 And God spoke all these words, as follows:

20:2 "I am YHWH your God, who brought you out of the land of Egypt, out of the house of slaves.

20:3 You shall have no other gods in my face.[1]

20:4 You shall not make for yourself an idol,[2] or any representation of what is in heaven above or of what is on the earth beneath or of what is in the water under the earth.

20:5a You shall not worship them

20:5b and you shall not serve them,

20:5c for I, YHWH your God, am a jealous God, who punishes the iniquity of the fathers on the children, up to the third or the fourth generations of those who hate me,

20:6 but who shows grace to thousands—to those who love me and who keep my commands.

20:7a You shall not use the name of YHWH your God disrespectfully,[3]

20:7b for YHWH will not treat as innocent anyone who uses his name disrespectfully.

20:8 Remember the Sabbath day, to sanctify it.

20:9a For six days you shall labor

20:9b and you shall work at all your business,[4]

20:10a but the seventh day is a Sabbath of YHWH your God.

---

1. The translation of עַל־פָּנָי is difficult. Usually rendered "before me," this translation seems to suggest that one may have other gods as long as they are secondary gods, "after" YHWH and not "before" him, so that YHWH is the primary deity. This is surely not the meaning of the Hebrew. Perhaps the closest analogy to the use of עַל־פָּנָי in this text is at 1 Kings 9:7, "the house that I have consecrated for my name I will send away from my face (אֲשַׁלַּח מֵעַל פָּנָי)." The idea is that something offensive to YHWH is right in front of his face. That is, any worship of another god is an affront to YHWH and is, in effect, an insult. This is best communicated by the English idiom, "in my face."
2. The word פֶּסֶל is from the root פסל, to "carve out," and it is perhaps the most neutral term in biblical Hebrew for an idol. Many Hebrew words for "idol" are highly derogatory (see Edward M. Curtis, "The Theological Basis for the Prohibition of Images in the Old Testament," *JETS* 28, no. 3 (1985): 278-80, for a survey of the more derogatory terms). But פֶּסֶל is simply descriptive, a "carved thing," because this text is not ridiculing idolatry (as is often the case in the prophets), but is giving a matter-of-fact prohibition.
3. The word תִשָּׂא (נשׂא) here means to take up something upon one's lips (i.e., to say it). לַשָּׁוְא ("to nothing") here means to treat something as cheap or to fail to give it respect.
4. The word מְלָאכָה can refer to any kind of personal business, such as trade (Ps. 107:23), official duties (Dan. 8:27), a craft or skill (Exod. 35:31; 1 Chron. 22:15), or simply some work that one needs to take care of (Prov. 24:27). It can also refer to temple service, but obviously that is not prohibited on the Sabbath.

20:10b Do not work at any business—not you or your son or your daughter, not your male or your female servant or your cattle or the resident alien whom you have[5] within your gate.

20:11a For in six days YHWH made the heavens and the earth, the sea and all that is in them,

20:11b and he rested on the seventh day;

20:11c therefore YHWH blessed the Sabbath day,

20:11d and he sanctified it.

20:12a Honor your father and your mother

20:12b in order that your days may be prolonged in the land that YHWH your God is giving to you.

20:13 You shall not commit homicide.[6]

20:14 You shall not commit adultery.

20:15 You shall not steal.

20:16 You shall not give testimony as a perjurer against your neighbor.[7]

20:17a You shall not desire[8] your neighbor's house;

20:17b you shall not desire your neighbor's wife or his male servant or his female servant or his ox or his donkey or anything that belongs to your neighbor."

Structure

The text of Exod. 20 does not specify how many commands we have here, but Exod. 34:28; Deut. 4:13; 10:4 all speak of the tables of the Law containing "ten words" (עֲשֶׂרֶת הַדְּבָרִים), and these are universally considered to be the ten commands making up Exod. 20:1–17 and its parallel, Deut. 5:6–21. The controversy over how the Ten Commandments ought

5. Lit. "your resident alien," but obviously the resident alien is not the property of the implied Israelite reader. The idea is that he cannot hire foreigners to do work on the Sabbath that the Israelite is not allowed to carry out.

6. The word רצח refers to killing a person violently, as an act of revenge, or without legal sanction, but it is not necessarily premeditated murder. It is regularly used to refer to the person who has committed accidental or involuntary homicidc (Num. 35:22–28). See the discussion in the commentary.

7. The setting is a judicial proceeding. ענה refers to the giving of testimony (Exod. 23:2). The עֵד־שֶׁקֶר is a perjurer (Deut. 19:18).

8. There is nothing wrong with the translation "covet" except that, since it is not a common word in modern English, its use here can give rise to legalistic wrangling about precisely what "covet" means and about what constitutes a violation of the command. The word חמד simply means to "desire." One is guilty of "coveting," as defined in this command, if one desires what belongs to another person.

to be divided is well-known, with different traditions enumerating the commands somewhat differently. Briefly, the different interpretations are as in Table 11.

<table>
<tr><th colspan="5">TABLE 11. THE DIVISION OF THE TEN COMMANDMENTS</th></tr>
<tr><th>Text</th><th>Judaism</th><th>Orthodox</th><th>Roman Catholic, Lutheran</th><th>Anglican, Reformed</th></tr>
<tr><td>20:2</td><td>1</td><td rowspan="2">1</td><td rowspan="3">1</td><td>Prologue</td></tr>
<tr><td>20:3</td><td rowspan="2">2</td><td>1</td></tr>
<tr><td>20:4–6</td><td>2</td><td>2</td></tr>
<tr><td>20:7</td><td>3</td><td>3</td><td>2</td><td>3</td></tr>
<tr><td>20:8–11</td><td>4</td><td>4</td><td>3</td><td>4</td></tr>
<tr><td>20:12</td><td>5</td><td>5</td><td>4</td><td>5</td></tr>
<tr><td>20:13</td><td>6</td><td>6</td><td>5</td><td>6</td></tr>
<tr><td>20:14</td><td>7</td><td>7</td><td>6</td><td>7</td></tr>
<tr><td>20:15</td><td>8</td><td>8</td><td>7</td><td>8</td></tr>
<tr><td>20:16</td><td>9</td><td>9</td><td>8</td><td>9</td></tr>
<tr><td>20:17a</td><td rowspan="2">10</td><td rowspan="2">10</td><td>9</td><td rowspan="2">10</td></tr>
<tr><td>20:17b</td><td>10</td></tr>
</table>

Judaism, following talmudic teaching, treats 20:2 as a command to believe in God, and combines 20:3–6 into a single command that prohibits all improper worship, whether of other deities or by means of idols. Eastern Orthodoxy combines 20:2–3 as a single assertion that one must worship only God, and treats 20:4–6 (against the worship of idols) as the second commandment. The Roman Catholic and Lutheran churches, following Augustine, treat all of 20:2–6 as the first commandment, and divide the prohibition against coveting at 20:17 into two parts, forming the ninth and tenth commandments. Anglicans and Protestants, as indicated in the catechism of the Book of Common Prayer and in countless Protestant expositions, generally treat 20:2 as a prologue, 20:3 as the first commandment, 20:4–6 as the second commandment, and after that follow the order adhered to in Judaism and Orthodoxy. This commentary follows the standard Anglican/Reformed division of the text.

Commentary

20:1. The brief assertion that God spoke “all these words” introduces the Book of the Covenant (20:1—24:8), the first systematic presentation of legal stipulations in the Torah. This text is the core of the requirements of the Sinai covenant to which Israel has pledged obedience. Numerous specific regulations that follow in the rest of Exodus as well as in Leviticus, Numbers, and Deuteronomy will comprise the full presentation of the requirements of the Sinai covenant. But the Book of the Covenant succinctly states Israel's obligations to God. Indeed, all of the rest of the legal material of the Torah could be considered an exposition of the Book of the Covenant, and the full Book of the Covenant could be considered an exposition of the Ten Commandments.

20:2. This verse does not command anything, and it should not be considered to be all or part of the First Commandment. Against the standard Jewish interpretation, it is hardly a charge to believe in God; the existence of God and the people's belief is simply assumed. Rather, this verse gives the basis for God's claims over the people of Israel: he is their God because they have accepted the terms of the covenant (Exod. 19:8), and he has a claim upon them because he redeemed them from Egypt. As such, this verse is prolegomenous to all the commandments and to the whole Book of the Covenant; God asserts that he legitimately has the right to make these demands of Israel.

20:3. Although it is understandable that one would link "You shall have no other gods before me" to the prohibition of idolatry, as is done in both Jewish and Roman Catholic interpretation, this command is in fact distinct from 20:4–6. One could, for example, worship another god for which there is no idol (such as Allah of Islam or Ahura Mazda of Zoroastrianism), and thus violate 20:3 without violating 20:4–6. As such, 20:3 stands alone as the First Commandment.

This command is popularly taken to be an assertion of monotheism or a demand that the Israelites adhere to monotheistic doctrine. A problem, however, is that there is no monotheistic exposition of the command (several commands—the second, third, fourth, and fifth—have exposition). More to the point, this verse never states that YHWH is the only God or that all other gods are delusions. This naturally raises the question of whether the commandment teaches "henotheism" (a belief in many gods but with devotion to only one) as opposed to monotheism (a belief that in fact only one God is real). Before addressing this question, one should note that all pagans were to some degree polytheists and to some degree "henotheists" in accordance with the above definition. That is, while a pagan happily believed in many gods, he or she often felt a stronger obligation to a single, patron deity. Thus,

Amun was especially honored in New Kingdom Egypt, and Marduk was celebrated as the god of Babylon. Even on the family level, people tended to devote themselves to one, or to a few, patron deities of the household. A pagan was free to worship other gods and indeed considered it a safe thing to do, but that pagan would always display special homage to the deities of his own state or family.

But one is asking the wrong question of the text if one asks whether Exod. 20:3 teaches henotheism or monotheism. The command is not a catechism, and it does not raise doctrinal or theoretical issues. That is, it simply does not address the question of monotheism. What it does is to demand absolute loyalty to YHWH. It does not matter whether or not the average Israelite could give a satisfactory apologetic for the proposition that YHWH exists but Baal is the work of human imagination. That Israelite is still commanded to serve YHWH alone and have nothing to do with any other deity. No deference to any other god, the sort of religious respect that a pagan would routinely give toward many gods other than his patron deity, was allowed to the Israelite. Any homage to any other god is done "in YHWH's face," that is, it constitutes a direct insult to YHWH. Other biblical passages establish monotheism theoretically, but this text makes the point that apart from the worship of YHWH, one must shun every religious belief and practice. We should also note that being a monotheist does not mean that one is obedient to this command. One may falsely believe in one God, as Muslims falsely believe that the one Allah of the Koran is the God of Abraham.

20:4–6. The prohibition of the making and worship of idols is, along with the Sabbath commandment, highly controversial in the Christian church. At the one extreme are churches that are filled with images of God, Jesus, angels and saints (Orthodox and, to a lesser degree, Roman Catholic churches are obvious examples). On the other extreme are churches that are not only devoid of icons but are artistically barren as well, having only plain, white walls and no artwork of any kind (traditional reformed and Baptist churches often follow this model). The latter groups argue that the command is straightforward enough; images are prohibited. The former tend to argue, first, that God in the incarnation demonstrated that deity could be represented in human form and, second, that they do not worship icons but venerate them and use them as means for the contemplation of the divine.

In order to deal with this, we must first ask what the text actually prohibits. First, it tells us that we must make no physical representation of God (or of a god). The word פֶּסֶל describes something that is hewn out of wood or stone, but in context and usage it plainly refers to an artistic representation of a deity. Second, it tells us that we must not "worship" any image. But we need to be careful here. The word "worship" in English means something like "to praise someone as a god." But the word תִּשְׁתַּחֲוֶה is not so purely theological; it simply means to bow down or otherwise make a physical show of obeisance. Such veneration may be legitimately offered to a human being (e.g., 2 Sam. 14:33). In such a case, the man so honored is not deified; he is only being shown respect. But what can be proper to offer to a living man under the right circumstances is never to be offered to an artistic object under any circumstances. That is, we should make no representations of God, and we should not make any gestures of respect or adoration to such images.

From that, it follows that there should be no artistic representations of God for Christians. This includes not only images of God the Father but also of Jesus Christ, as we believe him to be truly human and truly God. The argument that the incarnation legitimizes such icons is specious; Jesus is himself the legitimate image of God (Heb. 1:3), but this does not legitimate making images of him. One cannot have artificial images of the true image; this is no different from any other artificial image of God. To pose the issue historically: Is it possible to imagine that Paul, distressed at all the idols of Athens (Acts 17:16), would pull from his cloak an icon of Jesus, or of Mary and the baby Jesus, and tell the Athenians that this is what they should bow before? It is inconceivable. Paul did not so interpret the incarnation. Although in Jesus of Nazareth God was with us in human flesh, this in no way legitimizes making images of him.

From the second part of the commandment, it follows that we should not bow down before any artistic representation, be it of Jesus, a saint, or an angel. In this, it does not matter whether or not one affirms that the person represented is a god. It is the very fact of bowing before such images that is illegitimate. Even the pagans, at least the more sophisticated ones, would have understood that they were not actually worshipping the image but were worshipping the god through the image. But this does not make the activity any less illicit. And one cannot avoid the force of this by having only images of saints (and not of God) to kneel before. When the Egyptians deified a mortal (such as the Old Kingdom architect and physician Imhotep), they did not think of him as "God" as we understand the term. They merely thought of him as a good and wise mortal who had been elevated to a high status among the heavenly beings, and who could now be entreated for help. If a pre-Christian pagan could see a Christian kneeling before an image of Mary and making requests for aid, that pagan would have no doubt about what that Christian was doing:

he was calling upon his goddess. If the Christian were to counter that Mary is not a goddess, the pagan would rightly reply that the Christian simply does not understand the meaning of the word.

Does it follow then that no artistic work of any kind is legitimate, and that all churches should be the bare, white buildings of Puritanism? In my view, this, too, is an extreme position. Even the Israelite Tent of Meeting had numerous representations of cherubim (on the Ark of the Covenant and woven into the inner layer of the tent itself). But these were cherubim, not gods, and the people were not to bow down before them, address them, or in any way pay homage to them. Thus, the two tests of idolatry are: 1) Does the artwork represent God or a god? 2) Do people bow before the artwork (and especially, do they speak toward it, as though by speaking to it one can speak to the person it represents)? If the answer to either is Yes, then the object is an idol. It is the very act of homage to the image that makes it into an idol.

The sin of idolatry became the great stumbling block of Old Testament Israel. The Former and Latter Prophets mark it out as the centerpiece of evil and apostasy. Of all the commands in the Decalogue, the text attaches to this one its most powerful threat of punishment and promise of reward (20:5c–6), implying that a curse rests upon generations of those who break it.

20:7. There are two ways in which one may use God's name disrespectfully, and both are covered in the English word "swearing." One way is to swear an oath in YHWH's name, but to do it dishonestly. The Egyptian votive stele of Neferabu (New Kingdom) illustrates this. The author claims that he swore an oath in Ptah's name but did not keep it, and that he was struck blind for his impiety. He therefore warns the reader, "Beware of Ptah, Lord of Maat! / Behold, he does not overlook anyone's deed!"[9] Therefore, the notion that it was wrong to swear falsely in a god's name was familiar to Egyptians, and certainly the Israelites held to the same standard for oaths in YHWH's name. That is, if one invokes the name of YHWH in an oath but does it with the purpose of deceiving, it is one way of violating this command. The other is to use God's name flippantly, as an expletive (shouting "God!" or "Jesus!" when angry or surprised). The two types of offenses, swearing falsely and the use of God's name as an expletive, may be historically related, and this could explain why both are called "swearing" in English. That is, at one time a person in anger might have sworn something like, "By

9. "Votive Stela of Neferabu with Hymn to Ptah," translated by B. Gunn (*AEL* 2:110).

God, I am going to deal with this!" Eventually, this could be shortened to "By God!" and finally just to "God!" The latter way of abusing God's name, profanity, is much more common today, as people rarely take formal oaths. The exposition of the command makes the point that God does not regard this as innocent or harmless. We should note that there is a third way someone in the ancient world might have taken God's name in vain: by using it as a magical term to make a spell or incantation more potent. The Egyptians thought that there was great power in knowing a god's secret name; the goddess Isis in one myth gains power over Re by learning his secret name. Something like this may be occurring in Acts 19:13–16, where Jewish exorcists use the name of Jesus to try to gain control over demons.

20:8–11. The Sabbath command is unique to Israel in the ancient world, having no parallel in the other ancient Near Eastern law codes. Attempts at uncovering some extra-Israelite origin for the Sabbath idea have not been successful. Some have tried to link the idea to the Akkadian *šapattu*, a festival term associated with a phase of the moon, and others have sought to demonstrate a Kenite or Ugaritic origin for the Sabbath, but these efforts have persuaded few.[10] In the exodus narrative, the Israelites themselves had no awareness of a Sabbath concept until the manna incident of Exod. 16, so it is hardly likely that we will find the origin of the Sabbath outside of Israel.

The command to keep the Sabbath, like the command against idolatry, has divided the church, although not so clearly along denominational lines as the second commandment has (apart from the existence of Seventh Day Adventist churches). Some argue that we are bound to keep the Sabbath strictly, while others assert that the command is altogether obsolete or never applied to the Gentile church. Two factors complicate this question. First, what day, Saturday or Sunday, should we observe as the Sabbath? Second, what are we to make of the two versions of the Sabbath (comparing Deut. 5:15 to Exod. 20:11)? The Exodus version explains the Sabbath on the basis of the creation week, while the Deuteronomy version explains it by the exodus event.

There is no doubt that the Sabbath of ancient Israel corresponds to our Saturday, the seventh day of the week (strict Jewish observance carries it from Friday evening to Saturday evening). On the other hand, there is no doubt that the Christian church, from its inception,

10. Mark F. Rooker, *The Ten Commandments: Ethics for the Twenty-First Century,* NAC Studies in Bible & Theology (Nashville: B&H Academic, 2010), 75.

considered the first day of the week, Sunday, as "the Lord's day" and as a day for worship (Acts 20:7; 1 Cor. 16:2; Rev. 1:10; see also Justin Martyr, First Apology 67). There is no indication in the New Testament that the seventh day has special status in the church. The reason for the church's shift to the first day is obvious: it celebrates the resurrection of Jesus, which took place on a Sunday. More profoundly, the commemoration of Jesus's resurrection on Sunday anticipates the new creation of all things, the new heaven and earth, for which Jesus's resurrection is the "first fruits." Thus, as the Old Testament Sabbath looked back to the old creation, the Lord's Day looks back to Jesus's resurrection but also looks forward to the new creation.

However, although Exod. 20:11 states that Israel was to observe the Sabbath because YHWH rested on the seventh day of creation, Deut. 5:15 says that the basis for Sabbath observance is that "you were slaves in Egypt and YHWH your God brought you out of there." It is not clear why we have two versions of the command. It is, however, theologically significant.

The Deuteronomy version indicates that Israelites should take a weekly day of rest because they had been slaves in Egypt; a weekly Sabbath reminds them that they are no longer slaves and that they owe their freedom to YHWH. So understood, the Sabbath is a purely Israelite day of rest; it is a national holiday for this people alone. On the other hand, the linkage of the Sabbath to creation in Exod. 20:11 implies that the Sabbath principle is universal in nature. In other words, we see the Old Testament at one point speaking of the Sabbath as Israel's national day of rest (Deut. 5) and at another point as something that is, as it were, part of the structure of creation (Exod. 20). This, combined with the New Testament celebration of the Lord's Day, indicates that the weekly observance of a special day (Sunday) continues to have validity in the church. In short, basing the Sabbath in creation indicates that the principle of treating one day in seven as special has some validity for all humanity, even if certain particulars of the Sabbath are strictly for Israel and relate to Israel's exodus. The church, in maintaining the one-day-in-seven rule but focusing on the new creation in Christ, is legitimately making use of the Sabbath principle. We should note that there is one other difference, however; Israel's Sabbath is essentially a day of rest,[11] while the Lord's Day is essentially a day for gathering to worship.

---

11. This is true of Old Testament Israel. The emergence of the synagogue and of gathering there on the Sabbath is a later phenomenon. Of course, the

20:12. The command to "honor" parents essentially means one shows them the respect that they are due. The word for "honor" (כַּבֵּד) essentially means to regard someone as "weighty" (that is, not as a "lightweight" or as unimportant). Like the Latin term *gravitas*, it literally refers to heaviness but metaphorically implies dignity, authority, and high value in a person. The manner in which respect is shown toward parents will vary with circumstances. An adult does not show the kind of absolute obedience to parents that a ten-year-old child ought to show, and parents should not desire to direct the actions of adult children in the way that they ought to direct the behavior of younger children. On the other hand, a ten-year-old should not be financially responsible for parents in the way that an adult child is, should the parents fall into need (Mark 7:10–13).

Perhaps the most remarkable aspect of this command, however, is that as Paul says, it comes with a promise: "in order that your days may be prolonged in the land that YHWH your God is giving to you" (see Eph. 6:2). What is the connection between honoring parents and having a long life? First, we should observe that this is a proverbial truth; it is generally true, but it is not without exception. Clearly there are examples of good and respectful sons and daughters who die tragically young. But even as a proverbial truth, how is it that respect for parents contributes to a long life? The answer, I believe, is that parents are the first and foremost representatives of the authority structures of life. That is, those who respect their parents will not have trouble dealing with another authority in life, be it in government, business, the military, or society in general. From a habit of respecting parental authority, one learns that there are rules that govern life and that there are people who rightly are in a position to enforce the rules. Such a person will respect laws, school rules, and company policies as well as the police, teachers, and employers. He will not have in his company file the notation "has trouble with authority," and is therefore less likely to be fired. He will not be expelled from a university for disorderly behavior or cheating. More generally, such a person will understand that rules govern all of life, and will not do such things as trying to drive a car while intoxicated. In short, those who, out of their relationship to their parents, learn respect for authority avoid the calamities that befall people who do not, and so are far more likely to be healthy, at peace, and to live long.

Jewish institution of the synagogue in turn influenced the Christian concept of gathering for worship on the Lord's Day.

20:13. The verb רצח means to kill a person with violence. It does not necessarily mean to intentionally murder someone. The man responsible for accidental manslaughter in the cities of refuge legislation of Num. 35 is called הָרֹצֵחַ (Num. 35:12), "the one who committed רצח." Also, in that legislation the "avenger of blood" may lawfully kill (רצח) the one guilty of manslaughter should the latter leave a city of refuge (Num. 35:27). Since the word רצח is used both for the person guilty of accidental manslaughter and for the "avenger of blood," one might argue that any taking of human life violates this command, so that both capital punishment and participation in military action also fall under this prohibition. But other biblical texts indicate that taking life for these two reasons is valid; we cannot choose to reject one standard and accept the other unless we wish to argue that much of the Old Testament is morally misguided. But such a course would be self-defeating. In the final analysis, it would turn the entire Old Testament into a subjective conflict among competing moral visions, and the prohibition against killing would have no more moral authority than any competing viewpoint. Taking the moral teaching of the Bible as it stands, it is clear that one may kill if one is lawfully fighting in a war, or one may kill if one is the lawful representative of the state in carrying out capital punishment. Examples of both of these are so common in the Old Testament that neither needs illustration, and the slaying of people under these circumstances is not described with the verb רצח. Therefore, the prohibition of רצח in the Ten Commandments does not prohibit killing in warfare or for capital punishment. What, therefore, constitutes the committing of רצח, and what is specifically prohibited? The one guilty of manslaughter is said to have committed רצח not because he did or did not intend to kill but because he had no legal sanction from a government to kill. That is, he is not lawfully killing as an agent of the state. And in fact, the same is true of the "avenger of blood." If he kills (רצח) the one guilty of manslaughter, the avenger is carrying out a family vendetta. Thus, even though his action may be tolerated in a primitive society, it is a violent act of revenge and not an execution carried out by the state. Thus, the "avenger of blood" also commits רצח, even if this is the exceptional case in which רצח is tolerated and not punished by government action. In short, the word רצח means to "kill" and not strictly to "murder," but it carries the suggestion of violence and lawlessness, much like the English word "killer." The word does not apply to someone who takes life as the representative of the state (by analogy, we do not refer to soldiers who do their lawful duty as "killers"). There are, of course, other ethical issues that one could consider. Does the state sometimes take away life for wrong reasons? The answer certainly is Yes (waging a war of aggrandizement, or putting a person to death for having displeased a king). But the commandment does not go into these moral tangles; it only gives the most basic guideline: one should not take life without proper legal sanction.

20:14. The word נאף means to commit adultery; that is, it specifically refers to having a sexual relationship with a person in violation of an existing marriage (either one is married and has sexual relations with another person, or one has sexual relations with another person's spouse). See, for example, Lev. 20:10; Jer. 29:23; Hos. 4:13. We should note that betrothal is considered to be legally binding so that having sexual relations with a person other than the betrothed is also considered to be adultery. Also, the word נאף is sometimes used metaphorically for idolatry (Israel is committing adultery against YHWH by going to idols; Jer. 3:9). Still, נאף is not a generic word for sexual immorality, such as occurs when an unmarried man goes to an unmarried prostitute. For that, biblical Hebrew would use a word such as זנה (e.g., Lev. 21:9). We should be clear that this is not grounds for supposing that the Bible only forbids sexual acts that violate a marriage vow, or that sexual relations between two unmarried persons, even if they are consenting adults, is acceptable. To the contrary, Scripture emphatically prohibits all licentiousness (see Lev. 18:6–23; also, the daughter who "plays the whore" in Lev. 21:9 is plainly not married, and there is no reason to suppose that her partners are married, but she is clearly condemned as immoral). Similarly, any homosexual act between two persons is immoral, but it is not adultery. We must therefore ask why the Decalogue explicitly forbids adultery as opposed to more generically forbidding sexual immorality. The reason, I believe, is that marriage is foundational for the survival of the family and of society. It is not that other forms of sexual immorality are less evil. Rather, it is that the focus of the text is not on describing generically every kind of sin; the focus is on sins that destroy the fabric of socicty among the covenant people. There are other sexual sins, but the pastor who expounds on this verse should give special attention to the special place of marriage in human society and to how adultery destroys that institution.

20:15. The prohibition against stealing is one command about which there can be little confusion. Any method of taking the property of another person without that person's freely-given consent, be it by clandestine theft, armed robbery, fraud, or embezzlement, violates this command. By implication, the command asserts that the possession of private property is valid, since there can be no theft where there is no property. Thus, it indirectly opposes the idea of concentrating all wealth in the hands of the state, whether that state is called "the king" or, by the euphemism, "the people."

20:16. The central difficulty with this command is analogous to what we see in the prohibition of adultery. Just as the seventh commandment forbids a certain kind of sexual sin and does not deal with all sexual sin generically, so also this command specifically prohibits perjury (see translation notes to this verse and also compare 23:1). It is not a prohibition against every kind of lying. But as before, this does not mean that lying outside of the courtroom is morally acceptable (Lev. 19:11 alludes to the Decalogue but uses more generic language to prohibit all kinds of lying; see also Prov. 6:16–17). Once again, we must recall the purpose of the Decalogue. It is not simply a list of ten broad and generic types of evildoing. It is ten specific sins that will destroy the covenant community. As marriage is foundational to the family, so also a fair and equitable justice system is foundational to social coherence within the community. And the justice system depends entirely upon honest testimony; without that, no justice is possible because judges and juries are not omniscient. They depend upon witnesses in order to function. Thus, this command not only calls for honesty in giving testimony, but also by implication demands that people show respect for both the rule of law and also for basic principles of fairness.

20:17. The command against coveting is the only one that deals with a matter that is purely internal, an individual's thoughts and desires. The fact that another man's wife is included with house and cattle in the list of things that one might covet does not mean that the woman is regarded as mere property. It is true that the command is stated from the male perspective, but it is equally wrong for a woman to desire another woman's husband. The desirable items mentioned here (house, wife, slaves, and livestock) constitute a list of what a typical person in an ancient agricultural society might covet. Children are not in the list since, although many people desire children of their own, it is fairly rare for someone to desire someone else's children. A modern list might include someone else's spouse, house, car, salary, job, fame, power, or success.

The word for "covet" (חמד) simply means to "desire." A desire for something becomes coveting when its object is another person's possession or achievement. Obviously any desire can be emotionally and spiritually destructive if it is obsessive, but the focus of this command is not any desire at all but specifically on the desire for what actually belongs to another person. Thus, for example, a man might lawfully long to have a house, but if he desires a specific house belonging to another man, it is coveting. The term "covet" does not imply that the individual has actually taken any action to fulfill his desire; one can covet something and never do anything about it. A person who only covets has broken the Decalogue once; a person who covets and then steals what he covets has broken the Decalogue twice. Two significant aspects of coveting, therefore, are that the violation of the command takes place only inside one's head, and that the desire for something constitutes a violation of the command only if its object is the possession of another person.

What is the reason for this prohibition? First, this prohibition tells us that the Torah is concerned with the state of one's soul and not only with external acts of obedience. Second, evil in the heart is a precursor to external evil actions (murder, adultery, theft, and so forth), and someone who recognizes evil in his heart for what it is may be able to turn aside from committing overt acts of evil. Third, as Paul recognizes, this command enables us to see how deeply rooted evil is within our hearts (Rom. 7:7–12). This should help us to recognize self-righteousness for what it is—an act of self-deception—and prompt us to seek the mercy of God. Fourth, coveting shows a serious lack of charity, for when we covet someone else's possessions, we mentally treat that person as insignificant, not respecting the fact that the thing we desire actually belongs to him or her. This may be the most important moral issue raised by the command. The fundamental evil in coveting is not desire for the object but contempt for the owner of the object. Fifth, as with the others, there is a community focus with this command. A peaceful and harmonious society cannot exist where there is class warfare between the "haves" and the "have-nots." Covetousness creates a climate of envy and hostility, making it impossible for people to cooperate for the common good. Some politicians actually promote covetousness (in the form of wealth-envy and class warfare) in order to build a political base for themselves. Doing this, they promote a great evil.

Theological Summary of Key Points

1. The key theological points of the Decalogue are obviously the commands themselves. In addition, the commands essentially have three demands: loyalty to YHWH, moral integrity, and responsibility to the covenant community. The first two of these are obvious to any reader; the third has been overlooked. Devotion to God and avoidance of pagan practices is the first element that ensures the survival of the community, and it should be obvious that no society can endure if essential moral rules are widely and pervasively ignored. But also, as described above, the specificity of many of the commands indicates that the survival of the nation, and not a mere catalogue of moral principles, is in view here. Thus adultery and perjury, rather than other forms of evil involving sexual behavior or dishonesty, are singled out for prohibition. Even the prohibition of coveting, as pointed out above, has the purpose of preventing disharmony in society through jealousy and class warfare. The command to honor parents, moreover, creates an environment in which authority is respected and society can function. Thus, although honor for God and proper moral behavior are the goals of the commands, the purpose of the commands for the life of the community has greater explanatory power, enabling us to understand why certain things are prohibited.

2. We should also note that the Ten Commandments is the primary basis for the indictment of Israel for their failure to observe the covenant. As described by David Noel Freedman, the narrative of the Hebrew Bible is in some respects an exposition of Israel's violations of nine commands of the Decalogue,[12] as in Table 12.

TABLE 12. VIOLATIONS OF THE DECALOGUE IN THE NARRATIVE OF THE OLD TESTAMENT

Commandment	Violation
Idolatry	Exodus 32:1–8
God's Name	Leviticus 24:10–16
Sabbath	Numbers 15:32–36
Parents	Deuteronomy 21:18–21
Stealing	Joshua 7:11, 22–26
Murder	Judges 20:4–7, 43–47
Adultery	2 Samuel 11:1–4; 12:7–10
Coveting	1 Kings 21:1–4
Perjury	1 Kings 21:7–14, 20–24

12. David Noel Freedman, *The Nine Commandments: Uncovering a Hidden Pattern of Crime and Punishment in the Hebrew Bible* (New York: Doubleday, 2000).

3. Some commandments figure prominently in the New Testament narrative and theological exposition. Jesus's charge of hypocrisy directed against the Pharisees focuses on the command to honor parents (Matt. 15:1–9). Paul's discussion of sin and grace in Romans is founded in part on his reflections over coveting in his own experience (Rom. 7:7–25). A motive behind Paul's missionary work was the bondage of the nations to idolatry (Acts 17:16; 1 Thess. 1:9).

RESPECT FOR GOD (20:18–26)

After the Decalogue, each section of the Book of the Covenant focuses on giving proper respect to God or some human right or institution. In the first section, the focus is on respect for God, and this is shown both in the initial narrative (20:18–21) and in the subsequent rules governing proper worship (20:22–26).

Translation

20:18a And all the people were observing the sounds and the flashes and the sound of the trumpet and [how] the mountain was smoking:[13]
20:18b the people observed,
20:18c and they shook,
20:18d and they stood far away,
20:19a And they said to Moses,
20:19b "You speak with us
20:19c and we will pay [close] attention;[14]
20:19d but don't let God speak to us,
20:19e or we will die."
20:20a And Moses said to the people,
20:20b "Do not be afraid;
20:20c for God has come in order to test you,
20:20d and in order that the fear of him may be a vivid reality for you,[15]

---

13. This is a periphrastic clause in the pattern וְ + subject + participle, and it is offline, giving the background information to what follows. The series of *wayyiqtol* clauses gives exposition to what happened while they were watching.
14. The *weyiqtol* with paragogic ה here connotes intention or determination. It indicates that the people were strongly assuring Moses they would listen to him if he would act as intermediary.
15. It is difficult to capture the sense of תִּהְיֶה יִרְאָתוֹ עַל־פְּנֵיכֶם (lit., "the fear of him will be at your face"). A translation to the effect that the fear of God would be "with" them is too weak. The point is that it would be vividly experienced, like something that was right in their faces.

20:20e so that you may not sin."
20:21a And the people stood far away,
20:21b but Moses approached the thick darkness where God was.[16]
20:22a And YHWH said to Moses,
20:22b "Thus you shall say to the Israelites,
20:22c 'You observe that I speak to you from heaven.[17]
20:23a You shall not make alongside me gods of silver,[18]
20:23b and gods of gold you shall not make for yourselves.
20:24a You shall make an altar of dirt for me,
20:24b and you shall sacrifice on it your whole offerings and your peace offerings, your sheep and your oxen.
20:24c In every place where I cause my name to be remembered,
20:24d I will come to you
20:24e and I will bless you.
20:25a But if you do make an altar out of stones for me,
20:25b you shall not build it of cut stone;
20:25c if you wield your tool on it,
20:25d then you profane it.
20:26a And do not go up by steps to my altar,
20:26b so that your genitals[19] will not be exposed on it.'"

Structure

This section consists of both narrative and divine exposition of the laws of the covenant, but the two are bound together, as the narrative leads into the topic of the fear of YHWH, the main point of this section. That is, 20:18–21 should not be thought of as a narrative interruption or parenthetic insertion between the Decalogue and the remaining rules of the Book of the Covenant. Rather, the Book of the Covenant, like Deuteronomy, has both narrative and legislative instruction. The

16. The use of the offline pattern וְ + subject + verb makes this clause prominent in the narrative; Moses's walking into the darkness where God was a highly dramatic moment.

17. The *qatal* verbs here are not past tense but present; the *qatal* is used rather than the participle because it is not the process of their observing and God's speaking that is the point; it is the simple fact that these things are happening.

18. The Masoretic cantillation, which divides the verse after לֹא תַעֲשׂוּן אִתִּי, should not be followed. Interpreters often insert something like "other gods" as the object of the first clause (NASB, TNIV; but see NRSV), but that is forced and improbable. It is better to move the clausal break after אֱלֹהֵי כֶסֶף. Note also the chiastic structure of the verse as here translated.

19. Lit. "nakedness."

section is in two parts, with the standing back of the people serving as the lead-in to the two halves.

- I. The Words of the People and Moses (20:18–20)
  - A. The People Stand Back (20:18)
  - B. The People Make a Request and Moses Responds (20:19–20)
- II. The Words of YHWH (20:21–26)
  - A. The People Stand Back (20:21)
  - B. Items Used in Worship (20:22–26)
    - 1. Idols (20:22–23)
    - 2. Altars (20:24–26)

Commentary

20:18. The dread shown by the people is not to be regarded as inappropriate or as a sign of lack of faith. The quaking and burning of the mountain was plainly terrifying, and intentionally so. God had told Moses that his purpose in shaking the mountain was to instill in the populace a fear of God and a respect for Moses (Exod. 19:9), and it was working.

20:19. Out of their terror, the people call on Moses to be the mediator between themselves and God. This is a valid request; the theophany had demonstrated that God was not to be trifled with. Only Moses had been authorized to speak directly with God, and the Israelites come to realize what a fearful task that is. Moses's position as mediator will also allow him to serve as intercessor when the people sin (Exod. 32:9–14).

20:20. Moses assures the people that the terrors of the theophany have a redemptive spiritual purpose, that the people may be transformed by the power they see in the presence of God. Both frightening and unforgettable, the experience at Sinai was intended to dissuade them from sin.

20:21. The repetition of the assertion that the people stayed back transitions to the second part of this narrative, in which Moses ascends the mountain and receives instructions from God. The first statutes he receives, in keeping with the theophany narrative, relate to respect for YHWH himself.

20:22–23. Idolatry is the primary offense against YHWH. Two aspects of idolatry are indicated in the prepositional phrases "alongside me" (אִתִּי, lit. "with me") and "for yourselves" (לָכֶם). YHWH is understood to be present in his sanctuary, and any idol set up with him, even if it is intended to represent YHWH himself, is in fact YHWH's rival. Idols were putatively "for" the people, intended to be an aid to worship, but actually they are for the people in the sense that the idols, and not YHWH, serve as the actual gods of the people. They are also "for" the people in that they are objects of human manufacture that represent human desires about what God should be. Instead of having "designer gods," Israel is to worship the true God as he really is.

20:24–26. Apart from the avoidance of images, a specific ideology and proper decorum are to be reflected in the construction of altars. It is not clear whether the "altar of dirt" is literally just a pile of dirt or if it can be, like the altar of the Tent of Meeting, an ornate altar of bronze and wood that was to be filled with dirt to weight it down whenever the shrine was set up. To all appearances, v. 24 seems to envision a simple pile of dirt as the best of all altars. All human artifice is to be eschewed as a distraction from God, the object of worship. It may be that the bronze-sheathed altar of Exod. 27:1–8 was specifically for the central shrine, but that the command to have altars made of dirt related more specifically to outlying altars throughout the nation where people might make sacrifice to YHWH (such as the shrine on Mt. Carmel where Elijah made sacrifice [1 Kings 18:30], or the various sites at which Samuel sacrificed [1 Sam. 10:8; 16:5]). As an alternative to a pile of dirt, the Israelites might have an altar of stones, so long as the stones were uncut (Deut. 27:5). Such an altar would be little more than a heap of big rocks. The point is that elaborate religious structures are a diversion, causing people to focus more on their manmade places for worship than on God.

The Israelites are also told not to make an altar with steps. The stated reason is that if someone goes high up on steps, his genitals would be exposed beneath his tunic. This seems to be an odd reason; surely if the exposure of the priest's lower body was the concern, garments could be devised that kept him covered as he ascended the stairs. But probably there is more to it than this; the creation of a large, high altar, although intended to add dignity to the worship, would actually detract from focus on God and make the altar itself the focus. A priest who ascended such a high altar would draw attention to himself rather than to God and, depending on how well he was covered, may have made more of a spectacle of himself than he intended. Obviously such an incident would make a mockery of the worship of God, and it makes the point that all attempts to add to God's glory by human artifice are ultimately ridiculous if not blasphemous.

Theological Summary of Key Points

1. Moses here takes on the role of mediator between God and Israel. Theologically, this implies that the majesty of God is such that we cannot approach him directly, without a mediator. The great mediator between God and man is Christ (Heb. 12:18–24).

2. The lack of an image and the making of an altar of uncut stones are highly significant. People naturally feel that they must use art and architecture to convey the innate majesty of God. Ancient peoples found it inconceivable that one would construct a shrine to a god and not set up images of that god, and they believed that the shrine itself was to be as magnificently constructed as possible. The Parthenon of Athens, for example, was set high upon the acropolis of Athens, was grandly constructed of cut stone and stately stone pillars, and it had elaborate statuary in its frieze. Within the temple was a massive and richly decorated statue of the goddess Athena. And the Parthenon was in some ways modest compared to the massive complex of temples at Karnak in Egyptian Thebes. Rather than compete with such shrines, this text rejects such an ideology altogether.

3. The Bible proclaims a God who chooses to remain hidden and invisible. Artificial structures that supposedly augment his glory actually diminish it, since the worshipper confuses the temple and image for God himself, who is too great for the human mind to conceive. This is paradoxical; great altars atop a massive flight of stairs and constructed of finely cut stones substitute a limited and facile glory of human construction for the true glory of God. A crude altar of uncut stones more properly conveys the fact that humans cannot adequately portray God's majesty, thereby asserting God's glory more perfectly.

4. Presenting God's glory by a humble and paradoxical means has a parallel in the incarnation of Jesus Christ. One would expect God's Messiah to appear as an invulnerable demigod analogous to the Greek Hercules. But Jesus is born in a stable, lives as a humble man, and is crucified. In this, the weakness of God is greater than the strength of man and the folly of God is wiser than the wisdom of man (1 Cor. 1:25). We also note that the presence of God is to be realized by God's Spirit and not by icons and images (John 4:24; 1 Thess. 1:9). While the glory of God is primarily reflected in the incarnation, it is secondarily reflected in the lives of the people of the church (1 Pet. 2:5). This, rather than the church's architecture, is the true image of God on earth.

PART V

RESPECT FOR HUMAN LIFE (21:1–32)

Respect for human life includes both respect for the health, dignity, and well-being of persons and respect for their inherent right to life. It is more than just acknowledging that we should not commit murder. In this section, the Book of the Covenant touches upon many areas in which we need to show respect for human persons.

Translation

21:1 “And these are the ordinances which you are to set before them:
21:2a If you acquire a Hebrew slave,
21:2b he shall serve for six years;
21:2c but in the seventh he shall go out as a free man without condition or obligation.[20]
21:3a If he arrives alone,
21:3b he shall depart alone;
21:3c if he [arrives as] the husband of a wife,
21:3d then his wife shall depart with him.
21:4a If his owner should give him a wife,
21:4b and [if] she bears him sons or daughters,
21:4c [then] the wife and her children shall belong to her owner,
21:4d and he shall depart alone.
21:5a But if the slave should properly state,[21]
21:5b 'I love my master, my wife and my children;
21:5c I will not depart as a free man,'
21:6a then his master shall bring him to the magistrates,[22]

---

20. The word חִנָּם is often translated “without payment,” but it is broader than that. It means that the former slave has no obligations whatsoever, financial or otherwise, to his former owner.
21. The infinitive absolute with finite verb pattern here (וְאִם־אָמֹר יֹאמַר) appears to connote that the statement is freely made in accordance with legal procedures (i.e., without coercion, being of sound mind, etc.). In other words, the decision must be open and above any suspicion that the slave has been manipulated.
22. The MT has הָאֱלֹהִים, which normally means “God.” But the idea of bringing a man “to God” in a legal context seems rather odd. Is this a private religious act before God? Is it something conducted at the sanctuary? The former is unlikely because it is hard to see how a private ceremony could be legally binding. And the latter, if that were the intended meaning, should explicitly speak of the sanctuary. Sprinkle, *Covenant*, 59–60, suggests that הָאֱלֹהִים are teraphim representing the ancestors of the householder. As such, the slave is “adopted” into the family in the presence of the ancestors. In favor of taking this to refer to magistrates, we note that sometimes

21:6b and then he shall bring him to a door or a doorframe,

21:6c and his master shall pierce his ear with an awl.

21:6d And he shall serve him perpetually.

21:7a If a man sells his daughter as a female slave,

21:7b she is not to depart as the male slaves depart.

21:8a In a case where a master has selected [her] for himself [as a spouse], if [the woman] is disappointing in his eyes,[23]

21:8b then he shall let her be redeemed.

21:8c He does not have authority to sell her to a foreign people since he has been treacherous toward her.

21:9a If he selected her [as a spouse] for his son,

21:9b he shall deal with her in accordance with what is the proper treatment for a daughter.

21:10a If he gets another woman for himself,

21:10b he may not reduce her portion of meat, her clothing allowance, or her conjugal rights.

21:11a If he will not do these three [things] for her,

21:11b then she shall go out without condition or obligation;

21:11c there shall be no financial compensation[24] [for the man].

21:12a If someone strikes a man so that he dies,

21:12b he definitely must be put to death.

21:13a But in the case of someone who did not set out to kill[25] [the victim],

21:13b but God caused it to happen by his hand,

21:13c I will appoint you a place to which he may flee.

21:14a But if a man has behaved viciously[26] toward his neighbor, killing him by design,

21:14b from my very altar you must take him to die.

21:15 Whoever strikes his father or his mother definitely must be put to death.

21:16a If someone kidnaps a man and sells him,

אֱלֹהִים does have this meaning (Ps. 82:6). In addition, Targum Onkelos renders this with דייניא, "the judges." Finally, the context, in which the slave is making a formal statement (21:5), suggests that a court of law is in view.

23. The Hebrew of this clause is not especially difficult but its word order makes it somewhat unclear when rendered literally (a literal translation is, "And if [she is] bad in the eyes of her master who for himself appointed her").

24. Lit. "silver."

25. Lit. "he did not lie in ambush."

26. The word זיד here describes callous disregard for the rights and the person of the victim (Exod. 18:11). The verb describes cruel or arrogant behavior, and is apparently from a root meaning "to be hot" (Gen. 25:29).

21:16b or if [the victim] is found in his possession,
21:16c [the kidnapper] definitely must be put to death.[27]
21:17 Whoever curses his father or his mother definitely must be put to death.
21:18a And if [two] men have a fight
21:18b and one strikes the other with a stone or with [his] fist,
21:18c and [the injured party] does not die,
21:18d but he has to stay in bed,
21:19a if he can [at least] get up[28]
21:19b and can walk around outside on his staff,
21:19c then he who struck him shall not be subject to prosecution;
21:19d he shall only provide for the time [that the injured party] is unable to work,[29]
21:19e and shall be fully responsible to provide medical treatment.[30]
21:20a If a man should strike his male or female slave with a rod
21:20b and [the slave] dies by his hand,
21:20c he most definitely must face the appropriate punishment.[31]
21:21a But if [the servant] can get back on his feet in a day or two,
21:21b [the owner] will not be punished,
21:21c since it is his money.[32]
21:22a And if men struggle with each other,
21:22b and they strike[33] a pregnant woman,

27. The participle וְגֹנֵב is the subject of the verb מוֹת יוּמָת, and the *weqatal* verbs וּמְכָרוֹ וְנִמְצָא are functionally part of the subject phrase with the participle.
28. This second conditional clause indicates that although the injuries may have been fairly extensive, they did not result in paralysis.
29. Lit. "he shall give [for] his cessation."
30. The infinitive absolute with finite verb here suggests full legal responsibility to see to it that the injured man receives care and treatment until he recovers.
31. The verb נקם generally means to "avenge." But here in the phrase נָקֹם יִנָּקֵם it has a more technical legal meaning, "to suffer a punishment that is appropriate to the offense." For further discussion, see the commentary.
32. "Money" translates כֶּסֶף, which is more literally "silver." It is usually rendered "property," but it seems that the more appropriate term for human beings as property is נֶפֶשׁ (Gen. 12:5). The term "money" evaluates the event from a purely economic perspective: by injuring his slave, the owner has cost himself money in the form of lost labor.
33. Evidently the plural (וְנָגְפוּ) is used here because either the woman's husband or his adversary may have been the one who banged into the pregnant woman in the course of the struggle. In the confusion of a street fight,

21:22c so that her children come forth,[34]
21:22d but it is not a fatal injury,[35]
21:22e a fine will most definitely be assessed in accord with what the woman's husband may demand of him,
21:22f and he shall pay it in accordance with [his assessed] liability.[36]

---

it is not always clear what happened. Even so, the husband's adversary is considered liable (21:22e).

34. It is not clear whether her offspring comes forth alive or whether this is a miscarriage. The traditional Jewish view is that this is a miscarriage (Sarna, *Exodus*, 125). But יצא can be used of a live birth (Gen. 25:25). It is also unclear why the verb and subject are plural (וְיָצְאוּ יְלָדֶיהָ). Surely the text does not apply only to multiple births. One might suggest that the plural is generic, not specifying whether the child is male or female, but Hebrew generally does not use the plural in this manner. Stuart, *Exodus*, 491, translates this as, "but she is still able to have children." This rendition is, in my opinion, impossible. Perhaps the plural is used in order to imply that the same rules apply regardless of whether she bears one or more children at this incident.

35. The word אָסוֹן means "a fatal injury" and not simply, "an injury." See אָסוֹן, *HALOT*, 1.73, and also the usage in Gen. 42:4, 38; 44:29, where it plainly refers to a fatal incident and not just an injury. See also Samuel E. Loewenstamm, "Exodus XXI 22–25," *VT* 27, no. 3 (1977): 358. Unfortunately, it is not clear in this text whether the fatal injury is to the mother alone or if it can refer also to the death of the fetus. The LXX considers the injury to be to the child and not to the mother, seeing the alternatives as either that the child was not malformed (*μὴ ἐξεικονισμένον*) or was malformed (*ἐξεικονισμένον*). But this is wrong, since אָסוֹן does not mean "malformed" but "fatally injured." As such, the LXX evidence should not be regarded as decisive.

36. The clause וְנָתַן בִּפְלִלִים is very difficult. The noun פָּלִיל is traditionally rendered as "judge," but this meaning can be claimed for it only here and in Deut. 32:31, כִּי לֹא כְצוּרֵנוּ צוּרָם וְאֹיְבֵינוּ פְּלִילִים. But the Deuteronomy text, with "judges" as the meaning for פְּלִילִים, is almost inscrutable. With this meaning, it literally reads, "For their rock is not like our rock, and our enemies [are] judges." This is often taken to mean that even our enemies must judge, or concede, that our God is better than theirs (NIV, RSV), but that is frankly far-fetched (the NRSV follows the LXX and has, "our enemies are fools"). Some interpreters believe that בִּפְלִלִים should be emended to בִּנְפִלִים, "for the miscarriage" (פָּלִיל, *HALOT*, 3.932). Thus it would be translated, "and he shall pay a fine for the miscarriage." This interpretation assumes that the fetus has died but that the mother is uninjured. On the other hand, Houtman, *Exodus*, 3:162–3, argues that פללים of itself means "miscarried fetus" without recourse to emendation. In favor of treating פָּלִיל as having something to do with judgment, the root פלל

21:23a	But if it is a fatal injury,
21:23b	then you shall assess a life for a life.
21:24-25	[In personal injury cases, the rule shall be] an eye for an eye, a tooth for a tooth, a hand for a hand, a foot for a foot, a burn for a burn, a wound for a wound, [and] a bruise for a bruise.
21:26a	And should a man strike the eye of his male slave or the eye or his female slave
21:26b	and destroy it,
21:26c	he must let him [or her] go free on account of his eye.
21:27a	And if he knocks out a tooth of his male slave or the tooth of his female slave,
21:27b	he shall let him [or her] go free on account of his tooth.
21:28a	And should an ox gore a man or a woman
21:28b	and he [or she] dies,
21:28c	the ox definitely must be stoned
21:28d	and its flesh shall not be eaten;
21:28e	but the owner of the ox will not be prosecuted.
21:29a	But if an ox had a history of goring
21:29b	and warnings were given to its owner,
21:29c	and he had not been keeping it confined[37]
21:29d	and it should kill a man or a woman,

can mean to "arbitrate" (Piel) or to "intercede" (Hithpael). The situation is simpler if פְּלִילִים can mean, "assessment," as Sarna, *Exodus*, 125, suggests (see also Sprinkle, *Covenant*, 94). It would thus mean, "And he will pay a fine by a [court] verdict." But the usage in Deut. 32:31 speaks against this interpretation. It is more likely that Adele Berlin, "On the Meaning of פלל in the Bible," *RB* 96, no. 3 (1989): 345–51, is correct that the word פְּלִילִים implies liability or accountability. Interpreted in this manner, Deut. 32:31 means, "For their rock is not like our rock, and our enemies are accountable [for the lies they believe about their gods]." Similar usage appears in Job 31:11, where עָוֺן פְּלִילִים is a sin for which one must give account (see also Job 31:28). Another difficult occurrence is at Isa. 16:3, but פְּלִילָה could there be translated as "behave responsibly." Translating Gen. 48:11 (רְאֹה פָנֶיךָ לֹא פִלָּלְתִּי) as "I did not consider the seeing of your face [to be] probable" is also explicable under this interpretation (note that some English dialects also can use "liable" to mean "probable," as in "He is liable to come tomorrow"). The phrase וְנָתַן בִּפְלִלִים in Exod. 21:22f can therefore be translated as above.

37. In 21:29abc the verbless clause (שׁוֹר נַגָּח הוּא), the *weqatal* (וְהוּעַד), and the clause having וְלֹא with *yiqtol* (וְלֹא יִשְׁמְרֶנּוּ) each have a past imperfect meaning. The translation of clause types in Hebrew is heavily driven by context.

21:29e the ox shall be stoned
21:29f and its owner also shall be put to death.
21:30a If a financial penalty in lieu of execution[38] is determined for him,
21:30b then he shall pay the full amount that is determined for him for the redemption of his life.
21:31a Whether it gores a son
21:31b or it gores a daughter,
21:31c it shall be done to him as this legal principle [stipulates].
21:32a If the ox gores a male or a female slave,
21:32b the owner shall give his [or her] master thirty shekels of silver,
21:32c and the ox shall be stoned.

Structure

After the introductory verse (21:1), the text gives a series of commands that all center upon the value of human life.

I. Laws Governing Slaves and Manumission (21:2–11)
  A. A Male Hebrew Slave (21:2–6)
  B. A Female Slave (21:7–11)
II. Capital Offenses involving Violence toward Others (21:12–17)
  A. Homicide (21:12–14)
  B. Striking Parents (21:15)
  C. Kidnapping (21:16)
  D. Cursing Parents (21:17)
III. Personal Injury (21:18–32)
  A. A Fight between Free Men (21:18–19)
  B. Striking One's Slave (21:20–21)
  C. Injury to a Pregnant Woman (21:22–23)
  D. Governing Principle for Free Persons (21:24–25)
  E. Governing Principle for Slaves (21:26–27)
  F. Dangerous Livestock (21:28–32)

Commentary

21:2–6. The position of the laws of slavery so near the beginning of the covenant code is actually unusual. Joe Sprinkle has commented: "Slave laws end rather than begin the Laws of Hammurabi (§§278–82), and the Laws of Eshnunna place its most substantial slave laws at the end (§§49–52). Middle Assyrian laws only rarely deal with slaves at

38. So translating כֹּפֶר, which is here a financial payment given in order to ransom one's life from execution. Cf. Num. 35:31.

all."[39] No doubt the reason for this prominence of slavery laws in the biblical text lies in the central theme of Exodus, that YHWH has delivered Israel from slavery.

Laws concerning slavery actually deal with owning the life of another person. As such, these laws are placed with laws that concern such issues as homicide rather than later, among laws that deal with property. For us, the greatest difficulty is that slavery should be allowed in the Old Testament at all. We should recall, however, that slavery such as described here was a way of dealing with problems such as severe indebtedness and poverty. By slavery, a poor person could have shelter and food. No one would claim that the life of these slaves was easy, and the laws make clear that slaves did not have the status and rights of free persons. But it was not the same as, for example, the slavery that existed in pre-Civil War America, where people were kidnapped from their homes by slave traders, crammed into ships, and taken away to toil for the rest of their lives in a foreign land. That kind of slavery is strictly forbidden in the Bible (Exod. 21:16; Amos 1:6).

In this text, the slave is called a "Hebrew" rather than an "Israelite"; the choice of terms seems to hearken back to the time in Egypt, where the Israelite slaves were routinely called "Hebrews," and its use suggests that such a status is really not proper for an Israelite and that an Israelite who falls into slavery has lost something of his identity. As the people redeemed from servitude to Egypt, ideally they should have no slaves at all among their fellow Israelites.[40] But inevitably, such situations would arise. The text seeks to answer several questions. First, how long should the Hebrew slave serve? Second, may his wife and children, if he takes a wife while in slavery, leave with him when he is manumitted?[41] Third, what exceptions are there to these guidelines? The answer to the first is that he was to serve six years. The precise date for his release was not set (just that it was "in the seventh year"),

39. Joe M. Sprinkle, "Law and Narrative in Exodus 19–24," *JETS* 47, no. 2 (2004): 244.

40. See also Anthony C. Phillips, "The Laws of Slavery: Exodus 21.2–11," *JSOT* 30 (1984): 51–66.

41. Lev. 25:35–55 is in some respects different in its framing of the slavery laws. Adrian Schenker, "The Biblical Legislation on the Release of Slaves: The Road from Exodus to Leviticus," *JSOT* 78 (1998): 23–41, argues that the two texts complement one another. Exodus 21 concerns unmarried men and women who fall into slavery, but Lev. 25 concerns a man that falls into slavery who is already, at the time of his enslavement, a head of a household. Thus, Lev. 25 fills a gap in the legislation of Exod. 21.

but in an age without exact calendars the idea was that as soon as it was clear that he had served six years, he could go without any payment or further obligation.[42] The provision that he could take his family with him if he came with a wife is obviously fair, but it is harsh on both the slave and his wife that, if the master gave to him a slave woman as his wife during his service, both she and their children had to stay behind. The law, sometimes cruelly, dealt only in legal rights and obligations, not in how such standards might distress a person emotionally. We should note, however, that the law only stipulated the slave's rights; it did not imply that the owner was obligated to separate the family; he might go beyond the demands of the law and free the wife as well. In Roman times, the manumission of slaves by owners was fairly common, and we may well suppose that Israelite slave owners often displayed a similar generosity toward their slaves. An owner could free a slave before the six years was up, and he could release a slave's wife and children even when he was not obligated to do so.

There was another option for the slave: he might ask to be permanently bound to the household so that he might remain with his family and in the service of a master he had come to appreciate. After the slave had made up his mind to enter into permanent bondage he would go before magistrates to make his declaration. Then, the fact that he was bound to that house was dramatically portrayed in the slave's having his ear pierced upon the doorpost of the house. The doorpost is metonymy for the entire house, just as the "gate" of a city can be metonymy for the entire city. Therefore, he was symbolically attached to the household, and the hole in his ear was a permanent mark of his status. As the organ of hearing, the ear represents listening and obedience.[43] Also, the need to go before judges to make the arrangement formal gave protection to the slave. An unscrupulous master could not falsely claim that the slave had freely requested permanent slave status since a panel of judges could easily determine that this was not so.

21:7–11. A female Hebrew slave would not be released after six years because she would have nowhere to go and might have no recourse but

---

42. Deut. 15:12–15 is often taken to mean that all slaves were to be released in the sabbatical year, in which all debts were cancelled, but I do not believe that to be the case. It appears even in Deut. 15 that a slave was expected to work for six years regardless of when the sabbatical year of debt release came.

43. Sprinkle, *Covenant*, 55-6.

to engage in prostitution in order to survive (released male slaves were expected to be able to find work and provide for themselves). Also, although a female slave might be acquired strictly for household labor, at least sometimes the woman was purchased to be the wife or concubine of the owner or of his son. A young woman might be sold into this status by her family if they were impoverished and saw it as a means to make some money for themselves and also—one can only hope—to put her into a better situation. But a woman who was purchased for this purpose and then cast off would be wretched indeed; her owner/husband would have "broken faith" with her. The protection of such a woman's "conjugal rights" are not exclusively or even primarily concerned with her sexual desires. By being impregnated, she had the hope of a son who would care for her as she got older. A woman who was denied her rights could, if she chose and had an opportunity to improve her situation, leave freely.

21:12–17. This small section describing capital offenses has a kind of parallel structure, with two crimes against persons (murder and kidnapping) each followed by a violent action against parents. The basic rule, that deliberate murder is punishable by death, reaffirms the Noahic stipulation of Gen. 9:6. It is, however, given an exception clause: if the act was an accident, the perpetrator could flee to a designated place and there be given sanctuary. The assertion that "God caused it to happen" (21:13b) is a way of saying that it was an accident while acknowledging that all things are under the sovereignty of God. The rules governing sanctuary for the man who has committed accidental manslaughter are elaborated upon in the cities of refuge legislation (Num. 35:6–34).[44] The statement that a person who commits deliberate homicide should be dragged away even from God's altar (21:14b) alludes to the ancient and universal notion that the altar of a god was a

44. On the other hand, in light of the fact that the "place" of refuge is here not defined as a city, and since v. 14 describes someone seeking sanctuary at YHWH's altar, it is possible that the "place" of refuge in v. 13 was originally understood to be the altar of the central shrine. See Jeffrey Stackert, "Why Does Deuteronomy Legislate Cities of Refuge? Asylum in the Covenant Collection (Exodus 21:12–14) and Deuteronomy (19:1–13)," *JBL* 125, no. 1 (2006): 24-9. Taking refuge at YHWH's altar was obviously not a workable solution to the problem of accidental homicide, however, since a person could only remain clutching the horns of the altar for a short period of time. As such, the cities of refuge gave long-term sanctuary to those who legitimately had a claim to it.

place of sanctuary for a person whose life was threatened. The point is that there can be no sanctuary for such a crime.

The kidnapping described in v. 16 is done for the sake of selling a person into slavery. This was common in the ancient world, and it is here regarded as a heinous crime. The popular notion that the Bible approves of slavery needs careful qualification; the kind of slavery practiced in recent times, whereby African persons were kidnapped by Arabs, sold to Europeans, and transported to the New World, is absolutely forbidden in the Bible and even said to be worthy of the death penalty.

Crimes against one's own parents, whether striking them or cursing them, are regarded here as terrible acts of violence that are so perverse that they set the perpetrator completely outside of human society.

21:18–19. The situation here is one in which two men have a fight out of mutual antagonism and it is difficult to assign specific guilt to either. It does not refer to injury that comes about when someone simply ambushes an innocent person with violence, as in Jesus's parable of the Good Samaritan (Luke 10:30). In the latter case there is clear guilt, but in this Exodus text neither party is less guilty than the other and as such there is no judicial punishment. However, if one of the men in the fight loses self-control and injures the other more severely than can be considered acceptable for an ordinary street brawl, he must give compensation for lost wages and medical expenses incurred by the injured party.

21:20–21. This law involves a case of beating a slave. A slave was regarded as the property of the owner, and the owner had the right to beat the slave for poor performance of labor (this is not an employer-employee relationship, where no such right to corporal punishment exists). Corporal punishment for slaves, children, and students was universal in the ancient world, and failure to exercise it was regarded as an act of folly (see Prov. 23:13; 29:19). Nevertheless, a master could be temperamentally vicious or simply get out of control and take the beating too far. If the slave died, the owner was to be prosecuted, but the punishment is not prescribed in the law. This has caused a good deal of scholarly discussion, since it leaves unclear whether the master could be put to death for the offense. If this is the case, then the slave is no less a person at law than a free person. But the text itself seems vague on the issue of the punishment. The best solution is that of Raymond Westbrook, who sees a strong parallel in the Hammurabi laws §115–116.

> If a man has a claim of grain or silver against another man, distrains a member of his household, and the distrainee dies a natural death while in the house of her or his distrainer, that case has no basis for a claim.
>
> If the distrainee should die from the effects of a beating or other physical abuse while in the house of her or his distrainer, the owner of the distrainee shall charge and convict his merchant, and if (the distrainee is) the man's son, they shall kill his (the distrainer's) son; if the man's slave, he shall weigh and deliver 20 shekels of silver; moreover, he shall forfeit whatever he originally gave as the loan.[45]

This law indicates that if a person is "distrained" (taken into slavery for nonpayment of a debt) and is wrongfully put to death, the distrainer had to pay the appropriate penalty. Thus, if he had seized the debtor's son and put him into slavery, and the debtor's son was wrongfully put to death, then the distrainer's own son would be put to death. The biblical law probably envisages a similar situation. The slave is a "distrainee," and if he is wrongfully put to death, the distrainer would pay a penalty appropriate to the relationship between the distrainee and the debtor. The paying of an appropriate penalty, as Westbrook demonstrates, is the meaning of נקם here.[46] The distrainee could well be the son of the debtor; see 2 Kings 4:1–2. Thus, the biblical law does, in context, actually give some guidance regarding the penalty that the violent master would have to pay. Also, of course, a jury presumably had latitude in such a case. It is conceivable that if the debtor himself was the distrainee; if so, the violent master would be put to death. If the slave did not die, the financial loss incurred by the owner for lost labor is considered to be punishment enough (see translation note to 21:21c).

21:22–23. This law envisages a scene in an Israelite village in which two men are fighting and the wife of one runs out to assist her husband. The wife happens to be pregnant, and in the ensuing melee the woman is struck and goes into labor. If there is no fatal injury, the adversary of the husband might only have to pay a fine as determined by a jury, after it had considered the aggrieved husband's demands in light of what they know of the situation. If there is a fatal injury,

45. "The Laws of Hammurabi," translated by Martha Roth (*COS* 2.131.343).

46. Raymond Westbrook, *Studies in Biblical and Cuneiform Law* (Paris: J. Gabalda, 1988), 90–1.

the punishment could be as severe as execution ("life for life"; 21:23b). Unfortunately, an important detail about the law is unclear: it is impossible to tell whether the "fatal injury" is to the mother or the child. If the clause "her children come forth" (21:22c) implies a live birth, then the injury could apply to the child or the mother. That is, the mother could have died while, or after, giving birth, or the child could have come forth alive but then died afterward from having been born prematurely. But if "her children come forth" of itself describes a miscarriage, then it is a given that the child is dead, and the clauses about a "fatal injury" or the lack of the same can only apply to the mother. The latter interpretation is followed by the NRSV: "When people who are fighting injure a pregnant woman so that there is a miscarriage, and yet no further harm follows. . . ." In my view, we do not have enough information here to know which is meant.[47] Probably there is deliberate ambiguity in the text about the nature of the delivery and of any death that might follow in order to allow juries latitude in dealing with the varieties of cases that might arise. There is, however, more to be said.

This law has parallels in several ancient law codes, including Hammurabi and the "Hittite Laws." The most explicit and detailed version is in "The Middle Assyrian Laws"[48] §50–53:

> [If a man] strikes [another man's wife thereby causing her to abort her fetus, ...] a man's wife [...] and they shall treat him as he treated her; he shall make full payment of a life for her fetus. And if that woman dies, they shall kill that man; he shall make full payment of a life for her fetus. And if there is no son of that woman's husband, and his wife whom he struck aborted her fetus, they shall kill the assailant for her fetus. If her fetus was a female, he shall make full payment of a life only.
>
> If a man strikes another man's wife who does not raise her child, causing her to abort her fetus, it is a punishable offense; he shall give 7,200 shekels of lead.
>
> If a man strikes a prostitute causing her to abort her fetus, they shall assess him blow for blow, he shall make full payment of a life.
>
> If a woman aborts her fetus by her own action and they then prove the charges against her and find her guilty, they

47. See also Durham, *Exodus*, 324.

48. "The Middle Assyrian Laws" are found on tablets that date from the 11th century B.C. They were found in Assur, the Assyrian capital city, and are probably copies of original laws that date from the 14th century.

> shall impale her, they shall not bury her. If she dies as a result of aborting her fetus, they shall impale her, they shall not bury her. If any persons should hide that woman because she aborted her fetus [...][49]

The relevant Hammurabi laws (§209–214) are similar except that their penalties are not as severe and they do not mention deliberate abortion.[50] The Hittite laws (§17–18) prescribe financial penalties for "causing a woman to miscarry" but do not seem to be clear about the circumstances.[51] The biblical law is peculiar for having a hypothetical fight between two men and then having the pregnant woman insert herself into the brawl to assist her husband. Hammurabi and the Middle Assyrian laws, by contrast, simply and directly speak of a man who strikes a pregnant woman without reference to such a specific and peculiar circumstance.[52] Why does the Bible mention the fight, a detail that seems altogether unnecessary and even somewhat contrived, and why does it not speak more directly of striking a pregnant woman (that is, of striking her deliberately), as these other codes do?

I believe that the reason is that a woman who behaved in this way, diving into a brawl while pregnant, might be considered to have brought her troubles on herself. Such behavior would be foolish in the extreme; it practically invites serious medical complications. But this is the whole intent of the law: it is meant to drive home the lesson that a man must be very careful about violence in the presence of a pregnant woman, even when the woman herself is behaving irresponsibly. He would do better to flee the scene than to carry on with the fight knowing that he might cause serious injury to the woman and child. It is also significant that the law assumes that the other man, not the woman's husband, was responsible for the injury. In the eyes of the law, the other man has taken advantage of the presence of the pregnant woman to get an edge over his adversary, who now must try to protect his wife. Whether or not this is actually what happened in a given incident is not the point (the woman's husband may actually try to use her presence to his advantage). The implied warning, again, is that in such a situation the other man must break off from fighting and

49. "The Middle Assyrian Laws," translated by Martha Roth (*COS* 2.132.359).
50. "The Laws of Hammurabi," translated by Martha Roth (*COS* 2.131.348).
51. See "Hittite Laws," translated by Harry A. Hoffner, Jr. (*COS* 2.19.108).
52. Loewenstamm, "Exodus XXI," 354–5, observes that this provision "is unparalleled in ancient oriental laws, which invariably deal with the responsibility of one single person who did harm to the pregnant woman."

run away rather than risk a grievous outcome. Also, it is the duty of the other man to flee because the woman's husband can hardly withdraw and leave his wife in the fight. Put another way, a defendant under the Middle Assyrian laws might claim that the woman jumped into a fight between himself and her husband, and that as such any injury that came to her was not his fault. Such a defense is not allowed in the Book of the Covenant. Instead, a man's pregnant wife is to be regarded as sacrosanct at all times.

Christians look to this text for direction in the matter of abortion, desiring to determine whether or not the fetus is regarded as a person whose life and rights are protected under the law.[53] We need to be clear that abortion is not the topic of Exod. 21:22–23. Unlike the Middle Assyrian laws, the Book of the Covenant does not directly address the issue. But we can say that special protection is afforded to a pregnant woman and her unborn child in this legislation; no other kind of bystander at a village quarrel (an old person, a woman who is not pregnant, or a young child) is given such considerations. If nothing else, therefore, the law indicates that a strong instinct for protecting the unborn is appropriate. With good reason, the Christian church has always regarded abortion as immoral and repugnant.

21:24–25. The purpose behind the *lex talionis*, the standard "eye for an eye" rule for determining punishment in a personal injury case, is to provide fairness and justice in punishment.[54] The punishment should be neither too lenient nor too harsh but commensurate with the crime. These principles, however, should be understood as guidelines for juries and not as invariable rules. A jury might call for a lesser penalty or no penalty at all if, for example, the man who lost the eye was discovered to have been the aggressor and if the man who struck out his eye had good reason to fear for his life. Most importantly, this

---

53. Recent interpreters disagree over whether this text has direct application to abortion. Contrast Russell Fuller, "Exodus 21:22–23: The Miscarriage Interpretation and the Personhood of the Fetus," *JETS* 37, no. 2 (1994): 169–84, with Joe M. Sprinkle, "The Interpretation of Exodus 21:22–25 (*Lex Talionis*) and Abortion," *WTJ* 55, no. 2 (1993): 233–53.

54. The *lex talionis* has clear precedent in the laws of Hammurabi (trans. Roth [*COS* 2.131.348]) §196–198: "If an *awīlu* should blind the eye of another *awīlu*, they shall blind his eye. If he should break the bone of another *awīlu*, they shall break his bone. If he should blind the eye of a commoner or break the bone of a commoner, he shall weigh and deliver 60 shekels of silver." The *awīlu* are free persons or perhaps the lower nobility.

law was never meant to justify private retaliation, as in a feud between families. To claim the words "an eye for an eye" as grounds for taking vengeance is an abuse of this passage and counter to Jesus's teaching (Matt. 5:38–39).

21:26–27. The *lex talionis* does not apply in a case where a man knocks out the eye or tooth of his slave. In this case, the slave is manumitted in compensation for the lost eye or tooth. Again, this law is a principle; it does not mean that there were no other circumstances in which a slave might be freed in compensation for personal injury (for example, a jury might order the slave freed if the owner cut off the slave's finger). But loss of an eye or tooth would be far more common, since an angry owner is likely to strike a slave in the face. We thus have three rules governing the striking of slaves (see vv. 20–21). If an owner strikes a slave and he dies, the owner is prosecuted. If the slave is simply laid up for a while, there is no punishment for the owner; the owner suffers the loss of his slave's labor. If the slave suffers a permanent injury of some severity, he is released from bondage.

21:28–32. The basic rule is that an ox that gores a person must be stoned to death (it was treated as a murderer and was not eaten because it was defiled). The more difficult issue is whether the owner of the ox is accountable. The text answers this with what seems to be an absolute rule: if the ox was known to be dangerous and likely to gore someone, but the owner did not take steps to protect the public, then the owner is to be put to death. The text states that a death penalty would be imposed on the owner only if the bull had a reputation in the community for being dangerous and if the owner had been warned about it ("The Laws of Hammurabi" §251 has a similar stipulation[55]). But then Exodus gives a provision for having the owner pay a fine if the jury considers that to be appropriate. The reality, of course, is that any bull might at some time behave skittishly or dangerously. Also, the owner may have taken some steps to secure the bull, but there may be questions about whether he had taken sufficient measures. As such, the line between an owner who is absolutely innocent and one who is absolutely reckless is blurred, and there could be questions about whether the victim of the goring had been provocative or unreasonably careless. As such, the community is given latitude about what penalty to impose.

Interpreters have also puzzled over why the ox is put to death by

55. "Hammurabi," trans. Roth (*COS* 2.131.350).

stoning. As Westbrook has argued, the reason is surely not that the bull is being punished and formally executed, as though it had moral culpability on a level with human culpability for sin. Also, the bull is not killed by stoning because he is so dangerous that no one dare approach him (people who spent their entire lives handling livestock surely could have managed to kill the bull by ordinary means). Rather, an animal that was slaughtered in the normal way (with a knife) would have been killed using the same method as was used in a sacrifice. In fact, such a slaughtering of livestock effectively was a sacrifice. Being a manslayer, the bull could not be subjected to even an informal sacrifice. Furthermore, people would be more likely to think that they could eat a bull that had been slaughtered with a knife. A bull killed by stoning would not be nearly so attractive.[56] The fact that its blood had not been drained away would in fact render the meat unclean.

Verses 31–32 add provisions regarding the victim. First, the gender of the victim was irrelevant. It did not matter whether the person killed was male or female; the same rules for assigning a penalty applied. Second, it did not matter if the victims were children (as implied in the terms "son" and "daughter"); the same rules applied. Third, however, it mattered whether the victim was free or a slave. The previously-stated rules applied only when the victim was free; if he or she was a slave, a thirty-silver-shekel fee was imposed on the owner of the bull. For comparison, "The Laws of Eshnunna" stipulated a penalty of forty shekels for fatally goring a free person and fifteen shekels for fatally goring a slave (§54–55).[57] "The Laws of Hammurabi" §251–252[58] required a payment of thirty shekels for goring to death a member of the *awīlu* class (free persons, although the term might refer to aristocrats),[59] but twenty shekels if the victim was a slave. While one might argue that the Bible places higher value on the life of the slave, the higher penalties in the biblical text, coming from a later time, may only be a reflection of economic inflation. It is, at any rate, clear that the laws in Exodus are very similar to those from Mesopotamia and this indicates that the biblical laws naturally reflect their culture and context. Slaves did not have the same rights or status as free persons. When a fee was

56. Westbrook, *Cuneiform Law*, 83–8.

57. "The Laws of Eshnunna," translated by Martha Roth (*COS* 2.130.334). Eshnunna was an Amorite city of north Mesopotamia that flourished in the early 2nd millennium.

58. "Hammurabi," trans. Roth (*COS* 2.131.350).

59. Martha T. Roth, *Law Collections from Mesopotamia and Asia Minor,* Writings from the Ancient World 6 (Atlanta: Scholar's Press, 1997), 268.

imposed, it was apparently paid to the family of a free person or to the owner of a slave.

An enormous number of court documents describing trials and lawsuits have survived from the ancient Near East. And although the codes of Eshnunna and Hammurabi, like the Book of the Covenant, have laws related to the bull that gores someone, there is not a single example of a law case involving this in all the extant records from Mesopotamia. This implies that the goring bull was in fact a rare occurrence. Wells is probably correct that the laws about the goring bull are meant to provide legal principles that could be applied to all kinds of cases.[60] They were never intended to apply narrowly only to lawsuits involving bulls. In following the custom of using the hypothetical case of the goring bull to establish precedent for settling all kinds of disputes involving injury, the Book of the Covenant was adhering to a well-established ancient Near Eastern pattern.

Theological Summary of Key Points

Respect for persons includes, according to this text, at least the following aspects.

1. The law must protect the rights of those who by their status are more easily exploited. No one has less prestige than a slave. But even they had certain legal protections and rights afforded them. By extension, every person's dignity must be protected.

2. The ultimate assault on another person's innate rights is homicide. This is so heinous that it is punishable by death.

3. By analogy, any animal that kills a person must be destroyed, and its owner can be held liable and punished severely.

4. To kidnap a person for sale into slavery is scarcely less than murder. The victim is taken from family, with little or no hope of ever seeing them again, and is consigned to a life that will likely be short and miserable.

5. Gross disrespect for the dignity of a parent is so perverse that it warps the soul. Someone who does this will have no respect for any other person's rights and will be a menace to society.

---

60. Wells, "Exodus," 239.

6. All acts of violence are dehumanizing, but even these acts must be handled fairly and with justice. The law need not intervene in every conflict or redress a situation unless there is excessive violence or unless one party is the aggressor and the other the victim. In these cases, penalties should be carried out in such a way that justice is equally applied for both the victim and the accused, with punishment that is neither too lenient nor too harsh.

7. Pregnant women and the children they carry should be given special protection. Violence against a pregnant woman is so repugnant that one should never risk it. When done deliberately, such action draws down the punishment of God (Amos 1:13).

The principles in this text obviously have bearing on what we now call human rights. But we must be careful: in doing exposition of this passage we may include "rights" never envisioned in this or any other biblical text. There is, for example, no biblical "right" to an education or to healthcare. If one believes that these are rights and chooses to advocate them as such, one should not force these ideals onto the Bible. Thus, one should handle Exodus honestly when seeking to elucidate its teachings on human rights. First, one should proclaim the plain meaning of the text, but should extend it toward applicable situations in the modern world. One should warn against violence, demand that people respect the rights of all, and stress how important it is that we never assault parents physically or verbally. As a modern analogy to the goring ox, one could even speak of how perversely some indulge their aggressive dogs over against the rights and safety of neighbors. As Christians, however, we are to go beyond the basic legal requirements of Exodus and remember that anyone who hates his neighbor has also committed violence (of a mental kind), according to Matt. 5:21–22. It is not enough that we refrain from violence; we are commanded to love.

RESPECT FOR WHAT BELONGS TO ANOTHER (21:33—22:17)

The laws in this section concern disputes over property. The meaning of the individual stipulations is generally self-evident. One should recognize, however, that laws such as these are not meant to be exhaustive, covering every possible exigency, but exemplary, establishing precedent for dealing with analogous situations. Thus, the laws have wider significance than their most narrow, literal meanings.

Translation

21:33a “And if a man opens a pit,
21:33b or if he digs a pit
21:33c and he does not cover it over,
21:33d and an ox or a donkey falls down there,
21:34a the owner of the pit shall make restitution.
21:34b He shall give money[61] to its owner,
21:34c and the dead [beast] shall become his.
21:35a If one man’s ox attacks his neighbor’s ox,
21:35b and it dies, then they shall sell the live ox
21:35c and divide the money from its sale equally;
21:35d and they shall divide the dead [ox], too.
21:36a Or, [in case] it is known
21:36b that the ox had a prior history of goring,
21:36c and [if] its owner did not restrain it,
21:36d he shall make full restitution—ox for ox—
21:36e and the dead [ox] shall become his.
22:1a[62] If a man steals an ox or a sheep
22:1b and he slaughters it
22:1c or he sells it,
22:1d he shall make restitution of five oxen for the ox and four sheep for the sheep.
22:2a (If the thief is discovered in the process of breaking in
22:2b and he is struck
22:2c and he dies,
22:2d his [death] will not be [reckoned] as homicide.[63]
22:3a If the sun has risen on him,

---

61. Lit. “silver.” Coinage would not be invented until centuries after the exodus, and so it is somewhat anachronistic to speak of “money.” Items would be paid for with either precious metal weighed out or with some other valuable commodity, such as clothing. Silver was probably the most common form of currency, as it could be exchanged at set weights and so allowed for a degree of standardization. However, כֶּסֶף (“silver”) is probably used generically for any medium of financial exchange, just as לֶחֶם (“bread”) was used generically for “food.” Thus, the payment need not always have been literally in silver.
62. Exodus 22:1 in the English Bible is 21:37 in the Hebrew Bible, and thus through chapter 22 there is a one-verse difference between the English and Hebrew versification.
63. Lit. “he has no bloodshed.” The phrase אֵין לוֹ דָּמִים is used impersonally to mean that there is no homicide. See Num. 35:27.

22:3b his [death] will be [reckoned] as homicide[64].)[65]
22:3c [Otherwise, the thief] must make full restitution.
22:3d If he owns nothing,
22:3e then he shall be sold for his theft.
22:4a If the stolen property, whether a live ox or a donkey or a sheep, is in fact found alive in his possession,[66]
22:4b he shall make double restitution.
22:5a If a man purges a field or vineyard of vegetation by grazing,[67]
22:5b and releases his grazing animal [to roam freely]
22:5c and it wipes out the vegetation in another man's field,
22:5d he shall make restitution from the best of his own field and the best of his own vineyard.
22:6a If fire gets out of control
22:6b and it spreads to [the] hedgerows,[68]
22:6c and stacked grain or the standing grain or the field is consumed,
22:6d the man who started the fire shall make full restitution.
22:7a If a man gives his neighbor money or goods for safekeeping
22:7b and it is stolen from the man's house,
22:7c if the thief is caught,
22:7d he shall make double restitution.
22:8a If the thief is not caught,
22:8b then the owner of the house shall appear before God,
22:8c [to determine] if he has not [in fact] laid his hands on his neighbor's goods.
22:9a For every tort—over an ox, over a donkey, over a sheep, over clothing, over any lost thing about which one says,
22:9b 'This is mine,'[69]

64. Lit. "he has bloodshed."
65. The case of the thief who is caught in the act and is struck down (22:2a–3b[1a–2b]) and killed is a parenthetical aside within a larger legal text dealing with the crime of stealing. Otherwise, the abrupt transition in 22:3c(2c) makes no sense.
66. Lit. "in his hand."
67. The situation in 22:5–6(4–5) is that a man wants to purge all the vegetation from a field or vineyard in order to make a new planting. He may do this either by allowing his livestock to eat the plants or by burning the fields. In both cases, the verb בער is used. *HALOT* (1.145–6) treats these as two separate roots (בער [I] and [II]), but acknowledges that they may in fact be a single root.
68. Lit. "thorns" (קֹצִים), these are thorny shrubs used as hedgerows separating fields of different owners.
69. Lit. "This is that," or "This is it."

22:9c the claims of the two men shall go to God;
22:9d the one whom God condemns[70] shall make double restitution to his adversary.
22:10a If a man gives his neighbor a donkey, an ox, a sheep, or any animal for safekeeping
22:10b and it dies,
22:10c or it is injured,
22:10d or it is driven off—
22:10e [and if] there is no witness—
22:11a there shall be an oath before YHWH between the two of them
22:11b [to determine] if he has not [in fact] laid his hands on his neighbor's goods.
22:11c And its owner shall accept [the oath],
22:11d and [the other] shall not make restitution.
22:12a But if it was actually stolen from him,
22:12b [the thief] shall make restitution to its owner.
22:13a If it has actually been mauled [by a wild animal],
22:13b he must bring it as evidence.
22:13c In the case of a mauling, he shall not make restitution.
22:14a If a man borrows [something] from his neighbor,
22:14b and it is damaged,
22:14c or it dies—
22:14d [and if] its owner is not with it—
22:14e he shall make full restitution.
22:15a If its owner is with it,
22:15b he shall not make restitution.
22:15c If it is rented,
22:15d it came for its rent.
22:16a If a man seduces a virgin who is not engaged,
22:16b and he lies with her,
22:16c he must pay a full bride-price for her [to be] his wife.
22:17a If her father absolutely refuses to give her to him,
22:17b he shall pay money equal to the bride-price for virgins."

---

70. Lit. "whom [the] gods condemn," since the verse uses the plural form of the verb (אֲשֶׁר יַרְשִׁיעֻן אֱלֹהִים). Generally speaking, אֱלֹהִים with a plural verb means "gods" and not "God" (Judg. 9:9; Isa. 36:18; Jer. 2:28). There is another apparent exception to this rule (2 Sam. 7:23). It is conceivable on the basis of Ps. 82 that אֱלֹהִים here refers to human judges (NIV, TNIV), but that is unlikely. It may be that יַרְשִׁיעֻן should be emended with the Samaritan Pentateuch to a 3ms verb with a 3ms suffix, ירשיענו, giving "whom God condemns."

Structure

The laws here are divided into sections dealing with both deliberate and unintended acts that result in someone suffering financial loss of one kind or another.

I. Liability for Loss of Livestock (21:33–36)
II. Punishment for Theft of Livestock (22:1–4)
III. Liability concerning Agricultural Land (22:5–6)
IV. Personal Property Disputes (22:7–15)
V. Liability for the Loss of Virginity (22:16–17)

Commentary

21:33–36. A man might open a pit because he is digging a well or cistern, or he might intend it as a trap for wild animals. However, if he does not take measures to prevent other people's livestock from falling into it, he is liable for the financial loss. He has to pay the full market value for the animal, but since he has paid for it, the carcass is his to use as he wishes. Similarly, an owner of an ox that one may reasonably expect to be violent must take steps to prevent injury to another person's animals (for example, the owner of the goring ox might dehorn it). By analogy, anyone is liable for the financial loss suffered by a second party if the loss is caused by the negligence of the first party. Thus, the rule that applies to a goring ox would apply equally to a vicious dog.

22:1–4. The rules involving theft are fairly straightforward. If a person steals and disposes of the property, he must repay it: fivefold for an ox and fourfold for a sheep (the reason for the disparity is not clear, although Stuart suggests that it is because sheep are prone to wander and thus easier to steal[71]). If someone steals an animal but does not dispose of it, he must repay double (that is, he must return the original animal and give up one other of equal value). If the thief cannot repay, he is sold into slavery. These stipulations allow the courts certain latitude; the fact that different penalties are imposed in different circumstances suggests that the courts were to exercise some judgment in assessing penalties. In the midst of these rules, as a parenthesis, the law takes up the issue of violence done to the thief while he is committing robbery. The essential rule is that if it is night, and the man defending his property has no way of knowing how great the danger to himself is and therefore resists with maximum force, the property owner is considered guiltless even if the thief dies. But if the incident

71. Stuart, *Exodus*, 502.

took place in daylight and the jury can assess that the property owner was not in personal danger and acted out of vengeance, the property owner can be charged with homicide. Theft is not a capital offense, and no person, even the victim, has the right to act as judge and executioner. The insertion of this aside on homicide makes the point that we are here concerned with property, which should never be placed on the same level as human life.

22:5–6. After harvest, the ancient farmer might clean out the old vegetation from his fields by one of two methods. Either he could turn his livestock loose into the field to eat the plants, or he could set the field on fire. Whichever he did, he was to take care that his neighbor's fields were untouched or be willing to reimburse the neighbor out of his own harvest. The amount to be repaid is not set, since obviously only a jury, aware of the particulars of the case, could do that. The only stipulation in the law is that he must repay out of his best, and not his worst, crops.

22:7–15. This is a series of precedents for dealing with property disputes between two parties. In early Israel there were no banks, and many people would only have limited facilities for storing harvested grain or other goods. As such, sometimes private individuals would temporarily store other people's goods, produce or animals (no doubt for a fee). Also, a person might be hired to temporarily care for another's cattle or sheep, or sometimes someone might simply borrow another person's property. There were various reasons, therefore, that one party might have possession of another party's goods. A court case from Nuzi illustrates the kind of disputes that might arise. This one involved alleged negligence by a hired oxherd:

> Tehip-tilla son of Puhi-shenni went to court before the judges against Taia son of Warad-ahi, (saying): "Taia the oxherd of Tehip-tilla — he injured one ox." Said Taia: "his fellow(-ox) injured (this) ox out on the range." But the judges said to Taia: "Bring your witnesses to the effect that his fellow(-ox) injured (him) on the range." Taia said: "My witnesses are not there." The judges said: "(It is) you who injured him. Pay the equivalent of the ox." Tehip-tilla won the lawsuit and (the judges) ordered Taia (to pay) one ox (out) of (his) own herd.[72]

72. "The Goring Ox at Nuzi," translated by William W. Hallo (COS 3.121.270).

According to Exod. 22:7–15, if one man was lawfully and temporarily in possession of another's property but the property was lost or destroyed, various guidelines apply. If a third party stole or destroyed the property, no penalty is assessed against the temporary custodian (who presumably was not negligent). Also, if the property was lost while the owner was present and presumably supervising the use of his property, the temporary custodian is not liable. Otherwise, the temporary custodian is liable. If a situation involving property claims is ambiguous, so that it is one man's word against another, an oath before God settles the matter. If someone protests his innocence under such an oath, that oath must be accepted. But we should note that this is a last resort, to be employed when there are no normal methods for ascertaining the facts. A man who swore that he was the lawful owner of property would not have his oath accepted if there were witnesses to testify against him.

If two parties both swore to be the rightful owners of something, and there were no ordinary means of determining who was in the right, the case would be settled by God (22:9), but the means by which this was done is not specified. We cannot presume it would be done by Urim and Thummim, since people in outlying villages would rarely, if ever, have access to these high-priestly devices. Members of a local jury may have appealed to an itinerant prophet for direction (Saul and his servant sought out a certain "man of God," who turned out to be Samuel, for direction in seeking lost donkeys; 1 Sam 9:6). Pagans, of course, would employ various forms of divination, but this is not authorized for Israel. On the other hand, there is some allowance in the Old Testament for the casting of lots (Prov. 16:33). Many pagan property laws, moreover, were similar to what we see in Israelite law. Another case from the Nuzi archives describes how a certain man named Zigi claims to have deposited 30 seahs of barley with a man named Ilanu. Zigi claimed that Ilanu refused to return all of his barley. In the trial, Ilanu was able to produce witnesses in his behalf, and Ilanu also completed an obscure ritual that involved "the lifting of the gods." As such, Ilanu won the case.[73]

22:16–17. It seems odd to us that this law is included here among laws concerning property rights; we might expect to find it in a passage such as Lev. 18, which concerns sexual behavior. But the point of the law here is not sexual morality as such, but the property rights of the family of the virgin. Since she would marry when she came of age, she

73. The relevant text is cited in Wells, "Exodus," 241.

would be lost to the family and go to another. The financial compensation for this was the bride-price. A girl who was deflowered would fetch a lower bride-price, if any at all. Thus, the boy who deflowers her was to pay a full bride-price, as though she were still a virgin, and marry her, taking away her disgrace. If the girl's family considered the young man to be of bad character and did not want him to have their daughter, he still had to pay a bride-price. Note that this law concerns the girl who is not engaged; if she were engaged (to another man), it would be a case of adultery and altogether different (Lev. 20:10).

Theological Summary of Key Points

Beyond the obvious legal authority of these rules, this text implies certain theological and moral truths.

1. These laws are meant to instill in the people of Israel a respect for the property and rights of one another. We have an obligation to see to it that no one suffers financial loss through our dishonesty, irresponsible actions or indifferent attitude.

2. The laws imply that when humans are in contact with one another, invariably there will be conflict. As such, an equitable method for resolving property disputes is essential for society to function.

3. Property rights are real. Israel was never a communal society; the land and its cattle did not belong to "the people." They belonged to individual Israelites.

4. Property is never on a par with human life. One may kill a thief if one reasonably feels endangered by the thief, but one may not kill a person for the sake of a stolen sheep. The defense of human life is the highest moral law, and it trumps lower laws.

5. Religious acts, such as taking an oath, can be devices of evasion and dishonesty. As such, taking an oath in God's name does not overrule contrary evidence.

6. It is noteworthy that the text offers two forms of punishment: restitution and slavery. The latter strikes us as very harsh, but we should recall that slavery in Israel was, by law, temporary and not a lifelong sentence. There is no provision for punishment by imprisonment in these laws. Arguably, the biblical provisions give the criminal more dignity than do modern penal systems. By directly repaying or by working off his obligations, the Israelite had his value as a man reaffirmed, and he was not confined with thousands of other criminals. My own suspicion is that recidivism was much lower in ancient Israel than in modern society (it is obviously impossible to verify this since we have no data). The Old Testament code was not an especially draconian code. But its penalties, grounded in the principle of restitution, by design imparted lessons to miscreants about property rights.

7. Ultimately, this is a passage about integrity. In teaching this text to a Christian congregation, one would want to stress its moral lessons. That we should not steal, that we should always respect the property of others even where stealing is not the issue, and that we should seek out fair ways of resolving disputes are obvious lessons. A New Testament counterpart to this text may be the letter to Philemon, where Paul exhorts a Christian not to value his property above another man's soul. Property rights are important and should not be violated by individuals or governments, but they are not the highest of all values for the Christian.

RESPECT FOR HUMAN DIGNITY (22:18–27[17–26])

There are two ways we can abuse human dignity. The first is by involving ourselves in, and promoting, degrading behavior, and the second is by treating others in a disrespectful manner. Both are affronts to the fact that we are made in God's image.

Translation

22:18	"You must not allow a sorceress to live.
22:19	Whoever lies with an animal definitely must[74] be put to death.
22:20	Whoever sacrifices to the gods—[and] not to YHWH alone—shall be placed under the ban.
22:21a	You must not abuse an alien
22:21b	and you must not push him around,[75]
22:21c	for you were aliens in the land of Egypt.
22:22	You must not afflict any widow or orphan.

74. The infinitive absolute pattern מוֹת יוּמָת here implies that no other course of action is allowable.

75. The verb לחץ literally means to "push." It may be used literally of giving someone an unfriendly shove, or metaphorically for pushing an alien around with unjust and irrational legal or commercial restrictions.

22:23a If you afflict them[76] in any way,
22:23b [and] if they cry out in desperation to me,
22:23c I will most definitely hear their cry,[77]
22:24a and my anger will rage,
22:24b and I will kill you with the sword,
22:24c and your wives will become widows and your children orphans.[78]
22:25a If you loan money to my people, to the poor among you,
22:25b you are not to be like the moneylender to him;
22:25c you must not charge him interest.
22:26a If you actually take your neighbor's cloak as collateral,
22:26b you must return it to him as the sun begins to set,
22:27a for that is his only covering;
22:27b it is his garment for his skin.
22:27c In what shall he lie down?
22:27d And should it happen
22:27e that he should cry out to me,
22:27f I will hear.
22:27g For I am gracious.

Structure

The commands here focus on human dignity from two different angles. First, there are three actions that are so degrading and dehumanizing that they must be eliminated from Israel by the most severe means possible (execution). If such behavior were to flourish, Israel would not only fail to be the people of God, but they would hardly be human at all. Second, there are commands to protect three groups of vulnerable people. Both sets of commands arise from the conviction that a human being is in the image of God. The balance of two sets of three commands is probably intentional. Sins committed by a person and sins

76. Lit. "him." So also in 22:23bc, the 3ms suffix represents any widow or orphan.

77. This verse has three examples of a combination of the infinitive absolute with a cognate finite verb. They illustrate the difficulty of finding an appropriate translation and also show that the pattern must always be translated according to context. Thus, in 22:23b(22b), צָעֹק יִצְעַק seems to intensify the action ("cry out in desperation"). In 22:23c(22c), שָׁמֹעַ אֶשְׁמַע appears to indicate certainty ("I will most definitely hear"). In 22:23a(22a), עַנֵּה תְעַנֶּה is more difficult, but I believe that it reflects the language of a stern warning (thus, "If you afflict them in any way").

78. Since women as a rule had no economic power in ancient Israel, a child without a father was, in effect, an orphan.

committed against a person equally degrade that person's humanity. We are defiled by the evil we do and by the evil done to us.

I. Degrading Behavior Not to be Tolerated (22:18–20)
   A. Sorcery (22:18)
   B. Bestiality (22:19)
   C. Idolatry (22:20)
II. Prohibitions against Showing Disrespect to the Vulnerable (22:21–27)
   A. The Treatment of Aliens (22:21)
   B. The Treatment of Widows and Orphans (22:22–24)
   C. The Treatment of Borrowers (22:25–27)

Commentary

22:18–20. The three kinds of degrading behavior not to be allowed to thrive in Israel are sorcery, bestiality, and idolatry. Each of these reduces a person to a subhuman level and is an affront to the Creator. There are, of course, many other sins for which the Torah prescribes the death penalty, but the focus here is on behavior that brings a person down to a level of baseness that obliterates his or her humanity or personal dignity. It is not disrespect for human life but respect for it that demands that such persons be put to death.

The first of the three offenses, sorcery, involves humans working with magic and demonic forces in order to achieve their goals (gaining power, wealth, revenge, and so forth). Pagans, we should observe, also feared sorcerers and magic. In the Hittite laws §111, sorcery was a serious crime and had to be reported to the royal administration:

> [If] anyone forms clay for [an image] (for magical purposes), it is sorcery (and) a case for the king's court.[79]

Pagan means for dealing with sorcery, however, often involved a kind of counter-magic that was little better than the sorcery it was meant to thwart. For example, a Ugaritic text describes a ritual for invoking Horon in order to break the power of a sorcerer. It contains the following curse:

> Then (Horon) shall expel the sorcerer-accuser
> — Horon, the magician,
> and Galmu, the familiar.

79. "Hittite Laws," trans. Hoffner, Jr. (*COS* 2.19.114).

> Go, you shall founder . . . ,
> you shall find your tongue stammering,
> you shall be tightly bound(?).
> The god clothed you,
> the god has stripped you.[80]

But Horon himself was the god of sorcery,[81] and calling on him with magical ritual while uttering curses against an enemy was ultimately just another form of sorcery. As such, whoever invoked Horon in this manner to thwart a sorcerer would also be involved in such degrading behavior. The Book of the Covenant, by contrast, does not allow magic for any purposes, even for counter-spells.

The second of the offenses, bestiality, involves human sexual intercourse with animals. The degradation implied here is self-evident.

The third of the offenses, idolatry, has humans, the image of God, bowing before objects of wood and stone and metal. It is noteworthy that idolatry is included here. This activity was in fact very common in Israel, as it was in the entire ancient Near East, but it was no less heinous for being popular.

22:21. The alien could be "pushed around" in various ways. He might be denied the right to carry on certain trades, or forced to reside in isolated ghetto-like areas, or subjected to daily abuse, or simply seized and enslaved. The reminder that the Israelites were aliens in Egypt is double-edged. On the one hand, they must not dole out that kind of abuse since they know how bitter it is to receive such treatment. On the other hand, they were accepted into Egypt when they were desperate, during a time of famine, and they should show to others the same kindness that the pharaoh who knew Joseph showed to them.

22:22–24. The widow and the orphan were equally vulnerable in ancient Israel since neither had any economic power. Such people might be afflicted in a number of ways, including enslavement, sexual exploitation, verbal or physical abuse, or even by callous indifference. If they

---

80. "Ugaritic Incantation Against Sorcery," translated by Daniel Fleming (*COS* 1.96.302).

81. Karel van der Toorn, Bob Becking and Pieter W. van der Horst, eds. *Dictionary of Deities and Demons in the Bible,* 2nd ed. (Leiden: Brill, 1999), 425-6. Horon resided in the netherworld and was the chief of demons. Other texts, such as the Egyptian Harris Papyrus, refer to the practice of invoking Horon for protection from demons.

suffer such things and call on God, God's vengeance will be very severe. The text suggests that they do need to expressly appeal to YHWH in order for him to intervene on their behalf. The language of v. 24 is extraordinarily harsh, indicating how little tolerance God has for abuse of the poor.

22:25–27. Modern readers have difficulty with this text because the economies of the modern world and of ancient Israel are so different. Today, credit is routinely and almost universally used by businesses and individuals for major purchases and even for normal operating expenses. Rare is the person and rarer the business that makes large purchases with cash on hand. By contrast, in ancient Israel borrowing was done almost exclusively for emergencies only. The prohibition against charging interest probably concerns the fact that one should not take advantage of a person in distress; it is not concerned with charging interest as part of the routine of doing business, as such a practice was probably rare if not unheard of. Therefore, it is perhaps unwise to claim that charging interest on a home mortgage is forbidden in the Bible, since the banking industry and home mortgages as we know them did not exist when the Bible was written. In fact, money itself did not exist in Israel until the postexilic period. Prior to that, purchasing was done by barter or by weighing out silver. The only thing analogous to a business loan from biblical Israel was the making of investments in a trading venture, and it does not appear that this behavior was considered unethical (see Prov. 31:24; Eccl. 11:1–2; Matt. 25:27).[82] Having said that, one should not conclude that the modern practice of incurring enormous debt in order to make purchases is wise or is consistent with biblical ideals. One reason that the modern concept of financing purchases was so rare in ancient Israel is that people were, with good reason, uncomfortable about taking on debt. As I write these words, the world is in financial crisis precisely because individuals, businesses, and especially governments were only too willing to take on massive debt.

In this text, however, the main point is that one should not take advantage of or humiliate the person whose situation requires that he seek a loan. Charging interest exploits his need, and it appears that interest rates in the ancient world could be very high. Seizing personal

82. Borrowing on interest was much more common among the upper classes of ancient Rome, where men with political ambition were expected to indulge the crowds with extravagant and expensive largesse. Thus, for example, Caesar borrowed heavily from Crassus.

assets, such as the cloak in which he sleeps, not only imposes great suffering on him but humiliates him. The ideal is that by not charging interest and by not depriving him of the basic essentials for a normal life, the lender gives the borrower a chance to recover from his financial condition.

Theological Summary of Key Points

1. The people of God should be the most human of all people. With appropriate conduct, their dignity as the creatures made in God's image is fully maintained. But this dignity is lost through occult practices, through gross sexual misconduct, and through idolatry. Similarly, people are robbed of their dignity when not treated with respect and kindness, regardless of their economic or social status. The essential point is, just as we seek the restoration of our own human dignity by the grace of God, so also we should see in others—however broken they may be—a dignity that is worthy of merciful treatment from us.

2. We are commanded to renew and rebuild the image of God in ourselves and see the image of God in others. As such, all behavior that degrades the soul (and not just specifically the items listed here) should be resisted and avoided. Positively, the renewal of the mind is not just a matter of avoiding certain behavior but is a work of God in sanctification (Eph. 4:21–24). The demand to treat the poor with respect and kindness when lending them money relates well to Jesus's teaching, "Everything that you would want people to do for you, you should do the same for them" (Matt. 7:12).

RESPECT FOR THOSE TOWARD WHOM HONOR IS DUE (22:28–31[27–30])

Israel must not be negligent about showing respect to those in authority. In Israel, however, the highest authority is YHWH, and as such, the bulk of the text is taken up with matters that relate to God. Therefore, the focus here is not the religious life, but the proper demeanor of vassals toward their sovereign.

Translation

22:28a You must not speak disrespectfully[83] of God,
22:28b and you must not curse a ruler among your people.

83. The verb קלל is often translated "curse" and indeed it is frequently, as here, used in parallel to ארר, which plainly does mean "curse." However, the root idea of קלל is to be "small, lightweight, or insignificant," and thus

22:29a You must make no delay with respect to your harvest and your vintage.[84]
22:29b The firstborn of your sons you shall give to me.
22:30a This is what you shall do with your ox [or] with your sheep:
22:30b for seven days it shall be with its mother;
22:30c on the eighth day you shall give it to me.
22:31a You must be my holy people
22:31b and not eat meat [found] in the field—a mauled animal;
22:31c throw it to the dogs."

Structure

Respect is to be shown both to God and to human authorities by speaking of them with due respect. In addition, God is to be honored both by giving timely and appropriate sacrifices and by shunning loathsome behavior.

I. Respect in Speech (22:28)
II. Respect in Offerings (22:29–30)
III. Respect in Decorum (22:31)

Commentary

22:28. The two clauses of this verse show perfect parallelism, illustrating the fact that Hebrew parallelism is not confined to poetry. The focus is on speech concerning persons in authority, be they divine or human. The parallelism of the passage implies that verbal respect for God and for rulers springs from the same source: a basic respect for authority. Paul cited this verse in Acts 23:5, albeit perhaps somewhat ironically; he spoke of Ananias, who was functioning not as high priest but as "ruler" of Jerusalem.

---

it does not necessarily mean a formally pronounced curse. It can mean speech that is simply disrespectful.

84. The precise meanings of מְלֵאָתְךָ and וְדִמְעֲךָ are unknown. See the discussion in Sarna, *Exodus*, 140–1. In Num. 18:27, מְלֵאָה (which appears to literally mean "fullness") is used in respect to the wine vat, so it is clear that it does not exclusively refer to the grain harvest (the NIV translates it in Exod. as "your granaries"). See also Deut. 22:9, its only other occurrence, where it also relates to vintage. The word דֶּמַע is *hapax legomenon*, but many relate it to דִּמְעָה, "tear." The term could be a poetic reference to the "tears" of the grapes as they are trampled upon (that is, the grape juice), although this etymology is not certain. Therefore, it is possible that both terms relate to vintage. It seems likely, however, that מְלֵאָתְךָ more broadly refers to harvests of any kind.

22:29–30. The command "The firstborn of your sons you shall give to me" is given without any explanation. What does it mean to "give" one's son to YHWH? Similarly, what does giving the firstborn of the oxen or sheep entail? Is it sacrificed as a whole offering or as a fellowship offering? These laws are further developed in the larger teachings on the offering of firstfruits (Num. 18:8–13) and on the redemption of firstborn sons and animals (Num. 18:14–19; Deut. 15:19–23; see also Exod. 13:11–15). The firstborn son was apparently redeemed by a payment of five shekels to the sanctuary. The firstborn animals provided food for the priestly families, but Deut. 15 also indicates that the donating families could partake of the sacrificial meal (that is, the animal was given in a fellowship offering). But the purpose of this text in the Book of the Covenant is not to regulate the procedures for making offerings to God; its purpose is to insist that one must give God what is due to him in a timely manner, without delay or evasion. God is, in effect, the suzerain over the people, and they are to pay their tributes to him as they would to a great king. The stipulation that newborn animals should remain with the mother for seven days is healthier for the mother and also strengthens the calf or lamb, so that it is a better offering to YHWH and meal for the participants in the sacrifice.[85]

22:31. Meat that otherwise would be considered clean for human consumption (such as beef, lamb, or venison) is unclean if it is found dead, having been mauled by a wild animal that presumably fled when humans approached. This meat it suitable only for dogs. But again, the focus here is not on elucidating kosher laws as such. The focus of the text is seen in its opening clause ("You must be my holy people") in contrast to its closing clause ("throw it to the dogs"). Holiness is set against "dogs," and the implication is that by avoiding disgusting forms of food, one is showing respect for the person of YHWH, who has chosen Israel as his people. It is an affront to the covenant and a disgrace to the name of YHWH for God's people to behave like dogs. The idea that God's people should be holy so that they might honor God is especially developed in the Holiness Code of Lev. 17–26.

Theological Summary of Key Points

1. The essential demand of the text is that people show respect for the authorities with whom they are associated. But such behavior toward God and rulers arises from a general respect for authority, and it will show itself in many ways. A person who understands these

85. See Stuart, *Exodus*, 522.

principles will show respect for employers, teachers, business partners, as well as for government officials and ultimately for God. The clearest New Testament link to this text is Jesus's command that we "render to Caesar the things that are Caesar's, and to God the things that are God's" (Matt. 22:21). As in Jesus's teaching, the primary focus in Exodus is on our duty to God, but duty to human authorities is not to be neglected.

2. The specific laws given above should be regarded as illustrative and not as exhaustive. Thus, for example, a Christian should avoid viewing pornography not only because such behavior is intrinsically immoral but also out of respect for the name of Christ, in that it is a disgrace for a Christian to indulge in such behavior.

3. The structure of the text described above sets out the main ways in which respect for superiors is demonstrated. We must show respect for God and for authorities in our speech, and we must also be timely about our financial obligations to both. Similarly, our behavior, decorum, dress, and general demeanor should reflect well on those with whom we are associated. If, for example, a soldier behaves badly while out on the town, people do not say, "That man is a disgrace" but, "That soldier is a disgrace," and his actions reflect badly not only upon himself but also upon his unit and his superior officers. So also, a Christian should behave in a manner that reflects well on the church and on the name of God.

RESPECT FOR THE TRUTH (23:1–9)

This text is in many respects an exposition of the Ninth Commandment (20:16). It emphasizes respect for the truth in judicial and property rights, although it also deals with nonjudicial matters.

Translation

23:1a "You must not pass along a groundless rumor.

23:1b Do not join your hand with a wicked man by being a malicious witness.

23:2a You must not follow behind popular opinion[86] toward doing evil.

23:2b And you must not testify in a dispute in a way that veers [from the truth] in accord with how popular opinion twists [people's thinking].[87]

86. "Popular opinion" is lit. "many [people]" (רַבִּים).

87. The root נטה appears in this verse first as a Qal infinitive construct (לִנְטֹת) and then as a Hiphil infinitive construct (לְהַטֹּת). Both, in this context,

23:3 And you must not show partiality toward a poor man in his dispute.
23:4a If you come across your enemy's ox or his donkey wandering away,
23:4b you obviously have to return[88] it to him.
23:5a If you see the donkey of someone who hates you lying [helpless] beneath its load,
23:5b you must refrain from [your impulse to[89]] abandon him like that.[90]
23:5c Could you really abandon him like that?[91]
23:6 You shall not turn back the just case of the impoverished man among you in his dispute.
23:7a You must keep far from false testimony,
23:7b and do not kill the innocent or the righteous,
23:7c for I will not acquit the guilty.
23:8a You must not take a bribe,
23:8b for 'a bribe blinds those who see
23:8c and subverts the words of the righteous.'[92]

---

mean to "turn aside," but the Qal is intransitive and means to veer away (see 2 Sam. 2:19). By implication, the Qal here describes veering off from the truth. Alternatively, the Qal could be transitive with "justice" as the implied object (see Exod. 23:6). The Hiphil, however, is transitive, and it has the thoughts and opinions of people as its implied object. That is, the Hiphil, in effect, means to mislead or deceive (see Isa. 44:20; Job 36:18; Prov. 7:21).

88. The infinitive absolute construction here (הָשֵׁב תְּשִׁיבֶנּוּ) appears to set up a contrast between what a person may reason within himself, that he has no obligation to an enemy, and the moral truth, that even the rights of someone whom one does not like are to be respected. Thus, I have rendered it as "obviously," reflecting a contrast with self-serving, fallacious reasoning.

89. The verb "refrain" (חדל) here implies that there is a natural impulse that one must resist: to leave your enemy and his animal to their troubles.

90. "Abandon him like that" is lit. "from abandoning to him" (מֵעֲזֹב לוֹ).

91. The clause עָזֹב תַּעֲזֹב עִמּוֹ is difficult. Lit. this is, "You certainly must abandon it with him," that is, you must leave the donkey to his own devices. This plainly contradicts 23:5ab. A second possibility is to treat the verb as עזב (II), "to restore," rather than עזב (I), "to abandon." This is favored by Sarna, *Exodus*, 142, who compares it to Ugaritic *ʿdb*, "to prepare, set." The problem with this is that עזב (II) is quite uncertain and very late, appearing only in Neh. 3:8; 4:2(3:34), where it seems to mean to "restore" a ruined structure. Also, the pattern עזב עִמּוֹ in 23:5c parallels עזב לוֹ in 23:5b, suggesting that it has the same meaning. I therefore suggest that 23:5c should be regarded as a rhetorical question.

92. Although it is impossible to be certain, it appears that 23:8bc cites a common proverb. With minor variation in wording, Deut. 16:19 seems to

23:9a And you must not push an alien around;
23:9b you [of all people][93] know the experience of an alien,
23:9c for you were strangers in the land of Egypt."

Structure

This passage is nicely balanced, with instructions on giving testimony about others (vv. 1–2) set against instructions on rendering judgments (vv. 7–8), and these two are paired with commands not to show prejudice either in favor of (v. 3) or against (v. 6) the poor. After each set of judicial instructions, there is also a command regarding social behavior toward those whom one might be disposed against: the property of one's personal enemy (vv. 4–5) and the alien (v. 9).

I. Disputes and Legal Matters (23:1–3)
 A. Giving Testimony (23:1–2)
 B. Showing Bias in Favor of the Poor (23:3)
II. Dealing with an Enemy's Animal (23:4–5)
III. Disputes and Legal Matters (23:6–8)
 A. Showing Bias Against the Poor (23:6)
 B. Rendering Verdicts (23:7–8)
IV. Dealing with an Alien in the Community (23:9)

Commentary

23:1–2. Giving testimony about others, whether in a judicial or nonjudicial setting, is the focus here. To pass along a groundless rumor is to testify to something even though one has no direct, personal knowledge of the facts but is only repeating common hearsay. The command in 23:1b actually concerns conspiracy to commit perjury. The command of 23:2 concerns the manipulative power of popular sentiment; the witness can have his own testimony shaped by popular feelings and in turn can further inflame those same popular passions. But the facts as one knows them, and not what the crowd believes or wants to believe, should always govern one's words.

23:3. Although it is proverbial that the rich get better treatment in cases of law than do the poor, there can also be prejudice in favor of the poor. This is especially so when people operate out of a preconceived

---

cite the same proverb. We have similar cases in Proverbs, where the same axiom can be cited repeatedly with minor changes in wording.

93. The fronting of the conjunction and pronoun in this clause (וְאַתֶּם) sets up an implied contrast between the Israelites and the other peoples of earth.

agenda to do away with all social inequalities, or when there is popular sentiment to punish the wealthy (or, in modern society, wealthy businesses) for their very success. Whatever the motivation, discrimination in favor of the poor is no less evil than discrimination against the poor.

23:4–5. Superficially, these commands make the simple demand that one should not abandon to its fate a struggling or lost animal that happens to belong to a personal enemy. On a deeper level, these commands also focus on valuing the truth above one's personal likes and dislikes. The truth, in this case, is that the property lawfully belongs to another man and thus it should be returned to him, or that the animal is suffering and it is a duty to be helpful in such circumstances. We cannot allow our personal feelings to turn us from the simple facts of ownership and of our personal duties. We cannot have one set of moral standards for friends and another for enemies. Otherwise, truth is pliable and ethical duties are meaningless.

23:6. The phrase to "turn back the just case of the impoverished man" could mean that the poor man is literally turned away from the court, so that he never gets to make his case, but it also can mean to hear him plead his case but then dismiss it with evasive judicial pronouncements that distort the facts against the poor man. In either case, the poor man gets no justice because he lacks money and the attendant political power.

23:7–8. There are three basic commands here: do not accept "false testimony," do not wrongfully convict the innocent (especially if the crime is a capital offense), and do not take a bribe. Thus, the commands relate to the duties of jurors (that is, of citizens gathered in the city gate in an ancient Israelite setting). The jurors obviously are not culpable if they have made every effort to uncover the truth but were deceived outright by perjurers. But the effect of the commands is to impress upon jurors how weighty their duty is: they must be diligent about seeking the facts, and God will hold them culpable if they turn a blind eye to pertinent information. The warning against taking bribes seems so obvious as to be almost unnecessary, but bribes are not always given in an obviously conspiratorial manner (the word שֹׁחַד can simply mean "gift"). The juror must be cautious; he may have received what were to him simple gifts and favors and only later realize that he has been targeted for special treatment by someone who has a case to bring to the court and who expects preferential treatment.

23:9. This verse essentially repeats a command just given in Exod. 22:21. Why is it repeated here? The focus, in context, is again on one's need to acknowledge the truth. In this case, the truth is that the Israelites themselves were aliens in a foreign land, and thus they are in no position to behave arrogantly toward people in that situation in their land. If they reflect on the facts of their own history, they should be able to sympathize with the plight of the outsider. If they mistreat foreigners, they are being dishonest about their own history. Also, the present context suggests that one should not "push around" a foreigner in a judicial context. Jurors must be fair in hearing all cases and not be prejudicial against outsiders.

Theological Summary of Key Points

Respect for the truth is the most precious possession a person can have. It saves one from self-deception in one's own interest or in the interest of popular or deeply held prejudice. The issue naturally has great gravity in the law courts. If one distorts the truth because of a personal or popular prejudice, or indeed because of a bribe, then a terrible injustice can be perpetrated. But it also has significance for personal behavior: the fact that I do not like a person or the group from which he comes has no bearing on that person's rights or on my duties.

RESPECT FOR DIVINE PROVISION (23:10–19)

The regulations here concern the religious life of Israel especially as it is manifested in agricultural and dietary life. This involves the agricultural festivals, but not everything in this text concerns ritual and religious ceremony. The practice of leaving the land uncultivated was meant to honor God, for example, but was not ceremonial in nature.

Translation

23:10a "For six years you shall sow your land
23:10b and gather in its produce,
23:11a but in the seventh year you are to let it go
23:11b and leave it untended.[94]

---

94. The verb נטשׁ should not be translated as "to leave fallow" (נטשׁ, *HALOT*, 2.695–6; NASB) which is too much of a deliberate agricultural strategy to be appropriate here. Also, leaving land fallow does not necessarily mean not working the field at all; a fallow field might still be plowed or periodically purged of weeds by burning. נטשׁ implies complete neglect of the land (cf. נטשׁ in Prov. 1:8). One does no work in the field at all, and it becomes the common property of men and beasts, to take whatever food they can

23:11c And the poor of your people may eat [freely of it];

23:11d and whatever they leave the wild animals may eat.

23:11e You are to do likewise with your vineyard [and] your olive grove.

23:12a For six days you are to do your work,

23:12b but on the seventh day you are to observe Sabbath[95]

23:12c so that your ox and your donkey may rest,

23:12d and [so that even] the son of your female slave and the alien can catch his breath.[96]

23:13a And observe everything about which I have spoken to you.

23:13b And do not remind [people] of the name of other gods,

23:13c and do not let [such a thing] be heard from your mouth.

23:14 Three times in a year you shall celebrate a festival to me.

23:15a The Feast of Unleavened Bread [is the first that] you must observe.

23:15b For seven days you are to eat unleavened bread—as I commanded you—at the appointed time in the month Abib,

23:15c for in it you came out of Egypt.

23:15d And [the people] must not appear before me empty-handed.

23:16a And the Feast of the Harvest:

23:16b [it is] the first fruits of your work—what you sow in the field.

23:16c And the Feast of the Ingathering:

23:16d [it is] at the end of the year when you gather from the field [the fruit of] your work.

23:17 Three times in the year all your males shall appear before the Lord YHWH.

23:18a You shall not offer sacrifices that involve blood to me along with[97] leavened bread,[98]

23:18b and the fat of my feast must not remain until morning.

---

find. It is a temporary cessation of the command of Gen. 1:28 to "subdue" the earth.

95. The verb שבת means to "stop," and in this context one could justifiably supply something like "your labor" as the direct object. But it appears that the Qal of שבת comes to be used absolutely for "observing Sabbath," with all that this observation entails (see Exod. 34:21; 2 Chron. 36:21).

96. The root נפש fundamentally relates to the throat as the locus of breathing (or eating), and in this case the Niphal stem means to "breath freely" or "catch one's breath." It represents getting a break from hard exertion.

97. The preposition עַל is not spatial ("upon") in this case, but means "in addition to" or more simply, "with."

98. Lit. "You shall not sacrifice with leavened bread the blood of my sacrifice," but this is a case of cognate accusative, with "the blood of my sacrifice" having the meaning "sacrifices for me involving blood."

23:19a You must bring the best of the first fruits of your ground into the house of YHWH your God.
23:19b Do not boil a kid goat in its mother's milk."

Structure

This text has a parallel pattern, with cyclical events (Sabbaths and Festivals) set against warnings against improper behavior (transmission of pagan teachings and improper handling of foodstuff).

I. Cyclical Events: Sabbaths (23:10–12)
  A. Sabbath Years for the Land (23:10–11)
  B. Sabbath Days for People (23:12)
II. Warning: Prohibition against Transmitting Pagan Ideas (23:13)
III. Cyclical Events: Three Festivals (23:14–17)
IV. Warning: Prohibition against Dishonoring God in the Handling of Food (23:18–19)
  A. Rules about Offerings (23:18–19a)
  B. Boiling a Kid in its Mother's Milk (23:19b)

Commentary

23:10–11. As this text reads, it is not entirely clear how the system of leaving land uncultivated is to work. The law as given here does not explicitly state that every field in Israel was to be left uncultivated at the same time; conceivably, one could leave one field uncultivated in its seventh year while plowing and planting the other fields in one's possession. If this were the intended practice, the fields or vineyards left uncultivated would thus be rotated through the years. In this system, the owner would not bother at all with the uncultivated field during the sabbatical year of that field. This text, in fact, asserts that he is to let the poor and even wild animals go into it and take whatever they wish. The owner, if the fields were rotated in this manner, would live off of the produce of his other fields (the text actually says nothing about what people who were not poor were to eat during this time). However, later legislation (in Lev. 25:1–7; 18–22) indicates that every field in the country is to be left uncultivated at the same time. All people, including aliens and slaves, were to eat from the remains of the previous year's harvest, and nothing was to be harvested from the fields in the sabbatical year. This later legislation does not say anything about feeding the poor (whether they were to glean from the fields or be fed from the prior year's harvest). As such, one could conclude either that the Leviticus laws clarify the original intent of the Exodus laws or that they modify the Exodus laws in a manner that demands a universal agricultural sabbatical year. We should also note that Deut. 15:1–10 describes a sabbatical year system in which all debts owed by Israelites to one another are to be simultaneously cancelled, but that text does not describe a sabbatical year for the fields. Be that as it may, the important point the text makes here in Exodus is that Israel, as part of its agricultural routine, should show faith in God by leaving fields uncultivated and honor God by allowing the poor to gather whatever edibles they could find in those fields.

23:12. This verse reminds Israel of the importance of the Sabbath. Here, it is presented as an act of mercy for those who work the hardest (slaves and migrant workers from outside Israel). Elsewhere, the justification was either to commemorate creation (Exod. 20:11) or to remind Israel that they must not work like slaves again, as they had in Egypt (Deut. 5:15). Israel's agricultural life is the focus in this passage.

23:13. As an act of loyalty to YHWH, the people are not even to speak of pagan gods. This implies that they must not use the names in oaths, that they must not describe what the pagans believe about the gods, and that they must not tell the stories of their myths. In a culture that was saturated with paganism, as the ancient Near East was, the oral transmission of traditions and beliefs was the primary means by which devotion to the various cults was encouraged. Thus, refusal to speak of these things was a way of breaking the hold paganism held over people. By contrast, they were to constantly speak of the mighty acts of YHWH (Deut. 6:6–9). It is not surprising, we should note, that this rule comes in the midst of legislation that is concerned with laws relating to agriculture and how one should relate agricultural life to God. Pagan religion, and certainly that of the Canaanite variety, closely tied its agricultural cycle to the myths. Baal's battle with Mot famously represented the annual cycle of the seasons (the period of the storm god's death coinciding with the days of summer drought), much as the Persephone myth did for the Greeks. Ancient farmers would know and pass on all the myths and legends that tied seasons, rains, sunshine, and crops to the gods. But this was not to be done in Israel.

23:14–17. Israel classically celebrated seven major festivals: Passover, Unleavened Bread, Firstfruits, Pentecost (Feast of Weeks), Trumpets, the Day of Atonement, and Sukkoth (Tabernacles). This text only speaks of three festivals: Unleavened Bread, Harvest (equivalent to Pentecost), and Ingathering (equivalent to Sukkoth). Passover was already described at the plague on the firstborn (Exod. 12–13), so its omission here cannot be due to the fact that it did not yet exist. On the other hand, the

Day of Atonement is not mentioned until Lev. 16; it is reasonable to suppose that at this stage the Day of Atonement was unknown. Similarly, the Feast of Trumpets is not mentioned until Lev. 23:23–25 and Num. 29:1–6. Firstfruits, according to Lev. 23:9–14, took place every year in conjunction with the beginning of the Feast of Unleavened Bread. However, Firstfruits appears to have been more of an individually celebrated holy day; as farmers began their harvest, they would take the first cuttings of grain to hold up or "wave" before God in ritual thanksgiving. It is surely not the case that every farmer in Israel began his harvest on the same day; therefore, Firstfruits celebrations apparently took place individually throughout the period between Unleavened Bread and Pentecost. Also, the Firstfruits legislation is not given until Lev. 23. Therefore, the three festivals here are holy days requiring a national assembly (Passover took place in private homes, and Firstfruits was individually celebrated), and of course they do not include festivals that had not yet been inaugurated. These three festivals coincide with the three major events of Israel's agricultural cycle: Unleavened Bread comes at the approximate time of the beginning of the spring barley harvest, Pentecost comes at approximately the end of the wheat harvest seven weeks later, and Sukkoth comes at the end of the agricultural year, after the produce harvest and just before the winter rains. As such, national thanksgiving for the harvests is probably their purpose.

23:18–19a. Three statutes involving the use of food in ritual sacrifice are here laid out. First (23:18a), leavened bread is not to be offered with a blood sacrifice. Elsewhere, leavened bread is excluded from the Passover ceremony (see Deut. 16:2–4), but it is not clear that this command relates strictly to Passover. It seems to be more general, and it makes the point that Israelites should never offer leavened bread in a sacrificial ritual that involves blood (that is, when an animal is slain and its blood is smeared on the horns of an altar). Leavening can represent corruption, and thus it is incompatible with a blood sacrifice, an act of ritual purification. Second, the fat of a sacrificed animal is not to remain until the next day (it either had to be eaten, if permissible, or burned). Fat quickly turns rancid, and the decay and stench would be contrary to the holiness sacrifice is meant to communicate. Third, the people are to bring the best of their first fruits harvest as offerings, not the worst. The obvious point is not to dishonor God with inferior offerings. All these rules promote respect for the holiness of God in Israel's ritual life.

23:19b. The injunction against boiling a kid in its mother's milk is the basis for certain kosher regulations of Judaism that go far beyond the biblical requirement: they forbid any contact between a dairy product and meat. The purpose and origin of this rule in the Bible is uncertain. Moses Maimonides (1135-1204) argued that the practice of boiling a kid in its mother's milk originated in the cultic life of Canaanite paganism: "I think that most probably it is also prohibited because it is somehow connected with idolatry, forming perhaps part of the service or being used on the festivals of the heathen")[99]. But there is no evidence for the existence of such a rite among Canaanite pagans; the suggestion is pure speculation. At one time scholars supposed that a Ugaritic text mentioned boiling a kid in its mother's milk as part of a religious ritual, but that turned out to be a misreading of the text.[100] An alternative view is that the command prohibits placing dairy and meat products near each other or in the same containers because the milk would cause spoilage of the meat. Contemporary Cypriot women never put meat in a clay jar that had contained milk because bacteria-laden milk residue trapped in the pores of the pottery would quickly ruin the meat.[101] However, there is no evidence that Israelites or early Jews rigorously separated dairy and meat products; second temple literature mentions no such practice. Anyway, the command does not prohibit placing meat in a jar that had contained any dairy product; it specifically prohibits boiling a kid in its own mother's milk. And 19th and 20th century travelers among the Bedouin reported that these people would in fact boil a kid in its mother's milk.[102] The most reasonable solution is that the prohibition is in place because some desert people at the time actually boiled kids in their mother's milk as a matter of local cuisine, but that the Bible rejects the practice as inherently contrary to nature and inhumane. By analogy, the common biblical injunction against consuming blood (e.g., Deut. 12:15–16) does not refer to some obscure ritual but relates to the simple fact that some people in the ancient Near East did in fact use blood as an ingredient in food preparation.[103] This, too, is considered in the Bible to be inherently heinous and is therefore forbidden.

---

99. Moses Maimonides, *The Guide of the Perplexed of Maimonides*, Vol. 3, trans. M. Friedländer (London: Trübner & Co., 1885), 253.
100. See Wells, "Exodus," 246.
101. Gloria London, "Why Milk and Meat Don't Mix." *BAR* 34, no. 6 (2008): 66–9.
102. Edwin Firmage, "Zoology (Fauna)," in Freedman, *ABD* Vol. 6, 1128.
103. See Jean Bottéro, *Textes Culinaires Mésopotamiens* (Winona Lake: Eisenbrauns, 1995), 29. Akkadian tablets containing what are, in effect, recipes, the Yale Culinary Tablets, were examined by Bottéro, and he observes that

The placement of this prohibition here among various statutes about sacred times and offerings might imply that this, too, is related to some kind of Israelite offering. We note, for example, that meat from sacrifices was given to the priests, and the rule was that this meat was to be boiled (1 Sam. 2:13). Thus, there may have been a temptation to boil such meat in its mother's milk after a sacrifice. Even so, this does not mean that the practice occurred only at sacrifices. Furthermore, not every ordinance in this section is strictly cultic; the practice of letting the land lie uncultivated is done out of respect for God and as an act of faith, but it does not involve ritual life at the sanctuary. The same is probably true of the rule about boiling a kid. It is a simple dietary prohibition and was meant to instill in the people a basic humanity and decency in showing a kind of respect for the animals that they consumed.

Theological Summary of Key Points

Human beings, as philosophers are fond of saying, are contingent beings. Nothing brings out our basic dependency so much as our daily need for food. Like all ancient peoples, the Israelites closely related food and agriculture to religion. They did so in a manner that was quite distinct from the approach of the pagan world, however, and their laws are instructive for us.

1. We should not be so driven by desire for food or other material security that we seize every opportunity for gain. The Sabbath principle is first of all a lesson in trusting God, confident that he will provide for us even when we do not work every minute of the day or plow and sow every inch of ground.

2. Trust in God for success is joined to humane and compassionate treatment of subordinates. Because we trust God, we should not work subordinates as severely as possible or pay them as little as possible.

3. Trust in God for success also involves not turning to false gods. Many in the modern west may not be tempted to outright paganism, but many may look to various superstitions, such as horoscopes, for guidance in economic decisions. Farmers, investors, and other modern professionals can make decisions based on irrational superstitions.

---

the use of blood in food preparation is not unusual in these texts. The tablets are from the Old Babylonian period.

4. Christians do not have agricultural festivals of the sort the Israelites had. Even the traditional Christian calendar, with Advent, Lent, Easter, Pentecost, and so forth, is not agricultural in focus in the way that the Israelite festivals were. Our one analogous holiday, Thanksgiving, is not universal. The American and Canadian Thanksgiving holidays, for example, are celebrated at different times, and other cultures have similar but distinct holidays (Korea, for example, has an autumn harvest festival called Chuseok). But a day of thanksgiving for harvest and food is surely a valid thing for Christian churches, whether these celebrations are rooted in their home cultures or not. Such events build up community, in that they are times of joy and feasting, and remind us that the bounty of earth comes from God.

5. Food is necessary for life, but it can be improperly used or used in a manner that is not edifying. "All things are allowed to me, but not all things are beneficial. All things are allowed to me, but I will not be dominated by anything" (1 Cor. 6:12). Although we do not engage in animal sacrifice, we can dishonor God through food. We know that the body is God's temple, and we rightly apply that to sexual sin (1 Cor. 6:15–20), but it also applies to gluttony. Also, the fact that a specific food can be eaten (we are not under kosher laws) does not mean that it should be eaten. For example, one should refrain from eating food that gives offense to local believers (1 Cor. 8:13). Although cultures legitimately (and wonderfully) have different cuisines, it is legitimate to ask whether the eating of some kinds of food is simply bizarre or degrading. To boil a kid in its mother's milk is a perversion of nature.

THE BLESSINGS OF OBEDIENCE (23:20–33)

As the stipulations of the Book of the Covenant come to a close, YHWH declares what blessings will come to Israel through obedience. In contrast to Deut. 28, there is no list of curses for disobedience. The overall tone, despite the warnings in this text, is therefore optimistic.

Translation

23:20 "Be aware that[104] I am sending an angel before you to protect you along the way and to bring you into the place that I have prepared.
23:21a Be careful in his presence
23:21b and obey his voice.

104. The primary function of הִנֵּה here is that the audience should be aware of a fact. The fact that an angel is going before them is not necessarily something they would perceive.

23:21c Do not irritate[105] him,
23:21d for he will not forgive your transgression,
23:21e although[106] my name is with him.
23:22a But if you actually do obey his voice
23:22b and you do everything that I say,
23:22c then I will be an enemy to your enemies and an adversary to your adversaries.
23:23a For my angel will go before you
23:23b and he will bring you in to [the land of] the Amorites, the Hittites, the Perizzites, the Canaanites, the Hivites and the Jebusites,
23:23c and I will eliminate them.
23:24a You must not worship their gods,
23:24b and you must not give service to them,
23:24c and you must not follow their behavior.
23:24d Rather, you must utterly overthrow them
23:24e and smash to pieces their monumental sacred stones,
23:25a and you must give service to YHWH your God.
23:25b And [then] he will bless your bread and your water.
23:25c And I will remove sickness from among you.
23:26a There will not be a miscarrying or barren woman in your land;
23:26b I will make the number of your days attain their full allotment.[107]
23:27a I will send the terror of me before you,

105. This is usually emended to אַל־תַּמֵּר and translated "rebel," from מרה, but the MT has the Hiphil of מרר, to "embitter" or perhaps "irritate." Although the emendation is perhaps supported in the LXX (μη ἀπείθει), the MT is supported in the Vulg. (*nec contemnendum putes*). There being no compelling reason to emend, the MT is to be retained. As indicated in the Vulg. rendition, the verb may actually mean to "despise." But here it implies failure to show respect to a delegated authority and therefore irritating or angering that person.

106. It is often difficult to know how to translate כִּי, but in this case the concessive "although" seems better. There is no reason that the presence of the name should cause it to be impossible for the angel to forgive sin, since YHWH himself is forgiving and full of mercy (Exod. 34:6). Also, an angel by definition cannot forgive sin, as that is a divine prerogative. Thus, an explanatory translation ("because") is inappropriate. It is concessive, meaning that even though the name is present in the angel, he still does not forgive. That is, although the angel has some measure of divine authority—the name—he still does not have the authority to forgive.

107. "Attain their full allotment" is literally, "fulfill" (מלא, Piel stem). It here means to bring to fullness the number of days a mortal can be expected to live if not cut short by disease, violence, or some other calamity.

23:27b and throw all the people that come against you into disarray,
23:27c and I will make all your enemies turn [their] backs to you.[108]
23:28a I will send hornets before you
23:28b so that they will drive out the Hivites, the Canaanites, and the Hittites ahead of you.
23:29a I will not drive them out before you in a single year,
23:29b or the land will be desolate and the wild animals will be too many for you.
23:30a Little by little I will drive them out ahead of you,
23:30b until you become fruitful
23:30c and take possession of the land.
23:31a I will set your boundary from the *Yam Suph* to the Sea of the Philistines, and from the wilderness to the River [Euphrates];
23:31b for I will place the inhabitants of the land in your hands,
23:31c and you will drive them out ahead of you.
23:32 Do not make a covenant with them or with their gods.
23:33a They must not stay in your land,
23:33b or they would make you sin against me.
23:33c For you will perform service to their gods;
23:33d for it will be a snare to you."

Structure

The passage has a pattern of alternating topics, with two texts detailing promises of blessing sandwiched between three warnings. Since warnings come at the beginning, middle and ending of the full passage, the warnings are prominent. However, more text is devoted to the blessings, giving the overall passage an optimistic tone. As noted above, this text has only blessings and no curses (contrast Deut. 28).

I. Warnings to Listen to YHWH's Angel (23:20–21)
II. Blessings for Obedience to YHWH's Angel (23:22–23)
III. Warnings Against Worshiping the Gods of the Pagans (23:24–25a)
IV. Blessings for Obedience (23:25bc–31)
V. Warnings Against Worshiping the Gods of the Pagans (23:32–33)

Commentary

23:20–21. The identity of this angel is somewhat enigmatic. Sarna notes that traditional Jewish expositors are divided as to whether the

108. For the idiom נתן עֹרֶף, "to turn one's back," see 2 Chron. 29:6.

angel (or messenger) is heavenly or human,[109] but from the description, it appears that the angel must be a heavenly being. Many interpreters take this angel to be the "angel of YHWH" (that is, to be YHWH himself).[110] Against this, the angel here is introduced simply "an angel" (מַלְאָךְ) and is nowhere in this text called the angel of YHWH. The angel does have the "name" of YHWH with him. Analogous usage of the word for "with" (קֶרֶב), however, does not support the idea that this requires that the angel be identified as YHWH himself (see especially Jer. 14:9, where similar language is used of Israel).[111] Furthermore, judging from 23:21, this angel seems to lack either the authority or the disposition to forgive sin (he may lack both). This does not seem appropriate as a description of YHWH, who is abundantly forgiving (Exod. 34:6). This is consistent with what we see elsewhere in the Pentateuch, where angels are agents of wrath (most notably in the Sodom and Gomorrah episode; Gen. 19:1) or of protection (Exod. 33:2), but not of forgiveness. Furthermore, the people are told not to "irritate" or perhaps "despise" this angel (see translation note). This suggests that the Israelites might recognize that they are dealing with a subordinate being, and not YHWH himself, and conclude that they do not need to show the angel the same respect (compare the enigmatic Jude 8, which seems to describe speaking disrespectfully of angels). Finally, YHWH's threat in 33:2–3 to send only his angel with Israel and not to go himself makes no sense if this angel is in fact YHWH. Thus, it seems that this being is indeed an angel and not YHWH. It may be that we are uncomfortable with the idea that God would work through an angel and not always be directing things, as it were, in person. But we should not ignore the fairly straightforward implication of the text.

23:22–23. As the agent of YHWH, the directives of the angel are ultimately from YHWH himself, much as the words of a prophet are ultimately YHWH's words. It is probably in this sense that the "name" of YHWH is with the angel. As such, obedience to the angel is no different from obedience to YHWH, and both the angel and YHWH will protect Israel in this case. The benefit promised here is that Israel will be assisted by YHWH and his angel when the people invade Canaan. The process of conquering the land and eliminating the Canaanites

---

109. Sarna, *Exodus*, 147.
110. E.g., Stuart, *Exodus*, 542; Durham, *Exodus*, 335.
111. Jeremiah 14:9 has וְאַתָּה בְקִרְבֵּנוּ יְהוָה וְשִׁמְךָ עָלֵינוּ, "and you are among us, YHWH, and your name is upon us." Israel is plainly not the same as YHWH himself. See also Exod. 17:7.

would be, under the best of circumstances, a lengthy one (see vv. 29–30). As such, Israel's obedience would need to be equally consistent and persevering.

23:24–25a. Occupying the center position in this text, the injunction to shun entirely the paganism of the Canaanites and indeed to eliminate the Canaanites themselves is the primary means by which obedience to YHWH and his angel will be shown. Pagan idolatry is the primary, besetting sin of Israel, and it is in this context that Israel shows itself to be either faithful or apostate. The Israelites must not even preserve the "monumental sacred stones" of the Canaanites. Although there may have been a temptation to keep these objects as trophies of victory, they nevertheless would retain their power to remind and tempt Israel into the veneration of sacred objects.

23:25bc–31. The blessings promised to Israel include the following: essential material prosperity (that is, freedom from famine and drought; 25b), a general state of good health in the community (freedom from plague, 25c), fertility and good pregnancies, insuring healthy demographics (26a), good public health manifested in longevity (26b), and victory over enemies (27–28). In short, Israel will be healthy and vigorous internally and victorious externally. The promise that God will terrify Israel's enemies is not only a reward for faithfulness but an encouragement to be resolute in their refusal to compromise with local pagans. If they steadfastly fight pagans, God will assist them. The comment that the Canaanites would not be expelled all at once adds a note of realism; Israel must be ready for a long struggle and not suppose that eliminating an entire civilization would be quick and easy. The full extent of greater Israel would be from the *Yam Suph* (the Gulf of Aqaba), to the Sea of the Philistines (the southwestern corner of the Mediterranean Sea), to the Euphrates River in Syria. A domain of this size was not realized until the reign of David, and that for only a short time.

23:32–33. Israel was to have no relationship with the Canaanites, but instead was to drive them out. It is important to understand two aspects of this command. First, racism was not the issue. A covenant with the Canaanites is forbidden not out of anti-Canaanite bigotry but because of the moral and spiritual danger that the Canaanites carried with them. Idolatry, we must never forget, was Israel's primary area of failure. It was precisely to this that Canaanite culture, with its impressive temples and images, its store of myths and legends, its sacred groves and shrines with holy prostitutes, and its promise of prosperity, tempted the Israelites. It is not even correct to say that Israel was to drive out or destroy the Canaanites because they were pagans; Israel had no mandate to destroy pagans anywhere and everywhere. It is rather that Israel was to keep its homeland free of paganism. Canaanites who left the land would not be pursued.

Second, this is not a holy war analogous to the Islamic jihad. Unlike the Muslim warriors, Israel was not aiming to create a religious empire. There was no mandate to conquer lands so that the natives, under pressure and persecution, would eventually convert. There was no promulgation of Israelite religion by the sword. Furthermore, Israel had no authorization to conquer lands beyond the territory promised to the patriarchs, and thus it had no right to wage imperialistic wars of religion.

Theological Summary of Key Points

1. The reality, power, and presence of angels should not be despised or treated as pre-modern superstition. Angels are real, and it is valid to ask God, for example, to send his angels to watch over us, our loved ones, and others who are in danger. On the other hand, we should beware of the veneration of angels. We should not seek to communicate with them directly or make them into objects of contemplation. We should also remember that angels do not dispense grace. Angels cannot forgive sin.

2. The Sinai covenant strictly relates to Old Testament Israel alone, but it remains a fact that righteousness exalts any people. Severe punishment awaits the people who turn toward gross immorality or toward a false religion. By contrast, God shows patience and favor to a nation where, in some significant numbers, the people fear him and seek to live rightly.

3. Obedience to God needs to be sustained for a long period of time. Israel maintained a short burst of faithfulness to God, during the time of Joshua, but then it settled into the long disobedience of the Judges period. The results were terrible indeed.

4. Toleration of serious immorality and apostasy has very bad consequences. Israel was to avoid this by eliminating Canaanite culture entirely. We are not expected to do the same in our society, but this does not mean that we can be indifferent to the moral and spiritual danger posed by the influence others have over us (1 Cor. 15:33; Rev. 2:20).

PART V

THE COVENANT CEREMONY CONCLUDED (24:1–11)

At the close of the Book of the Covenant comes a description of the ceremony of its ratification. This indicates that the terms are now fixed and that obedience to its terms is now obligatory.

Translation

24:1a But to Moses he said,
24:1b "Come up toward YHWH, you and Aaron, Nadab and Abihu and seventy of the elders of Israel,
24:1c and worship from a distance.
24:2a And Moses alone shall approach toward YHWH,
24:2b but the others[112] must not approach,
24:2c and the people must not ascend with him [at all]."
24:3a And Moses came back
24:3b and he recounted to the people all the words of YHWH and all the ordinances;
24:3c and all the people answered with one voice
24:3d and they said,
24:3e "All the words which YHWH has spoken we will do!"
24:4a And Moses wrote out all the words of YHWH.
24:4b And he arose in the morning,
24:4c and he set up[113] at the bottom of the mountain[114] an altar and twelve monumental sacred stones for the twelve tribes of Israel.
24:5a And he commissioned [some of] the young men of the Israelites,
24:5b and they offered whole offerings
24:5c and they made peace offering sacrifices of bulls to YHWH.
24:6a And Moses took half of the blood
24:6b and he put [it] in bowls,
24:6c and the [other] half of the blood he sprinkled on the altar.
24:7a And he took the Book of the Covenant

---

112. Lit. "they."

113. The verb בנה is generally translated as "build," but that is misleading here, as it would seem to indicate precision building with the use of a chisel and hammer, and this is explicitly forbidden. The twelve monumental stones (מַצֵּבָה), traditionally translated as "pillars," would have been no more than large, oblong stones stood up on end. Thus, "set up" is more appropriate for בנה here.

114. The phrase "beneath the mountain" (תַּחַת הָהָר) obviously does not mean that the altar was in a subterranean chamber under the mountain, and a translation such as, "at the foot of the mountain," is legitimate. However, in using תַּחַת ("under"), instead of something like, "before the mountain," the text conveys the image of the mountain of God looming over Israel.

24:7b and he read [it] in the hearing of the people.
24:7c And they said,
24:7d "All that YHWH has spoken we will do,
24:7e and we will pay attention!"
24:8a And Moses took the blood
24:8b and he sprinkled [it] on the people,
24:8c and he said,
24:8d "Look[115]: the blood of the covenant that YHWH has made with you, [which is] in addition to[116] all these words."
24:9 And Moses and Aaron, Nadab and Abihu, and seventy of the elders of Israel moved up.
24:10a And they saw the God of Israel.
24:10b And under his feet there was something like a brickwork of lapis lazuli;[117]
24:10c [it was] like heaven itself for purity.
24:11a And he did not stretch out his hand against the leaders of the Israelites;
24:11b and they saw God,
24:11c and they ate
24:11d and they drank.

Structure

The Book of the Covenant concludes with a statement of the ceremonial ratification of the covenant. It neatly divides into two larger and two smaller segments. First, the narrative describes the people's formal acceptance of the covenant, followed by a short statement to the effect that Moses set the terms in a written text. This fixes the terms of the covenant; in modern terms, it "puts it in writing." Second,

115. The word הִנֵּה is used here to draw the people's attention to an important fact: it is blood, and not just words, that binds Israel to YHWH.

116. This preposition (עַל) is often translated as "according to all these words," but that is a peculiar preposition to use for such a meaning. The normal way to express this would be with כְּ, as in Exod. 8:9(13) וַיַּעַשׂ יְהוָה כִּדְבַר מֹשֶׁה, "and YHWH did according to the word of Moses." This usage of כְּ + דָּבָר is very common. It is best to give עַל in this context its much more common translation, "in addition to." The point is that YHWH has made his covenant with Israel both by means of the words of the covenant and by means of a covenant ritual of blood.

117. The identification of stones and minerals in the Bible is always difficult, but this is plainly a blue stone of some kind. It is either sapphire, a semi-precious gem, or lapis lazuli, a beautiful blue rock. See סַפִּיר, *HALOT*, 2.764.

the ceremony of covenant ratification is described, followed by Moses's brief assertion that the blood of the covenant has sealed the agreement and made it binding. After this, a covenant meal concludes the ceremony, and references to the activity of Moses and Aaron, Nadab and Abihu, and seventy of the elders of Israel at 24:1, 9 make something of an inclusio, delimiting the text.

I. The People's Agreement to the Covenant Terms Reconfirmed (24:1–3)
II. The Text of the Covenant (24:4a)
III. The Ceremony of Covenant-Making (24:4b-8b)
IV. The Blood of the Covenant (24:8cd)
V. The Covenant Meal (24:9–11)

Commentary

24:1–3. The formal procedure of ratifying the covenant begins. First, as in any ceremony, the positions for various participants are set. The mass of Israelites stands furthest back from YHWH, while Moses Aaron, Nadab, Abihu and seventy elders of Israel come forward to form a representative delegation before YHWH. Aaron, Nadab and Abihu are priestly representatives of Israel, while the seventy elders are there as lay representatives of all the tribes. But only Moses is allowed to come directly before YHWH and speak with him. Moses recounts the words of the covenant so that the people fully understand what they are agreeing to, and as before (19:8), they solemnly affirm their allegiance to the covenant and its obligations. Earlier, they had agreed to the covenant in principle, and now they agree to its actual stipulations. As before, their statement that they would do all that God commands is not to be understood as a legalistic or self-righteous boast; it is simply acceptance of the covenant terms. Had they not accepted, they could not have been God's people at all.

24:4a. Moses wrote out the words of the covenant, the terms that the people had just accepted, so that its stipulations would be fixed in writing. This is analogous to a modern, written contract.

24:4b-8b. The covenant ceremony evidently took place over two days. On the second day, twelve stones were set up as memorial stones to the agreement between YHWH and the twelve tribes. Probably they were positioned around the altar Moses had made. Then, as was common in the ancient world, a sacrifice was made in order to ritually confirm the covenant. Young men from Israel were specially commissioned to assist in this sacrifice. They were not chosen because there were as yet no priests in Israel; Aaron, Nadab and Abihu already had that role even though they, as yet, did not have their priestly vestments and formal investiture under the terms of the covenant (see Exod. 28). Rather, the young men were probably representatives of all the tribes.[118] They symbolically placed all the tribes under the covenant obligation, because all the tribes participated in the covenant sacrifice. The chosen representatives were said to be "young." This may have been partly for practical reasons; they would have the physical strength to handle the animals and carry out the sacrifices. But it may also have been symbolic; they represented the future of Israel. In the ceremony, Moses used part of the blood of the sacrifice to sprinkle over the altar, symbolizing YHWH's obligations under the covenant, and he used part of the blood to sprinkle the people, symbolizing Israel's obligations under the covenant. The covenant was thus fully bilateral, with both YHWH and Israel assuming toward one another a covenant commitment with specific duties. This contrasts with the Abrahamic covenant, where only YHWH, in the form of smoke and fire, passed between the pieces of the sacrificed animals (Gen. 15:17). In other words, the Abrahamic covenant is a unilateral commitment by God, but the Sinai covenant places Israel under covenant obligations—with dire consequences should they fail to keep them.

24:8cd. As the counterpart to the written text of 24:4a, Moses here reminds Israel that the sacrificial blood has solemnized the ratification of the covenant, and thus they are now fully obligated to keep it.

24:9–11. Two elements mark the closing of the covenant ceremony. First, there is a vision of YHWH's glory. It is a beautiful and peaceful apparition, appearing to be finely-crafted ashlars made of sapphire. It is explicitly declared to be heavenly. It is emblematic of the divine presence but it is not threatening, in contrast to the smoke, earthquakes, fire and thunder that had earlier enshrouded Sinai. Although the Sinai covenant includes a threat of judgment, it is not God's desire that his relationship to his people be characterized by threats and terror. The

118. Ernest W. Nicholson, "The Covenant Ritual in Exodus XXIV 3–8," *VT* 32, no. 1 (1982): 81, argues that נְעָרִים is a technical term here and that the "young men" are subordinate cultic personnel. However, the full phrase אֶת־נַעֲרֵי בְּנֵי יִשְׂרָאֵל suggests that these are men drawn from all of the tribes of Israel for this special ceremony rather than their being subordinate members of a body of priests.

peaceful nature of the scene made explicit in the comment that even though the seventy elders were closer to YHWH than would otherwise be allowed (they had evidently crossed the boundaries around the mountain), they were not struck dead (24:11a). Second, there is a communal meal. Just as the ideal is for Israel to be at peace with God, so also peace with God is ideally to lead to celebration, abundance, and unity for Israel.[119]

Theological Summary of Key Points

1. In salvation history, this text represents a solemn and critical moment. Israel has formally entered into a covenant with God. He is their God and they are his people, and as such they are a favored people and special possession of God. But their status depends upon their upholding of their duties under the covenant. Should they break the covenant, special punishment rather than special protection is all that they can expect. The subsequent history of Israel, starting with the golden calf episode and going through all of the episodes of apostasy in subsequent generations (as described and condemned by the prophets), tells how they finally came under the full condemnation of God and received all the punishments stipulated in the covenant.

2. The distinction between the bilateral Sinai covenant and the unilateral Abrahamic covenant is critically important. The Abrahamic covenant is God's commitment to create a nation for himself and ultimately to bring blessing to the world through that nation (Gen. 12:1–3). The Sinai covenant is, in effect, a pedagogue (Gal. 3:23–24), meant to guide and preserve Israel the nation as they await the fulfillment of all the promises. God would fulfill the commitments made under the Abrahamic covenant regardless of Israel's apostasy, but under the terms of the Sinai covenant, that apostasy would cost Israel dearly. Thus, although obviously historically related, the two covenants are radically different.

3. Elements of this text are taken up elsewhere in the Bible. The vision of the glory of God at Exod. 24:10 is taken up in Ezekiel's vision of the divine presence (Ezek. 1:26) and in John's vision of the heavenly

119. Ernest W. Nicholson, "The Interpretation of Exodus XXIV 9–11," *VT* 24, no. 1 (1974): 77–97, needlessly wrenches vv. 9–11 from their context and asserts that this text has no connection to the covenant ratification ceremony. Also, he roots this text in pilgrimages to Sinai (Ernest W. Nicholson, "Origin of the Tradition in Exodus XXIV 9–11," *VT* 26, no. 2 [1976]: 148–60).

Jerusalem (Rev. 21:19). The seventy elders of the Sinai covenant have a counterpart in the seventy men whom God sent to assist Moses, and who prophesied, according to Num. 11:14–17, 25). The beneficent quality of the presence of God here, in contrast to the terrors of fire and thunder earlier at Sinai, has an echo in the experience of Elijah, who came to Mt. Sinai and found that God was present not in fire and earthquake but in a quiet voice (1 Kgs. 19:11–12).

4. Christians naturally want to see a connection between the blood of Christ and the blood of Old Testament covenant sacrifices. But one must be careful here. The blood of Christ is redemptive (analogous to the Passover lamb) and expiatory (analogous to the sacrifices of the Day of Atonement). The sacrifice enacted here is neither; it is a sacrifice solemnizing a suzerain-vassal relationship and fixing the duties of each party. More specifically, it is a warning of death. Blood was sprinkled on the Israelites as a symbolic forewarning that, should they break the covenant, they would be put to death, just as the sacrificial animals had been put to death, and that their blood would flow, just as there was now blood sprinkled on their bodies. A more appropriate analogy is in the fact that a Christian, in conversion, profession and baptism, is committing himself or herself to a life of discipleship to Christ. When Christians memorialize Jesus's blood of the new covenant in the Eucharist, they remind themselves that under this covenant they also are to take up the cross.

PART VI

The Worship of God (24:12–31:18)

This section of Exodus, after introductory material in 24:12–18, describes the Tent of Meeting, the shrine that is at the center of Israel's worship of YHWH. As such, this division of the book has the concept of worship as its central focus. It is important to understand that the point of these texts is not to give a full blueprint of the tent and its furnishings. The main point is that YHWH spoke to Moses and told him what he wanted.[1] Certain details are emphasized not because they are architecturally critical for the structure but because they are theologically important. Many purely structural details are left out, and any reconstruction of the Tent of Meeting is hypothetical in nature.

BY REVELATION (24:12–18b)

The place of Moses as the lawgiver and intercessor between YHWH is at the center of this passage. But as the introduction to the Tent of Meeting legislation, it also makes the point that worship is to be carried out in a manner that is in accord with divine revelation.

Translation

24:12a And YHWH said to Moses,

1. See Rolf P. Knierim, "Conceptual Aspects in Exodus 25:1–9," in *Pomegranates and Golden Bells: Studies in Biblical, Jewish, and Near Eastern Ritual, Law and Literature in Honor of Jacob Milgrom*, ed. David P. Wright, David N. Freedman and Avi Hurvitz (Winona Lake: Eisenbrauns, 1995) 113–124.

24:12b "Come up into the heights of the mountain[2] to me,
24:12c so that you can be present[3]
24:12d while I give[4] you the stone tablets with the law and the commandment that I have written for their instruction."
24:13a And Moses and Joshua his assistant got up,
24:13b and Moses ascended into the mountain of God.
24:14a But to the elders he had said,[5]
24:14b "Wait here for us
24:14c until we return to you.
24:14d And of course, Aaron and Hur are with you;
24:14e Anybody who has an issue to raise[6] can approach them."

Sixth Poem: Glory on Sinai

Stanza 1

24:15a And Moses ascended into the mountain,
וַיַּ֥עַל מֹשֶׁ֖ה אֶל־הָהָ֑ר 1-3-3

24:15b And cloud covered the mountain.
וַיְכַ֥ס הֶעָנָ֖ן אֶת־הָהָֽר׃ 1-3-3

24:16a And the glory of YHWH dwelt on Mount Sinai,
וַיִּשְׁכֹּ֤ן כְּבוֹד־יְהוָה֙ עַל־הַ֣ר סִינַ֔י 1-3-5

24:16b And the cloud covered it for six days;
וַיְכַסֵּ֥הוּ הֶעָנָ֖ן שֵׁ֣שֶׁת יָמִ֑ים 1-3-4

24:16c And he called to Moses
וַיִּקְרָ֧א אֶל־מֹשֶׁ֛ה 1-2-2

24:16d On the seventh day from within the cloud.
בַּיּ֥וֹם הַשְּׁבִיעִ֖י מִתּ֥וֹךְ הֶעָנָֽן׃ 0-2-4

2. "Into the heights of the mountain" translates הָהָ֫רָה, (lit. "toward the mountain" or "mountain-ward"). Since they were already on some part of the mountain, this can only refer to the high interior of the mountain.
3. Lit. "there."
4. The imperative with conjunction in 24:12c (וֶהְיֵה) and the *weyiqtol* in 24:12d (וְאֶתְּנָה) each represent purpose. They are to be understood as coordinated purposes rather than sequential actions, and thus the translation "while."
5. This line is offline and contrastive, giving background information. From context the Qatal verb אמר has to be understood as pluperfect.
6. Lit. "whoever is a lord of words."

Stanza 2

24:17a And the appearance of the glory of YHWH:
וּמַרְאֵה֙ כְּב֣וֹד יְהוָ֔ה 0-2-3

24:17b Like a consuming fire on the mountain top
כְּאֵ֥שׁ אֹכֶ֖לֶת בְּרֹ֣אשׁ הָהָ֑ר 0-2-4

24:17c Before the eyes of the Israelites!
לְעֵינֵ֖י בְּנֵ֥י יִשְׂרָאֵֽל׃ 0-1-3

Stanza 3

24:18a And Moses came within the cloud;
וַיָּבֹ֥א מֹשֶׁ֛ה בְּת֥וֹךְ הֶעָנָ֖ן 1-3-4

24:18b And he ascended into the mountain.
וַיַּ֣עַל אֶל־הָהָ֑ר 1-2-2

Structure

As indicated above, this text is probably best analyzed as in two parts, a prose account of Moses's calling to go up to YHWH followed by a poetic account of his ascent. Obviously enough, the entire text could be treated as prose, as it generally is. There are, however, a number of reasons for treating 24:15–18ab as poetry.

1. The six lines of stanza 1 parallel each other in that each one begins with a *wayyiqtol* verb, except the last (24:16d), which closes the stanza.

2. The six lines of stanza 1 are arranged in a parallel A–B– A'–B'–A''–B'' pattern, as demonstrated below. While it is true that parallelism can occur in prose, this is a much more elaborate pattern than one would normally see in prose.

A: Moses goes up mountain (24:15a)
  B: Cloud covers mountain (24:15b)
A': YHWH on mountain (24:16a)
  B': Cloud covers mountain six days (24:16b)
A'': YHWH calls Moses (24:16c)
  B'': On seventh day from the cloud (24:16d)

3. While the three lines of stanza 2 (24:17abc) are a single nominal clause, they could also certainly be prose. In this context, however, these lines furnish a strong contrast to the activity of the *wayyiqtol* verbs that make up the rest of the poem, and give a dramatic portrayal

of how frightening the mountain looked to the Israelites. This contrast highlights the courage and special position of Moses, just as the verbless nature of these lines subtly suggests Israel's passivity in contrast to his labors. But such vivid language and arrangement of clause types is more in keeping with poetry than with prose.

4. The two lines of stanza 3 (24:18ab) are a classic bicolon with both syntactic and semantic parallelism.

5. The poem has an inclusio structure, with 24:18b echoing 24:15a.

6. The poem meets all the poetic constraints. Following the cantillation, at only one point is there a break at a slightly unusual spot, 24:16c, which ends with a *tevir*.

As such, the structure of the text is as follows:

- I. Prose Account of Moses's Ascent (24:12–14)
  - A. YHWH's Instruction to Moses (24:12)
  - B. Moses's Ascent (24:13)
  - C. Moses's Instructions to Israelites (24:14)
- II. Poetic Portrayal of Moses's Ascent (24:15–18ab)

In an ancient text, it is not unusual to have a prose account and a poetic account of the same event. The two principal Egyptian sources for information on Ramesses II at the battle of Kadesh are the "Poem" and the prose "Bulletin."[7]

Commentary

24:12–14. Of itself, there is nothing in the opening clause of v. 12, "And YHWH said to Moses," that indicates that there is a major structural division here. However, the subsequent narrative—the extensive set of instructions regarding the construction of the shrine—sufficiently marks this as a new stage in the book. As described above (Excursus: The Sequence of Events in and after Exodus 19), there was probably a considerable gap of time between the ratification ceremony and the revelation described here.

The brief narrative gives us two pieces of background information that will be relevant later. First, Joshua accompanied Moses and apparently waited for him while he was with YHWH. We are therefore not surprised to learn that Moses encountered Joshua on his way back down from the mountain (Exod. 32:17). Second, Aaron and some others

7. See Richard D. Patterson, "Victory at Sea: Prose and Poetry in Exodus 14–15," *BSac* 161, no. 641 (2004): 42–54.

were left behind as recognized leaders. Thus, the people went to Aaron when they wanted to build the golden calf (Exod. 32:1). This text also makes the point that on the mountain Moses received specific laws from God. The content of those laws, the construction of the Tent of Meeting and priestly vestments, follow.

24:15–18ab. The poetic account of the ascent of Moses is not strictly necessary, as the fact that Moses went up to YHWH is already given in the prose version of events. As suggested above, however, the poem strongly accentuates the distinctive role of Moses as the intercessor between God and Israel. He alone is willing and able to brave the terrors of Sinai in order to meet with YHWH, and it is done for Israel's sake. Notice that Joshua is not mentioned in the poetic version; mention of other persons would distract from the focus on the role played by Moses. His unique position, as described here, prepares the reader for Moses's courageous and vital intercessory role at the golden calf incident (Exod. 32:9–14).

Theological Summary of Key Points

1. Moses the man of God, the lawgiver, and the intercessor for Israel is the key person in this narrative and a central figure for biblical theology. It may be that sometimes we Christians are so fixed on the subordination of Moses to Christ that we fail to see the significance and greatness of Moses himself. The whole of the Israelite faith, and their very survival as a nation, goes back to Moses. The account of Moses going up alone to Sinai, leaving a passive Israel behind, shows how exalted he had become before God and Israel. Perhaps if we better appreciate Moses, we will have all the greater appreciation for Christ.

2. We have already seen the significance of the 6 + 1 pattern in Exodus. The Song of the Sea is in seven stanzas, with six stanzas describing events at the sea and their consequences and the seventh being a longing for arrival at the sanctuary of God, the Holy Land. The journey to Sinai, similarly, has six ordeals followed by a seventh stage, the arrival at the mountain. Here, Moses has six days of being held back by thick cloud, but he is finally ushered into God's presence on the seventh. The pattern is used for the Sabbath principle and for divine revelation, and both are manifest here. It is no surprise that Gen. 1:1–2:3, essentially a revelation of God's work in creation prior to entering his rest, is also in the 6 + 1 pattern.

3. The worship of God is always to be in accord with revelation. This does not mean that there is no room for cultural distinctions or for varieties of worship style. However, worship must include all that biblical precedent and teaching demand (in the Christian context, this includes songs and words of praise, Scripture reading, prayer, proclamation, and the Eucharist), and it must exclude all that is forbidden (for example, the use of an image of God).

WITH REVERENCE (24:18c—25:40)

In the texts that follow we have the instructions for making the tent, its furnishings, and the vestments. Any Bible dictionary will give readers an artist's reconstruction of these objects. This can be helpful, but it can also be misleading. Many details about these items are left out of the biblical account, and every reconstruction of the Tabernacle involves trying to decipher the biblical instructions, working with analogies from the ancient Near East and from later Judaism, and some guesswork.

In order to understand the instructions, one needs a basic orientation to the layout of the sanctuary. The Tent of Meeting was nearly rectangular, with longer north and south sides. Its doorway faced toward the east. The interior had two chambers. The eastern part—the first chamber as one entered the tent—was the "holy place" containing the menorah, the incense altar, and a table for a daily bread offering. Going through the holy place, one came to the "holy of holies." It was the inner sanctum and occupied the western, back part of the tent, and it contained the Ark of the Covenant. A screen separated the holy place from the most holy place. Outside of the entrance, on the east side of the tent, were a wash basin and an altar. The whole area was fenced in by a screen, with the courtyard entrance on the east side.

The first objects described in the narrative are the Ark of the Covenant, The table of the bread of the Presence, and the menorah. These are to be in or near the inner sanctuary, the holy of holies, and as such they are the most sacred objects in the Tent of Meeting. They represent aspects of the character of God, and are meant to inspire reverence.

Translation

24:18c And Moses was on the mountain for forty days and forty nights,
25:1 and YHWH spoke to Moses, as follows:
25:2a "Tell the Israelites
25:2b that they should collect a contribution for me;

25:2c you must raise my contribution from every man whose heart moves him.

25:3-7 And this is the contribution that you are to collect from them: gold and silver and bronze and blue and purple and scarlet and linen and goat hair[8] and tanned ram's hide and *tahash* leather[9] and acacia wood and oil [suitable] for lighting[10] and spices [suitable] for the anointing oil and for the fragrant incense, and stones of carnelian[11] and [other] stones [suitable] for setting in the ephod and the breastpiece.

25:8a And they shall make a sanctuary for me,

25:8b and I will be present among them.

25:9 You must make [it] precisely in accord[12] with the pattern of the Tabernacle and the pattern of all its furnishings that I am showing you.

25:10 They are to construct a box [that is, an "ark"][13] of acacia wood two and a half cubits long, and one and a half cubits wide, and one and a half cubits high.

25:11a And you are to overlay it with pure gold—

25:11b you are to overlay both the interior and the exterior—

---

8. עִזִּים, the plural of עֵז, "goat," is used for goat hair as a material for fabric.
9. The meaning of תַּחַשׁ (תְּחָשִׁים) is uncertain; it is often translated as "porpoise skin" on the basis of an Arabic cognate. But this is unlikely; the porpoise (or "sea cow," or "manatee," as some have rendered it) is unclean and thus should not be used on the sanctuary. It is more likely that this is some variety of tanned leather. It could be cognate to Akkadian *dušû*, and refer to leather tanned like the *dušû* stone (N. Kiuchi, "תַּחַשׁ," *NIDOTTE*, 4.287). But the precise meaning is lost, and we can only transliterate the word, assuming it to be a kind of tanned leather.
10. This is oil of a quality that will produce minimal smoke when burnt, as is needed for lamps. The preposition לְ in this verse does not only describe the purpose for which the material is to be used, but implies that the material must be appropriate for its use.
11. The exact translation of שֹׁהַם has long been a matter of conjecture; according to *HALOT* (4.1424), most recent research indicates that carnelian is the most likely meaning.
12. The expression כְּכֹל אֲשֶׁר ("like all which") implies a precise following of the plans.
13. This is the Ark of the Covenant, but we should realize that the word אֲרוֹן simply means "box," and that in fact "ark" is an archaic English word for a box. Out of regard for the fact that "Ark of the Covenant" has come a fixed term in English, I hereafter translate it as "ark."

25:11c and you are to frame it with gold molding at the edges.[14]
25:12a And you are to cast four gold rings for it
25:12b and you are to set them at its four legs: two rings on one side of it and two rings on the other side of it.
25:13a And you are to make poles of acacia wood
25:13b and you are to overlay them with gold.
25:14 And you are to put the poles into the rings on the sides of the ark, to carry the ark with them.
25:15a The poles are to remain in the rings of the ark;
25:15b they are not to be removed from it.
25:16 And you are to place the testimony that I shall give you into the ark.
25:17 And you are to make a place of atonement[15] of pure gold, two and a half cubits long and one and a half cubits wide.
25:18a And you are to make two cherubim of gold—
25:18b make them of hammered work at the two extremities of the place of atonement.
25:19a And make one cherub at one extremity and one cherub at the other extremity;
25:19b you shall make the cherubim as an affixture to the place of atonement[16] at its two extremities.
25:20a And the cherubim are to be spreading [their] wings upward, covering the place of atonement with their wings,
25:20b and their faces are to be toward one another
25:20c while [at the same time][17] the faces of the cherubim are to be [bent down] toward the place of atonement.

---

14. Lit. "and you shall make on it a gold molding around." The expression סָבִיב with עשׂה throughout the Tabernacle construction narrative means to put something at the edges of an object.
15. The word כַּפֹּרֶת is lit. "atonement," and it here is a technical term for the place where blood was sprinkled to make atonement. The traditional translation is "mercy seat."
16. The translation "as an affixture to the place of atonement" is lit. "from the place of atonement" (מִן־הַכַּפֹּרֶת). It means that the cherubim were to be permanently attached to the place of atonement. Throughout the description of the Tabernacle furnishings, the preposition מִן is often used to describe how a decorative element is affixed to a larger piece. It does not imply that the decorative element and the larger piece were made at the same time from a single lump of gold.
17. The two clauses in 25:20bc have a chiastic structure (with the faces of the cherubim heading the first clause and at the end of the second clause). In this case, this pattern implies that the two situations are simultaneous:

25:21a And you are to set the place of atonement on top of the ark,
25:21b and you are to set the testimony which I will give to you in the ark.
25:22a I will meet with you there,
25:22b and from above the place of atonement, from between the two cherubim that are upon the Ark of the Testimony, I will tell you everything that I intend to command you with regard to the Israelites.
25:23 And you are to make a table of acacia wood, two cubits long and one cubit wide and one and a half cubits high,
25:24a and you are to overlay it with pure gold
25:24b and you are to frame it with gold molding at the edges.
25:25a And you are to frame it with a one handbreadth border at the edges,
25:25b and you shall frame it with gold at the edges of the border.
25:26a And you are to make four gold rings for it,
25:26b and you are to place the rings on the four corners that are at its four legs.
25:27 The rings shall be close to the border as housings for the poles to carry the table.
25:28a And you are to make the poles of acacia wood
25:28b and you are to overlay them with gold,
25:28c and the table is to be carried with them.
25:29a And you are to make its dishes and its bowls and its jars, as well as its libation vessels, with which to pour [libations];
25:29b you shall make them of pure gold.
25:30 And you are to set on the table the bread of the Presence before me perpetually.
25:31a And you are to make a menorah of pure gold.
25:31b And you are to make the menorah—its base and its shaft—of hammered work;

---

the cherubim face each other while also looking down at the place of atonement.

25:31c its blossoms—[18] its calyxes and its petals[19]—shall be affixed to it.

25:32 Six branches shall go out from its sides; three branches of the menorah from its one side and three branches of the menorah from its other side.

25:33a Three almond-shaped blossoms (with calyx and petals) are to be in the one branch,

25:33b and three almond-shaped blossoms (with calyx and petals) are to be in the opposite branch;

25:33c [make it] like that for the six branches going out from the menorah.

25:34 But in the menorah [stand itself you must set] four almond-shaped blossoms with calyx and petals.

25:35a For the six branches coming out of the menorah,[20] a bulb-like knob[21] shall be attached[22] under the [first] pair of branches,

25:35b and a bulb-like knob shall be attached under the [second] pair of branches,

25:35c and a bulb-like knob shall be attached under the [third] pair of branches.

25:36a Their bulb-like knobs and their branches are to be joined together;

25:36b all of it shall be a single hammered work of pure gold.[23]

---

18. This is usually translated "bowl" or "cup," which are indeed legitimate translations of גָּבִיעַ. In this case, however, the term is probably botanical and refers to a "blossom," since the word is described as something that has both calyx and petals. The common term for "flower" is צִיץ (which has the by-form צִיצָה). This appears to be a generic word for "flower," and it can refer to the whole plant or at least the stem and blossom. There is also the grape flower, the נִצָּה. But גָּבִיעַ, as used here, seems to refer strictly to a blossom, that is, to the calyx and petals. It is not a "cup" that is separate from the flower motif, and it is purely decorative. It is not a cup that holds a liquid.
19. This is usually translated as "buds (כַּפְתּוֹר) and flowers (פֶּרַח)." But it is clear that there was one כַּפְתּוֹר and one פֶּרַח at each location. It is more likely that this is one flower, with כַּפְתּוֹר being the calyx and פֶּרַח being the petals in bloom. So also NRSV.
20. For the sake of clarity and English style this prepositional phrase has been moved from 25:35c to 25:35a.
21. This word, כַּפְתּוֹר, is the same word translated as "calyx," the bulbous part of the blossom motif. Here, however, it appears to be a join between the main shaft and a branch, a place where the metal is thicker and bulbous in shape to make it stronger.
22. The word מִמֶּנָּה (lit. "from her") is another example of מִן describing how a decorative element is attached to a larger piece.
23. This describes the finished product and not necessarily the construction method. It does not require that the workman began with one lump of

25:37a	And you are to make its lamps—seven [of them].
25:37b	And [the menorah] shall lift up its lamps
25:37c	And it shall shed light on the space in front of it.
25:38	And its wick trimmers[24] and their fire pans[25] [are to be] of pure gold.
25:39	[The whole menorah,] with all these utensils, shall be made from a talent of pure gold.
25:40	See to it that you make [everything] after the pattern that was shown to you for them on the mountain."

Structure

The structure of the entire Tent of Meeting directive is quite straightforward, as it moves from one object to be constructed to the next. In this section, we see the following elements.

I. General Instructions (24:18c–25:9)
II. The Ark of the Covenant (25:10–22)
III. The Table of the Bread of the Presence (25:23–30)
IV. The Menorah (25:31–40)

Commentary

24:18c–25:9. The text opens with a general introduction to the topic of the Tent of Meeting and its furnishings. Moses stayed on the mountain for forty days receiving instruction from God. This may represent a prolonged period of communion with God; it does not necessarily indicate forty days of pure instruction. The text also stipulates that the people were to provide the necessary raw materials by contributions in kind (see also 35:23). Exodus tells us that the Israelites did not leave Egypt empty-handed (12:35); they obviously had a great deal of gold and silver. But one may wonder at the implication that they had at their disposal all of the fabric, hides, and bronze necessary for making the tent complex.

---

gold and hammered it until it was the finished menorah. It does, however, require that the finished product be a single work of hammered gold with no other material used for foundation or joins.

24. מֶלְקָחַיִם is lit. "tongs." It would not seem to be a snuffer, a cone-shaped instrument for putting out a candle, but a tool for trimming the wicks of the menorah lamps. So also TNIV.

25. On the basis of Lev 10:1, it appears that the מַחְתָּה is a small vessel capable of holding a small fire, either for burning incense (i.e., a censer) or for carrying fire to another place. Here it is the latter and is used for lighting the menorah lamps.

As people who had lived in settled villages in Egypt for generations, it is not likely that they had large quantities of tents or tent-making supplies on hand. But Exodus does not assert that the Israelites brought all these raw materials from Egypt. If they passed through Midian, as seems certain, they may have traded for material en route. Since they needed tents for themselves, they would have had a high incentive to acquire such tent-making materials. In addition, since they did come out of Egypt with great wealth, the expense would not have been a major issue. The battle with the Amalekites (17:8-16), moreover, suggests that they were not isolated from contact with other nations while en route. We may thus presume that they purchased the raw materials they needed for their own tents and that they had plenty to spare. The stated purpose for constructing the tent was so that God could dwell among them (v. 8). The tent had to made according to God's specifications (v. 9).

25:10–22. The Ark of the Covenant, the symbolic throne of God, has first place in the entire description of the tent and its furnishings. The word "ark" is an old English word that means "box" (Noah's "ark" was also essentially a great box). No one was allowed to touch the ark, and therefore its carrying poles were to remain in the rings of the ark (25:14–15; see 2 Sam. 6:3-8). The ark contained a copy of the Ten Commandments or perhaps of the entire Book of the Covenant. It is thus often called the "Ark of the Testimony." The covering for the ark, the place of atonement (or "mercy seat"), served as the symbolic place of God's presence (1 Sam. 4:4) and as the place where blood would be sprinkled on the Day of Atonement (Lev. 16:15). The description of the ark's construction is thorough and needs little explanation. We cannot be sure about the appearance of the cherubim, however, since no description is given beyond the fact that they had wings. Evidently the Israelites of this time had a common conception of how cherubim ought to be portrayed. For us, cherubim are, like all angels, winged anthropomorphic beings (a conception based in Greco-Roman art). But this may not be how cherubim were depicted on the ark (and it is surely not correct to think of these beings as winged, naked babies, creatures that some call "cherubs" but which are in fact "putti"). For the Israelites, cherubim may have been composite zoomorphic figures analogous to the huge Assyrian winged bulls from the palace of Khorsabad (now in the British Museum). Indeed, these hybrid creatures served as spiritual guardians and gatekeepers, much as the biblical cherubim do, and the Akkadian term for these beings is *kāribu*, a term probably cognate with כְּרוּב.[26] Descriptions of angelic beings that surround the throne of God in Ezek. 1:5-12 and Rev. 4:6-7 suggest that zoomorphic depictions are more in line with the ancient Israelite conception. But in fact, we do not know what the cherubim on the ark looked like.

25:23–30. The description of the table of acacia wood is for the most part readily comprehensible. The one difficulty is with the "border" that was one handbreadth wide (about 3 inches or 7.6 cm) and that went all around the table. One cannot tell if it extended horizontally outward on the sides or was set vertically around the legs as a reinforcement. Probably it was the latter, since setting this border out horizontally would seem to serve no purpose and would itself be quite fragile and liable to be broken off. One must recall that this was part of a portable structure that would be frequently moved from place to place, and thus durability was of prime importance. The table was set in the holy place and had fresh bread placed on it every day (25:30). This was not done in order to feed God (a pagan practice; see Ps. 50:12); it was a symbolic thanksgiving and prayer for divine provision. This was the bread David ate while fleeing Saul (1 Sam. 21:2-6; Mark 2:26). It is difficult to know what was the function of "dishes," "bowls," "jars," and "libation vessels" (25:29) beyond the obvious fact that the latter was used for libations. Even that, however, is somewhat mysterious since 30:9 forbids libations on the altar of incense. Apparently there were some licit libations in the Tent of Meeting, but they were not to be poured on the altar of incense.

25:31–40. Because we have some fairly ancient depictions of the temple menorah, and because it survives to this day as a symbol of Judaism, the menorah is for us the easiest of all the sanctuary objects to imagine. In Jerusalem today there is a reconstruction of the temple menorah; it is housed in glass and stands opposite the temple mount. Ancient pictures of the menorah are found in tile floors, coins, bas-relief synagogue carvings, and other artwork. When the Romans sacked the second temple in A.D. 70, they carried away the great menorah, and this is depicted on the Arch of Titus in Rome. On the other hand, the menorah depicted there differs in some respects from descriptions of the second temple menorah found in rabbinical sources and Josephus.[27] Furthermore, Moses's menorah was not necessarily the same as the second temple menorah, and the Exodus description leaves out many

26. See כְּרוּב, *HALOT*, 2.497.
27. Sarna, *Exodus*, 164.

details. For example, and in contrast to our standard image of the menorah, the text does not stipulate that the six side lamps should all be level with one another and at the same height. In fact, no dimensions are given for the menorah at all. We need to be careful, therefore, not to project later conceptions of the menorah into this description. A few facts should be remembered.

First, a menorah is a lampstand; it is not itself a lamp. The lamps (which held the oil, wicks, and fire) may have been detachable ceramic lamps. Second, although some believe that the "blossoms" held oil, the term גָּבִיעַ, although it literally means "bowl," is probably purely botanical here, describing the almond flower motif (see translation notes to 25:31c). These flowers themselves appear to me to be purely decorative. That is, they adorned the menorah for aesthetic and perhaps symbolic reasons; they did not serve as oil reservoirs (ancient lamps always had their own oil containers). There were three such motifs on each branch, except for the central shaft, which had four. Thus, the almond blossoms were possibly affixed at various points along the sides of the branches, like actual blossoms, and it is hard to see how they could have fed oil to the lamps, presuming that the lamps were at the end of each branch. On the other hand, the modern reconstruction in Jerusalem puts the almond motifs at the end of each branch, stacked inside of each other, but still apparently purely decorative. But even this strikes me as unlikely, since the result looks nothing like almond blossoms. At any rate, aspects of the appearance of the original menorah are lost to us. Practically, the lampstand provided light for the priests; we must never forget that this was its essential function even as we seek to interpret its symbolism.

Opinions differ concerning the meaning or theological significance of the menorah. It may have represented Israel as a tree standing before God (Jer. 11:16; Hos. 14:6; Ps. 52:8). On the other hand, the tree in these texts is usually an olive tree, while the blossoms on the menorah are those of the almond. Stuart speculates on how the menorah may simultaneously represent both an olive tree and an almond tree, suggesting both divine provision and divine deliverance for Israel,[28] but I do not think his construction works. Some interpreters see a tree of life motif in the menorah.[29] This is possible, but the text itself makes nothing of it, here or anywhere else. The idea of the menorah, a tree-like

28. Stuart, *Exodus*, 578-80.
29. E.g., Sarna, *Exodus*, 165.

stand for burning lamps, could be a reflection of Moses's experience of the burning bush.[30]

In terms of what the text itself emphasizes, two factors stand out. First, the menorah was a beautiful object, made of solid gold and decorated with images of almond blossoms. Second, it had six branches coming off of a single, central column, for a total of seven lamps. In this, it conforms to the pattern of 6 + 1 seen in the creation narrative and at several points in Exodus. The significance of these two features is explored below.

Theological Summary of Key Points

1. The instructions for the construction of the Tent of Meeting and its furnishings came out of a prolonged period—40 days—of Moses's communion with God. That is, they came out of a profound experience with, and reverence for, God. Reverence is above all else what the shrine is meant to communicate to the people. Israel is to be in awe of YHWH, the God who is among them. For us, the point is no different. We, too, need to first of all think of worship as a time for revering God, and do all that we can to promote that attitude in worship services.

2. The Ark of the Covenant, being the throne of God, being symbolically guarded by cherubim, and being isolated in the holy of holies, indicates that God is scarcely approachable by sinful mortals. But the ark has a place of atonement on its cover, indicating that God does allow humans to approach him if there is a true act of propitiation and expiation. Hebrews 9 takes up this symbolism and tells us that Jesus, our high priest, has once and for all made atonement for sin and has opened the way for mortals to approach God.

3. In contrast to every pagan temple, the inner sanctuary is marked by one glaring omission: there is no image of the god. Instead of an

30. The similarity between the burning bush and the menorah is noted by Nicolas Wyatt, "The Significance of the Burning Bush," *VT* 36, no. 3 (1986): 361–5, but he uses it as a basis for a rather far-fetched piece of source criticism, dating the hypothetical J after the even more elusive E. See also Bernard P. Robinson, "Moses at the Burning Bush," *JSOT* 75 (1997): 119-21. Robinson suggests that Num. 8:4, which states that Moses made the menorah in accordance with the "appearance" (מַרְאָה) that YHWH showed him, may actually indicate that the burning bush was the archetype for the menorah.

idol, there is the Ark of the Covenant—an empty throne. Paradoxically, however, the lack of an image throws more focus on God himself. That is, we are to worship God and not allow ourselves to be distracted by the props. Contemplating that there was no image of YHWH in the tent, Israelites were, in effect, reminded to focus on God himself. It goes without saying that we, too, should focus on God and not on the props of worship during church services.

4. The table of the bread of the Presence reminds us that all provision is from God and that we should constantly give thanks to God, just as bread was constantly set upon the table.

5. Apart from any symbolism that may be involved in the menorah, it is clearly intended to be a very beautiful lampstand. The arrangement of seven branched lamp-holders, the gold from which it is made, and the decorative almond blossoms all bespeak an object that adds beauty to its utilitarian function. The implication is that worship of YHWH is beautiful, since the beauty of the menorah reflects the glory of God. In short, the beauty itself, and not what the gold or almonds supposedly represented, is the point.

6. The 6 + 1 pattern for the stems and central trunk of the menorah reflects the Sabbath principle seen in the creation narrative. This is also found in the structure of the Song of the Sea and in the narrative of the journey to Sinai, as described above. Finally, Moses had six days of waiting in the mist before he was ushered into YHWH's presence on the seventh day (24:16). In all of these, the ideal is one of entering into God's presence and his rest. Thus, the menorah, standing before the holy of holies and casting its light, symbolizes access into the presence of God and his rest.[31]

WITH AWARENESS OF SIN AND OF HOLINESS (26:1—27:21)
The text next proceeds to the structures that enclose the Ark of the Covenant: the tent itself and the courtyard fence. In addition, it

---

31. It is possible that the seven lamps of the menorah also represent the seven planets (for the ancients, the seven planets were the seven visible heavenly bodies that moved in the sky: the moon, the sun, Mercury, Venus, Mars, Jupiter, and Saturn). If so, the menorah indicates that the holy place, the outer sanctum, is a microcosm of the lower heavens. But the Old Testament elsewhere never shows any interest in the planets, even in the creation narrative, and thus I hesitate about making this connection.

describes the altar of burnt offering, which, like the other elements, is symbolic of God's holiness and, conversely, of the sin that keeps God and humanity apart.

Translation

26:1a "And as for the tent-sanctuary, make [it] with ten sheets of linen of tightly spun thread[32] with blue and purple and scarlet;

26:1b you are to make them [in the pattern of] cherubim (a work requiring a craftsman[33]).

---

32. The word מָשְׁזָר is often translated as "twisted," but that makes it sound as though it were wrung like a mop or twisted like a sheet to be used as a rope. שֵׁשׁ מָשְׁזָר is obviously some kind of linen material, but the precise meaning is difficult to fathom. שׁזר is used in Middle Hebrew to refer to twisting many threads over one another (שׁזר, *HALOT*, 4.1496). Taking that as our clue, the word מָשְׁזָר must refer to the process of spinning the thread or yarn. Of course, all linen is made of thread that has been spun. We must look further to see what it means here. The word שֵׁשׁ is an Egyptian loanword for linen. It is often translated as "fine linen," but there is not, as far as I can tell, any justification for the notion that it is particularly fine. Egyptian iconography gives us many examples of clothing made with linen, and the aristocrats wore a fine linen indeed, but this does not mean that the word שֵׁשׁ itself connotes a weave from a light thread. In fact, the fine linen of aristocratic clothing was so light and sheer that it is difficult to see how it could have served as tent fabric, notwithstanding that the Tent of Meeting had other fabrics over it. More than that, the linen for the Tent of Meeting had to serve as a foundation for a great deal of needlework that was woven in, and this was not true of Egyptian clothing (which was typically all white and pleated, but not embroidered). In Ezek. 27:7, שֵׁשׁ describes the linen used for a sail with patterns woven into it; surely a sail would have to be made of a fabric strong enough to withstand the winds and would not be made of the sheer material that aristocratic ladies wore. To be sure, שֵׁשׁ can be used of a more luxuriant linen (Ezek. 16:13), but this only makes the case that, of itself, שֵׁשׁ can refer to many kinds of linen. In short, the word שֵׁשׁ simply means "linen" and does not imply anything about the thickness of the thread of the linen or about the type of weave it has. To return to שֵׁשׁ מָשְׁזָר: it seems that מָשְׁזָר implies that the spin of the thread was the distinctive thing about this linen. I suggest that it is linen made from thread that has been tightly spun, perhaps from more than the usual amount of flaxen fibers, to give it additional strength, and thus the translation above.
33. The tent-sanctuary description in Exodus frequently includes a construct chain composed of מַעֲשֵׂה and a noun or a substantive participle referring to an occupation. These include מַעֲשֵׂה רֹקֵם ("the work of an embroiderer"), מַעֲשֵׂה אֹרֵג ("the work of a weaver"), מַעֲשֵׂה חָרָשׁ ("the work of a gem cutter"),

26:2a The length of each sheet is to be twenty-eight cubits,
26:2b and the width of each sheet four cubits;
26:2c [this] one [set of] measurements applies to all the sheets.
26:3a Five sheets are to be joined to one another,
26:3b and [then the other] five sheets are to be joined to one another.
26:4a And you are to make loops of blue on the edge of the sheet at the far end of the [first] set,
26:4b and in the same way you are to make [loops] on the far edge of the sheet in the second set.
26:5a You are to make fifty loops in the one sheet,
26:5b and you are to make fifty loops at the end of the sheet that is in the second set;
26:5c the loops are to be [placed] opposite each other.
26:6a You are to make fifty clasps of gold,
26:6b and you are to join the sheets to one another with the clasps
26:6c so that the tent-sanctuary will be a single piece.
26:7a And you are to make sheets of goats' hair for a canopy over the tent-sanctuary;
26:7b you are to make eleven sheets of this kind.
26:8a The length of each sheet is to be thirty cubits,
26:8b and the width of each sheet four cubits;
26:8c [this] one [set of] measurements applies to the eleven sheets.
26:9a And you are to join the five sheets as a separate set and the six sheets as a separate set,
26:9b and you are to double over the sixth sheet towards the front end of the tent.[34]
26:10a And you are to make fifty loops on the edge of the sheet that is outermost in the [first] set,
26:10b and fifty loops on the edge of the [corresponding] sheet of the second set.
26:11a And you are to make fifty clasps of bronze,
26:11b and you are to put the clasps into the loops
26:11c and you are to join the tent together,

מַעֲשֵׂה חֹשֵׁב ("the work of a craftsman/designer"), and מַעֲשֵׂה רֹקֵחַ ("the work of a perfumer"). The most logical explanation for this little pattern is that it is describing a task that required a worker with highly specialized skills.

34. This is often translated as, "at the front of the tent" (ESV, TNIV, NASB, etc.). But this makes no sense, as it would place the fold in the sixth sheet at the tent's doorway, in the front. It is clearly at the back of the tent (Exod. 26:12). Thus, the sixth sheet is the last one of all, and it is folded back toward the front of the tent, rather than placed at the front.

26:11d so that it will be a single piece.

26:12 And as for the excess that is left over in the sheets of the tent: the half-sheet that is left over is to form an extra layer[35] at the back of the tent-sanctuary.

26:13 The cubit on one side and the cubit on the other, of what is left over in the length of the sheets of the tent, are to be excess at the sides of the tent-sanctuary on one side and on the other, to cover it [fully].

26:14 And you are to make for the tent a covering of tanned rams' hide and at the top a covering of *tahash* leather.

26:15 And you are to make the frames for the tent-sanctuary out of upright[36] acacia trees.

26:16a The length of each frame is to be ten cubits

26:16b and the width of a single frame[37] is to be one and a half cubits.

---

35. "Form an extra layer" translates תִּסְרַח, lit. "will be excess." The verb סרח also appears in Ezek. 17:6, where it is used of a vine that grows excessively. The verb does not mean "hang over" (ESV), but to be an extra amount. It cannot hang over, because it is actually bent back upwards from the backside toward the front.

36. The word עֹמְדִים plainly modifies עֲצֵי שִׁטִּים, and not הַקְּרָשִׁים, and thus it describes the kind of material the frames are to be made of, not the finished product. עֲצֵי שִׁטִּים עֹמְדִים, "standing acacia trees" would appear to refer to trees that are tall and straight, able to furnish a pole for the tent frames.

37. The word קֶרֶשׁ cannot mean "board," as it is often translated (e.g., NASB) and against Homan, *To Your Tents*, 137–47. First, although some acacias can get fairly large, it would be very difficult to obtain acacia boards of this dimension (approximately 18' × 2', or 5.5m × 0.6m) in quantity, and none is indigenous to the area of Israel's sojourn. The Egyptians, when they needed large pieces of lumber, traded for cedar from Lebanon. This would not have been necessary if acacias of such large size had been available more locally. Second, if boards of this size could be produced, they would invariably warp when stood up on end (vertically) and be impossible to use for a structure with any beauty or symmetry. Third, a structure made of beams of this size would not be a tent but a building. Fourth, there are analogies from the ancient world for tented structures made with a framework of poles (for example, the pavilion of Queen Hetepheres of 4th dynasty Egypt [see Shaw, *Oxford Egypt*, 96]). Fifth, the proper word for a "plank" or "board" is לוּחַ, (*HALOT*, 2.522–23) not קֶרֶשׁ. The word means "frame," and it describes a lightweight section made of thin poles of acacia word. The word קֶרֶשׁ is used in the Old Testament only to describe the frames of the Tent of Meeting, except at Ezek. 27:6, where it describes the ribs of a ship (not the deck, contrary to a number of versions).

26:17a [There are to be] two stiles[38] for each frame, each one fitted with crossbars[39] to its counterpart;

26:17b that is what you are to do for all the frames of the tent-sanctuary.

26:18 And you are to make the frames for the tent-sanctuary [with] twenty frames for the south side.

26:19 And under the twenty frames you are to make forty bases of silver, two bases under one frame for its two stiles and two bases under another frame for its two stiles.

26:20–21 And for the second side of the tent-sanctuary, on the north side, [make] twenty frames, and their forty bases of silver; two bases under one frame and two bases under another frame.

26:22 And for the back of the tent-sanctuary, to the west, you are to make six frames.

26:23 And you are to make two frames to serve as corner-pieces of the tent-sanctuary at the back.

26:24a They are to be twins[40] (separate stiles) at the bottom,

26:24b but they are joined together at its top,[41] [going] into the one ring;[42]

26:24c it is to be that way for both of them.

---

38. The word יָדוֹת (lit. "hands") is usually translated as "tenons," but this tells us nothing at all, as it is not clear what pieces the "tenons" joined together. From the description, in which there are two יָדוֹת per frame, with one יָד standing over each base, it seems evident that the יָדוֹת are the stiles of the ladder-like frames.

39. The verb שׁלב occurs only here and in Exod. 36:22, but it is the denominative of שָׁלָב, the rung or crossbar of a ladder. Thus, the verb tells us that the two stiles are to be held together by means of crossbars, as is done in a ladder.

40. "Twins" is the literal translation for תֹּאֲמִים. It means that there are two separate and identical stiles at the bottoms of the corner pieces.

41. The line וְיַחְדָּו יִהְיוּ תַמִּים עַל־רֹאשׁוֹ is literally, "and together they are whole at the top." This verse and its parallel in 36:29 are the only two places where תָּם ("whole, complete") appears in the plural in the Bible. The plural is obviously used because there are two stiles, but it does not mean that each stile is complete of itself. Instead, תַמִּים implies that the two become "whole," a single piece, when they go into the one ring. The ESV properly renders the clause as "joined at the top." There is also a bit of wordplay in that the two stiles are "twins" (תֹּאֲמִים) at the bottom but "whole" (תַמִּים) at the top.

42. These corner pieces had an "A" shape, with two matching pieces separate at the bottom but coming together at the top and fitted into a single "ring," a metallic join. This is the only possible way to understand this verse; other renditions are not only wrong as translations but unintelligible. For example, the TNIV has the bewildering: "At these two corners they must

26:24d [These frames] are to form the two corners.

26:25 And there are to be eight frames with their bases of silver, sixteen bases: two bases under one frame and two bases under another frame.

26:26–27 And you are to make crossbars of acacia wood, [with] five for [each of] the frames[43] of one side of the tent-sanctuary, and five crossbars for [each of] the frames of the other side of the tent-sanctuary, and five crossbars for [each of] the frames of the side of the tent-sanctuary at the back, toward the west.

26:28 And the middle bar is to be in the middle of the frames, [as measured] from one end [of a stile] to the [other] end [of that stile].[44]

26:29a And you are to overlay the frames with gold and make their rings of gold [as] housings for the crossbars,

26:29b and you are to overlay the crossbars with gold.

26:30 And you are to erect the tent-sanctuary according to the plan for it that you were shown in the mountain.

26:31a And you are to make a veil of blue and purple and scarlet and linen of tightly spun thread (a work requiring a craftsman);

26:31b he should make it in a cherubim pattern.

26:32 And you are to hang it on four posts of acacia [that are] overlaid with gold, [having] their hooks [made of] gold, [and standing] on four bases of silver.

26:33a And you are to hang up the veil under the clasps,

26:33b and you are to bring in the Ark of the Testimony there on the inner side of the veil,

26:33c and the veil is to serve as your partition between the holy place and the holy of holies.

---

be double from the bottom all the way to the top and fitted into a single ring."

43. Although it is conceivable that a single set of five crossbars went across all the frames, this is most unlikely. Each pole would have had to be at least 60' (18.28 m) in length. It would be difficult to find and shape such poles, to say nothing of keeping them from breaking. It is far more likely that these are the rungs or crossbars that hold each individual frame together.

44. It is again conceivable that this is to be one enormous pole that passes through all of the frames on one side, but it more likely means that it is the middle or third rung (or crossbar) of one individual frame, and that it is to be set precisely at the center point of each of the two stiles, as measured from one end of the stile to the other.

26:34	You are to put the place of atonement[45] on the Ark of the Testimony in the holy of holies.
26:35a	You are to set the table outside the veil, and the menorah opposite the table on the side of the tent-sanctuary toward the south;
26:35b	and you are to put the table on the north side.
26:36	You are to make a screen for the doorway of the tent of blue and purple and scarlet and linen of tightly spun thread (a work requiring an embroiderer).
26:37a	You are to make five posts of acacia for the screen and overlay them with gold, [having] their hooks [of] gold;
26:37b	and you are to cast five bases of bronze for them.
27:1a	And you are to make the altar of acacia wood, five cubits long and five cubits wide.
27:1b	The altar is to be square,
27:1c	and its height is to be three cubits.
27:2a	And you are to make its horns upon its four corners.
27:2b	Its horns are to be affixed to it,
27:2c	and you are to overlay it with bronze.
27:3a	And you are to make its buckets for removing its ashes, as well as its shovels and its basins and its forks and its fire pans;
27:3b	you are to make all its utensils of bronze.
27:4a	And you are to make for it a grating—a network of bronze—
27:4b	and on the network, at its four corners, you are to make four bronze rings.
27:5a	And you are to place it under the sheathing[46] of the altar, towards the bottom,

45. The LXX has κατακαλύψεις τῷ καταπετάσματι τὴν κιβωτὸν ("you shall cover the ark with the curtain"), indicating that the LXX *Vorlage* was פָּרֹכֶת ("curtain") and not the similar כַּפֹּרֶת ("place of atonement"). See Daniel M. Gurtner, "'Atonement Slate' or 'Veil'? Notes on a Textual Variant in Exodus XXVI 34," *VT* 54, no. 3 (2004): 396–8.

46. The meaning of כַּרְכֹּב, which appears only here and at Exod. 38:4, is unknown, although it is often translated as "ledge." It is difficult to visualize, however, how the network with its four corners could sit beneath a ledge, nor is it clear what its function would be. Some suggest that it held the fire of the altar (Durham, *Exodus*, 375–6), but this is impossible for two reasons. First, the purpose of the fire on the altar was to consume pieces of a sacrificed animal. But this would be done on the altar, not under it. Second, if the grating held a fire and if the fire were under the wooden structure of the altar, the intense heat would destroy the wood, notwithstanding the bronze covering. Later stone altars contained no firebox in a lower part; the fire was put on top. It appears that the network was

27:5b so that the network will be halfway up the altar.
27:6a And you are to make poles for the altar—poles of acacia wood—
27:6b and you are to overlay them with bronze.
27:7a Its poles are to be inserted into the rings,
27:7b so that the poles are to be on the two sides of the altar when it is carried.
27:8a And you are to make it hollow with planks.
27:8b Just as he showed you on the mountain,
27:8c so they are to make [it].
27:9a And you are to make the court of the tent-sanctuary.
27:9b On the south side [there are to be] screening curtains for the court of linen of tightly spun thread one hundred cubits long for the one side.
27:10a And it is to have twenty posts,[47]
27:10b and they are to have twenty bronze bases;[48]
27:10c the hooks of the posts and their bands are to be of silver.
27:11a In the same manner, for the length of the north side, there are to be screening curtains one hundred [cubits] long.
27:11b And it is to have twenty posts
27:11c and they are to have twenty bronze bases;
27:11d the hooks of the posts and their bands are to be of silver.
27:12a And as for the width of the court on the west side, there are to be screening curtains of fifty cubits.
27:12b And it is to have ten posts
27:12c and they are to have ten bronze bases.
27:13 The width of the court on the east side is to be fifty cubits.
27:14a The screening curtains for the [one] side are to be fifteen cubits.
27:14b And it is to have three posts
27:14c and they are to have three bases.
27:15a The screening curtains for the other side are to be fifteen cubits.

---

actually for strengthening and stabilizing the altar. Such a function seems implied by the fact that this is where the rings for the carrying poles were attached. The translation "covering" is suggested by an Ethiopic word that may be cognate, *kababa* ("to enclose"; כַּרְכֹּב, *HALOT*, 2.498). I have rendered it "sheathing" because it appears to refer to the bronze overlay that covered the wooden altar. That is, it appears that the altar consisted of a hollow, wooden box on four legs. The box had a sheathing (כַּרְכֹּב) of bronze. Below that, the four legs were stabilized with the network and the rings for the carrying poles were set in the legs at the level of the network.

47. Lit. "and its pillars are twenty."

48. Lit. "and their bases are to be twenty [of] bronze."

27:15b And it is to have three posts

27:15c and they are to have three bases.

27:16a For the gate of the court there is to be a screen of twenty cubits, of blue and purple and scarlet and linen of tightly spun thread (a work requiring an embroiderer).

27:16b And it is to have four posts

27:16c and they are to have four bases.

27:17a All the posts around the court are to be banded with silver.

27:17b their hooks are to be of silver

27:17c and their bases are to be of bronze.

27:18a The length of the court is to be one hundred cubits,

27:18b and the width is to be fifty cubits at each end,[49]

27:18c and the height is to be five cubits of linen of tightly spun thread,

27:18d and their bases are to be of bronze.

27:19 All the utensils of the tent-sanctuary [used] in all its service, and all its pegs, and all the pegs of the court, are to be of bronze.

27:20a And you are to command the Israelites

27:20b that they bring you pure oil of beaten olives for the light, to make a lamp burn, continually.

27:21a In the Tent of Meeting, outside the veil that is before the testimony, Aaron and his sons are to manage it from evening to morning before YHWH.

27:21b [This is to be] a perpetual statute throughout their generations, for those who are of the Israelite line.

Structure

Having described the principal furnishings, the text moves on to describe the tent, the altar, and the courtyard.

- I. The Tent (26:1–37)
  - A. The Tent Layers (26:1–14)
  - B. The Tent Framework (26:15–30)
  - C. The Veil, the Placement of Furnishings, and the Doorway (26:31–37)
- II. The Altar (27:1–8)
- III. The Courtyard (27:9–18)
- IV. Various Supplies (27:19–21)

Commentary

26:1–14. In interpreting the instructions for the construction of the

49. The MT has the somewhat obscure חֲמִשִּׁים בַּחֲמִשִּׁים, “fifty in fifty.”

Tent of Meeting, one must bear in mind two facts. First, it is in fact a tent; it is not a building. Some reconstructions of the tent portray it as a building having walls of solid wood and covered in gold. This is impossible for several reasons. The acacia trees are not big enough to supply such lumber, and if they existed, such broad, lengthy wooden boards when stood on end would warp badly. Also, unless the "bases of silver" under such beams were truly massive, necessitating large-scale excavation at every camp site, they would never be able to hold steady these massive boards of wood and gold when stood upright. Furthermore, the whole point of a tent is that it is to be portable. Massive beams covered in gold would be terribly heavy and highly impractical for moving from place to place, to say nothing of the weight of the massive silver bases such a construction would require. In reality, many modern reconstructions of the Tent of Meeting are plainly retrojections based on Solomon's temple. But Solomon's temple was a permanent structure of stone and heavy timber. Such a structure needs to be vertical, as stone is very strong under pressure but very weak under tension. As such, it is at its strongest when vertical. For a tent, stability can be achieved in one of two ways. Either the tent poles can be tilted and somehow joined, as in a teepee, or the tent poles can be vertical but held in place by the tension of guy lines set opposite one another and by the tension of the tent fabric itself when taut. Also, and in contrast to a monumental building, a tent needs to be as lightweight as possible.

The second feature of the Tent of Meeting description is that many details are left unstated. For example, no dimensions are given for the veil that is to separate the holy of holies from the holy place. Nothing is said about ropes that would keep the tent sheets taut and secure it on windy days. The tent had four layers; careful and detailed instructions, with all dimensions, are given for the lower two layers, but no information is given about the size or manner of construction of the upper two layers. No explanation is provided for how the four layers of the tent related to each other: were they simply laid on top of each other, like sheets and blankets on a bed, or were the upper layers somehow suspended above the lower layers? No doubt the Israelites had become very familiar with tents in their now itinerant lifestyle, and they would have learned more about tents and tent construction when purchasing materials from the Midianites and others. One may assume that many details are left out since the missing information could be filled in with common knowledge or common sense. Therefore, we should understand that the tent instructions only focus on details that are distinctive and religiously significant.

This, in fact, helps to explain a curious feature about this text: there are many details left out, but instructions that are given are often repeated in what seems to be needless redundancy. But the point is to stress what has special meaning, not to state what is obvious or universal in tent making.

The fabric covering for the Tabernacle was in four layers: the lowest, of tightly-woven linen; the second, of goat hair; the third, of tanned ram hides; and the fourth, of some kind of leather. Measurements throughout the account are given in cubits; for simplicity's sake one may treat the cubit as equal to 18 inches (45.7 cm) although in fact the actual cubit used could have been longer or shorter than that.

Ten curtains, or sheets of fabric, made up the linen layer. Each sheet was of tightly woven linen (that is, a strong, not delicate, weave) and, using blue, purple, and scarlet thread, had a design of cherubim worked into it (v. 1). Each sheet was 28 cubits (42' or 12.8 m) long and 4 cubits (6' or 1.8 m) wide. It appears that two sets of five sheets were stitched together along their long sides, creating two very large pieces, each one 20 cubits × 28 cubits (30' × 42', or 9.1 m × 12.8 m). One 28-cubit side of each of these two large pieces had 50 loops of blue yarn worked into it, allowing the two pieces to be joined together by 50 gold clasps at the 50 loops on each piece. This linen layer, when the two large pieces were joined by the gold clasps, would have been 40 cubits (60') long and 28 cubits (42') wide. When set up with the tent poles, the front edge went up to the front opening of the tent but did not drape over it. The back edge of the linen layer, however, did drape down the back side of the completed tent. As such, the join where the loops and metal clasps were located did not sit directly above the center point, dividing the tent into two equal halves. Rather, it was closer to the back side of the tent. The veil separating the inner holy of holies at the back from the holy place was situated below this row of clasps. As such, the holy of holies was smaller than the holy place.

The second tent layer, made from the wool of goats, was constructed in the same manner as the first except that it had eleven curtain panels instead of ten, and each panel was 30 cubits (45' or 13.7 m) long instead of 28 cubits. It had two large sections of six and five sheets, and these were joined with rings of bronze instead of gold. It was thus 44 cubits × 30 cubits (66' × 45', or 20.1 m × 13.7 m).

No details are given on how to construct the third and fourth, or outermost, layers (26:14). Presumably their construction was similar to that of the linen and goat's-wool layers. They may have been, and probably were, larger than the first two layers—and perhaps they were much larger. The meaning of the term for the fabric of the outermost layer (תַּחַשׁ) is uncertain. Many interpreters believe that it refers to the hides of some kind of sea mammal.[50] This is possible, but these animals are unclean; leather from cattle tanned by a special process seems more likely. I have thus translated it as "*tahash* leather," acknowledging that the actual material used is unknown. In Ezek. 16:10, תַּחַשׁ is used for the leather of sandals, suggesting that whatever it was, תַּחַשׁ was a kind of leather and was highly durable.

26:15–30. The tent had a wooden framework that could be broken down, packed up and moved from place to place. The framework was made up of a series of individual "frames." They are double-tent-pole devices, each of which is actually made of two long poles or stiles held together by five crossbars or rungs in a ladder-like construction. Each frame was 10 cubits long (15' or 4.6 m) and 1.5 cubits wide (27" or 68.6 cm). As described in the translation note to 26:16b, these cannot be solid boards or planks, contrary to a number of modern translations (e.g., NASB, HCSB). The acacia tree is too small to provide boards of such enormous size, and even if such boards could be obtained, if they were stood vertically on end and side-by-side, the boards would warp terribly and the overall appearance would be atrocious. These pieces were instead empty frames made of two long, narrow, parallel wooden rails held together by shorter wooden pieces, somewhat as the rungs of a ladder hold together its two stiles. From 26:26, we learn that each frame had 5 rungs or crossbars holding together its two stiles, with the middle or third crossbar set right in the middle of the length of the two stiles (see translation notes at 26:26–28). I do not believe that the text means that there were lengthy poles that ran the entire length of each side. The poles that made up these ladder-like frames were probably quite thin, both because of expense (they had to be covered in gold) and because of weight (one would want the parts of a tent to be lightweight and portable). The framework was a tent skeleton and not solid walls; one could have easily seen through it when it was not covered. Since the tent frames were made of lightweight poles, the "silver bases" (26:19) in which they sat could have been very small and lightweight. They were probably small stakes with indentions at the top into which the poles were set.

50. This is based on a proposed etymological connection between תַּחַשׁ and the Arabic *tuḫas*, "porpoise." See תַּחַשׁ, *HALOT*, 4.1720–21. The HCSB oddly has "manatee," but manatees are not found anywhere in the region of the Red Sea.

The tent had twenty frames on its north and south sides, and six frames on its western or back side. There were also two corner frames at the back corners, one at the northwest corner and one on the southwest corner. The description of these two corner pieces is critical for understanding the structure of the whole tent. Verse 24 says that the stiles of these corner pieces were separated at the bottom but joined at the top, indicating that they had a triangular A-shape instead of a rectangular ladder-shape. Artistic conceptions of the tent always show the tent as rectangular with vertical walls, but this is not possible. These triangular corner frames joined the north and south sides to the west side. This means that all the sides had to slope inward toward the top. If we assume that the corner pieces were isosceles triangles with bases of 1.5 cubits and sides of 10 cubits (basing our dimensions on those of the rectangular frames), then allowing for the slope, the framework roof would have been 9.94 cubits (14.9' or 4.54 m) from the ground. That is, the frames would have been 10 cubits long but, because of the slope, the tops of the frames would be slightly less than 10 cubits from the ground. The width of the Tabernacle at the bottom would be 2.12 cubits (3.18' or 0.97 m) wider than at the top, and at the west wall the bottom edge would be set back from its top edge by 1.06 cubits (1.59' or 0.485 m).

The traditional shoebox-shaped tent would have to have perfectly vertical walls in order to be aesthetically pleasing. It is difficult to understand how the walls could be kept vertical without the extensive use of guy-lines, and these would be problematic in themselves (they would interfere with the draping of the linen tent layer). If the structure tilted to one side or the other, the whole tent would look like a shanty. It would be not only ugly but seem to be the work of foolish or inept builders. This is hardly what one wants for the holy abode of God. A tent with sloping walls would, I think, be far easier to set up than the traditional shoebox-shaped Tent of Meeting seen in most artistic renditions. If, as I suspect, there were bars going across the top that connected the frames of the north side to those of the south side, the structure would be more stable than one with vertical walls, and there would be no danger that the whole thing would lean to one side or the other. At any rate, the traditional shoebox-shaped reconstruction simply disregards the triangular corner pieces of 26:24. This alone indicates that the reconstruction is inaccurate.

I assume that the frames stood side-by-side and edge-to-edge and had no overlap. This contrasts with the view of Richard Friedman, who has a reconstruction of the Tabernacle that does make use of overlapping frames, resulting in a total length of 20 cubits for the Tabernacle.

Friedman believes that the lower tent layers were completely doubled over, with the fold in the linen layer being at the point where the two large pieces were joined with fifty gold clasps. He places this fold with its fifty gold clasps at the front to the Tabernacle, where they would form a golden archway that went around the front entrance. That idea is attractive, but the veil of the holy of holies sat directly beneath the clasps, making this arrangement impossible.[51] So then, assuming that the frames do not overlap, the length of the Tabernacle at the top of the tent framework was 30 cubits (20 × 1.5 cubits), or 45' (13.7 m), in length. But the bottom length of the Tabernacle, because of the flaring out due to the triangular corner pieces, was 31.06 cubits (46.59', or 14.2 m). The Tabernacle width would be 9 cubits (15', or 4.6 m) at the top and 11.12 cubits (16.68', or 5.08 m) at the bottom.

The lower, linen layer of the tent spanned the length from the top front edge of the framework to its top back end (30 cubits [45', or 13.7 m]) with an additional 10 cubits (15', or 4.6 m) for going down the back wall. The gold rings were 20 cubits (30', or 9.15 m) from the top front edge and 10 cubits (15', or 4.6 m) from the top back edge. The linen layer would have been placed on the framework with its decorative face on the bottom so that a priest inside the tent could look through the frames and see the cherubim on the linen. The back side of the linen would have been to the outside, on top. It was covered by the second, woolen layer, and unseen. The linen layer, at 28 cubits (42', or 12.8 m) in width, would not have reached the ground on the north and south sides, as height of the two sides plus the top width of the Tabernacle (10 + 10 + 9 cubits) would be 29 cubits (43.5', or 13.26 m). Thus, the linen tent layer would fall 9" short of covering the framework on the north and south sides, although it would reach just to the ground on the west (back) side.

The woolen (goat hair) layer was 30 cubits (45', or 13.7 m) wide. It would have been flared out from the north and south sides of the framework and staked down, allowing for some space between it and the linen layer on the sides (26:13). There is a problem with the extra, eleventh sheet of the goat hair fabric. It is plainly stated to be at the

51. See Richard E. Friedman, "Tabernacle," in Freedman, *ABD* Vol. 6, 298. Friedman's solution to the problem of the veil and the rings is to prefer the LXX, which he says places the veil not "under the rings" but "under the frames." But this is not correct; the LXX of 26:33 says that the veil is ἐπι τοὺς στύλους ("upon the posts"), in agreement with 26:32, although it is true that the LXX of 26:33 does not mention the rings. Even so, there is no reason to prefer the LXX here.

back of the tent in 26:12, but it seems to be at its front in 26:9 as that verse is rendered in many translations (ESV: "and the sixth curtain you shall double over at the front of the tent"). A possible solution, as indicated in the translation above, is that 26:9 should be rendered, "You shall join the five sheets to the six sheets, and you shall double the sixth sheet back toward the front side of the tent." So understood, the eleventh sheet was at the back of the Tabernacle but doubled over towards the front. A problem, of course, is that it is not clear how this fold was done or what its purpose was. Perhaps it was folded and staked in such a manner that it gave extra protection to the back side of the tent, where holy of holies was situated. My own suspicion is that the tent-dwellers of this time would have known precisely what kind of fold was intended.

We do not know how the third and fourth tent layers of tanned rams' hide and of *tahash* leather were constructed or pitched. We are given no details at all about their sizes. We should not assume that the outer two layers were simply draped over the under two layers. Not only would this have been unsightly, it would have added weight and strain to the gold-plated frame poles and perhaps have made the whole structure less stable. It may be that other poles and guy lines supported these external layers, so that there was one tent of two layers (the linen and the goat's-wool) within another tent of two layers (the rams' hide and *tahash* leather). However it was done, it was probably based on some common understanding of how to construct a multi-layered tent, so that detailed instructions on this point would be unnecessary and outside of the main purpose of the text. In contrast to the inner (linen) layer of the tent, which was embroidered with cherubim and carried theological significance, the outer layers were purely utilitarian—they protected the inner parts of the tent from the elements. As such, they are given no particular attention in the text.

How was stability achieved with this tent? My own opinion is that there must have been guy lines at various points. There may also have been horizontal joins—thin poles—at the tent ceiling between frames on the north side and those on the south side. These would have added necessary stability and, combined with the sloping structure of the frames and guy lines, would have allowed for a tent that was both lightweight and stable. Or, the tent fabric itself may have provided tension stability, if the upper ends of the poles protruded through holes in the tent fabric, as is common in traditional tents. Again, many details of basic tent construction are left unstated, and we do not know what principles they applied.

26:31–37. The interior veil was of the same design as the linen tent layer, having cherubim patterns in blue, purple, and scarlet. It was held in place by four gold-plated posts of acacia wood with gold hooks. The veil was attached to these gold hooks and placed below the gold clasps of the linen tent layer. The clasps would have formed a golden archway at the border between the holy place and the holy of holies, with the veil there also separating the two divisions of the tent. Other than that, nothing is said about the veil; its dimensions are conspicuously absent. The instructions for making the screen before the entrance are quite cursory as well; they describe only the materials used for construction. Other details are apparently left to widely understood principles.

27:1–8. Israelite altars of stone have been found at Beersheba and Arad. These indicate that the standard Israelite altar was, as described in this text, more-or-less cube-shaped and had four horn-like projections at the top corners. The altar of the Tabernacle was to be portable, unlike the stone altars of Arad and Beersheba, and therefore it had to be lightweight. Thus, it was made with boards and it was hollow. It may have been filled with sand when it was set up to add stability; when it was to be moved, the sand would be emptied out. Contrary to popular opinion, the horns of the altars were not used to tie down the sacrificial animals. Some the altars are so large that it would be exceedingly difficult to get a live bull up on the altar, and at any rate the horns do not flair out in such a way as to allow them to hold a rope; they typically go straight up, and they are rather short, so that any rope put around them would come right off. The horns were for ceremonial purposes, for daubing blood onto for the sake of making ritual atonement (Exod. 29:12; Lev. 8:15). Furthermore, animals in Israelite ritual were not killed on altars, but in proximity to altars (Lev. 1:11; 3:13). When a burnt offering was consumed in fire on top of an altar, it was cut into pieces first (Lev. 1:6–9). This avoided the problem of hauling a full-sized dead bull up onto the altar, and it also meant that a smaller fire could be used. A great conflagration, such as would be needed for burning up an adult animal, would destroy the altar itself. In order to preserve the altar from damage from the heat, it is probable that the fire box was up quite high and removed from the wooden supports of the altar.

27:9–18. Most of the details of the construction of the courtyard barrier are self-explanatory. The Tabernacle area was holy, and people were not allowed to approach it casually, and for this reason it had to be fenced off. The Tabernacle was set in a courtyard of 100 × 50 cubits (150' × 75', or 45.7 m × 22.85 m). This was surrounded by a fence made with linen sheets of fabric. Certain details are left somewhat obscure, and others are left out altogether. Most surprisingly, there is no indication of how high the screen was supposed to be. The sheets were to be of linen, but there is no indication of coloring with blue, purple, and scarlet threads. Therefore, they were presumably plain, although there is no specific command to this effect. The sheets that screened the gateway did have blue, purple, and scarlet threads worked into them, but there is no indication that cherubim figures were to be set into this embroidery. We do not know if the screening sheets were to be hung directly upon the silver hooks that were on the posts, or if there were lines that were strung from one hook to the next, with the sheets hung on the lines (I suspect the latter is correct). We also do not know if the screens were to be secured at the bottom to prevent them from blowing in the breeze. We do not know how large or how heavy the bronze bases for the posts were; they were apparently stakes with holes set into their tops for securing the posts. Apart from giving the dimensions for the courtyard and the number of posts, the text repeatedly emphasizes that the poles were to have silver bands and hooks and that the bases were to be of bronze.

27:19–21. The lamps of the menorah were to burn with an eternal flame. This contrasted with the fire of the altar of burnt offering, which was only lit as needed. Since the menorah stood inside the Tabernacle, only the priests could approach it to tend it.

Theological Summary of Key Points

We have seen that the text often leaves a great deal of information out while sometimes repeating other pieces of instruction several times over. The repetition may be partially stylistic, but it also may serve to throw emphasis on significant information. That is, purely structural issues are up to the tentmakers to work out, and the instructions say nothing about them. But details that are important for conveying the message and meaning of the Tent of Meeting are explicitly and repeatedly stated. Thus, even though our picture of the Tent of Meeting complex is incomplete and partially hypothetical, we can surmise the theologically meaningful portions of the text by focusing on what the text actually says. That is, we should base our theology on what the text emphasizes and not on theoretical reconstruction.

1. The external barrier around the courtyard, with its linen shielding, its silver hooks and its poles set into bronze stakes would have suggested dignity. But above everything else, it was a barrier, telling the Israelite that YHWH was holy and that no one could cross through the sacred ground that surrounded his tent.

2. The altar outside the tent, with its bronze exterior and its fire for consuming the carcasses of sacrificial victims, would have suggested to the observer that God is a consuming fire, like YHWH of the burning bush on Mt. Sinai, and would have warned the individual that human corruption cannot stand in God's presence. No human, not even an Aaronic priest could approach God without atonement.

3. The leather outer layers of the tent no doubt made for the largest single tent in the entire Israelite encampment, and its exterior covering, whatever *tahash* leather actually was, certainly implied that the best quality of material was used for the sheltering of YHWH's shrine. But here, too, the central message was one of a barrier. Looking at it from afar, the average Israelite only saw the dark and perhaps somewhat forbidding tent exterior. He had no glimpse of the beauty within. Told of the exquisite workmanship of the inner layer and of the sacred furnishings of the tent, he understood that there was a beauty that adorned the inner sanctuary that he would never see. He understood that God had great glory that he was cut off from, and he depended on the priest to go into the tent to represent him and his family to God.

4. Whatever the external two tent layers looked like, entering the Tent of Meeting itself would have been visually stunning. The priest, going into the holy place, would enter a chamber illuminated by the soft light of the seven lamps of the menorah. As his eyes adjusted, the fine linen inner tent with its colorful tapestry of cherubim would have suggested entry into heaven, where the angels in splendor were in attendance upon God. The tent frames of gold, reflecting the lamps, would have seemed to twinkle like stars and would have suggested a glorious hallway towards God's throne room. The screen before the holy of holies, with its cherubim, would have suggested an angelic honor guard standing between the priest and YHWH. The priest thus would have a sense of being in the earthly representation of the outer chamber of God's heavenly abode.

5. There was probably a cosmic dimension to this. That is, the outer chamber represented the lower heavens (what we would call the physical heavens) and the inner chamber, the holy of holies, would represent the upper heaven, God's abode. The Tent of Meeting was a microcosm of the created universe and of the heavenly throne room that was above the created universe. That is, God's glory fills all of creation, but there is yet a heavenly throne room that is above and beyond the physical universe. The Tent of Meeting is a smaller version of this cosmic reality. It is also the place where God who dwells in the highest heavens can be present or immanent in the world.

The overall message of this aspect of the tent complex is that God is holy. The barriers between the people and the interior of the tent, as well as the altar of burnt offering, all indicate that because of sin, people are kept apart from God. For the Christian, the barriers that separated the Israelites from the holy of holies remind us that in Christ the barrier is removed and that we have access to God (Matt. 27:51). Even so, we should not fail to take away an important message in the tent structure: that God is holy, that we should fear God, and that in worship, we should approach in reverent respect and also with constant brokenness of heart and repentance, knowing that we have no right of ourselves to approach God.

UNDER A PRIESTHOOD (28:1—29:37)

The vestments of the high priest and the ceremony of his ordination take up an enormous amount of the text of Exodus (80 verses, or more than the entire account of the *Yam Suph* and accompanying Song of the Sea [14:1—15:21], at 52 verses). This suggests how important the priesthood was in Israel's religion.

Translation

28:1 "And you—bring near to yourself from among the Israelites your brother Aaron and his sons with him to function as a priest for me—Aaron, Nadab and Abihu, Eleazar and Ithamar, Aaron's sons.

28:2 And you are to make holy garments of glory and of splendor for Aaron your brother.

28:3a And you are to speak to all the wise[52] men whom I have filled with a spirit of wisdom,

28:3b so that they will make Aaron's garments to consecrate him, in order for him to function as a priest for me.

52. It is understandable that some would want to render חָכָם here as "skillful," as that is appropriate for the context. On the other hand, it is important to see that in the Bible, skills also constitute "wisdom."

28:4a And these are the garments that they are to make: a breastpiece and an ephod and a surplice and a checkered tunic, a headdress and a sash,

28:4b and they shall make holy garments for your brother Aaron and his sons, in order for him to function as a priest for me.

28:5 And they shall make use of the gold and the blue and the purple and the scarlet and the linen.

28:6 And they are to make the ephod of gold, of blue and purple [and] scarlet and linen of tightly spun thread (a work requiring a craftsman).

28:7a Two shoulder pieces are to be affixed at its two ends,

28:7b that it may have pieces affixed to it.[53]

28:8 And the *ephudah* band[54] that [goes] upon it, [being] of the same kind of workmanship [as the ephod]—of gold, of blue and purple and scarlet and linen of tightly spun thread—is to be affixed to it.

28:9a And you are to take two carnelian stones

28:9b and engrave on them the names of the sons of Israel.

28:10 Six of their names are to be on the one stone and the names of the remaining six are to be on the other stone, according to their genealogical records.[55]

28:11a In a work requiring a gem cutter in the engraving of a signet, you are to engrave the two stones with the names of the Israelites;

28:11b you are to mount them in filigree settings of gold.

28:12a And you are to put the two stones on the shoulder pieces of the ephod [to serve as] memorial stones for the sons of Israel,

28:12b and Aaron is to bear their names before YHWH on his two shoulders for a memorial.

28:13–14a And you are to make filigree settings of gold and two chains of pure gold.

---

53. The clause וְחֻבָּר is lit. "that it may be joined." This seems to make little sense; surely the point is not that the ephod is to be joined to itself by two shoulder pieces. It would not seem to refer to the joining of the two shoulder pieces to the ephod since the text has just described that feature of the ephod (חֹבְרֹת). It is more likely that the Pual *weqatal* וְחֻבָּר indicates that the ephod is to have things joined to it by means of the shoulder pieces. This is precisely what the following verses describe.

54. The word אֲפֻדָּה is some kind of decorative accessory for the ephod, as its name indicates. The word חֵשֶׁב relates to the verb חשׁב, "weave," and seems to be a kind of band.

55. While תּוֹלְדוֹת is most precisely understood to be genealogical records of descendants from a common ancestor, here it may refer to the birth order of the twelve patriarchs.

28:14b You are make them twisted, made like a rope,
28:14c and you shall put the rope-chains on the filigree settings.
28:15a And you are to make a breastpiece of judgment (a work requiring a craftsman).
28:15b You are to make it like the work of the ephod;
28:15c you are to make it of gold, of blue and purple and scarlet and linen of tightly spun thread.
28:16 It is to be square [when] folded double:[56] a span in length and a span in width.
28:17a And you are to mount upon it four rows of stones;
28:17b the first row is to be a row of ruby, topaz and emerald;
28:18 and the second row is to be a turquoise, a sapphire and a moonstone;
28:19 and the third row is to be a jacinth, an agate and an amethyst;
28:20a and the fourth row is to be a beryl and a carnelian and a jasper.[57]
28:20b Their settings are to be in gold filigree.
28:21a The stones are to be, corresponding to the names of the sons of Israel, twelve—corresponding to [the number of] their names.
28:21b Each is to have its signet-style engraving, corresponding to its name;
28:21c they are for the twelve tribes.
28:22 And you are to make on the breastpiece twisted chains, made like a rope, in pure gold.
28:23a And you are to make on the breastpiece two rings of gold,
28:23b and you are to attach the two rings to the two [top] corners[58] of the breastpiece.
28:24 And you are to attach the two ropes of gold to the two rings at the [top] corners of the breastpiece.
28:25a And you are to attach the [other] two ends of the two ropes to the two filigree settings,
28:25b and [so] attach them to the shoulder pieces of the ephod, at the front of it.
28:26a And you are to make two [more] rings of gold

56. The idea seems to be that a single piece of fabric was folded double and sewn as a pouch. When folded and sewn, it was square in shape.
57. The precise identity of each of the twelve stones is impossible to ascertain, and the translations will vary.
58. Lit. "ends." It obviously has to be the top corners since it would flip over if attached by its bottom corners.

28:26b and you are to set them on the two [bottom] corners[59] of the breastpiece, on its inside edge, next to the ephod.
28:27a And you are to make two [more] rings of gold,
28:27b and you are to attach them to two shoulder pieces of the ephod, [affixed] to the bottom part, opposite its front side, beside the seam [that is] above the *ephudah* band[60] of the ephod.
28:28a And they are to bind the breastpiece by its rings to the rings of the ephod with a blue cord, for [the breastpiece] to be near the decorative work of the ephod,
28:28b and thus the breastpiece will not come loose from the ephod.
28:29 And Aaron will always carry the names of the Israelites in the breastpiece of judgment over his heart when he enters the holy place, for a memorial before YHWH.
28:30a And you are to affix the Urim and the Thummim to the breastpiece of judgment, and they shall be over Aaron's heart when he goes in before YHWH;
28:30b and Aaron will always carry the [breastpiece of] judgment of the Israelites over his heart before YHWH.
28:31 And you are to make the surplice of the ephod completely blue.
28:32a And its head-opening is to be in the middle;
28:32b around its opening there shall be a hem (a work requiring a weaver), as [is used in] the [collar] at the [head] opening of light body armor,[61]

---

59. From context, it is most reasonable that these gold rings attached to the bottom corners of the breastpiece. They held the blue cord, which only stabilized the breastpiece. The gold chain, that bore the weight, would have been attached at the upper corners.
60. It appears that the חֵשֶׁב is woven (from the root חשב, which originally meant "to weave"), and that it had to be fastened on to the ephod as a belt (Exod. 29:5). This would seem to be the same item that is called an "*ephudah* band" in v. 8.
61. The word תַּחְרָא appears only here and in Exod. 39:23. It is often translated as "coat of mail" on the basis of the targum, but this translation calls to mind anachronistic images of medieval coats of mail, and it is not at all clear how that kind of armor/mail illustrates the point. Some believe that the word refers to a kind of Egyptian leather, *dḥr*, and it could refer to the leather binding around the edge of an Egyptian wicker shield. But this derivation is not certain, and there is evidence for translating תַּחְרָא as "coat of mail" in the Samaritan textual tradition (see Jeffrey M. Cohen, "Samaritan Authentication of the Rabbinic Interpretation of *Kephî Taḥrā'*," *VT* 24, no. 3 [1974]: 361–366). Sarna, *Exodus*, 182, compares תַּחְרָא to the leather collar worn by Egyptian charioteers with their armor, as depicted

28:32c so that it will not be torn.
28:33–34 And you are to make on its [lower] hem pomegranates of blue and purple and scarlet, [going] all around on its hem, and [with] bells of gold between them all the way around (a golden bell and a pomegranate, a golden bell and a pomegranate, [going] all the way around the [lower] hem of the surplice).
28:35a And it shall be on Aaron when he officiates,
28:35b and its sound shall be heard when he enters and leaves the holy place before YHWH,
28:35c so that he will not die.
28:36a And you are to also make an emblem[62] of pure gold
28:36b and shall engrave upon it a signet-style of engraving,
28:36c 'Holy to YHWH.'
28:37a And you are to fasten it to a blue cord,
28:37b and it will go on the headdress;
28:37c it is to be toward the front of the headdress.
28:38a It is to be on Aaron's forehead,
28:38b and Aaron shall [by that] bear the guilt attached to the holy things that the Israelites consecrate, for the sake of all their holy gifts;
28:38c and it shall always be on his forehead, for them to have favor before YHWH.
28:39a And you are to weave the tunic of linen,
28:39b and you are to make a headdress of linen,
28:39c and you are to make a sash (a work requiring an embroiderer).
28:40a And for Aaron's sons you are to make tunics;
28:40b and you are to make sashes for them,
28:40c and you are to make headbands of glory and of beauty for them.
28:41a And you are to put them on Aaron your brother and on his sons with him.
28:41b And you shall anoint them
28:41c and ordain them
28:41d and consecrate them,
28:41e that they may function as priests for me.

---

in a relief of Thutmose IV. The word must refer to some specific item that had a hem that illustrated how the hem of the ephod head-opening was supposed to look. It seems that Sarna's solution is the best available.

62. The word צִיץ is literally "flower," but here it is some kind of decorative piece or symbolic emblem made of gold. It was probably not a flat plate, however, as some versions imply (e.g., ESV), since צִיץ implies some kind of three-dimensional structure.

28:42a	And you are to make linen undergarments for them to cover [their] genitals;
28:42b	they are to go from the abdominal area to the thighs.
28:43a	And they are to be on Aaron and on his sons when they enter the Tent of Meeting, or when they approach the altar to officiate in the holy place,
28:43b	so that they do not incur guilt
28:43c	and die.
28:43d	It is to be an eternal statute for him and for his descendants after him.
29:1a	And this is the protocol that you are to follow with them to sanctify them to function as priests for me.
29:1b–2a	Take one bull and two rams without blemish, and unleavened bread and unleavened cakes mixed with oil, and unleavened wafers spread with oil
29:2b	(you are to make them of fine wheat flour).
29:3a	And you are to put them in one basket,
29:3b	and you are to present them in the basket along with the bull and the two rams.
29:4a	And you are to present Aaron and his sons to the doorway of the Tent of Meeting,
29:4b	and you are to wash them with water.
29:5a	And you are to take the garments,
29:5b	and you are to clothe Aaron with the tunic and the surplice of the ephod and the ephod and the breastpiece,
29:5c	and gird him with the woven belt of the ephod.
29:6a	And you are to set the headdress on his head
29:6b	and put the holy diadem on the headdress.
29:7a	And you are to take the anointing oil
29:7b	and pour it on his head
29:7c	and anoint him.
29:8a	And you are to present his sons
29:8b	and clothe them with tunics.
29:9a	And you are to gird them, Aaron and his sons, with sashes,
29:9b	and you are to bind headbands on them,
29:9c	and they shall have the priesthood by a perpetual statute.
29:9d	And you are to ordain Aaron and his sons.
29:10a	And you are to present the bull before the Tent of Meeting,
29:10b	and Aaron and his sons are to lay their hands on the head of the bull.
29:11	And you are to slaughter the bull before YHWH at the entrance of the Tent of Meeting.

29:12a And you are to take some of the bull's blood
29:12b and put [it] on the horns of the altar with your finger;
29:12c and you shall pour out all the blood at the base of the altar.
29:13a And you are to take all the fat that covers the internal organs and the lobe of the liver and the two kidneys and the fat that is on them,
29:13b and offer them up in smoke on the altar.
29:14a But you are to burn the flesh of the bull and its hide and its refuse in a fire outside of the camp.
29:14b It is a sin offering.
29:15a And you are to take the one ram,
29:15b and Aaron and his sons are to lay their hands on the head of the ram;
29:16a and you are to slaughter the ram
29:16b and take its blood
29:16c and sprinkle it all around upon the altar.
29:17a And you are to cut the ram into pieces,
29:17b and wash its entrails and its legs,
29:17c and place [them] with its pieces and its head.
29:18a And you are to offer up in smoke the whole ram on the altar.
29:18b It is a whole offering to YHWH;
29:18c it is a soothing aroma;
29:18d it is an offering by fire to YHWH.
29:19a And you are to take the other ram,
29:19b and Aaron and his sons are to lay their hands on the head of the ram.
29:20a And you are to slaughter the ram,
29:20b and take some of its blood
29:20c and put [it] on the lobe of Aaron's right ear and on the lobes of his sons' right ears and on the thumbs of their right hands and on the big toes of their right feet,
29:20d and you are to sprinkle the blood all around upon the altar.
29:21a And you are to take some of the blood that is on the altar and some of the anointing oil,
29:21b and you are to sprinkle [it] on Aaron and on his garments and on his sons and on his sons' garments with him.
29:21c And he and his garments shall be holy and, along with him, his sons and his sons' garments.
29:22–23 And you are to take the fat from the ram and the fat tail, and the fat that covers the internal organs and the lobe of the liver, and the two kidneys and the fat that is on them and the right thigh—for it is a ram of ordination—and, from the basket of unleavened bread

that is before YHWH, one round loaf of bread and one thick loaf of bread [with] oil and one wafer,

29:24a and you are to put all these in the hands of Aaron and in the hands of his sons,

29:24b and you are to wave them as a wave offering before YHWH.

29:25a And you are to take them from their hands,

29:25b and you are to offer them up in smoke on the altar in addition to the burnt offering for a soothing aroma before YHWH;

29:25c it is an offering by fire to YHWH.

29:26a And you are to take the breast of Aaron's ram of ordination

29:26b and wave it as a wave offering before YHWH.

29:26c And it shall be your portion.

29:27 And you are to sanctify the breast of the wave offering and the thigh of the contribution[63] that was waved and that was presented from the ram of ordination, from the one that was for Aaron and from the one that was for his sons.

29:28a And it shall be a perpetual rule for Aaron and his sons [that it is to be] from the Israelites,

29:28b for it is a contribution;

29:28c and [so] a contribution shall come from the Israelites—from the sacrifices of their peace offerings, their contribution to YHWH.

29:29 And the holy garments of Aaron are to be for his descendents after him, for their anointing and their ordination.

29:30 For seven days the priest from his descendents who takes his place is to put them on when he enters the Tent of Meeting to minister in the holy place.

29:31a And you are to take the ram of ordination

29:31b and boil its flesh in a holy place.

---

63. The precise etymology and meaning of תְּרוּמָה is debated. See, for example, the lengthy discussion and bibliography in תְּרוּמָה, *HALOT*, 4.1788–90. In this context, one might argue that it connotes lifting something up as a wave offering, particularly if it is derived from רוּם, "to be high." Exod. 29:27 makes the strongest case for it being a wave offering since שׁוֹק הַתְּרוּמָה, "the thigh of the תְּרוּמָה," is used in parallel with הַתְּנוּפָה, "breast of the wave offering." But it may be that here שׁוֹק הַתְּרוּמָה is a wave offering not because of the meaning of תְּרוּמָה but because of context, which specifies that it is elevated before YHWH. In many other contexts תְּרוּמָה seems to mean no more than "contribution" and to have no connection to the wave offering (Exod. 25:2–3; 30:13-15; 35:5,21,24; etc.). It is of course possible that all contributions were ceremoniously lifted up before YHWH. Even so, it appears that "contribution" is the best translation, and that one should not connect this word specifically to the wave offering.

29:32 And Aaron and his sons are to eat the flesh of the ram and the bread that is in the basket at the entrance of the Tent of Meeting.
29:33a And they are to eat those things by which atonement was made to ordain and to sanctify them;
29:33b but no one else is to eat [them],
29:33c because they are holy.
29:34a But if any of the flesh of ordination or any of the bread remains until morning,
29:34b then you are to burn the remainder in a fire;
29:34c it shall not be eaten,
29:34d because it is holy.
29:35a Thus you are to do for Aaron and for his sons, according to all that I have commanded you;
29:35b you shall ordain them [over a period of] seven days.
29:36a And each day you are to offer a bull, a sin offering, for atonement.
29:36b And you are to purify the altar when you make atonement for it,
29:36c and you are to anoint it to sanctify it.
29:37a For seven days you shall make atonement for the altar
29:37b and consecrate it;
29:37c and the altar shall be most holy—
29:37d whatever touches the altar shall be holy."

Structure

This text is lengthy, but the essential structure is very simple.

- I. Construction of the Priestly Vestments (28:1–43)
  - A. Introduction to the Construction of the Vestments (28:1–5)
  - B. The Ephod (28:6–14)
  - C. The Breastpiece of Judgment (28:15–30)
  - D. The Surplice (28:31–35)
  - E. The Headdress (28:36–38)
  - F. The Tunic (28:39–41)
  - G. The Undergarments (28:42–43)
- II. Ordination of the Priests and the Altar (29:1–37)
  - A. Preparation (29:1–4)
  - B. The Robing of Aaron and Sons (29:5–9)
  - C. A Bull as a Sin-Offering (29:10–14)
  - D. A Ram as a Whole Offering (29:15–18)
  - E. A Ram as an Ordination Offering (29:19–26)
  - F. Rules for Future Ordinations (29:27–30)
  - G. The Ordination Meal (29:31–34)
  - H. The Week of Sanctification (29:35–37)

Commentary

28:1–43. The description of the priestly vestments is exceedingly complex and made more confusing by virtue of the many individual elements that we are unfamiliar with. In order to make sense of the data, we should begin with an overview of the essentials of the high priest's dress. At the lowest layer the priest wore linen undergarments that went from the waist to the thighs (28:42). Above this was a linen tunic (28:39), a garment analogous to a long nightshirt. The tunic was the basic garment for men and women in the ancient world, and a sash was normally tied around the waist (see v. 4 and Lev. 8:7). Above his tunic the priest wore a large, blue surplice, fringed with decorative pomegranate embroidery and bells around the lower hem. This is the "surplice of the ephod" of 28:31-35. Over this surplice was the ephod itself, which was something like an apron, and it had two shoulder pieces mounted on it. These shoulder pieces extended down in front and perhaps in back to somewhere around the middle of the priest's chest and back. Also attached to the ephod, just below the bottom edge of the shoulder pieces and therefore apparently at about the bottom of the ribcage, was a woven belt called an *ephudah*. In the middle of the priest's chest, attached to the ephod shoulder pieces by chains of pure gold and cords of blue yarn, was a breastpiece that was a kind of pouch. On his head, the priest wore a headdress, and on the headdress was a golden emblem saying, "Holy to YHWH."

28:1–5. Aaron was to be the first high priest of the Tent of Meeting, and his four sons Nadab, Abihu, Eleazar and Ithamar were to be subordinate priests. Nadab and Abihu would be struck down by God for sacrilegious behavior (Lev. 10:1–2). The materials of the priests' garments included materials also used for the inner layer of the Tent of Meeting (v. 5). In both cases, the linen, gold, and colored embroidery indicated the purity and beauty of the presence of YHWH.

28:6–14. The ephod is listed first because it is the item most closely associated with priestly office. The definition of ephod, however, is somewhat obscure. Gideon made a golden ephod which became a kind of idol to the Israelites (Judg. 8:24–27); this makes it sound like an ephod is a solid object, like a figurine. But here in Exodus, the ephod is plainly an item of clothing. But Judges does not say that Gideon's ephod was solid gold (similarly, the "houses of ivory" of Amos 3:15 are not built of solid ivory). Probably Gideon's ephod was an expensive and richly embroidered sacred garment which was eventually displayed in a shrine and became an object of adoration. The ephod obviously covered at least the upper part of the body, since it had shoulder pieces. In any case, an ephod was a garment associated with the priestly office. Most likely, it was something like an apron. On the ephod, there were two shoulder pieces, and each shoulder piece had a semi-precious red stone (possibly carnelian[64]) with the names of six tribes of Israel inscribed on them, so that on the two together all twelve names were inscribed. This reflects the fact that the priest was Israel's representative before God at the sanctuary. The shoulder pieces were probably not at all like military shoulder boards of today, which are small and sit directly on top of the shoulders. They were probably attached to the ephod at the shoulder but extended in the front well below the left and right collarbones and down toward the shoulder blades in the back. This is fairly clear from the account of how the breastpiece was attached to the shoulder pieces, as described below. The ephod also had some kind of woven band called an "*ephudah* band." The nature of the *ephudah* band is difficult to determine, beyond that it was colorfully decorated and, judging from its name, an accessory that was distinctive to the ephod. It was apparently something like a band or belt. Also, it seems to have been located at the middle or lower part of the ephod, with its top near the lower edges of the two shoulder pieces. Thus, it was probably at the bottom of the rib cage or at the waist.

28:15–30. These shoulder pieces, as mentioned above, apparently extended in the front to about the middle of the chest. Attached to the shoulder pieces of the ephod was the breastpiece. This was a square pouch about 8" × 8" (25 cm × 25 cm). Two gold rings on upper corners of the breastpiece were attached by golden braided chains to gold rings mounted high up on the shoulder pieces. These chains supported the weight of the breastpiece, but blue cords secured the lower part of the breastpiece to a lower part of the shoulder pieces at spots near the top of *ephudah* band (this indicates that the shoulder pieces extended downward). The blue cords required a second pair of gold rings, at the lower corners of the breastpiece, that would be attached to yet another pair of gold rings on the lower parts of the shoulder pieces. Thus, there were four gold rings on the breastpiece (one at each corner) and two gold rings on each of the two shoulder pieces (one ring high on each shoulder piece and one ring down low). The lower rings may have been on parts of the two shoulder pieces that went down behind the priest's back. The blue cord (28:28) would have attached there, passed around

64. See שֹׁהַם, *HALOT*, 4.1424. The precise identity of the stone is unknown, but based on Akkadian cognates, it was reddish in color.

to the front side of the priest, and then been attached to the lower rings of the breastpiece, making it secure.

The breastpiece was large enough that it would have covered much of the priest's chest. The text specifies that it was over the priest's heart (Exod. 28:30; this is one of the few times in the Bible that "heart" is used in a purely physiological sense). On the breastpiece were twelve precious stones, each symbolic of a tribe of Israel. Inside the pouch were the Urim and Thummim. These were the sacred stones that were used for casting lots, doing a kind of licit divination when seeking an answer from God (Num. 27:21). Their very existence is somewhat surprising, since other common forms of divination (such as haruspicy [looking at the liver of a sacrificed animal] and belomancy [drawing arrows from a container]) were not practiced, or at least sanctioned, in Israel.[65] No one knows how the Urim and Thummim worked; even the meanings of the names is obscure (some speculate that they respectively mean "light" and "dark"). One possibility is that they were flat like coins, each with a white side and a dark side. When tossed like coins, if both came up white, the answer was Yes; if both came up dark, the answer was No. If one was white but the other was dark, that meant that God was not answering (1 Sam. 28:6). This arrangement does allow for three possible answers (positive, negative, and no answer), while most other proposals only allow for a "Yes" or "No." But we do not really know what they looked like or how they worked. Considering the casual way in which the Urim and Thummim are mentioned here (with no explanation of what they are and no instructions on how to make them), it appears that they already existed before the making of the priestly vestments. They never appear in the Old Testament narrative after the time of David, and Ezra 2:63 indicates that in the early postexilic period they were already lost.

28:31–35. The surplice worn over the priest's tunic (but under the ephod) was apparently quite long, coming down to near the feet. No reason is given for the blue color, and one should not arbitrarily attach theological significance to the color. Perhaps the ringing bells symbolically alerted YHWH of the priest's coming when he approached the tent so that he would not enter unannounced and so incur God's wrath (wearing the bells would be analogous to knocking before entering and

65. Prov. 16:33 and 18:18 appear to speak more favorably of the use of lots.

thus be a sign of respect).[66] The pomegranate was a decorative element frequently associated with priestly objects (see 1 Kgs. 7:18–20).

28:36–38. Other than that it is made of linen, there is no description of the headdress at all. All emphasis is on the emblem attached to the headdress that says, "Holy to YHWH." This emblem, sitting above the priest's forehead, is analogous to the uraeus worn on the pharaoh's crown. The emblem was not a snake, however; the Hebrew term used (צִיץ; "flower") suggests that it could have been floral in appearance. Aaron would by that emblem "bear the guilt attached to the holy things." This is a bit enigmatic, but the idea seems to be as follows: The Israelites had consecrated all the sacred items for service to YHWH, but they polluted those things by their own impurity. Aaron, in going before YHWH with polluted holy things, risked being destroyed by God. But the emblem "Holy to YHWH" marked him as sacred to God and therefore allowed to enter the tent and officiate, notwithstanding the defiling sins of Israel. In short, it seems that the emblem was for Aaron's protection, enabling him to officiate before YHWH even as he bore the sin of the nation. In this way, symbolically, the sin was understood to be forgiven.[67] In this manner, the offerings made by the Israelites through Aaron would be accepted.

28:39–41. For most Israelites, a woolen tunic was probably much more commonly worn than linen. Egyptians regularly wore linen, but Israelites had to contend with a true winter, whereas Egyptians did not. Also, Israelites were shepherds, but Egyptians were farmers; thus, the former had wool readily available where the latter had flax. But wool is hot and causes people to sweat, and it is difficult to whiten. As such, linen was much to be preferred for the priest, whose appearance was to convey the idea of purity.

28:42–43. We may presume that the wearing of linen undergarments was quite rare in Israel (the average peasant probably had none at all, except perhaps a loin cloth worn under his tunic. For the priest, however, it was essential that his "nakedness" not be exposed. Carelessness

66. Many theories have been given as to why the high priest wore bells, but they are all little more than guesses. See Cornelis Houtman, "On the Pomegranates and the Golden Bells of the High Priest's Mantle," *VT* 40, no. 2 (1990): 223–29, for other theories. One should not be dogmatic about interpreting the symbolism.

67. The verb נשׂא means both to "bear" and to "forgive."

about how the priest presented himself to God would be tantamount to blasphemy.

29:1–37. In modern ecclesiastical polity, we think of ordination as conferring a status; one is an "ordained minister" regardless of whether or not one serves as a pastor in a church. In ancient Israel, one was ordained to service at a specific shrine. In this text, there is no indication that Aaron is chosen to be a priest; he evidently already is one. Israel clearly already had priests (Exod. 19:24), and there is no indication of a question, or of a divine decree, about the selection of Aaron. It seems that everybody, including YHWH, simply understands that Aaron is the priest. But the office to which Aaron is ordained is not the status of being a priest; he is ordained for service at a specific place, the central shrine of Israel at the Tent of Meeting. The sacrifice for ordination included a bull, two rams, and unleavened bread. Aaron wore all the vestments of the high priest, but his sons, ordained as subordinate officiants for the tent, wore less elaborate vestments (thus they had headbands instead of the headdress that Aaron wore [29:6, 9]). The blood of the sacrifices symbolically atoned for the sin of Aaron and his sons, and it consecrated them to service.

29:1–4. The sacrificial animals, the unleavened bread, and Aaron and his sons were presented before YHWH. Aaron and his sons were perhaps ritually stripped and washed, signifying that they brought nothing with them, that their whole persons were consecrated to the service of the sanctuary, and that they were ritually cleansed.

29:5–9. The ceremonial dressing of Aaron and his sons in the vestments obviously indicates that they were assuming their duties and that they were taking on a new identity and rank. The anointing with oil also marks the individual's induction into a high office, and it may also imply empowerment by the Spirit of God for that task. David received the Spirit when Samuel anointed him (1 Sam. 16:13), and the same was also true of Saul (1 Sam. 10:1–10). On the other hand, several judges seem to have received the Spirit apart from any anointing with oil (Judg. 3:10; 6:34; 11:29; 13:25). The only people specifically said to have received an endowment of the Holy Spirit in Exodus are the craftsmen who constructed the tent and the other sacred objects (Exod. 28:3; 31:3; 35:31). Therefore, we should be hesitant about asserting that the anointing with oil implies *ipso facto* that the priests had a special endowment of the Spirit.

29:10–14. The bull is sacrificed as a sin offering for Aaron and his sons, so that they not be ritually defiled and therefore disqualified for the work of a priest. There is special legislation for a sin offering for a priest. If the sin offering is for a layman, a lamb or two pigeons were sacrificed (or if the person were very poor, grain was offered), but the meat was given to the priests as their food provision (Lev. 5:1–13). In the case of a priest, however, the sin offering was to be a bull, and after the ritual at the altar, all that remained of the animal was to be burned outside the camp. Because of the gravity attached to the priest's duties at the shrine and because purity was essential, the sacrifice had to be a bull. And because the sacrifice atoned for the priest's guilt, he could not eat of it. Thus, the ritual here follows the normal practice for a sin offering for a priest. In this ceremony, the sacrifice of the bull did not consecrate the priest to service at the tent; instead, it ceremonially removed the guilt and pollution that otherwise would have disqualified him.

29:15–18. This ram is offered as a whole burnt offering (עֹלָה). Even though the sin offering of vv. 10–14 was entirely burnt up, it was not a whole burnt offering. The carcass of the sin offering was burnt up outside the camp, but the ram of the whole burnt offering described here was burnt at the altar. The whole offering is a general act of propitiation and worship offered to God. It, in effect, ceremonially removes the guilt of the people and priests as a whole and allows the entire ordination process to go forward. Like the sin offering, however, this whole burnt offering was propitiatory and did not of itself consecrate Aaron and his sons to service at the tent.

29:19–25. The second ram is the sacrifice of ordination; this is the animal that actually consecrates the priests to their duties at the tent. Aspects of the symbolism of this sacrifice are somewhat obscure, but we may suggest that at least some elements are fairly clear in meaning. When the priests laid their hands on the ram (v. 19), this was not a transfer of guilt, for this ram was not a sin offering. Rather, the slaughtering of the ram was a way of consecrating it totally to God, analogous to how a firstborn animal was consecrated to God by sacrificing it (Exod. 13:12). When Aaron and his sons put their hands on the ram, they were symbolically being totally consecrated to YHWH along with the ram. That is, they metaphorically died with the animal and now belonged wholly to YHWH. The earlobe, thumb, and big toe (v. 20) represented the whole person, and placing blood on these parts consecrated the entire body to God's service. The act of waving parts of the animal and some of the unleavened bread before YHWH was a ceremonial presentation of those parts to God, perhaps with the parts standing for the whole, as these parts were consumed in the fire. It is not clear why these specific parts (the liver, kidneys, their fat, and the right thigh) were chosen to be elevated before YHWH.

29:26–28. This section introduces the "breast of the wave offering," an item not mentioned previously among the pieces to be waved before YHWH. Moses, as the officiant, received this portion of the meat for himself (the rest of the meat was for Aaron and his sons; see vv. 31–34). The nation as a whole was to provide the animals for the ordination ceremony. It would be unjust for the priests to have to pay for the sacrificial animals since their service was for the nation and not themselves. Worse, it would suggest that a man could buy the office of priest.

29:29–30. The vestments are not the personal property of any priest but are to be handed down from one generation to the next. The notice that the son of Aaron who succeeds him to the high priesthood is to wear the vestments for seven days is somewhat obscure. Apparently he was to wear it for that period as a way of formally taking on the office of high priest; that is, by wearing it for seven days straight his identity would be melded to the identity of high priest. After that, he would only wear all the vestments when duties at the shrine required it.

29:31–34. The meat that was not used in the wave offering was to be boiled and serve as a meal for Aaron and his sons. This perhaps completes the ritual begun by having the priests lay their hands on this ram. Eating this ram more fully merged the identity of the ram with the priests. They identified with it in its consecration to YHWH, and so became consecrated to YHWH themselves.

29:35–37. There is here another reference to a seven-day period connected to the ordination of the priests. However, it is not seven days of wearing the vestments (vv. 29–30) but seven days of making sin offerings for the altar and also of anointing with oil. The sacrifices removed any impurity, and the oil consecrated it. This consecration of the altar apparently only had to be done the one time, when it first came into use, in order to make it into a holy object. Successors of Aaron would have to undergo the seven days of wearing the vestments but apparently did not repeat the seven days of sin offerings for the altar.

Theological Summary of Key Points

1. Some aspects of the priest's vestments were obviously symbolic and carried a transparent meaning. The stones with the names of the Israelite tribes on them, for example, plainly represented the tribes of Israel (28:9-12); they indicated that the high priest stood before YHWH as Israel's representative. But it is precarious for us to postulate a theological meaning for every color, metal, or object described here. We run the risk of turning the vestments into an allegory. The danger is that we will interpret each item as it suits us without any real warrant from the text. It is enough to simply understand that the vestments portrayed the purity, splendor and beauty of holiness.

2. A dread of the holiness of God pervades the text. The numerous sacrifices, the requirement to wear the bells and the emblem on the forehead that said "Holy to YHWH" all imply a fear of arousing YHWH's anger by bringing impurity before him. The obvious point is that those who would seek to serve God must maintain their purity.

3. The representation of Israel's tribes two times, first on the carnelian stones on the shoulder pieces, and second on the twelve stones on the breastpiece, show that the whole purpose of a priest is to represent others. Humans need an intercessor between themselves and God. Thus, we Christians rejoice that Christ our high priest intercedes for us. We also rightly speak of a "universal priesthood of believers," but we should understand that this is a duty, not an honorific title. It implies going before God in behalf of others.

4. Above everything else, this text tells the Israelites that there is only one licit way to approach God at the Tent of Meeting: through the priesthood of Aaron. It indicates that the institutions for worshipping God are established by God himself. They are not human innovations, and no one has the right to skirt these sanctioned institutions, as Korah and his followers discovered to their ruin when they tried to usurp the position of Aaron (Num. 16). Thus, for Israel, the ordained means of approaching God is both personal (the Aaronic priest) and institutional (the whole Tent of Meeting complex). For Christians, analogously, the one access to God is the person of Christ and the one institution ordained by God for his worship is the church, as it was built by Christ himself (Matt. 16:18). There is no other name under heaven whereby we may be saved than that of Christ (Acts 4:12). And Christians may disagree over the precise definition of "church," but there can be no grounds for private worship or for a hyper-separatist, isolationist ecclesiology.

IN CONSTANT COMMUNION (29:38—46)

Daily sacrifices and offerings at the Tabernacle symbolically removed spiritual pollution and insured that the site was kept perpetually holy. More than that, it created a bond between YHWH and Israel and was a means for their coming to know him.

Translation

29:38 "Now this is what you are to offer on the altar: two one-year-old lambs each day, without fail.

29:39a The one lamb you are to offer in the morning

29:39b and the other lamb you are to offer at twilight.

29:40 And [you are to offer] with the first lamb a tenth [of an ephah] of fine flour mixed with one-fourth of a hin of beaten oil, and one-fourth of a hin of wine for a drink offering.

29:41a The other lamb you are to offer at twilight,

29:41b and you are to offer it with the same grain offering and the same drink offering as in the morning, for a soothing aroma, an offering by fire to YHWH."

Seventh Poem: The Song of the Tent

Stanza 1.1

29:42a Constant burnt offerings throughout your generations;
עֹלַ֤ת תָּמִיד֙ לְדֹרֹ֣תֵיכֶ֔ם 0-2-3

29:42b The entrance of the Tent of Meeting before YHWH:[68]
פֶּ֥תַח אֹֽהֶל־מוֹעֵ֖ד לִפְנֵ֣י יְהוָ֑ה 0-2-5

Stanza 1.2

29:42c Where I will meet with you,
אֲשֶׁ֨ר אִוָּעֵ֤ד לָכֶם֙ שָׁ֔מָּה 1-4-4

29:42d By speaking to you there,
לְדַבֵּ֥ר אֵלֶ֖יךָ שָֽׁם׃ 0-3-3

29:43a And there I will meet with the Israelites!
וְנֹעַדְתִּ֥י שָׁ֖מָּה לִבְנֵ֣י יִשְׂרָאֵ֑ל 1-3-4

Stanza 1.3

68. The first two lines do not form complete clauses but are sentence fragments. Syntactically, they are an example of *casus pendens*, announcing the topic of the poem before any full clauses are given.

29:43b And it will be sanctified by my glory:
וְנִקְדַּשׁ בִּכְבֹדִי׃ 1-2-2

29:44a I will sanctify[69] the Tent of Meeting and the altar,
וְקִדַּשְׁתִּי אֶת־אֹהֶל מוֹעֵד וְאֶת־הַמִּזְבֵּחַ 1-3-4

29:44b And Aaron and his sons I will sanctify as my priests.
וְאֶת־אַהֲרֹן וְאֶת־בָּנָיו אֲקַדֵּשׁ לְכַהֵן לִי׃ 1-4-5

Stanza 2.1

29:45a And I will dwell in the midst of the Israelites,
וְשָׁכַנְתִּי בְּתוֹךְ בְּנֵי יִשְׂרָאֵל 1-2-4

29:45b And I will be their God!
וְהָיִיתִי לָהֶם לֵאלֹהִים׃ 1-3-3

Stanza 2.2

29:46a And they will know that I am YHWH their God,
וְיָדְעוּ כִּי אֲנִי יְהוָה אֱלֹהֵיהֶם 1-4-4

29:46b Who brought them out from the land of Egypt
אֲשֶׁר הוֹצֵאתִי אֹתָם מֵאֶרֶץ מִצְרַיִם 1-4-5

29:46c That I may dwell in their midst.
לְשָׁכְנִי בְתוֹכָם 1-2-2

Stanza 2.3

29:46d I am YHWH their God!
אֲנִי יְהוָה אֱלֹהֵיהֶם׃ פ 0-3-3

Structure

Contrary to most renditions, which take this entire text as prose, I believe that verses 29:42–46 are poetry. The song is a celebration of the Tent of Meeting as a place of constant communion between YHWH and Israel via the sacrifices offered there daily.

I. Prose: Stipulations Regarding the Daily Sacrifices (29:38–41)

---

69. The *weqatal* of 29:44a is epexegetical of 29:43b. The ו + X + *yiqtol* of 29:44b marks it as bound to 29:44a (note also the chiastic construction of 29:44). As such, all of 29:44 amplifies or expounds upon 29:43b, which asserts that YHWH will sanctify the shrine.

II. Poetry: Celebration of Israel's Communion with YHWH (29:42–46)

The following poetic elements can be observed in the poem:

1. All lines conform to normal breaks according to the poetic constraints and cantillation marks. Line 29:46b is somewhat unusually terminated by *tifha*, but the accent has subordinate disjunctives within its domain, strengthening the case that it is a line break. I do, however, differ with the MT at several points regarding strophic divisions, as my strophes do not always agree with the placement of the *sof pasuq*.

2. There are two stanzas and a total of six strophes in fourteen lines. Each stanza begins with a bicolon (1.1; 2.1) and follows this with a tricolon (1.2; 2.2). The first stanza has a second tricolon (1.3), but the second stanza ends the song with a monocolon (2.3). It is normal for a Hebrew poem to end by breaking a pattern.

3. Each tricolon focuses on a specific benefit for Israel conferred by the daily sacrifice at the sanctuary.
   - The tricolon at 1.2 focuses on YHWH meeting with Israel to speak to them. It creates an inclusion, using the verb יעד in the first and third lines.
   - The tricolon at 1.3 focuses on YHWH's sanctification of the sanctuary and priesthood for Israel.
   - The tricolon at 2.2, and indeed the whole of the second stanza, focuses on the covenant bond, that YHWH is "their God."

4. There are instances of various poetic tropes (repetition, dependence, and inclusion) within the poem.
   - The tricolon at 1.2 repeats שׁם ("there") in every line.
   - The tricolon at 1.3 repeats קדשׁ ("sanctify") in every line.
   - The tricolon at 2.2 uses dependence rather than repetition (29:46c is dependent on 29:46b, and 29:46b is dependent on 29:46a). But אלהיהם ("their God") is repeated three times in the second stanza.
   - The first stanza repeats a pattern to mark strophe termination. Strophe 1.1 ends with לְ attached to a construct chain of two words (לִפְנֵ֥י יְהוָֽה), as does strophe 1.2 (לִבְנֵ֖י יִשְׂרָאֵ֑ל). Strophe 1.3 is a variation on this, having two words, each beginning with לְ (לְכַהֵ֥ן לִֽי). Even the progression of words that end these three strophes ("YHWH," "Israel," and "priest for me") seems deliberate, marking the special status of Israel before God.
   - Another pattern of three words appears in the first stanza. It

speaks of the Tent of Meeting (מוֹעֵד) at 29:42b, and from the same root employs the verb יעד in the Niphal in אִוָּעֵד ("I will meet") at 29:42c and in וְנֹעַדְתִּי ("and I will meet") at 29:43a.

- The second stanza also has an inclusio, using שׁכן ("dwell") at 29:45a followed by an assertion at 29:45b that YHWH is "their God," while 29:46c also uses שׁכן and follows this at 29:46d with an assertion that YHWH is "their God."

Commentary

29:38–41. The prose legislation gives a straightforward legal requirement: a lamb is to be sacrificed every morning and another every evening. They are burnt offerings, and thus their carcasses are cut up and entirely burnt on the fire, and a grain offering and libation are to be burned with the lambs. A "hin" is a liquid measurement of volume. It was one-sixth of a "bath," suggesting that a hin was about one gallon (3.8 l).

29:42–46. The significance of the act is brought out in the poem. The mood is positive and joyful, and it celebrates the significance of the Tent of Meeting: YHWH is present with Israel. He instructs them, sanctifies the sanctuary and its priests, and maintains the covenant relationship—that he is their God. So understood, the ritual is not burdensome, but a realization of the promise that Israel will be unique among the nations, a treasured possession and holy people belonging to YHWH (Exod. 19:5).

Theological Summary of Key Points

1. The covenant people needed constant communion with God. For Israel, this was demonstrated in the daily sacrifices. For us, consistent worship and prayer, both corporate and private, are no less vital. One cannot experience the blessings of knowing God, of sanctification, and of the assurance that we belong to him if we do not regularly come before him.

2. Worship and its requirements are not meant to be irksome or tedious. Most of us cannot imagine having to slaughter two lambs every day. But for Israel, this duty was not imposed in order to weary them with stringent religious requirements; it was an opportunity for Israel to begin and end every day by standing before God. In the same way, we should not look upon activities of worship as burdensome.

3. As Christians, we tend to look down on the Old Testament sacrificial system as something horrible, that we are only too glad to be away from. While we do rejoice in the once and final sacrifice of Christ, we should understand that from within, the Old Testament law was not an affliction but a great privilege and an opportunity for Israel to experience God among them. What we have now in the new covenant is greater, but in its time and place, the worship code of the Law was a blessing from God.

WITH PRAYER (30:1–10)

An altar of incense was to be set within the holy place so that incense could burn before YHWH day and night. This represents a constant appeal for divine favor.

Translation

30:1a	"And you are to make an altar as a place for burning incense;
30:1b	you are to make it of acacia wood.
30:2a	Its length is to be a cubit,
30:2b	and its width is to be a cubit,
30:2c	it is to be square,
30:2d	and its height is to be two cubits;
30:2e	its horns are to be affixed it.
30:3a	And you are to overlay it with pure gold, all around its top and its sides, and on its horns;
30:3b	and you are to make a gold molding at its edges.
30:4a	And you are to make two gold rings for it under its molding:
30:4b	you are to make [them] on its two side walls—on its two sides [and not on the front and back[70]]—
30:4c	and they shall serve as housings for poles with which to carry it.
30:5a	And you are to make the poles of acacia wood
30:5b	and overlay them with gold.
30:6	And you are to put this altar in front of the veil that is near the Ark of the Testimony, facing the place of atonement that is over [the Ark of] the Testimony, where I will meet with you.
30:7a	Aaron is to burn fragrant incense on it;
30:7b	he is to burn it every morning when he takes care of the lamps.
30:8a	When Aaron lights the lamps at twilight, he shall burn incense.
30:8b	Incense is perpetually [to burn] before YHWH throughout your generations.
30:9a	And you are not to offer any foreign incense upon it, or burnt offering or meal offering;

70. The redundancy of stating that the rings are to be on the sides is probably meant as a way of emphasizing that the rings are not to be on the front and back.

30:9b and you are not to pour out a drink offering on it.
30:10a And Aaron is to make atonement on its horns once per year;
30:10b he is to make atonement on it with the blood of the sin offering of atonement once a year throughout your generations.
30:10c It is most holy to YHWH."

Structure

The section is in two parts.

I. The Structure and Placement of the Incense Altar (30:1–6)
II. Duties at the Incense Altar (30:7–10)

Commentary

30:1–6. The instructions for making the altar of incense are quite straightforward and need no elucidation. At two cubits in height (about 36" or 91.5 cm), it would be at a convenient height for working with the burning incense. Incense altars have been found at various archaeological sites; the most famous are the pair of limestone incense altars found at the shrine of Israelite Arad. These were smaller than the Tent of Meeting altar, one being about 0.4 m and the other 0.5 m tall.

The greatest enigma about the Tent of Meeting incense altar is why its description is placed here and not with the instructions for building the menorah and table for bread offerings (25:23–40). Various suggestions have been offered, but the simplest may be that since there was a morning and evening sacrifice, as described in 29:38–46, this seemed the proper place for describing the twice-daily offering of incense. Both the sacrifices and the incense were burnt and sent a fragrant plume up to God (the verb קטר is used for causing either incense or an animal sacrifice to burn and send smoke into the sky). Also, the instructions for making the incense itself are nearby, at 30:34–36.

30:7–10. The text does not say whether the incense was burned directly on top of the altar or whether special, portable burners were brought in and placed on top of the altar. A priest normally carried burning incense in a censer (מַחְתָּה), but that was used when he was standing and officiating (Num. 16:17–18). He may have brought the censer into the holy place and set it on the incense altar, or he may have put the burning contents into a receptacle on the altar. Regardless, the main points are that incense was to burn perpetually, being refreshed every morning and every night, and that this altar was for this purpose only. The incense used at the altar was of a special blend; no other incense could be used, and the sacred blend of incense could not be used for any other purpose (Exod. 30:34–38). The horns were present so that the altar could be ceremonially cleansed every year by daubing sacrificial blood on them.

Theological Summary of Key Points

1. Like the morning and evening sacrifice, the constant burning of incense in the holy place represented Israel's constant worship of YHWH, while at the same time conveying the fact that YHWH was Israel's God.

2. The fundamental question we must ask is what the burning of incense implied or represented in the minds of the Israelites. Most references to the burning of incense simply state that it was to be done or was done; nothing is said as to why it was done or what it signified. Several passages, however, do give us hints. After the rebellion of Korah, Dathan, and Abiram and their associates, YHWH told Moses that he was going to wipe out the entire assembly, and a plague immediately struck. Aaron, at Moses's direction, put incense in his censer and ran into the assembly, standing between the living and those who had already died. His burning of incense "made atonement" for Israel and stopped the plague (Num. 16:44–50[17:9–15]). In this case, "make atonement" cannot be the provision of a substitutionary sacrifice; even so, the priestly incense was somehow propitiatory for the people and so gained forgiveness for them. Psalm 141:2, similarly, asks God to accept the psalmist's prayers "like incense" and like "the evening sacrifice." This makes sense when we realize that an essential idea of these sacrifices is that they send up fragrant odors that are "sweet smelling" or soothing and appeasing to God. When God warns of disasters that will befall Israel should they break the covenant, he says that he will turn from them and no longer smell their pleasing aromas (Lev. 26:31). In Revelation, burning incense before God is three times said to represent the "prayers of the saints" (5:8; 8:3, 4). In all these cases, the incense represents the seeking of God's favor for his people. It may be a plea for forgiveness, as in Numbers. In Revelation, the prayers are for the relief of the persecuted church, and when an angel throws the censer to earth, there is an earthquake and thunder (Rev. 8:5). Fundamentally, therefore, incense is an appeal for divine help and favor, and its most obvious counterpart in Christian spirituality is prayer.

WITH PURITY (30:11—31:18)

The instructions for building the Tent of Meeting close with an apparently random set of instructions on various topics. The dominant theme, however, is that Israel is to worship God with purity. This is most evident in the command to construct the bronze basin for cleansing and in instructions concerning perfumes that would infuse the shrine with a beautiful fragrance. A special tax serves to discourage the defiling of the people through conducting a census.

Translation

30:11 And YHWH also spoke to Moses, as follows:
30:12a "If[71] you take a census of the Israelites to count them,
30:12b each one of them must give a ransom for himself to YHWH, when you count them,
30:12c so that there will be no plague among them when you count them.
30:13a This is what everyone who undergoes the census is to give: half a shekel according to the shekel of the sanctuary
30:13b (the shekel is twenty gerahs;
30:13c half a shekel [is given] as a contribution to YHWH).
30:14 Everyone who undergoes the census, from twenty years old and upward, is to give YHWH's contribution.
30:15 The rich are not to pay more and the poor are not to pay less than the half shekel that one gives as YHWH's contribution to make atonement for your lives.
30:16a And you are to take the atonement money from the Israelites
30:16b and provide it for the service of the Tent of Meeting,
30:16c and it will be for the Israelites a memorial before YHWH, to make atonement for your lives."
30:17 And YHWH spoke to Moses, as follows:
30:18a "And you are to make a basin of bronze, with its base of bronze, for washing.
30:18b And you are to put it between the Tent of Meeting and the altar,
30:18c and you are to put water in it.
30:19 And Aaron and his sons are to wash their hands and their feet in it.
30:20a When they enter the Tent of Meeting, they shall wash with water,
30:20b so that they will not die;
30:20c or when they approach the altar to officiate by offering up in smoke an offering by fire to YHWH.
30:21a And they shall wash their hands and their feet
30:21b so that they will not die;
30:21c and it shall be a perpetual statute for them, for Aaron and his descendants, throughout their generations."

---

71. In administrative law כִּי at the beginning of a conditional clause purely means "if." That is, it does not mean "when" and is certainly not an implied command. See Exod. 21:2, 37; 22:4–6, 9; 23:4, etc.

30:22 And YHWH spoke to Moses, as follows:

30:23–24 "And you, take the finest of spices: five hundred [shekels] of myrrh resin,[72] and half as much cinnamon spice[73] (two hundred and fifty [shekels]), and two hundred and fifty [shekels] of calamus[74], and five hundred [shekels] of cassia,[75] [weighed] according to the shekel of the sanctuary, and a hin of olive oil.

30:25a And you are to make of these a holy anointing oil, a mixture of perfume (a work requiring a perfumer);

30:25b it shall be a holy anointing oil.

30:26–28 With it you are to anoint the Tent of Meeting and the Ark of the Testimony, and the table and all its utensils, and the menorah and its utensils, and the altar of incense, and the altar of whole offering and all its utensils, and the basin and its stand.

30:29a And you are to also sanctify them

30:29b that they may be most holy.

30:29c Everything that touches them shall be holy.

30:30a And you are to anoint Aaron and his sons,

30:30b and sanctify them to function as priests for me.

30:31a And you are to speak to the Israelites, saying,

30:31b 'This is to be my holy anointing oil throughout your generations.

30:32a It is not to used for [the ordinary] anointing of a person's body,

---

72. Myrrh is obtained from the sap of the tree *Commiphora myrrha*, native to the Arabian Peninsula. It flows as a liquid sap when extracted, but it hardens when exposed to the air. It is here called מָר־דְּרוֹר, often translated as "liquid myrrh" (ESV, NRSV, TNIV), but this is misleading, since the English reader would assume that it exists in a liquid state. Even if the name is related to דרר, perhaps meaning to "ooze" or to "flow," that refers only to its process of extraction, not to the state in which it exists when stored or put to use.
73. A number of translations render בֹּשֶׂם as "sweet-smelling cinnamon" (e.g., ESV), but this is an example of the etymology fallacy. The word בֹּשֶׂם may be derived from a root that means "to season" and perhaps "to be fragrant," but of itself the word only means a "spice" (it sometimes refers specifically to balsam). The word בֹּשֶׂם does not evaluate the smell of cinnamon (as "sweet-smelling") and probably it is not even specifying a type of cinnamon; it simply identifies it as a spice.
74. The phrase וּקְנֵה־בֹשֶׂם, "and reed-spice," implies that this is a spice derived from a reed. It is probably calamus, a spice derived from the south Asian wetland reed commonly known as "sweet flag."
75. The translation for קִדָּה here, "cassia," comes from the Vulgate and must be regarded as uncertain. Cassia is similar in flavor to cinnamon and is often used as a cheaper substitute for cinnamon.

30:32b and you are not to make [any] like it in the same proportions.
30:32c It is holy,
30:32d [and] you are to treat it as holy.[76]
30:33 Anyone who makes a perfume like it or who puts any of it on an unauthorized person shall be cut off from his people.'"
30:34a And YHWH said to Moses,
30:34b "Get spices—stacte[77] and onycha[78] and galbanum[79]—and pure frankincense.
30:34c These are to be in equal parts.
30:35 And with it you are to make perfumed incense (a work requiring a perfumer) salted, pure, [and] holy.
30:36a And you are to pulverize some of it to a powder,[80]
30:36b and you are to put part of it before the testimony in the Tent of Meeting where I will meet with you.
30:36c You are to treat it as absolutely holy.[81]
30:37a The incense that you are to make—you are not to make [any] in the same proportions for yourselves.
30:37b You are to treat it as holy [and] for YHWH.
30:38 A man who makes [incense] like it to use as fragrance is to be cut off from his people."
31:1 And YHWH spoke to Moses, saying:
31:2a "Look!
31:2b I have called by name Bezalel, the son of Uri, the son of Hur, of the tribe of Judah.
31:3–5 I have filled him with the Spirit of God, [manifested] in wisdom,[82] in understanding, in knowledge, and in every [kind of] skill, to

76. Lit. "holy it will be to you."
77. The precise nature of נָטָף is unknown. The translation "stacte" is derived from the LXX *στακτήν*.
78. The שְׁחֵלֶת is traditionally thought to be "onycha," a fragrance derived from a part of the snail and widely used in the ancient world. The LXX translates שְׁחֵלֶת as *ὄνυχα*. On the other hand, שְׁחֵלֶת, *HALOT*, 4.1462, suggests possible botanical etymologies for the term. Thus, we cannot be sure precisely what שְׁחֵלֶת is.
79. There is a clear etymological relationship between the Hebrew חֶלְבְּנָה and the English translation "galbanum" (and also the Greek *χαλβάνην* of the LXX). Galbanum is yellowish in color due to the presence of sulfur and is said to be foul-smelling.
80. Lit. "And you are to beat to powder some of it with crushing."
81. Lit. "holy of holies it will be to you."
82. It is probably best to take רוּחַ אֱלֹהִים as that with which Bezalel was filled and to take בְּחָכְמָה etc. as the domain of activity in which this filling

devise artistic designs, to work in gold, and in silver, and in bronze, and in the cutting of stones for mounting, and in the carving of wood, in order to do every [kind of] craft.

31:6a And I—take note[83]—have appointed with him Oholiab, the son of Ahisamach, of the tribe of Dan.

31:6b and I put wisdom in the hearts of all who are wise,

31:6c–11a so that they may make all that I have commanded you: the Tent of Meeting, and the Ark of Testimony, and the place of atonement that is upon it, and all the furniture of the tent, and the table and its utensils, and the pure [gold] menorah and all its utensils, and the altar of incense, and the altar of whole offering and all its utensils, and the basin and its stand, and the woven garments, and the holy garments for Aaron the priest, and the garments of his sons [used] for functioning as priests, and the anointing oil, and the spiced incense for the holy place.

31:11b They are to make [them] in accordance with everything I have commanded you."

31:12 And YHWH said to Moses the following:

31:13a "And you, speak to the Israelites as follows:

31:13b 'Despite all of that,[84] you are to keep my Sabbaths;

31:13c for that is a sign between me and you throughout your generations for [you] to know

31:13d that I am YHWH your sanctifier.

---

displays itself. In simple English terms, the בְּ can be translated here as "[manifested] in."

83. The word הִנֵּה here marks something important, to which the speaker draws the hearer's attention.

84. "Despite all of that" is admittedly a pleonastic translation of אַךְ, more literally "but" or "except." But it brings out the fact that what follows is somehow in contrast to what has gone before. English versions typically either ignore the particle (NRSV) or translate it incorrectly (the ESV has "above all"). Notwithstanding אַךְ, *HALOT*, 1.45, the particle always implies contrast and is not simply "surely." Examples cited where it seems to be simply emphatic ("surely") are misleading. In 1 Kgs. 22:32, when the Syrians shout אַךְ מֶלֶךְ־יִשְׂרָאֵל הוּא, they mean, "Now that's the king of Israel," in contrast to all the other warriors in chariots. When Laban says to Jacob (Gen. 29:14) אַךְ עַצְמִי וּבְשָׂרִי אָתָּה, he means, "You really are my bone and my flesh," meaning that although Jacob arrived as a total stranger, his story has convinced Laban of his identity. In other examples, the implied contrast is even more obvious or explicit (Gen. 7:23; 9:4–5; 18:32; 20:12; 23:13; Exod. 10:17; 12:16; 21:21; Lev. 11:4; Num. 18:3; Judg. 6:39; 10:15; Jer. 5:5; 34:4).

31:14a And you are to keep the Sabbath,
31:14b for it is holy to you.
31:14c Anyone who profanes it is certainly to be put to death;
31:14d for if anyone does any work on it,
31:14e that person is to be cut off from among his people.
31:15a For six days work is to be done, but on the seventh day there is a Sabbath day of rest,[85] holy to YHWH.
31:15b Anyone who does work on the Sabbath day is certainly to be put to death.
31:16 And the Israelites are to observe the Sabbath by keeping the Sabbath throughout their generations as a perpetual covenant.
31:17a It is a sign for all time between me and the Israelites.
31:17b For in six days YHWH made heaven and earth,
31:17c but on the seventh day he ceased
31:17d and caught his breath.'"[86]
31:18 And he gave to Moses, when he had finished speaking with him upon Mount Sinai, the two tablets of the testimony—tablets of stone written by the finger of God.

Structure

This text lays out matters relating to providing for the ongoing worship at the Tent of Meeting but ends, somewhat surprisingly, with an extended exhortation to keep the Sabbath just before the concluding verse. The structure of the passage is obvious, each section being marked by a narrative comment that "YHWH spoke to Moses."

I. The Census and Sanctuary Tax (30:11–16)
II. The Bronze Laver (30:17–21)
III. The Anointing Oil (30:22–33)
IV. The Incense (30:34–38)
V. The Construction Foremen (31:1–11)
VI. The Sabbath (31:12–17)
VII. The Tablets of the Testimony (31:18)

85. The phrase שַׁבַּת שַׁבָּתוֹן is a technical term for a complete cessation of labor in observation of Sabbath. See Daniel C. Timmer, *Creation, Tabernacle, and Sabbath: The Sabbath Frame of Exodus 31:12–17; 35:1–3 in Exegetical and Theological Perspective* (Göttingen: Vandenhoeck & Ruprecht, 2009), 47-51.

86. This is a bold anthropomorphism, in which even YHWH is portrayed as working so hard that he needs to take a break to catch his breath. On נפשׁ, see Exod. 23:12.

Commentary

30:11–16. A census is an administrative measure of information gathering for the sake of governance. That is, by gathering data about a population, a central authority is better able to control it. A census would be preparatory for organizing the state, for going to war, or for implementing taxes. Being a means of maintaining dominance over the people, a census enhances the power of the centralized government and so removes the covenant people from direct allegiance to God.

Against some modern interpreters,[87] the census was not solely for military purposes. The language of Exod. 30:14, "everyone who crosses over to the lists" (כֹּל הָעֹבֵר עַל־הַפְּקֻדִים), describes the mechanics of taking a head-count and is not an actual mustering for going into battle. So also, translations such as the TNIV are misleading in rendering אֶת־מִסְפַּר מִפְקַד־הָעָם at 2 Sam. 24:9 as "the number of the fighting men," since this suggests that it is purely a military matter and is in preparation for launching a war (the NASB is more accurate with its rendition, "the number of the registration of the people"). In Israel as in the Roman Empire, a census would be taken under the direction of military commanders because those were the national government officials. There were very few non-military "government" employees as we understand the concept. Although a census had obvious military applications, and although men over age twenty were also liable to militia service (analogous to how every citizen of republican Rome was liable for military service), the census, of itself, has broader administrative and taxation purposes than just going to war. So, for example, the census taken in the year Jesus was born (Luke 2:1) had administrative purposes and was a tool of control and taxation, but clearly the intent was not to enroll Jewish subjects into the Roman army. 2 Samuel 24 never suggests that David was planning a military campaign, much less that this was the reason his census was regarded as a sin. And in fact the census did have broad non-military repercussions, as Solomon radically reorganized the state in a manner that infringed upon ancient tribal identities and borders in the aftermath of David's census (1 Kgs. 4:7–20; see also 2 Chr. 2:17, which explicitly states that Solomon made use of David's census data). The placement of David's census at the end of the narrative of his reign is, I believe, meant to link it to the restructuring of Israel carried out under Solomon. Put another way, military aggrandizement is one of the bad results, but not the only bad result, that can come of a census. The taking a census is, of itself, offensive to Israel's identity as the people of YHWH unless

87. E.g., Stuart, *Exodus*, 635-6.

YHWH himself commands it, as happened only during the wilderness sojourn. At any rate, in Exodus it is the census itself, not any particular military application of it, that the text speaks of.

Here in Exodus, where taking a census is not forbidden by God, the people must pay a poll tax for the sanctuary in order to avoid a plague. This is strictly a poll tax (paid equally regardless of one's status or income) and not a graduated tax because each Israelite (that is, each male over age twenty) is equally a member of the covenant community, and the tax must reflect that. The tax, moreover, is a ransom for each man's life. Thus, there are no exemptions for economic hardship or any other reason. The half-shekel tax is specified to be calculated from the "sanctuary shekel," or twenty gerahs, in distinction from other denominations of the shekel weight (a Mesopotamian shekel, for example, weighed 24 giru, the giru being the Akkadian analogy for the gerah). One gerah was a little over half a gram.[88] The tax would therefore be a little over 5 grams (roughly the weight of the 25¢ coin, the "quarter," in US currency, but in pure silver).[89] This amount of silver would in fact be a fairly heavy burden for the average yeoman peasant. Joseph was sold into slavery for twenty shekels (Gen. 37:28), the penalty for the accidental death of another man's slave is thirty shekels (Exod. 21:32), and Jeremiah bought a field for seventeen shekels (Jer. 32:9). Land and slaves were major expenses, purchases that many peasants in fact could never afford. As such, a half-shekel would be much more than small change.

It is important to recognize that this text does not command or even recommend a census; it is purely a concession. But whenever they do take a census, the poll tax was to be imposed in order to avoid the plague that would strike them because of their implied turn from being a simple covenant people toward being a nation with a centralized government. Practically speaking, this law would have the result of making a census extraordinarily unpopular, and that is probably the intended effect; that is, the tax is meant to discourage rulers from taking a census.

In discussing the purpose of this law, therefore, we must set aside two common interpretations that are plainly wrong. First, it was not, as Durham suggests, imposed for the upkeep of the sanctuary.[90] If that

88. Sarna, *Exodus*, 196.

89. It may have been slightly heavier than this, since there is evidence that the Israelite shekel was unusually heavy in comparison to the shekel of other nations. See Wells, "Exodus," 257–8.

90. Durham, *Exodus*, 402.

had been its purpose, it would have been commanded, not set in a conditional structure, and some kind of timeframe would have been given (for example, that the census and tax should take place every year or every seven years). On the other hand, against Sarna, it was not a one-time tax imposed to pay for the construction of the sanctuary.[91] Contributions for its construction were voluntary (35:21–29), and the language of 30:16 (עַל־עֲבֹדַת אֹהֶל), that it is for the "service of the sanctuary" indicates that if imposed, the tax went to the ordinary upkeep and expenses of the sanctuary, not to its construction. The actual import of this law, therefore, is the opposite of what it may first appear. It looks like a tax imposed by God on the nation for the purpose of maintaining the services at the temple. In fact, it is a discouragement to taking a census. The preferred means of getting material provision for the sanctuary, as described elsewhere in Exodus, is by voluntary contributions (25:2; 35:5). Therefore, the census tax is not a standard way of providing financial resources for the sanctuary. It was imposed to make restitution for the offense of conducting a census and serves to discourage such activity.

30:17–21. Nahum Sarna observes that the instructions regarding the bronze laver are not included among the construction texts for the Tent of Meeting, the altar, and the other furnishings because the laver was used only to prepare the priest for worship, not for worship itself. The laver played no role in the actual rituals of the shrine. Also, the laver was not used in the ordination of Aaron and his sons because that ceremony required the washing of their entire bodies; the laver was used only for washing the hands and feet.[92] In the daily activities of the priests, the hands and feet had to be regularly washed because the hands touched sacred objects and the feet trod the sacred ground in and around the tent. Curiously, the description of the vestments of the priests makes no provision for shoes or sandals. Does this mean that they went barefoot? On the analogy of Moses at the burning bush, this is certainly possible. At any rate, the laver is a provision for the priests, enabling them to keep their hands and feet clean and so to avoid defiling sacred things.

30:22–33. The "hin" (about one gallon) of olive oil was the base for making the anointing oil. Apart from its ritual purposes, ancient people used anointing oils as perfumes to make the body more fragrant, for

91. Sarna, *Exodus*, 195.
92. Ibid., 197.

treating injury and illness, for general massage, for managing the hair, and as a kind of liquid soap. Since the formula for making the sacred oil is here public knowledge, it was necessary to explicitly forbid the making of this particular blend for common usage. The formula described here does make use of expensive ingredients (cinnamon was probably imported from India or even China), but other than that is not extraordinary. As such, the special nature of the anointing oil is preserved by decreeing that it could be put to no other use. This blend was used for both people and things that were consecrated to holy service.

30:34–38. Incense was widely used in the temples of the ancient world in places as diverse as India, Mesopotamia, Egypt, Greece, and Rome. Hence, its use in the sanctuary of YHWH is not unique. Also, people may have burned it in their homes for the simple pleasure of its fragrance or as an insect repellent. As such, the incense used in the Tent of Meeting is made distinctive by adhering to a specific formula and by forbidding the use of this type of incense elsewhere. Houtman observes that ancient people relied heavily on the sense of smell, using it to distinguish healthy from unhealthy environments and even recognizing other people by their smell (Gen. 27:27). That being the case, it was important that YHWH's sanctuary had a fragrance that was wholesome, pleasant, and altogether distinctive. The odor of the unique incense was one of the things that marked it as the house of YHWH.[93]

31:1–11. The men chosen to superintend the work of making all the sacred objects were not priests, and not even Levites. Bezalel was of the tribe of Judah and Oholiab was of the tribe of Dan. In them, the Spirit of God would show itself in the extraordinary skill with which they would make the tent and its furnishings, as well as the vestments, and it was for that reason that they had the Spirit. Elsewhere, the Spirit was manifested in ecstatic prophesying (Num. 11:25–26; 24:2–9). Thus, there may be here something analogous to the New Testament concept of the gifts of the Spirit, whereby different people experience the filling of the Spirit, but it shows itself in different ways and for different purposes. In the broader context of this narrative, the main points are that God himself had provided the necessary people to do the work of making the tent and that his

93. Cornelis Houtman, "On the Function of the Holy Incense (Exodus XXX 34–8) and the Sacred Anointing Oil (Exodus XXX 22–33)," *VT* 42, no. 4 (1992): 458–65.

Spirit had sanctified those men, authorizing them for participation in such a holy work.

31:12–17. An admonition to keep the Sabbath here is quite unexpected; it is what we would expect to see in the Book of the Covenant (and indeed there is an admonition to observe Sabbath at 23:12). But why is there an extended and indeed stern warning about the Sabbath day here? A probable explanation is found in the fact that the exhortation begins with the contrastive, "But for all of that" (אַךְ; see translation note to 31:13b). This section is preceded by the full instructions for building the Tent of Meeting and its furnishings, and more narrowly, at 30:11—31:11, by instructions regarding various provisions to be made for the service at the sanctuary. The implied point is that the commands to build the sanctuary and to make provision for it do not supersede the command to observe the Sabbath. In short, despite everything that had to be done, construction work was not to be done on the Sabbath, and Israelites were not to violate Sabbath under the justification that their extra labor provided the income to help maintain the sanctuary. Behind this is the greater theological point that God was the one who provided for Israel and the sanctuary. Keeping Sabbath is a way of trusting God. We should note that Sabbath is not a special day of worship in the Old Testament analogous to the Lord's Day for the church. As such, the issue here is trust in God's provision, not setting aside a day for going to worship services.

31:18. As a bridge to chapter 32, the notice that YHWH gave Moses the two stone tablets prepares the way for 32:19, where Moses breaks the tablets. In this context, however, this speaks of a final provision of God: the stone tablets of the Decalogue, the heart of the Book of the Covenant, binding Israel to YHWH. It is this covenant that legitimates the entire Tent of Meeting complex.

Theological Summary of Key Points

1. The overarching topic in this section is purity. The poll tax, if a census is taken, is to go to the sanctuary, but the preferred method of providing for its financial needs is through tithes and offerings. But the point of the tax is to avoid the defilement and subsequent plague that taking a census would cause. The people are also to make the bronze laver, the means for the priests to wash their hands and feet and so remain ritually clean while officiating at the sanctuary.

They are also to provide for the regular supply of anointing oils and incense.

2. God provided Israel with skilled craftsmen who could oversee the work of construction, and he had, above all, given the covenant, the basis for the whole operation of the sanctuary. The people, in turn, should provide contributions for the construction and upkeep of the Tent of Meeting. In doing this, they must not violate the Sabbath but must trust God to provide for their needs. The point is that Israel must not defile itself by working on the Sabbath; doing this would nullify the worthiness of their contributions.

3. The priest's washing of hands and feet is symbolic of the need to keep one's deeds (hands) and one's walk (feet) pure before God. This is especially true for those who are in God's service, as the priests were.

4. The implied warning against taking a census was a reminder that Israel was to exist not as a "state" but as the tribes of YHWH. Ideally, YHWH alone should have been their king. There is ever a conflict between the kingdom of God and the kingdoms of this world, and the latter finds expression most clearly in the power of the state. A census, which is a step toward a centralized state, would inevitably weaken the ideal of Israel as a people whose only allegiance was to their God.

5. The covenant, symbolized by the tablets of the Law, was the foundation for Israel's ceremonial or "cultic" relationship to God. Apart from the covenant, the Tent of Meeting had no meaning. Thus, when Israel broke the covenant, the legitimacy of the sanctuary came to an end (so Ezek. 10, where the glory of YHWH abandons the Jerusalem temple). This is anticipated in the very next section, the episode of the golden calf.

PART VII

Sin And Restoration (32:1–40:38)

The final major division of Exodus describes Israel's great sin, the making of the golden calf, and its aftermath. This was a complete violation of the covenant that they had just ratified with YHWH. With the covenant terminated, YHWH is prepared to destroy Israel, or at least to abandon them. Were it not for Moses's intervention, Israel's story would have abruptly come to an end.

THE BESETTING SIN (32:1–8)

The golden calf episode, no less than the crossing of the *Yam Suph*, is an archetypal event of Exodus.[1] The one demonstrates YHWH's power to save Israel, and the other demonstrates Israel's proclivity toward apostasy in the one crucial area of idolatry. This episode is thus the paradigm for Israel's greatest failing, the sin that would dominate the nation until the exile.

Translation

32:1a And the people saw that Moses delayed coming down from the mountain,
32:1b and the people congregated around Aaron
32:1c and said to him,

1. The text was also very important in early Judaism. For histories of Jewish interpretation up through the talmudic period, see Karla R. Suomala, *Moses and God in Dialogue: Exodus 32–34 in Postbiblical Literature,* Studies in Biblical Literature 61 (New York: Peter Lang, 2004) and Pekka Lindqvist, *Sin at Sinai: Early Judaism Encounters Exodus 32* (Turku, Finland: Åbo Akademi University, 2008).

32:1d "Get up!
32:1e Make us gods[2] who will go before us!
32:1f Because this guy[3] Moses, the man who brought us up from the land of Egypt—we do not know what has happened to him."
32:2a And Aaron said to them,
32:2b "Yank[4] off the gold rings that are in the ears of your wives, your sons, and your daughters,
32:2c and bring [them] to me."
32:3a And all the people yanked[5] off the gold rings that were in their ears
32:3b and brought [them] to Aaron.
32:4a And he took [the gold] from their hand,
32:4b and he shaped it with a tool[6]
32:4c and made it into a calf made from poured metal.[7]

---

2. The word אֱלֹהִים most often has the singular meaning, "God," but the plural verb יֵלְכוּ indicates that the noun here is understood to be plural (so also the form אֵלֶּה אֱלֹהֶיךָ ["these are your gods"] in 32:4). Even so, we cannot be sure that the people understood themselves to be embracing a plurality of gods. After all, they use the term in reference to the single golden calf. Possibly the plural forms, like the calf itself, simply indicate that they adopted a pagan outlook on religion, where a single god can have a plurality of identities and many gods can be at times merged into one.
3. The word זֶה here implies contempt, as in the American idiom, "this guy."
4. The verb פרק plainly implies violence ("yank off" or "tear off"). It is not clear why Aaron used such language; perhaps it implies frustration both with the people and with Moses's absence.
5. This use of פרק (Hithpael) would seem to indicate the mindless enthusiasm with which the people went about pulling off their earrings.
6. The word חֶרֶט means "stylus" in Isa. 8:1, a meaning that is not appropriate here unless fine metalwork is meant. It is possible that it refers to some kind of metalworking tool, however. On the other hand, it could be an alternative form of חָרִיט, "sack," and here refer to a mold. It is impossible to be sure which is correct.
7. The noun מַסֵּכָה is probably from נסך (I), "to pour out," and is used to describe an object made of metal cast in a mold. Durham, *Exodus*, 415-6, takes it to be from נסך (II), "to weave," and takes it to mean "shaped sheathing," but this is not persuasive to me. Scholars speculate over whether the calf was a cast metal object all of gold or had a gold overlay on a wooden frame, as was common. In light of the fact that the text says nothing about the use of wood or any substratum, one may argue that the image was all of gold. But probably the gold was in fact a veneer over a wooden model. The mention of only the gold is perhaps for rhetorical purposes, to make the point that the people wanted an image that was beautiful and expensive—a treasured national idol. The gold of the donated rings did, after all, have

32:4d And they said,
32:4e "These are your gods, O Israel, who brought you up from the land of Egypt."
32:5a And Aaron saw [it][8]
32:5b and he built an altar before it.
32:5c And Aaron called out;
32:5d he said,[9]
32:5e "Tomorrow [shall be] a feast to YHWH!"
32:6a And they rose early the next day,
32:6b and they offered whole offerings
32:6c and presented peace offerings.
32:6d And the people sat down to eat and drink,
32:6e and they rose up to revel.[10]
32:7a And YHWH spoke to Moses:
32:7b "Go down![11]
32:7c For your people, whom you brought up from the land of Egypt, behave corruptly![12]
32:8a They quickly turned off from the way that I commanded them.
32:8b They made for themselves a calf made from poured metal,
32:8c and they worshiped it
32:8d and sacrificed to it
32:8e and said,
32:8f 'These are your gods, Israel, who brought you up from the land of Egypt!'"

Structure

The narrative of the making of the calf is in two parts, describing the actions of the people first and then the response of YHWH. This short

---

to be melted down before it could be used to gild the idol. Therefore, the use of נסך (I), "to pour out," does not decisively show that the image was of solid gold.

8. The *wayyiqtol* of ראה itself indicates a response to a prior situation (as in Gen. 1:4), but it also serves to mark the equivalent of a paragraph division (as in Gen. 6:5, where it is preceded by the Masoretic paragraph marker פ).
9. This is an epexegetical *wayyiqtol*.
10. The verb צחק is lit. "to laugh." It is here a bacchanalian, or wild and ecstatic, form of worship. Such religious celebration also characterized certain Egyptian feasts.
11. The word לֵךְ is here an auxiliary to רֵד and need not be thought of as a separate clause.
12. The *qatal* שִׁחֵת has a present meaning here.

text, however, is built around an entire series of actions or requests and the responses to them, and we should observe this pattern in full, as below.

- I. Israel Makes the Calf (32:1–6)
  - A. First Round of Events (32:1–4)
    1. Israel Makes a Request (32:1)
    2. Aaron Responds with a Request for Gold (32:2)
    3. Israel Responds by Giving Gold (32:3)
    4. Aaron Responds by Making an Idol (32:4abc)
    5. Israel Responds with a Cultic Chant (32:4de)
  - B. Second Round of Events (32:5–6)
    1. Aaron Observes the Calf, Makes an Altar, Calls for Worship (32:5)
    2. Israel Responds with Hedonistic Worship (32:6)
- II. YHWH Responds (32:7–8)

Commentary

32:1–4. The text does not tell us how long Moses had been gone, but apparently it was long enough that the people were ready to believe that they would never see him again. They naturally go to Aaron, a priest of the community and the designated leader in Moses's absence (Exod. 24:14). Their desire for an idol is based in a pagan sense that the image is reassurance of a divine presence; absent the image, the people are in dread that they have no supernatural protection. It is important to see that the making of the calf, while from one perspective an act of gross apostasy and rebellion, was from another perspective an act driven by a need for reassurance and even by a misguided piety. Even so, the desire for the image expresses itself with words of contempt ("this guy Moses") and has as its outcome a full-fledged pagan rite of Dionysian revelry. Aaron responds to their request by asking for earrings. As coinage did not yet exist, earrings were a convenient way for the average person to carry a small quantity of gold. We are told nothing of what motivated Aaron to yield to their request; he simply did what they asked and made them a god in the form of a calf.

Bovine deities are very common in both Egyptian and Canaanite religion. In the former, the Apis bull was the earthly manifestation of the god Ptah (one pair of Egyptian figurines, from the 26th dynasty, depicts a ruler kneeling before a bull[13]), and the cow was the zoomorphic representation of the fertility goddess Hathor. In the latter, the

13. A photograph can be found in Shaw and Nicholson, *Dictionary*, 35.

senior Canaanite god El was regularly called a "bull." Thus, the choice of a bull image is not surprising. The image is sometimes taken to be indicative of a fertility cult, but this is not necessarily correct. It may have been more martial in nature.[14] In the Old Testament, although YHWH is often metaphorically associated with various animals (e.g., the eagle [Exod. 19:4], the lion [Hos. 13:7]), he is never associated with the bull in any except illicit shrines. The bull image, therefore, is quintessentially pagan, and it results in the cultic cry, "These are your gods, O Israel, who brought you up from the land of Egypt!"

32:5–6. In the second round of events, Aaron looks at the now completed bull idol and decides it needs to be consecrated with an altar, sacrifices, and a sacred assembly. Again, we are told nothing of his motivations behind his actions, and it is best not to speculate beyond the fact that he obviously believed that a sacred object needed a ceremony of consecration. Aaron does refer to the consecration ceremony as a sacrifice to YHWH, showing that in his mind the making of the idol did not imply turning from YHWH. This did not justify the making of the idol, however, and it did nothing to mitigate the evil progression of events. This ceremony of consecration had certain superficial similarities to the ritual for the consecration of priests and the Tent of Meeting described above (for example, both involved whole offerings; see 29:18, 25). But the outcome was radically different. In contrast to the solemnity and focus on purity at the consecration of the Tent of Meeting, the consecration of the bull idol degenerated into revelry. The precise nature of the revelry is not described, and we should not make it out to be as bad as possible, imagining that the whole nation was in orgiastic hysteria, with everyone engaging in open sex and drunkenness. The text does not say that, although plainly it was bad enough (32:25). The critical point, however, is not in how bad the revelry was, but in the mere fact that there was idol worship.

32:7–8. In his response to the situation, YHWH portrays this purely as an act of apostasy and disobedience. The issues of why the idol was made, or of who said or did what, are irrelevant. In describing their corrupt behavior, however, God does not dwell upon or even mention the revelry of their worship. Instead, he says that they made, sacrificed

14. This is the position of J. Gerald Janzen, "The Character of the Calf and its Cult in Exodus 32," *CBQ* 52, no. 4 (1990): 597–607. But the distinction between a martial god and a fertility god is probably not to be too strongly drawn. A single god could have characteristics of both.

to, and worshipped an image. The idolatry itself is the great sin. One curious thing about God's speech is that he normally speaks of himself in terms like, "I am YHWH who brought you out of the land of Egypt" (Exod. 3:10, 17; 6:6; 12:17; 20:2; etc.). Here, talking to Moses, he says, "For your people, whom *you* brought up from the land of Egypt, behave corruptly!" (emphasis added). Apart from any humorous associations we might make (comparing this to the angry husband who says to his wife, "Look what your son did!"), we should understand that the language is important. First, like the words of the angry husband, these words convey YHWH's exasperation. Second, they imply that Moses's leadership is urgently needed, and indeed that Israel is so hopelessly corrupt that Moses can scarcely leave them alone without their falling into some form of malfeasance. Finally, this language speaks of a bond between Moses and Israel. That bond will be tested to its fullest in the next episode, when Moses must intercede for Israel before an angry God.

Theological Summary of Key Points

1. We noted above that the making of the calf proceeded from a desire for reassurance of divine presence and protection. Rarely do people fall into apostasy or superstition simply because they have a perverse desire to defy God. Christians may similarly fill their homes or churches with icons out of a desire for a tangible sign of a spiritual presence. But the fact that the deed is not driven by the most wicked of motives does not lessen the seriousness of either the sin or its result.

2. When the people succumbed to the desire for an idol, it was not long until they were fully paganized, making their shrill cultic cry ("These are your gods, O Israel, who brought you up from the land of Egypt") and engaging in a mindless revelry of worship. It is difficult for anyone to hold the line at a little idolatry; it comes to dominate one's entire religious life. The sequence of requests and responses that make up vv. 1–6 illustrate the progress towards this paganism. Simply put, one thing leads to another.

3. We should also note that Israel's cultic cry undermined the whole point of the exodus; its purpose was to bring glory to YHWH who redeemed them. But the cry attributes the exodus to the bull-god and so robs YHWH of his due honor. This, too, is always the outcome of idol usage in worship.

4. At the same time, the bull-god is presented by Aaron, and no doubt accepted by the people, as a legitimate representation of YHWH (32:5e).

This is consistent with Israelite idolatry throughout their history; they never thought of themselves as apostates, but always believed that their images were acceptable as signs of homage to YHWH. They believed that when they merged YHWH and Baal it was a permissible syncretism and not a preference of Baal over YHWH. Apostasy rarely presents itself as apostasy. In our day, similarly, the various ways that the church strays from simple fidelity to the gospel never advertises itself as a turning aside from the faith.

5. Many interpreters have noticed the parallel between the golden calf episode and the paradigmatic sin of Jeroboam the son of Nebat, who made the two calf shrines at Dan and Bethel (1 Kgs. 16:26; 21:22; 2 Kgs. 10:29; etc.). This is certainly valid, but more broadly the episode points to the fact that idolatry became the particular and "besetting" sin for Israel. Throughout the rest of the history of Israel and in all of the preaching of the prophets, right up to the time of the exile, this would be the one sin above all others that dominated Israel and constituted its most consistent manner of breaking the covenant with YHWH. Individuals, families, and entire nations have characteristic flaws that consistently drag them down. For Israel, this flaw was idol worship. For us, whether as individuals or as communities, the besetting sin may be something different. But we will not be able to confront it if we do not identify it.

6. The sequence of requests and responses illustrates how people can drag one another downward into ruin. The people encouraged Aaron to make "gods" for them, and he in turn encouraged them to participate in the act by making contributions of gold. Aaron built the altar and called for a ceremony to consecrate the bull image, and the people responded by turning the ceremony into a full pagan revel.

7. People need consistent and reliable leadership to keep them from going in the wrong direction. Whatever Aaron's intentions were, he was a weak leader, unable to resist a popular impulse toward evil. The leadership belonged to Moses because he was, in fact, the only person who could lead them effectively.

THE INTERCESSOR (32:9–35)

Although they do not realize it, the very existence of the Israelites now hangs in the balance. Moses is a true intercessor, standing between YHWH and Israel. He first has the task of assuaging YHWH's anger, so that he doesn't destroy the nation. After that, he must restore order to

Israel—and especially do away with their idol and the worship around it—so that YHWH is not provoked further.

Translation

32:9a And YHWH said to Moses,
32:9b "I have seen this people
32:9c and, face it,[15] this is a stiff-necked people.
32:10a And now let me alone
32:10b so that my anger can burn against them
32:10c and I can destroy them,
32:10d and I will make a great nation from you."
32:11a And Moses assuaged the anger[16] of YHWH his God:
32:11b he said,[17]
32:11c "Why, YHWH, does your anger burn against your people, whom you brought out from the land of Egypt with great power and with a strong hand?
32:12a Why should the Egyptians say,
32:12b 'With evil [intent] he brought them out to kill them in the mountains and to eliminate them from the face of the earth'?
32:12c Turn away from your furious anger
32:12d and relent about the calamity in store for your people!
32:13a Remember your servants Abraham, Isaac, and Israel, to whom you swore by yourself, and to whom you said,
32:13b 'I will multiply your descendants as the stars of the heavens,
32:13c and all this land—as I said[18]—I will give to your descendants,
32:13d and they shall inherit [it] forever.'"
32:14 And YHWH relented about the calamity that he spoke of inflicting on his people.
32:15a And Moses turned
32:15b and went down from the mountain with the two tablets of the

15. The particle וְהִנֵּה here calls on Moses to face a painful truth, and that truth will be the basis for YHWH's suggestion that the whole nation be annihilated.

16. The clause וַיְחַל מֹשֶׁה אֶת־פְּנֵי יְהוָה is lit. "And Moses weakened the face of YHWH." The idea is that when one weakens or softens a stern, unyielding face, one is getting that person to be more placable and forgiving.

17. This is an epexegetical *wayyiqtol*, and in fact all of 32:11bc–14 is an exposition of 32:11a. That is, 32:11a states that Moses turned aside God's anger, and what follows tells how he did it.

18. Taking אֲשֶׁר אָמַרְתִּי to be equivalent to כַּאֲשֶׁר אָמַרְתִּי.

testimony in his hand, tablets that were written on both sides, written on this side and that.
32:16a The tablets were God's work,
32:16b and the writing was God's writing engraved on the tablets.
32:17a And Joshua heard the sound of the people's shouting,
32:17b and he said to Moses,
32:17c "It sounds like a war in the camp."
32:18a And he said,
32:18b "There is no sound of the paean over victory;
32:18c there is no sound of desperate war cries of men facing defeat.
32:18d But I hear a sound of [mindless] ululating."[19]
32:19a And it came about,

---

19. The root ענה (IV) in the Qal means to "cry out" or "sing." It can refer to a celebratory victory song (famously at 1 Sam. 18:7 and parallels; also Jer. 51:14). It is also used for a song of praise to God, as at Exod. 15:21 (the Song of the Sea, celebrating Egypt's defeat); Ps. 147:7; 119:172; and Ezra 3:11. Isaiah 13:22 uses it for the yapping of hyenas. It occurs in the Piel here and at Isa. 27:2 (where it is used like the Qal) and in the Ps. 88 superscript (where it is part of an obscure tune title). In general, the term in both the Qal and Piel connotes a celebratory song, often used after a victory or some other achievement. From this, the phrase קוֹל עֲנוֹת גְּבוּרָה in 32:18b to refer to a victory song is perfectly intelligible. However, the phrase קוֹל עֲנוֹת חֲלוּשָׁה in 32:18c is peculiar. The verb ענה (IV) indicates excited singing or shouting, and it is generally celebratory. This phrase is often taken to be a song of lament by the defeated, but I do not think that ענה would be used with such a meaning. If it were a lament over defeat, one would normally use a verb such as ספד ("lament"). A more literal translation of קוֹל עֲנוֹת חֲלוּשָׁה would be "sound of singing/response of weakness." It is therefore not the mourning of the defeated but the desperate war cries of men facing defeat. But the Piel usage of קוֹל עַנּוֹת at Exod. 32:18d is even more obscure. It has no noun object, unlike the prior two lines. Various emendations have been proposed (see ענה [IV], *HALOT*, 2.854), none of them being particularly compelling. It is of course possible that some word has dropped out after קוֹל עַנּוֹת, but most suggestions are purely speculative and thus of no value. The LXX rendition of this phrase, *φωνὴν ἐξαρχόντων οἴνου* ("the sound of those who chant of wine"), is possible but is probably an interpretive expansion and not based on a different *Vorlage*. But the Piel of a root can describe an action that is repeated over and over and when used in this manner need not have an explicit direct object (such as the Piel of הלך). That is probably the idea of קוֹל עַנּוֹת here. It is the hyper-excited chanting of a song or ditty, probably with a great deal of repetition and little intelligible content. I have tried to capture this notion of mindless repetition with "ululating," and this may be precisely what was involved.

32:19b as Moses came near the camp,
32:19c that he saw the calf and [the] dancing.
32:19d And Moses's anger burned,
32:19e and he cast the tablets from his hands
32:19f and shattered them at the foot of the mountain,
32:20a and he took the calf that they had made
32:20b and he burned [it] with fire.
32:20c And he ground [everything] to dust,[20]
32:20d and he scattered [the dust] over the surface of the water,
32:20e and he made the Israelites drink.
32:21a And Moses said to Aaron,
32:21b "What did this people do to you,
32:21c that you have brought a great sin upon them?"
32:22a And Aaron said,
32:22b "May my lord's anger not burn!
32:22c You know the people,
32:22d that they are prone to evil.
32:23a And they said to me,
32:23b 'Make for us gods who will go before us;
32:23c for this guy Moses, the man who brought us up from the land of Egypt, we do not know what has become of him.'
32:24a And I said to them,
32:24b 'Whoever has any gold, let them yank it off.'
32:24c And they gave [it] to me,
32:24d and I threw it into the fire,
32:24e and this calf came out."
32:25a And Moses saw that the people were out of control—

It was not "singing" in the sense of harmonious melody-making, but was pagan, ecstatic, and ultimately monotonous.

20. The Hebrew does not provide a direct object for the verb טחן ("grind"). That is, it does not specify whether Moses ground up just the calf or both the calf and the tablets of the Law. Translators assume that because the calf is mentioned in the nearer clause, it must be the direct object. However, it is possible to take 32:19d–20b as an account of the destruction of the sacred objects, and then take 32:20cde to be a specific ritual of a judicial punishment applied to the people some time later that day. If this is the intent, then the calf is not the only direct object of the verb. By supplying "everything" as the object of טחן, I have tried to be as ambiguous as the Hebrew, since it could refer to just the calf, or to the calf and the tablets.

32:25b for Aaron had let them get out of control, to the point of being a laughingstock[21] among their enemies—

32:26a and Moses stood in the gate of the camp.

32:26b And he said,

32:26c "Anyone for YHWH, to me!"

32:26d And all the Levites collected about him.

32:27a And he said to them,

32:27b "Thus says YHWH, the God of Israel,

32:27c 'Every man, set his sword by his thigh,

32:27d and make two sweeps[22] across the camp from gate to gate,

32:27e and kill every man his brother, and every man his friend, and every man his neighbor.'"

32:28a And the Levites did as Moses said,

32:28b and about three thousand men from the people fell that day.

32:29a And Moses said,

32:29b "Dedicate yourselves today to YHWH—for every man has been against his son and against his brother—to give yourselves a blessing today."

32:30a And it came about on the next day

32:30b that Moses said to the people,

32:30c "You have committed a great sin.

32:30d And now I shall go up to YHWH.

32:30e Perhaps I can make atonement for your sin."

32:31a And Moses returned to YHWH,

32:31b And he said,

32:31c "Alas! This people has committed a great sin!

32:31d They made[23] a god of gold for themselves!

32:32a And now, if you would only forgive their sin—

32:32b but if it is not to be,

---

21. The word שִׁמְצָה is *hapax legomenon*, and its meaning is thus not certain. It is generally thought to be related to שֶׁמֶץ (a "whisper"), found in Job 4:12; 26:14. Janzen, "Character," 602-3, argues that שִׁמְצָה refers to whispers of fear among the nations; Israel's intent is that they should tremble when they hear that Israel is coming with a great bull-god at their head. But even if one follows Janzen in his supposition that the bull cult concerned a martial rather than a fertility god, this interpretation of שִׁמְצָה is not persuasive. It more likely refers to derisive whispering.

22. Lit. "go across and return" (עִבְרוּ וָשׁוּבוּ). In this case, עבר means to make a military-style sweep across the camp, and שׁוּב means to repeat an action. Thus, they were to sweep through the camp twice, going out once and coming back once.

23. An epexegetical *wayyiqtol*.

32:32c erase me from your book that you have written!"
32:33a And YHWH said to Moses,
32:33b "I will erase from my book whoever sinned against me.
32:34a But now go,
32:34b lead the people where I told you.
32:34c Yes, my angel will go before you,
32:34d but on my day of giving punishment, I will punish them for their sin."
32:35a And YHWH struck the people [with plague][24]
32:35b because they made the calf—the one that Aaron made.

Structure

Two moments of intercession by Moses for Israel bracket this text. Between these, Moses visited the camp to try to restore discipline and so turn aside the divine fury. In the camp, he confronted the people's apostasy and went about restoring order. There are five different episodes involving Moses's activity in to the camp, as described below.

I. Moses's First Intercession (32:9–14)
II. Moses in the Camp (32:15–29)
  A. Moses Returns to Camp (32:15–19c)
  B. Moses Destroys the Tablets and the Calf (32:19d–20b)
  C. Moses Grinds Up the Tablets and Makes the People Drink (32:20cde)
  D. Moses Confronts Aaron (32:21–24)
  E. Moses Gets the People Under Control (32:25–29)
III. Moses's Second Intercession (32:30–35)

Commentary

32:9–14. In theory, God could have destroyed Israel and still been faithful to his covenants. Israel had already violated the Sinai covenant and so God was under no obligation to keep them as his people, and wiping out the nation of Israel would not of itself violate God's oath to Abraham (Gen. 12:1–3). Moses was, after all, a descendent of Abraham, and a new nation raised up from Moses would also be of the line of Abraham, Isaac, and Jacob. In telling Moses to step aside, God made it clear that Moses was the only thing standing between Israel and destruction. But Moses accepted this responsibility and became the great intercessor for the people. He argued along several lines. First, Moses reminded YHWH (against 32:7) that it was not Moses

24. Plague is implied in the verb נגף when God is the subject.

but YHWH who brought Israel out of Egypt. This whole program of redeeming Israel from Egypt was YHWH's and it was for the sake of YHWH's greater purposes; YHWH would undercut his own designs if he abandoned Israel now (3:11c). Second, destroying Israel now would do the opposite of God's stated purpose of gaining glory among the nations through the great deliverance of Israel. Instead, the name of YHWH would be besmirched as evil (contrast 32:12b with 7:5 and 14:18). Third, Moses simply appealed for mercy (32:12cd). Fourth, citing Gen. 26:4, Moses, in effect, argued that God would be violating the spirit and intent (if not the letter) of his promises to the patriarchs by killing the Israelites now, even if he did raise up a generation later through Moses. In short, Moses appealed to God's greater plans, to God's glory, to God's compassion, and to God's promises. He did not make any excuses for the Israelites, and he did not suggest that their sin did not merit God's severest punishment. Moses was successful, and "YHWH relented."

32:15–19c. The description of the two tablets is meant to convey what treasures they were, being texts written by God himself. This, in turn, sets the stage for the breaking of the tablets, a ritual act that demonstrated how heinous Israel's violation of the covenant was. As Moses and Joshua approached the camp, they heard the cultic shouting of the people; it was a frenzied speech something like battle cries. Again, we should not focus on the analogy of the wild party with drunken revelry and orgies (although there could have been some of that, too). The noise, possibly like ululation, was primarily a cultic celebration of their new god. Whatever sexual immorality that might have taken place, the main point of the narrative is not sexual misconduct (and in fact such behavior is not explicitly mentioned). The real issue is their thoroughgoing paganism.

32:19d–20b. Moses arrived in the camp. The first action that the text describes is his destruction of the two religious objects. The first was the most genuinely sacred object of all, the tablets of the covenant. The second was a pseudo-sacred object: the golden calf. Whatever the actual sequence of events was (this issue is discussed below), giving first place to the breaking of the tablets and the burning of the calf vividly makes the point that the covenant is broken and that the idol is a blasphemy. The text describes the tablets in some detail, noting that they had been engraved by YHWH himself and that they had inscriptions on both sides (many stone or clay tablets from the ancient world would be engraved on one side only, since the tablet was likely to be ruined or broken if one tried to engrave both sides). There were two copies, which probably means that symbolically one was for God and the other for Israel (it was a covenant, and thus analogous to a contract or a treaty, in which both parties get a copy). For all these reasons, and not least because they were the fundamental terms of the covenant, these tablets were inexpressibly valuable. And yet Moses cast them to the ground, breaking them. While Moses was no doubt angry (32:19d), one should not take the breaking of the tablets as a rash act, done quickly in fury and soon regretted. Rather, this was a symbolic statement that Israel had so thoroughly violated the covenant—in effect, before the ink on the contract was even dry—that they had rendered the covenant void. Moses, seeing for himself the apostasy of the people, realized the gravity of the situation and communicated it in the speech-act of breaking the covenant documents.

The burning of the calf obviously communicated that it was pagan and worthy of destruction. No significance attached to it by virtue of the offerings made in order to consecrate it could change the fact that it was a religious lie. One may wonder how an object of gold could burn. It plainly had parts that could burn, probably including a wooden base and wooden core over which the golden sheathing was fashioned.

32:20cde. In the translation above, I have noted the possibility that the destruction of the tablets and the calf are presented as one act and that the grinding of the two objects (not just the calf) was a second, separate act. Readers have long been perplexed that Moses first burned up the calf and then ground it up. Presumably, if the core of the calf was made of wood, then there would be almost nothing left to grind up after it had been consumed in a fire. One does not normally speak of "grinding" ashes. On the other hand, if the calf was solid gold, that would be very difficult to grind to a fine powder (as the text states) without an enormous amount of time and labor, not to mention the necessary tools for grinding metal. If it, in fact, was solid gold and was first burned and then ground to dust, then apparently it was partially melted so as to disfigure it, and then the gold was ground up. But the problem of grinding a metal object to dust still remains.

Loewenstamm resolved the difficulty by pointing to a Ugaritic mythological text in which the goddess Anat burned the god Mot in fire, ground him up, spread him over a field, and then allowed the birds to eat his flesh. Obviously these acts could not all be carried out in such a sequence; there would have been nothing left for the birds to eat. But this is hyperbole for a total destruction; it is not to be taken literally, and Loewenstamm suggests that the burning, grinding, and drinking of the calf-dust is meant in the same way.[25] A significant difference, however, is that the Ugaritic text takes place in a mythological realm where such logical inconsistencies are commonplace; the golden calf narrative concerns the real world and physical objects. As such, one expects the narrative to be coherent. At the same time, it is possible that the narrative has a bit of hyperbole, as described below.

David Frankel argues that it was the tablets and not the calf that was ground up.[26] Since the tablets were of stone, and since they were broken and not burnt up, it is easy to comprehend how they could have been smashed into small pieces, fragments, and dust. More significantly, drinking water with the dust of the broken commandments is consonant with what we see elsewhere in Torah. In the Sotah, the ritual for testing a woman charged with adultery, the accused was required to drink holy water with dust from the floor of the Tent of Meeting mixed in (Num. 5:17). In both cases, the dust from a sacred object (the tablets, or the Tent of Meeting floor) is used in the ritual. The two examples are not exactly alike; the Sotah is meant to determine a woman's guilt, and it is not clear that this was the point of what Moses did (although it is possible that the process was a means of separating ringleaders and committed pagans from the rest of the people). At the least, forcing the Israelites to drink water into which the dust of the broken covenant had been poured was a way of making them confront what they had done. More significantly, it anticipates an ideal that will be developed later in the prophets, that idolatrous Israel is the equivalent of an adulterous wife, a woman who breaks her covenant with her husband (Ezek. 16; 23; Hos. 1–3).

A difficulty with this view, however, is that Deut. 9:21 expressly speaks of Moses grinding up the calf ("I took the calf that you had made and burned it with fire and crushed it with a thorough pulverizing, until it was ground to dust, and I cast its dust into the stream that ran down from the hill country"). It is important to note that the Deuteronomy account appears to arrange events for rhetorical purposes, not adhering to strict chronology when there is reason to organize a narrative differently. Thus, the sequence of events in Deuteronomy implies that Moses

25. Samuel E. Loewenstamm, "The Making and Destruction of the Golden Calf," *Bib* 48 (1967): 481–90; and Loewenstamm, "The Making and Destruction of the Golden Calf: A Rejoinder," *Bib* 56 (1975): 330–43.

26. David Frankel, "The Destruction of the Golden Calf: A New Solution," *VT* 44, no. 3 (1994): 330–9. Frankel also develops the idea that the ritual has a parallel in the Sotah (pp. 335-7). I do not agree with his view that 32:20ab is an interpolation (pp. 337-9); in my opinion, this is unnecessary.

first broke the tablets (9:17), then fasted for forty days before YHWH while interceding for Israel and Aaron (9:18–20), and then burned the calf (9:21). The Exodus sequence is that Moses first entered the camp and broke the tablets (32:19), then burned the calf, then had the people drink the water with dust sprinkled on it (32:20), then confronted Aaron (32:21–24), then restored order in the camp with the aid of the Levites (32:25–29), and then, on the next day, made intercession before YHWH (32:30–34). This period of intercession (32:35—34:27) lasted for forty days (34:28), but it came only after Moses had destroyed the calf and restored order to the camp. Of the two versions, the Exodus sequence is far more likely. It is impossible to imagine that Moses would leave the calf idol intact for forty days in the middle of the Israelite camp while he interceded with YHWH. The Deuteronomy sequence makes YHWH's anger and Moses's intercession more prominent by moving it forward in the retelling of events, but this is done for rhetorical purposes, not in order to provide a strict chronology. Even the Exodus version, however, may not be purely chronological. For example, it is reasonable to suppose that Moses restored order to the camp before he lined up the whole nation for the drinking of the water.

At the same time, both Exodus and Deuteronomy stress that the calf was finely ground. Thus, even if the tablets were also ground up, there is focus in both narratives on the grinding of the calf. The reason is not difficult to fathom. Just as Israel's making of the calf is the paradigm example of Israel's besetting tendency toward idolatry, so Moses's thorough pulverization of the calf is a paradigm for how the Israelites ought to deal with idols: they should burn them, break them apart, grind them to pieces, and trample them into the dust (Exod. 34:13; Deut. 7:5; 12:3). It is in this sense that the account of how Moses burned, ground, smashed, and pulverized the golden calf and then dumped its remains into a stream (as described in Deut. 9:21) may be slightly hyperbolic. That is, Moses is presented as doing everything to the golden calf that Israel should do to all idols in general, but this does not mean that they needed to do all of these things to every idol. For example, a stone idol that had been thoroughly broken apart did not also need to be burned and ground up, and a wooden idol that was burned to ashes did not also need to be smashed.

It is important to note that, although Deut. 9:21 is extravagant in its description of Moses's obliteration of the idol, it says nothing about having the Israelites drink the water into which the dust was placed. Indeed, if one were to read only the Deuteronomy account, one would assume that the ashes were dumped into a mountain stream as a way of washing them away forever. This is plainly the implication of casting its dust into the "stream that ran down from the hill country." The Deuteronomy verse portrays what Exodus simply calls "the water" as a mountain stream that would carry the very dust of the calf into oblivion. This is consistent with the overall message of Deuteronomy: idols are to be obliterated.

In Exod. 32:20, however, Moses "scattered [the dust] on the surface of the water and made the Israelites drink." This is parallel to the Sotah ritual as described by Frankel, and it suggests that the water that they drank had the dust of the two tablets in it. The ritual would have both demonstrated their violation of the covenant and suggested the analogy of idolatrous Israel to an adulterous wife.

Both of the Pentateuchal interpretations are valid: Israel is the guilty covenant-breaker (Exodus) and Moses's actions are the paradigm for what is to be done to idols (Deuteronomy). But can these two presentations be reconciled?

My own reconstruction of events—admittedly a hypothetical one—is as follows: First, Moses arrived at the scene and confronted Aaron in order to get the facts about what was happening. Then he restored order with the aid of the loyal Levites. It is hard to imagine Moses's conducting the water ritual while the people were still out of control or while the Levites were sweeping through the camp killing people. This further supports the idea that 32:19d–20b should be separated from 32:20cde and regarded as a distinct episode. At some point in this sequence Moses broke the tablets and destroyed the calf. Both of these acts should be regarded as carried out deliberately and even ritualistically, not as the acts of an enraged Moses flailing away at everything around him. Breaking the tablets showed Israel that the covenant was broken; destroying the idol showed how idols ought to be treated. Since the idol burned, it is likely that it was wooden with a golden sheathing overlaying it. Pulverizing the ashes that remained would not require true grinding, but it is called a "grinding" to make the point that every idol should be thoroughly ruined. The tablets of stone were subjected to a normal crushing and grinding, and everything was cast in to a stream that ran through the camp. I have no idea how fast the stream was running, and in any case that is not significant. As a stream, it carried away the remains of the idol; as a body of water, it served the purposes of the drinking ritual. Whether the waters literally carried away the dust of the idol or whether every person literally ingested rubble from the tablets is not the point. The acts were rituals, and it is the symbolism that mattered.

As an aside, one notices that there was a stream of water in the camp, indicating that Mt. Sinai was not in a barren, dry wilderness.

This further demonstrates that it was not in the southern Sinai Peninsula.

32:21–24. When confronted by Moses, Aaron attempted to deflect blame from himself and onto the people. Even so, what he said was fundamentally correct (although overly self-exonerating) until 32:24de, where he makes the ludicrous claim that he simply tossed gold into the fire and the calf popped out. Aaron is left looking pathetic. Even so, notwithstanding his central role in the affair, he was not singled out for punishment. Perhaps his humiliation was punishment enough.

32:25–29. Verse 25 indicates that Moses was afraid that Israel would become an object of derision and scorn to its enemies. The concern was not over the nation being caught in embarrassing behavior but over its being viewed as militarily impotent. Israel would not be a laughingstock to their enemies because they were involved in the worship of the bull, even if that worship involved orgiastic behavior. Such activity was not unusual in the ancient world, where pagan worship was universal and was often frenetic. Rather, Israel would be a laughingstock because they had lost all order and control. They had degenerated quickly into a mob, and no nation fears an army made up of an undisciplined, leaderless mob.

Having interceded for Israel, Moses here seems very vindictive. Sending out armed men to sweep through the camp to kill people apparently at random was, to say the least, severe. But it is important to see that this was not an act of punishment; their only punishment from Moses was their having to drink the water with the dust in it (YHWH punished them with a plague; 32:35). The sweep through the camp was done because the people were out of control, being wholly caught up in the frenzy of ecstatic celebration. It is analogous to using severe force to stop a riot. The Levites were to make two sweeps through the camp not in order to kill as many as possible but because that is what was required to regain full control of the situation. The command that everyone should kill his brother, friend or neighbor does not mean that they should kill everyone in the camp; it means that they should not spare anyone out of kinship or friendship. The presence of the Levite volunteers is evidence that not everyone got swept up in the worship of the bull.

32:30–35. Having seen how bad the idolatrous worship was in Israel, Moses knew that he had to go back and intercede for Israel yet again. Here we see the true heart of Moses: his desire to save the people was so great that he offered his own life, telling God that he was not willing to live longer (much less raise up a new people) if God would not forgive Israel. And Moses was successful. God told Moses that he would continue to lead Israel by his "angel." God still punished Israel with a plague because the nation was still full of stubborn and apostate people, as subsequent events would show. Similarly, when YHWH said, "I will erase from my book whoever sinned against me," the point was not that he was unwilling to forgive, but that he knew those in Israel who were his own and those who were not, and he would deal with them individually in the course of time. Nevertheless, the episode ended with YHWH, by the plague, showing Israel how close they came to complete annihilation. The plague also served to bring the Israelites to their senses, with the result that they were much more remorseful in the next chapter.

Theological Summary of Key Points

1. We have noted that Moses appealed to God's greater plans, to his glory, to his compassion, and to his promises. In other words, Moses said that God should forgive Israel because he is merciful and because this is consistent with his larger purposes. Moses did not dispute the fact that, by the letter of the covenant, God was within his rights to destroy Israel. For us, forgiveness depends on God's completed program for humanity in Christ, and also upon his basic compassion and faithfulness. We never seek forgiveness on the grounds of our worthiness or importance, or on the grounds that our sins are excusable.

2. The matter of God changing his mind raises questions of importance. Did God not foreknow that he would not destroy Israel? If so, was he pretending to be angry and at the point of killing all the people? To these questions, the answers have to be that God did indeed foreknow that he would not here destroy Israel, but also that God's threat was not a pretense. It is not even correct to speak of God's anger as "condescension," as if God were not really enraged enough to destroy Israel but only acted as he did in order to communicate anger. In other words, he showed anger in a manner that people would understand, but he did not really "feel" such great anger or intend to act upon it. This is not an honest reading of the text. To the contrary, the threat must be taken as real and serious. If Moses had not interceded, God really would have killed them all. This seems paradoxical, and indeed it is. It derives from the fact that being human, we cannot possibly understand the mind of God or know what it is like to be omniscient.[27] But the paradox

27. Some attempt to resolve exegetically the problems posed by this passage by trying to explain God's intent (e.g., Jonathan Master, "Exodus 32 as an

this text presents us with is the paradox that Christians confront every time they pray: they believe that God knows all (including what he is going to do in the future), but they pray anyway. Arguably, all prayer could be a waste of time since God already knows both what he will do and the content of our prayers. But in fact we do pray, and we do so with the conviction that our prayers matter and that they actually move God to do things he otherwise would not have done. The doctrine of divine omniscience and the conviction that prayer moves God are equally true.

3. This episode also raises questions about the compassion of God. Is Moses more merciful than God? How is it that a human must dissuade God from destroying an entire people? But this only raises another paradox that Christians already instinctively accept. God is compassionate, and yet God is wrathful toward sin and sinners. God is patient, and yet he is also moved to show patience toward a person when others intercede. The fact that God responds to our intercession does not make us more compassionate than God. But it does imply that we have a great gift and responsibility.

4. One might argue that intercession is in one sense unnecessary since God is already going to behave compassionately, but that God wants us to make intercession so that we can learn to be compassionate by the very act of praying for others. But this cannot be the whole reason for praying for people. Although interceding for others, especially for our enemies, does train us in compassion (Matt. 5:44), we must also affirm that our intercession does something good for the people for whom we pray. We pray for them because we believe God will respond by helping them and not just because the act of praying is good for us. Intercession does involve actually moving God to be more forbearing or gracious toward others. Jesus is our great high priest who intercedes for us, and he is well beyond the point of being trained in righteousness. Yet he still intercedes, because we need it. In similar fashion, we should pray for others because they need it.

Argument for Traditional Theism," *JETS* 45, no. 2 (2002): 585–98, arguing that God was inviting Moses to intercede). While I appreciate the desire of such efforts (directed at combatting errors such as "open theism"), I do not find the arguments persuasive or helpful. It is better, I think, simply to take the text at face value while also adhering to biblical teaching on the omniscience of God, and then to understand that we cannot and need not explain the mind of God.

5. Whatever difficulties we may have with the notion that God changed his mind, we should not miss the high status to which the text elevates Moses, the man who loved Israel so much that he offered his life for the nation. By his fearless intercession, he saved Israel. He is a forerunner of Christ and a model for us.

6. Moses's private intercession with God is also analogous to Christ's heavenly intercession in that the people of Israel did not even know it was happening or that they needed it. So also, our survival depends on Christ's intercession, even when we are wholly unaware of it.

7. Israel was the people of the covenant, but when they broke that covenant, their status as the chosen people became meaningless, as indicated by Moses's breaking of the tablets of the Law. Paul points out that one can be of Israel in the flesh but not in the heart (Rom. 2:28). Similarly, our claim to be people of the new covenant is vacuous if we live in disobedience. As James said, "Faith without works is dead" (Jas. 2:26).

8. If my interpretation of the breaking of the tablets and the burning of the calf is correct, Moses ritually demonstrated to Israel two fundamental facts about idol worship. First, it is the primary and most thorough offense against the covenant that Israel can commit. All sin is sin, but when Israel worships idols, it smashes the covenant. By idolatry, the covenant becomes as meaningless as a marriage vow after one spouse has committed adultery. Second, Moses demonstrated what Israel ought to do to idols. For us who are Christian, the essential lesson is that the single most important issue is our loyalty to Christ. All else is secondary, and everything that causes us to stumble in this regard should be cast away, even if it is our own right eye (Mark 9:47).

REPENTANCE AND MERCY (33:1—34:9)

Although YHWH has forgiven Israel and will not destroy them, he announces that he cannot go with them, lest he destroy them on the way. This provokes repentance in the Israelites and another round of intercession by Moses.

Translation

33:1a And YHWH spoke to Moses:
33:1b "Go up from here,[28] you and the people whom you have brought up

28. Taking לֵךְ as an auxiliary to עֲלֵה.

from the land of Egypt, to the land about which I swore to Abraham, Isaac, and Jacob, saying,
33:1c 'I will give it to your descendants.'
33:2a And I will send an angel before you
33:2b and I will drive out the Canaanite, the Amorite, the Hittite, the Perizzite, the Hivite and the Jebusite.
33:3a [Go] to a land flowing with milk and honey,
33:3b although I will not go up among you, for you are a stiff-necked people,
33:3c and I could obliterate you on the way."
33:4a And the people heard this harsh message,
33:4b and they went into mourning,
33:4c and no one put on his jewelry.
33:5a YHWH also had said[29] to Moses,
33:5b "Say to the Israelites,
33:5c 'You are a stiff-necked people;
33:5d Were I to go up in your midst for one moment,
33:5e I would obliterate you.
33:5f And now, remove your jewelry from you,
33:5g and then I will know what I will do with you.'"
33:6 And the Israelites went without their jewelry from the time at Mount Horeb [and subsequently].
33:7a And Moses used to take[30] [his] tent[31]
33:7b and pitch it outside the camp, at some distance from the camp,
33:7c and he would call[32] it "the tent of meeting."
33:7d And it came about
33:7e that everyone who was seeking YHWH would go out to the tent of meeting that was outside the camp.
33:8a And the routine was[33] that as soon as Moses went out to the tent,
33:8b all the people would get up,

29. The ordinary *wayyiqtol* וַיֹּאמֶר would normally be a simple past tense in a sequential narrative, "and YHWH said." Context, however, implies that the verb must be pluperfect. See commentary for further discussion.

30. The *yiqtol* יִקַּח is imperfective here. Its use tells us that this is offline, background information, and that it refers to an activity that was continued during the timeframe of the narrative context.

31. Lit. "the tent," but the use of the article is unusual since this is the first reference to this tent. It apparently refers either to Moses's own tent or to some specific tent set aside for Moses to use for his encounters with YHWH.

32. The *weqatal* וְקָרָא is imperfective and has the same nuance as יִקַּח in 33:7a.

33. Note the imperfective use of וְהָיָה.

33:8c and every man would stand at the entrance of his tent,
33:8d and stare after Moses until he entered the tent.
33:9a And whenever[34] Moses entered the tent
33:9b the pillar of cloud would descend
33:9c and would remain at the entrance of the tent.
33:9d And YHWH would speak with Moses.
33:10a And all the people would see the pillar of cloud standing at the entrance of the tent,
33:10b and all the people would arise,
33:10c and each one would worship at the entrance of his tent.
33:11a And YHWH would speak to Moses face-to-face,
33:11b just as a man speaks to his equal.
33:11c And Moses would return to the camp,
33:11d and his servant Joshua, the son of Nun, a young man, would not depart from within the tent.[35]
33:12a And Moses said to YHWH,
33:12b "Look here!
33:12c You are saying to me,
33:12d 'Lead up this people!'
33:12e But you do not let me know whom you will send with me.
33:12f And you say,
33:12g 'I know you by name,
33:12h and also, you have found favor in my eyes.'
33:13a And now, if indeed I have found favor in your eyes,
33:13b let me know your ways
33:13c that I may know you,
33:13d in order that I may find favor in your eyes.
33:13e And look here!
33:13f This nation is your people!"
33:14a And he said,
33:14b "My presence will go [with you],
33:14c and I will give you rest."
33:15a And he said to him,
33:15b "If your presence is not going [with us],
33:15c do not lead us up from here.
33:16a For by what means, in that case, could it be known that I and your

34. This translation of וְהָיָה again reflects the imperfective nature of this part of the narrative.

35. This obviously does not mean that Joshua never left the tent. He served as its caretaker, probably when it was pitched but not in use by YHWH and Moses.

people have found favor in your eyes when you are not going with us?
33:16b And would I and your people be any different from all the people who are upon the face of the earth?"
33:17a And YHWH said to Moses,
33:17b "I will do also this thing of which you have spoken,
33:17c for you have found favor in my eyes
33:17d and I know you by name."
33:18a And Moses said,
33:18b "Show me your glory!"
33:19a And he said,
33:19b "I will make my goodness [that is, all kinds of my wonderful benefits[36]] pass before you,
33:19c and will proclaim the name of YHWH before you;
33:19d and I will favor those whom I favor,
33:19e and I will be compassionate toward those for whom I am compassionate."[37]
33:20a And he said,

---

36. The expression כֹּל טוּב occurs elsewhere in the Old Testament at Gen. 24:10; Deut. 6:11; 2 Kgs. 8:9; Neh. 9:25. In every case, it refers to all kinds of good things: gifts, the produce of the land, treasures, and so forth, and it is often translated "all kinds of good things." Elsewhere, טוּב refers to farm products (Gen. 45:18; Isa. 1:19), material prosperity (Job 21:16), and happiness that comes from material prosperity, although that prosperity often is a blessing from YHWH and may be eschatological (Deut. 28:47; Neh. 9:35; Jer. 31:12; Hos. 3:5). In all of these, טוּב implies material goods, albeit almost always described as from God. A distinctive usage, and closer in meaning to this text, is Ps 25:7, where the psalmist appeals for forgiveness on the basis of YHWH's טוּב. Here in Exod. 33:19, the term טוּב is certainly not just material prosperity, but it must imply the many benefits YHWH bestows (as opposed to abstract perfection as an internal quality of YHWH). There is a beauty and simplicity to the translation "goodness," but without qualification, the reader will miss the fact that it implies numerous and varied benefits.

37. The NJPS translation, "I will proclaim before you . . . the grace that I grant and the compassion that I show," is attractive and certainly easier to interpret. It is supported by Sarna, *Exodus*, 214, and in a modified form by Stuart, *Exodus*, 798. But it is not possible. Against Stuart, for example, 33:19d cannot mean, "I will show grace in being gracious," because the relative אֶת־אֲשֶׁר must be taken as a pronominal direct object. A close analogy to וְחַנֹּתִי אֶת־אֲשֶׁר אָחֹן is at Exod. 16:23: אֵת אֲשֶׁר־תֹּאפוּ אֵפוּ ("what you will bake, bake"), which, although it reverses the sequence of main verb and relative pronoun, is grammatically the same.

33:20b "You are not able to see my face,
33:20c for no human will see me
33:20d and live."
33:21a And YHWH said,
33:21b "Now then, there is a place by me,
33:21c and you can stand at the rock [there].
33:22a And it will happen like this: as my glory passes by,
33:22b I will set you in the cleft of the rock
33:22c and cover you with my hand until I have passed by.
33:23a And I will remove my hand
33:23b and you will see my back,
33:23c but my face will not be seen."
34:1a And YHWH said to Moses,
34:1b "Chisel out two stone tablets like the former ones,
34:1c and I will write on the tablets the words that were on the previous tablets that you shattered.
34:2a And be ready in the morning,
34:2b and come up in the morning to Mount Sinai,
34:2c and present yourself there to me on the top of the mountain.
34:3a No man is to come up with you,
34:3b and no man is to be seen on the whole mountain.
34:3c Even the flocks and the herds must not graze on [the ground] leading up to that mountain."
34:4a And Moses[38] chiseled out two stone tablets like the previous ones,
34:4b and he rose up early in the morning
34:4c and went up to Mount Sinai,
34:4d just as YHWH had commanded him,
34:4e and he took two stone tablets in his hand.
34:5a And YHWH descended in the cloud
34:5b and stood there with him.
34:5c And he called upon the name of YHWH.
34:6a And YHWH passed by in front of him,
34:6b and he proclaimed,

Eighth Poem: YHWH! YHWH!

Stanza 1

34:6c YHWH! YHWH!
יְהוָה יְהוָה 2-2-2

38. "Moses" is transposed for clarity from the next clause, 34:4b.

Stanza 2.1

34:6d Compassionate and gracious God,
אֵל רַחוּם וְחַנּוּן 0-2-3

34:6e Slow to anger, and rich in grace and faithfulness!
אֶרֶךְ אַפַּיִם וְרַב־חֶסֶד וֶאֱמֶת׃ 0-2-5

Stanza 2.2

34:7a Maintaining grace for thousands,
נֹצֵר חֶסֶד לָאֲלָפִים 1-3-3

34:7b Forgiving iniquity, transgression and sin!
נֹשֵׂא עָוֺן וָפֶשַׁע וְחַטָּאָה 2-4-4

Stanza 3.1

34:7c But he does not grant blanket amnesty;[39]
וְנַקֵּה לֹא יְנַקֶּה 1-1-2

---

39. The translation of וְנַקֵּה לֹא יְנַקֶּה is difficult but critically important. The text is usually translated something like, "but who will by no means clear the guilty" (ESV). This creates a significant problem: if the guilty person is not in some sense cleared of guilt and released from punishment, there is no forgiveness. Such a translation of 34:7c does not qualify but flat-out contradicts the previous lines, which speak emphatically of YHWH's forgiving nature. If God will "by no means clear the guilty," then all of us are lost. In the Niphal stem, נקה generally means to be free of guilt, obligation or liability to punishment (Gen. 24:8; Exod. 21:19; Judg. 15:3; Prov. 11:21). In the Piel, נקה normally has a personal direct object; it means to release someone from deserved punishment, or even to indulge that person's sin (Exod. 20:7; 1 Kgs. 2:9; Jer. 30:11; 46:28; Ps. 19:13[12]; Job 9:28; 10:14). Here, however, there is no direct object (וְנַקֵּה לֹא יְנַקֶּה); the addition of "the guilty" to the standard translation is gratuitous. The verb is used absolutely; it means to "grant amnesty." The cognate infinitive absolute, moreover, implies a complete, blanket, or absolute amnesty. A "blanket amnesty" would be pure indulgence; it is forgiveness where there is no repentance and perhaps also forgiveness that exempts people from suffering any consequences whatsoever. So understood, not granting a blanket amnesty does not contradict the fact that YHWH is forgiving, but it does preclude forgiveness where there is no repentance, and it opens the possibility for YHWH to deal out limited retribution while still forgiving the sin.

34:7d Avenging the iniquity of fathers
פֹּקֵ֣ד ׀ עֲוֺ֣ן אָב֗וֹת 1-2-3

Stanza 3.2
34:7e On the children and on the grandchildren,
עַל־בָּנִים֙ וְעַל־בְּנֵ֣י בָנִ֔ים 0-2-3

34:7f On the third and on the fourth generations.
עַל־שִׁלֵּשִׁ֖ים וְעַל־רִבֵּעִֽים׃ 0-2-2

34:8a Moses hurriedly bowed low toward the earth
34:8b and he worshiped.
34:9a And he said,
34:9b "If, my Lord, I have found favor in your eyes,
34:9c my Lord should go with us—
34:9d even though the people are stiff-necked—
34:9e and pardon our iniquity and our sin,
34:9f and take us as your own possession."

Structure

This is a lengthy text, but it moves seamlessly from one episode to the next. Furthermore, it is all of a single theme, the repentance of Israel and Moses's appeals for mercy. The oracle poem (34:6–7) celebrates YHWH's mercy and, apart from its importance as a revelation to Moses, serves as a grand conclusion to the account. Thus, 33:1—34:9 should be regarded as a unified text.

I. God's Decree and Israel's Response (33:1–6)
  A. First Cycle (33:1–4)
  B. Second Cycle (33:5–6)
II. Background: The Tent (33:7–11)
III. Moses's First Intercession and Request (33:12–23)
  A. First Cycle (33:12–14)
  B. Second Cycle (33:15–23)
IV. Moses and the Glory of YHWH (34:1–9)
  A. Preparation for the Revelation (34:1–34:6ab)
  B. The Song of YHWH's Benefits (34:6cde–7)
  C. Moses's Second Intercession (34:8–9)

The song at 34:6cde–7 has three stanzas, the first being a monocolon (almost a title), the second having four lines in two bicolon strophes, and the third also having four lines in two bicolon strophes. The second stanza speaks of YHWH's mercy, and the third warns of his wrath. Formally, several tropes are evident. For example, the signal for the start of the third stanza is that line 34:7c begins with a conjunction; all the other lines begin with asyndeton. Strophe 2.1 is a bicolon in which both lines start with א, and strophe 2.2 is a bicolon in which both lines start with a Qal active participle beginning in נ. In strophe 3, both lines of the second bicolon begin with עַל.

Commentary

33:1–6. In both cycles of vv. 1–4 and 5–6, YHWH sends word to the Israelites through Moses that they are a stubborn people, so that he cannot remain among them or he would obliterate them for their sin. After that, the people grieve and remove their jewelry. In the first cycle, however, YHWH announces that they may make their way to the Promised Land, and he uses the standard language for bringing them into Canaan (33:2b–3a; cf. 3:8, 17; 13:5; 23:23). But in the second cycle, at 33:5, YHWH tells them to remove their jewelry, something he does not do in the first cycle. It appears, therefore, that there was actually only one message from YHWH to Israel through Moses and only one act of removing the jewelry, since it makes no sense for God to command them to remove the jewelry after they had already done so. But why break the narrative into two cycles instead of using just one, continuous sequence? It appears that the purpose is to interrupt YHWH's announcement at 33:3bc, that they are a stubborn people, with the people's response of mourning and removing their jewelry. Then, after the command to get rid of the jewelry in v. 5, the text announces again that they did it. In short, the people are portrayed as responsive to YHWH, both being grieved at having sinned against him and obedient to his decree. This structure gives greater attention to the sorrow and obedience of the people than a simple narrative would have done.

The removal of the jewelry, moreover, has greater significant than is apparent at first sight. Although Egyptians wore jewelry for cosmetic purposes, they also routinely decorated jewelry with images of gods and hieroglyphic religious texts meant to have an apotropaic function. That is, the jewelry served as amulets meant to ward off evil spirits and misfortune. A common motif was the eye of Horus, an image thought to have powerful magic. Egyptians even had jewelry with magical signs related to the realm of the dead; it was thought that the magic contained in the amulets could help them negotiate the dangers of the underworld.[40] It can hardly be doubted that the Israelites, having just

40. David, *Handbook*, 121, 327–8.

come out of Egypt, wore the same kind of jewelry and for the same purposes. This means that getting rid of the jewelry was not just a matter of personal vanity; it was primarily a matter of eliminating the paganism that literally clung to them. In addition, we should not underestimate what a major step this was for the Israelites. Ancient peoples depended upon their amulets for their safety. Without them, they felt defenseless, believing that they and their families were open to attack from malicious spirits. Even today in many places, there are people who would not think of riding in a car without an amulet to protect them from the evil eye. Going without their amulets required real faith in YHWH.

This text also alludes to the angel who will go before Israel, a figure already mentioned in 23:20–21. As in that text, the angel is not YHWH himself but a subordinate being. In fact, YHWH will not be among them at all, he says, since he could not tolerate their evil and would strike out to destroy them. This section therefore has tension built into it. On the one hand, YHWH has announced that Israel is so stubbornly sinful that he cannot abide among them; on the other, Israel has mourned and stripped itself of its amulets, having no hope of supernatural protection if YHWH is not with them. Once again, Moses must step in to resolve the crisis.

33:7–11. The "tent of meeting" described here is difficult to make sense of. In this account, it appears to be a small, nondescript tent that was pitched away from the camp and to which Moses would retreat for private consultation with YHWH. But the same name, "tent of meeting" (אֹהֶל מוֹעֵד) also designates the great worship center described at length in Exod. 26–27.[41] The great sanctuary tent was pitched in the middle of the camp, not outside of it. Three solutions can be proposed for this problem.

First, it could be that the great sanctuary tent of Exod. 26–27 was where official worship took place but that when Moses went out to meet God for instructions, he retreated to a small, simple tent that was outside the camp. Its small size is suggested by v. 7, which implies that Moses could single-handedly carry it out and set it up as needed (although in fact he had Joshua as his assistant). If an Israelite had a special enquiry to bring before YHWH, he would take it to Moses, who would meet God in this small tent outside the camp. In this

41. The sanctuary tent of Exod. 26–27 (commonly called the "Tabernacle") is called the אֹהֶל מוֹעֵד over one hundred times, as at Exod. 27:21; 28:43; 29:30; 30:26; Lev. 1:3; Num. 3:7–8.

interpretation, there were actually two "tents of meeting" functioning throughout Israel's wilderness experience. In favor of this interpretation, it is unlikely that sacred items such as the Ark of the Covenant would be deposited in a location outside the camp. Also, one might argue, Moses himself could not proceed at will into the holy of holies of the great sanctuary, and thus some other place was needed for him to go to for an encounter with YHWH. One could also argue that the small tent of meeting was created specifically in response to the sin of the golden calf.[42] Against this interpretation, there is no evidence elsewhere for the separate and continuous existence of a small "tent of meeting" alongside the great Tent of Meeting.[43] Also, Moses did not need to proceed all the way inside the holy of holies of the great tent sanctuary in order to receive a word from God, and thus it is hard to see the need for a second tent. More than that, we cannot really say that Moses could not proceed into the holy of holies. If any man might have been an exception to this rule, it would have been he. Finally, against the view that the small tent was created in response to the golden calf sin, it is impossible to escape the force of the imperfective verbs in vv. 7–8, implying as they do that the small tent of meeting already existed prior to the making of the calf.

The second possibility is that the "tent of meeting" described here is in fact the great Tent of Meeting of Exod. 25–31. The argument is that in response to the people's sin the tent sanctuary was temporarily moved outside the camp, or that even if it was actually still in the middle of the encampment, a great distance was placed between it and the people's tents. In this interpretation, there never was a secondary, smaller "tent of meeting." However, the narrative sequence plainly indicates that the great Tent of Meeting was not built until after the golden calf episode (Exod. 35–39). Also, it is very unlikely that Israel would station their main shrine with all of its sacred furnishings in an

---

42. Wells, "Exodus," 261.

43. Stuart, *Exodus*, 694-7, believes that the two tents functioned simultaneously. He argues that the second, smaller tent of meeting is mentioned in Num. 11:16–17, 24–26; 12:1–8; Deut. 31:14–15; but I see no reason for those texts to refer to anything but the central sanctuary tent. For example, Num. 11:26 mentions that two men remained in the camp while others went to the Tent of Meeting. But this does not mean that the tent was at this time outside the camp; it only means that the two men did not pass through the barrier into the courtyard of the Tent of Meeting. Also, all of these episodes involve "cultic" (ceremonial) acts that perforce would have been performed at the main sanctuary.

isolated spot. And no matter what the distance, a shrine in the middle of the camp is not outside the camp.

A third possibility is that the small tent of meeting only existed until the main shrine was completed, after which the use of the smaller tent was discontinued. This is the most persuasive solution. From the storyline of Exodus, it is fairly clear that the golden calf episode and its aftermath took place prior to the building of the great Tabernacle, which is not described until 35–39. This implies that Moses could not have gone to the great Tent of Meeting at the time of chapter 33, outside the camp or anywhere else, for the simple reason that it did not exist. In addition, confusion about the name is unnecessary. "Tent of Meeting" is a purely functional title, referring to whatever tent was recognized as the one that YHWH would use for his encounter with Moses. It is analogous to how "Air Force One" is the call sign for any airplane that carries the President of the United States. By analogy, Solomon worships at a tent at the high place of Gibeon that is actually called "God's Tent of Meeting that Moses the servant of YHWH made in the wilderness" (2 Chron. 1:3). But the older Tent of Meeting was almost certainly destroyed by the Philistines at Shiloh (Ps. 78:60). And yet the Gibeon tent could be called Moses's "Tent of Meeting" precisely because it functioned in that role.

It appears that the small tent of meeting would, as needed, be set up on the lower slopes of Mt. Sinai,[44] probably beyond the border that the Israelites were allowed to cross[45] but still well within their view, so that they could observe at a distance and show respect when the divine presence descended on the tent. The great tent sanctuary, when finished, had the same name ("Tent of Meeting") transferred to it, and the use of the previous tent ceased. As already mentioned, the pitching of the small tent outside the camp was not a response to the golden calf episode. It was routine to put this tent outside the camp well before the calf incident, as indicated by the imperfective verbs that are used throughout this section. Also, vv. 7–8 are plainly background information. That is, they tell us that setting up the tent outside the camp was a standing practice before the calf incident. Since the smaller tent of

44. Comparing 33:21 to 34:2 suggests that this tent is on Mt. Sinai.

45. Sarna, *Exodus*, 211, misinterprets 33:7e to mean that any Israelite could go right up to the tent. This would be a gross violation of holiness. Verse 33:7e only means that Israelites could approach it (to a designated spot or distance, apparently). It is not that they could walk right up and, as it were, knock on the door. Were that the case, there would have been no reason for the tent to be routinely pitched away from the camp.

meeting had no formal priestly structure and no barriers (that is, no priestly "cult" to safeguard its holiness), it would have been improper to set it right among all the other tents, where it would be profaned. At any rate, the main point of this brief excursus in the Exodus narrative is that Moses had direct access to God and received clear and unambiguous messages from him (33:11).

Mark Wessner observes a chiastic structure to this passage.[46] Slightly modifying his analysis, the text can be diagrammed as follows:

A Moses pitched tent outside camp; people come out to the tent (33:7)

B Everyone rose and stood at entrance of his tent (33:8)

C Pillar of cloud at entrance of the tent (33:9abc)

D YHWH spoke with Moses (33:9d)

C' Pillar of cloud at entrance of the tent (33:10a)

B' Everyone rose and worshipped at entrance of his tent (33:10bc)

A' Moses returns to the camp; Joshua remains with the tent (33:11)

The central position of 9d indicates the main point is the direct access Moses had to YHWH. This section has two functions in the narrative. First, it explains how Moses was able to enter into direct negotiations with YHWH about YHWH's announced intention not to go forth with Israel. Only Moses could have done this, as only he had such access to YHWH. Second, it explains how it was that Moses met God out in a place of wilderness, where there were great rocks and crags (33:21), since the tent was outside of the camp (and almost certainly was on Sinai itself).

33:12–34:3. Like 33:1–6, the dialogue at 33:12–34:3 seems to be two overlapping cycles. As it stands, the text seems to suggest that Moses continued pressing God to go with them even after God already said that he would do so (33:14–15). But this is probably a deliberate literary

46. Mark D. Wessner, "Toward a Literary Understanding of Moses and the Lord 'Face to Face' (פָּנִים אֶל־פָּנִים) in Exodus 33:7–11," *ResQ* 44, no. 2 (2002): 112.

technique, emphatically asserting that Moses pleaded earnestly and effectively for YHWH to stay with Israel.[47] It is, in effect, saying, "Moses made this appeal (33:12–13) and YHWH agreed (33:14). And Moses made this appeal (33:15–16), and YHWH agreed to that one, too (33:17)." In short, Israel's survival depended on the intercession of Moses more than they could ever know. Moses's requests also have a chiastic structure, with his requests for YHWH to give him a more complete assurance that God is with him forming the outer brackets (33:12e–13c and 33:18), and his requests that YHWH not abandon Israel forming the inner brackets (33:13f and 33:15–16).

33:12–14. Moses begins his intercession in this text with two claims on YHWH, both headed by the imperative רְאֵה ("look here!"). The first, 33:12–13d, is based in Moses's personal relationship to YHWH. He claims that YHWH evidently has faith enough in Moses to make him the leader ("You are saying to me, 'Lead up this people!'"), and that YHWH asserts that Moses enjoys God's personal favor ("And you say, 'I know you by name'"). Nevertheless, Moses argues, YHWH is withholding vital information from him. Yahweh has not told Moses anything about this angel who will go with Israel ("But you do not let me know whom you will send with me"). The request "Teach me your ways" simply means that in some vital sense Moses does not understand what YHWH is doing. That is, this is not a request for an advanced class in theological doctrine; it is simply that Moses is bewildered at how things are turning out after the triumph of the exodus. Israel has committed gross sin, the covenant seems defunct, and YHWH is threatening to abandon the people. Things could hardly be worse! Moses is left in the middle wondering what to do. It is true that the "ways" of God normally refer to his commandments (Deut. 8:6; 10:12; etc.), but the usage here is more akin to Isa. 55:8, where YHWH says, "For my plans are not your plans, nor are your ways my ways." That is, the "ways" are God's hidden intents and purposes, carried out in a manner that is often counterintuitive and may even seem like folly. Thus also, for Paul, the wisdom of God in the cross seems like foolishness to people (1 Cor. 1:18–2:16). Moses is asserting that he is sure that God has something planned to make this all turn out for good, but he doesn't know

47. William H. Irwin, "The Course of the Dialogue between Moses and Yhwh in Exodus 33:12–17," *CBQ* 59, no. 4 (1997): 629–36, sees irony in the dialogue, arguing that Moses and YHWH are talking at cross-purposes and that this illustrates that Moses spoke with YHWH as with a friend, where communication may be less than perfect.

what it is. Thus, "Show me your ways" means something like, "What do you have in mind here, Lord? I am more than a little bewildered."

The second claim on YHWH concerns Israel: "This nation is your people!" (33:13f). YHWH has bound himself to Israel, and he cannot abandon them now, Moses claims. God, in a terse response (v. 14), accedes to Moses's last request and states that he will go with Israel, reversing his earlier decision to send only his angel.

33:15–17. Moses again presses YHWH not to abandon them, but as suggested above, this repetition may be literary structuring rather than the actual flow of the conversation. At any rate, he asserts that there is no point in Israel going anywhere if YHWH does not go with them. In that event, Israel is just another one of the nations, and their proceeding to take the Promised Land would be a hollow fulfillment of the promises to the patriarchs. The goal of God having a people for himself would fail. YHWH accepts this reasoning; he will go with them (vv. 15–17).

33:18–20. At this point, the dialogue takes an unexpected turn as Moses asks YHWH to show him his glory (v. 18). What was Moses asking for, and why did he ask for it? A typical interpretation is that Moses was looking for some kind of special, mystical experience with God. Some suggest that Moses was asking for what no man should seek, a direct vision of God, and thus that he was politely refused, with the consolation that he got an acceptable but limited vision of God. But it is not at all clear why Moses would do this; his main concern was for reassurance that God would not abandon either him or Israel. A desire for a mystical experience is no more apposite in this situation than a desire for a doctrinal seminar. He is not seeking Faustian knowledge of the secret things of God.[48] Furthermore, Moses long ago knew that no one could see God's face and live (Exod. 3:6). It is odd in the extreme that he would in this context ask for an experience that he had always known was illicit and deadly. And in fact Moses did not ask to see God's face. He asked to see his glory, and Israel with Moses had already seen God's glory twice (Exod. 16:10; 24:16–17). The request was therefore not extravagant.

Furthermore, the previous visions of YHWH's glory came at a time

48. Propp, *Exodus 19–40*, 606, completely misses the point with his comment, "Moses' persistent desire to see Yahweh emblematizes a common human sense of alienation from the divine. . . . Mythology is replete with cautionary tales of heroes who presume to obtain a full vision of a god."

of crisis (when Israel was desperate for food, at Exod. 16) and when Israel became bound to YHWH (immediately after the covenant ratification ceremony at Exod. 24). The request to see YHWH's glory is therefore not from a desire for a private mystical experience but more concretely springs from a need that God reassure him, by another visible manifestation of his presence, that YHWH was Israel's God and that he would see Israel and Moses through this crisis.[49] God responds that he will show Moses all his "wonderful benefits" (כָּל־טוּבִי; see translation note to 33:19b).

We therefore must ask why God determines to show Moses his "wonderful benefits," what that implies, and why God felt it necessary to add the caveat that Moses would not be able to see his face. The answer, I believe, begins with the understanding that the "wonderful benefits" was actually more than Moses had asked for, not less. Moses's desire for reassurance was justifiable, but rather than meet the request by another transient glimpse at YHWH's visible splendor (his "glory"), YHWH gives Moses a more profound understanding of the divine character. This consists of a deeper awareness of YHWH's goodness and of how that goodness works itself out in compassion and acts of blessing for people. And because God exceeded Moses's request, he had to qualify his statement by saying that there are yet aspects of God that Moses cannot behold. Furthermore, when God says in v. 20 that Moses would not be able to see his face, he is not implying that Moses had actually asked for that (contrary to many interpretations). YHWH's caution that no one can see his face is a secondary qualification; it is not God's primary answer (interpreters often read the text as though the assertion that no one could see God's face were the first words out of YHWH's mouth). But to paraphrase freely, God is actually saying, "I'll do better than to show you my glory as you have seen it; I'll show you all of my wonderful benefits. But of course, I can't go so far as to show you my face; no one can see that."[50] The point that no one can see God's face and live is of secondary importance; it qualifies the nature of the anticipated revelation and is a clarification of what

---

49. J. Gerald Janzen, *Exodus,* Westminster Bible Companion (Louisville: Westminster John Knox Press, 1997), 247, reads the text correctly when he comments, "If God would again let Moses see his glory, he would know that all was well." But then Janzen veers off course by adding, "This time he asks more than is possible."

50. Against, for example, Durham, *Exodus*, 452: "What Moses asks, however, is more than Yahweh is willing to grant." J. Carl Laney, "God's Self–Revelation in Exodus 34:6–8," *BSac* 158, no. 629 (2001): 39, is similar.

follows, explaining that there is some ultimate experience of seeing the essential nature and power of God that humans cannot bear to see, even though they can in some lesser sense "see God." This distinction among various degrees of seeing God, there being some final, extreme vision that no mortal can endure, is maintained right into the New Testament, which declares that no one except the only-begotten Son has seen God at any time, although we lesser beings can see the glory of God (John 1:14–18).

Two more items of importance in this text concern why YHWH says he will call out his name and why he speaks of being compassionate toward those for whom he has compassion (33:19). The name, YHWH, is the identity by which he is known as Israel's God and how he is manifested in the world. The name, therefore, is closely tied to his "wonderful benefits." YHWH will reveal that his name is manifested in Israel not to instill fear of wrath but primarily as a promise of forgiveness and blessing.

The matter of God's showing favor toward those whom he favors can be taken in a capricious sense, as though God were saying, "I'll show compassion whenever and on whomever I please." It is of course true that God has the right to show compassion as he chooses, but the point here is not so much God's freedom, much less his capriciousness, in election. Rather, it is that he is abundantly compassionate toward his own. The sentence structure of the Hebrew focuses on God's action of being compassionate and not on the process of choosing to whom he will show compassion.[51] Furthermore, the relative clauses "those whom I favor" and "for whom I am compassionate" refer to Israel, God's people, and are not an open-ended statement about anyone toward whom God might feel a kind impulse. A legitimate paraphrase would be, "If I have chosen someone (that is, Israel) for favor, well then, you can believe that I will show them favor, and if I have chosen for someone (Israel again) compassion, then I will most definitely be compassionate toward them." In other words, the main point is that God will indeed show favor and compassion to Israel, just as Moses desires. YHWH is saying that his favor and compassion for Israel will just keep coming and coming, because he has chosen them for that. The statements are not sudden, out-of-the-blue pronouncements on God's freedom in election, even though that freedom is somewhat foundational here. The point is that because God chose Israel to receive his compassion, they

51. In וְחַנֹּתִי אֶת־אֲשֶׁר אָחֹן the main verb is fronted. Contrast this against Exod. 16:23, אֵת אֲשֶׁר־תֹּאפוּ אֵפוּ ("bake what you will bake"), where the relative clause is fronted and the focus is on choosing what you want to bake.

could not escape it if they wanted to. He is determined to show compassion to them.

33:21–23. As mentioned above, since we know that the tent was outside the camp, its situation near a great rock (v. 21) and away from people is comprehensible. This text, with v. 20, is highly anthropomorphic in how it speaks of God (his face, his hand, and his back). The essential idea is that the power, purity, and holiness of God are so great no one can withstand the full impact of the divine presence (his "face") and survive. Therefore, God must set a shield (his "hand") between himself and Moses (similarly, the rock somehow shields Moses from the energy of the divine presence). Instead of the "face," Moses experiences only a part of the divine presence, the "back." Understood in context, the "back" does not represent anything except that it is less than the full expression of YHWH's being and presence. God's showing his "back" rather than his "face" to Moses is analogous to shining a powerful flashlight away from someone instead of directly into his eyes. Or, to stay with the biblical metaphor, if we see someone's face, we feel we have truly seen what that person looks like. But if we have only seen someone from behind, we can generally say whether the person was male or female, tall or short, and perhaps catch a few other details such as hair color or skin color. We would not claim without qualification that we have "seen" someone, however, unless we have seen that person's face. Thus, when Moses saw God's "back" but not his "face," he had a limited but real encounter with the person of God. But we should not let our imagination run amok with this text in order to create some theological counterpart to the "back," as though it symbolized some attribute of God or had some secret significance. For example, one should not think that the back represents the future, and more specifically that it refers to Christ (an interpretation proposed by Tertullian).[52] Such an approach is no more than an allegorical reading of later theology into the text; it does not arise from the passage. When YHWH puts Moses into the cleft of a rock, covers Moses's face with his hand, and then shows him God's "back," the text is communicating that Moses at that moment sees as much of the glory and essence of God as any human being can possibly bear to see. That is, this is a revelation of God that surpasses the previous displays of God's glory given in Exod. 16 and 24.

34:1–34:6ab. Three factors indicate that the covenant with Israel is

52. Gowan, *Theology*, 235.

about to be renewed. First, of course, Moses is to bring up two tablets, like the two that he broke, so that YHWH can write the words of the covenant on them. This is not a different covenant, since the tablets are replacements and not a new set with different terms. Second, the admonition that no one is to come up on Sinai recalls 19:12–13 in the preparations for the initial making of the covenant. Third, YHWH descends in a cloud, similar to the smoke and fire of 19:18. In other words, the same ceremonial rules are put in place, and the same covenant terms are written on identical tablets, and YHWH makes a similar theophany; this all demonstrates that it is a renewal of the same covenant.[53]

34:6cde–7. This text can be called a song of YHWH's benefits and grace even though the final stanza (34:7cdef) focuses on his refusal to grant blanket amnesty (see translation note to 34:7c). But the warnings about punishment are a qualification and not the main point; that is, YHWH is indeed gracious and forgiving, but this does not mean that he is indulgent or that one can take his mercy for granted. The grace of YHWH, as described in the song, includes the following:

- רַחוּם ("compassionate"): This speaks of a gut-level, emotional reaction of sympathy and tender-hearted mercy. It is related to רֶחֶם ("guts, womb"), and has a counterpart in the Greek *σπλάγχνον* and the related verb *σπλάγχνίζομαι*, a term often associated with the compassion of Jesus (Mark 6:34; 8:2; Luke 7:13).
- חַנּוּן ("gracious"): From the root חנן, this connotes responding favorably to someone's desire for mercy, help or forgiveness. Thus we often see appeals such as Ps. 51:3(1) חָנֵּנִי אֱלֹהִים ("Be gracious to me, God"). As such, it implies not just a kind disposition but a proclivity to respond favorably to cries for help or forgiveness.
- אֶרֶךְ אַפַּיִם ("slow to anger"): Literally translated, this is the peculiar idiom "long of nose," where "nose" refers to being hot-tempered or easily angered. Thus, "long of nose" is the opposite of being "short-tempered." It implies that YHWH's immediate response to an affront is forbearance rather than retaliation.
- רַב־חֶסֶד וֶאֱמֶת ("rich in grace and faithfulness"): On חֶסֶד ("grace"),

53. Some interpreters take the absurd view that the covenant here is a different covenant, not the same as the one given in Exod. 19–24. See, for example, William J. Dumbrell, "Paul and Salvation History in Romans 9:30—10:4," in *Out of Egypt: Biblical Theology and Biblical Interpretation*, ed. Craig Bartholomew (Grand Rapids: Zondervan, 2004), 298-9.

see below. The word אֱמֶת ("faithfulness") implies that something is dependable, solid, has integrity, and stands in contrast to something that fails when needed most (the "bruised reed"). In this context, it means that when one needs mercy, one can rely upon YHWH.

- נֹצֵר חֶסֶד לָאֲלָפִים ("maintaining grace for thousands"): Many translations are proposed for חֶסֶד ("loyal love, lovingkindness, kindness, goodness"). In my view, it refers to a disposition of kindness that is the closest Hebrew equivalent to the New Testament idea of χάρις ("grace"). That is, it is a mercy that is undeserved and freely given. In maintaining חֶסֶד for thousands, YHWH is demonstrating that his grace is inexhaustible.
- נֹשֵׂא עָוֹן וָפֶשַׁע וְחַטָּאָה ("forgiving iniquity and transgression and sin"): The verb נשׂא when used with "sin" as its object means to carry away the sin; that is, the word essentially means "forgive." It is used here with three different terms as its object: "iniquity and transgression and sin." The point is that YHWH forgives all manner of immorality, disobedience, indiscretion, rebellion, or more generically, sin. There are no degrees or types of sin that are beyond YHWH's power or willingness to forgive. YHWH forgives sin of every kind and shape.

The qualification, that YHWH offers no blanket amnesty, means that he does not indulge sin. The unrepentant person cannot escape punishment under a general amnesty; that person remains unforgiven. Forgiveness, moreover, does not necessarily imply release from all consequences for one's actions, although it does mean that one will not pay the full penalty that God would otherwise impose, and it also means that one will, in the end, experience redemption. The fact that the punishment extends for generations does not mean that God will continue to punish members of subsequent generations even if they turn from the evil of their fathers (see Ezek. 18). It means that the punishment can be very severe, with repercussions on generations yet unborn. Again, however, the main point of the oracle is that YHWH is merciful; the final stanza is a qualification and not the fundamental lesson.

34:8–9. Moses at the end of the revelation of YHWH's wonderful benefits has a much deeper understanding of God. His response is to fall down before God and plead yet again for mercy for Israel. This does not mean that he is still not convinced of God's willingness to go with Israel or that he doubts God's compassion—that would be a very odd response to the revelation. To the contrary, he understands these things better than ever. But because he now has such a clearer vision of God, he also has a clearer apprehension of the repugnance of evil and of the need for the mercy of God. As such, he can only appeal again for grace.

Theological Summary of Key Points

1. The repentance of the Israelites is genuine and profound. As described above, a pagan felt naked before the evil spirits without the protection of amulets, and the Israelite removal of their jewelry was a turning away from magic and a casting of themselves upon the mercy of YHWH. Had they refused to remove the jewelry, the paganism would have clung to them and YHWH would have had to make good on his threat not to go with them. Their mourning and their actions are marks of true repentance and are deeds that provoke divine mercy.

2. There is an analogy between Moses's experience with YHWH here and that of Elijah when he made a pilgrimage to Mt. Sinai (1 Kgs. 19:8–18). In both cases, the men sought out YHWH after doing battle with the idolatry of the Israelites. Both were seeking encouragement, although Moses was interceding for Israel and Elijah was complaining against Israel. Both seem to have expected to gain insight or strength from a miraculous display of YHWH's power (Moses with the glory of YHWH, and Elijah with the wind, fire, and earthquake). Both encountered YHWH in an unexpected message (Moses hearing the "goodness" of YHWH and Elijah hearing the small whisper). For both men, Israel's paradigmatic men of God, their greatest encounter with YHWH involved experiencing not his power but his goodness.

3. Moses's prayers have a directness and honesty even as he seems to argue with God, saying "Look here!" Nothing is gained by holding back from God one's discouragement, confusion, or even dismay at how things are turning out.

4. Moses again demonstrates the importance of the intercessor. People are weak and prone to do things to offend God. As such, the intercession needs to be as consistent as their behavior is inconsistent. Hebrews 7:25 teaches that Christ "forever lives to make intercession for us," implying that Christ lives forever as a constant intercessor for his wayward people. The experience of Moses and Israel models for us why this is necessary.

5. God's mercy, kindness, benefits, and goodness form the core of the Israelite understanding of the divine nature. Israelites turn back to this essential description of YHWH, citing parts of Exod. 34:6–7, on many different occasions (Num. 14:18; Isa. 48:9; Jer. 32:18; Joel 2:13; Jon. 4:2; Nah. 1:3; Ps. 86:15; 103:8; 145:8; Neh. 9:17). The heart of Israel's faith is that God is good and merciful.

COVENANT RENEWAL (34:10–27)

YHWH fully yields to Moses's intercession. He renews the covenant with Israel and affirms that he will go with them and continue to do great miracles for them. In the renewal of the covenant, however, he reaffirms that they must be zealous to guard themselves against the one sin that has a hold upon them: idolatry.

Translation

34:10a And [God] said,
34:10b "Take note that I am making a covenant [renewal].[54]
34:10c Before all your people I will perform miracles that have not been created in all the earth or among any of the nations.
34:10d And all the people among whom you live will see the work of YHWH,
34:10e for it is an awesome thing that I am doing with you.
34:11a Abide by what I command you this day.
34:11b After all, I am about to drive out before you the Amorite, and the Canaanite, the Hittite, the Perizzite, the Hivite and the Jebusite.[55]
34:12a Be careful that you do not make a covenant[56] with the inhabitants of the land into which you are going,

---

54. The clause is הִנֵּה אָנֹכִי כֹּרֵת בְּרִית. YHWH is not initiating a new or different covenant; the stipulations are the same as already given at Sinai, and thus this is a covenant renewal and not simply the making of a covenant. It is sometimes argued that כרת בְּרִית always refers to initiating a covenant where one did not already exist, but that הקים בְּרִית is a renewal or modification of an already existing covenant (William J. Dumbrell, *Covenant and Creation: An Old Testament Covenantal Theology* [Exeter: Paternoster, 1984], 42-43). But this is plainly wrong; in this case, it is self-evident that the Sinai covenant of Exod. 19–24 is being renewed. For that matter, there are cases where הקים בְּרִית refers to making a covenant that has no precedent (e.g., Gen. 6:18, the first appearance of בְּרִית).
55. The list of nations whom YHWH will dispossess for Israel appears in Exod. 3:8, 17; 13:5, 11; 23:23, 28; 33:2; 34:11.
56. This alludes to Exod. 23:32, the command not to make a בְּרִית ("covenant") with the inhabitants of the land.

34:12b or it will become a snare[57] in your midst.
34:13a For you are to tear down their altars
34:13b and smash their monumental sacred stones[58]
34:13c and cut down their Asherim.
34:14a For you are not to worship any other god,
34:14b because YHWH, whose name is Jealous, is a jealous God.[59]
34:15a Otherwise, you might[60] make a covenant with the inhabitants of the land
34:15b and they would behave like a harlot with their gods,[61]
34:15c and they would sacrifice to their gods,
34:15d and someone might invite you
34:15e so that you would eat of his sacrifice.[62]
34:16a And you would take some of his daughters for your sons,
34:16b and his daughters would behave as harlots with their gods,
34:16c and they would provoke your sons to behave as harlots with their gods.
34:17 And you are not to make for yourself gods made from poured metal.[63]
34:18a And you are to observe the Feast of Unleavened Bread.
34:18b For seven days you are to eat unleavened bread—as I commanded you—at the appointed time in the month of Abib.
34:18c For in the month of Abib you came out of Egypt.[64]
34:19 Every firstborn from the womb belongs to me—all your male[65] livestock, the firstborn cattle and sheep.

57. This alludes to Exod. 23:33, יִהְיֶה לְךָ לְמוֹקֵשׁ ("[worshipping the gods of Canaan] will be a snare to you").
58. This alludes to Exod. 23:24, a command to tear down מַצֵּבֹתֵיהֶם ("their monumental sacred stones").
59. The warning that YHWH is a jealous god appears in Exodus only here and at 20:5.
60. See the usage of פֶּן in Exod. 13:17.
61. The comparison of idolatry to prostitution, although common elsewhere in the Old Testament, appears in Exodus only at 34:15–16.
62. The fear that the Israelites may be enticed to join in the worship festivals and sacrifices of the Canaanites appears only here in Exodus.
63. The term מַסֵּכָה ("[a god] of poured metal") is first used in 32:4 in reference to the golden calf.
64. The Feast of Unleavened Bread is mentioned numerous times in Exodus, but 34:18, with minor modifications, is a verbatim quotation of 23:15. Thus, 34:18 must be regarded as taken from the Book of the Covenant and not from the earlier legislation on this feast.
65. The MT has תִּזָּכָר, which appears to be a Niphal *yiqtol* form of זכר ("remember"). It is evidently a scribal error for הַזָּכָר ("the male"). See LXX

34:20a And you are to redeem with a lamb the firstborn from a donkey;
34:20b but if you do not redeem [it],
34:20c then you are to break its neck.
34:20d And you are to redeem all the firstborn of your sons.[66]
34:20e And no one is to appear before me empty-handed.[67]
34:21a And you are to work for six days,
34:21b but on the seventh day you are to rest;
34:21c [even] at plowing time and during harvest: you are to rest.[68]
34:22 And you are to celebrate the Feast of Weeks with the first fruits of the wheat harvest, and the Feast of Ingathering at the turn of the year.[69]
34:23 Three times per year all your males are to appear before the Lord YHWH, the God of Israel.[70]
34:24a For I will drive out nations before you and enlarge your borders,[71]
34:24b and no one is going to covet your land when you go up to appear before YHWH your God three times per year.
34:25a And you are not to offer the blood of my sacrifice with leavened bread.
34:25b And the sacrifice of the Feast of the Passover is not to be left over until morning.[72]

---

and Vulg. Sarna, *Exodus*, 218, suggests that it may be a verb זָכָר meaning "to drop a male." Thus, the NJPS has, "from all your livestock that drop a male as firstling." But he acknowledges that no other such occurrence exists, and that this apparent verb תִּזָּכָר is feminine, whereas its subject מִקְנְךָ is masculine. As such, this proposed translation of the unemended text is less persuasive than a simple emendation of the text.

66. This legislation concerning the redemption of the firstborn male animals and firstborn sons is adapted from 13:11–13.
67. This injunction (וְלֹא־יֵרָאוּ פָנַי רֵיקָם) is a verbatim quote of 23:15.
68. The Sabbath command appears numerous times in Exodus (16:26; 20:9–11; 23:12; 24:16), but this form of the command, with the injunction to rest even during plowing and harvest season, is unique in Exodus.
69. Exod. 34:22 alludes to 23:16, but 23:16 uses "Feast of Harvest" to refer to what 34:22 calls the "Feast of Weeks."
70. Except that it appends the words אֱלֹהֵי יִשְׂרָאֵל ("the God of Israel") and uses אֶת־ instead of אֶל־, Exod. 34:23 is a verbatim quotation of 23:17.
71. This probably alludes to Exod. 23:31, which speaks of YHWH expanding גְּבֻלֶךָ, "your (Israel's) territory."
72. Exod. 34:25 loosely quotes 23:18, the most significant difference being that 23:18 commands that the "fat of my feast" (חֵלֶב־חַגִּי) not be left till morning, where 34:25 more specifically speaks of not allowing the Passover sacrifice to remain until morning.

34:26a And you are to bring the beginning of the first fruits of your ground into the house of YHWH your God.
34:26b And you are not to boil a young goat in its mother's milk."[73]
34:27a And YHWH said to Moses,
34:27b "Write down these words,
34:27c for under these terms I make a covenant with you and with Israel."

Structure

This text, in which YHWH reaffirms his commitment to the Sinai covenant, is laid out as a modified or simplified covenant text, with a prologue, set of stipulations, and provision for maintaining the terms of the covenant.

I. Prologue (34:10–11)
II. Stipulations (34:12–26)
  A. Separation from Paganism (34:12–17)
  B. Acts of Piety (34:18–26)
III. Instructions for Covenant Documents (34:27)

Commentary

34:10–11. YHWH declares that he will renew the covenant with Israel. Notably, this is a private revelation to Moses and not a covenant-making ceremony (the people of Israel have no role whatsoever). Only YHWH acts in this case; the people do not make a vow of obedience and there is no ceremony analogous to that of Exod. 24. This is because the people have broken the covenant, and YHWH would be in his rights to abandon them and the covenant immediately. He, not they, is the wronged party. As the injured party, he must unilaterally decide whether or not he will enforce his rights under the terms of the covenant. Thus, this is not the making of a new covenant between YHWH and Israel; it is simply YHWH's declaration that he will continue to consider the covenant to be in force even though he could, if he chose, declare Israel to be in breach of covenant and walk away from it. More than that, God shows himself to be gracious (and to have fully yielded to Moses's intercession) in his declaration that he will yet perform great wonders among them. He will, after all, go with them, and will do yet mightier works in the future than he had done in the past. Israel is fully forgiven and restored.

Unlike other covenant prologues (Exod. 20:2; Deut. 1:1–4:40), this prologue does not look to the past but to the future. This, too, is an act

73. Exod. 34:26 is a verbatim citation of 23:19.

of grace, since a retrospective look would entail an overt mention of the recent and painful events of the golden calf. Instead, the forward-looking prologue is optimistic: YHWH will go with Israel, do great miracles, and drive out the nations before them.

34:12–26. We here have the covenant stipulations. As indicated in the notes to the translation above, the stipulations mentioned in this covenant renewal are almost entirely drawn from the last two parts of the Book of the Covenant at 23:10–19 and 20–33. However, the order is reversed, with 34:12–17 (warnings against idolatry) drawing heavily upon 23:20–33 and with 34:18–26 (injunctions about the Sabbath and other rituals) drawing heavily upon 23:10–19.[74] The order is reversed because, in light of the golden calf, the need to exhort Israel to flee paganism is more urgent, and it has first place.

But it is also important that 34:14 draws upon the first and second commandments at 20:3–5, the very beginning of the Book of the Covenant.[75] Thus, the stipulations of 34:12–26 really draw together the entire Book of the Covenant, starting with the Ten Commandments at 20:3 and going through to the end of its code of laws at 23:33. In short, the reader is to understand 34:12–26 as a summary of the Book of the Covenant and as a renewal of the charge to keep its stipulations. One should not regard 34:12–26 as the most important parts of the Book of the Covenant; rather, they represent its beginning and end and thus represent the whole thing.

On the other hand, the specific texts that are cited, and the order in which they are cited, are important. The stipulations of 34:12–17 focus on the need for Israel to avoid idolatry, paganism, and any interaction with pagans that might entice them into such activity. The reason for this is not hard to apprehend; Israel has just emerged from the golden calf episode, and it is clear that this is a tendency toward which they

74. Cf. Shimon Bar-On, "The Festival Calendars in Exodus XXIII 14–19 and XXXIV 18–26," *VT* 48, no. 2 (1998): 163, on the comparison of Exod. 23:14–19 to 34:18–26: "To my mind, any unprejudiced consideration of the large number of virtually identical provisions cannot lead to any conclusion other than that the two calendars of feasts are actually one and the same text. The accepted view of these two passages as belonging to two different documents—J and E—representing two literarily independent formulations, would seem not to be the result of objective study of the two texts themselves but rather of the scholarly necessity to sustain the classical documentary hypothesis." Bar-On develops his own theory about the redaction history of Exod. 34:18–26, but his starting point is well-taken.

75. I consider the Decalogue to be part of the Book of the Covenant.

are tempted. Therefore, they must make every effort to keep themselves from such temptations.

Several new elements appear in this exhortation; they serve as a kind of expositional midrash on the Book of the Covenant. One is the command to destroy the Asherim, which are here mentioned for the first time (the Book of the Covenant does command that they destroy מַצֵּבֹתֵיהֶם, the pagans' monumental sacred stones, at 23:24). The Asherim were poles sacred to the goddess Asherah, a fertility deity, mother goddess, and consort of the god El. Asherah poles were apparently ubiquitous in the land. They were probably not exactly images of the goddess but sacred poles meant to demarcate a place as sanctified to Asherah. In the Middle Bronze Age, Asherah is often depicted with a palm tree or a palmetto tree. With the passage of time, the depiction of the tree became more stylized, until it was essentially just a pole.[76] As such, poles were apparently used in the land to represent sacred trees and sacred ground. Unfortunately, the Israelites would not be able to resist their allure. The famous Kuntillet ʿAjrud inscription (from an 8th century B.C. Israelite site in the northern part of the Sinai Peninsula) reads "to YHWH of the Teman and his asherah."[77] At least some Israelites by syncretism folded the worship of Asherah into the Israelite faith and turned her into the consort of YHWH.

Also, the word מַסֵּכָה, referring to an idol "of poured metal" is not found in the Book of the Covenant but appears in the narrative at 32:4 to describe the golden calf. The word can be regarded as an allusion to that episode. That is, Israel is clearly, but not too harshly, told not to repeat the golden calf episode.

In addition, the text introduces at 34:15 the idea that worship of idols is a kind of prostitution (using the word זנה, to "fornicate" or "behave as a prostitute"). This language has multiple applications. First, it creates the metaphor of Israel as the bride of YHWH, turning away from him to go after other lovers. This would be developed later in the prophets, most notably in Hosea 1–3. Second, it alludes to the actual sacred prostitution that took place at the pagan sanctuaries. Israel would first fall into this snare at the Baal of Peor cult (Num. 25). Third, it portrays the intermarriage of Israelites and pagans as illicit, on a level with going to a prostitute, and thus the stern warning at 34:16.

---

76. Othmar Keel and Christoph Uehlinger, *Gods, Goddesses, and Images of God in Ancient Israel,* trans. Thomas H. Trapp (Minneapolis: Fortress, 1998), 153.

77. "Kuntillet ʿAjrud: Inscribed Pithos 2," translated by P. Kyle McCarter (*COS* 2.47B.171).

The commands of 34:18–26, as mentioned above, draw heavily upon 23:10–19. They focus on distinctive elements of Israelite worship: on the Sabbath, on three sacred festivals (Unleavened Bread, the Feast of Weeks, and the Feast of Ingathering), and on the redemption of the firstborn.[78] This emphasis, too, is a response to Israel's proclivity toward idolatry. Israel should focus on the faithful observance of its own religious rites; in doing this, it is much less likely to be drawn into paganism.

34:27. Moses is commanded to write down the words of the covenant as they are the stipulations that govern the covenant. This, the provision for the writing down of the rules of the covenant, is a formal element in a covenant text. But again, this is a summary and reaffirmation of the whole Book of the Covenant. It is not implying that any rule from the Book of the Covenant not specifically mentioned here is no longer in force.

Theological Summary of Key Points

1. This text is the consummation of all the intercession by Moses and of the declaration of the compassion of YHWH at 34:6–7. The crisis of the golden calf is ended and Israel's status as the people of the covenant is fully renewed, with YHWH again willing to travel among them. This sets the pattern for many generations to come, with Israel constantly falling into idolatry but YHWH remaining faithful to the covenant, punishing them but calling them back. It is the full realization that God truly is compassionate and slow to anger.

2. The stipulations of the renewal are a warning for Israel to get free from its besetting sin of idolatry. For us, they imply that we should be aware of how powerful a besetting sin can be and how we must take steps to escape it.

3. This text provides the model of a negative inducement (stern admonitions about the dangers of paganism) and a positive inducement (admonitions to worship YHWH rightly and keep his festivals, so that

78. The injunction of 34:20e, that one should not appear before YHWH empty-handed (i.e., without an offering) should be regarded as a separate admonition in this context. That is, it is not related to the law of the redemption of the firstborn, as the firstborn law has no connection to the annual festivals but would be fulfilled in any household whenever there was a firstborn male.

paganism will be less of a temptation). We are to escape evil by both fear of the punishment and attraction toward the good. Faithful worship and prayer enable us to escape temptation and sin.

4. From the standpoint of Old Testament theology and salvation history, this text sets the stage for the rest of the history of Israel up until the exile. Israel entered into covenant with YHWH at Exod. 19–24. Israel's status as the covenant people (and their very existence) was threatened by the golden calf of Exod. 32, but Moses's intercession and the revelation of the compassion of YHWH allowed the covenant to be reaffirmed rather than abandoned. However, a central theme of Israel's history, idolatry as a snare to Israel and a test of the forbearance of God, is set in motion. This will become a dominant strain of the Old Testament story.

VEILED GLORY (34:28–35)

Translation

34:28a And he was there with YHWH for forty days and forty nights;
34:28b he did not eat bread
34:28c and he did not drink water.
34:28d And he wrote on the tablets the words of the covenant, the Ten Commandments.
34:29a And it came about, when Moses was coming down from Mount Sinai
34:29b (and the two tablets of the testimony were in Moses's hand as he was coming down from the mountain),
34:29c that Moses did not know
34:29d that the skin of his face glowed[79] because of his speaking with him.

79. Interpreters have long been perplexed by the choice of the verb קָרַן for "glow" or "shine," since the word is evidently related to the noun קֶרֶן, "horn." Some translations, following the Vulgate, actually indicated that Moses had horns, and this gave rise to Michelangelo's much-copied statue of the horned Moses. But if Moses's head sprouted horns, it is hard to see why the text would speak of them coming from his skin. The LXX translates this as *δεδόξασται ἡ ὄψις τοῦ χρώματος τοῦ προσώπου αὐτοῦ*, "the appearance of the color of his face was glorified." William H. Propp, "The Skin of Moses' Face—Transfigured or Disfigured?" *CBQ* 49, no. 3 (1987): 375–86, suggests that it means that Moses's skin became blistered and then calloused through what was, in effect, radiation burns, but that the thickened, horny skin made him better able to withstand the power of the divine radiance. Hugo Gressmann, *Mose und seine Zeit; ein Kommentar zu den Mose-Sagen* (Göttingen: Vandenhoeck & Ruprecht, 1913), 246-51,

34:30a And Aaron and all the Israelites saw Moses,
34:30b and the skin of his face glowed!
34:30c And they were afraid to come near him.
34:31a And Moses called to them,
34:31b and Aaron and all the rulers from the congregation came back to him,
34:31c and Moses spoke to them.
34:32a And after that, all the Israelites approached,
34:32b and he gave them all the commands that YHWH had enunciated to him on Mount Sinai.
34:33a And Moses finished speaking with them,

---

argues that it refers to a horned, cultic mask that Moses wore. Karl Jaroš, "Des Mose 'strahlende Haut': Eine Notiz zu Ex 34:29, 30, 35," *ZAW* 88 (1976): 275–80, argues that Moses wore a mask with horns, but that P suppressed the idea by introducing the shining face. Against Gressmann, see especially Menahem Haran, "The Shining of Moses' Face: A Case Study in Biblical and Ancient Near Eastern Iconography," in *In the Shelter of Elyon: Essays on Ancient Palestinian Life and Literature in Honor of G. W. Ahlström*, ed. W. Boyd Barrick and John R. Spencer (Sheffield: *JSOT* Press, 1984), 160-5. But scholars have wondered why, if the meaning is that Moses's face glowed, the text does not use the Hiphil of אור, to "give light." But that word is actually functional, meaning to "provide illumination" so that people can see (Gen. 1:15; Exod. 13:21; Num. 8:2; Isa. 50:11; 60:19; etc.), although it can metaphorically mean to give light in the sense of showing approval or favor (Num. 6:25). Had the text used this word, it would be like saying that people used Moses's face for a flashlight! In my view, the use of קרן arises from the fact that in both ancient and modern imagery, a radiant body like the sun is depicted with pointed, horn-like projections coming from it. Thus, the horn-like projections from the Statue of Liberty represent a glowing head. In fact, our word "radiant" is from the Latin *radiare*, "to shine," which is itself probably derived from radius, a "rod" like the spoke of a wheel, which in turn may be related to the Greek ἄρδις, a "sharp point," like an arrowhead or a horn. Furthermore, the Sumerian word *si* is used for both horns and the radiance of the sun (Seth L. Sanders, "Old Light on Moses' Shining Face," *VT* 52, no. 3 (2002): 403; Sanders himself wrongly concludes from this that Moses becomes a kind of semi-divine figure, but the lexocographic analogy is helpful). Thus, we have in Hab. 3:4, קַרְנַיִם מִיָּדוֹ לוֹ ("horns [that is, beams of light] come from his hand"). In addition, Num. 27:20 states that Moses was to impart some of his "splendor" (הוֹד) to Joshua, his successor. This is not simply "authority" but a radiance of divine glory, and this usage has parallels in ancient Near Eastern literature (see Haran, "Moses' Face," 165-8). In short, the term means that Moses's skin was glowing.

34:33b and he put a veil[80] over his face.
34:34a But whenever Moses went in before YHWH to speak with him, he would remove[81] the veil until he came out.
34:34b And he would come out,
34:34c and he would tell the Israelites what commands he was receiving.
34:35a And the Israelites would see the face of Moses—
34:35b that the skin of Moses's face glowed.
34:35c And Moses would replace the veil over his face until he went in to speak with him.

Structure

This text is in two parts. The first describes the specific episode in which Moses, having interceded with YHWH and having secured the covenant renewal and YHWH's promise not to abandon his people, descended to tell the people what had happened. On this occasion, having been in communion with YHWH, Moses's face was glowing with the glory of God. The second part of the text describes Moses's routine practice in the aftermath of this episode, that he covered his face with a veil to cover its radiance.

I. The Afterglow of the Presence of God (34:28–33)
II. The Subsequent Use of the Veil (34:34–35)

Commentary

34:28–33. Moses's communion with God left an imprint upon him in the form of a radiant glow, a reflection of the glory of YHWH. This is accounted for by the prolonged period of time he spent with God (forty days), by the intensity of his communion (Moses fasted the whole time), and by the nature of the revelation given to him (the goodness and wonderful benefits [טוּב] of YHWH [33:19–34:7]). We should understand that what Moses experienced was the mercy of YHWH; that was the content of the revelation, and that was the significance of YHWH's decision to renew the covenant with Israel rather than to enforce his rights by either destroying Israel or abandoning them. The glow on Moses's face reflected YHWH's compassion; it was not a reflection of

80. The word for veil (מַסְוֶה) is used exclusively for the veil over Moses's face and is found only in this passage. It is not related to the curtain (פָּרֹכֶת) that separated the holy place from the holy of holies (see, for example, Exod. 26:33). Thus, one should not draw an analogy between the two.
81. The *yiqtol* יָסִיר here represents habitual action.

the raw power,[82] much less of the wrath, of YHWH. Nor was it meant to give new credentials to Moses.[83] Nor did it mark Moses as a kind of demigod.[84] His face glowed because he had been in close proximity to the glory that is the love, faithfulness, and saving righteousness of God. It is this truth that Paul explains in 2 Cor. 3 (see below Excursus: Paul's Interpretation of Moses's Veil).

Moses proceeded down the mountain holding the rewritten tablets of the covenant and he announced to Israel what had happened: God had renewed the covenant, had reaffirmed his requirements, and had pledged not to abandon them but to go with them. Moses did not realize, however, that his face glowed. Aaron and the people were of course alarmed at this and drew back, but Moses was able to gather them to himself to relay his message from YHWH. It appears that he did not don the veil until after he completed his message about the covenant renewal (34:33).

34:34–35. Afterwards, Moses maintained the practice of concealing the glow of his face with the veil, but he always removed it when before YHWH. Even about this, however, the text is somewhat unclear, since the Israelites continued to see the glow of his face (v. 35ab). Does this mean that the Israelites could see little bits of light shining out from behind the veil? Possibly, but it is more likely that he took off the veil when giving a public proclamation of YHWH's word to them, and that he put it back on when going about his ordinary business. Also, the text does not say anything directly about why Moses wore the veil. But the explanation is so obvious that it hardly needed stating: having a leader

82. At 33:20, YHWH indicates that there is a kind of divine radiance, a full encounter with the power of God, that no mortal can withstand and that is fatal. But God specifically and deliberately did not show Moses such a self-revelation. Moses was not endangered or harmed, and his own subsequent glowing face (34:30–35) did not endanger or harm anyone. It is therefore illegitimate to conclude from 33:20 that Moses's glowing face was somehow dangerous.
83. The supposition of Durham, *Exodus*, 468, and Stuart, *Exodus*, 735-6, that the glowing face was meant to reestablish the authority of Moses is certainly wrong. By this point in the narrative, Moses's authority is not in question, and the Israelites are highly submissive (33:5–6), and the text never implies that the glowing made them realize that Moses really was God's spokesman.
84. This is the position of Morgenstern, "Bloody Husband," who believes that legend has elevated Moses to the point of being almost the equal, and sometimes the superior, of YHWH.

whose face shone like a lamp was more than a little weird. Some people would find it frightening and disturbing, while others would want to stare at Moses as though he were some kind of freak. Thus, for his own peace of mind and theirs, he covered it.[85]

Theological Summary of Key Points

1. One cannot experience the power of the grace of God in one's life without spending a prolonged period of time in God's presence. Moses engaged in a fast of forty days (a pattern that was emulated by Jesus) and, in effect, remained in prayer, appealing to God and interceding for Israel. In this, he found himself experiencing firsthand the "goodness" of YHWH. The glow on his face demonstrated the profound presence of God's grace within him. For us, there is no shortcut to God's presence.

2. Moses's face was a living representation of the benediction in Num. 6.25: "May YHWH make his face shine on you, and may he be gracious to you" (יָאֵר יְהוָה פָּנָיו אֵלֶיךָ וִיחֻנֶּךָּ). Although the Israelites do not seem to have realized it, they were seeing in Moses's shining face a visible manifestation of the blessings and kindness of YHWH.

3. Moses's mother had said that he was "good," like the first creation of humanity (Exod. 2:2; see commentary above), and here Moses is a man in God's image like no other. His face, like YHWH's, radiated God's nature and goodness. Of Jesus, similarly, it is said, "In him was life, and the life was the light of humanity" (John 1:4) and "[He] is the radiance of [God's] glory and the visible representation of his being" (Heb. 1:3).

4. Moses came down the mountain as an emissary of good news: YHWH had chosen to continue the Sinai covenant and would not abandon Israel. This day was as great a day as the Passover and departure from Egypt or as the crossing of the *Yam Suph*. Israel's sin was forgiven! By analogy, the greatest words a paralyzed man could hear were not "Rise and walk" but, "Friend, your sins are forgiven" (Luke 5:18–25).

---

85. Against Scott J. Hafemann, *Paul, Moses, and the History of Israel: The Letter/Spirit Contrast and the Argument from Scripture in 2 Corinthians 3* (Peabody: Hendrickson, 1996), 223 (see also Hafemann, "The Glory and Veil of Moses in 2 Cor 3:7–14: An Example of Paul's Contextual Exegesis of the OT—A Proposal," *HBT* 14, no. 1 [1992]: 31–49), there is no suggestion in the text that Moses veiled his face to protect the Israelites from seeing the glory of God because seeing it would mean their deaths. They did in fact see it (Exod. 16:10), and they did not die.

5. The people did not know what to make of Moses' shining face and were disturbed or astonished at it. But the real point here is not the physical shining of Moses's face; it is the power of God to transform a human being. Many people hardly know what to make of true godliness and grace in a person's life and countenance. It is strange, disturbing, or frightening.

Excursus: Paul's Interpretation of Moses's Veil
Paul refers to Exod. 34 in the course of his correspondence with the Corinthian church at 2 Cor. 3, and he specifically refers to Moses's glowing face and the veil. But Paul's interpretation has many difficulties. The Greek is elliptical and allusive, and translators have not been careful in their renditions of Paul's vocabulary. In fact, the Greek text of 2 Cor. 3 is poorly served in standard translations. As it appears in English versions, Paul says that Moses put on the veil so that the Israelites would not see that the glow in his face was fading away.[86] But

86. Among English translations, for example, see the renditions of *εἰς τὸ τέλος τοῦ καταργουμένου* from 2 Cor. 3:13 in the RSV, NRSV, NJB, NIV, TNIV, NASB, and CEV, where the verb is either explicitly or implicitly taken to mean "fade." The interpretation of *καταργουμένου* as a fading away is supported by E. Bernard Allo, *Saint Paul, Seconde Épître aux Corinthiens* (Paris: J. Gabalda, 1956), 89-91; Philip E. Hughes, *Paul's Second Epistle to the Corinthians: The English Text with Introduction, Exposition and Notes* (Grand Rapids: Eerdmans, 1962), 109; Linda Belleville, *2 Corinthians* (Downers Grove: InterVarsity, 1996), 104; and Francis Watson, *Paul and the Hermeneutics of Faith* (London: T & T Clark, 2004), 293. Rudolf Bultmann, *The Second Letter to the Corinthians.* trans. Roy A. Harrisville (Minneapolis: Augsburg, 1985), 85, also seems to take it this way, commenting that the Israelites "were not to notice that Moses' *δόξα* was at an end." Others recognize that "fade away" is an impossible translation but seem to have great difficulty providing a coherent interpretation. Victor P. Furnish, *II Corinthians,* AB (New York: Doubleday, 1984), 207, asserts that Paul is claiming that Moses put on the veil so that the Israelites would not see the end of "the entire ministry of the old covenant," but the veil certainly did not have this function; it was not meant to hide the end of the old covenant. See also Jan Lambrecht, *Second Corinthians,* (Collegeville: The Liturgical Press, 1999), 52. Simon J. Kistemaker, *Exposition of the Second Epistle to the Corinthians* (Grand Rapids: Baker, 1997), 118-9, translates the line as "the end of what was set aside" but then stumbles trying to explain what this means, finally suggesting (wrongly) that Exodus teaches that the Israelites could not look at the glow because they had guilty consciences. The ESV translation, "the outcome of what was being brought to an end," is equally opaque. Hafemann, "Glory and

this would be deceitful, and there was no good reason for Moses to do it.[87] More significantly, Exod. 34 never implies that he was trying to conceal a fading of the glow. In fact, Exod. 34 never indicates that the glow was fading at all. According to many translations of 2 Cor. 3:14, moreover, the veil is some kind of inability to understand Torah that can only be removed "in Christ." But in Exodus the veil is purely a practical measure for dealing with the discomfort people had in looking at Moses' shining face. Overall, Paul's interpretation of Moses's actions, as indicated by English translations of 2 Cor. 3, is arbitrary if not absurd from the standpoint of what Exodus actually says.[88] It is, perhaps, for all of these reasons that New Testament scholars often treat 2 Cor. 3 as though it really had little to do with Exod. 34,[89] having no point of contact beyond the fact that Paul alludes to Moses's veil and glowing face.[90]

Veil," 40, argues strongly against a meaning such as "fade" at v. 13, but suggests that the veil "brought the glory of God to an end in terms of that which it would accomplish if not veiled, i.e., the judgment and destruction of Israel." But it is difficult to imagine how the verse could possibly be translated with such a meaning.

87. Mitzi L. Minor, *2 Corinthians,* (Macon: Smyth & Helwys, 2009), 75-6, suggests that Paul means to portray Moses as duplicitous, but Minor herself is aware that Moses is a "hero" for Paul, and so she suggests that Paul's presentation of Moses as a fraud is mere "rhetoric" and not "theology." But this hardly helps to settle the issue.

88. Jason C. Meyer, *The End of the Law: Mosaic Covenant in Pauline Theology* (Nashville: B & H Academic, 2009), 96–7, for example, argues that Moses donned the veil because he wanted to harden the Israelites' hearts. As a reading of Paul, this interpretation is wrongheaded, not seeing that the veiling is the result, not the cause, of the Israelites' hard hearts. Exod. 34, moreover, certainly does not indicate that Paul donned the veil to harden the Israelites' hearts.

89. Furnish, *II Corinthians*, 230, argues that apart from Moses's dazzling face (and later the veil), the exposition in 2 Cor. 3:7–11 is based on Paul's own remarks and not on the text of Exodus.

90. But an exception to the rule of separating Paul's interpretation from the intent of Torah is Watson, *Hermeneutics*, 291-6, who asserts that Moses in Exod. 34 actually is deceiving the Israelites, making them believe that the shining is permanent, and that Paul perceives Moses's deceitfulness. Watson's conclusion is that "*the veiling of Moses' face signifies the fact that, apart from Christ and its own indirect testimony to Christ, the Torah itself promotes a belief in its own enduring and unsurpassable authority*. . . . [Torah] conceals the fact of its own transitoriness, thereby encouraging a belief in its permanence and a disbelief in the gospel's claim

Within Exodus, the shining of Moses's face comes at a climactic and indeed very positive moment. At Sinai, God had offered the covenant to Israel, the promise that they would become his "special possession" (19:5–6). Israel accepted, and Moses received the Book of the Covenant (Exod. 19—23). Israel reaffirmed its desire to enter into covenant with YHWH, and the covenant was ratified (Exod. 24). At this point, Moses received the guidelines for making the Tent of Meeting (Exod. 25—31). Since Israel was now YHWH's special possession, he would sojourn among them in the Tent. In Exod. 32:1–6, however, Israel engaged in idolatry and paganism, an act that was flagrantly in violation of the terms YHWH had laid down. YHWH therefore intended to end the covenant and destroy them, but Moses dissuaded him (32:7–14). Moses restored order and destroyed the idol, but YHWH now declared that he would not go with Israel but only send his angel instead (32:33—33:3). Moses set about making intercession again, this time appealing for YHWH not to abandon Israel in their journeys. YHWH at last agreed, and he renewed the covenant (34:11–28). At this point, with the covenant fully renewed and YHWH committed to going with Israel, the building of the Tent of Meeting could commence (Exod. 35). Meanwhile, however, Moses had seen the glory of God and had come back to the camp with a glowing face. As context indicates, Moses was not looking for an esoteric knowledge of God or for an experience that would make him a spiritual superhuman. He was seeking reassurance of God's favor for himself and Israel. The revelation of the glory was more than he asked for (not less), because he saw "all" of God's "goodness." The experience and revelation was of God's mercy and favor, and the glowing face reflected this. What, then, does Paul make of this?

Paul composed his interpretation of Moses's veil in the context of

---

that God's definitive self-disclosure occurs not at Sinai but in the raising of Jesus" (emphasis original). This is entirely wrong. The most natural interpretation of Exod. 34 is that Moses put on the veil because the people found his face disturbing, not because Moses was trying to trick them. Exodus hardly presents the Sinai covenant as enduring, not least in the fact that it narrates how grossly Israel violated it, so that it was almost cancelled (and Israel was almost annihilated) at the very time of its inauguration (Exod. 32). Certainly Exodus, with its unending recital of Israel's failures, does not present Torah as sufficient and not needing a further divine intervention. Finally, if Torah were as Watson describes it, then Paul's opponents would not have a veil over their hearts at all, but would be reading Torah exactly as intended. Their only failing would be that they, unlike Paul, did not catch Torah in its deceitfulness. But Paul's point is not that Torah and Moses have pulled the wool over their eyes.

his ongoing conflict with Judaizers, teachers who asserted that gentile Christians, in order to be truly incorporated into the people of God, had to become proselytes, taking upon themselves all the regulations of Judaism (such as kosher dietary laws, observance of Jewish festivals, and above all, circumcision for the males).[91] In contrast with what we see in Galatians or Romans, however, where Paul explicitly deals with circumcision and other requirements for proselytes, his response in 2 Cor. 3 is primarily a response to the claims of his opponents, the Judaizing teachers, to have more credibility than Paul himself has. These teachers flourished their credentials, "letters of recommendation" (2 Cor. 3:1), and apparently made much of the fact that Paul had no such credentials. But Paul had no need for such documents; the Corinthians themselves were his credentials (2 Cor. 3:2). Having made a distinction between a written text (ἐπιστολὴ) and the work of God, he extends this line of argument, moving from the credentials of the false teachers (written documents) to the substance of their ministry (the written text of Torah). They are teachers of the "letter" (γράμμα), that is, of Torah, but he is a minister of the Spirit under the new covenant (v. 6). This leads into the premise for all that follows, Paul's contention that the Spirit gives life but the letter kills (v. 6b).

91. There are today alternative views about the origin and doctrine of the false teachers in Corinth. Belleville, *2 Corinthians*, 34, summarizes the various major views, including the ideas that they were Jewish charismatics or proto-Gnostics. There are also various eccentric views, such as Dalton 1987, that the opponents in 2 Cor. 3 are gentile Judaizers, and Duff 2004, who reinterprets the controversy over the law. But in reality it seems that Paul's opponents were the same kind of Judaizers he encountered repeatedly in his ministry. These teachers are focused on Torah (called by Paul in 2 Cor. 3 "the letter," the "ministry of condemnation," "that which is about to be made null," "Moses," and simply "the old covenant"). This strong emphasis on Torah is inexplicable if Paul's opponents did not use that as the basis for their teaching, and there is no indication that their interpretation of Torah was outside of mainstream Judaism. The lack of focus on issues such as circumcision here in 2 Cor. is best explained by the fact that Paul is not at this point dealing with that specific teaching, but is instead concerned to show that he, and not his opponents, rightly understands and teaches the Scriptures. Furthermore, it is not special pleading to suggest that Paul may have already dealt with larger theological issues involving Torah, circumcision, and justification in prior correspondence with Corinth. If he had not, his harsh description of Torah as the "ministry of condemnation" (given here without explanation) would be hard to understand.

A major problem with interpreting 2 Cor. 3 is how loosely *καταργέω*, a verb of critical importance in this passage, is handled by translators. The verb essentially means "to make idle or inoperative," and in a legal context means to render a law or a process inoperative, that is, to nullify it.[92] Translators of the New Testament, however, have often rendered it as "destroy," "come to an end," or, in 2 Cor. 3, as "fade away." These meanings are not attested elsewhere, however, and in no case does such a translation actually fit the context.

In the New Testament, *καταργέω* occurs at Luke 13:7; Rom. 3:3, 31; 4:14; 6:6; 7:2, 6; 1 Cor. 1:28; 2:6; 6:13; 13:8, 10, 11; 15:24, 26; 2 Cor. 3:7, 11, 13, 14; Gal. 3:17; 5:4, 11; Eph. 2:15; 2 Thess. 2:8; 2 Tim. 1:10; Heb. 2:14. In the Lukan text, it refers to making fertile ground idle by leaving a nonproductive fig tree in place. In Paul, it is used in various discussions of justification. In Rom. 6:6, for example, Paul uses *καταργέω* to assert that the body of sin "is made inoperative" by the cross. The verb does not mean that the body is "destroyed" or "done away with"[93] by the cross; it means that through the cross the flesh loses its power to dominate us, "so that we may no longer be enslaved to sin." Romans 7:2 illustrates the legal use of *καταργέω*, in that a woman's obligations to fidelity to her husband are nullified when the husband dies. In Gal. 3:17, Paul argues the law that was introduced 430 years after the covenant with Abraham could not "nullify" (*καταργέω*) the promise.

A number of passages, in the eyes of translators, demand a meaning such as "destroy" or "remove." For example, 1 Cor. 6:13 is often taken to mean that God will "destroy" food and the stomach (e.g., NRSV, ESV, and NIV). But this is incorrect (why or when would God "destroy" food and the stomach?), and it misses the whole point. The meaning is that in the eschaton human life will no longer be sustained by the natural means currently employed, by "food and stomach." God will cause the old rules that governed life to "cease to function" (*καταργέω*). That being the case, and since Christians are supposed to have their focus on the resurrection, they should not be overly dominated by concerns over food and the stomach now. An analogous example is the use of *καταργέω* in 1 Cor. 13:8–11, which states that when the perfect means of knowing God has come (the direct encounter with him in the

92. This meaning is illustrated in classical texts by Euripides, *Phoenissae* 751-753 and Strabo, *On Machines* 4.6. The LXX also conforms to this meaning, using *καταργέω* at Ezra 4:21; 5:5; 6:8.

93. As in the ESV, which translates *καταργέω* as "might be brought to nothing," or the TNIV, which translates it as "might be done away with."

resurrection), then all other modes of knowing him (prophecy, tongues, and the like) will be "nonfunctional."[94]

Another noteworthy usage is at 2 Thess. 2:8, which speaks of the "lawless one" whom "the Lord will remove by the breath of his mouth and will nullify (*καταργέω*) by the visible manifestation of his arrival." The Lord will indeed "remove" the lawless one, but the verb for that is *ἀναιρέω*, and it is accomplished by divine command ("the breath of his mouth"). What *καταργέω* communicates is the nullifying of all the pretenses of the antichrist figure, the lawless one, and this is accomplished by the mere arrival of Christ. That is, when the true Messiah appears, the claims of the false one will be nullified indeed.

In 2 Cor. 3, *καταργέω* is often translated as "fade away" (vv. 7, 13), "come to an end" (v. 11), or "be removed" (v. 14), but none of these meanings is really valid for this verb, and it should be self-evident that it is odd to have the same verb in the same context used with such different meanings. Verse 11 most clearly sets forth the meaning of the term for this chapter in stating that if "the thing that was being nullified" (*τὸ καταργούμενον*) had glory, then "the thing that abides" (*τὸ μενον*) must have much greater glory. These terms refer, respectively, to the old covenant, which was to be legally nullified, and the new covenant, which was to remain in force forever.[95]

Similarly, v. 7 does not mean that the glow on Moses's face was "fading away." Literally translated, it speaks of "the being-annulled glory" (*τὴν δοξαν . . . τὴν καταργουμένην*). But, again, the thing "being annulled" is the old covenant. The line could legitimately be paraphrased to say that the Israelites could not bear to gaze into Moses's face because of the "old covenant glory" that it possessed. Paul's main point is that even the old covenant, something that was due to be nullified, had glory so great that the Israelites were unwilling to look at it.

Verse 13 is difficult, but it does not mean that Moses put on a veil so that the Israelites would not see the glow on his face fade out. Like v. 11,

---

94. The verb *καταργέω* does not mean "cease" in v. 8 even though it is used in proximity to *παύομαι* ("cease"). Here and in Rom. 4:14, Paul uses parallel structures with words that are semantically analogous but that are by no means synonymous: *καταργέω* ("be inoperative"), *κενόω* ("be empty"), *παύομαι* ("cease"), and *πίπτω* ("fall"). The verbs communicate similar underlying truths, but they are no more synonyms in Greek than are their counterparts in English.

95. The verbs *μένω* and *καταργέω*, respectively, refer to the terms of a treaty either remaining in force or being annulled. An example of the verbs used in this manner is at Herodotus 4.201.3.

v. 13 uses *τὸ καταργούμενον* in reference to the old covenant. The end of v. 13 could be translated, "so that they not gaze forever (into Moses's face) right up to the end of the thing being nullified (that is, to the end of the old covenant)." The verse thus literally means that he put on the veil so that they would not keep on staring at the glow on his face forever, until the end of the old covenant. But it is not meant to be taken so literally; it simply means, in agreement with what Exod. 34 indicates, that Moses put on the veil so that people would not be fixated on staring at it. But there is more to it than this. Paul deliberately uses this peculiar language in order to exploit the ambiguity of the word *τέλος*, which can mean both "end" and "purpose." This means that the verse could also be translated, "so that they not gaze into the purpose of the thing being nullified (that is, into the purpose of the old covenant)." That purpose was to bring people into the knowledge of God, so that they would experience his transforming presence. Because the people were so focused upon the physical phenomenon of Moses's glowing face, they could not grasp what it signified, which was the power of an encounter with the grace of God. And because they were so upset by his face, Moses had no choice but to put on the veil. The veil was thus a metaphor of their inability to grasp the point of being in the covenant, to know God.

Finally, *καταργέω* appears in v. 14 in a clause that is usually translated something like "because only in Christ is (the veil) removed" (*ὅτι ἐν Χριστῷ καταργεῖται*). But *καταργέω* does not mean "remove." It refers again to the nullifying of the old covenant. And in this context, *ὅτι* does not mean "because" but "that." *Ὅτι* points to what, because of the veil on their hearts, the Judaizers cannot see: that the new covenant has nullified the old. The latter part of v. 14 should be translated, "To this day, the same veil remains over the reading of the old covenant, not uncovering (the fact) that it (the old covenant) is nullified in Christ." That is, the Israelites of Moses's day could not see the glory of the grace of God in Moses's face, and Paul's opponents could not see it when they read Moses's book.

The translation for the chapter that I would suggest, therefore, is quite different from what one usually sees. With supplied words in italics, it is as follows:

> ***1*** Do we begin again to commend ourselves, or do we need, as some do, letters of recommendation to you or from you? ***2*** Our letter of recommendation is none other than you, written on our hearts, known and read by all people. ***3*** It is evident that you are a letter from Christ written under our ministry not in ink but in the Spirit of the living God, *and* not on tablets

of stone but on tablets of heart and *living* flesh. ***4*** This is the kind of confidence we have through Christ toward God! ***5*** *It is* not that we of ourselves are sufficient to claim something, as though *it were* of our own *making*, but our sufficiency is from God, ***6*** who has made us sufficient to be ministers of a new covenant, *one that is* not of letter but of Spirit. For the letter kills, but the Spirit gives life.

7 Now if the ministry of death, engraved in letters on stone, came about with glory, so that the Israelites could not gaze at Moses's face because of the glory of his face—*the old covenant* glory that was in process of becoming null and void— ***8*** how could the ministry of the Spirit not have even more glory?
9 For if there was glory in the ministry of condemnation, by how much more does the ministry of righteousness exceed it
in glory? ***10*** For in fact, when the *new covenant had its* turn, the thing that had been glorified *(the old covenant)* turned out to have no glory on account of the *new covenant's* surpassing
glory. ***11*** For if the *dispensation* that was in process of becoming null and void went through a period of glory, how much more will the dispensation that remains in force *abide* in glory?

12 So then, having such a hope, we employ much boldness:
13 *we do* not *do* as Moses *did*, who would place a veil over his face so that the Israelites would not stare *at his face* forever, until the very end of—and into the purpose of—that which was in process of becoming null and void, *the old covenant.*
14 But *the real problem was not the veil; it was that* "their minds were hardened."

This is evident in the fact that, right up to the present day, the same veil remains over the reading of the old covenant, not uncovering *the fact* that in Christ *the old covenant* is null and
void. ***15*** But *in contrast to the prior veil over Moses's face*, to this day whenever Moses is read a veil lies over their hearts.

16 On the other hand, "whenever he turns toward the Lord *YHWH*, the veil is removed." ***17*** Now "the Lord *YHWH*" *here refers to* the Spirit, and "where the Spirit of the Lord *YHWH* is, *there is* freedom." ***18*** And all of us, mirroring in an uncovered face the glory of the Lord *Jesus, becoming a reflection that bears* the authentic image *of God*, are transformed by

God's glory into *God's* glory, as the counterpart to the glory that shone from Lord *YHWH the* Spirit.

The structure of 2 Cor. 3 is as follows:[96] First, Paul turns to the claims of his opponents, who possess letters of recommendation and claim on that basis that Paul has less authority than they do. Paul counters that the Corinthians themselves are his letters of recommendation. Furthermore, he makes a comparison: having contrasted the physical epistles that his opponents possess with the writing the Spirit does on the human heart, he then contrasts the letter of the law that kills, with the Spirit that gives life (vv. 1–6). Second, Paul asserts that the old covenant had very great "glory," but that the new covenant has far greater glory. This is based in the meaning of "glory" that Paul derives from Moses's experience in Exod. 33–34. This "glory" was not primarily a bright glow or some other physical manifestation of splendor. Instead, it was God's transformative grace. Moses's glowing face was merely evidence of an encounter with the goodness of God. But this glory was in the context of the old covenant, something Paul calls the "ministry of condemnation" and "the ministry of death." But the new covenant, by nature, is a ministry of life and grace, and therefore it has far greater glory. Thus, it is foolish, now that the new covenant has come, to follow a ministry that is based upon the "letter" that was "subject to cancellation," the old covenant (vv. 7–11). Third, the passage contrasts Moses's veiling of his face before the Israelites (vv. 12–15) with his unveiling of his face before YHWH (vv. 16–18). In the former case, Paul speaks of two counterparts: the ancient Israelites, whose hardened hearts kept them from understanding the significance of Moses's face and forced him to put on the veil (vv. 12–14a), and Paul's opponents, who likewise have hardened hearts that have effectively given them an internal veil when they read Moses (vv. 14b–15). Both parties, the ancient Israelites and Paul's opponents, are unable to perceive or experience the goodness of God. Fourth, the final section (vv. 16–18) also speaks of two counterparts: Moses unveiled in the presence of the Lord, and new covenant believers unveiled in the presence of the Lord. Both parties experience the transformative glory.

To summarize, Paul asserts that in Exod. 33–34 Moses encountered all the goodness of God, that is, his glory, in the context of his intercession before YHWH. This caused his face to glow, and this was evidence of his having been in the presence of divine mercy, goodness, and grace. This occurred, however, in the context of the old covenant,

96. For simplicity's sake, this excursus treats 2 Cor. 3 as a discreet text.

a dispensation that was characterized by condemnation and was destined to be annulled. But if even the old covenant, a ministry of death, had such glorious grace, how much greater is it in the new covenant, a covenant founded in mercy and which will never be superseded? In Moses's day, however, the Israelites could not see the meaning of Moses's glowing face. They were, in fact, disturbed by it, and Moses had to cover it with a veil. Paul's opponents, who seek to continue the old covenant, also cannot recognize the greater glory of the new covenant; it is as though the veil was on their hearts. Those who turn to Christ in the new covenant, however, are like Moses in the tent before YHWH with an unveiled face. They receive and reflect the transformative glory of God. In all of this, Paul's interpretation is perfectly in harmony with what Exod. 33–34 describes.

GIVING (35:1—36:7)

Now that the covenant has been renewed and the golden calf incident has been put behind them, Israel can build the Tent of Meeting complex. If Moses had not by his intercession persuaded YHWH to accompany Israel, there would be no need for the Tent of Meeting.

Translation

35:1a And Moses assembled the whole congregation of the Israelites,
35:1b and he said to them,
35:1c "These are the things that YHWH has commanded [you] to do:
35:2a For six days work is to be done, but on the seventh day you are to have a holy Sabbath day of rest for YHWH;
35:2b anyone who does work on it shall be put to death.
35:3 And you are to not kindle a fire in any of your dwellings on the Sabbath day."
35:4a And Moses spoke to all the congregation of the Israelites, as follows:
35:4b "This is the command that YHWH has given, as follows:
35:5a 'Take from among you an offering for YHWH.
35:5b–9 Anyone who has a willing heart should bring something as an offering to YHWH: gold and silver and bronze and blue and purple and scarlet and linen and goat hair and tanned ram's hide and *tahash* leather and acacia wood and oil [suitable] for lighting and spices [suitable] for the anointing oil and for the fragrant incense, and stones of carnelian and [other] stones [suitable] for setting in the ephod and the breastpiece.[97]

97. Although 35:5b–9 and 35:10b–19 are extraordinarily long, each is a single clause.

35:10a Let every man with a wise mind among you come,

35:10b–19 so that he can make all that YHWH has commanded: the tent-sanctuary with its canopy and its covering, its hooks and its frames, its crossbars, its posts, and its bases; the ark and its poles, the place of atonement, and the sheet of the screen; the table and its poles, and all its utensils, and the bread of the Presence; and the light-giving menorah and its utensils and its lamps and the oil for the light; and the altar of incense and its poles, and the anointing oil and the fragrant incense, and the screen over the entrance at the entrance of the tent-sanctuary; the altar of whole offering and the bronze grating that belongs to it, its poles, and all its utensils, the basin and its stand; the screening curtains of the court, its posts and its bases, and the screen for the gate of the court; the pegs of the tent-sanctuary and the pegs of the court and their lines; the woven garments for officiating in the holy place, the holy garments for Aaron the priest and the garments of his sons, in order [for them] to function as priests.'"

35:20 And all the congregation of the Israelites departed from Moses.

35:21a And everyone whose heart moved him and everyone whose spirit provoked him to good will came.

35:21b They brought the offering for YHWH for the work of the Tent of Meeting and for all its service and for the holy garments.

35:22a And the men came, as well as the women[98]—all who had willing hearts.

35:22b They brought brooches and earrings and rings and necklaces (all articles of gold).

35:22c And every man who [came] made a wave offering of gold to YHWH.

35:23 And every man with whom was found blue and purple and scarlet and linen and goat hair and tanned ram's hide and *tahash* leather brought them.

98. The expression וַיָּבֹאוּ הָאֲנָשִׁים עַל־הַנָּשִׁים is somewhat unusual. It could be taken to mean, "And the men came on account of the women" (see Gen. 20:3), but this makes no sense in context. Propp, *Exodus 19–40*, 661, suggests that it means that the men went to their wives to receive the women's donations of jewelry. That is, it was the men who actually carried the donations to the work site. This is a creative solution, but it has no analogy in Hebrew usage that I can see. The most reasonable interpretation is the most common, that עַל here means "in addition to." One may compare Jer. 44:20, "and Jeremiah said to all the people, both the men and the women" (וַיֹּאמֶר יִרְמְיָהוּ אֶל־כָּל־הָעָם עַל־הַגְּבָרִים וְעַל־הַנָּשִׁים).

35:24a Everyone who could make an offering of silver and bronze brought [it as] the offering to YHWH.

35:24b And every man with whom was found acacia wood for any work of the project brought [it].

35:25a And every woman of wise heart spun with her hands,

35:25b and they brought what they had spun: the blue and the purple [and] the scarlet and the linen.

35:26 And all the women whose hearts moved them spun the goat hair with wisdom.[99]

35:27–28 And the leading men brought the carnelian stones and the setting stones (for the ephod and for the breastpiece) and the spice and the oil (for light and for the anointing oil and for the fragrant incense).

35:29 Every man and woman whose heart moved him or her to bring [something] for all the work that YHWH through Moses had commanded to be done—the Israelites—brought [it as] a freewill offering to YHWH.

35:30a And Moses said to the Israelites,

35:30b "Look!

35:30c YHWH has called by name Bezalel the son of Uri, the son of Hur, of the tribe of Judah.

35:31–33 And he has filled him with the Spirit of God, for wisdom, for understanding and for knowledge and for every [kind of] skill, to devise artistic designs, to work in gold, and in silver, and in bronze, and in the cutting of stones for mounting, and in the carving of wood, in order to do every [kind of] skilled craft.

35:34 He also has put teaching ability into his heart—both he and Oholiab, the son of Ahisamach, of the tribe of Dan.

35:35 He has filled them with a wisdom of heart [that enables them] to do [every kind of] work: of an engraver and of a designer and of an embroider in blue and in purple [and] in scarlet and in linen, and of a weaver, as men who do every [kind of] work and as designers.

36:1 And Bezalel and Oholiab and every man of wise heart, to whom YHWH has given in those matters wisdom and understanding in order to know how to do all the work in the construction of the sanctuary, are to make [it] in accordance with all that YHWH has commanded."

36:2 And Moses summoned Bezalel and Oholiab and every man of wise heart, in whose hearts YHWH had placed wisdom—everyone whose heart moved him to offer his services for the work, in order to do it.

36:3a They received from Moses the entire offering that the Israelites had brought to do the construction work of the sanctuary.

---

99. Taking בְּחָכְמָה with what follows (contrary to the MT accentuation).

36:3b And [the Israelites] still brought[100] to him freewill offerings every morning.
36:4 And all the wise men who were doing all the work of the sanctuary came, each from the work which he was doing,
36:5a and they said the following to Moses:
36:5b "The people are bringing more than enough for the construction work that YHWH commanded [us] to do."
36:6a And Moses issued a command,
36:6b and a proclamation was circulated throughout the camp, as follows:
36:6c "No man or woman is to continue to do any work for the sanctuary offering."
36:6d And the people were restrained from bringing [offerings].
36:7 For the [contribution] effort had been sufficient—more than sufficient—for getting all the work done.

Structure

This section is a straightforward account of the collection of an offering of materials for constructing the Tent of Meeting and also of the appointment of overseers for the work. There is a parallel pattern in this text, with three passages related to work (35:1–3; 35:10–19; 35:30–36:3a) each followed by a passage related to the offering (35:4–9; 35:20–29; 36:3b–7). The parallel parts suggest that work (with due attention paid to the Sabbath) and contributions are equally important for the building and maintenance of YHWH's shrine.

I. Restatement of the Sabbath Regulation (35:1–3)
II. The Command to Collect an Offering (35:4–9)
III. The Command to Gather Qualified Workers (35:10–20)
IV. The Collection of the Offering (35:21–29)
V. The Appointment of Bezalel and Oholiab over the Work (35:30–36:3a)
VI. The Great Success of the Offering (36:3b–7)

Commentary

35:1–3. The most peculiar thing about this restatement of the Sabbath regulations is that it is here at all. We would not expect that the first thing after the story of the golden calf and its aftermath would be a repetition of the command to keep the Sabbath. But in fact, as

100. The ו + X + *qatal* formation (וְהֵם הֵבִיאוּ) here gives an offline statement that sets up the background for the narrative that follows. It therefore marks a break in this narrative and begins a new subsection.

Daniel Timmer points out, exhortations to observe the Sabbath appear at 31:12–17 and 35:1–3 and therefore frame the whole golden calf narrative of Exod. 32–34. This suggests that Sabbath is a key to understanding the whole of Exod. 32–34, and indeed to understanding the entire book.[101] The primary significance of Sabbath is that it points to the obtaining of "rest" in the presence of God. This goes back to the creation narrative, where the whole of the created cosmos is portrayed as a sanctuary, and humanity is by the Sabbath invited to enjoy the person of God through worship (Gen. 1:1–2:3). We have also seen that the Song of the Sea (Exod. 15) has a structure that parallels the creation narrative. It culminates in the hope for Israel to enter the "sanctuary" of the Promised Land. They would there enjoy God's rest. With the making of the Sinai covenant, God was to sojourn with Israel in the Tent of Meeting, allowing Israel to enjoy the divine presence, that is, to enjoy the "rest" of having YHWH in their midst.

Thus, the instructions for the Tent of Meeting and its furnishings (Exod. 25–31) follow directly upon the making of the Sinai covenant (Exod. 24), and the instructions conclude with an admonition to observe the Sabbath at 31:12–17. However, the golden calf threatened all of this, first nearly bringing about Israel's destruction, and then leaving Israel faced with the possibility of having to move toward the land without having YHWH among them. At the end of Moses's intercession, as described above, Israel was fully restored and the covenant renewed. As such, the possibility of enjoying the presence of YHWH among them, "entering his rest," is again open to Israel. The commands to begin the building of the Tent of Meeting therefore commence with an exhortation to observe the Sabbath. By doing this, Israel will demonstrably practice the "rest" that covenant offers, and they will show that they understand that cessation from labor and dependence upon YHWH are essential for understanding the true meaning of having God dwell among them.

Interpreters have naturally wondered why this exhortation to keep the Sabbath specifies that they are to kindle no fires on that day, and even what the command actually entails. The standard talmudic interpretation is that people are not to kindle fires, an activity which does involve a significant amount of work, but that they are allowed to use fire so long as it was kindled prior to the beginning of Sabbath. On the other hand, the sectarian Karaite school asserted that Jews were not allowed to use fire at all. The latter is a truly ascetic approach, as it would entail having no light in the darkness, no warmth in the cold,

101. Timmer, *Creation*.

and no allowance for any kind of cooking. It is not surprising that the standard rabbinic view of the Talmud prevailed.[102] As for why this command is given, W. H. Propp makes three suggestions. First, the work of the hearth may be a synecdoche for all domestic labor. Second, the use of combustion, which may be considered as a kind of technology, is inherently contrary to the concept of Sabbath. Third, the use of fire may evoke the first work of creation, God's making of light (Gen. 1:3–5).[103] Thus, the command may, by implication, call Israel to join God in his Sabbath rest.

35:4–9. The items to be collected are in three categories. The first group includes what in the ancient world was almost a form of currency, precious metals and fabric or clothing (see Judg. 14:19, where Samson, using clothing as currency, pays what he owes on a bet). As such, these items would have been given to the Israelites by the Egyptians at the time of the exodus, as the text indicates (Exod. 12:35). A second group consists of items that could have been locally manufactured by the Israelites themselves. Yarn or thread, for example, could be spun from wool (35:25). A third group included items that may have been subject to spoilage, or would have been difficult to carry in large quantities, or would have simply been too exotic for the Israelites to have on hand. In these categories would be the "*tahash* leather and acacia wood and oil [suitable] for lighting and spices [suitable] for the anointing oil," as well as perhaps certain dyes for the yarn. These materials were possibly purchased from the Midianites. Everything in the list would have been of high value; the Israelites were not to build the Tent of Meeting from cheap materials.

34:10–20. This part of the text is set within an inclusio, with 34:10a stating that Moses addressed the whole congregation of Israel, and 34:20 stating that the congregation departed from before Moses. The inventory of everything that was to be made anticipates 36:8—39:43, where all of the elements of the Tent of Meeting are actually built.

35:21–29. This part of the text, like 34:10–20, is also set within an inclusio structure. It asserts at 35:21–22a and at 35:29 that both men and women came with willing hearts. The tone of this passage suggests that the people worked with skill, eagerness, and excitement. This indicates that the Tent of Meeting was well-built, having been

102. Sarna, *Exodus*, 222.
103. Propp, *Exodus 19–40*, 659-60.

made by people who knew what they were doing and who cared about their work. As Propp observes, the comment in v. 21 that the people were prompted by their hearts to generosity contrasts strongly with what was said in the plague narrative about Pharaoh's heart: he was spiteful and grasping where they were enthusiastic and giving.[104]

35:30–36:3a. Echoing 31:1–11, the passage repeats the fact that Bezalel and Oholiab were chosen to oversee the work. The text essentially makes two points about these men. The first is that they were highly skilled, and the second is that they were empowered by God for this specific task. Natural talents and supernatural anointing of God to a task are not necessarily opposed to one another. On the one hand, God did not choose unskilled workers and supernaturally enable them to do the job. On the other hand, Bezalel and Oholiab could not have been truly successful had they not been empowered and directed by the Spirit of God.

36:3b–7. The enthusiasm and willingness of the people was such that they had to be told to stop giving. They did not have to be cajoled or browbeaten into making contributions, and they were not lazy about doing the work. It is worth noting that Exodus does not always criticize the behavior of the Israelites. It also points toward and celebrates instances of their faith and obedience.

Theological Summary of Key Points

1. The last point in the narrative before the golden calf was YHWH's instructions to Moses about the making of the Tent of Meeting (Exod. 25–31). YHWH was their covenant God, and as such, he would need the tent to dwell among them. The golden calf had put all this at risk, but Moses's intercession had averted the crisis (32–34). Thus, as soon as the account of Moses's acts of intercession is concluded, the narrative immediately moves into an account of the making of the tent. The tent is a visible demonstration of the reality of forgiveness.

2. Knowing, worshipping, and enjoying God are a key element of the message of Exodus, and this is brought out through the theme of the Sabbath. It is not meant to be a burden, but a reminder that the reason for the Exodus was that Israel may become God's special possession from all the nations, that they may have God among them, and that they may experience the relief from toil that only God can provide. In order for Israel to grasp and experience this lofty theological concept,

104.Ibid., 660-1.

however, they needed to do something very simple and practical: observe Sabbath in their ordinary lives. It is the simple, daily acts of prayer, devotion and faith that allow us to experience the godliness and peace that the Bible offers.

3. Love for God and for the work of God can be demonstrated in two ways. First, by taking part in some specific work, and second, by contributing financially to that work.

4. "God loves a cheerful giver" (2 Cor. 9:7). The account of the people's enthusiasm and generosity testifies to the reality of their faith. Here, more than anywhere else, they show themselves to be God's people. They also vindicate the wisdom of Moses in interceding so intensely in their behalf.

OBEDIENCE: BUILDING THE SANCTUARY (36:8–39:43)

This section describes the construction of the Tent of Meeting. It not only records the fulfillment of the commands of Exod. 26–31 but is for the most part a verbatim repetition of that text (the main difference being that the verbs here are all past tense). Where the Hebrew is essentially identical to the parallel passage in 26–31, I have not repeated the translation notes.

Translation

36:8a And all the men of wise heart among those who were doing the work made the tent-sanctuary with ten sheets of linen of tightly spun thread and of blue and purple and scarlet.
36:8b He made them [in the pattern of] cherubim (a work requiring a craftsman).
36:9a The length of each sheet was twenty-eight cubits
36:9b and the width of each sheet four cubits;
36:9c all the sheets had the same measurements.
36:10a And he joined [the first] five sheets to one another
36:10b and he joined [the other] five sheets to one another.
36:11a And he made loops of blue on the edge of the sheet at the far end of the [first] set,
36:11b and in the same way he made [loops] on the edge of the last sheet in the second set.
36:12a He made fifty loops in the one sheet
36:12b and he made fifty loops at the end of the sheet that was in the second set;
36:12c the loops were [placed] opposite each other.

36:13a And he made fifty clasps of gold
36:13b and he joined the sheets to one another with the clasps,
36:13c so the tent-sanctuary was a single piece.
36:14a And he made sheets of goat hair for a canopy over the tent-sanctuary;
36:14b he made eleven sheets of this kind.
36:15a The length of each sheet was thirty cubits
36:15b and the width of each sheet was four cubits;
36:15c [this] one [set of] measurements applied to the eleven sheets.
36:16 And he joined the five sheets as a separate set and the six sheets as a separate set.
36:17a And he made fifty loops on the edge of the sheet that was outermost in the [first] set,
36:17b and he made fifty loops on the edge of the [corresponding] sheet of the second set.
36:18 And he made fifty clasps of bronze to join the tent together so that it would be a single piece.
36:19 And he made a covering for the tent of tanned rams' hide, and at the top a covering of *tahash* leather.
36:20 And he made the frames for the tent-sanctuary out of upright acacia trees.
36:21a The length of each frame was ten cubits
36:21b and the width of a single frame was one and a half cubits.
36:22a [There were] two stiles for each frame, each one fitted to its counterpart;
36:22b that is what he did for all the frames of the tent-sanctuary.
36:23 And he made the frames for the tent-sanctuary [with] twenty frames for the south side.
36:24 And he made forty bases of silver under the twenty frames; two bases under one frame for its two stiles and two bases under another frame for its two stiles.
36:25–26 And for the second side of the tent-sanctuary, on the north side, he made twenty frames and their forty bases of silver, with two bases under each frame.[105]
36:27 For the back of the tent-sanctuary, to the west, he made six frames.
36:28 And he made two frames for the corners of the tent-sanctuary at the back.
36:29a They were twins (separate stiles) at the bottom,
36:29b but they were joined together at its top, [going] into the one ring;
36:29c that is how he made both of them for the two corners.

105. Lit. "two bases under one frame and two bases under one frame."

36:30 And there were eight frames with their bases of silver: sixteen bases, with two under every frame.[106]

36:31–32 And he made crossbars of acacia wood: five for [each of] the frames of one side of the tent-sanctuary, and five crossbars for [each of] the frames of the other side of the tent-sanctuary, and five crossbars for [each of] the frames of the tent-sanctuary for the back, toward the west.

36:33 And he made the middle crossbar [of each] to pass right through the frame from one end to the other.

36:34a And he overlaid the frames with gold and made their rings of gold [as] housings for the crossbars,

36:34b and he overlaid the crossbars with gold.

36:35a And he made the veil of blue and purple and scarlet, and linen of tightly spun thread (a work requiring a craftsman);

36:35b he made it in a cherubim pattern.

36:36a And he made four posts of acacia for it,

36:36b and he overlaid them with gold.

36:36c and their hooks were gold,

36:36d and he cast four bases of silver for them.

36:37–38a And he made a screen for the doorway of the tent, of blue and purple and scarlet, and linen of tightly spun thread (a work requiring an embroiderer) and its five posts and their hooks.

36:38b And he overlaid their tops and their bands with gold.

36:38c And their five bases were bronze.

37:1a And Bezalel made the ark of acacia wood.

37:1b Its length was two and a half cubits,

37:1c and its width one and a half cubits,

37:1d and its height one and a half cubits.

37:2a And he overlaid it with pure gold on the interior and the exterior,

37:2b and he framed it with a gold molding at the edges.

37:3 And he cast for it four rings of gold on its four feet: two rings on one side of it and two rings on the other side of it.

37:4 And he made poles of acacia wood and overlaid them with gold.

37:5 And he put the poles into the rings on the sides of the ark, for carrying it.

37:6 And he made a place of atonement of pure gold, two and a half cubits long and one and a half cubits wide.

37:7a And he made two cherubim of gold;

37:7b–8a he made them of hammered work at the two extremities of the place

106. Lit. “two bases, two bases under one frame.”

of atonement—one cherub at the one extremity and one cherub at the other extremity.

37:8b He made the cherubim as an affixture to the place of atonement at the two extremities.

37:9a The cherubim had [their] wings spread upward, covering the place of atonement with their wings,

37:9b and their faces were turned toward each other [while at the same time] the faces of the cherubim were toward the place of atonement.

37:10 And he made the table of acacia wood, two cubits long and a cubit wide and one and a half cubits high.

37:11 And he overlaid it with pure gold, and framed it with a gold molding at the edges.

37:12a And he framed it with a one-handbreadth border at the edges,

37:12b and he framed it with gold at the edges of the border.

37:13a And he cast four gold rings for it

37:13b and placed the rings on the four corners that were at its four legs.

37:14 The rings were close to the border as housings for the poles to carry the table.

37:15a And he made the poles of acacia wood

37:15b and overlaid them with gold, for carrying the table.

37:16 And he made the utensils that were on the table—its dishes and its bowls and its jars, as well as its libation vessels, with which to pour [libations]—of pure gold.

37:17a And he made the menorah of pure gold.

37:17b And he made the menorah—its base and its shaft—of hammered work;

37:17c its blossoms, its calyxes and its petals were affixed to it.

37:18 Six branches went out from its sides; three branches of the menorah from one side of it and three branches of the menorah from its other side.

37:19a Three almond-shaped blossoms (with calyx and petal) were in the one branch,

37:19b and three almond-shaped blossoms (with calyx and petal) were in the opposite branch;

37:19c it was like that for the six branches going out from the menorah.

37:20 But in the menorah were four almond blossoms (with calyx and petal);

37:21a for the six branches coming out of the lampstand,[107] a bulb-like knob was attached under the [first] pair of branches,

---

107. This is transposed from 37:21c.

37:21b and a bulb-like knob was attached under the [second] pair of branches,
37:21c and a bulb-like knob was attached under the [third] pair of branches.
37:22a Their bulb-like knobs and their branches were joined together;
37:22b all of it was a single hammered work of pure gold.
37:23 And he made its seven lamps with its wick trimmers and its fire pans of pure gold.
37:24 [The whole menorah,] with all its utensils, was made from a talent of pure gold.
37:25a And he made the altar of incense of acacia wood.
37:25b Its length was a cubit,
37:25c and its width was a cubit
37:25d (it was square)
37:25e and its height was two cubits;
37:25f its horns were affixed it.
37:26a And he overlaid it with pure gold, all around its top and its sides, and on its horns;
37:26b and he made a gold molding at its edges.
37:27 And he made two gold rings for it under its molding on its two side walls—on its two sides [and not on the front and back]—as holders for poles with which to carry it.
37:28a And he made the poles of acacia wood
37:28b and overlaid them with gold.
37:29 And he made the holy anointing oil and the pure, spiced incense (a work requiring a perfumer).
38:1 And he made the altar of whole offering of acacia wood, five cubits long, and five cubits wide, square, and three cubits high.
38:2a And he made its horns on its four corners.
38:2b Its horns were affixed to it,
38:2c and he overlaid it with bronze.
38:3a And he made all the utensils of the altar, the buckets and the shovels and the basins, the forks and the fire pans;
38:3b he made all its utensils of bronze.
38:4 And he made for the altar a grating—a network of bronze—under its covering, reaching halfway up.
38:5 And he cast four rings on the four ends of the bronze grating as housings for the poles.
38:6a And he made the poles of acacia wood
38:6b and overlaid them with bronze.
38:7a And he placed the poles into the rings on the sides of the altar, for carrying it.

38:7b And he made it hollow with planks.

38:8 And he made the basin of bronze, with its base of bronze, from the mirrors of the women with duty assignments—the ones who were assigned duties at the entrance of the Tent of Meeting.[108]

38:9a And he made the court.

38:9b For the south side the screening curtains of the court were of linen of tightly spun thread, one hundred cubits [in length].

38:10a Their twenty posts and their twenty bases were bronze;

38:10b the hooks of the posts and their bands were of silver.

38:11a For the north side [the screening curtain was] one hundred cubits [in length].

38:11b Their twenty posts and their twenty bases were bronze;

38:11c the hooks of the posts and their bands were of silver.

38:12a For the west side [there were] screening curtains of fifty cubits in [length].

38:12b Their posts were ten [in number]

38:12c and their bases were ten [in number];

38:12d the hooks of the posts and their bands were silver.

38:13 [The length] of the east side was fifty cubits.

38:14a The screening curtains for the [one] side [of the gate were] fifteen cubits [in length];

38:14b their posts were three [in number]

38:14c and their bases were three [in number].

38:15a And on the other side, the two sides of the gate of the court being balanced,[109] the screening curtains were fifteen cubits [in length].

38:15b Their posts were three [in number]

38:15c and their bases were three [in number].

38:16 All the screening curtains all around [the limits] of the court were of linen of tightly spun thread.

38:17a The bases for the posts were bronze,

---

108. The description of the women (הַצֹּבְאֹת אֲשֶׁר צָבְאוּ פֶּתַח אֹהֶל מוֹעֵד) is paralleled in 1 Sam. 2:22 (אֶת־הַנָּשִׁים הַצֹּבְאוֹת פֶּתַח אֹהֶל מוֹעֵד). The verb צבא most commonly means "to fight." It can refer to an organized army (e.g., Num. 31:42), or it can refer to YHWH fighting against his enemies (Isa. 31:4). In the latter case, however, the idea of a regimented army may still be present, since in the same verse YHWH is called יְהוָה צְבָאוֹת, "YHWH of the (heavenly) armies." In Num. 4:23; 8:24, צבא is used of Levites on duty at the Tent of Meeting. The Levitical usage may refer to the fact that while on duty the Levites wore distinctive clothing and that they served at regular, assigned times. Thus, they were regimented like soldiers.

109. Lit. "from this and from this to the gate of the court," the idea is that the two sides mirrored each other.

38:17b the hooks of the posts and their bands were silver,
38:17c and the sheathing of their tops was silver,
38:17d and all the posts of the court were banded with silver.
38:18a The screen of the gate of the court was of blue and purple and scarlet and linen of tightly spun thread (a work requiring an embroiderer).
38:18b And the length was twenty cubits
38:18c and the height was five cubits, corresponding to the screening curtains of the court.
38:19a Their posts were four [in number]
38:19b and their bases were four [in number and] bronze;
38:19c their hooks were silver,
38:19d and the sheathing of their tops and their bands was silver.
38:20 All the pegs of the tent-sanctuary and [at the edges] all around the court were bronze.
38:21a These are the records for the tent-sanctuary, the tent-sanctuary of the testimony, that were recorded by the command of Moses.
38:21b [It was] a task for the Levites [as carried out] under the direction of Ithamar the son of Aaron the priest.
38:22 And Bezalel the son of Uri, the son of Hur, of the tribe of Judah, made everything that YHWH had commanded Moses.
38:23 With him was Oholiab the son of Ahisamach, of the tribe of Dan, an engraver and a craftsman and a weaver in blue and in purple and in scarlet, and linen.
38:24 All the gold that was used for the work, in all the work of the sanctuary, including the gold of the wave offering, was 29 talents and 730 shekels, according to the sanctuary shekel.
38:25 The silver [received from] those of the congregation who were counted was 100 talents and 1,775 shekels, according to the sanctuary shekel.
38:26 [It was] a beka per head (half a shekel, according to the sanctuary shekel), for everyone who crossed over to [join] those who were counted, from twenty years old and upward, for 603,550 men.
38:27 And the hundred talents of silver were for casting the bases of the sanctuary and the bases of the veil: one hundred bases for the hundred talents, a talent for a base.
38:28a And he made the 1,775 [shekels] into hooks for the posts
38:28b and overlaid their tops
38:28c and banded them.[110]
38:29 The bronze of the wave offering was 70 talents and 2,400 shekels.

---

110. The use of the two *weqatal* forms in וְצִפָּה and וְחִשַּׁק is difficult to account for.

38:30–31 And with it he made the bases to the entrance of the Tent of Meeting and the bronze altar and the bronze grating attached to it, and all the utensils of the altar, and the bases all around [the limit of] the court and the bases of the gate of the court, and all the pegs of the tent-sanctuary and all the pegs all around [the limit of] of the court.

39:1a And from the blue and purple and scarlet they made woven garments for ministering in the holy place,

39:1b and they made the holy garments that were for Aaron,

39:1c just as YHWH had commanded Moses.

39:2 And he made the ephod of gold, [with] blue and purple and scarlet and linen of tightly spun thread.

39:3 They hammered out gold sheets and sliced [them] into threads to be worked in with the blue and the purple and the scarlet and the linen (a work requiring a craftsman).

39:4a And [on the] shoulder pieces they made attachments;

39:4b [it was] joined at its two ends.

39:5a And the skillfully crafted *ephudah* that was affixed to it was of similar workmanship, of gold, of blue and purple and scarlet and linen of tightly spun thread,

39:5b just as YHWH commanded Moses.

39:6a And they did the work with the carnelian stones [chosen for] gold filigree settings;

39:6b they were given signet engravings with the names of the Israelites.

39:7a And he placed them on the shoulder pieces of the ephod [as] memorial stones for the sons of Israel,

39:7b just as YHWH commanded Moses.

39:8 And he made the breastpiece (a work requiring a craftsman) like the work of the ephod: of gold, blue and purple and scarlet and linen of tightly spun thread.

39:9 They made the breastpiece to be square when folded double: a span long and a span wide when folded double.

39:10a And they mounted four rows of stones on it.

39:10b The first row [was] a row of ruby, topaz, and emerald;

39:11 and the second row, a turquoise, a sapphire and a moonstone;

39:12 and the third row, a jacinth, an agate, and an amethyst;

39:13a and the fourth row, a beryl, a carnelian, and a jasper.

39:13b Their settings were in gold filigree when they were mounted.

39:14a The stones were for the names of the sons of Israel;

39:14b they were twelve, corresponding to their names, each one engraved with the signet of its name for the twelve tribes.

39:15 And they made on the breastpiece twisted chains, made like a rope, in pure gold.

39:16a And they made two gold filigree [settings] and two gold rings,
39:16b and they put the two rings on the two ends of the breastpiece.
39:17 And they attached the two gold cords to the two rings at the ends of the breastpiece.
39:18a And they attached the [other] two ends of the two ropes to the two filigree settings
39:18b and attached them to the shoulder pieces of the ephod at the front of it.
39:19 And they made two gold rings and placed [them] on the two ends of the breastpiece, on its inside edge, next to the ephod.
39:20 And they made two gold rings and set them at the bottom part of the two shoulder pieces of the ephod, opposite its front side, beside the seam [that is] above the woven belt of the ephod.
39:21a And they bound the breastpiece by its rings to the rings of the ephod with a blue cord, for [the breastpiece] to be near the decorative work of the ephod,
39:21b and so that the breastpiece would not come loose from the ephod,
39:21c just as YHWH commanded Moses.
39:22 And he made the surplice of the ephod all of blue (a work requiring a weaver).
39:23a And the opening of the surplice was in the center, as [is used in] the [collar] at the [head] opening of light body armor, with a hem all around its opening,
39:23b so that it would not be torn.
39:24 And they made pomegranates of spun blue and purple and scarlet on the hem of the surplice.
39:25a And they made bells of pure gold,
39:25b–26a and they placed the bells between the pomegranates all around on the hem of the surplice, between the pomegranates (bell and pomegranate, bell and pomegranate) all around on the hem of the surplice for officiating in the service,[111]
39:26b just as YHWH had commanded Moses.
39:27–29a And they made the tunics of linen (a work requiring a weaver) for Aaron and his sons, and the headdress of linen, and the headbands of linen, and the undergarments of linen of tightly spun thread, and the sash of linen of tightly spun thread, and of blue and purple and scarlet (a work requiring an embroiderer),
39:29b just as YHWH commanded Moses.
39:30a And they made the emblem of the holy diadem of pure gold,

111. This is exceedingly redundant; the text may be corrupt.

39:30b and they wrote an inscription on it, an engraved signet, "Holy to YHWH."
39:31a And they attached a blue cord to it for fastening it to the headdress above,
39:31b just as YHWH commanded Moses.
39:32a And all the work of the tent-sanctuary, the Tent of Meeting, was completed
39:32b and the Israelites did in accordance with all that YHWH had commanded Moses.
39:32c So they made [it][112]
39:33–41 and they brought the tent-sanctuary to Moses: the tent and all its furnishings, its clasps, its frames, its crossbars, and its posts and its bases; and the covering of tanned rams' hides, and the covering of *tahash* leather, and the screening veil; the Ark of the Testimony and its poles and the place of atonement; the table, all its utensils, and the bread of the Presence; the pure [gold] menorah, with its lamps set in a row, and all its utensils, and the oil for the light; and the gold altar, and the anointing oil and the fragrant incense, and the veil for the entrance of the tent; the bronze altar and its bronze grating, its poles and all its utensils, the basin and its stand; the screening curtains for the court, its posts and its bases, and the screen for the gate of the court, its cords and its pegs and all the implements for the service of the tent-sanctuary, for the Tent of Meeting; the woven garments for conducting services in the holy place and the holy garments for Aaron the priest and the garments of his sons, for functioning as priests.
39:42 In full accord with everything that YHWH commanded Moses, the Israelites did all the work.
39:43a And Moses saw all the work and indeed, they had done it.
39:43b As YHWH had commanded,
39:43c so they had done.
39:43d And Moses blessed them.

Structure

This section tells of the construction of the Tent of Meeting and is divided according to the individual elements of the tent complex.

I. The Tent Covering (36:8–19)
II. The Tent Framework (36:20–38)

---

112. This apparently orphaned clause (כֵּן עָשׂוּ) should be placed with the next sentence.

III. The Ark of the Covenant (37:1–9)
IV. The Table for the Bread Offering (37:10–16)
V. The Menorah (37:17–24)
VI. The Altar of Incense (37:25–29)
VII. The Sacrificial Altar (38:1–8)
VIII. The Courtyard (38:9–20)
IX. Summary of Materials Used for the Tent (38:21–31)
X. The Vestments (39:1–32)
XI. Conclusion (39:33–43)

Commentary

This section of Exodus tells of the construction of the Tent of Meeting. It is almost a verbatim repetition of 25:10–30:10, the instructions for building the tent complex, except that the verb tenses are in the past and the order of the elements of the tent complex is somewhat altered. For example, in the instructions, the Ark of the Covenant is given first (25:10–22). In the account of its construction, however, it is third (37:1–9), after the accounts concerning the making of the tent fabric (36:8–19) and its framework (36:20–38). The reordering of the elements is probably not very significant. In the original instructions, the guidelines for building the Ark of the Covenant no doubt were given first because it is theologically the most important item. The account of the construction, however, may follow a more chronological order, perhaps describing what work crews were first organized. Since the weaving and stitching of so much fabric would certainly have been highly time consuming, that crew may have started its work first.

Of greater importance is the question of why the text is so repetitive. For modern students of the Bible, reading the description of the Tent of Meeting just one time through is difficult enough. Why is the whole thing repeated? A possible explanation may be found in the epigraphic discoveries from Babylonia and from Ugarit.

From the Old Babylonian Empire, we have an inscription from Samsuiluna, the son and successor of Hammurabi, whose reign was c. 1749–1712 B.C. He states that the god Shamash directed him to restore the temple called Ebabbar, and he makes use of repetition in describing the divine commission and how he fulfilled it. A portion of the inscription demonstrates the use of slavish repetition to describe obedience to a divine commission.

> He commanded me . . . to return (the temple) Ebabbar to its place; to raise the head of the *ziqqurrat*, his lofty *gegunû*, like the heavens; to cause the deities Shamash and Aya to enter

> their abode pure in happiness and joy. . . . I restored Ebabbar. I raised the head of the *ziqqurrat*, his lofty *gegunû*, like the heavens; I caused the deities Shamash, Aya and Adad to enter their abode pure in happiness and joy.[113]

Ugarit was a city-state that ruled a Late Bronze Age kingdom situated on the Mediterranean coast of the Levant and to the north of Phoenicia. The city and its palace were discovered in 1928 at Ras Shamra in northwestern Syria. Most importantly for scholars, it contained a large cache of cuneiform clay tablets. These tablets reveal Ugarit to have been a cosmopolitan center with a strong literary tradition; the texts included examples of five different scripts and nine languages.[114] Most significant among these were the numerous texts in the local language, Ugaritic, which were written in a distinctive, alphabetic cuneiform. Decipherment of the texts showed that the people of Ugarit spoke a northwest Semitic language that had many affinities to Phoenician and Hebrew. Although not strictly Canaanite, the Ugaritic texts provided a valuable window into Canaanite culture. Chronologically, culturally, and linguistically, the Ugaritic texts are very close to Exodus and thus are more relevant than the Old Babylonian material. Many Ugaritic texts were administrative, being records of governance and commerce. In addition to these texts, however, there were a number of important religious and mythological documents found. Among these were two major texts, the Myth of Baal and the Epic of Kirta.

The Myth of Baal tells of the god's battles with the gods Yamm and Mot and of his death and ultimate triumph. It also tells of the construction of his palace, a concept that has an obvious parallel in the construction of the Tent of Meeting for YHWH. The account of the building of Baal's palace, which includes information about its builders and its materials, has some formal parallels to the biblical account, but these are not strong enough or significant enough to draw any firm conclusions. One stylistic device that partially emerges in the Baal myth, however, is similar to what we see in the Exodus account of the building of the Tent of Meeting—instructions may be repeated verbatim. For example, the instructions for the making of the palace as given by the god El to the goddess Asherah are as follows:

---

113. Text cited in Wells, "Exodus," 264–5; see also *COS* 1.86.260–61.
114. Rainey and Notley, *Sacred Bridge*, 101.

Let them announce to Mighty Baʿlu:
Summon an (entire) caravan to your house,
 wares to your palace;
Let the mountains bring you massive amounts of silver,
 (let) the hills (bring you) the choicest gold,
 let them bring you magnificent gems.
Then build a house of silver and gold,
 a mansion of purest lapis-lazuli.[115]

The goddess Anat then conveys this message to Baal:

Girl ʿAnatu laughs,
 raises her voice and shouts aloud:
You have good news, Baʿlu!
 I bring you good news!
They may build for you a house like (those of) your brothers,
 a court like (those of) your kin.
Summon an (entire) caravan to your house,
 wares to your palace;
Let the mountains bring you massive amounts of silver,
 (let) the hills (bring you) the choicest gold,
Then build a house of silver and gold,
 a mansion of purest lapis-lazuli.[116]

Detailed instructions on the building of the palace and its construction process do not appear in the Baal myth, in contrast to what we see in the construction of the Tent of Meeting. There is clearly, however, a preference for repeating a directive verbatim.

This tendency is more marked in the Kirta myth, and this text does have a detailed command and obedience pattern, albeit not one that involves temple construction. Kirta is an epic poem that tells the story of its eponymous hero Kirta (also spelled Keret), king of a city called Bêtu-Ḫubur. The story begins with this man in Job-like fashion having lost all of his family, including multiple wives, to various calamities. Weeping and mourning over his perished loved ones, Kirta falls asleep, and the god El appears to him in a dream and offers him great dominion and power. Kirta replies that such things are meaningless to him so long as he possesses no heir; what he really wants is a woman who can bear him many children. Specifically, he wants the

115. "The Baʿlu Myth," translated by Dennis Pardee (*COS* 1.86.260).
116. Ibid.

maid Ḥurraya. El responds by giving Kirta a lengthy and detailed set of instructions on how to proceed. He begins:

Wash and rouge yourself,
 wash your hands to the elbow,
 your fingers to the shoulder.[117]

Continuing his instructions, El gives Kirta specific, lengthy directions on the sacrifices and prayers Kirta should make before setting out on his campaign, on provisioning his city, on gathering and preparing his army, on making the journey to the city of ʾUdmu, on laying siege to the city, and on making negotiations with its king to obtain the maid Ḥurraya. The text then states that Kirta awoke and realized it was a dream omen sent by El. The epic then states:

He washed and rouged himself,
 washed his hands to the elbow,
 his fingers to the shoulder.[118]

In the lines that follow, as in the above sample, everything El had commanded is repeated almost verbatim. That is, the text demonstrates how fully Kirta obeyed El's instructions by slavishly repeating all of the previous lines, except that what had been imperatival and in the second person in El's directions ("Wash and rouge yourself") is put into the past tense and the third person in Kirta's obedience ("He washed and rouged himself"). In line after line of the poem, everything El had commanded is restated from the perspective of fulfillment. For example, in his instructions and predictions on laying siege to the city, El had said:

Occupy the cities,
 invest the towns.
The women gathering wood will flee from the fields,
 from the threshing-floors the women gathering straw;
The women drawing water will flee from the spring,
 from the fountain the women filling (jugs).[119]

117. "The Kirta Epic," translated by Dennis Pardee (*COS* 1.102.334).
118. Ibid., 335. Pardee's translation of the full Kirta Epic (that is, of all that is extant) appears in *COS* 1.102.333–43.
119. Ibid.

The fulfillment is described as follows:

> He occupied the cities,
> invested the towns.
> The women gathering wood fled from the fields,
> from the threshing-floors the women gathering straw;
> The women drawing water fled from the spring,
> from the fountain the women filling (jugs).[120]

As a result of following El's directions, Kirta is successful in his siege and obtains the maid Ḥurraya. In the larger structure of the epic, however, Kirta's exact fidelity to El's instructions becomes even more important. He is eventually struck with a severe illness for failure to honor a vow to the goddess Asherah, but El responds by fashioning a healer to save him from death's door. The implied lesson is that El was faithful to Kirta because Kirta had so faithfully obeyed El.

Exodus follows the same literary technique, as illustrated by comparing 26:4–8 to 36:11–15. See Table 13 below.

Ugarit was in the literary and cultural mainstream of the Late Bronze Age northwest Semitic world. It is therefore reasonable to take the lengthy repetition in Kirta as conventional for this culture at this time and not as an aberration. We have no Ugaritic literature from later periods for the simple reason that Ugarit was destroyed at about the beginning of Iron I, c. 1200 B.C. In biblical literature, however, we have a great many later texts. It is striking that this kind of command and fulfillment narrative, making massive use of repetition, is not found in those later texts.

This evidence points toward two conclusions. First, the tent construction narrative follows a literary convention that was still employed in the Late Bronze Age. By contrast, this use of repetition lacks clear counterparts in biblical texts from the Iron Age or later. This suggests an early provenance for the tent narrative. Second, the main point of all the verbatim repetition in the Exodus tent narrative, as in the Kirta Epic, is that the divine commands were carefully followed. This, clearly, is the intended message of the lengthy and detailed account of how the Israelites built the tent complex. They followed YHWH's instructions to the letter.

Since the physical construction and theological significance of the various components of the tent complex have been discussed above, the reader is referred to the relevant portion in the commentary on Exod.

120. Ibid., 336.

25–31. Unlike Kirta and Exodus, I will not repeat everything I have said!

36:8–19. Concerning the fabric coverings for the tabernacle, see the comments on 26:1-14.

36:20–38. Concerning the tabernacle framework and its structure, see the comments on 26:15-30.

37:1–9. Concerning the Ark of the Covenant and cherubim, see the comments on 25:10-22.

37:10–16. Concerning the table for the bread offering, see the comments on 25:23-30.

37:17–24. Concerning the lampstand, see the comments on 25:31-40.

37:25–29. Concerning the altar of incense, see the comments on 30:1-10.

38:1–8. Concerning the sacrificial altar, see the comments on 27:1-8. New information is added at v. 8, however. First, we learn that the bronze basin and its stand were made from the bronze of the women's mirrors. In the ancient world, mirrors were commonly made of bronze or copper; the face of the mirror would be highly polished to allow for a reflection. Such a mirror, dating to c. 1980 B.C., was found in Egypt. Its handle was decorated with the head of Hathor, goddess of fertility.[121] Exodus tells us that the Israelites devoted a great deal of bronze for constructing the tent complex (see 38:29–31). It is not clear why it here gives special attention to the fact that the laver was made with the women's mirrors. Stuart suggests that metal used in a mirror would be of very high quality.[122] But it is not clear that hand mirrors really were made of exceptionally pure metal, and at any rate one would think that the bronze altar, and not a washing basin, would be singled out for being made of the finest bronze if the purity of the metal were the point. The notice about the donation may be here simply to memorialize the generosity of the women, who were willing to give up a small, personal luxury in order to contribute to the construction of this part of the sanctuary.

121. David, *Handbook*, 17.
122. Stuart, *Exodus*, 767.

TABLE 13. REPETITION IN THE TENT CONSTRUCTION NARRATIVE	
Exodus 26:4–8	**Exodus 36:11–15**
And you are to make loops of blue on the edge of the sheet at the far end of the [first] set,	And he made loops of blue on the edge of the sheet at the far end of the [first] set,
and in the same way you are to make [loops] on the far edge of the sheet in the second set.	and in the same way he made [loops] on the edge of the last sheet in the second set.
You are to make fifty loops in the one sheet,	He made fifty loops in the one sheet
and you are to make fifty loops at the end of the sheet that is in the second set;	and he made fifty loops at the end of the sheet that was in the second set;
the loops are to be [placed] opposite each other.	the loops were [placed] opposite each other.
You are to make fifty clasps of gold,	And he made fifty clasps of gold
and you are to join the sheets to one another with the clasps	and he joined the sheets to one another with the clasps
so that the tent-sanctuary will be a single piece.	so the tent-sanctuary was a single piece.
And you are to make sheets of goats' hair for a canopy over the tent-sanctuary;	And he made sheets of goat hair for a canopy over the tent-sanctuary;
you are to make eleven sheets of this kind.	he made eleven sheets of this kind.
The length of each sheet is to be thirty cubits,	The length of each sheet was thirty cubits
and the width of each sheet four cubits;	and the width of each sheet was four cubits;
[this] one [set of] measurements applies to the eleven sheets.	[this] one [set of] measurements applied to the eleven sheets.

A second issue is the question of who these women were. A common view is that these were essentially cleaning women who washed the sacred utensils and priestly vestments, policed the courtyard, and so forth. Their activity is described with the verb צבא, "to perform a duty." The use of this verb at Num. 4:23 supports this interpretation, since that verse introduces the duties of the Gershonites, who were Levites charged with carrying the sheets, the ropes, and the leather goods of the Tent of Meeting. As such, the women's duties were probably fairly mundane and did not involve actual priestly activity. But we really do not know what they did; the idea that they did clean-up duty is pure guesswork. Some have detected a hint of sacred prostitution in the descriptions of the women serving at the sanctuary entrance,[123] but that is not possible. Apart from the fact that such a thing was contrary to the whole ethos of the Tent of Meeting (see 1 Sam. 21:4), the report that the sons of Eli were sleeping with the women who served at the tent (1 Sam. 2:22) implies they were doing something that was regarded as an aberration and as a corrupt abuse of their authority, not something that fulfilled a sacred duty. Whatever these women did, they clearly were not prostitutes.

38:9–20. Concerning the courtyard, see the comments on 27:9-18.

38:21–31. This text summarizes the work of Bezalel and Oholiab and gives an account of the amount of gold and silver used in the construction. Such a careful accounting of how the raw materials were used establishes the fact that there was no deception or corruption. No one enriched himself from the Tabernacle offerings. See also 31:1–11.

39:1–32. Concerning the priestly vestments, see the comments on 28:1-43.

39:33–43. These verses summarize the construction process to make the point again that all was done according to God's instructions. The conclusion to the text, vv. 42–43, strongly emphasizes the theme of obedience and blessing.

Theological Summary of Key Points

1. As indicated above, the main point of this text, apart from the fact that the Tent of Meeting complex was built, is that Israel fully obeyed all of YHWH's instructions. For the reader, there is a kind of lesson

123. See Durham, *Exodus*, 487.

even in the apparent tedium of the repetition. Doing everything that one is commanded to do, not skipping anything and not taking short-cuts, can be a long and tiresome job. But it is the right thing to do—especially when the commands come from God.

2. In taking time to enunciate the fact that every element of the tent complex was built according to instructions (the furnishings, the fabrics, the poles, the vestments, etc.), the text reinforces in the reader's mind how important it is that every aspect of worship be carried out properly. Every element of the tent complex conveyed a message of holiness. If, for example, everything had been built except the screen that separated the Tent of Meeting courtyard from the rest of the camp, the shrine would have been defiled and unusable. In the service of God and the spiritual life, no aspect can be omitted as superfluous.

3. The methodical account of the building of the tent complex contrasts with the rapid construction of the golden calf and its altar and with the subsequent chaos of pagan worship. Israel sinned in building one sacred object. Israel found redemption in building another sacred object. Their obedience was characterized by diligence and generosity, but it was also an exact counterpart to the enthusiasm they displayed in their sin.

A WALK AFTER GOD (40:1–38)

The Tent of Meeting is set up and becomes the center of Israelite worship and the abiding place of YHWH.

Translation

40:1 And YHWH spoke to Moses, saying,

40:2 "On the first day of the first month you are to set up the tent-sanctuary—the Tent of Meeting.

40:3a And you are to place the Ark of the Testimony there,

40:3b and you are to screen the ark with the veil.

40:4a And you are to bring in the table and set its arrangements in order,

40:4b and you are to bring in the menorah and put up its lamps.

40:5a And you are to set the gold altar of incense before the Ark of the Testimony.

40:5b And you are to put in place the screen for the entrance to the tent-sanctuary.

40:6 And you are to place the altar of whole offering in front of the entrance of the tent-sanctuary—the Tent of Meeting.

40:7a And you are to set the basin between the Tent of Meeting and the altar

40:7b and you are to put water in it.
40:8a And you are to set up the court all around [the perimeter]
40:8b and you are to put in place the screen for the gateway of the court.
40:9a And you are to take the anointing oil
40:9b and anoint the tent-sanctuary and all that is in it,
40:9c and you are to sanctify it and all its furnishings.
40:9d And it shall be holy.
40:10a And you are to anoint the altar of whole offering and all its utensils,
40:10b and you are to sanctify the altar.
40:10c And the altar shall be most holy.
40:11a And you are to anoint the basin and its stand,
40:11b and you are to sanctify it.
40:12a And you are to have Aaron and his sons approach the entrance of the Tent of Meeting,
40:12b and you are to wash them with water.
40:13a And you are to clothe Aaron in the holy garments,
40:13b and you are to anoint him,
40:13c and you are to sanctify him,
40:13d that he may function as a priest for me.
40:14a And you are to have his sons approach,
40:14b and you are to clothe them in tunics,
40:15a and you are to anoint them,
40:15b just as you anointed their father,
40:15c that they may function as priests for me.
40:15d And their anointing will be[124] for them [a sign of] a perpetual priesthood throughout their generations."
40:16a And Moses did everything exactly as YHWH commanded him;
40:16b thus he acted.
40:17a And it came about in the first month of the second year, on the first [day] of the month,
40:17b that the tent-sanctuary was erected.
40:18a And Moses raised the tent-sanctuary
40:18b and he set its bases in place,
40:18c and he set up its frames,
40:18d and he inserted its crossbars,
40:18e and he raised its posts.
40:19a And he spread the tent canopy over the tent-sanctuary
40:19b and he put the outer covering of the tent on top of it,
40:19c just as YHWH commanded Moses.

124. The pattern וְהָיְתָה לִהְיֹת is absolutely without parallel in the Hebrew Bible. It is difficult to make sense of, and may be a scribal error.

40:20a And he retrieved and placed the testimony into the ark,

40:20b and he attached the poles to the ark,

40:20c and put the place of atonement on top of the ark.

40:21a And he brought the ark into the tent-sanctuary,

40:21b and he set up the screening veil,

40:21c and he screened off the Ark of the Testimony,

40:21d just as YHWH commanded Moses.

40:22 And he put the table in the Tent of Meeting on the north side of the tent-sanctuary, outside the veil.

40:23a And he set the arrangement of bread in order on it before YHWH,

40:23b just as YHWH commanded Moses.

40:24 And he placed the menorah in the Tent of Meeting, opposite the table, on the south side of the tent-sanctuary.

40:25a And he put up the lamps before YHWH,

40:25b just as YHWH commanded Moses.

40:26 And he placed the gold altar in the Tent of Meeting in front of the veil.

40:27a And he burned spiced incense on it,

40:27b just as YHWH commanded Moses.

40:28 And he set up the screen of the entrance for the tent-sanctuary.

40:29a And he set the altar of whole offering at the entrance of the tent-sanctuary—the Tent of Meeting,

40:29b and he offered on it the whole offering and the meal offering,

40:29c just as YHWH commanded Moses.

40:30a And he placed the basin between the Tent of Meeting and the altar

40:30b and he put water in it for washing.

40:31 And from it Moses and Aaron and his sons washed their hands and their feet.

40:32a When they entered the Tent of Meeting, and when they approached the altar, they would wash,

40:32b just as YHWH commanded Moses.

40:33a And he set up the court all around the tent-sanctuary and the altar,

40:33b and he put up the screen for the gateway of the court.

40:33c And Moses finished the work.

40:34a And the cloud covered the Tent of Meeting,

40:34b and the glory of YHWH filled the tent-sanctuary.

40:35a And Moses was not able to enter the Tent of Meeting

40:35b because the cloud abided on it

40:35c and the glory of YHWH filled the tent-sanctuary.

40:36 And throughout all their journeys, whenever the cloud rose up from over the tent-sanctuary, the Israelites would set out.

40:37a But if the cloud would not rise up,

40:37b then they did not set out until the day that it did rise up.
40:38a For the cloud of YHWH was on the tent-sanctuary by day
40:38b and fire was in it by night in the sight of all the house of Israel throughout all their journeys.

Structure

The final chapter of Exodus is almost entirely taken up with an account of the initial setting up of the Tent of Meeting.

- I. God Commands that the Tent Complex Begin its Function (40:1–15)
    - A. The Setup and Sanctification of the Tent Complex (40:1–11)
    - B. The Sanctification of the Priests (40:12–15)
- II. Moses Obeys (40:16–33)
- III. The Glory of YHWH Fills the Tent (40:34–35)
- IV. Israel Journeys with YHWH (40:36–38)

Commentary

40:1–33. This chapter is almost entirely a report of YHWH's command to set up the Tent of Meeting and the fulfillment of that command. First God tells Moses to set up the tent complex (vv. 1–15), and then Moses does it (vv. 16–33). Unlike 36:8—39:43, which essentially repeats the directions on the building of the tent found in chapters 25—29, this chapter does not contain a great deal of verbatim repetition. It does have enough repetition to demonstrate to the reader that the instructions of God were all followed. For example, 40:6 says, "And you are to place the altar of whole offering in front of the entrance of the tent-sanctuary—the Tent of Meeting." Moses's obedience is related in 40:29a: "And he set the altar of whole offering at the entrance of the tent-sanctuary—the Tent of Meeting." Still, repetition is not the key element in the report of the fulfillment of YHWH's commands, and in fact the command and its fulfillment are at many points complementary but not overlapping. Compare, for example, the brevity of the command with the elaborate account of its fulfillment at 40:2–3 and 40:17–22, as given in Table 14.

But sometimes the command is more elaborately given than is the account of its fulfillment. For example, vv. 9–11 give instructions for the consecration by anointing of the tent, its furnishings, the utensils, the altar, and the basin, but this is not mentioned at all in the fulfillment account. Similarly, the instructions in vv. 12–15 call for Aaron and his sons to be washed and then consecrated with a holy anointing. This, too, is not mentioned in the fulfillment except for a passing comment that the priests routinely washed themselves before approaching the tent (vv. 31–32). Clearly the two accounts are complementary, and the text is not concerned to demonstrate exact fulfillment of the instructions by having the fulfillment account repeat the content of the command, as was done in Exod. 35–41.

TABLE 14. BRIEF COMMAND AND ELABORATE FULFILLMENT	
40:2–3	**40:17–21**
2 On the first day of the first month you are to set up the tent-sanctuary—the Tent of Meeting.	**17a** And it came about in the first month of the second year, on the first [day] of the month,
	17b that the tent-sanctuary was erected.
	18–20 And Moses raised the tent-sanctuary and he set its bases in place, and he set up its frames, and he inserted its cross-bars, and he raised its posts. And he spread the tent canopy over the tent-sanctuary and he put the outer covering of the tent on top of it, just as YHWH commanded Moses. And he retrieved and placed the testimony into the ark, and he attached the poles to the ark, and put the place of atonement on top of the ark.
3a And you are to place the Ark of the Testimony there,	**21a** And he brought the ark into the tent-sanctuary,
3b and you are to screen the ark with the veil.	**21b** and he set up the screening veil,
	21c and he screened off the Ark of the Testimony,
	21d just as YHWH commanded Moses.

What, then, is distinctive in this command and fulfillment account? It is surely the heavy emphasis on the person of Moses himself. In the fulfillment, almost every action is described as though Moses personally carried out the command. The text obviously does not mean for us to understand that Moses literally raised the tent by himself or moved in all the furniture by himself. He did it through subordinates. But the initiation of the service of the Tent of Meeting is described as the crowning achievement of his work in behalf of Israel: he has initiated the service at the place where YHWH meets Israel. The tent is identified as the work of Moses. From that point on, the tent shrine where Israelites will encounter YHWH will not simply be the "Tent of Meeting" but will be the "Tent of Meeting that Moses, the servant of YHWH, made" (2 Chron. 1:3).

40:34–35. The cloud at the Tent of Meeting attests to the presence of YHWH. God had affirmed to Moses that he would not abandon Israel but would accompany them (33:12–17), and the cloud was tangible proof that the promise was not broken. Also, the account of the revelation of the goodness of God had asserted that no man could withstand the power of the full divine presence (33:20). The fact that Moses could not enter the tent when the cloud was upon it demonstrates the intensity of YHWH's presence. That is, God was fully present at the tent in the midst of Israel. He had not abandoned Israel during their journey.

40:36–38. The book closes on a positive note. God was with Israel and guiding them; Israel journeyed through the wilderness in the presence of YHWH. Later, Israel would experience a crisis of faith at Kadesh-barnea, the refusal to invade Canaan that would lead to a forty-year experience in the wilderness (Num. 13). But that is not in view here. Instead, the time in the desert is portrayed as idyllic; Israel walks with God, and they see the manifestation of his presence at his tent in the middle of the camp. It is this vision of the wilderness that is behind Hosea's account of YHWH's renewal of love to Israel at 2:14(16):

> So then, I shall be wooing her,
> and taking her into the wilderness,
> and speaking to her heart.

Theological Summary of Key Points

1. There is a striking similarity between the language used at the end of the creation narrative and the language used at the conclusion of the making of the Tent of Meeting, as has been pointed out by A. Leder.[125]

> Thus the heavens and the earth were finished [כלה] (Gen. 2:1)
>
> So all the work on the Tent of Meeting was finished [כלה] (Exod. 39:32)
>
> And on the seventh day God finished [כלה] the work he had been doing (Gen. 2:2)
>
> And so Moses finished [כלה] the work (Exod. 40:33)
>
> And God saw [וַיַּרְא אֱלֹהִים] everything he had made, and indeed [הִנֵּה] it was very good (Gen. 1:31)
>
> And Moses saw [וַיַּרְא מֹשֶׁה] the work, and indeed [הִנֵּה] they had done it just as the Lord had commanded (Exod. 39:43)
>
> And God blessed [וַיְבָרֶךְ] the seventh day (Gen. 2:3)
>
> And Moses blessed [וַיְבָרֶךְ] them (Exod. 39:43)
>
> and he sanctified [קדשׁ] it (Gen. 2:3)
>
> consecrate [קדשׁ] (the tabernacle and the altar) (Exod. 40:9–10).

The remarkable similarity of language suggests that the sanctuary is meant to be a microcosm of the created cosmos. In biblical theology, the abode of God is beyond the physical heavens. The sky or "firmament" is above earth, and above the sky is the upper "waters," and above that is God in the highest heavens. The physical heavens are not God's temple, but are a kind of antechamber to the heavenly sanctuary. Thus, in Ezek. 1:22–28, a "firmament" (sometimes translated as "dome," and representing the sky) was situated above the four living creatures (representing the earthly creation). Above the firmament was a throne with a brightly shining human figure seated upon it (representing God). The Tent of Meeting mirrored this. In its holy place, the cherubim embroidered into the inner tent fabric and the many

125. Arie C. Leder, "The Coherence of Exodus: Narrative Unity and Meaning," *CTJ* 36, no. 2 (2001): 267.

points of light reflected off the gold framework were a model of the heavenly antechamber. The holy of holies and the Ark of the Covenant corresponded to the high sanctuary of God that is beyond the physical creation. God, who is enthroned in the sanctuary of the upper heavens, at the same time sojourned on earth among the Israelites in a tent sanctuary. This establishes that YHWH, the God of Israel, is the one true deity, the maker of heaven and earth. If anyone wishes to come to the creator, he or she must worship Israel's God. The gods of the nations are just idols.

2. Yet another striking feature of the comparison is that Moses effectively has the role in Exod. 40 that God has in Gen. 2:1–3. That is, in all the parallels, Moses is the subject of the verbs in Exod. 40 where God is the subject in Gen. 2. This is consistent with how Moses dominates the fulfillment report of Exod. 40; it reads as though Moses personally and single-handedly did all the work of setting up the tent and establishing the worship of God. The text means for us to understand that Moses is the true human founder of Israel and that he is without an equal among all the Old Testament heroes of faith who walked with God.

3. Furthermore, the theology of "rest," the ideal of finding fulfillment and repose in the presence of God, is suggested by the linkage between the sanctification of the seventh day of creation and the sanctification of the Tent of Meeting. In all of humanity, the one place where people can walk with God and participate in the Sabbath rest inaugurated at creation is at the Tent of Meeting. Such communion with God is not to be found in the temples of Egypt or in any other shrines and holy places among the nations. The place of rest and salvation for humanity is in Israel: "salvation is from the Jews" (John 4:22). And Israel continues to be the place of salvation, for it is the Israelite Messiah, who was the living Tent of Meeting, that walked among us (John 1:14[126]).

4. The presence of God in all his glory is implied by the descent of the cloud upon the Tent of Meeting. As described in the commentary above, the fact that the fullness of deity was there is suggested by Moses's inability to approach the tent at that time. In Exod. 40, this is a work of grace; God has responded to Moses's intercession and will go with Israel in their journeys. However, not every such event is a matter of mercy and forgiveness. A remarkable parallel appears in Rev. 15:8:

126. Note the use of *ἐσκήνωσεν* in John 1:14.

"And the temple was filled with smoke from the glory of God and from his power, and no one was able to enter the temple until the seven plagues of the seven angels were completed." This is followed by the seven bowls of wrath in Rev. 17. Comparing the two passages, the implication is that one may either dwell alongside the full glory of God as part of his people, or one may face the fury of his full presence as part of the number of those who will not repent.

Excursus: Exodus 32–40 as a Spiritual Pilgrimage

The order of the narrative of Exod. 32:1—40:38, from the golden calf episode until the completion of the Tent of Meeting, describes the literal pilgrimage of Israel in their often tumultuous walk with God. This story sets forth a pattern, however, that is also applicable to every believer in his or her pilgrimage of faith. This is not an allegory; it is a demonstration of how the experience of Israel is prototypical for the experience of weak and failing human beings who seek to follow God. We can therefore suggest that each major stage of the narrative has a typological significance.

As a prologue to the pilgrimage, of course, we could speak of the act of coming to God, the beginning of a covenant relationship with him. For Israel, this took place in the acceptance and ratification of the Sinai covenant (Exod. 19–24). From that point forward, they were the people of God. For us, it takes place when we enter the new covenant in Christ. But our study of pilgrimage concerns those who have come to God and are his people; we are not here considering the matter of how one comes to know God in the first place. This is a study of the walk of faith of the people of God.

Following the structure of the Exodus account, that pilgrimage has the following pattern.

1. The Besetting Sin (32:1–8). The first thing Israel does as the newly-formed people of God is make the golden calf. This part of the narrative focuses, obviously enough, upon idol worship. The fact that Israel begins its pilgrimage with this particular sin is telling. This was the one sin that would cling to Israel throughout its history until the exile, and it is the great sin that the law and the preexilic prophets focus upon above all others. Deuteronomy, for example, is dominated by warnings against idolatry. No other evil (murder, adultery, stealing, and so forth) receives anything like the amount of attention that is devoted to warnings against the making and worshipping of idols. When Israel enters the land, Moses warns, they must carefully obey all of the laws of YHWH, and the first way they must demonstrate their obedience is by destroying the shrines, images, altars, and Asherah poles of Canaan (Deut. 12:1–3). In the recitation of accursed persons of Deut. 27:11–26, the head of the list is the one who makes an idol (v. 15). If any person or persons, be it a prophet, a family member, or even an entire city, should promote the worship of other gods, those persons are to be entirely exterminated (Deut. 13). When future generations would wonder why the Israelites were destroyed and driven from their land, the answer would be simply that they served other gods (Deut. 29:22–28). The golden calf story establishes the fact that idolatry was the greatest moral and spiritual peril they faced. Israel committed other sins in the wilderness, but only at the calf did YHWH come near to destroying all the people. And despite everything they suffered for it, idolatry was the sin that they could not escape. It was to them an addiction. The pilgrimage lesson is that we all must know our besetting sins. Each of us has weaknesses of many kinds, but there are sins that truly dominate us and that we cannot escape apart from the grace of God. We should add that although all sin is destructive, the greatest offense to God is disloyalty to our covenant with him. We can betray the faith even without an idol. The pilgrimage of faith therefore begins with an awareness of the peril of the sins that cling to us.

2. The Intercessor (32:9–35). When Israel, still worshipping the calf, was not even aware that they were in danger of being annihilated by God, Moses was already interceding for them. Moses then came down and confronted and punished them, but above all he continued to intercede for them, pleading that YHWH not abandon them. In the narrative sequence of Exodus, this is highly significant. The beginning of the process of restoring Israel was entirely out of their hands. They were not able to control it, and indeed initially they did not know of their need for it. The intercessor had to stand between them and their punishment if they were to have any hope of deliverance. The Christian is reminded of Paul's teaching that the Spirit and Christ make intercession for us (Rom. 8:26–34). We recall also that Christ, in his role as our high priest, is constantly interceding for us (Heb. 7:25). The lesson is that our ability to continue in our pilgrimage is not of us; it all depends upon the intercessor. Indeed, our survival depends upon the intercessor even before we repent of our sin. The pilgrimage is possible only by grace.

3. Repentance and Mercy (33:1—34:9). Confronted by Moses and told of God's threat to abandon them, the people did indeed mourn and repent. This was reflected above all in their abandonment of their jewelry, an act which, as suggested in the commentary, was a forsaking of the protection afforded by the amulets, charms, and images of deities engraved on Egyptian jewelry. The Israelites would have believed that such charms gave them real spiritual shields, and casting that jewelry from themselves was a way of demonstrating the reality of their sorrow over their idolatry and their determination to place their faith in YHWH alone. For the believer, the lesson is that he or she must turn away from the besetting sin. This includes both heartfelt brokenness and taking concrete steps to escape the power of the specific sin.

4. Covenant Renewal (34:10–27). YHWH, having yielded to Moses's intercession and having announced that he would neither destroy nor abandon Israel, renewed the covenant. In the course of the renewal, he restated in abbreviated form the Book of the Covenant, but with more prominence given to the sin of idolatry. The covenant renewal itself was purely an act of YHWH; Israel was not involved in the process, and there was no ceremony analogous to the original making of the covenant in Exod. 24. The reason is that Israel had broken the covenant. It was YHWH's prerogative to announce either that Israel was in breach of the covenant and would be abandoned or that he would forgive them and remain with them as their God. They had no say in the matter, and thus were not involved in the renewal of the covenant. On the other hand, this does not mean that there was nothing for them to do at all at this stage. The restatement of the Book of the Covenant in Exod. 34 was a reminder to them of what their obligations were under the covenant. For the believer, this remains a critical part of the pilgrimage of faith. We must ever remind ourselves of our duties to God. It is good to recognize our besetting sin, our need for an intercessor, and the requirement that we repent. But we must also ever learn and learn again what is expected of us. We will never be faithful if we forget the terms of the covenant.

5. Veiled Glory (34:28–35). Moses came back to Israel, having been assured of YHWH's forgiveness and having seen the vision of his glorious goodness, and he announced the good news that God would not abandon Israel. And having had this great experience of the grace of God, Moses's face glowed. The people, however, drew back, being bewildered and disturbed by the shining of his face. Paul, in 2 Cor. 3, perceives in this their inability to comprehend the grace of God. They could not understand the wonderful significance of Moses's face, that it reflected the love and goodness of God. Moses had to veil his face in order to avoid disorder and confusion in the camp. For us who are under the new covenant, the lesson is that we should follow the example not of the Israelites but of Moses, who would go before YHWH in the tent and there experience his transformative glory with an unveiled face (2 Cor. 3:18). It is good to hear the law, that is, the list of all that God requires of us, but it is better yet to commune with him and to remain in his presence. Doing that, we are remade in his image and reflect his glory.

6. Giving (35:1—36:7). With the episode of the golden calf resolved, Israel could set about the task of building the Tent of Meeting. This would have been pointless apart from Moses's intercession. There would have been no need for a Tent of Meeting if YHWH would not go with them. But YHWH was going with them, and they needed to construct his tent. The narrative of the construction begins with an account of the call for donations and of how Israel responded—with great generosity and enthusiasm. This, too, is a mark of true repentance. In the pilgrimage of faith, giving of one's possessions to the work of God is not optional. It is essential: where our treasures are, there our hearts will be also. Those who will not give will never serve God rightly or grow in grace.

7. Obedience: Building the Sanctuary (36:8—39:43). With the materials collected, Israel set about the task of actually building the Tent of Meeting. The lesson for us is simple and straightforward. Those who would wish to be God's people must carry out his commands. Most particularly, they must work to see that the structures in which his glory is to reside are actually brought to completion. In the new covenant, this is not physical buildings but the lives and souls of people: "and you like living stones are being built into a spiritual house to offer, as a holy priesthood, spiritual sacrifices acceptable to God through Jesus Christ" (1 Pet. 2:5). But whether it is the building of the great Tent of Meeting in the wilderness or the building of people into a holy priesthood, the task requires work, dedication, and obedience.

8. A Walk after God (40:1–38). The Tent of Meeting finished, YHWH came and dwelt among them and went with them in all their travels. Exodus ends on a poignant note: "For the cloud of YHWH was on the tent-sanctuary by day and fire was in it by night in the sight of all the house of Israel throughout all their journeys" (40:38). The point for us, simply enough, is to follow God.

In summary, therefore, the pilgrimage of faith is straightforward. If we are God's people, we must recognize what sins beset us and trip us up. From that, we must recognize that our salvation depends upon our intercessor and on the grace of God. We must repent, learn again to pay heed to God's requirements, and seek the transformative presence of God so that we may be renewed in God's image. Beyond that, we must set our treasure in heaven through the simple act of giving, we must do the work of the gospel, and we must follow God.

APPENDIX
The Songs of Exodus

This commentary has suggested that Exodus contains a number of previously unrecognized songs or poems (for the Israelites, these two words designated the same thing). The commentaries for each of the texts have sought to demonstrate why these passages may be considered to be poetry. A drawback to such a presentation, however, is that analysis makes it difficult to see the works as poems, as they are laden with notes and comments. It may be helpful to see these songs apart from any context and without notations. They are as follows:

A BITTER CURSE (5:21)

The first poem is a curse; such an imprecation might naturally take poetic form in the ancient world. This poem seems to have no obvious liturgical function. It would, however, be a vivid reminder of how Moses was viewed in the early days of his leadership over Israel.

> May YHWH look upon you and may he judge
> You, who have made us a stench
> In the eyes of Pharaoh and in the eyes of his servants,
> By putting a sword in their hand to kill us.

I AM YHWH (6:2–8)

The song that I have called "I am YHWH" is, in context, an oracle meant to encourage Moses, who has fallen into despair over the apparent failure of his mission. It has, however, obvious liturgical significance. In two stanzas and employing six quatrains it reminds Israel of the historical continuity between the promises to the patriarchs (the first stanza in three quatrains) and their coming redemption and subsequent reception of the land as their inheritance (the second stanza in three quatrains, with the inclusio lines, "I am YHWH"). Most importantly, it recites God's self-designation as YHWH, emphasizing what is the name by which Israel's God is to be forever known.

I am YHWH.

And I appeared to Abraham, to Isaac, and to Jacob
As El Shaddai.
But my name is YHWH.
Did I not make myself known to them?

And also I set up my covenant with them,
To give to them the land of Canaan,
The land of their sojourning,
In which they sojourned.

And also I heard the groaning of the Israelites,
Whom the Egyptians were enslaving,
And I remembered my covenant.
Therefore, say to the Israelites:

I am YHWH.

And I will bring you out from under the heavy labor of the
Egyptians,
And I will deliver you from their service,
And I will redeem you with an outstretched arm
And with great judgments.

And I will take you as my people,
And I will be your God.
And you will know that I am YHWH your God,
Who brings you out from under the heavy labor of the Egyptians.

And I will bring you to the land
That I lifted my hand in an oath
To give to Abraham, to Isaac, and to Jacob,
And I will give it to you as a possession.

I am YHWH.

THE SONG OF THE SEA (15:1–18)

This is the one text of Exodus that is universally recognized to be a song. Like "I am YHWH," its focus is on how the deity known as YHWH has delivered Israel and made them to be his own people. As described in the commentary, it is in seven strophes, and the first six of these are in a parallel structure (A-B-A-B-A-B). The last strophe, like the seventh day of creation, leads into the Sabbath rest with YHWH in his sanctuary.

I will sing to YHWH for he is thoroughly majestic!
The horse and its rider he has hurled into the sea!

Yah is my strength and protection,
And he has become my salvation.

This is my God, and I will praise him!
This is the God of my father, and I will exalt him!

YHWH is a man of war!
YHWH is his name!

He cast Pharaoh's chariots and his army into the sea!
The best of his officers were plunged into the *Yam Suph*.

The deeps began to cover them;
They sank down to the depths like a stone!

Your right hand, YHWH, is magnificent in power!
Your right hand, YHWH, vanquishes enemies;

By the abundance of your majesty you bring those who rise
against you to ruin.
You release your fury; it consumes them like straw.

And by the blast of your nostrils waters were stacked up;
Flowing waters stood up in a heap;
The murky depths at the heart of the sea were churned up.

The enemy said, "I will pursue; I will overtake;
I will divide plunder; my appetite will be filled with them;
I will draw my sword; my hand will dispossess them."

You blew with your wind; sea covered them!
They vanished like lead in the magnificent waters!

Who is like you among the gods, YHWH?
Who is like you, magnificent in power?

Feared in the midst of the praises given to you!
A worker of wonders!

You stretch out your right hand; earth swallows them!
You lead by your grace a people whom you have redeemed.
You guide them by your strength to your holy pastureland.

The peoples hear; they tremble!
Agony grips the inhabitants of Philistia!
Next, the chiefs of Edom are terrified;
And as for the leaders of Moab—trembling starts to seize them!
All melt away—the inhabitants of Canaan!

Let terror and dread fall upon them!
At the great power of your arm, let them be dumb as stone!
Until your people cross over, YHWH!
Until this people whom you redeemed cross over!

May you bring them and plant them on the mountain of your
inheritance:
A specific place that you made for you to inhabit, YHWH;
A sanctuary, Lord, which your hand has specified.

May YHWH reign forever and ever!

YHWH YOUR HEALER (15:25–26)

This song is an oracle from YHWH and, like many such texts, is poetry. It celebrates the lesson of the waters of Marah and has as its focus the last line, that Israel's God is YHWH their healer. This liturgical recitation is a counterpoint to the Song of the Sea, the celebration of the destruction of the Egyptian forces. It asserts that by obedience to his commands Israel can experience YHWH not as destroyer, as Egypt experienced him, but as healer.

There he made for them a statute and ruling,
And there he tested them and said,

"If you will listen carefully to the voice of YHWH your God,
And do what is right in his eyes,
And pay attention to his commands,
And keep all his statutes,

Then all of the disease that I set upon Egypt
I will not set upon you;
For I, YHWH, am your healer."

THE SONG OF THE COVENANT (19:3–6)

This is another oracle and is thus another song. It recounts YHWH's offer to Israel, through Moses, of a covenant relationship with himself. It has an abiding liturgical function, reminding worshippers of the exodus story that was prior to the covenant event, of their responsibility under the covenant, and of the covenant benefits that belong uniquely to Israel.

Thus you shall say to the house of Jacob
And tell the Israelites:

You have seen what I did to Egypt!
I carried you on eagles' wings
And I brought you to me.

And now, if you will genuinely listen to my voice,
And keep my covenant,

Then you will be my possession chosen from all peoples
Although all the earth is mine.
But you will be to me as a kingdom of priests
And a holy nation.

These are the words
That you shall speak to the Israelites.

GLORY ON SINAI (24:15–18)

This song uses the idea of a "cloud on the mountain" as a kind of leitmotif to epitomize the glory of YHWH that was present at the ratification of the covenant. It is also framed in the inclusio structure of Moses ascending the mountain and entering the cloud. It celebrates Moses as the great mediator and lawgiver, and by reference to six days and then a seventh it repeats the pattern of "6 + 1" that is derived from the creation narrative and that is presented again in the seven strophes of the Song of the Sea. It thus associates Torah, the word of God received by Moses, with the Sabbath rest principle. At the same time, the recollection of the cloud on the mountain recalls the terrors of Sinai. It carries an implied warning against breaking the covenant.

And Moses ascended into the mountain,
And cloud covered the mountain.

And the glory of YHWH dwelt on Mount Sinai,
And the cloud covered it for six days;

And he called to Moses
On the seventh day from within the cloud.

And the appearance of the glory of YHWH:
Like a consuming fire on the mountain top
Before the eyes of the Israelites!

And Moses came within the cloud;
And he ascended into the mountain.

THE SONG OF THE TENT (29:42–46)

This song celebrates the Tent of Meeting as the tangible manifestation of the reality of the covenant with Israel: YHWH has made his dwelling with his people. It is another oracle song in that it is a first-person recitation of the words of YHWH. It also proclaims the glories of the Israelite priesthood and sanctuary: it is there and through the priesthood that YHWH encounters his people and receives their worship. It is also the culmination of the work of YHWH first proclaimed in the "I am YHWH" song: he had intended to deliver Israel from Egypt and make them into his own people, and this song celebrates the fulfillment of that purpose. With words of the last line, "I am YHWH their God!" it looks back to the "I am YHWH" song

Constant burnt offerings throughout your generations;
The entrance of the Tent of Meeting before YHWH:

Where I will meet with you,
By speaking to you there,
And there I will meet with the Israelites!

And it will be sanctified by my glory:
I will sanctify the Tent of Meeting and the altar,
And Aaron and his sons I will sanctify as my priests.

And I will dwell in the midst of the Israelites,
And I will be their God!

And they will know that I am YHWH their God,
Who brought them out from the land of Egypt
That I may dwell in their midst.

I am YHWH their God!

YHWH! YHWH! (34:6–7)

This song, recited by YHWH to Moses as he passed by the cleft in the rock, celebrates YHWH as, first and foremost, merciful and only secondarily as a punishing God. At the same time, it implicitly recalls the episode of the golden calf, Moses's intercession, and Israel's near destruction at YHWH's hands. This song became the most famous and frequently recalled of all of the songs of Exodus (see Num. 14:18; Ps. 86:15; 103:8; 145:8; Joel 2:13; Jonah 4:2; Nah. 1:3; Neh. 9:17). It was a constant reminder to Israel that YHWH is fundamentally compassionate and forgiving, but that obstinate and flagrant disobedience brings ruin.

YHWH! YHWH!

Compassionate and gracious God,
Slow to anger, and rich in grace and faithfulness!

Maintaining grace for thousands,
Forgiving iniquity, transgression and sin!

But he does not grant blanket amnesty;
Avenging the iniquity of fathers

On the children and on the grandchildren,
On the third and on the fourth generations.

SUMMARY AND CONCLUSION

The songs of Exodus celebrate YHWH's power and goodness as well as the glory that Israel has as YHWH's covenant people. There is also heavy emphasis on the name YHWH. Even the initial song, "A Bitter Curse," is given in YHWH's name. In addition, the song collection recites liturgically the entire exodus story. It begins in bitterness, with both Israel and Moses deeply discouraged. It proceeds to YHWH's intention to redeem all of his promises to the patriarchs by delivering Israel from Egypt and by making this people into his own nation, as recited in "I am YHWH." It then recalls the plagues on Egypt and the great deliverance in the "Song of the Sea." After that, "YHWH your Healer" alludes to the journey to Sinai and emphasizes Israel's special relationship to God: he is their healer and is not to them a bringer of plagues. After this, the oracular "Song of the Covenant" recalls the offer of the covenant to Israel and all that this offer entails. The song "Glory on Sinai" then alludes to the covenant ratification and the glory that was seen on the mountain. The "Song of the Tent" then recalls a matter that is a major focus of Exodus, the making of the Tent of Meeting with its implication that YHWH dwells among his people. Finally, as mentioned above, the song "YHWH! YHWH!" alludes to the golden calf, to Moses's intercession, and to Israel's reinstatement. It is not, I think, overly speculative to suggest that the songs have both liturgical and pedagogical functions. They may well have served both as Israel's early hymnody and as a succinct but poetic means for recalling the story and lessons of the exodus.

BIBLIOGRAPHY

Addinall, Peter. "Exodus III 19B and the Interpretation of Biblical Narrative." *VT* 49, no. 3 (1999): 289–300.

Albright, William F. "Northwest-Semitic Names in a List of Egyptian Slaves from the Eighteenth Century B.C." *JAOS* 74 (1954): 222–33.

Alexander, T Desmond. "The Composition of the Sinai Narrative in Exodus XIX 1–XXV 11." *VT* 49, no. 1 (1999): 2–20.

Allen, James P. *Middle Egyptian: An Introduction to the Language and Culture of Hieroglyphs*. Cambridge: Cambridge University Press, 2000.

______. "The Speos Artemidos Inscription of Hatshepsut." *Bulletin of the Egyptological Seminar* 16 (2002): 1–17.

Allen, Leonard. "Archaeology of Ai and the Accuracy of Joshua 7:1–8:29." *ResQ* 20, no. 1 (1977): 41–52.

Allen, Leslie. *Psalms 101–50, Revised*. WBC 21. Nashville: Thomas Nelson, 2002.

Allen, Ronald B. "The 'Bloody Bridegroom' in Exodus 4:24–26." *BSac* 153 (1996): 259–69.

Allo, E. Bernard. *Saint Paul, Seconde Épître aux Corinthiens*. Paris: J. Gabalda, 1956.

Armour, Robert A. *Gods and Myths of Ancient Egypt*. Cairo: American University in Cairo Press, 2001.

Ashby, G. W. "The Bloody Bridegroom: The Interpretation of Exodus 4:24–26." *ExpTim* 106, no. 7 (1995): 203–5.

Assmann, Jan. *Moses the Egyptian: The Memory of Egypt in Western Monotheism*. Cambridge, MA: Harvard University Press, 1997.

Auffret, Pierre. "The Literary Structure of Exodus 6.2–8." *JSOT* 27 (1983): 46–54.

BIBLIOGRAPHY

Baines, John, and Jaromír Málek. *The Cultural Atlas of the World: Ancient Egypt*. rev. ed. New York: Checkmark Books, 2000.

Baker, Darrell D. *The Encyclopedia of the Egyptian Pharaohs*. Oakville: Bannerstone Press, 2008.

Bard, Kathryn A. *From Farmers to Pharaohs: Mortuary Evidence for the Rise of Complex Society in Egypt*. Sheffield: Sheffield Academic Press, 1994.

Bar–On, Shimon. "The Festival Calendars in Exodus XXIII 14–19 and XXXIV 18–26." *VT* 48, no. 2 (1998): 161–95.

Barré, Michael L. "'My Strength and My Song' in Exodus 15:2." *CBQ* 54, no. 4 (1992): 623–37.

Batto, Bernard F. "The Reed Sea : *Requiescat in Pace*." *JBL* 102, no. 1 (1983): 27–35.

Beard, Mary. *The Fires of Vesuvius: Pompeii Lost and Found*. Cambridge, MA: Harvard University Press, 2008.

Beckerath, Jürgen von. "Theban Seventeenth Dynasty." In *Gold of Praise: Studies on Ancient Egypt in Honor of Edward F. Wente*, edited by Emily Teeter and John A. Larson, 21–26. Chicago: University of Chicago, 1999.

Beit–Arieh, Itzhaq. "Fifteen Years in Sinai." *BAR* 10, no. 4 (1984): 26–54.

Beitzel, Barry J. "Exodus 3:14 and the Divine Name: A Case of Biblical Paronomasia." *TJ* 1 (1980): 5–20.

Belleville, Linda. *2 Corinthians*. IVP New Testament Commentary 8. Downers Grove: InterVarsity, 1996.

Ben-Tor, Amnon. "Hazor." In Stern, *NEAEHL* 2:594–606.

Berlin, Adele. "On the Meaning of פלל in the Bible." *RB* 96, no. 3 (1989): 345–51.

Beuken, W. A. M. "Exodus 16:5, 23: A Rule Regarding the Keeping of the Sabbath?" *JSOT* 32 (1985): 3–14.

Bietak, Manfred. *Avaris: The Capital of the Hyksos: Recent Excavations at Tell el–Dabʿa*. London: British Museum, 1996.

______. "Canaanites in the Eastern Nile Delta." In *Egypt, Israel, Sinai: Archaeological and Historical Relationships in the Biblical Period*, edited by Anson F. Rainey, 41–56. Tel Aviv: Tel Aviv University, 1987.

______. "Comments on the Exodus." In *Egypt, Israel, Sinai: Archaeological and Historical Relationships in the Biblical Period*, edited by Anson F. Rainey, 163–72. Tel Aviv: Tel Aviv University, 1987.

Bimson, John J. *Redating the Exodus and Conquest*. 2nd ed. Sheffield: Almond, 1981.

Biology News Net. "UCSD study finds anthrax toxins also harmful to fruit flies." Biology News Net. Accessed 4/23/2014. http://www.biologynews.net/archives/2006/01/31/ucsd_study_finds_anthrax_toxins_also_harmful_to_fruit_flies.html.

Blackman, Aylward M. *Gods, Priests and Men: Studies in the Religion of Pharaonic Egypt.* London: Kegan Paul International, 1998.

Bottéro, Jean. *Textes Culinaires Mésopotamiens.* Winona Lake: Eisenbrauns, 1995.

Breasted, James Henry. *Ancient Records of Egypt.* Chicago: University of Chicago, 1906.

Bright, John. *A History of Israel.* Philadelphia: Westminster, 1959.

Bromiley, Geoffrey W., ed. *International Standard Bible Encylopedia, Rev.* Grand Rapids: Eerdmans, 1982.

Bultmann, Rudolf. *The Second Letter to the Corinthians.* Translated by Roy A. Harrisville. Minneapolis: Augsburg, 1985.

Burleigh, Nina. *Mirage: Napoleon's Scientists and the Unveiling of Egypt.* New York: HarperCollins, 2007.

Callaway, Joseph A. "New evidence on the conquest of 'Ai.'" *JBL* 87, no. 3 (1968): 312–20.

Carson, D. A. "Matthew." In *The Expositor's Bible Commentary*, Vol. 8, edited by Frank E. Gaebelein, 1–599. Grand Rapids: Zondervan, 1984.

Cassuto, Umberto. *A Commentary on the Book of Exodus.* Translated by Israel Abrahams. Jerusalem: Magnes, 1967.

Childs, Brevard S. *The Book of Exodus: A Critical, Theological Commentary.* OTL. Philadelphia: Westminster, 1974.

Christensen, Duane L. *Deuteronomy 1:1–21:9, revised.* 2nd ed. WBC 6a. Nashville: Thomas Nelson, 2001.

Coats, George W. "Moses in Midian." *JBL* 92, no. 1 (1973): 3–10.

Coborn, John. *The Atlas of Snakes of the World.* Neptune City: T.F.H. Publications, 1991.

Cohen, Jeffrey M. "*Hatan Damim*: The Bridegroom of Blood." *JBQ* 33, no. 2 (2005): 120–6.

______. "Samaritan Authentication of the Rabbinic Interpretation of *Kephî Taḥrā'*." *VT* 24, no. 3 (1974): 361–366.

Cole, R. Alan. *Exodus: An Introduction and Commentary.* TOTC. Downer's Grove: InterVarsity, 1973.

Collins, John J. *Introduction to the Hebrew Bible.* Minneapolis: Fortress, 2004.

Cox, Dorian G. C. "The Hardening of Pharaoh's Heart in Its Literary and Cultural Contexts." *BSac* 163, no. 3 (2006): 292–311.

Craigie, Peter C. "An Egyptian Expression in the Song of the Sea (Exodus XV 4)." *VT* 20, no. 1 (1970): 83–6.

Cross, Frank Moore, Jr., and David Noel Freedman. *Studies in Ancient Yahwistic Poetry.* Grand Rapids: Eerdmans, 1975.

Currid, John D. *Ancient Egypt and the Old Testament.* Grand Rapids: Baker, 1997.

Curtis, Edward M. "The Theological Basis for the Prohibition of Images in the Old Testament." *JETS* 28, no. 3 (1985): 277–87.

David, Rosalie. *Handbook to Life in Ancient Egypt.* Oxford: Oxford University Press, 1998.

______. *Religion and Magic in Ancient Egypt.* London: Penguin, 2002.

Davies, Eryl W. "A Mathematical Conundrum: The Problem of the Large Numbers in Numbers I and XXVI." *VT* 45, no. 4 (1995): 449–69.

Davies, Graham I. "Hebrew text of Exodus 8:19 (Evv 23): An Emendation." *VT* 24, no. 4 (1974): 489–92.

______. *The Way of the Wilderness: A Geographical Study of the Wilderness Itineraries in the Old Testament.* SOTSMS 5. Cambridge: Cambridge University Press, 1979.

Davies, John A. *A Royal Priesthood: Literary and Intertextual Perspectives on an Image of Israel in Exodus 19.6.* JSOTSup 395. London: T & T Clark, 2004.

Dever, William G. *Who Were the Early Israelites and Where Did They Come From?* Grand Rapids: Eerdmans, 2003.

Dozeman, Thomas B. *Commentary on Exodus.* ECC. Grand Rapids: Eerdmans, 2009.

______. *God at War: Power in the Exodus Tradition.* New York: Oxford University Press, 1996.

______. "The *yam-sûp* in the Exodus and the Crossing of the Jordan River." *CBQ* 58, no. 3 (1996): 407–16.

Dumbrell, William J. *Covenant and Creation: An Old Testament Covenantal Theology.* Exeter: Paternoster, 1984.

______. "Exodus 4:24–26: A Textual Re–Examination." *HTR* 65, no. 2 (1972): 285–90.

______. "Paul and Salvation History in Romans 9:30—10:4." In *Out of Egypt: Biblical Theology and Biblical Interpretation*, edited by Craig Bartholomew, 286–312. Grand Rapids: Zondervan, 2004.

Durham, John I. *Exodus.* WBC 3. Waco: Word Books, 1987.

Dyer, Charles H. "The Date of the Exodus Reexamined." *BSac* 140, no. 559 (1983): 225–43.

Enns, Peter. *Exodus: From Biblical Text to Contemporary Life.* NIV Application Commentary. Grand Rapids: Zondervan, 2000.

______. *Inspiration and Incarnation: Evangelicals and the Problem of the Old Testament.* Grand Rapids: Baker, 2005.

Exum, J. Cheryl. "'You Shall Let Every Daughter Live': A Study of Exodus 1:8–2:10." *Semeia* 28 (1983): 63–82.

Faulkner, Raymond O. *A Concise Dictionary of Middle Egyptian.* Oxford: Griffith Institute, 1999.

Fee, Gordon D. *God's Empowering Presence: The Holy Spirit in the Letters of Paul.* Hendrickson: Peabody, 1994.

Fensham, F. Charles. "The Dog in Ex. XI 7." *VT* 16, no. 4 (1966): 504–507.

Ferris, Paul W., Jr. "The Manna Narrative of Exodus 16:1–10." *JETS* 18, no. 3 (1975): 191–99.

Firmage, Edwin. "Zoology (Fauna)." In Freedman, *ABD* Vol. 6, 1109–1167.

Foerster, Gideon. "Jericho." In Stern, *NEAEHL* 2:674–97.

Food and Agriculture Organization of the United Nations. "Desert Locust Information Service of FAO: Locust FAQs." Accessed 4/23/14. http://www.fao.org/ag/locusts/oldsite/LOCFAQ.htm.

Foster, Karen Polinger, Robert K. Ritner and Benjamin R. Foster. "Texts, Storms, and the Thera Eruption." *JNES* 55, no. 1 (1996): 1–14.

Frankel, David. "The Destruction of the Golden Calf: A New Solution." *VT* 44, no. 3 (1994): 330–9.

Franzmeier, Henning. "Sherds, Clay and Clean Water." *Ancient Egypt* 8, no 6 (2008): 45–49.

Freed, Rita E., Yvonne J. Markowitz and Sue H. D'Auria, eds. *Pharaohs of the Sun: Akhenaten, Nefertiti, Tutankhamen.* Boston: Museum of Fine Arts, Boston in association with Bullfinch Press / Little, Brown, 1999.

Freedman, David Noel, ed. *The Anchor Bible Dictionary.* New York: Doubleday, 1999.

______, ed. *Eerdmans Dictionary of the Bible.* Grand Rapids: Eerdmans, 2000.

______. *The Nine Commandments: Uncovering a Hidden Pattern of Crime and Punishment in the Hebrew Bible.* New York: Doubleday, 2000.

______. *Pottery, Poetry, and Prophecy: Studies in Early Hebrew Poetry.* Winona Lake: Eisenbrauns, 1980.

Fretheim, Terence E. *Exodus.* IBC. Louisville: John Knox, 1991.

Freud, Sigmund. *Moses and Monotheism.* Translated by Katherine Jones. New York: A.A. Knopf, 1939.

Friedman, Richard Elliott. "Tabernacle." In Freedman, *ABD* Vol. 6, 292–300.

Fritz, Glen A. *The Lost Sea of the Exodus: A Modern Geographical Analysis.* Ann Arbor: UMI Dissertation Services, 2006.

Frolov, Serge. "The Hero as Bloody Bridegroom: On the Meaning and Origin of Exodus 4,26." *Bib* 77 (1996): 520–23.

Fuller, Russell. "Exodus 21:22–23: The Miscarriage Interpretation and the Personhood of the Fetus." *JETS* 37, no. 2 (1994): 169–84.

Furnish, Victor Paul. *II Corinthians.* AB. New York: Doubleday, 1984.

Garfunkel, Zvi. "The Nature and History of Motion along the Dead Sea Transform (Rift)." In *The Jordan Rift Valley*, by Aharon Horowitz, 627–651. Lisse: A. A. Balkema Publishers, 2001.

Garland, David E. *2 Corinthians.* NAC. Nashville: Broadman & Holman, 1999.

Garr, W. Randall. "The Grammar and Interpretation of Exodus 6:3." *JBL* 111, no. 3 (1992): 385–408.

Garrett, Duane A. *Amos: A Handbook to the Hebrew Text.* Waco: Baylor University Press, 2008.

______. *Hosea, Joel.* NAC. Nashville: Broadman, 1997.

______. *Rethinking Genesis: The Sources and Authorship of the First Book of the Pentateuch.* Grand Rapids: Baker, 1991.

Geller, Stephan A. "Manna and Sabbath: A Literary–Theological Reading of Exodus 16." *Int* 59, no. 1 (2005): 5–16.

"Geographiae Expositio Compendiaria." In *Geographi Graeci Minores,* Vol. 2. Edited by Karl Müller. Parisiis: Firmin Didot et sociis, 1882.

Geraty, Lawrence T. "Heshbon." In Stern, *NEAEHL* 2:626–30.

Gesenius, Wilhelm, E. Kautzsch, and A. E. Cowley. *Gesenius' Hebrew Grammar.* 2nd English Edition. Oxford: Oxford University Press, 1982.

Gianotti, Charles R. "The Meaning of the Divine Name YHWH." *BSac* 142, no. 565 (1985): 38–51.

Glueck, Nelson. *The Other Side of the Jordan.* Cambridge, MA: American Schools of Oriental Research, 1970.

Goedicke, Hans. *The Speos Artemidos Inscription of Hatshepsut and Related Discussions.* Oakville: Halgo, 2004.

Goldingay, John. "The Significance of Circumcision." *JSOT* 88 (2000): 3–18.

Goldwasser, Orly. "How the Alphabet was Born from Hieroglyphs." *BAR* 36, no. 2 (2010): 36–50.

Gonen, Rivka. "The Late Bronze Age." In *The Archaeology of Ancient Israel*, edited by Amnon Ben-Tor, translated by R. Greenberg, 211–57. New Haven: Yale University Press, 1992.

Good, Edwin Marshall. "Exodus XV 2." *VT* 20, no. 3 (1970): 358–9.

Gordon, Cyrus Herzl, and Gary Rendsburg. *The Bible and the Ancient Near East.* New York: W. W. Norton, 1997.

Gorospe, Athena Evelyn. *Narrative and Identity: An Ethical Reading of Exodus 4.* Leiden: Brill, 2007.

Gowan, Donald E. *Theology in Exodus: Biblical Theology in the Form of a Commentary.* Louisville: Westminster John Knox, 1994.

Gray, Mary P. "The *Ḫâbirū*-Hebrew Problem in the Light of the Source Material Available at Present." *HUCA* 29 (1958): 135–202.

Gressmann, Hugo. *Mose und seine Zeit; ein Kommentar zu den Mose-Sagen.* Göttingen: Vandenhoeck & Ruprecht, 1913.

Grimal, Nicolas. *A History of Ancient Egypt.* Translated by Ian Shaw. Oxford: Blackwell, 1992.

Groll, Sarah Israelit. "The Egyptian Background of the Exodus and the Crossing of the Red Sea: A New Reading of Papyrus Anastasi VIII." In *Jerusalem Studies in Egyptology*, edited by Irene Shirun-Grumach, 173–92. ÄAT 40. Wiesbaden: Otto Harrassowitz, 1998.

______. "Historical Background to the Exodus: Papyrus Anastasi VIII." In *Gold of Praise: Studies on Ancient Egypt in Honor of Edward F. Wente*, edited by Emily Teeter and John A. Larson, 159–62. Chicago: Oriental Institute, 1999.

Gurtner, Daniel M. "'Atonement Slate' or 'Veil'? Notes on a Textual Variant in Exodus XXVI 34." *VT* 54, no. 3 (2004): 396–8.

Hafemann, Scott J. "The Glory and Veil of Moses in 2 Cor 3:7–14: An Example of Paul's Contextual Exegesis of the OT—A Proposal." *HBT* 14, no. 1 (1992): 31–49.

______. *Paul, Moses, and the History of Israel: The Letter/Spirit Contrast and the Argument from Scripture in 2 Corinthians 3.* Peabody: Hendrickson, 1996.

Hallo, William W., ed. *The Context of Scripture.* 3 vols. Leiden: Brill, 2003.

Haran, Menahem. "The Shining of Moses' Face: A Case Study in Biblical and Ancient Near Eastern Iconography." In *In the Shelter of Elyon: Essays on Ancient Palestinian Life and Literature in Honor of G. W. Ahlström*, edited by W. Boyd Barrick and John R. Spencer, 159–73. JSOTSup 31. Sheffield: *JSOT* Press, 1984.

Harbach, Ralph E., Bruce A. Harrison, Adel M. Gad, Mohamed A. Kenawy, and Sherif El-Said. "Records and Notes on Mosquitoes (Diptera: Culicidae) Collected in Egypt." *Mosquito Systematics* 20 (1988): 317–342.

Harding, Keith A., and Kenneth R. G. Welch. *Venomous Snakes of the World: A Checklist.* New York: Pergamon Press, 1980.

Hawkins, Ralph K. "Propositions for Evangelical Acceptance of a Late–Date Exodus–Conquest: Biblical Data and the Royal Scarabs from Mt. Ebal." *JETS* 50, no. 1 (2007): 31–46.

Hays, Christopher. "'Lest Ye Perish in the Way': Ritual and Kinship in Exodus 4:24–26." *HS* 48 (2007): 39–54.

Hendel, Ronald. "The Exodus in Biblical Memory." *JBL* 120, no. 4 (2001): 601–22.

Hertog, Cornelis G. den. "The Prophetic Dimension of the Divine Name: On Exodus 3:14a and its Context." *CBQ* 64, no. 2 (2002): 213–28.

Hobson, Christine. *Exploring the World of the Pharaohs.* London: Thames and Hudson, 1987.

Hoffmeier, James K. *Ancient Israel in Sinai: The Evidence for the Authenticity of the Wilderness Tradition.* Oxford: Oxford University Press, 2005.

______. "Egypt, Plagues in." In Freedman, *ABD* Vol. 2, 374–378.

______. *Israel in Egypt: The Evidence for the Authenticity of the Exodus Tradition.* Oxford: Oxford University Press, 1996.

______. "What is the Biblical Date for the Exodus? A Response to Bryant Wood." *JETS* 50, no. 2 (2007): 225–47.

Hoffner, Harry A., Jr. "Hittites." In *Peoples of the Old Testament World*, edited by Alfred J. Hoerth, Gerald L. Mattingly and Edwin M. Yamauchi, 127–55. Grand Rapids: Baker, 1994.

Holladay, John S., Jr. *Cities of the Delta, Part III: Tell el-Maskhuta.* American Research Center in Egypt Reports. Malibu: Undena, 1982.

Holladay, William. "Hebrew Verse Structure Revisited (I): Which Words 'Count'?" *JBL* 118, no. 1 (1999): 19–32.

______. "Hebrew Verse Structure Revisited (II): Conjoint Cola, and Further Suggestions." *JBL* 118, no. 3 (1999): 401–16.

Homan, Michael H. *To Your Tents, O Israel! The Terminology, Function, Form and Symbolism of Tents in the Hebrew Bible and the Ancient Near East.* Leiden: Brill, 2002.

Hoop, Raymond de. "The Colometry of Hebrew Verse and the Masoretic Accents: Evaluation of a Recent Approach (Part 1)." *JNSL* 26, no. 1 (2000): 47–73.

______. "The Colometry of Hebrew Verse and the Masoretic Accents: Evaluation of a Recent Approach (Part II)." *JNSL* 26, no. 2 (2000): 65–100.

Horowitz, Aharon. *The Jordan Rift Valley.* Lisse: A. A. Balkema Publishers, 2001.

Hort, Greta. "The Plagues of Egypt." *ZAW* 69, no. 1–4 (1957): 84–103.

______. "The Plagues of Egypt." *ZAW* 70, no. 1 (1958): 48–59.

Hostetter, Edwin C. "Puti-el." In Freedman, *ABD* Vol. 5, 561.

Houlihan, Patrick. "Spellbound: Charming the Snake & the Scorpion." *Ancient Egypt* 3, no. 6 (2003).

Houtman, Cornelis. *Exodus.* Translated by Johan Rebel and Sierd Woudstra. Historical Commentary on the Old Testament. Kampen: Kok, 1993.

______. "On the Function of the Holy Incense (Exodus XXX 34–8) and the Sacred Anointing Oil (Exodus XXX 22–33)." *VT* 42, no. 4 (1992): 458–65.

______. "On the Meaning of *Ûbāʿēṣîm Ûbāʾăbānîm* in Exodus VII 19." *VT* 36, no. 3 (1986): 347–52.

______. "On the Pomegranates and the Golden Bells of the High Priest's Mantle." *VT* 40, no. 2 (1990): 223–29.

Hughes, Philip Edgcumbe. *Paul's Second Epistle to the Corinthians: The English Text with Introduction, Exposition and Notes.* Grand Rapids: Eerdmans, 1962.

Humphreys, Colin J. *The Miracles of Exodus: A Scientist's Discovery of the Extraordinary Natural Causes of the Biblical Stories.* New York: HarperCollins, 2004.

______. "The Number of People in the Exodus from Egypt: Decoding Mathematically the Very Large Numbers in Numbers I and XXVI." *VT* 48, no. 2 (1998): 196–213.

Ions, Veronica. *Egyptian Mythology.* New York: Peter Bedrick Books, 1968.

Irwin, Brian P. "Yahweh's Suspension of Free Will in the Old Testament: Divine Immortality or Sign-Act?" *TynBul* 54, no. 2 (2003): 55–62.

Irwin, William H. "The Course of the Dialogue between Moses and Yhwh in Exodus 33:12–17." *CBQ* 59, no. 4 (1997): 629–36.

Janzen, J. Gerald. "The Character of the Calf and its Cult in Exodus 32." *CBQ* 52, no. 4 (1990): 597–607.

______. *Exodus.* Westminster Bible Companion. Louisville: Westminster John Knox Press, 1997.

Jaroš, Karl. "Des Mose 'strahlende Haut': Eine Notiz zu Ex 34:29, 30, 35." *ZAW* 88 (1976): 275–80.

Kantor, Mattis. *Codex Judaica: Chronological Index of Jewish History.* New York: Zichron, 2005.

Katzenstein, H. J. "Philistines." In Freedman, *ABD* Vol. 5, 326–328.

Keel, Othmar, and Christoph Uehlinger. *Gods, Goddesses, and Images of God in Ancient Israel.* Translated by Thomas H. Trapp. Minneapolis: Fortress, 1998.

Keil, C. F., and F. Delitzsch. *Commentary on the Old Testament.* Electronic Edition from Oaktree Software. Edinburgh: T. & T. Clark, 1866–1891.

Kemp, Barry. "The Amarna Project: What Kind of City was Amarna?" *Ancient Egypt* 8, no. 6 (2008): 33–38.

Kennedy, J. S. "The Migration of the Desert Locust (Schistocerca gregaria Forsk.). I. The Behaviour of Swarms. II. A Theory of Long-Range Migrations." *Philosophical Transactions of the Royal Society of London.* Series B, Biological Sciences 235, no. 625 (1951): 163–290.

Kirkpatrick, T. W. *The Mosquitoes of Egypt.* Cairo: Government Press, 1925.

Kistemaker, Simon J. *Exposition of the Second Epistle to the Corinthians.* Grand Rapids: Baker, 1997.

Kitchen, Kenneth A. "Egpyt, History of (Chronology)." In Freedman, *ABD* Vol. 2, 321–331.

______. "From the Brickfields of Egypt." *TynBul* 27 (1976): 137–47.

______. *On the Reliability of the Old Testament.* Grand Rapids: Eerdmans, 2003.

______. *Pharaoh Triumphant: The Life and Times of Ramesses II, King of Egypt.* Warminster: Aris & Phillips, 1982.

Kline, Meredith G. *Treaty of the Great King; the Covenant Structure of Deuteronomy: Studies and Commentary.* Grand Rapids: Eerdmans, 1963.

Knauf, Ernst Axel. "Seir." In Freedman, *ABD* Vol. 5, 1072–73.

Knierim, Rolf P. "Conceptual Aspects in Exodus 25:1–9." In *Pomegranates and Golden Bells: Studies in Biblical, Jewish, and Near Eastern Ritual, Law and Literature in Honor of Jacob Milgrom*, edited by David P. Wright, David N. Freedman and Avi Hurvitz, 113–124. Winona Lake: Eisenbrauns, 1995.

Knight, George A. F. *Theology as Narration: A Commentary on the Book of Exodus.* Grand Rapids: Eerdmans, 1976.

Kochavi, Moshe. "Rabud, Khirbet." In Stern, *NEAEHL*, 4:1252.

Koehler, L., W. Baumgartner, and J. J. Stamm. *The Hebrew and Aramaic Lexicon of the Old Testament*. Translated and edited under the supervision of M. E. J. Richardson. 4 vols. Leiden: Brill, 1994-1999.

Kosmala, Hans. "Bloody Husband." *VT* 12, no. 1 (1962): 14–28.

Kugel, James. *The Idea of Biblical Poetry: Parallelism and its History.* Baltimore: Johns Hopkins University Press, 1998.

Kunin, Seth Daniel. "The Bridegroom of Blood: A Structuralist Analysis." *JSOT* 70 (1996): 3–16.

Lachs, Samuel T. "Exodus IV 11 : Evidence for an Emendation." *VT* 26, no. 2 (1976): 249–50.

Lambrecht, Jan. *Second Corinthians.* SP. Collegeville: The Liturgical Press, 1999.

Laney, J. Carl. "God's Self–Revelation in Exodus 34:6–8." *BSac* 158, no. 629 (2001): 36–51.

Leder, Arie C. "The Coherence of Exodus: Narrative Unity and Meaning." *CTJ* 36, no. 2 (2001): 251–69.

Lemche, Niels Peter. "Habiru Hapiru." In Freedman, *ABD* Vol. 3, 6–10.

Lemmelijn, Bénédicte. *A Plague of Texts? A Text-Critical Study of the So-Called 'Plagues Narrative' in Exodus* 7:14–11:10. Leiden: Brill, 2009.

Lesko, Barbara. *The Great Goddesses of Egypt.* Norman: University of Oklahoma Press, 1999.

Levy, Thomas E., and Thomas Higham, eds. *The Bible and Radiocarbon Dating: Archaeology, Text and Science.* London: Equinox, 2005.

Lewis, Brian. *The Sargon Legend: A Study of the Akkadian Text and the Tale of the Hero Who Was Exposed at Birth.* Cambridge, MA: American Schools of Oriental Research, 1980.

Lichtheim, Miriam. *Ancient Egyptian Literature: A Book of Readings.* Vol. 2, *The New Kingdom*. Berkeley: University of California Press, 1973.

Lindqvist, Pekka. *Sin at Sinai: Early Judaism Encounters Exodus 32.* Turku, Finland: Åbo Akademi University, 2008.

Livingston, David P. "Location of Biblical Bethel and Ai Reconsidered." *WTJ* 33, no. 1 (1970): 20–44.

Lockshin, Martin L., ed., trans. *Rashbam's Commentary on Exodus: An Annotated Translation.* Atlanta: Scholar's Press, 1997.

Loewenstamm, Samuel E. "An Observation on Source–Criticism of the Plaguepericope (Ex. VII–XI)." *VT* 24, no. 3 (1974): 374–8.

______. "Exodus XXI 22–25." *VT* 27, no. 3 (1977): 352–60.

______. "The Lord is my Strength and my Glory." *VT* 19, no. 4 (1969): 464–70.

______. "The Making and Destruction of the Golden Calf." *Bib* 48 (1967): 481–90.

______. "The Making and Destruction of the Golden Calf: A Rejoinder." *Bib* 56 (1975): 330–43.

London, Gloria. "Why Milk and Meat Don't Mix." *BAR* 34, no. 6 (2008): 66–9.

Loretz, Oswald. *Habiru-Hebräer: Eine Sozio-Linguistische Studie über die Herkunft des Gentiliziums ibrî vom Appelativum Habiru.* Berlin: Walter de Gruyter, 1984.

Macintosh, A. A. "Exodus 8:19, Distinct Redemption and the Hebrew Roots פרה and פדד." *VT* 21, no. 5 (1971): 548–55.

Magen, Itzhak. "Shechem." in Stern, *NEAEHL,* 4:1345–59.

Magonet, Jonathan. "The Rhetoric of God: Exodus 6.2–8." *JSOT* 27 (1983): 56–67.

Maimonides, Moses. *The Guide of the Perplexed of Maimonides.* Vol. 3. Translated by M. Friedländer. London: Trübner & Co., 1885.

Mann, Thomas W. "The Pillar of Cloud in the Reed Sea Narrative." *JBL* 90, no. 1 (1971): 15–30.

Master, Jonathan. "Exodus 32 as an Argument for Traditional Theism." *JETS* 45, no. 2 (2002): 585–98.

Mathewson, Daniel B. "A Critical Binarism: Source Criticism and Deconstructive Criticism." *JSOT* 98 (2002): 3–28.

Mazar, Amihai. *Archaeology of the Land of the Bible: 10,000–586 B.C.E.* New York: Doubleday, 1992.

McCarthy, Dennis J. "Exod 3:14: History, Philology and Theology." *CBQ* 40, no. 3 (1978): 311–22.

McConville, J Gordon. "Deuteronomy's Unification of Passover and Maṣṣôt: A Response to Bernard M. Levinson." *JBL* 119, no. 1 (2000): 47–58.

McEntire, Mark. "A Response to Colin J. Humphreys's 'The Number of People in the Exodus from Egypt: Decoding Mathematically the Very Large Numbers in Numbers I and XXVI.'" *VT* 49, no. 2 (1999): 262–4.

Mendenhall, George E. "Covenant Forms in Israelite Tradition." *BA* 17, no. 3 (1954): 50–76.

______. "Midian." In Freedman, *ABD* Vol. 4, 815–818.

Mertz, Barbara. *Red Land, Black Land: Daily Life in Ancient Egypt.* New York: William Morrow, 2008.

______. *Temples, Tombs & Hieroglyphs: A Popular History of Ancient Egypt.* New York: William Morrow, 2007.

Meshel, Ze'ev. "Wilderness Wanderings: Ethnographic Lessons from Modern Bedouin." *BAR* 34, no. 4 (2008): 32–29.

Meyer, Jason C. *The End of the Law: Mosaic Covenant in Pauline Theology.* Nashville: B & H Academic, 2009.

Middelkoop, Pieter. "The Significance of the Story of the 'Bloody Husband' (Exodus 4:24–26)." *SEAJT* 8, no. 4 (1967): 34–8.

Minor, Mitzi L. *2 Corinthians*. Smyth & Helwys Bible Commentary. Macon: Smyth & Helwys, 2009.

Miserey, Yves. "Égypte: la chronologie des dynasties revue au carbone 14." *Le Figaro.* June 18, 2010. http://www.lefigaro.fr/sciences-technologies/2010/06/18/01030-20100618ARTFIG00607-egypte-la-chronologie-des-dynasties-revue-au-carbone-14.php.

Mitchell, T. C. "The Meaning of the Noun *ḤTN* in the Old Testament." *VT* 19, no. 1 (1969): 93–112.
Morgenstern, Julian. "The 'Bloody Husband' (?) (Exod 4:24–26) Once Again." *HUCA* 34 (1963): 35–70.
______. "Moses with the Shining Face." *HUCA* 2 (1925): 1–28.
Morschauser, Scott. "Potters' Wheels and Pregnancies: A Note on Exodus 1:16." *JBL* 122, no. 4 (2003): 731–33.
Müller, W. W. "Havilah (Place)." In Freedman, *ABD* Vol. 3, 82.
Na´aman, Nadav. "Habiru and Hebrews: The Transfer of a Social Term to the Literary Sphere." In *Canaan in the Second Millennium B.C.E.*, 252–74. Winona Lake: Eisenbrauns, 2005.
Nicholson, Ernest W. *Exodus and Sinai in History and Tradition.* Richmond: John Knox, 1973.
______. "The Covenant Ritual in Exodus XXIV 3–8." *VT* 32, no. 1 (1982): 74–86.
______. "The Interpretation of Exodus XXIV 9–11." *VT* 24, no. 1 (1974): 77–97.
______. "Origin of the Tradition in Exodus XXIV 9–11." *VT* 26, no. 2 (1976): 148–60.
O'Connor, Michael P. *Hebrew Verse Structure.* Winona Lake: Eisenbrauns, 1980.
Oakes, Lorna, and Lucia Gahlin. *Ancient Egypt: An Illustrated Reference to the Myths, Religions, Pyramids and Temples of the Land of the Pharaohs*. New York: Hermes House, 2002.
Olyan, Saul M. "Exodus 31:12–17: The Sabbath according to H, or the Sabbath according to P and H?" *JBL* 124, no. 2 (2005): 201–9.
Oren, Eliezer D. "The 'Ways of Horus' in North Sinai." In *Egypt, Israel, Sinai: Archaeological and Historical Relationships in the Biblical Period*, edited by Anson F. Rainey, 69–120. Tel Aviv: Tel Aviv University, 1987.
Parker, Simon B. "Exodus XV 2 Again." *VT* 21, no. 3 (1971): 373–9.
Patterson, Richard D. "Victory at Sea: Prose and Poetry in Exodus 14–15." *BSac* 161, no. 641 (2004): 42–54.
Phillips, Anthony C. J. "A Fresh Look at the Sinai Pericope, Part 1." *VT* 34, no. 1 (1984): 39–52.
______. "A Fresh Look at the Sinai Pericope, Part 2." *VT* 34, no. 3 (1984): 282–94.
______. "The Laws of Slavery: Exodus 21.2–11." *JSOT* 30 (1984): 51–66.
______, and Lucy Phillips. "The Origin of 'I AM' in Exodus 3.14." *JSOT* 78 (1998): 81–4.

Pratico, Gary. "Where Is Ezion–Geber? A Reappraisal of the Site Archaeologist Nelson Glueck Identified as King Solomon's Red Sea Port." *BAR* 12, no. 5 (1986): 24–35.

Pritchard, James B., ed. *Ancient Near Eastern Texts Relating to the Old Testament.* 3rd ed. with supplement. Princeton: Princeton University Press, 1969.

Propp, William H. C. *Exodus 1–18: A New Translation with Introduction and Commentary.* AB 2. New Haven: Yale University Press, 1999.

______. *Exodus 19–40: A New Translation with Introduction and Commentary.* AB 2A. New York: Doubleday, 2006.

______. "The Origins of Infant Circumcision in Israel." *Hebrew Annual Review* 11 (1987): 355–70.

______. "The Skin of Moses' Face—Transfigured or Disfigured?" *CBQ* 49, no. 3 (1987): 375–86.

______. "That Bloody Bridegroom (Exodus IV 24–6)." *VT* 43, no. 4 (1993): 495–518.

Protist Information Server. "Protist Images: Euglena sanguinea." Accessed April 23, 2014. http://protist.i.hosei.ac.jp/PDB/images/Mastigophora/Euglena/sanguinea/index.html.

Provan, Iain W., V. Philips Long, and Tremper Longman III. *A Biblical History of Israel.* Louisville: Westminster John Knox Press, 2003.

Rainey, Anson. "Shasu or Habiru: Who were the Early Israelites?" *BAR* 34, no. 6 (2008): 51–5.

______, and R. Steven Notley. *The Sacred Bridge: Carta's Atlas of the Biblical World.* Jerusalem: Carta, 2006.

Reader, Colin. "Pharaoh's Gold." *Ancient Egypt* 9, no. 2 (2008): 15–21.

Redford, Donald B. *Egypt, Canaan, and Israel in Ancient Times.* Princeton: Princeton University Press, 1992.

Reed, Stephen A. "Perizzite." In Freedman, *ABD* Vol. 5, 231.

Reis, Pamela Tamarkin. "The Bridegroom of Blood: A New Reading." *Judaism* 40, no. 159 (1991): 324–31.

Rendsburg, Gary A. "An Additional Note to Two Recent Articles on the Number of People in the Exodus from Egypt and the Large Numbers in Numbers I and XXVI." *VT* 51, no. 3 (2001): 392–6.

______. "The Date of the Exodus and the Conquest/Settlement : The Case for the 1100s." *VT* 42, no. 4 (1992): 510–27.

Richter, Sandra L. "The Place of the Name in Deuteronomy." *VT* 57, no.3 (2007): 342–66.

Robinson, Bernard P. "Zipporah to the Rescue: A Contextual Study of Exodus IV 24–6." *VT* 36, no. 4 (1986): 447–61.

______. "Israel and Amalek: The Context of Exodus 17:8–16." *JSOT* 32 (1985): 15–22.

______. "Moses at the Burning Bush." *JSOT* 75 (1997): 107–22.

Rohl, David M. *A Test of Time: The Bible from Myth to History.* London: Century, 1995.

Rooker, Mark F. *The Ten Commandments: Ethics for the Twenty-First Century.* NAC Studies in Bible & Theology. Nashville: B&H Academic, 2010.

Roth, Martha T. *Law Collections from Mesopotamia and Asia Minor.* Writings from the Ancient World 6. Atlanta: Scholar's Press, 1997.

Russaw, Kimberly D. "Zipporah and Circumcision as a Form of Preparation: Cutting Away at the Comfort Zone." *JITC* 31, no. 1–2 (2003–4): 103–12.

Russell, Brian D. *The Song of the Sea: The Date of Composition and Influence of Exodus 15:1–21.* Studies in Biblical Literature 101. New York: Peter Lang, 2007.

Ryken, Philip Graham. *Exodus: Saved for God's Glory.* Preaching the Word. Wheaton: Crossway, 2005.

Sailhamer, John. *An Introduction to Old Testament Theology: A Canonical Approach.* Grand Rapids: Zondervan, 1995.

Sanders, Seth L. "Old Light on Moses' Shining Face." *VT* 52, no. 3 (2002): 400–6.

Sarna, Nahum M. "Exploring Exodus: the Oppression." *BA* 49, no. 2 (1986): 68–80.

______. *Exodus: The Traditional Hebrew Text with the New JPS Translation, Commentary.* The JPS Torah Commentary. Philadelphia: Jewish Publication Society, 1991.

Sasson, Jack M. "Circumcision in the Ancient Near East." *JBL* 85, no. 4 (1966): 473–76.

Schenker, Adrian. "The Biblical Legislation on the Release of Slaves: The Road from Exodus to Leviticus." *JSOT* 78 (1998): 23–41.

Scolnic, Benjamin E. "From Bloody Bridegroom to Covenant Rite: *Brit Milah*—The Perspective of Modern Biblical Scholarship." *Conservative Judaism* 42, no. 4 (1990): 12–20.

Shanks, Hershel. "Two Early Israelite Cult Sites Now Questioned." *BAR* 14, no. 1 (1988): 48–52.

Shaw, Ian, ed. *The Oxford History of Ancient Egypt.* Oxford: Oxford University Press, 2000.

______, and Paul Nicholson. *The Dictionary of Ancient Egypt.* New York: Harry N. Abrams, 1995.

Shea, William. "Exodus, Date of the." In Bromiley, *ISBE*, 1.230–38.

Shortland, A. J. "Shishak, King of Egypt." In *The Bible and Radiocarbon Dating*, edited by Thomas E. Levy and Thomas Higham, 43–54. London: Equinox, 2005.

Shreckhise, Robert. "The Problem of Finite Verb Translation in Exodus 15.1–18." *JSOT* 32, no. 3 (2008): 287–310.

Silverman, David P., ed. *Ancient Egypt*. Oxford: Oxford University Press, 1997.

Simkins, Ronald A. "Seir." In *Eerdmans Dictionary of the Bible*, edited by David Noel Freedman, 1179. Grand Rapids: Eerdmans, 2000.

Simpson, William Kelly, ed. *The Literature of Ancient Egypt: An Anthology of Stories, Instructions, Stelae, Autobiographies and Poetry*. 3rd ed. New Haven: Yale University Press, 2003.

Sivertsen, Barbara J. *The Parting of the Sea: How Volcanoes, Earthquakes and Plagues Shaped the Story of Exodus*. Princeton: Princeton University Press, 2009.

Slivniak, Dmitri M. "The Golden Calf Story: Constructively and Deconstructively." *JSOT* 33, no. 1 (2008): 19–38.

Smith, Henry Preserved. "Ethnological Parallels to Exodus iv.24–26." *JBL* 25, no. 1 (1906): 14–24.

Soliman, M. M., S. M. Abdel-Mogheeth, I. M. El-Azizy, and N. A. M. Morad. "The Environmental Impact of the Rainfall-Runoff upon Groundwater Quality in Wadi Sudr, South Sinai." In *Environmental and Groundwater Pollution: Proceedings of the International Conference on Water Resources Management in Arid Regions (WaRMAR)*, edited by M. M. Sherif, V. P. Singh and M. Al-Rashed, 65–72. Lisse: A. A. Balkema, 2002.

Spalinger, Anthony John. *War in Ancient Egypt: The New Kingdom*. Oxford: Blackwell, 2005.

Sprinkle, Joe M. *The Book of the Covenant: A Literary Approach*. JSOTSup 174. Sheffield: *JSOT* Press, 1994.

______. "Law and Narrative in Exodus 19–24." *JETS* 47, no. 2 (2004): 235–52.

______. "The Interpretation of Exodus 21:22–25 (*Lex Talionis*) and Abortion." *WTJ* 55, no. 2 (1993): 233–53.

Stackert, Jeffrey. "Why Does Deuteronomy Legislate Cities of Refuge? Asylum in the Covenant Collection (Exodus 21:12–14) and Deuteronomy (19:1–13)." *JBL* 125, no. 1 (2006): 23–49.

Stern, Ephraim, ed. *The New Encyclopedia of Archaeological Excavations in the Holy Land*. Jerusalem: Israel Exploration Society and Carta, 1993.

Stern, Philip D. "The Origin and Significance of 'The Land Flowing with Milk and Honey.'" *VT* 42, no. 4 (1992): 554–7.

Stuart, Douglas K. *Exodus*. NAC 2. Nashville: Broadman & Holman, 2006.

Suomala, Karla R. *Moses and God in Dialogue: Exodus 32–34 in Postbiblical Literature.* Studies in Biblical Literature 61. New York: Peter Lang, 2004.

Taher, Ayman Wahby. "The Mummy of Hatshepsut Identified." *Ancient Egypt* 8, no. 2 (2007): 10–13.

Thiele, Edwin Richard. *The Mysterious Numbers of the Hebrew Kings: A Reconstruction of the Chronology of the Kingdoms of Israel and Judah.* Grand Rapids: Eerdmans, 1965.

Thompson, Thomas L. "How Yahweh Became God: Exodus 3 and 6 and the Heart of the Pentateuch." *JSOT* 68 (1995): 57–74.

Timmer, Daniel C. *Creation, Tabernacle, and Sabbath: The Sabbath Frame of Exodus 31:12–17; 35:1–3 in Exegetical and Theological Perspective.* Göttingen: Vandenhoeck & Ruprecht, 2009.

Toombs, Lawrence E. "Shechem." In Freedman, *ABD* Vol. 5, 1174–1186.

Toorn, Karel van der, Bob Becking, and Pieter W. van der Horst, eds. *Dictionary of Deities and Demons in the Bible.* 2nd ed. Leiden: Brill, 1999.

Turell, Michael J, and Gregory B. Knudson. "Mechanical Transmission of Bacillus anthracis by Stable Flies (*Stomoxys calcitrans*) and Mosquitoes (*Aedes aegypti* and *Aedes taeniorhynchus*)." *Infection and Immunity* 55, no. 8 (1987): 1859–1861.

Tyldesley, Joyce A. *Hatchepsut: The Female Pharaoh.* London: Penguin Books, 1998.

______. *Ramesses: Egypt's Greatest Pharaoh.* London: Penguin, 2001.

USA Today. "Egypt swarms with locusts." Accessed 4/23/14. http://www.usatoday.com/news/world/2004-11-17-locusts_x.htm.

Van Seters, John. *A Law Book for the Diaspora: Revision in the Study of the Covenant Code.* Oxford: Oxford University Press, 2003.

Vaux, Roland de. *The Early History of Israel.* Translated by David Smith. London: Darton, Longman & Todd, 1978.

Vermès, Géza. "Baptism and Jewish Exegesis: New Light from Ancient Sources." *NTS* 4, no. 4 (1958): 309–19.

Walters, Joseph A. "Moses at the Lodging Place: The Devil is in the Ambiguities." *Encounter* 63, no. 4 (2002): 407–25.

Waltke, Bruce K. *An Old Testament Theology: An Exegetical, Canonical, and Thematic Approach.* Grand Rapids: Zondervan, 2007.

______. "Palestinian Artifactual Evidence Supporting the Early Date of the Exodus." *BSac* 129, no. 513 (1972): 33–47.

______, and Michael O'Connor. *An Introduction to Biblical Hebrew Syntax.* Winona Lake: Eisenbrauns, 1990.

Watson, Francis. *Paul and the Hermeneutics of Faith.* London: T & T Clark, 2004.

Watterson, Barbara. *The Gods of Ancient Egypt.* London: Sutton, 1984.

Weinfeld, Moshe. *Deuteronomy and the Deuteronomic School.* London: Oxford University Press, 1972.

Wells, Bruce. "Exodus." In *Zondervan Illustrated Bible Backgrounds Commentary*, edited by John H. Walton, 1:160–283. Grand Rapids: Zondervan, 2009.

Wessner, Mark D. "Toward a Literary Understanding of Moses and the Lord 'Face to Face' (פָּנִים אֶל־פָּנִים) in Exodus 33:7–11." *ResQ* 44, no. 2 (2002): 109–16.

Westbrook, Raymond. *Studies in Biblical and Cuneiform Law.* Paris: J. Gabalda, 1988.

______. "What is the Covenant Code?" In *Theory and Method in Biblical and Cuneiform Law: Revision, Interpolation and Development*, JSOTSup 181, edited by Bernard M. Levinson, 15–36. Sheffield: Sheffield Academic Press, 1994.

White, J. E. Manchip. *Ancient Egypt: Its Culture and History.* New York: Dover, 1970.

Wilson, Ian. *The Exodus Enigma.* London: Weidenfield and Nicolson, 1985.

Wilson, Robert R. "The Hardening of Pharaoh's Heart." *CBQ* 41, no. 1 (1979): 18–36.

Wolters, Al. "Not Rescue but Destruction: Rereading Exodus 15:8." *CBQ* 52, no. 2 (1990): 223–40.

Wood, Bryant G. "The Biblical Date for the Exodus is 1446 BC: A Response to James Hoffmeier." *JETS* 50, no. 2 (2007): 249–58.

______. "Did the Israelites Conquer Jericho? A New Look at the Archaeological Evidence." *BAR Electronic Archive*. Vol. 19.2. March/April 1990.

______. "The Rise and Fall of the 13th Century Exodus–Conquest Theory." *JETS* 48, no. 3 (2005): 475–89.

Wright, David P. *Inventing God's Law: How the Covenant Code of the Bible Used and Revised the Laws of Hammurabi.* Oxford: Oxford University Press, 2009.

______, David N. Freedman, and Avi Hurvitz, eds. *Pomegranates and Golden Bells: Studies in Biblical, Jewish, and Near Eastern Ritual, Law, and Literature in Honor of Jacob Milgrom.* Winona Lake: Eisenbrauns, 1995.

______ and Richard N. Jones. "Leprosy." In Freedman, *ABD* Vol. 4, 277–82.

Wyatt, Nicolas. "The Significance of the Burning Bush." *VT* 36, no. 3 (1986): 361–5.

Yurco, Frank. “End of the Late Bronze Age and other crisis periods: A Volcanic Cause?” In *Gold of Praise: Studies on Ancient Egypt in Honor of Edward F. Wente*, SAOC 58, edited by Emily Teeter and John A. Larson, 455–463. Chicago: University of Chicago, 1999.

Zertal, Adam. “Has Joshua’s Altar Been Found on Mt. Ebal?” *BAR* 11, no. 1 (1985): 26–43.

______. “Israel Enters Canaan—Following the Pottery Trail.” *BAR* 17, no. 5 (1991): 29–49, 75.